DUNGEON, FIRE AND SWORD

DUNGEON, FIRE AND SWORD

THE KNIGHTS TEMPLAR IN THE CRUSADES

JOHN J. ROBINSON

Brockhampton Press

This edition published in 1999 by Brockhampton Press,
a member of Hodder Headline PLC Group

First published in 1994 by
Michael O'Mara Books Limited

A CIP catalogue record for this book is available from the British Library.

ISBN 1 86019 952 6

Printed and bound in Great Britain by Creative Print and Design (Wales), Ebbw Vale

Table of Contents

PART THREE: Torture and Trial

"Faith of our fathers, living still
In spite of dungeon, fire and sword..."

FREDERICK W. FABER (1814-1863)

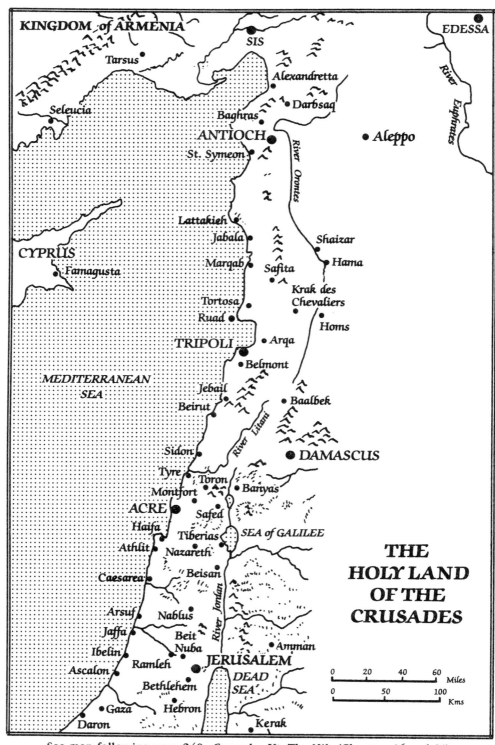

KINGDOM of ARMENIA

EDESSA

SIS

Tarsus

Alexandretta

Seleucia

Baghras

Darbsaq

ANTIOCH

Aleppo

St. Symeon

River Orontes

River Euphrates

Lattakieh

Jabala

Shaizar

CYPRUS

Marqab

Safita

Hama

Famagusta

Krak des Chevaliers

Tortosa

Ruad

Homs

TRIPOLI

Arqa

MEDITERRANEAN SEA

Belmont

Jebail

Beirut

Baalbek

River Litani

Sidon

DAMASCUS

Tyre

Toron

Montfort

Baniyas

ACRE

Safed

Haifa

Tiberias

SEA of GALILEE

Athlit

Nazareth

Caesarea

Beisan

THE HOLY LAND OF THE CRUSADES

River Jordan

Arsuf

Nablus

Jaffa

Beit Nuba

Amman

Ibelin

Ascalon

Ramleh

JERUSALEM

Bethlehem

DEAD SEA

Gaza

Hebron

Daron

Kerak

| 0 | 20 | 40 | 60 | Miles |
| 0 | | 50 | 100 | Kms |

See map following page 240, *Crusades Up The Nile* (Chapters 16 and 21).
See map following page 398, *The Siege of Acre 1291* (Chapter 27).

Introduction

ANYONE WHO BELIEVES that historical research is drudgery has never delved into the past of the military monastic order known as the Knights Templar. Its story in the great Crusades, even when recounted by somber church chroniclers, is high adventure.

The order was organized in the aftermath of the First Crusade, when a small band of knights took vows of poverty, chastity, and obedience to dedicate their entire lives to the protection of pilgrims to the Holy Land. At first they just guarded the pilgrim roads to Jerusalem, but over the years they grew to become the largest standing army in the Christian kingdom. They took their name from their headquarters in a captured mosque built on the site of the ancient Temple of Solomon, on the Temple Mount in the Holy City.

Their selfless dedication earned the approval of all Christendom. Saint Bernard of Clairvaux became their most enthusiastic champion, and soon a flood of gifts enriched the Knights Templar with manors, mills, and markets throughout Europe, along with vast estates and castles in the Holy Land. Predictably, their pride quickly grew to match their wealth. In time, the prelates and princes who had once extolled the Templar virtues became jealous of the treasure that the order had accumulated—in such abundance that the employment of its surplus funds had made the Knights Templar the major bankers of the Christian world.

The Templars operated under the personal protection of the popes so long as the struggle for the Holy Places of Jesus Christ continued, as it did for almost two hundred years. Over twenty thousand military monks fought and died in the sacred quest. Even a number of the order's grand masters died on the battlefields, where the Knights Templar crossed swords with Turks and Kurds, Arabs and Egyptians. As the invading Christians were ultimately pushed back to the shores of the Mediterranean Sea, there were countless awesome examples of courage and faith. After the loss of one of their inland castles, the Templar garrison was offered life and freedom if the knights would abandon Christianity to embrace Islam. All of them, over two hundred Knights of the Temple, chose to kneel before their Muslim executioners and lose their heads, rather than lose their faith.

As Christians were forced out of one walled city after another, and eventually out of the Holy Land altogether, the Templars were the last to leave. They had castles that the Muslims never succeeded in taking, but in the end there were no Christian pilgrims for them to protect, no Crusader leaders to support. They simply abandoned their last fortresses.

Once the Crusades were lost, the Templar purpose was lost, although much of the order's wealth remained. With their own coffers drained through incessant wars, Christian monarchs looked at the Templar treasure with envy, but none with more aggressive greed than Philip IV of France.

In league with Clement V, a French pope largely under his control, Philip plotted to bring down the Templar order with charges of heresy, the one crime that would permit confiscation of its extensive properties. To implement his plan, King Philip ordered the arrest of every Templar in France at the same time, at dawn on Friday the Thirteenth in October of 1307. The agonizing torture to extract confessions of heresy began that same unlucky day.

A papal bull went out to all the Catholic monarchs, commanding them to arrest and torture the Knights Templar within their domains. Some obeyed, some flouted the pope's orders, and some had their local Templars tried and found innocent, but by then the venerable military order was effectively shattered. Templars who retracted the confessions made under torture were judged to be "relapsed heretics," eligible to be burned at the stake. Fifty-four Templars were burned alive on one morning in Paris.

Years of imprisonment and torture by the Inquisition went by, until Pope Clement V officially disbanded the Knights of the Temple in 1312. Their grand master, Jacques de Molay, was held in miserable confinement for two more years in Paris, then led in chains to a high platform in front of the majestic cathedral of Notre Dame. He was ordered to make his confessions of guilt to the crowds of assembled clergy, nobles, and commoners who had been gathered to hear him. Instead, the aging, courageous grand master seized the moment to shout out the innocence of the Knights Templar. He was hustled from the platform by his enraged captors, to be burned at the stake before the day was over.

Even as the executioners lit the wood piled at his feet, de Molay continued to cry out the innocence of his order. Legend has it that he also cried out a curse on Pope Clement V and King Philip IV, calling on them to meet him at the throne of God before the year was out. Both pope and king died within weeks, giving strength to that legend, which was only the first of many. Succeeding generations speculated on the whereabouts of missing Templar treasure, their missing ships, the fugitive knights who had eluded their captors and were never found. Stories grew of clandestine bands of surviving Templars, of other Templar knights who fought for Robert Bruce against Edward II of England, even of a secret succession of underground grand masters that allegedly exists to this day.

Templar memory has been embellished or sullied by centuries of writers. The medieval minnesinger Wolfram von Eschenbach gave the Templars a role in the legend of the Holy Grail. Sir Walter Scott cast them as sinister villains. A book published during the last decade speculated on the Templars as the guardians of a holy royal bloodline emanating from Jesus Christ. A recent novel from Italy finds a secret society founded by the Templars that is plotting to rule the world.

With such continuing interest, which all too often shrouds the Templars in an aura of myth and magic their story does not require, there appears to be a need for a factual narrative history of the ancient order. I have chosen to concentrate this book on the warrior-monks in their role as warriors, not as monks, and even less as bankers and farmers. One Templar said it for me when he expressed his frustration at being in Britain instead of Bethlehem: "We are preceptors of sheep!" He wanted to be at the center of action in the Holy Land, and so do we. The essence of the Knights Templar lies in their adventures in the Crusader states, not in raising barley in Britain or grapes in Gascony, nor even in their part in the wars against the Moors in Iberia.

To put the Templars in a crusading context it is necessary to fit them in with the people and politics of the Middle East, the men they fought with and the men they fought against. The story is filled with familiar peoples such as the Armenians and Georgians, the Druzes of Lebanon and the Azeri Turks of Azerbaijan. Familiar men are there: Richard the Lion Heart of England, St. Louis of France, Frederick Barbarossa of Germany. Even St. Francis of Assisi is there, as he joins a crusading army in Egypt—neither the first nor the last to believe that a reasonable man can bring peace to the Middle East in friendly discussions. Marco Polo arrives to ask for holy oil from the Church of the Holy Sepulcher to take as a gift

to Kublai Khan. In his travels across the Kurdish lands north of
Mesopotamia, he observes "fountains" of black oil coming from
the ground.

The Mongols turned loose by Genghis Khan arrived, after cutting a bloody path across modern Iran, Iraq, and Syria. They were
finally stopped by an Egyptian army on the west bank of the Jordan
River. That defeat motivated the Mongols to send ambassadors to
the Holy See and to the monarchs of Europe, unsuccessfully seeking
a Christian alliance against the Muslims. They asserted a great
influence on the Crusades, but not as much as the Egyptian Mamelukes who had stopped them, nor as much as the most memorable
Muslim leader of them all, the Kurdish Sultan Saladin.

Our story calls for an understanding of the beliefs and the
structure of the Templars' Muslim enemies. The First Crusade at
the end of the eleventh century succeeded largely because of conflicts between Muslim factions that called themselves Sunni and
Shiite. The new Templar order had to learn the make-up of the
Muslim world as it took up residence in the al-Aqsa Mosque on
the Temple Mount.

So this book becomes two books in one, a history of the Knights
Templar and a history of the Holy Land, to present their impact
on each other. It is important to bear in mind that a full understanding of the Templar order cannot be achieved by seeing it only
as a part of the major Crusades. Those great invasions involved
multinational armies with twenty thousand to a hundred thousand
men, forces to which the Templars could provide welcome assistance and even guidance, but in which a few hundred knights, no
matter how dedicated, could not be the principal military factor.
It was in the long years between those Crusades that the standing
army of Knights Templar came into their own. Then they were the
strongest military force available to hold the Muslim enemy at bay,
which they did through the defense of their castles, direct engage-
ments in the field, and diplomatic missions to the Islamic courts.
Crusaders were military pilgrims, who came to fight and go home.
The Templars were military monks, committed to remain in the
Holy Land to consolidate the gains, or to clean up the mess, after
the Crusaders had fulfilled their vows and then sailed away from the
scene of their triumphs or tragedies.

For that reason, there are two centuries of history here, to be
condensed into one volume. It's rather like booking a round-the-
world tour, only to be informed that just one bag may be taken.
One ponders a mountain of possibilities to select those items likely
to be most useful on the journey ahead.

Although many months have been spent checking and double-checking facts set forth by centuries of historical writers who frequently disagree, I have been acutely conscious of the need to provide a smoother path through the dense jungle of names, dates, and places. In that regard, I have been frequently advised that I am wrong to avoid footnotes, because they give any book a ring of credibility. My reaction is the same one I experienced as a child when foul-tasting medicines were forced upon me with the assurance that their offensive taste was proof of their efficacy. The purpose of the footnote is to present additional information perhaps not pertinent to the time frame, or to acknowledge a source, but it is placed at the bottom of the page for the nonsensical notion that there it will not interfere with the flow of narrative. I am asked to lose my place, drop my eyes to the bottom of the page, then find my place again. I prefer to work to find a way to simply slip attribution or related information into the story.

In prior publication I received a number of letters citing historians who appeared to disagree with some point I had made. I can only defend myself by stating that when, for example, two European historians differ with each other, and Arab chroniclers disagree with both of them, I can only ponder a while, then pick the point of view that seems to make the most sense. Ancient chroniclers are the most difficult to draw upon, because they usually wrote to please a pope, or to cater to a king.

Another practice of which I am a sworn enemy is the propensity to pepper works of history with quotations in other languages, with no accompanying translation. The reader is apparently assumed to have a ready command of Latin, Greek, French, and Medieval English. I don't, although I draw heavily on an unpaid translator in the person of my wife, whose knowledge of Latin and French has saved me hours of digging to find translations.

Finally, in the interests of easier understanding, I have taken the liberty of occasionally using modern designations such as Iran and Iraq instead of Persia and Mesopotamia, and have located activities in areas identified as Lebanon or Yugoslavia, even though those nations didn't exist at the time. All this simply because I write not to preach, or to teach, but to share what I love. I just don't want confusion to dampen the excitement and wonder of the story of the legendary knights.

Finally, if we are saddened a bit by the unfolding realization that ancient ethnic rivalries and prejudices are still not laid to rest after centuries of conflict, we can at least reflect on the unbridled brutality of that feudal age and take comfort in the fact that we have indeed come a long way.

As our story opens, the Church of Rome is engaged in two

major struggles for papal supremacy, one with the Christian rulers of Europe and the other with the Greek Orthodox Church embraced by the Byzantine Empire centered at Constantinople, which did not recognize any biblical justification for a pope. Its chance came when the Byzantines appealed to Rome for military assistance to hold back the encroaching Turks. The pope could solve two problems at once by sending the militant nobles away from Europe to rescue Byzantium, an act certain to cause the Greek Church to recognize the supremacy of the Roman, under the religious banner of a great Crusade to rescue from the Muslims the Holy Places sacred to the memory of Jesus Christ. That was the beginning of the Crusades, in the eleventh-century atmosphere of faith, avarice, and antagonism.

PART ONE

The First Crusade and the Birth of the Temple

1

Holy War
1052 to 1099

O N A SABBATH DAY in the middle of the eleventh century, the patriarch of the Greek Orthodox Church was celebrating a solemn mass in the great basilica of Hagia Sophia in Constantinople, as three booted men entered the church and stomped down the center aisle to the high altar. The leader slammed a document down on the altar at which, without saying a word, they turned and marched out. The three men were cardinals, princes of the Church of Rome. The document was a decree of the Roman Pope Leo IX, which declared the excommunication of the emperor of Byzantium and all the patriarchs, priests and monks of the Orthodox Church, as well as all of the citizens of the Eastern Roman Empire. The choice was eternal damnation or submission to the overlordship of the Church of Rome.

It was just the latest antagonistic event in the unrelenting conflict between the Holy See and the Orthodox Church. Ever since the split of the Roman Empire in the fourth century, the two centers of Rome and Constantinople had maintained an incessant hostility, both secular and religious. Each claimed to be the true inheritor of Caesar, and each claimed to be the One True Church, according to the will of God. The Eastern Church simply wanted to be left alone to worship God in its own way, but the Roman Church was more aggressive. The pope demanded that the whole world recognize his exclusive right to men's minds as the viceroy of St. Peter and of Jesus Christ Himself. That primacy of the Roman Church was about to be more clearly defined by the Cluniac monk Hildebrand, who took the Throne of Peter as Pope Gregory VII. Gregory dramatized the fact that the bishop of Rome had a separate role above the bishops of the world by restricting the title of papa, or pope, to the bishop of Rome, forbidding the use of that title by anyone else on earth. He went further. Frequently, nobles paid homage to a bishop by kissing his foot. Now Gregory declared that henceforth only the foot of the pope would be kissed by princes, and not voluntarily as an act of respect, but as an enforceable canonical requirement.

As to the divine right of kings, its very divinity meant that it flowed from God to earthly rulers only through the medium of Christ's vicar on earth. In Gregory's view, it was in the power of the pope to bestow or remove that divine right. The pope, therefore, had the power to command citizens of any country to abandon their allegiance to any secular ruler and the power to depose any king or emperor. Reason said that this must be, because spiritual power came directly from God, while secular power was born in original sin.

As a monk, Gregory had taken a vow of celibacy, and he now not only repeated earlier decrees against clerical marriage, but reinforced them. At that time over 50 percent of the Catholic priests in Europe were married, so Gregory's decrees were not well received, even by the bishops. In England, at the Council of Winchester in 1076, the assembled bishops approved the marriage of "residential" priests, those with village parishes or attached as chaplains in castles. In response to the reluctant attitude of the clergy, Gregory sent out legates to enforce his law. All married priests were to set aside their wives. If they did not, they were forbidden to exercise any priestly functions, and the laity were to shun their ministries.

As part of his program to gain ascendancy over the Eastern Christians, Gregory cultivated a friendly relationship with the emperor of Byzantium, Michael VII. The young emperor responded because he needed all the friends he could get. He had asserted his claim to the throne when his father-in-law, the emperor Romanus Diogenes, had been wounded in battle and taken prisoner by the encroaching Seljuk Turks. After his wounds were healed, the Turks set him free. Finding that he had been supplanted by his son-in-law Michael, Romanus tried to regain the throne, but now was taken prisoner by his own people. He was subjected to the standard method in Byzantium (and Venice) for rendering a deposed ruler ineffective without killing him: He was sentenced to be blinded. The executioners were so ferocious in putting out Romanus's eyes, however, that he died a few days later. His friends and relatives were furious and immediately comprised a faction opposed to the young Michael VII, a faction that included the house of Comnenus, the former ruling family.

At the same time, the Eastern Empire lost its last possessions in Italy to the Normans under Robert Guiscard, perhaps inspired by their duke, who had conquered all England just seven years earlier. In 1073, the Turks erupted into Asia Minor, pushing back the Byzantine borders in the same year in which Guiscard and his Normans took Sicily. Pope Gregory encouraged the Normans in Italy because the lands they conquered immediately changed allegiance from the Orthodox Church to the Roman.

Losing lands to the east and to the west, Michael VII tried diplomacy to stabilize the situation. He proposed that the child daughter of Robert Guiscard be betrothed to his own infant son, the heir to the empire. Pope Gregory enthusiastically supported the proposed match, which would make a Roman Catholic the Empress of Byzantium.

In the meantime, it appeared that Michael VII was totally ineffective at staving off the erosion of the Eastern Empire, and in 1078 a provincial governor named Nicephorus rose in revolt. Michael didn't even put up a fight. Instead, he retired to a monastery, putting aside his wife to do so. A practical lady, and one of the most beautiful in the land, she offered her hand to the new emperor, which he accepted. Furious at these developments, Pope Gregory's wedding gift to the new emperor was a decree of excommunication. Within months another revolt was launched, this time by a Byzantine army general who had made a deal with the Turkish sultan Suleiman. The general failed to take Constantinople, but the arrangement had permitted Suleiman to walk right into Bithynia and take the sacred Christian city of Nicaea, which he made his new capital, less than a hundred miles from Constantinople.

With events apparently moving inexorably toward the eclipse of Byzantium, fierce quarrels erupted between the emperor Nicephorus and the Comneni faction. Finally, the old royal family made its move, declared Nicephorus deposed, and proclaimed Alexius Comnenus the new emperor. Pope Gregory excommunicated him, too.

Back home, Gregory had problems of his own. He was not satisfied with the order of things, in which the German Holy Roman Emperor reigned supreme in the temporal world, with the pope supreme only in the spiritual. With his power derived directly from God, surely the pope alone should be supreme, with all other mortals on levels beneath him. One custom that stood in the way of his supremacy was that of lay "investiture." This was the right of kings, princes, and other noblemen to appoint bishops and abbots, who commanded the large religious landholdings in their domains, which in any given area might range from 20 to 40 percent of the land surface. Such appointees owed fealty to the lay rulers who had favored them with their benefices, although "favored with" often meant "sold," as religious appointments became an important source of income for local rulers.

Gregory determined to stop the sale of benefices, a practice called "simony" after Simon Magus, the first recorded purchaser of a spiritual office. The pope decided that henceforth all appointments would be made by the Holy See and not by any layman, no matter how highly placed. This would be a great blow to the secular princes and would mean that the fortunate cleric would owe fealty not to his lay lord, but to the pope alone. The pope introduced his new decree to the world in a council of bishops in 1074. The temporal world was rocked by this new assertion of papal power and the loss of income it would bring. In 1075, Gregory was kidnapped from the altar at the Basilica of St. Mary Major and taken to a house in the suburbs, where he was beaten and insulted until rescued by citizens of Rome the next morning.

Unshaken in his convictions, the pope called another council in 1076. He pronounced the ban on lay investiture in stronger terms, making it clear that not even the Holy Roman Emperor himself could name so much as a subdeacon in his own territories. With this declaration, Gregory was claiming direct and autocratic control by the pope of about one-third of all of Christian Europe. The Holy Roman Emperor, Henry IV, was just twenty years old, but had no intention of giving up one particle of his traditional rights and privileges. He ignored the papal decrees. Gregory wrote to Henry, demanding a notarized written confession of his sins against the Church. Henry's response was to call a council of his own at Worms, at which Gregory was declared to be deposed. Gregory's reaction was to excommunicate Henry and his followers. He declared that Henry was now without power and should be rendered allegiance by no man in any matter of any kind, thus effectively turning the German emperor into a nonperson, with no temporal or spiritual existence.

Henry had underestimated the spiritual power, which he realized as his bishops and nobles began to desert him. Finally, his own people gave him an ultimatum: Have the ban of excommunication removed before February 2, 1077, or be abandoned by all his subjects. Gregory announced that he was coming to Germany to establish order, and Henry immediately headed south to intercept him. Their paths crossed near Mantua, where Gregory was lodged in the castle of Canossa. On January 25, Henry climbed up to the castle in the biting cold, dressed in sackcloth, with his feet bare, as a true penitent. He pleaded for the pope to receive him, but he had to be taught a lesson first. Gregory kept him shivering in the freezing courtyard for three days and three nights, then finally admitted him to the papal presence.

Henry was forgiven and the bans against him lifted, in exchange for his public promise to obey the pope in all things. Then the pope demonstrated for all that he had acted only in accordance with God's will. Taking a piece of consecrated bread from the altar, he called upon God to make the bread stick in his throat and choke him to death if he was guilty of any wrongdoing. He swallowed the bread with ease, and the assembly went wild with cheers and shouts. They had actually witnessed with their own eyes that God had given His approval to this blessed pope's actions.

The pope, however, had done a little underestimating of his own. He may have thought Henry spent all those hours in the freezing courtyard with his mind full of repentance and contrition, but it appears that what Henry's mind was really full of was all-out revenge. It was not long in coming.

Back in Germany, Henry got rid of the disloyal around him, strengthened his army, then invaded Italy and laid siege to Rome. Gregory fled to Hadrian's Mausoleum, a massive circular structure that had been reworked into the papal fortress of Castel Sant'Angelo. Eventually, Gregory was rescued by the Normans under Robert Guiscard, who also took advantage of the expedition to burn and pillage the Holy City. The Normans took Gregory south to Salerno, where he lived in exile until his death in 1085.

Off in Constantinople, the emperor Alexius, still stinging under the ban of excommunication laid upon him by Gregory VII, received the news of the conflicts with great interest. He arranged an alliance with Henry IV, contributing funds to help his campaign against the pope, and closed all of the Roman churches in the Eastern Empire. Gregory's rescue and protection by the same hated Normans who had robbed Byzantium of its Italian possessions simply added to the pope's image as the arch enemy of the Orthodox Church.

Henry had a council appoint a pope of his choosing, Archbishop Guibert of Ravenna, who was installed in Rome as Clement III. Upon Gregory's death in exile, with the anti-pope Guibert in Rome, the cardinals still loyal to the Church elected the abbot of the Benedictine abbey of Monte Cassino as Pope Victor III. A frail man, Victor had no chance to accomplish anything before his death less than two years later. It was not until March 1088 that the cardinals could agree upon the next pope. He was Odo de Lagery, the shrewd cardinal-bishop of Ostia, who took the papal name of Urban II.

The new pope could see nothing about him but political and spiritual desecration. The strongest ruler in western Christendom was not only the strongest temporal enemy of the Roman Church, but was in league with the emperor of Byzantium, the strongest spiritual enemy of the Roman Church. The anti-pope Guibert sat on the Throne of Peter. The revenues of the Church had dropped to almost nothing. It was a situation calculated to plunge any ordinary man into despair, but Urban II was no ordinary man and no ordinary pope. Although fixed and determined in his purpose, he did not seek to achieve it with the arrogance of a Gregory VII. He was persuasive, conciliatory, courteous, and compromising. In that day and age, gentleness and courtesy put other men off their guard. Urban gradually earned the support of more and more of the independent princes. Spain was all for him. The clergy in France gradually came under his complete control. He encouraged Henry IV's son Conrad in his complaints, to the point that he revolted against his father.

In 1089, Urban lifted the ban of excommunication that Gregory had placed on the Emperor Alexius, which elicited a friendly response from that monarch. By 1093 Urban was able to return to Rome to take up residence in the Lateran Palace. He had avoided repeating Gregory's aggressive claims for superiority over all temporal rulers. As a result, even though the princes of Europe were still constantly in conflict with one another, the papacy had survived and now enjoyed a position of respect. Urban II had a view of the posture and supremacy of the Roman Church that was just as strong as Gregory's, but his approach was different. He was biding his time, waiting for the right event. His opportunity came from the east, in the form of a letter from the emperor Alexius.

The emperor needed help. Although the Byzantine Empire was still wealthy, it just did not have the population base to supply the troops required to protect the Balkans, the Danube territories, and Asia Minor, much less the capital itself, so Alexius had to rely on mercenaries. He had recruited nomadic tribesmen from the steppes, Norman adventurers, even Anglo-Saxon refugees from the conquest of England. The Normans had turned against him and Alexius desperately needed experienced fighting men. With nowhere else to turn, he appealed to the pope in the name of their common Christianity. In his correspondence Alexius recited a litany of Turkish atrocities: Christian boys were crudely circumcised, then held so that their blood would fall into the baptismal font; women and girls were abused like animals; Turkish soldiers committed the sin of sodomy on captured Christian men of every rank "and, O misery, something that has never been seen or heard of before, on bishops." Early in the year 1095 the pope called for the first formal council of his reign, to be convened in March at Piacenza. There Urban permitted the envoys from the emperor Alexius to present their plea for soldiers to take up the Christian cause in Asia Minor, but there was little enthusiasm for the prospect within the council.

For Urban II, however, the opportunity was just too great to be dismissed. As a plan formed in his mind, the plight of the Eastern Empire seemed almost like a gift from God. In one plan lay so many benefits. He envisioned a Holy War, a war in the service of God. The Christians would take possession of the Holy Land which had been wrenched from Byzantium by the fanatical followers of Muhammad, and restore it to Christian control, or better still, to Roman control. A common goal that put European Christians all on the same side would curtail their never-ending fights among themselves. Land would be available for the younger sons of the nobility, for now that laws of primogeniture were taking hold, all but the eldest sons were landless and turning into adventurers and near-bandits. The Church would have to play the lead role because men of many nations would be involved, and as a result all would recognize the leadership and primacy of Holy Mother Church. And surely the rescue of the Holy Places, as well as the protection of the Eastern Empire and of the Eastern Church, could be met with no level of Byzantine gratitude less than their acknowledgment of the total supremacy of the Roman pontiff who had effected it all.

That summer Urban traveled across France, testing the temperament of nobles and clerics, assessing the measures to be taken, formulating his plan. He sent letters to bishops throughout the principalities of France and neighboring countries, directing them to come to Clermont for a great council. About three hundred clerics answered the call to the Council of Clermont, which began on November 18, 1095. Allowing plenty of time for stragglers to arrive, it was proclaimed that all should attend a public session on Tuesday, November 27, at which time the pope would make a momentous announcement.

The crowd that assembled for the great event was so large that the cathedral could not hold them all, so the session was moved to a field outside the city. A high platform was built to raise the papal throne above the crowd.

There was no underlying anger against the Muslims, about whom almost nothing was known in Europe, except on the Iberian Peninsula. (As an example of just how little was known, the Greek emperor had described atrocities by tribes of nomadic Turks on the Syrian border, tribes the Greeks called *Sarakenos*. The word became *Saracenus* in Church Latin, and was misunderstood as a reference to all followers of Muhammad. In every subsequent papal bull and encyclical, the mistake lived on as the entire Muslim population of Turks, Arabs, Persians and Egyptians was referred to as the "Saracens". On the other side, some Muslims would decide that all Crusaders were French, and all Latin Christians would be referred to as the "Franj.") Christians in the Holy Land were permitted to practice their religion, and there was no barrier to pilgrims visiting the Holy Places. They had to pay a toll to enter Jerusalem, but they also had to pay a toll to pass through the gates of London or Paris. As for the "Saracen" rulers of Palestine, they had no problem with the presence of either Orthodox or Latin Christians in their territory, whether as pilgrims or as permanent residents. The Benedictine Rule prevailed among Roman clerics in Palestine, and was followed by a small order that was permitted to maintain a hostel or "hospital" for Christian pilgrims in Jerusalem. It had been founded about twenty years earlier, in 1075, by citizens of the Italian city of Amalfi. The order was dedicated to St. John the Compassionate, sometimes called St. John the Alms-giver, a seventh-century Patriarch of Alexandria known for his pious works of charity.

With such religious tolerance on the part of the Muslim rulers of Jerusalem, and with access to the Holy Places for Christian pilgrims, it was going to take some skillful effort on the part of the pope to stir up the people of Europe to the point that they would leave their homes to risk their lives in a foreign land.

Urban II was up to the task, and as he rose to address the crowd he employed all of the propaganda techniques the job required. He inspired hatred for the Muslims by allegations of horrible physical atrocities worked upon helpless Christians. He appealed to his listeners' quest for glory by comparing the proposed conflict with the victories of Charlemagne over the pagans. He held out the promise of land, catering to the frustrations of the noninheriting younger sons of the nobility: "Wrest that land from the wicked race, and subject it to yourselves. That land which the scripture says 'floweth with milk and honey.'" He held out the ultimate reward, an eternity in paradise, by declaring that all who died in this Holy Crusade would receive instant absolution and the total remission of sins. As Urban completed his inflammatory oration there were cries of *"Deus lo volt!"* ("God wills it!"). The entire audience took up the chant, and it became the battle cry of the First Crusade. Adhemar de Monteil, Bishop of le Puy, was the first to kneel before the papal throne to plead for permission to go with the host to the Holy Land.

Urban was pleased with the enthusiasm let loose by his call for a Holy War, but now needed to give it substance. He reassembled his bishops, and regulations were adopted. Any man who took the vow to join the Crusade must fulfill that vow or risk excommunication. Any man who went on the Crusade, but returned home before its mission was accomplished, would be excommunicated. Every man who took the vow was to wear a cross made of red cloth sewn to his surcoat as a public declaration of his vow. Those who feared for their possessions while away on Crusade could leave them for safekeeping with their local bishops, who would be held responsible for their safe and complete return. Those not physically fit were to be discouraged from participation.

All were to be prepared to leave the following summer by August 15, the Feast of the Assumption, when the southern harvests would be in and available to supply the armies. The various military factions could take different routes to the east, but they were to gather at Constantinople to launch their common campaign.

Above all, the Crusade would need a leader, and since all the world must know and recognize that this was to be an army of God controlled by His Holy Church, that leader must be a religious leader, responsible only to the pope. The papal choice was Bishop Adhemar of le Puy (his being the first to kneel before the pope at Clermont was probably arranged in advance).

Urban II was French, and most of the leaders who answered his call were of the French nobility, although the Germans and the Normans of southern Italy were well represented. Genoa agreed to help with men and shipping. Godfrey de Bouillon, duke of Lower Lorraine, sold and mortgaged his lands to finance a fighting force that he would command. Count Raymond of Toulouse assembled a force at his own expense. Robert Guiscard's son, Prince Bohemond of Taranto, declared for the cross, as did Duke Robert of Normandy, Count Robert of Flanders, and Hugh of Vermandois, the brother of the king of France. Success appeared to be assured. The emperor Alexius had asked for some help: He was about to be swamped.

In Constantinople, the news that the request for a few thousand mercenaries was being answered by the approach of whole armies, including about fifteen thousand knights, was met with alarm. Somehow they must be contained and directed right through the empire across to Asia Minor. If they weren't fed, they would forage and take what they wanted. Food stores were assembled and rushed to points the Crusaders were expected to pass. Those measures undoubtedly helped, but there was no effective way to contain entire armies on the move who practiced their skills in pillage and rape on the citizens of the empire. As the Christian armies gathered outside Constantinople, they were constantly reminded by the Greeks of the rich lands and the fabulous treasures that awaited them across the Bosphorus, as an incentive for them to move on.

Finally, the Crusaders were ferried across the straits and moved overland to their first bittersweet victory. After laying siege to the ancient city of Nicaea and fighting off counterattacks on their rear by the Turkish cavalry, they had the city at the point of surrender. It was a shock to awake one morning to find the banner of the emperor of Byzantium flying over the walls. The commander had surrendered to Alexius during the night, preferring the diplomacy-oriented Byzantines to the ferocious army of Latin Christians. The Crusaders were deprived of the loot, the captives, and the ransoms they had expected. Feelings against the eastern emperor were high. Alexius soothed the Latin leaders with lavish gifts, but stirred them up again when he demanded an oath of allegiance to himself as the price of his ongoing cooperation. The emperor especially wanted returned to him the great walled city of Antioch, which the Crusaders would have to take to clear their path to Jerusalem. Some were reluctant, some were angry, but the emperor's supplies were vital, and his armies would be the only protection at their backs. If the war turned against them, Alexius controlled the escape routes, whether by land or sea. Finally, the absence of alternatives made the decision for them, and they agreed to swear fealty to the emperor. For Alexius, the oaths would be binding forever. For the Latin Crusaders, their oaths were good for as long as it took to get out of the trap they were in.

Bishop Adhemar constantly reminded them that they had not yet achieved their sworn objectives, and at last a portion of the crusading army turned south toward Jerusalem under the leadership of the bishop, with the military command entrusted to Raymond of Toulouse. Others, led by Godfrey de Bouillon and Prince Bohemond, soon followed. They were attacked and harassed along the way, but managed to arrive in time to participate in the siege of Antioch.

The Muslim ruler of Antioch had not interfered in any way with those of his subjects who preferred to practice their faith in Orthodox Christianity. They had been allowed to operate their churches unmolested, under their own resident patriarch. Now, with the approach of the Crusader army, things changed. The patriarch was thrown into a dungeon, and the Christian leaders were ejected from the city. The great Orthodox Cathedral of St. Peter was closed to Christians and converted into use as a stable for the Muslim cavalry that was called in to help defend the city.

The Crusaders were awestruck at their first view of Antioch, a walled and heavily fortified metropolis a mile wide and three miles long. Doubtful of their ability to take the city by storm, they settled down for a long siege. They camped before Antioch for months, suffering from severe shortages of food and water, while the Turks taunted them from time to time by hanging the patriarch over the walls in a cage. The Crusaders sat before those walls from October until June, but it was not force of arms alone that achieved the final victory. Word had come to Bohemond weeks before that an officer in the Turkish army, an Armenian Christian named Firuz, who had been converted to Islam, was prepared to sell out the city of Antioch for a price. He had been disciplined by a Turkish superior and wanted revenge. Negotiations went on until Bohemond almost lost interest, but then word arrived that the traitor would turn over the city the very next night, when he was to be in command of two adjoining towers. He was even prepared to hand over his son as a hostage to guarantee his performance. Apparently Firuz had finally made up his mind to move upon discovering that his wife was cuckolding him with a Turkish officer.

True to his word, Firuz saw to it that the Crusaders were permitted to put ladders to a tower window. Sixty knights made the climb, then moved along the wall to take the second tower. Ladders were placed on the wall between the towers and enough Crusaders entered the city to take and open two separate gates. The Crusader army, waiting in the dark, swarmed into the city. Eight months of frustration were unleashed in the slaughter of civilians as well as soldiers, with no consideration for sex or age. The Christians in the city joined in the butchery. It took a long time to kill them all, but by nightfall of the next day every Turk in Antioch was dead. As the leader who had engineered the victory, Bohemond successfully asserted his right to rule the captured city, over the objections of Count Raymond of Toulouse.

When the army had turned south to Antioch, one Crusader had decided to leave the group to pursue his own hopes for land and treasure. Had he stayed at home, history would probably never have heard of Baldwin, the youngest brother of Godfrey of Bouillon. Godfrey was duke of Lower Lorraine and his brother Eustace was Count of Boulogne, but there were no lands for young Baldwin. He wouldn't need them, because his family had decided that Baldwin would be trained for the Church. After some years of study, however, he abandoned that life and chose to live the life of a knight at the court of Godfrey, with no one realizing the ambition that burned inside him. He took the Crusader's vow with Godfrey because there were no other prospects ahead of him, but now the Crusade opened new opportunities, which he was quick to seize. He was very mindful of Urban II's admonition that the Crusaders should take for themselves those lands that scripture said "floweth with milk and honey."

Baldwin could see no material benefit to himself in marching south to be a minor factor in the siege of Antioch, so he decided to head east toward the Euphrates River, on an expedition of adventure. He had no large following in the Christian armies, but was able to enlist about a hundred loot-hungry armored knights to accompany him.

As he traveled east toward Mesopotamia (modern Iraq), Baldwin was not entering Muslim lands, but those of the Armenians of the Separated Church, long dominated by the Orthodox Byzantines, whom the Armenians regarded as heretics. Three Christian cultures were about to clash, but at first the Armenians regarded the approaching Roman Catholic knights as their long-sought liberators. The population cheered them as they passed through, and some Armenian troops joined Baldwin on his march. Prince Thoros of Edessa, a principality to the east of the Euphrates, was burdened by the constant threat of Turkish strongholds to the north and east, and he got a message to Baldwin urging him to come all the way through to Edessa.

By winter, Baldwin had reached the Euphrates River, having captured two Turkish fortresses along the way. Short of trusted men of his own, he gave command of the captured bases to Armenian nobles, thereby enhancing his growing reputation as the liberator of the Armenians.

Thoros was now in a state of panic. Word had reached him that Kerboga, the vicious emir of Mosul, was assembling an army that he would lead to the relief of Antioch. Edessa was directly in his path, and the Armenians on both sides of the river could look forward to wholesale massacre. Messengers from Thoros had miscalculated. He thought of Baldwin as a mercenary whose services were for hire, but Baldwin, with dreams of a kingdom of his own, wanted much more than pay. Finally, an embassy arrived from Thoros with a proposal that could make that fantasy a reality. In exchange for his help, Thoros would legally adopt Baldwin, who would then be his only son and heir. Further, they would immediately begin to rule jointly. For Thoros, half a country was better than none.

Baldwin accepted the offer and set off to Edessa, accompanied by eight knights. Arriving on February 6, 1098, while the siege of Antioch was still bogged down and the threat of a relieving force under Kerboga lay heavy in the air, Baldwin was greeted by Prince Thoros and the Christian Armenian population as their savior. Thoros acted quickly to keep his part of the bargain with a public ceremony of adoption. There was nothing Christian about the proceedings, as the participants acted out an ancient pagan allegorical ritual of birth. Thoros and Baldwin, stripped to the waist, were clothed in one double-size garment. After rubbing their naked chests together, Baldwin came out of the garment, to symbolize his coming out of the body of Thoros. After going through exactly the same ceremony with the princess, he emerged as their legal son and heir.

The status of Baldwin as co-ruler gave the Armenian population the courage to do something they had previously discussed only in whispers. They hated Thoros, not only for his greed, which manifested itself in high taxation, but because he had left their Separated Armenian Church to join the despised Greek Orthodox Church, in order to curry favor with the emperor of Byzantium. They rose in revolt, confident that they would have a better ruler in Baldwin. Thoros turned to his co-ruler for protection, but Baldwin, who probably knew about the revolt in advance, advised him to surrender to the people. Deserted by his palace guards, Thoros attempted to escape through a window, only to be beaten and slashed to death by the angry mob waiting below, who enthusiastically confirmed Baldwin as their sole ruler. To consolidate that position, Baldwin used the treasure of Edessa to attract support for his new kingdom, and a number of crusading knights, on their way to support the siege of Antioch, turned aside for the more immediate benefits of Baldwin's generosity.

This influx of Frankish knights, who were given positions of authority and gifts of Armenian lands, incited some Armenian nobles to attempt a second revolt, this time against Baldwin the upstart. Unfortunately for them, the plot was revealed before it could erupt, and Baldwin reacted swiftly and brutally. The two ringleaders were seized and blinded. Other leaders of the group were sentenced to have their noses or feet cut off. The wealthy nobles involved were permitted to buy their way out of blindness or mutilation with the payment of exorbitant fines. That money rebuilt Baldwin's treasury but shattered the power of the nobles, who were reduced to near-poverty.

Now firmly in control, Baldwin styled himself as count of Edessa, establishing the first of the four great Latin Christian principalities that would make up the kingdom of Jerusalem. He had quickly reached what even he might have thought of as the zenith of power, but there was greater glory in store. With his daring and ruthless determination, perhaps it was inevitable that Baldwin would later take his place in the royal succession as a future king of Jerusalem.

Although Jerusalem was only ten days' march away, the Crusaders in Antioch settled down for a full year, perhaps because an epidemic, which now appears to have been typhoid, took the life of the papal legate, Bishop Adhemar of le Puy. The leadership was left to the competing secular lords, without the papal voice that had held them together in common cause. Bishop Adhemar had been a diplomat, working to hold disputes between temporal leaders to a minimum and treating the Orthodox clergy with respect and generosity, resembling his lord the pope in his ability to handle men who didn't want to be handled. From now on, it would be rough-and-tumble.

A diplomat would have been useful in dealing with the envoys that came to the Crusaders from the Shiite rulers of Egypt. The Egyptians had taken Jerusalem from the Sunni Turks just a few months earlier, while the Turks were occupied with fending off the Crusader invasion. They suggested to the Christian leaders that since the Turks were their common enemy, they should work together. The government at Cairo would welcome and guarantee the safety of all Christian pilgrims to the Holy Places. Their overtures were rejected. The Crusaders demanded nothing less than total conquest, and made ready to move on Jerusalem fully fifteen months after their arrival before the walls of Antioch. Turks or Egyptians, it made no difference to the crusading leaders. All Muslims were infidels, and all infidels were the enemies of Christ and his Church.

The Crusaders marched south, but without Prince Bohemond, who was determined to keep and build his new principality of Antioch. They took a number of towns and villages as they proceeded, but the most excitement was generated by their occupation of the almost totally Christian town of Bethlehem. Having actually rescued the birthplace of the Savior, the invaders were imbued with a new wave of religious fervor. A message arrived from the emperor Alexius, offering to join them for the assault on Jersualem if they would wait for his arrival. If anything, that message spurred the Crusaders to greater speed, and at last, on June 7, 1099, they found themselves before the walls of Jerusalem.

Upon the approach of the Crusaders, the Egyptian governor of Jerusalem had destroyed or poisoned the water wells around the city and had driven away the flocks surplus to his own needs. All of the Christians in the city were told to leave, not as an act of mercy, but to place the additional burden of their needs for food and water on the invaders. One of the ejected Christians was Gerard, master of the Amalfi hostel in the city, who immediately approached the Christian leaders to share all he knew of the layout and the defenses of Jerusalem. His intelligence was most welcome.

The siege of Jerusalem lasted for about six miserable weeks. No one had warned the Crusaders about the heat, particularly unbearable to men who had to wear clothing under armor, with no shade to keep the sun from beating down on that armor all day long. No one had told these men, used to the heavily forested areas of Europe, that there was no timber around Jerusalem for the construction of siege engines. The material had to be brought from the coast or from the forests of Samaria, requiring as many as sixty Muslim prisoners to carry a single beam. They had not expected to travel a twelve mile round trip for water for themselves and their animals.

Chroniclers state that the Crusader army in front of Jerusalem numbered about twelve hundred knights and twelve thousand foot soldiers. At just two meals per day, the army would have required food for over twenty-six thousand meals every single day, not counting the needs of the civilian Christians dependent upon them. Then, after six weeks of agonizing physical discomforts, multiplied by severe deficiencies in food and water, word came from Cairo that the Egyptians were marshalling a large force to relieve the city. A feeling of despair and panic ran through the Christian army.

As if in answer to their prayers, a priest in the Christian camp reported that he had had a vision. The good bishop Adhemar of le Puy had appeared to him and given him the conditions under which the Crusaders would be granted the victory. First, they were to put aside all sinning, all selfish ambitions, and all quarrels among themselves. Next, they were to fast and pray for three days. On the third day they were to process in humility with bare feet around the walls of God's holy city. With all of these conditions met, God would grant them the victory within nine days. The vision was accepted as valid, and the leaders ordered the entire army to comply. After two days of fasting, they shed their footwear and began the two mile walk around the city. Up on the walls, the Egyptian defenders looked down on the barefoot Crusaders with shouted taunts and laughter, urinating on crosses held up in view of the penitent marchers.

Fortunately, the prophecy was helped along by a surge of activity to complete three siege towers. To roll them up to the walls at the selected positions, it was first necessary to fill in portions of the great ditch or dry moat in front of the wall. This was done, but at great cost; a constant barrage of stones and unquenchable Greek fire was rained down on the Christians by the defenders on the wall. By the evening of July 13 the army was ready and began to roll the giant siege towers into position. Raymond of Toulouse positioned his tower at the wall first, but could not get his men across the bridge from the tower to the wall. Godfrey de Bouillon had his tower against the north wall by morning and dropped the bridge to the top of the wall. Hand to hand combat went on for hours, but by noon Godfrey had men on the city wall. Other men beat their way over the bridge to support them, and soon Godfrey commanded enough of the wall to permit the safe use of scaling ladders to bring more and more men to him. When he had a large enough party, he sent them to open the Gate of the Column (the Damascus Gate near Solomon's Quarries), and the main Crusader force poured into the city. Jerusalem had been taken on the ninth day, as the prophecy had promised.

Seized by a frenzy of vengeful blood lust after weeks of suffering outside the walls, the victorious Crusaders cut their way through the streets, breaking open houses, shops, and mosques and butchering every man, woman, and child they could find.

One of the reports to the pope read, "If you would hear how we treated our enemies at Jerusalem, know that in the portico of Solomon and in the Temple our men rode through the unclean blood of the Saracens, which came up to the knees of their horses."

Word spread that the local Muslims sometimes swallowed their gold as the surest way to hide it, and thereafter disemboweling became a common practice in the search for plunder.

Hoping to avoid the maniacal slaughter, the Jews crowded into their principal synagogue to give notice that they were not Muslims. The Crusaders burned down the synagogue, killing them all. The priest Raymond of Aguilers, in writing about the mutilated corpses that covered the Temple area, quoted Psalm 118: "This is the day the Lord has made. Let us rejoice and be glad in it."

The one merciful gesture in the insane bloodbath came from Raymond of Toulouse, after his men had encircled the citadel of the city known as the Tower of David. The Egyptian emir in charge offered to surrender if Raymond would guarantee a safe conduct out of Jerusalem for himself and his troops. Raymond agreed and walked the extra mile, providing an armed escort all the way back to the safety of the coastal city of Ascalon for the defeated defenders of the Tower. They did not forget that a man could stake his life on the personal honor of Raymond of Toulouse.

An interesting aftermath of the First Crusade lay in the treatment of the little order that had run the Amalfi hostelry for pilgrims. In gratitude for their information and assistance, and in the flush of victory, they were rewarded with gifts of treasure and grants of land. They were able to expand their operations under the enthusiastic sponsorship of the new Christian rulers. By about 1130, their new prior, a French nobleman, would decide that they should do more than just provide lodging and care for pilgrims. They would accept knights into their order and have a military arm that would fight for the Holy Land, calling themselves the Order of the Hospital of St. John of Jerusalem, the "Hospitallers." But that was all in the future. The immediate need was for the leading Crusaders to pick a ruler for the newly conquered Christian kingdom.

2

The Kingdom of Jerusalem
1100 to 1118

WHATEVER INSTRUCTIONS Pope Urban II had given his legate with regard to the ultimate control and government of Jersualem, they had died with the good Bishop Adhemar of le Puy. Nor could the pope be consulted: He died only two weeks after the conquest of Jerusalem, before news of the Christian victory could reach him. The pontiff may have envisioned the Holy Land as a papal state, but now the secular Crusaders saw themselves as the victors to whom the spoils belonged.

The French nobles saw Jerusalem as the basis for a feudal kingdom, with the surrounding lands held in fiefdom in the same system they were familiar with at home. They decided to begin by electing a sovereign, but the priests among them objected. Even if a secular kingdom was called for, how could a king be chosen and crowned without the guidance of a patriarch of the Church? The clerics' complaint was discussed politely and rejected totally.

The new king was to be selected from a group narrowed down to four great nobles. Of the eligible four, Robert of Normandy and Robert of Flanders declined to be considered, since they planned to go home as soon as Jerusalem was secure. Of the remaining two candidates, Raymond of Toulouse was thought by some to be the clear choice, in consideration of his age, wealth, and experience, but he was not popular among the Christian leaders. Raymond was a pompous, arrogant man, much taken with his own importance. His overbearing attitude had been a constant source of annoyance throughout the entire Crusade. Some condemned him for his unilateral decision to allow the Egyptian garrison to escape unharmed from the Tower of David. Most important, the nobles did not want a leader like Raymond, who would most certainly interfere in whatever plans they might have for themselves.

The fourth candidate was Godfrey de Bouillon, a man of a different stripe. A raging tiger on the battlefield, Godfrey was an intensely pious, humble creature at home. As some of the nobles sounded out Godfrey's own people, they learned that even Godfrey's own chaplains felt that he was overzealous in his piety. He spent hours at a time on his knees. He carried his prayers of thanksgiving to such tedious lengths that often his staff had to eat their meals cold or unappetizingly overcooked. Godfrey de Bouillon seemed the ideal choice: His ferocity in storming the walls of Jerusalem and his high birth and exemplary moral standards would make him an attractive leader to present to the Christian world, while his preoccupation with religious observances should keep him nicely distracted from the duties of government. That would be a very satisfactory state of affairs for greedy vassals who did not really want to be governed. Thus Godfrey de Bouillon, duke of Lower Lorraine, became the first ruler of the kingdom of Jerusalem, but not as king. True to the nobles' evaluation of him, Godfrey accepted the authority and responsibility entrusted to him, but would not accept a royal title. No man, he declared, should be called a "king" in Christ's own city. Nor should any man wear a crown of gold where Christ had worn a crown of thorns. Godfrey asked to be known as the *Advocatus Sancti Sepulchri,* Defender of the Holy Sepulcher.

With the secular government in place, the barons were prepared to address the leadership of the Church. They decided to select a patriarch for Jerusalem and bestowed the position on a man who must have been the least suitable candidate available. Arnulf Malecorne was a priest who had never held any position in the Church hierarchy, but he was well liked by the Normans and Lorrainers who now controlled Jerusalem. They considered him a good companion and easily overlooked Arnulf's inability to resist the temptation of worldly pleasures, including attractive women. His departures from his priestly vows were so frequent and so flagrant that they had served as the inspiration for a number of lewd poems and songs in the army. The most concrete barrier to Malecorne's advancement, however, was his illegitimate birth: Church law strictly forbade making a bastard a bishop.

In his favor, Arnulf was chaplain to Robert, duke of Normandy, and had been of service to Robert's father, William the Conqueror. He had also acted as tutor to William's daughter Cecilia, who had pressured her brother Robert into promising that one day he would make Arnulf a bishop. Best of all, Arnulf was not a man who would be likely to intrude into secular affairs.

Not that the new patriarch didn't enjoy his power, but he was careful to exercise it only in ecclesiastical matters. The Latins applauded his action in forcibly ejecting the Greek Orthodox priests from the Church of the Holy Sepulcher. Those priests had hidden a major portion of the cross on which the Savior had died and would not reveal its hiding place. As Arnulf's prisoners, they finally broke down when faced with the very real threat of hideous torture and took the patriarch to the section of the church wall in which they had sealed the holy relic. Arnulf triumphantly took possession of the True Cross, which instantly became the most valuable object in all Christendom.

What none of them realized yet was that just before he died Pope Urban II had appointed a replacement for the deceased legate, Adhemar of le Puy. He was Daimbert, archbishop of Pisa, and he was already on his way to the Holy Land, accompanied by a fleet of Pisan followers. Daimbert was a controversial figure. He had caused trouble wherever he was sent and had been the subject of serious accusations in Spain for liberally helping himself to Church funds. On the other hand, Daimbert was an excellent organizer, a champion of Church rights, and a strong advocate for papal supremacy. He had no doubts as to his new duties: The Holy Land belonged to the Church, and the pope had designated Archbishop Daimbert of Pisa to rule over it. His arrival would spell trouble.

Up to that point, the only troubling news came from the western frontier. The threat of an approaching Egyptian army had spurred the Crusaders to accelerate their efforts to take Jerusalem, and now word arrived that the Egyptian army was continuing its advance. Reports spoke of a host of over fifty thousand men under the personal leadership of al-Afdal, the vizier of Egypt.

A mounted troop under Godfrey's brother Eustace was sent to reconnoiter from Jerusalem to the coast, to ascertain the location and strength of the enemy. Fortunately, Eustace managed to capture some of the vizier's advance scouts, who were subjected to the usual painful interrogation process until they revealed all they knew. A messenger was sent to tell Godfrey that al-Afdal was apparently not alert for combat but was relaxing in camp, waiting for Egyptian ships to arrive with military supplies before his march on Jerusalem. Godfrey was urged to muster the Crusader forces for a surprise counterattack.

The Christian nobles had dispersed after Godfrey's election, to look after the lands they had been given, but they recognized the common danger. It took them a few days to gather their followers and reassemble, but on August 11, less than four weeks after their victory over Jerusalem, the Crusaders were again ready for battle.

About twelve hundred knights, with nine thousand men-at-arms and infantry, began their march to the coast to meet a Muslim army that outnumbered them five to one.

At dawn the next day the Christian scouts found the Egyptian army camped near the sea outside the walled city of Ascalon. Godfrey took the left wing, facing the city. Raymond of Toulouse commanded the right wing that would drive along the shore. The center was divided among the followers of Robert of Flanders, Bohemond's nephew Tancred, and Robert of Normandy. Experienced now in working together, they took their positions with speedy efficiency and launched the charge as soon as they were in place. For the first time, the True Cross was borne in front of them to solicit God's favor against the unbelievers.

For the unsuspecting Egyptians, many of whom were still asleep, the sudden onslaught was devastating. Scrambling out of their tents to see what the pandemonium and shouting were about, most of them had no time to don their protective armor or to reach their horses. Robert of Normandy rode right for the vizier's magnificent pavilion and personally cut down the standard bearer who tried to stop him. Al-Afdal, shielded by his bodyguards, managed to gain the refuge of the city, but his army was lost. A large group of Egyptian soldiers sought safety in a dense grove of sycamore trees, which the Christians surrounded and set ablaze. Fugitives trying to escape the fire were hacked down with sword or ax, so none survived. Those fleeing along the shore were killed or driven into the sea to drown.

It was a resounding victory for the Christian army, and the loot was more than any of them had ever seen before. The chests brought on campaign by al-Afdal and his emirs were broken open to reveal hoards of gold coins, precious stones, and magnificent silk robes. There was so much plunder that the entire Christian army couldn't carry it all. They loaded as much as they could of the most valuable treasure, then set fire to what was to be left behind.

The tragedy of the battle was that the victors missed the greatest prize of all, the city of Ascalon. It was a fatal error that would eventually be corrected only at the cost of thousands of Christian lives. Ascalon would have been a convenient port through which to bring pilgrims and supplies to Jerusalem. It would have provided protection for the Crusaders from further Egyptian incursions. It would have opened up the entire Palestinian coast to the Christians, and it was theirs for the taking, thwarted only by a side of Godfrey de Bouillon that no one had seen before.

The merchant leaders of Ascalon, much more inclined to be ruled by Latin Christians than by the antagonistic Egyptian Shiites, could foresee high potential for profitable trade. They agreed among themselves that they would turn their city over to the Crusaders, but they had to deal first with an overriding concern. They had heard vivid details of the senseless butchery at Jerusalem and dreaded the possibility of a similar madness being loosed on them. How could one trust such blood-crazy people? On the other hand, they had played host to the garrison that had been permitted to leave the Tower of David on the word of Raymond of Toulouse, who had gone so far as to send an escort of his own troops to guarantee their safe passage to the sea. There was one Christian noble, at least, whose word could be trusted.

An envoy came to the Crusaders, offering to surrender the city of Ascalon on the sole condition that such surrender would be made to no one other than Raymond of Toulouse, who would be asked to guarantee the safety of the citizens of the city. The condition was firm and not open to discussion or negotiation. The Christian nobles were delighted at the prospect of this valuable, bloodless victory that would give Jerusalem its own seaport. All, that is, except Godfrey de Bouillon, who took the condition as an unforgivable personal insult. The barons pleaded with him, only to learn that piety is no guarantee of humility. If Ascalon was to be a part of the kingdom of Jerusalem, that relationship must begin by recognizing the unquestioned personal supremacy of the Defender of the Holy Sepulcher. They must make their surrender only to Godfrey de Bouillon.

The citizens of Ascalon would not budge, nor would Godfrey. To make things worse, envoys came from the Muslim seaport city of Arsuf, to the north on the other side of Jaffa. The leaders of Arsuf also agreed to surrender to the Christians, but only to Raymond of Toulouse. Godfrey, offended to the point of rage, sent them home. Raymond of Toulouse was also enraged, but at Godfrey's behavior.

The consequence of Godfrey de Bouillon's obstinate pride was that Ascalon remained in Muslim hands for another fifty years. When it was finally conquered by military action, it took a dreadful toll in Christian lives, some of them represented by the headless bodies of Knights Templar hanging from the walls.

Robert of Flanders and Robert of Normandy agreed that Godfrey had aborted the whole concept of the Crusade. It should be for the glory of Jesus Christ, not for the glory of the impoverished duke of Lower Lorraine. To keep their own vows, they prayed at the Church of the Holy Sepulcher, visited Christ's birthplace at Bethlehem and bathed in the waters of the Jordan River. Their vows fulfilled in every part, they announced that they were going home and would take their armies with them. Raymond, who wanted no more to do with Godfrey de Bouillon, decided to head north with his forces, not homeward bound, but to carve out a principality of his own from the Muslim lands that the Crusaders had passed by in their push to get to Jerusalem. Godfrey's cousin Baldwin of Le Bourg went with Raymond, seeing no future for himself at Jerusalem, not dreaming that he would one day sit on the throne that Godfrey had established.

Bohemond's nephew Tancred stayed with Godfrey de Bouillon, but not for long. He was unhappy with his role at Godfrey's court and had watched his uncle Bohemond and Godfrey's younger brother Baldwin of Edessa carve out territories of their own. That was the route Tancred was determined to follow for himself. On that quest, he rode out of Jerusalem with just twenty-four knights, accompanied by a handful of mounted servants and men-at-arms. He headed up into Galilee, striking first at the city of Nablus.

Tancred's raid was a masterpiece of unintentional good timing. He was riding into an area that had been cut off from Egyptian support by the defeat at Ascalon, while to the other side the emir of Damascus was fully occupied with internal troubles. Tancred's small force took Nablus with ease, then turned to the larger city of Tiberias. The Muslim soldiers fled upon the news of Tancred's approach. From Tiberias, which he was to make the capital of his new principality of Galilee, Tancred reached out to scoop up Nazareth and Mount Tabor, then one small town after another. He got word to Jerusalem that there was plenty of land and loot to share with knights who would join him. The opportunity to exchange boredom for booty was irresistible. Godfrey watched with growing concern as knights and men-at-arms left his capital to join Tancred, the new self-styled prince of Galilee.

Godfrey de Bouillon, who had conducted himself as all-powerful in the matter of the surrender of Ascalon, now had to face the humbling realities that were to plague the kingdom of Jerusalem throughout its two centuries of existence. Crusaders were militant pilgrims. They took a crusading vow, came to fight, and then went home. The armies that would successfully take over Muslim territory would leave behind a resident Christian community that might not be strong enough to hold the new lands against attack.

The other reality was the the Christian barons, when functioning without a strong ruler, would happily turn on each other for personal gain. Godfrey would have liked to be that strong ruler, but he found himself in command of a mere three hundred knights and two thousand soldiers. That was not a large enough standing army to provide any semblance of security. It was imperative that the Christian nobles work together. Godfrey prayed hard, but to the north Christians were already in conflict with each other.

The arrival of Archbishop Daimbert with the Pisan fleet at Antioch had appeared to be a genuine godsend to Prince Bohemond. He longed to take the nearby Greek coastal city of Lattakieh, which would give Antioch a much-needed port, but he could not take a city that could be supplied by sea and thus withstand a siege for years. He needed a navy to blockade the port, and here with Daimbert was just the fleet to do the job.

Bohemond quickly arrived at an agreement with the archbishop and the Pisans over the division of the anticipated spoils of Lattakieh, and the blockade was effected. Bohemond felt no guilt in breaking his oath to the emperor of Byzantium, while the archbishop felt completely justified in attacking any group that called itself Christian but rejected the true faith by refusing to acknowledge the supremacy of the pope.

A few days later, the homeward bound crusading leaders from Jerusalem arrived at the town of Jabala, near Lattakieh. They were appalled to learn that Bohemond was attacking fellow Christians and, still worse, doing it with the aid of an archbishop. Even more alarming, such a serious rift between the Latins and the Greeks might easily deprive the departing Crusaders of the help they needed from the Greek emperor to get back to their own lands in Europe, whether by land or sea. They sent for Archbishop Daimbert to explain himself.

Whatever pride Daimbert may have felt in his elevation to the rank of archbishop and to the lofty post of papal legate, he was now in the presence of *real* power. He found himself being angrily chastised by the count of Toulouse, the count of Flanders and the duke of Normandy, all men of great wealth and extensive lands and able to wield substantial influence in Rome. It was a situation calling for adaptability. Daimbert offered his accusers no argument, apologized profusely, and assured them that the Pisan blockade would be withdrawn immediately. With the blockade gone, and under threats from three angry noblemen with armies at their backs, Bohemond discovered that he, too, could adapt, and he abandoned his campaign against Lattakieh.

The city was relieved and grateful. The gates were opened to the three Crusader leaders and the banners of Flanders and Normandy were raised next to that of the Byzantine emperor, to show that Lattakieh was under their protection. To give substance to his gratitude, the Greek governor of Cyprus provided ships to take the two Roberts to Constantinople, where the emperor assisted them in their homeward journey.

Daimbert was anxious to move on to Jerusalem to assume his new power, and Bohemond decided to escort him. It was not good politics to continue to neglect his crusading vow, and besides, the kingdom of Jerusalem itself was a not unlikely reward. Godfrey de Bouillon had no children, and there were strong rumors of his rapidly failing health. His new friend, the papal legate, was certain to exercise considerable influence over the appointment of God-frey's successor. Bohemond announced his intention to travel to Jerusalem with Daimbert toward the end of the year, to attend Christmas services in the Church of the Holy Sepulcher.

Off in Edessa, Godfrey's brother Baldwin had heard those same rumors about Godfrey's health, and he had a more direct connection to the royal succession. His older brother Eustace had returned to France, so now Baldwin was Godfrey's closest relative in the Holy Land. No law decreed that the throne of Jerusalem was hereditary, but custom was strong. Baldwin informed Bohemond that he would be joining him in his pilgrimage to the Holy City.

The long passage through what was still Muslim territory was not easy, with shortages of food and water and with Muslim raiders picking off the stragglers, but the pilgrims finally reached Jerusalem on December 21. Godfrey was delighted to greet them, but the patriarch Arnulf was distressed by the arrival of a papal legate. His fears were justified just after Christmas when Archbishop Daimbert, with strong support from Bohemond, got the nobles' approval of his assertion that Arnulf's election had been illegal. Arnulf's patron, Robert of Normandy, had gone home, so he had no strong backing of his own. Arnulf was deposed, and Daimbert of Pisa was unani-mously approved as the true patriarch of Jerusalem. Godfrey knelt in front of the patriarch to pay his homage to the Church.

Bohemond also knelt before Daimbert, and Tancred, prince of Galilee, rode to Jerusalem to offer his homage as well. Archbishop Daimbert misunderstood their motives. Godfrey was truly recog-nizing the supremacy of the Church, while the two princes were asserting that they did not hold their crowns as vassals of Godfrey. Daimbert was disturbed that Baldwin of Edessa had not knelt before him. Did this Baldwin not recognize any power above his own? Did he not recognize the supremacy of Holy Mother Church? He was a man of proven ambition and would bear watching.

Daimbert saw the kingdom of Jerusalem as a papal province, with himself as the sole and proper ruler. Through the months ahead he spent every spare moment with Godfrey, continually making the point that Jerusalem was the city of Jesus Christ and should not have a secular government. Godfrey should surrender the kingdom to God and to Christ's vicar on earth, whose legate was Daimbert of Pisa. Godfrey did not disagree with him, and with Daimbert's help he changed his will to leave the kingdom to the patriarch of Jerusalem, who from then on watched Godfrey's declining health with intense interest.

A fleet arrived from Venice, and arrangements were made to divide with the Venetians any conquests made with their help. The nobles agreed on Acre as the main target, to be assaulted on land by the forces of Godfrey and Tancred while the Venetian fleet would attack from the sea and blockade the port. By now Godfrey was confined to his sickbed in Jerusalem, too ill to accompany his army. Patriarch Daimbert went with the army in order to have a hand in the division of the plunder when the victory over Acre would come, so he was not in Jerusalem on July 18, 1100, when Godfrey finally succumbed to a quiet, painless death.

One of Godfrey's vassals in Jerusalem, who was also a good friend of Godfrey's brother, Baldwin of Edessa, moved quickly, probably through prearrangement. He sent men to occupy the Tower of David and dispatched messengers to Edessa to inform Baldwin of Godfrey's death. He did not send any messengers to the army, which had changed its target from Acre to the smaller city of Haifa, and sent no message to Patriarch Daimbert.

A Venetian in Jerusalem sent the news to his own fleet, so the Venetian admiral took a galley to meet with Tancred and Daimbert, to see if Godfrey's passing was going to alter their joint plans. Daimbert was convinced that no one in Jerusalem would contest Godfrey's will, but just to be certain he sent a messenger to Jerusalem with instructions for his followers to take the Tower of David and hold it for Daimbert's return. When word came back that Godfrey's men had already taken the Tower and had sent for Baldwin of Edessa, Daimbert sent a letter to Bohemond at Antioch. He asked Bohemond to prevent any attempt by Baldwin of Edessa to come to Jerusalem, with open warfare if necessary.

Bohemond didn't get the letter and wouldn't get any for years to come. He had made one raid too many to increase his holdings at the Muslims' expense and had just been captured. The only strong power capable of blocking Baldwin's path to the throne of Jerusalem was now in chains in a Muslim dungeon.

When Baldwin was given the news in Edessa, he sent for his cousin Baldwin of Le Bourg, whom he invested as count of Edessa but as vassal to himself, as the expected king of Jerusalem. Baldwin set out for Jerusalem with a bodyguard of nine hundred knights supported by infantry, traveling through the Christian towns to rally support for his claim to the throne. In the lands in between, the Muslims repeatedly attacked him, resulting in some fierce battles with losses that cut his little force in half, but they did not stop Baldwin's march to the holy city.

On November 9, 1100, Baldwin marched into Jerusalem to the cheers of the citizens, who greeted him as their new ruler. Two days later Baldwin, who did not share his brother Godfrey's attitude toward titles, took the crown of gold and became King Baldwin I of Jerusalem. Daimbert, defeated in his bid for power, moved from his palace in Jerusalem to the monastery on nearby Mount Sion to engage in pious exercises while awaiting his fate. He was relieved to learn that, for the present at least, Baldwin I was quite willing that he continue as patriarch of Jerusalem. Baldwin agreed that with Prince Bohemond in captivity, Tancred should rule as prince of Antioch. As part of the arrangement Tancred relinquished his principality of Galilee to the kingdom of Jerusalem.

Baldwin I was the man the moment required. Without him, there might never have been any real kingdom of Jerusalem. His flamboyant but successful adventures during the First Crusade were well known, which gave hm the aura of a man to be respected, even feared. He was compulsively ambitious but predictable, a man who never made a frivolous or ill-considered threat or promise. As an aggressive, hands-on ruler determined to defend and to expand his kingdom, he spent as much time in the saddle as on the throne.

Baldwin knew the importance of the coast and of trade. Merchants meant income. They didn't go home as soon as a fight was over, but took advantage of times between battles to strengthen their grip on trade and on their property. Baldwin eagerly made agreements with the merchants of Genoa and Venice, whose ships provided his kingdom with all the force of a substantial navy. With their cooperation he soon took the southern coastal cities of Arsuf and Caesarea, with his eye on additional Egyptian ports to the north.

Baldwin I did not permit encroachments on the landward side of his kingdom, but he led raids far to the east, into the land the French Crusaders called *Oultrejourdain,* "Across-the-Jordan." On one such raid, he waited until nightfall to pounce on a sleeping caravan. He captured it easily, pleased with the extensive plunder. When he received word that one of the prisoners was the wife of an important sheikh, and in an advanced stage of pregnancy, King Baldwin visited her in person. He had a tent set up for her and had the richest carpets and cushions selected from the loot of the caravan. He ordered that she be provided with food, water, and attendants, with two she-camels to provide milk for the expected child. Preparing to leave, he took off his own rich royal mantle and draped it over the wide-eyed young woman.

When the Christians left, the despondent sheikh came to the

site to look for his wife's body. When he found her safe, saw the rich furnishings and provisions and even the king's own robe, he was overwhelmed. He swore a sacred oath of gratitude to this chivalrous king. The sheikh's loyalty to his solemn oath would later save Balwin's life.

While King Baldwin of Jerusalem was occupied with building his kingdom, the Egyptians, as might be expected, were planning to tear it down. Early in the fall of 1101 an army of thirty thousand Egyptians marched past Ascalon on their way to Jerusalem. Informed too late to call in other forces, Baldwin had to defend the city with only the small force he had at hand, which meant the Christians were outnumbered twenty-five to one. Fortunately, all of the Christians were experienced in battle, while most of the Egyptians were not, having been drafted for this campaign. With the enemy close at hand, Baldwin made a brief speech to his men. As remembered by his chaplain, Baldwin summed up the life-and-death importance of the impending battle. In essence, he said, "Should you be slain, you will earn a martyr's crown. Should you be victorious, you will win immortal glory. As for flight, forget it. France is too far away!" Baldwin led the charge himself, with Bishop Gerard bearing the True Cross. The fighting was fierce, and the Christian front was so small that many in the horde of Egyptians couldn't get to it. Bloodied by the unrelenting strokes of the armored Crusaders, the Muslim front broke, and before long the entire Egyptian army was retreating at full speed to the safety of Ascalon. Baldwin, fully aware of the danger of having his small army spread out, shouted that death would be the punishment for any man who broke away in pursuit of plunder.

Eight months later the Egyptians came again, this time with an army of twenty thousand made up of Arabs and black Sudanese, both of whom were better fighters than the men of the first expedition. Baldwin rode out, again grossly outnumbered. This time the enemy was not massed, so that at Baldwin's charge they moved around to trap him in a huge circle. Baldwin saw the trap coming and rode off the field to seek shelter in the nearby small walled city of Ramleh.

During the night a lone Arab approached the city wall and demanded that he be taken to Baldwin. Not fearful of one man alone, the guards opened the gate to him and summoned an escort to take him to the king. In response to Baldwin's questioning look the Arab identified himself as the sheikh whose pregnant wife had been so chivalrously cared for by Baldwin during the raid into Oultrejourdain the prior year. In keeping with his vow of eternal gratitude, the sheikh had come to warn Baldwin that the Egyptian army was under orders to take up positions throughout the night, so that by dawn Ramleh would be completely surrounded. If Baldwin was to save his life, he must leave immediately, while there was still a chance to get through the Muslim lines.

It was good advice, which Baldwin followed promptly by ordering the saddling of his favorite horse, a magnificent Arabian called Gazelle, which was famous for its speed. Baldwin was spotted in the darkness galloping through the enemy lines, but none of the men who chased him was on a beast that could even approach the lightning speed of the king's horse as he rode for his life.

The Egyptian wars had emptied Baldwin's treasury, so he decided to get a loan from patriarch Daimbert. With revenues from lands and villages that had been given to the Church, gifts from Europe, and a steady stream of cash gifts from pilgrims, the Church appeared to be the primary place to which to turn for funds. The patriarch respectfully declined the king's petition, asserting that the church treasury held only two hundred marks, which was needed for the maintenance of the clergy. The king was doubtful, but helpless. Then word came to him that an Italan nobleman, Count Roger of Apulia, had sent a gift of one thousand gold marks to the patriarch, designating that it be divided equally between the Church, the Amalfi hospital and the kingdom of Jerusalem. Patriarch Daimbert claimed to know nothing about the gift.

The deposed bishop Arnulf, happy for the chance to get back at his enemy Daimbert, did know about the gift, and told Baldwin where to look for that money, and a lot more. Investigation revealed that Daimbert had pocketed the entire sum. Further investigation produced a total of twenty thousand gold marks that the patriarch managed to skim off for himself out of Church funds. Archbishop Daimbert was removed as patriarch of Jerusalem.

Two years later the Egyptians came again, but by now Baldwin had outposts to warn of their approach, so had time to summon the knights and soldiers of Galilee to join him. They would still have been grossly outnumbered, but providence intervened in the form of two hundred ships arriving from Europe bearing thousands of pilgrims, whose numbers included knights from France, Germany, and England. They were delighted to have the opportunity to take up arms against the infidel, a chance for glory that they had not anticipated. In the battle that followed, the Egyptians were decisively beaten by a much larger army than they had been led to expect.

Not forgetting his plans for the coast, Baldwin sought an alliance with a Genoese fleet in 1104, and with its help took the important Egyptian port city of Acre. The other Christian ports were at points of relatively shallow water, but Acre boasted the best protected deep-water harbor on the coast. The extra benefit was that Baldwin now had the full support of Genoa, which established a major naval and trading base at Acre.

In August 1105 a new Muslim army entered the kingdom of Jerusalem, this time made up of Sunni cavalry from Damascus and Shiite infantry from Egypt, brought together by their common Christian enemy. Baldwin met them near Ramleh, the town from which he had escaped on his swift Arabian horse. The Muslim cavalry followed its usual tactic of riding in close, firing arrows into men and horses, then galloping off too quickly for the heavy horses of the Christian knights to catch them. Baldwin, seeing his knights falling, turned away from the infantry to concentrate all his efforts on the harassing Sunni cavalry. The horsemen finally broke and ran, with no thought for the safety of the Shiite infantry they were leaving stranded. The Muslims on foot were brave enough, but stood no chance against the massive horses and armored men who crashed into them again and again. Most of the Egyptians died in their ranks.

Baldwin's success at Acre encouraged him to seek a similar naval alliance with the combined fleets of Genoa and Pisa for an attack on the great coastal city of Beirut, which was taken in May 1110. Six months later a similar alliance resulted in the capture of Sidon. Baldwin's power now extended well to the north, and he had new, richer lands to distribute to those who would agree to come to the Holy Land to take service under his banner.

Raymond of Toulouse had not gone back to Europe, but during Baldwin's reign had been the guest of the emperor of Byzantium at Constantinople. Still eager for a principality of his own in the Holy Land, Raymond returned with his army and managed to take the city of Tortosa, north of Tripoli. When Raymond of Toulouse died in 1109, his cousin Count William-Jordan took over the campaign and captured the inland town of Arqa, so that Tripoli was effectively surrounded. In July 1109 the Christians finally took the city of Tripoli and set up the last Crusader state, the county of Tripoli. Christians now effectively controlled the coast from Egypt to Cilicia (or Lesser Armenia, in modern Turkey).

In 1118 Baldwin took an expedition into Egypt itself to the great delta of the Nile. No Egyptian soldier had been able to bring him down, but the germ of an unidentified disease did it easily. The strange malady quickly took over his whole system and, a few weeks later, took his life.

His cousin Baldwin of Le Bourg of Edessa traveled to Jerusalem for the royal funeral. From the day he arrived he was hailed as the new king of Jerusalem. He was crowned King Baldwin II on April 14, 1118, following the Easter Sunday service. A few weeks later he would change the course of crusading history by giving his royal blessing to a new religious order of warrior monks, knights who took sacred vows to live and die for the True Cross.

3

The Knights of the Temple
1118 to 1139

$\mathcal{H}$UGH DE PAYENS, a knight of the lower nobility of Champagne, approached King Baldwin II with a completely new concept, born of its time and place. He and eight other knights had joined together to dedicate their entire lives to the service of the Holy Land. The extraordinary aspect of this little band was that its members had evidenced their dedication by approaching the patriarch of Jerusalem to take the same triple vow that was common to monastic orders, the perpetual vows of poverty, chastity, and obedience. All three of those pledges were precisely opposed to the life goals of the secular medieval knight.

The knight fought for a price, usually a piece of land and the people who worked it. In exchange he pledged war service to the man who gave him the land, for a specified number of days each year. He loathed the concept of poverty. He needed money for horses, armor, weapons, and servants. He needed money for his own household. If he fought beyond the contract period, he negotiated for pay. He was always on the lookout for loot. He learned as part of his informal training that common soldiers could be killed freely, but that he must not kill men of obvious rank and wealth unless absolutely necessary to save his own life. Such men were too valuable to die. Their capture and the ransoms they would bring were a major objective of the battlefield. If the captive was a poor knight whose family could not afford to purchase his freedom, there were always his sword, his ax, his shield, his armor, his horse, all items of value that enriched his captor. A defeated knight, on the other hand, might find himself totally destitute. Unable to fulfill his feudal contract with his lord, he could lose his land. It happened to many. Much has been written about the disgrace of the *ronin,* the Japanese samurai with no lord to serve, but the destitute European knight was no better off. Only if he had armor, weapons and horses could he serve his lord. The very word ''knight'' derived from *knecht,* a servant.

As for chastity, the twelfth century was long before the age of chivalry, and even when it arrived the knight's chivalrous conduct toward women was limited to those of his own class. All others were fair game, from the women on his own lands to those on lands taken from others. Chastity was for children, not for fighting men. That monks gained respect for taking such a vow is a measure of how difficult the state of chastity was known to be. The monk or hermit who tortured his body with hair shirts and whips to drive out evil thoughts was painfully driving out thoughts of sex. If he found himself with an erection he had physical proof that Satan was taking control of his mind and body. The only proper remedy was to inflict pain upon his body until that evil indicator went away. It was part of the mystique of monasticism, and a big part of the mystery was how any man could willingly embrace such a way of life. Chastity was the opposite of what the lusty knight longed for, especially in the great emotional upheaval that occurred at the end of a battle. The knight under accumulated stress often sought the relief of sex, with no importance attached to whether his partner was willing or not.

As for obedience, the medieval knight was obedient only when he had to be, or when he saw some personal advantage. If the feudal world had to be summed up in just three words, they would be *strong, stronger, strongest.* As the alternative to helplessness, men pledged themselves to a strong man who would shelter and protect them in return for their obedience, a portion of their income, and military service. Those strong men were pledged to men still stronger, until the pyramid came to its point in a sovereign lord, who might be a count, a duke, or a king, depending upon the extent of his independent power. Obedience was extracted not by a pledge, or trust, or loyalty, but as the result of raw fear of the punishment that disobedience could bring. To tell a noble that you were not afraid of him was a personal insult and frequently led to a challenge.

At that time, fear was the fountainhead of government control throughout the world. Off in China the emperor ended his orders with ''Hear, and *tremblingly* obey!'' In Japan, it was so important to express fear to ensure personal safety that an entire language style was developed to convince a superior that he generated terror: the fast breathless speech we see in Japanese movies, almost always coming from people on their knees. Rulers wanted to be feared, not loved, and that feudal attitude carried over into the Church, where "Fear God" meant exactly that: Be terrified of the punishments God can bring down on you. The clergy had a difficult time describing the precise joys of heaven, but it had an inexhaustible supply of loathsome details to identify the agonies of hell.

As to secular punishments, except in the special cases to be kept secret, they were very public, so that the lesson learned from watching a whipping, a branding, or a mutilation would be passed on to others. Platforms were erected so that everyone could have a clear view of a man having his bones broken with iron rods, and the bodies of the executed were often left dangling in a marketplace until they fell apart, a display also posted outside city gates to let visitors know that this was a place to stay in line. Obedience was not a virtue, but a safety precaution.

That a group of secular knights took such vows in that age was remarkable, especially since they were not going to disappear behind the walls of a monastic cloister but planned to patrol the roads of Jerusalem fully armed, ready to fight any enemy to protect the Christian pilgrims to the Holy Places of Jesus Christ. Such a service was sorely needed, since the number of pilgrims had grown to the point that they had become a substantial business. They spent money, they brought gifts. They paid tolls to enter city gates or to use the roads. The owners of the ships that brought them paid a tax based on the amount of their fare. Pilgrims bought religious merchandise, some as easy to deliver as bottles of water from the Jordan River. Other items, such as fraudulent holy relics, were more difficult to produce and authenticate, but extraordinarily profitable. The greatest danger to that growing source of revenue was the threat to every pilgrim's life and property.

Only the Christian cities were guarded, and only the cities were safe. All the deserts, plains, and rocky hills between them were a no-man's-land. Merchants would hire guards to protect their caravans, and the wiser pilgrims would attach themselves to a larger party, but most pilgrims were blithely innocent. Their mere arrival on the actual soil of the kingdom of Jerusalem lit a spark of euphoria. Never had they felt the protection of God more than while traveling in Christ's own land, and never were they more wrong. Arab and Egyptian marauders were constantly on the search for plunder and for prisoners to sell to the slave traders. Most pilgrims walked, making it easy for bandits to ride ahead to set an ambush, while others were simply ridden down or taken in their sleep. The roads to Jerusalem, Bethlehem, Nazareth, and the River Jordan were strewn with the bones of the fallen faithful, bleaching in the bright sun.

Not the least of those hurt by the Muslim bandits was the Church. It was expected that Christian pilgrims, especially the increasing number of penitents who had been ordered to make the pilgrimage to earn the remission of their sins, would bring gifts to lay on the altars of the Church of the Holy Sepulcher and the other shrines memorializing the life of Christ. Only anger and frustration could result from those Christian contributions being diverted to the purchase of jewelry for some Bedouin sheikh's favorite wife, but there had appeared to be no solution. It could only have been with enthusiasm that the patriarch of Jerusalem received and heard the vows of those nine dedicated knights, who would fight to restore and maintain that flow of silver and gold.

A problem that de Payens's group had was to find a means of support. They needed a place to live for themselves and their servants, stabling for their horses, and food for all. That is why Hugh de Payens approached Baldwin II, soliciting his royal patronage. The housing and the supplies they were asking was much less than the usual knight's plea for land and revenues. The king would favor any proposition that would increase his meager standing army, and these were all battle-proven warriors who had been fighting in the Holy Land for years. In answer to their petition he assigned to them a portion of the al-Aqsa Mosque on the Temple Mount, a structure said to have been built on the site of the original Temple of Solomon. It has been rebuilt several times over the centuries and still stands today. (It made headlines in October 1990 when young Muslim worshipers coming out of the al-Aqsa Mosque allegedly threw rocks at the Jews worshiping at the Western Wall immediately below them, an act that led to retaliatory gunfire and death.) It was from this headquarters location that the group ultimately took its name, *Pauperes commilitones Christi Templique Salomonis,* the Poor Fellow-Soldiers of Christ and the Temple of Solomon. The members became known as the Knights of the Temple and later, by the name most popular, the Knights Templar.

Although the Knights of the Temple would have had occasional revenue from the possessions of the bandits they killed or captured, the king must also have given them some kind of subsidy to cover their substantial expenses. A knight required at least two horses: a muscular, heavy war-horse that would carry a man, his armor, and his heavy weapons into battle, and a lighter horse on which to travel. Each knight required at least one attendant who helped him with his armor and carried extra weapons and his master's heavy shield, which the knight wore in battle secured by a strap around his neck and shoulders. With one hand required to hold his lance, sword, ax, or mace, and one hand needed to control his horse, he had no choice but to hang his thick shield around his neck when actually engaged in fighting. The shield, known in French as the knight's *escu,* was thus carried by his shield-bearer, or *escuier,* a term that entered the English language as "esquire." Only later would the esquire be an apprentice knight: In the early Templar period, the attendant was a sergeant or man-at-arms, who required at least one horse of his own. Knights also would have needed packhorses to carry supplies on the road and servants to tend the pack animals, care for the spare horses, and cook the food. Although there is no record of the actual numbers, the starting group of nine knights would have meant an establishment of twenty-five to thirty men, with forty to fifty horses.

There is no documentation to show that the Templars took in additional members during their first nine years, but there is also no documentation that they did not. There does exist, however, evidence that their services earned the approval of King Baldwin II. In 1127 Baldwin II wrote a letter to the most influential churchman in Europe, Bernard (later St. Bernard), abbot of Clairvaux, who was generally respected as the "second pope." The suggestion probably came from Hugh de Payens, who was a cousin of Bernard, and from André de Montbard, one of the nine founding Templars, who was Bernard's uncle. Baldwin asked Bernard of Clairvaux to use his considerable influence to intercede with Pope Honorius II. Hugh de Payens was coming to Rome to ask for official papal sanction of his military order and to ask the pope to provide it with a formal Rule to govern the life and conduct of the Knights Templar. Baldwin was loud in his praise of the Templars, but nowhere near as loud as Bernard was to become in their behalf.

It is almost impossible to overstate the importance of Bernard of Clairvaux's role in the establishment of the Templar order. He was a man on fire with zeal, but too physically frail to seek outlets for his talents and obsessions on the battlefields of secular war. He chose instead to fight on the broader spiritual battlefields of the Church. He joined the Cistercian order at the age of twenty-one, and with the persuasive power that would soon make him famous he recruited his own father, four brothers, an uncle, and a number of others to declare for the cloth with him. Backing his powers of oratory with a genius at organization, in a little over five years Bernard had established the abbey of Clairvaux, had become its abbot, and had set up over sixty-five "daughter" houses, whose complements of monks he recruited himself.

Just twenty-eight years old when he got the letter from Baldwin II, Bernard was already the most powerful voice in Christian Europe. He exerted an influence that almost amounted to control over Pope Honorius II, who was his former pupil. At heart, Bernard was a reformer who wanted to purify the Church, to drive it closer to the morality taught by Jesus Christ, and to destroy its enemies.

Bernard leaped with enthusiasm at the concept of an order of knights functioning under monastic vows. His enthusiasm went beyond merely gaining papal approval; It extended to taking a hand in shaping the order. He defined its aims and ideals in a Rule to govern the conduct of the new order, taking the opportunity to put his personal stamp on an army of God. Descended from generations of French knights, Bernard could now experience the vicarious satisfaction of creating and giving direction to a military force that his frail body would not permit him to join on the field of battle.

When Hugh de Payens arrived at the papal court with his companions, he found that his saintly cousin Bernard had paved the way. The papal welcome was warm and complimentary. Honorius called for a special council to be convened during the following year at Troyes, the capital of Champagne, to grant the Templars their wish. Hugh and André de Montbard met with Bernard while waiting for the council. It was very much a family reunion, where Bernard could assure his cousin and his uncle that they would have all they dreamed of, and more, for their military order.

The order also had the full support of the count of Champagne, whose vassals made up the order's leadership. His was the first response to Bernard's call for gifts of land and money for the Templars, with a grant of land at Troyes. This became the base for a new concept, that of "preceptories" throughout Europe. These establishments in each Christian country acted as provincial supply bases to support Templar operations in the Holy Land. They recruited new members, instructed them in the Rule, and even gave them basic training in fighting together, something of a new idea to the medieval military. The officers in charge, the "preceptors," were charged with extracting the maximum revenues from the Templar properties, which came to include farms, orchards, and vineyards, and gradually extended to include mills and bakeries, market franchises, and even whole villages. Those revenues, after expenses, were forwarded to Jerusalem. Frequently they were used to fill requisitions for heavy war-horses, weapons, armor, and military supplies such as iron and arrow shafts. They provided tools for masonry and other crafts, and even timbers for siege engines, ships, and buildings, which were not readily available in the scrub-covered plains and hills of the Holy Land.

That whole complex and affluent structure was made possible by the exhortations of Bernard of Clairvaux, followed by Hugh de Payens's subsequent visits to the Christian courts. The king of France was quick to respond with gifts of land, and the highest nobility of France followed his example. Traveling on to Normandy, de Payens was received by King Stephen of England, who enriched the new order with gifts of both money and land and made arrangements for Hugh's visits to the nobles of England and Scotland. Stephen's wife Matilda contributed the valuable English manor of Cressing in Essex. The Templars would add to it over the years until it ranked as one of their most productive agricultural properties. Just how productive can be demonstrated by the incredible size of the barns built to hold the crops produced on the manor (as this is being written, the County Council of Essex is in the final stages of preparing this impressive feature of Cressing Temple for public view, so that visitors will soon be able to stroll through the largest timber-framed medieval barns in all of Europe).

To the Christians in Spain, the Muslim threat was not a tale carried home by troubadors, but the threat of conquest and death on their doorsteps every day. Fighting the Moors in Spain was a major concern of the Christian rulers, who were delighted to hear every detail of Hugh de Payens's descriptions of the new order, not because of relief for the Holy Land, but because it could provide support for their own wars against the infidel. Gifts of land and castles came fast in a land where a Templar could be recruited today and ride into battle tomorrow.

Bernard gave as much attention to attracting men as he did to collecting property. He urged young men to take up the Templar sword, comparing the Templar's holy way of life, so pleasing to God, to the degenerate ways of the secular knights, whose lives were dedicated to vanity, adultery, looting, and stealing, with many sins to atone for. The dedication to Christ, to a life of chastity and prayer, to a life that might be sacrificed in battle against unbelievers, was enough penance to atone for any sin or any number of sins. On that basis, Bernard appealed to *sceleratos et impius, raptores et homicidas, adulteros,* "the wicked and the ungodly, rapists and murderers, adulterers," to save their own souls by enlisting as Knights of the Temple. That guaranteed absolution was also a way out for those suffering under decrees of excommunication. The taking of the Templar oath would evidence submission to the Church, and the supreme penance of a lifetime at war for the True Cross would satisfy God's requirement for punishment of the contrite.

Another pool of recruits was provided by the poor knights, who lacked the funds to acquire horses, armor, and weapons. All of those things would be given to them upon their entry, along with personal attendants and servants. They were certain of adequate food and a place in which to live. Their self-respect, no matter how low it might have sunk, would be instantly restored.

It quickly became apparent that the vow of poverty was a bond on the individual, not on the order as a whole. The Templar knight could have no personal possessions and had to content himself with what the new Templar Rule gave to him: three horses, clothing, a white robe, chain mail, a helmet, and equipment for his horses, with the requisite sword, shield, lance, knife, battle-ax and mace, not to mention a list of personal gear, such as bedding and eating utensils. Taken altogether, what a Templar recruit received upon joining was so expensive that it would be ridiculous to try to make it fit any medieval definition of "poverty." (A heavy war-horse cost roughly the equivalent of four hundred days' pay for a free laborer.)

Along with all that, the new Templar got pride. The clothing he had before might have shamed him because it was threadbare and worn. He might have envied the richer dress of his peers, but the clothing he got from the Templar order was suitable for any occasion, to be worn with pride even at the courts of kings and emperors. He also had friends, comaraderie, and a sense of belonging to a proud army commanded by the Holy Father himself. The Templars provide one of the earliest examples of *esprit de corps* (a term that we should bear in mind means exactly the opposite of "humility"). Of course, the Christian sovereigns might regret the enlistment of upright, loyal knights from among their vassals, but they were happy to see the conversion, and especially the absence, of the ungodly, the rapists, the murderers, and the heretics in their territories. Those recruits must certainly have had an impact on the conduct and the councils of the order, comprising as they did an element of the angry, the independent, the aggressive, and the resentful.

The Rule that Bernard had in mind for the new order was modeled on the Rule of St. Benedict of Nursia. Based on the vows of poverty, chastity, and obedience, it also called for regulations of diet, extensive daily prayers, and time alone in meditation and devotions in an atmosphere deliberately separated from the world of nonmembers. Some of its provisions simply would not do for men who were supposed to fight, not sit, and who would function in the center of secular activities. Accordingly, the Templars were permitted more meat on their tables and were forbidden rather than encouraged to fast, which would sap their strength. They had daily prayers, but they also had daily military duties, such as the inspection of their horses and equipment, to be certain that they were ready on a moment's notice to answer the call to battle. Exemptions were specified, so that no Templar keeping watch on the wall would ever be called down to the chapel to say his prayers.

The Rule called for full and immediate obedience of the Templar knight to his superiors. No battle commander has time to explain every order, so the Templar was trained to move quickly without question, a unique contribution to military behavior that is now universal. Nor were the highest officers exempt from that discipline. The Templar marshal for Ireland chose to be insubordinate to the master for England, and was confined in the little penitential cell built into the walls of the Temple church in London until he starved to death.

Sex, of course, was a preoccupation of the medieval Church. For the Church every aspect of sex, from lustful looking to enthusiastic participation, was at the instigation of Satan. St. Thomas Aquinas would write that all sexual contact was sinful. Sex in marriage was less sinful than sex outside it, but was still a sin. St. Augustine's attitude was much more condemning. He called for the abolition of all sexual congress, even in marriage. When it was pointed out to him that without sex there would be no babies, so that the human race would die out in a single generation, his response was that such a result would be the supreme benefit to all souls. With every human being gone from the earth, the conditions would be right for the coming of the City of God. A Templar knight fighting for the True Cross must obviously be free from all Satanic control, so every aspect of sexual behavior was forbidden to him, with every temptation to be avoided.

A Templar could not embrace or kiss his own mother or sister. He was not allowed to be alone in the company of any woman of any age. He was not permitted to be in a house where a woman was giving birth. Nor was sex with other men overlooked, perhaps because of a man Bernard detested and condemned as *un succube et un sodomite,* "a feminine demon and a homosexual," who was known to some of his fellow churchmen by the derisive nickname of Flora. His unabashed life as a practicing homosexual had not prevented his being named the bishop of Orleans, although his presence at the Council of Troyes may have provoked Bernard to emphasize the prohibition of homosexual activity within the Templar order. In addition to a white lambskin girdle to be worn always as a reminder of his vow of chastity, the Templar had to wear sheepskin drawers at all times, even when he went to bed, or perhaps especially when he went to bed. The dormitory was required to have a lamp burning all night as a deterrent to nocturnal visiting. The Templar was never to allow another person to see his naked body, not even another Templar. That rule did not interfere with bathing, for the Templar was never to bathe his body. (Although it may not have been intentional, the rule never to remove his sheepskin drawers and not to bathe for years on end in a blistering hot climate may have helped the Templar knight to adhere to his vow of chastity, since the sweaty filth of his body and the resultant stench must have held sexual invitations to a minimum.)

One item of Bernard's Rule for the Templars brought an unexpected benefit. The knights were ordered to crop their hair short but to let their beards grow, in contrast to the current European vanity of long hair and a clean-shaven face. Facial hair at that time was an important Middle Eastern symbol of virility and masculinity, and to an extent still is. Those today who do not emulate the beards of the Saudi Arabians and the Shiite Imams of Iran still cling to the bushy mustaches of Iraq, Syria, and Turkey. At the time of the Crusades, the smooth-faced Christians appeared feminine and disgraceful to their adversaries. One chronicler noted that when a Muslim emir brought his children to his tent to present to visiting Christian nobles, his little daughter burst into tears of terror and clung to her father. She had never seen grown men with hairless faces in all her life. To her, they looked weird and ugly. Her father agreed, but courtesy would prevent his expression of his opinion. Perhaps no story illustrates the importance of a beard to a Middle Easterner at that time more than the incident in which Baldwin I, then Count of Edessa, cleverly manipulated that tradition to his own advantage.

Soon after Baldwin's assumption of the sovereignty of Edessa, he married the daughter of the wealthy Armenian prince Gabriel. At one point Baldwin was in a serious cash crunch. He tried to get a loan from his father-in-law, but was flatly refused. Baldwin, who had let his beard grow in deference to the customs of his Armenian subjects, hit upon a plan. He told his father-in-law that he needed thirty thousand gold bezants to pay his retainers and soldiers, having made a sacred oath to them that if they were not paid promptly he would disgrace himself by shaving off his luxuriant beard. The prince was horrified, conscious only of the humiliation and the derision that would be heaped upon him if he had a clean-shaven son-in-law in his family. He agreed to give Baldwin the money, but only on condition that Baldwin swear his solemn oath to never again, under any circumstances, make a pledge that could cost him his beard. This perhaps will help to explain one reason why the Templars in the Holy Land were considered by the Muslims to be a breed apart, the manliest and therefore the most to be respected of all the Christian Crusaders.

The Rule, as might be expected, was amended, added to, and sometimes set aside during the course of the next 180 years, but the power structure remained inviolate. The master in any country had autocratic control over the Templars in his area, unless the grand master was present. The grand master was in total control. Although he might occasionally seek the advice of his officers, he alone had the decision-making power. He could delegate or withdraw authority at his own discretion. He could temporarily set aside or alter the Rule at any time if he felt that circumstances called for a change.

The Templar Rule would function well in its internal governance of the order, but the Templars could not unilaterally impose their status on the world in which they functioned. Such a definition, if it was to have the force of law, must come from a higher authority. When it came, it put all of Christendom on notice that this military order was to have rare privileges.

Within ten years Pope Innocent II would issue the bull *Omne datum optimum,* bestowing "Every great gift" on the Templar order. It exempted the Templars from all authority on earth, secular or temporal, except that of the pope himself, the highest pinnacle of independence a Christian body could possibly achieve, since no one would ever be free of the supremacy of Christ's Vicar on Earth. Now the Templars could collect tithes, but didn't have to pay them. No one could ask a Templar to swear an oath. No one could demand any change in their Rule. No monarch could impose his own civil law on the Templars. No bishop, archbishop, or cardinal could give them orders or interfere with their activities. They could even get rid of any priest who didn't suit them. The bull read in part: " . . . you shall have your own clerks and chaplains, to keep in your house and under its jurisdiction, without reference to the Diocesan bishop, by direct authority of the Holy Church of Rome. These chaplains shall undergo a novitiate of one year, and should they turn out troublesome or simply useless to the house, you shall be at liberty to send them away and appoint better priests. And these chaplains shall not meddle in the government of the Order."

The evil of sex was used as the reason to grant the Templars the right to have their own churches and cemeteries, for not even in death should the Templar have to mix with men who "frequented" with women: " . . . Further do we grant you the right to set up sanctuaries in the precincts of any Templar domain, that you may there attend divine services, and also be interred. For it is indecent and dangerous for the souls of the professed Brethren of the Temple, that they should rub shoulders with sinful persons and frequenters of women."

It annoyed the rest of the Church that the Templar order, except on rare occasions, was exempt from paying tithes and taxes, on the basis that all of its funds were used to fight for Christ.

Indeed, building and maintaining fortifications, and keeping them manned and supplied, required a river of revenues, and the Templars demonstrated ingenuity in finding new sources of money.

They took in "associate" members who lived or fought with them for a time in exchange for gifts to the order. They bought or built their own ships, with their own war galleys to protect them, and with this maritime fleet they brought their own supplies from Europe and transported pilgrims to Jerusalem for a fee. On the farms and plantations they acquired in the Holy Land they developed crops that could be used for export, so that their ships would not have to return empty to Europe. One of those products came from their fields of sugarcane, with the juice reduced to sugar at a factory in Acre. With not much other than wild honey to satisfy the natural craving for sweets, the European markets readily took every pound of sugar they could get. (Sometimes shipments included a local product made by boiling sugar into crystalline lumps to be sucked on, a product that the Arabs called *al-Kandiq,* a word that was Anglicized into "candy.") To a European society used to clothing limited to either leather or wool, they shipped textiles woven of Middle Eastern cotton. They occasionally carried the fine cotton cloth from Kurdistan, where it was prepared by the weavers of Mosul, called the *Mosulin,* whose name got to Europe as "muslin." They bought a very loosely woven cotton fabric made by the people around one of their southern castles. That special cloth, woven by the people of Gaza, came to be known as "gauze."

With surplus funds accumulating, the Templar order drifted into financial services, always with a "gift" or other provision for Templar profit. The easiest of those services was safe deposit. Since the Templars at each major location carefully guarded their own treasure, it required no extra effort to do the same for others. Although there were a few reports of theft, the Templar treasure house was consistently the most secure depository available. That service grew to offering security for the treasuries and even the crown jewels of France and England. Absolutely the most secure way to transport money was with Templar receipts. Money moving by land was at the mercy of robbers, and money moved by sea could be lost to pirates or to Mediterranean storms. With the Templars, whose far-flung bases provide the first example of "branch banking," the money need not move at all. A deposit could be made with the treasurer in Paris, then the receipt presented for collection to the treasurer in Jerusalem. The safety was well worth the "gift" the Templars required for this service.

Regular income was generated from the welcome service of money-changing in the Holy Land. Nineteen different languages were spoken by the Christians of the First Crusade, but there were far more forms of coinage than there were languages, a problem the Templars solved for newly-arrived pilgrims.

As to loans, the Church laws against usury made it difficult, if not illegal, for lenders to exact interest. The Templars would accept a gift of land, commodities, or even privileges as interest, but it was never called by that name. They seem to have invented, or at least popularized, the concept of interest deducted in advance. They gave a man four thousand gold pieces, but the loan document stated only his promise to repay a loan of five thousand, with no reference to interest. Another popular transaction was a mortgage in which there was no interest, but the Templars took the revenues from the property until the mortgage was repaid. It was much the same as purchasing the property now with an agreement to sell it back later at the same price. One can only imagine the economic havoc that would result today if mortgage lenders agreed to finance an office building, apartment complex or shopping mall only on the basis that the lender keeps 100 percent of the rents and revenues until the mortgage is totally paid off from some unrelated source. With ingenuity, surplus capital, and a whole army to back their moves to collect and foreclose, the Templars became for a time the foremost banking house in Europe, just as a revenue-producing sideline to their basic military objectives.

One interesting aspect of the Templar financial services is their usefulness in helping to put aside the contention of some historians that the Templars were simple sword-bearing illiterates of the lower nobility, in reality just a pack of brutal body bashers. Their banking activities called for careful record keeping and accurate correspondence and document preparation, plus an earned reputation for efficiency and trustworthiness. Many rulers, including several popes, delegated to the Templars the responsibility of collecting, holding, and dispersing tax revenues. The Templars were frequently called upon to act as emissaries, ambassadors, and administrators. Some even acted as administrators of the pope's own household and finances, as evidenced by a Templar named Bernard and another named Franco, who were borrowed from the order to act as personal chamberlains to Pope Alexander III.

More direct application of that efficiency was in the world of military affairs. Wars fought a thousand miles from home called for logistical skills that were almost unknown back in Europe. The Templars carefully planned for food and war supplies in the field, including the vital transport of water where required, necessities frequently overlooked or underestimated by visiting Crusaders. They entered the armament manufacturing business using both employees and slave craftsmen to turn out supplies that would take too long to bring from Europe. The Templar castle of Safed for example, had a normal complement of archers of three hundred men. If each archer shot just ten arrows per day during a thirty day siege, the Templars of Safed would have needed ninety thousand arrows on hand. The best chain mail was made of flattened rings (to leave as small a hole as possible in the center of the ring), with each little loop held together with rivets. A calf-length chain hauberk required thousands of loops and took weeks to make, with more time needed to make the leggings, foot coverings and mittens. To equip one hundred recruits with armor meant an impressive battery of armorers. For the chain mail, the weapons and spurs, the bits and horseshoes for their horses, the Templars maintained forges in the Holy Land and in Europe, including two on Fleet Street near the London Temple.

Every secular knight received some individual training, but the Templars were drilled to fight together. They had training fields on which to practice maintaining a line during the charge and to wheel or turn about on command. Those maneuvers seem hardly worth mentioning now, but in their day they were revolutionary. Feudal armies were mobs with no feel for acting in concert with other men. (This disciplined technique was far more advanced among the Arabs, however, and some English Crusaders apparently decided that Muslim foot soldiers had learned to move together because they often danced together to the beat of cymbals and drums. They took those dances home in an attempt to teach their own peasant soldiers to act in concert with their fellows. The memory of those attempts to turn mobs into military units lives today at British festivals, where groups of men known as Morris Dancers dance in lines with bells on their legs and sticks as weapons. Few watching them relate the Morris Dances to the "Moorish dances" from which they came.)

On the battlefield, Templars rallied around a battle standard called the Beauséant. In medieval French the expression was a charge, a battle cry that the Templars shouted to each other, meaning "Be noble!" or "Be glorious!" The banner consisted of a solid black square above a solid white square, the black signifying the worldly sin-ridden life they had left behind, the white symbolizing the purity of a life spent fighting for Christ. The standard was not a flag that drooped down its pole, but a vertical banner with rods top and bottom to hold it rigid so that it required no breeze to be seen. Its principal function was as a rallying point. In an armored charge of heavy horse, the knights were often separated after the impact on the enemy line, and it was difficult to rein the massive war-horses to a walk after the exhilaration of the gallop. The answer was to look for the Beauséant and ride to it to regroup.

Another lesson learned on the battlefield was the advantages of light cavalry. The Muslim light cavalry could move much faster than the heavy horses of the Christian knights and so was better suited for advance scouting, for foraging, for picking off stragglers, and for screening the movements of the army in the field. In pursuit and maneuver, the heavy cavalry was no match for the light.

The Templar answer was to have both. They recruited light cavalry from the men born of European fathers and native mothers, a cross known as *poulains*. They called these light cavalry units Turcopoles (perhaps a compound of Turco-Poulains). While the knights used their swords mainly for hacking, much as though they were axes with three-foot blades, the Muslims used two types of swords with curved blades. One style had the sharp edge outside the curve, for slashing, while the other had its cutting edge on the inside of the curve to drag the blade along the opponent's body while riding by, making a long, deep "draw cut." Both styles had sharp points for thrusting from horseback. If the European straight blade was driven into an enemy, the opposing actions of the falling body and the moving horse would tend to wrench the sword from the rider's hand, while the curved blade of the Muslim would tend to free itself by arcing out of the body as the rider moved on. The advantages of the lighter cavalryman and his curved sword were not lost on the Christians, so that one day every European army would include light cavalry, and the curve would become the identifying feature of the cavalry saber.

The Templars Rule stated that all Templar clothing, weapons and tack must be entirely without decoration, concentrating on quality rather than show. The final effect of that policy would have been to make the appearance of the armed Templar one that was all business. Unlike the individual who greedily dropped out of the fight to grab a piece of attractive loot such as a jeweled sword or dagger, the Templar was not permitted to take any personal plunder. Whatever loot there was went to the Templar treasury, so it was not difficult to enforce the rule that prohibited looting until the field commander gave the word. A secular knight would also stop fighting and surrender if he found himself outnumbered or wounded. He let himself be taken prisoner because he could be redeemed and save his life by payment of a ransom. The Templar Rule strictly prohibited the use of the order's funds for the ransom of Templars taken prisoner, with the result that captured Templars were usually killed. For the Templar on the battlefield, the prohibition against ransom meant fighting to the bitter end, even if he was wounded. Nor could he retreat under any circumstances except in response to a direct order, an order that was never to be given unless the Templars were outnumbered by at least three to one. His fighting, however, was not to glorify himself for his prowess. The Templar motto, probably a contribution of Bernard of Clairvaux, made that point clear. It was *Non nobis Domine, non nobis, sed nomine tuo, da gloriam,* "Not unto us, Lord, not unto us, but to thy name give glory."

Another Templar contribution to military evolution was the delegation of authority and departmentalization. The grand master was the commander-in-chief. The seneschal was his chief executive officer. The treasurer handled finances. The marshal was the field commander, although the grand master would assume that role personally if he was in the field (a number of grand masters were to die from wounds received in battle). Roughly equivalent to today's quartermaster, the officer in charge of weapons, equipment, and clothing was the draper, while the officer in charge of the light cavalry was the turcopoler.

As to the total body of Templars, they were divided into three classes. First were the knights, who had to be drawn from the knightly class. Initiation into the order did not make a man a knight, but rather made the knight a monk. Their robes were white. The sergeants or mounted men-at-arms were drawn from the bourgeoisie, and had to be free-born. They were assigned two horses each, and their chain mail was not as long nor as complete as that of the knights. They could act as squires, guards, stewards or in any other position, and were addressed as "Brother." They wore robes of black or brown. The remaining class, the smallest, was the Templar priests, who acted as chaplains but were often assigned to other tasks, such as letter writing and record keeping, to take advantage of their literacy. They wore green robes, and also wore gloves at all times to keep their hands clean for "when they touched God" in serving Holy Communion. (The Templars had not yet been granted the splayed red cross *patee* that became their easily recognized symbol, but it would come to them just a few years later when Bernard of Clairvaux called up the Second Crusade.)

As a final note on their Rule, although the Templar order came to relish its own privacy with secret meetings, secret initiations and, secret correspondence, the individual knight was permitted no secrets and was not even permitted a level of personal privacy. He was not permitted to have any debts, which would put him under an obligation to an outsider, and was forbidden to act as a godfather, even to children of his own family, to prevent the possibility of any future obligations. The Rule was revealed to him just a bit at a time on a "need to know" basis, nor could he discuss with anyone, not even a brother Templar, any part of the Rule that had been exposed to him. He was restrained by strict punishments from discussing Templar business with an outsider, especially the proceedings of any Templar meeting or initiation. He was not to concern himself with the administration of the order, unless promoted to do so. His only concern, his only purpose in his new life, was to fight the infidel.

The question has often been raised as to how the Roman Catholic Church could ever have come up with the idea for a monastic order that would have a license to kill, at a time when every clergy-man and every monk was forbidden to spill blood. Perhaps the best answer is that the Church did not come up with the idea. It was born in a group of knights. Theologians rarely come up with really new concepts, but display their talents best when called upon to justify actions already taken or decisions already made. Bernard of Clairvaux explained the anomaly to his own satisfaction by stating that killing a nonbeliever was not "homicide," the killing of a man, but "malecide," the killing of an Evil One. The whole truth would have to include the fact that for the first Templar knights, who formed a brotherhood of men to kill for Christ, the idea was as much a product of their culture as of their Catholicism.

In 1118, northern Europe had not been Christian for very long, and the conversion of the pagans was by no means complete. If a ruler agreed to convert to Christianity, thereupon ordering hun-dreds of thousands of subjects to do the same, it should not be thought that those people understood the religion they had been ordered to embrace. It would take many generations of infrequent visits by untrained priests to get the message through to them. There was not a single university in all of Christian Europe at the time, so religious training was not received at a seminary, but from a kind of apprenticeship. When a priest did make contact with the people, he conducted services in a language they did not understand, and the result was a frequent folk-blending of their old gods with the new. We are over eight hundred years beyond that time and still preserve in our folk customs the Christmas evergreens of the Teutonic worshipers and the holly and mistletoe of the Druids, just as we preserve the naturist fertility symbols of the rabbit and the gaily-colored egg at Easter time. How much stronger and more complex those remembrances were in the twelfth century we can only imagine, but it is interesting to note that when Richard Wagner, in the latter half of the nineteenth century, wrote his operatic cycle, *Der Ring des Niebelungen* (the Ring Cycle), and other works, no one in his country was puzzled by the tales of the Norse Valkyries or *Gotterdammerung,* the Twilight of the Gods. Nor were they in the next century when Adolf Hitler cited the ancient Teutonic deities. We must remember that the Vikings brought their religion to Britain and established such an extensive occupation of western France that they were finally legally recognized, and the Norsemen became the Normans. Their ancient beliefs would recognize, even honor, an order of fighting men willing to die for their God. Such a concept was a basic part of the old religion and lingered long after Christianity laid claim to their souls. To thoroughly understand the Templars it is worthwhile, if not absolutely necessary, to take a brief look at the old religion, which had held believers all across northern Europe.

The principal Norse god was Odin, or Woden. His son Thor was a war god, the Thunderer, who wielded a mighty hammer, presented in a symbolic form that looked much like the T-shaped Tau cross of Christianity. Odin's son Tiw was the god of battles. Odin lived in a great hall or palace called Valhalla, and from his throne he could observe the whole world beneath him.

One of Odin's principal concerns was to prepare for Ragnarok, the Twilight of the Gods, when the evil spirits, demons, and giants of heaven and earth would attack Valhalla to destroy the gods. To prepare for that day, he collected about him all of the heroic fighters of the earth. As any battle took place, Odin sent his messengers, warlike virgins called the Valkyrior (or Valkyries), whose name means "The Choosers of the Slain." They rode to the battlefield in armor, carrying spears, to select the bravest, most heroic of the fighters to be slain so that their souls could join Odin at Valhalla. When a brave fighter died, his friends on earth did not say "He is in heaven now," but "Now he will fight for the gods."

At Valhalla, the highest level of life after death, the hero left the hall every day to fight. He might be mutilated or killed, but as evening came he was made whole and healthy again in time for a great feast in Odin's hall, where brave deeds were recounted and the bravest fighters on that day were singled out for praise. Full of all the boar's meat and mead he could hold, the warrior went to his bed, only to rise in the morning to take up his weapons to go out to fight again. That was the northern European concept of the delights and rewards of heaven, the right to fight hand-to-hand every day for all eternity. Such was the creed that respected fighting above all other skills, and for a warlike people that belief was impossible to suddenly abandon for the forgiving sweetness of Christianity. As they did learn about their new religion, the avenging God of the Old Testament held more appeal for some than the loving God of the New, and they tenaciously clung to many of their old beliefs. The Church struggled and preached and thundered, but could not totally stamp out the feelings deep inside that the good fighter was beloved of God, and that fighting was the most manly and noble occupation for men. That belief nurtured the feudal concept, and the folk memory of the old faith guaranteed the appeal of a war band of brothers-in-arms who would fight and die for God, especially at a time when the Church was still struggling to wipe out the residual worship of the gods of war, without complete success. People clung to the old ways, and to a degree they still do.

The very concept of the holy Crusade had provided a way for the ingrained love of war to coexist with their Christian faith. If the fighting couldn't be stopped, at least it might be channeled toward a goal that God and his Church could approve. That concept had been one expression of the genius of Urban II.

There was an ancient legend of the Church that a professional acrobat had joined a monastic brotherhood, where his great physical skills were totally shut off. His gymnastics were his only real talent, so one day while alone in the chapel he had decided to exercise his one skill in the sight of God. He leaped and flipped and somersaulted in front of the altar, until at last his agile body dropped to the floor exhausted and perspiring. His abbot, who had been watching in the darkened doorway, started into the chapel to chastise and punish the wayward monk for his ridiculous behavior, but was stopped by the shock of what happened next. The statue of the virgin next to the altar had begun to move! The Holy Mother stepped from her pedestal and walked to the collapsed monk. She knelt beside him, and with the edge of her robe wiped the sweat from his face, smiling at him in complete approval. God loved a man who gave the best of himself, whatever that might be.

That's what the Knights of the Temple were doing. Jesus Christ could never have given them their love for war and the drive to perfect their lethal skills on the battlefield, but in the concept of a life fighting for the True Cross, the opposing pulls on their minds and hearts became one, giving what was left of their lives a glorious purpose. To become a Knight of the Temple, a Knight for Christ, put their faith and their instincts on the same course. To devote their major talent, and their major enthusiasm, to the service of God was a profound satisfaction that solved a deep problem in that time of secular and religious transition. They had no knowledge of psychology; they knew only that they were happy.

For the Templar recruits, many from rural areas, there must have been the additional appeal of exotic new lands and customs. Very likely, as would happen for centuries to come, during the weeks at sea the younger men would sit listening to the older, experienced men who had tales to tell of the land the French Crusaders called

Outremer, "over the sea." They would learn about the swarthy men with whom they would soon be locked in battle, men who called their god *Allah* and were governed every day of their lives by the teachings of a prophet named Muhammad.

We need to share some of that learning to better appreciate the adventures that lie ahead.

4

Allahu Akbar!

THE PROPHET MUHAMMAD did not build the Kaaba at Mecca, nor did he originate the concept of Allah, the creator of the world. Both existed for centuries before him. What the Prophet did was to explain the nature of God and of God's Law (*Shari'a*). He purified the concept of God by stripping away the icons, images, and symbols of hundreds of animist gods and goddesses that in his time were worshiped and fought over by the Arab people.

Kaaba in Arabic means "cube," which aptly describes the fifty-foot-high temple in the center of the western Arabian trading city of Mecca, where Muhammad was born. Its origins had been lost long before the coming of the Prophet, but tradition says that the Kaaba was built by Abraham. At the time of Muhammad's birth about A.D. 570 it was filled with idols and relics that, according to one historian, represented 367 different deities, all under a supreme being who was God, or in Arabic, *Allah.* The polytheism was very profitable for Mecca, because a wide variety of worshipers had manifold reasons for making their pilgrimages to prostrate themselves before their own gods. They brought funds to pay their living expenses in the city, and animals and farm products to sell in the local market. They bought salt, spices, cloth, and weapons to take home with them. The merchants of Mecca enjoyed a steady stream of revenues, so it is easy to understand why the business community would frown on anyone who denounced all those gods, thus threatening to reduce the steady flow of pilgrim profits.

Although poor, Muhammad's family was part of the Qaraish, one of the strongest clans in the area. Raised by relatives because his parents were dead, Muhammad may have had boyhood experiences that influenced his later revelation that hideous tortures in hell were waiting for those sinners who mistreated orphans.

Growing up surrounded by the traders, Muhammad, while still a young man, was employed by a wealthy widow named Khadija, who operated caravans into Arabia and Syria. Khadija was very pleased with her handsome, well-spoken young employee and rapidly entrusted him with more responsibility. Her approval went beyond business, and the two were married when Muhammad was about twenty-five years old, fifteen years younger than his affluent wife. One of the couple's daughters, named Fatima, married a young cousin named Ali, who was later to become a key figure in the new religion. For years Muhammad led their caravans to other cities and other peoples, always ready to engage in discussions, always ready to listen.

He met both Jews and Nestorian Christians, asked probing questions about their beliefs, and was intrigued by their frequent references to holy books that governed their faiths. In the city of Yathrib, about 275 miles north of Mecca, Muhammad became friendly with several Jewish merchants. The city, whose population was about 50 percent Jewish, was later to shelter the Prophet in his time of greatest personal danger.

Muhammad's thoughts were drawn increasingly toward the conflicts within the local religions. The religious leaders did nothing to condemn or even curb the corruption and immorality around them. The polytheists, who agreed with each other about almost nothing, had confused and obscured the supremacy of Allah, the almighty God. Muhammad was profoundly troubled and began to wander off by himself to meditate.

He left his home in Mecca one night in A.D. 610 to seek the solitude of a cave in the nearby mountains. As he meditated, he was suddenly surrounded by a radiant light in which the Archangel Gabriel appeared to him, ordering him to proclaim the true word of God. Allah had chosen him to teach the people. Muhammad confided only in his wife, who believed the truth of his experience completely and gave her husband her full support. The Prophet received more divinely inspired visitations, until one night he was exhorted to take the message to the whole world that there is no God but God. Allah is not just the *supreme* God, He is the *only* God. Allah has no consorts, no offspring, no alternate manifestations.

Thus was born the First Pillar of the Islamic faith, the assertion of belief, or *shahada*. It is heard in the calls to prayer and from the lips of every worshiper every day of his life: *La ilaha illa Allah: Muhammad rasul Allah*. ("There is no God but God: Muhammad is the messenger of God.")

As might be expected, Muhammad's first converts were from

among the poor and the slaves. Muhammad's condemnation of polytheism was not good for business, and those who suffered financially from his conversions were bitterly resentful, but he did find believers among his relatives and friends. Abu Bekr, who would become Muhammad's father-in-law, and the Prophet's son-in-law Ali were among the most fervent of his followers. The enemies he created, however, far outnumbered the converts.

Muhammad stayed in Mecca, in spite of the growing antagonism, because his wife's substantial business was based there. After her death, however, he moved to a nearby smaller town to spread his message from God, but his words were met with stinging insults and angry rejection. One day he was stoned by a mob of town ruffians and went back to Mecca, where, even if he was shunned, he was not physically abused. It was during this period of rejection and despair that Muhammad experienced another religious revelation. Some claim that it was actual, while others say that it happened in a dream, but all Muslims recognize its importance to their faith. It was this experience that held the most personal interest for the Knights Templar.

One night the Prophet was awakened by the Archangel Gabriel, who led him to the Kaaba. There outside the Temple was a magnificent snow-white winged beast, half mule and half donkey. Muhammad was ordered to mount, and as he sat in the saddle the beast, whose name was Buraq, unfolded its mighty wings and flew upward, soaring north into the starry night. As Buraq descended, Muhammad recognized the city of Jerusalem. He was taken to the Temple Mount and set down by a temple on the west side, on the abandoned site of the ancient Temple of Solomon. Inside the temple he met all the prophets who had preceded him. There was Moses, tall and thin, with curly hair. Here was Jesus, of medium height, with straight hair and freckles. Muhammad was most struck upon meeting Abraham, for as he said later, "Never have I seen a man who looked more like myself!"

The prophets invited Muhammad to refresh himself with a choice of wine or milk. He chose the milk. Gabriel told him that he had made a wise choice for himself and his followers, for from that night forward wine was forbidden to them. He was then led from the temple to a great rock in the center of the Mount, on which was resting a ladder. Muhammad was told to climb the ladder and he obeyed, ascending past all the strata of hell and heaven to the very throne of Allah. On the way, the angel Malik, the Keeper of Hell, lifted the lid of the flaming pit to show Muhammad the punishment accorded the abusers and robbers of orphans. The prophet reported that those sinners were ugly, with lips like camels. "In their hands were fiery coals which they put into their mouths to pass through their bodies and come out of their rectums.''

Moving higher past the levels of heaven, Muhammad saw unbelievably beautiful maidens with red lips and sparkling eyes, who catered to every desire of those whose virtuous lives had earned for them an eternity in paradise. When he recounted his mystic nocturnal journey to followers, a few left the Prophet in disbelief, deciding that his mind was slipping. Others accepted the revelation as conclusive evidence that Muhammad was indeed the chosen of God.

The Prophet's experience earned for Jerusalem its place as the third most holy location to men of the faith. The Temple Mount became revered under a name that identified its sanctity, the *Haram-es-Sharif,* the Sacred Sanctuary. In A.D. 691 the caliph Abd al-Malik decided to honor the celestial temple described in the seventeenth sura (chapter) of the Koran as the mosque then most distant from Mecca:

> Glory to God
> Who did take His Servant
> For a Journey by Night
> From the Sacred Mosque [the Kaaba]
> To the Farthest Mosque
> Whose precincts we did bless...

Abd al-Malik built a great mosque on the site of the Temple of Solomon, the location of the temple of the prophets in the night journey of Muhammad. He gave it the name it had been given in the Koran, "the Farthest Mosque," or in Arabic, the *al-Aqsa.* This was the al-Aqsa Mosque that King Baldwin II assigned to the newly-formed Knights Templar, on the site from which they took their name. The caliph also built a beautiful domed mosque at the center of the Mount, in reverence of the spot where the ladder had rested on the great rock. Some believed that this was the same rock on which Abraham had been prepared to sacrifice his son. It was called *Qubbat al-Sakhra,* the Dome of the Rock. Although rebuilt and reworked from time to time, both buildings still stand as houses of Islamic worship on the Temple Mount in Jerusalem.

After his transcendental night ride, Muhammad began to make a written record of his instructions from God. His collection of writings, divided into 114 chapters, or *suras,* was called *al-Qur'an,* "to be read"; in English it is called the Koran. The writings were not just to be read, they were to be explicitly obeyed in total submission, for which the Arabic term is *Islam.* The follower, a *Muslim,* is "one who submits." Muhammad's injunction that the Koran be reproduced only in Arabic not only prevented theological disputes created by translation errors and inadequacies but provided a great common bond for all the peoples who came to follow him. His exhortation that the Book was to be read by all the faithful was a strong force for literacy, a stand exactly opposite to that taken by the Roman Church, which ordered that the Holy Bible was *not* to be read by any except those with specific authority to do so. Muhammad said that a man must read God's word and gain direct understanding. The Roman Christian Church said that the layman, with his limited knowledge, must not try to understand God's word, and must let the Church interpret its meaning. Muhammad said that there is nothing and no one between the worshiper and God. No intercessor was necessary and none permitted, not even the Prophet himself. The Roman Church said there was no contact with God *except* through its intercessor the pope, the *Pontifex Maximus,* who held the keys to the kingdom of Heaven. The differences between the Muslim and Christian beliefs and practices were so fundamental that most missed the most fundamental point of all— that with the roots of their faith deep in the Old Testament, they both worshiped the same God.

As Muhammad gradually revealed the word of Allah, he began to teach the moral code that God required of his followers. They were to desist from all stealing, lying, cheating, and fornication. They were to stop murdering their unwanted infant daughters. Each revelation gained new converts—and new enemies among the merchants of Mecca as the nomadic pilgrims welcomed Muhammad's orders to stop throwing their money away on gifts to false priests serving false gods. He told them that their pilgrimages to do homage before idols and images were offensive to the one True God and that they would find more favor with Allah and save their money if they would simply stay home and pray.

While the steadily mounting opposition to Muhammad in Mecca grew uglier and more threatening, his teachings were enjoying success and attracting followers in the trading city of Yathrib. He gained such a positive reputation there that a delegation from Yathrib met with him in secret to invite him to establish his base in their city and to bring his followers with him. Their city was being torn apart by two Arab factions, and they felt that Muhammad's compassion, his respect for justice, and especially his skills at reasoning and oratory might bring him success as the mediator who could bring peace.

The idea was appealing because the Quraish of Mecca had become menacing to the point that Muhammad feared for his life. He ordered his followers to move to Yathrib, but to leave over a period of several weeks in groups of four or five to avoid alerting their enemies. The migration to the safety of Yathrib began, and finally the Prophet was forced to join his followers when he learned of an assassination plot to kill him as he left his house. His son-in-law Ali wrapped himself in Muhammad's green cloak and stretched out on his bed. The Prophet fled the city with the faithful Abu Bekr. As the assassins waiting outside his house peered through the windows, they thought they were seeing him on his bed. They waited for hours with swords drawn while Muhammad pushed hard on his eight-day flight to Yathrib. In Islamic history this flight of Muhammad and his followers is remembered as the "migration," *Hijra*, or Hegira. From it came the pillar of Islam called the *hajj*, the pilgrimage to Mecca that every Muslim is expected to make at least once in his lifetime. When he has done so, he may add the honorific *hajji* to his name.

The year of the Hegira was A.D. 622, *Anno Domini*, "In the Year of Our Lord." From now on Islam would govern its calendar by the great migration, so that the following year of A.D. 623 became 1 *Hijria*, or in English 1 A.H., "After the Hegira." The city of Yathrib was revered by followers as the place where Muhammad found protection. It was known thereafter as *Madinat al-Nabi*, the City of the Prophet, and came to be called simply The City, or *Medina*. The great mosque at Medina is the second holiest place in Islam.

It was greed, not an interest in theology, that induced the Crusaders to learn about and plan for the annual pilgrimage to Mecca, which the Prophet had decreed should be made in the twelfth month of the Muslim calendar, the *Dhu al-Hijjah*. Their motivation was identical to that which inspired the Bedouin and other Arab bandits to attack the Christian pilgrims to Jerusalem, which in turn had inspired the founding of the Knights Templar. Pilgrims almost always carried supplies, expense money and gifts. The month of the Muslim pilgrimage thus became a kind of human hunting season, when the Christians of Galilee, the Transjordan and Judea stalked the roads, passes, fords, and oases on the popular paths to Mecca, ready to pounce on the pilgrims who were not likely to be professional soldiers.

In Yathrib the Prophet did not enjoy unqualified success as a mediator between the rival tribes. He actually created a new rivalry between those who were his followers and those who were not. He was safe, but not successful, because his great ambition to cleanse the holy Kaaba of corruption had only led to his own flight for his life. The people of Mecca were still antagonistic to him and to his converts. In frustration, Muhammad exposed a side of himself never before seen. He decided to strike back at the leaders in Mecca by striking at their purses, an agonizing wound for merchants anywhere.

In A.D. 624 Muhammad gathered a group of about three hundred aggressive followers and led them in a mounted attack on a great Quraish caravan guarded by almost a thousand men. He lost only fourteen men in this first decisive military victory, and so had no trouble attracting others among his converts to join him on a series of profitable raids. Determined to end the depredations, the rulers of Mecca assembled an army of ten thousand men to take Medina and put an end to the Prophet Muhammad and his offensive religion.

Whether it was the Prophet's own idea or whether he copied something he had heard about on his travels we do not know, but while the Meccans were recruiting their forces, Muhammad had his people build a series of deep ditches around Medina, a technique completely new to contemporary Arab warfare.

When the Meccan army approached the ditches, they found themselves at too great a distance to inflict any real damage with their short bows, yet they were fearful of advancing down into and across the hazardous, steep-sided ditches, either on their camels or on foot. They raged and hurled screaming threats, but they didn't attack. Even as they turned for the long march home, leaving Medina unharmed, the story was starting to spread with lightning speed throughout Arabia. More and more converts elected to follow this man who indeed seemed to be favored by Allah.

After a couple of years of inconclusive fighting, a truce was agreed upon between Mecca and Medina. Then the Meccans broke the truce by attacking a tribe that had converted to Islam. This time it was Muhammad who was able to assemble an army ten thousand strong, an army that fought for God and His Prophet. They took Mecca with no trouble, and Muhammad reentered the city of his birth as its ruler. He ordered his followers to remove and destroy the abominable idols in the Kaaba, then had them cleanse and purify the ancient building. After his order had been carried out, Muhammad entered the temple to pray. Thus did the Kaaba at Mecca become the holiest place in all Islam, the primary objective of the *hajj*. It became the *quibla*, the "niche of God" toward which the whole Muslim world, from then until now, would turn in prayer five times a day for a lifetime, for generation after generation.

In 630 Muhammad went back to Medina, where he continued to set down his revelations during the remaining two years of his life. When complete, the Koran set forth God's commands as to belief, prayer ritual, moral conduct, charitable works, and matters of law. It was from these writings and from the experiences of the Prophet's lifetime that the Five Pillars of Faith emerged, the central core of Islam.

As already mentioned, the First Pillar is *shahada,* the testimony of faith in the overriding principle that there is no God but God, and that Muhammad is the Messenger of God. Muhammad had clarified the ancient commandment from "Thou shalt have no other gods *before* me" to "There is no God *except* me!" This basic belief made the Christian concept of a Triune God of Father, Son, and Holy Spirit totally unacceptable to Muslims. Allah had no offspring. Muhammad recognized Jesus of Nazareth as a genuine prophet, beloved of God, and venerated his mother Mary and the virgin birth. But he denied that Jesus was God or the Son of God. He also denied that Jesus died on the cross. That made the central claim of the Christian Crusades a sham in the eyes of devout Muslims, who believed that these crazy people had come to die for nothing.

The Second Pillar of Islam is *salah,* prayer, a ritual to be observed only in the Prophet's native Arabic tongue. Prayers are to be offered at dawn, at noon, at mid-afternoon, at sunset (when the new day begins), and in the evening. Preparation includes ritual ablutions, washing the face, hands, and forearms. Muhammad knew the conditions of the desert, so an exception was provided for times when there was no water available, or when supplies were dangerously low. At such times, the ritual ablutions could be performed symbolically with sand instead of water. The devout remove their shoes and, if possible, stand and kneel on a rug reserved for that purpose. Obviously, the prayers may be said anywhere, in a tent or in a hotel suite, but on Friday, the Muslim Sabbath, special effort is to be made to reach a mosque for a communal *salah.*

The Third Pillar of Islam is *zakah,* the alms tax, because the Koran absolutely requires acts of charity. Allah looks with special favor on those who give to those less fortunate than themselves. The *zakah* in some Muslim states is collected exactly like a national tax, with the government in charge of its distribution. In other areas it is collected by the Muslim community, which decides for itself where it will do the most good. A poor woman begging on a street or by a city gate may be regarded by some as a nuisance, but to the truly devout she performs an important function by providing the opportunity to earn a blessing from God whenever a few coins are dropped in her lap. Many fundamentalist Christians like to emphasize the point that good works have absolutely nothing to do with salvation. To a Muslim, they are vital.

The Fourth Pillar is *sawm,* the sacrifice of fasting. The most important and longest period of fasting in Islam commemorates the first revelation to Muhammad in his lonely mountain hideaway. It usually takes the name of the ninth month of the Islamic calendar, the period of the fast, so is called Ramadan. For the entire month during the daylight hours the Muslim refrains from eating, drinking, smoking, and sexual relations. In an urban area, sunrise and sunset may be announced on radio or television, but the traditional method in rural areas is to hold up a piece of white yarn and a piece of black. If there is enough light to tell them apart, it is still daylight. If the eye cannot detect the difference in color, the sun has set.

Over the centuries the adjustment to Ramadan has caused many Muslims to turn their daily lives inside out for the month. They sleep during the day, then work, play, and feast at night. I was in the old city of Fez in Morocco during Ramadan, which was like a ghost town in the daylight hours. At sundown, shops opened, restaurants fired up their stoves, bonfires blazed, and the children ran and played in the streets.

The end of Ramadan is signaled by the appearance of the new moon, the slender crescent that has become the worldwide symbol of Islam. This explains why the Islamic international relief organization, which can hardly call itself by the Christian name of Red Cross, is called the Red Crescent. Many Christians, in their condemnation of Muhammad as the Antichrist and agent of Satan, made any Islamic symbol an automatic symbol of the Devil, including the crescent moon. In the Islamic world the coming of the new moon heralding the end of the month-long fast is celebrated with three days of *Id al-Fitr,* the Breaking of the Fast, a happy time of feasting, gifts, and extra voluntary almsgiving.

The Fifth Pillar is the *hajj,* the pilgrimage to Mecca. Every Muslim has the obligation to make the ritual journey at least once, unless prevented by circumstances such as an illness or handicap. The pilgrimage recalls Muhammad's flight to Medina, but has its traditional roots in pilgrimages said to have been made by Abraham. The primary destination of the pilgrimage is the Great Mosque at Mecca, where the courtyard holds the sacred Kaaba and the nearby holy well of Zem-Zem. The pilgrims circle the Kaaba seven times, struggling through the crowd to touch or kiss a small, mysterious black stone set in the side. The origin and purpose of the stone are long-forgotten, but its very existence is sacred. The pilgrims observe days of ritual, including the gathering of stones to throw at a pillar representing Satan and a run between two hills, followed by drinking from the sacred well of Zem-Zem in memory of the Old Testament story of Hagar's search in the desert for water for her son, Ismail.

On the fourth day, a ritual takes place that is especially important because it is duplicated on that same day by every Muslim family in the world. It is called *id al-Adha,* the Feast of the Sacrifice, in remembrance of Abraham's willingness to obey God in all things, even to the sacrifice of his beloved son, Isaac. The festive meal is prepared, but not all of it is eaten by the family. A share of every meal must be given to the homeless and the poor. The portion given is the sacrifice. The part eaten is the celebration of Abraham's submission and God's mercy.

It was the cash taken on the pilgrimage for this feast, as well as for almsgiving and living expenses, that made the pilgrim caravans such an attractive target for Crusader attacks. For many pilgrims, of course, other perils plagued them on the long journeys to Mecca. They climbed through bleak, high mountain passes and crossed vast, scorching deserts, through country toally alien to them. Many pilgrims died along the way. (This fact did not escape the atheistic communist hierarchy in the Soviet Union in later years. They used it during the oppressive totalitarian regime as just one more point to reinforce their efforts to stamp out the Muslim faith within the U.S.S.R. A few years ago I made a visit to an elementary school in the Muslim republic of Tadzhikistan. A classroom of ten-year-olds was decorated with the usual crayon drawings done by the students. One picture caught my eye because of a bright yellow sun dominating the scene. I could identify palm trees, but not the crude figures scattered among them. My Russian guide explained, "On the ground are dead men and dead camels. This picture shows the evil law of Muhammad that makes men die of thirst trying to get to Mecca.")

The Five Pillars of Islam defining the faith could be expected to provide a strong common bond for all Muslims and help them to achieve and maintain complete unity, but the written word cannot be free of the changes caused by different interpretations and teachings. So it has been from time to time with Christianity, and so it was with Islam.

It was the deep split dividing the adherents of Islam that made possible the victories of the First Crusade. At that time there was no thought of cooperation between the Shiite empire of Egypt on one side and the Orthodox Sunni Muslims of Syria on the other. Thus the land between, the Holy Land, was vulnerable to any attack from an invader. Once the two sides were joined together they became like the two handles of a nutcracker, with the Crusader states in the middle. A working knowledge of the sects of Islam became vital as a basis for Templar diplomats, anxious to keep the Islamic divisions from joining forces against the Christians.

The great rift had begun soon after the death of the founder of the faith. When Muhammad died in 632, it was his friend and father-in-law Abu Bekr who made the announcement: "O, Muslims! If any of you have been worshiping Muhammad, then I will tell you that Muhammad is dead. But if it is God that you worship, let me tell you that God is living and will never die!"

In selecting a man worthy to take Muhammad's place as the

leader of Islam, his followers adhered to ancient tribal tradition. The elders and important sheikhs, meeting to select a man of maturity, character, and wisdom to guide them, quickly chose Abu Bekr, who became the first caliph (*khalifa*), or "successor." Their choice was aided by the fact that Abu Bekr was related to the Prophet by marriage and was a member of his own family clan, the Hashim.

As frequently happens, a number of followers in more distant areas, such as the Bedouin nomads, decided that there was no authority without the Prophet and began to drift away. Some even became militantly antagonistic and had to be brought under control. The aging Abu Bekr selected a younger, more vigorous man for the task, a skilled fighter named Khalid ibn-al-Walid, whose string of victories for the faith would earn him the title of "Sword of Allah." Khalid swiftly and brilliantly defeated all of the enemies of Islam in Arabia in the first *jihad,* or War for the Faith.

The victorious Muslim soldiers were exhilarated by their triumphs and eager for more opportunities to prove with their swords the supremacy of Allah. They broke out across the northern border of Arabia, crossed Syria into Iraq, and took the city of Hira on the Euphrates. Now well supplied and enriched with plunder, the Muslim army, mounted on camels, turned back in an unprecedented march across the Syrian desert to capture the Byzantine city of Damascus.

Caliph Abu Bekr died during that campaign, to be succeeded as caliph by Umar ibn-Khattab, also a father-in-law to Muhammad and a member of his Hashimite clan. Umar displayed unexpected talents for organization and encouraged the *jihad.* Khalid added to his reputation for valor by defeating a Byzantine army in the field, then went on to capture Jerusalem in 640. At the same time, another Muslim army was well on its way to the conquest of Persia.

The next prize the Muslim warriors went after was Egypt, the jewel in the crown of the Byzantine colonies. The fertile Nile valley was the most heavily populated region in the Middle East, leading out to the Mediterranean and to port cities that had become highly profitable trade centers. Now mounted on swift Arabian horses as well as the desert-oriented camels, the Arab army galloped across the Nile delta with one sweeping victory after another, taking the walled port city of Alexandria in 646. The Muslim holdings, which had begun with the single city of Medina, had grown into a country, and were now exploding into an empire stretching from Egypt to Afghanistan.

Once again a caliph died during a military campaign when Umar was murdered by a Persian slave. With the selection of Umar ibn-Khattab's successor, the stage was set for the rupture of Islam. The man picked was the elderly Uthman ibn-Affan. Already in his seventies, the new caliph took immediate steps to secure as many riches as possible for his own family during the lifetime remaining to him. Uthman ibn-Affan was not of Muhammad's Hashimite clan, but from a clan called the Umayyad. The Hashimites watched as the highest posts in the new government were given to members of the Umayyad, who were sent to rule over conquered cities and provinces, while the Prophet's own people were totally cut out of the leadership of the religious movement that had begun with them. The jealousy and resentment threatened to degenerate into civil war, but the disputes were brought to a halt for a time beginning in 656, when Caliph Uthman ibn-Affan was murdered by a son of Abu Bekr.

Muhammad's fourth *khalifa* was Ali-ibn-Abi-Talib, the cousin who had married the Prophet's daughter Fatima. The inter-clan animosity surfaced again when Caliph Ali asked for the resignation of all Umayyad officials, whom he intended to replace with his own Hashimite supporters. Muawiza, the new head of the Umayyad clan, flatly refused to give up his power as governor of Syria, and civil war became a reality.

After months of petty fighting the two massed armies confronted each other on a wide plain in Iraq. As they clashed and then parted to regroup, it was clear that Ali's army would have the victory. Then occurred a strange event in the chronicles of military and Islamic history. The leaders of Muawiza's losing army collected every copy of the Koran that could be found. The pages were torn out and distributed to every man. When the forces faced each other again, Muawiza's men all carried pages of sacred scripture impaled on their swords and lances, which were pointed upward, not toward the enemy. Their words rang out: "Our weapons are raised only for God. Let God decide this conflict!" The clash of weapons was not heard, as Ali's bewildered men hesitated to attack when striking the enemy blades would mean slashing the divine revelations of the Prophet.

The heat of the expected combat cooled into unfocused disorder. Both sides looked for direction to their leaders, who decided to appoint delegates to settle the issue. The delegations agreed that neither Ali nor Muawiza should remain as caliph, and both should stand aside so that a new caliph could be chosen. Ali refused the settlement, convinced that he was the only possible legitimate successor. Arguments continued, but not the war. The two sides eventually went home, leaving the main issue unresolved.

Ali would have won the war on the battlefield, but he lost it through his behavior. His followers began to desert him because they felt that his manhood had deserted him first. Men argued that

Ali had shown only weakness, and fighting men are always angry to have an assured victory talked away by politicians. No one knew which side the murderer was on, but the still unresolved split in Islam took shape when an angry man ran his sword through Ali, who was walking to a mosque to pray.

Muawiza now declared himself to be the true caliph. He called upon all Muslims to follow him and announced that his son Yazid would succeed him as caliph. Muhammad had said nothing about the leadership of Islam being hereditary, but to many Muslims it solved the problems of succession that had resulted in the murder of three of the first four caliphs. They accepted Muawiza, who thus founded the dynamic Umayyad dynasty of the caliphate.

The Umayyad caliphs moved their headquarters away from the Prophet's family at Medina and Mecca to the Syrian city of Damascus. From there they planned the Muslim conquests that built their empire. To the east, their horsemen moved all the way across Afghanistan into India. To the west, they conquered the North African lands all the way to the Atlantic coast. When they reached the coast, curiosity prompted them to send scouting parties across the narrow strait into southern Spain. Reports came back that the ruling Visigoths, who centuries earlier had wrested the land from the Romans, did not appear to be prepared for war. In 710, ships were gathered to carry an army of seven thousand Muslims onto the continent of Europe under the Berber general Tariq, a former slave. Tariq landed his army near a monumental rock rising nearly fourteen hundred feet above the water, so they named the rock the Mount of Tariq, *Jabal Tariq,* a name that would evolve over the course of history into Gibraltar.

When all of Spain had fallen to Muslim might, they pushed on to investigate a fair land on the other side of the Pyrenees. Liking what they saw, an army was organized to invade France, advancing as far as the city of Bordeaux. Charles Martel, a French leader whose grandson would become the emperor Charlemagne, rallied the towns and tribes to put together an army to stem the tide of Islam. In October 732 they met near the city of Tours. The Muslim army was all mounted, while the French were almost all on foot, so Martel elected to take a defensive role. The two armies stared at each other for a week until Abd-al-Rahman, the Muslim ruler of Spain who was in command, grew impatient with the delay and ordered the charge.

The French foot soldiers, armed with spears, should have been overwhelmed by the horses and camels crashing into them, but they were fighting for their lives and their homes and fiercely held their ground. Neither side would yield, and only the coming of darkness forced the Muslims to fall back, leaving more dead on the field than they had ever anticipated. Fortunately for the French, one of those bodies was that of the Muslim leader Abd-al-Rahman.

The next morning the French took their positions again, battered but resolute, ready to receive another Muslim charge. It never came. Scouts sent out by Martel reported that the enemy had retreated under cover of darkness. The Battle of Tours had turned the tide, preventing Europe from becoming another Islamic nation. Charles Martel's exalted reputation as the decisive battle's victorious hero reached such proportions that he was able to found a dynasty.

Meanwhile, there had been no Charles Martel to hold the Muslims in check as they flooded into Central Asia. They marched all the way to the Aral Sea, seizing the fabled cities of Bokhara and Samarkand. By the time the First Crusade was launched, the Muslim empire stretched from Spain across North Africa, into Iraq and Armenia, and through Persia and Central Asia to the Indus River. Much more of the world's surface was Muslim than was Christian, and there were millions more men who followed the caliphs than followed the pope.

Back when the caliph Ali was murdered, a number of his followers rejected the Umayyad claim to the caliphate. They clung to the belief that Muhammad would have wanted the disputed leadership bestowed on the husband of his beloved daughter Fatima. They formed the *Shiat Ali,* the Party of Ali, from which they came to be known as the Shiites. The sect exists to this day, although very much a minority. Claiming no more than 15 percent of the total Muslim population of the world, they still number about sixty million. Taking root first in Persia, now called Iran, they have remained the dominant religious and political force in that country, making up almost 50 percent of the Iranian population. Shiites are led by *Imams,* or teachers. The most famous—and notorious—imam in recent times was the Ayatollah Khomeini. At the time of the First Crusade, there was a Shiite caliph in Egypt, but that position would be wiped out during the crusading period.

The infallibility of the imams' teachings comes from Allah, to Muhammad, to Ali. Husayn, the grandson of Muhammad and son of Ali and Fatima, established a bloodline of succession that provided nine of the first twelve Shiite imams. Most of them met violent deaths through murder, death in battle, or execution for treason. The twelfth imam, however, who also was named Muhammad, disappeared into a cave in the year 878. Imam Muhammad's mysterious absence provides the basis for a messianic belief that he will one day return, just as many Christians believe Jesus Christ will return, before the end of the world. The imam Muhammad is awaited as the Mahdi, The Expected One.

Several times throughout the centuries a leader has appeared who claimed to be the Mahdi. By far the most famous was Muhammad Ahmed Ibn Seyyid Abdullah, who proclaimed himself to be Mahdi in 1881 and rose to power in the Sudan. His followers murdered the English general Charles "Chinese" Gordon at Khartoum, but were finally put down in the last great British cavalry charge at Omdurman in 1898, recently enough to have been witnessed by the young Winston Churchill.

The Shiites, frequently identified as the "fundamentalist" or "radical" Muslims, branched off into over seventy different divisions or sects. Of these, a major division was based on the belief that it was not the twelfth imam but the seventh, named Ismail, who was the Expected One. As a result, the adherents to this belief, called the Ismailis, became preoccupied with the number seven, endowing it with spiritual, mystical, and even magical properties.

One of the sects that sprang from the Ismailis was feared more than any other Muslim faction, because it claimed the right to murder anyone who stood in its way. The sect was founded by an Ismaili missionary who led his followers in the capture of their first fortress at Alamut, in Persia, less than ten years before the First Crusade was launched.

Legend claims that it was at Alamut that the leader of the sect had a private garden of infinite beauty, with the sparkling fountains so precious to the desert dweller and a selection of the most beautiful and most sexually accomplished young women in the land. A young member of the sect would be given hashish to numb his mind to the point of unconsciousness. When he awoke, he found himself in the fabled garden, where the beautiful young ladies fed him morsels of the most delicious foods. They treated him to every sexual delight he had ever heard of, and to some that he had never even imagined. As the day progressed, more and more hashish would be pressed upon him until he passed out again.

When he woke the next morning to his usual surroundings he was encouraged to recount his drug-induced adventure. After he had spelled out the unbelievable delights, he was told that he had been favored by Allah by being given a tiny glimpse of the highest level of heaven reserved for those martyrs who die for their faith. For such loyalty and devotion to God, the delights he had experienced so briefly were available for all eternity. Now he longed for nothing more in this world than the chance to die in the service of Allah.

In answer to his plea, he was given intense training to kill an enemy of God, who would be identified for him by the leader of the sect, called by chroniclers the grand master. Thus would he earn eternal bliss in paradise, because his would be a suicide mission.

His mind and heart must be set on a successful kill and not at all on his own escape. He learned the techniques of the dagger: where and how deep to strike, and how to circumvent armor. He was taught the use of poisons. He was instructed in the use of disguises and, if necessary, instructed in other religions, including Christianity, in order to be able to pass himself off convincingly as a member of the victim's own faith.

With a corps of such young men ready to kill and die, the grand master had a weapon that was often as powerful as an entire army. It inspired such fear that even the greatest rulers would think twice before going against the wishes of the grand master.

Based on their alleged use of hashish to trick the young followers, or perhaps just to give them courage, the sect became known as the *Hashshashin*. It proved to be a difficult word for the Crusaders, who took it into Church Latin as the *Assassini,* and into English as the Assassins, giving a sinister new word to the language.

In truth, the Garden of Paradise legend is probably just that, nor would such elaborate trickery have been necessary. There has never been a shortage of young Shiite Muslims ready to die for their faith, as has been dramatically proven in our own time. The Shiite group in Lebanon called the Hezbollah did not hesitate to have one of its members drive a truckload of explosives at full, suicidal speed into a Marine barracks in Lebanon. As we shall see, the Assassins were finally stopped by the Mongols in Persia and by the Egyptians in Syria, but the Ismaili sect lives to this day, with hundreds of thousands of adherents who call their leader the Agha Khan.

The tales of sexual delights in the Islamic heaven intrigued Europeans, whose Christian concept of heaven was totally devoid of even thoughts of sexual contact. They exaggerated the already exaggerated stories brought home to them, culminating perhaps in Gibbon's description. In his *Decline and Fall of the Roman Empire* he revealed that even on the lowest level of the Islamic paradise the celestial euphoria would include orgasms that lasted for a thousand years:

"Seventy *Houris,* or black-eyed girls of resplendent beauty, blooming youth, virgin purity, and exquisite sensitivity, will be created for the use of the meanest believer; a moment of pleasure will be prolonged to a thousand years, and his [sexual] faculties will be increased a hundred-fold to render him worthy of felicity."

Another sect evolving from the Ismailis was the Qarmations. Membership required going through an initiation rite, and although based on the Koran, the teachings were relaxed sufficiently to admit men of all religions or races. The Qarmations were active in organizing formal guilds of craftsmen before that structure became popular in Europe. In his book, *Islam, Beliefs and Practices,* C.E. Farah says, "Some authorities believe that their concept and organization of the guilds within a fixed ceremonial and ritualistic structure led to the rise of Freemasonry, with its clear reflections of Arabo-Islamic influences, and the Medieval guild system."

The Druzes, still active today in the mountains of Lebanon, have their own identity for the Muslim messiah. They await the return of the Shiite caliph of Egypt, al-Hakim, who met death in a plot engineered by his own sister, after he had publicly questioned her chastity. The Druzes are best known for exercising their religion in the strictest secrecy. They hold their services on Thursdays, usually on top of a high hill from which it is easier to detect the approach of strangers. Scholars ache for information, but to a Druze there is nothing more sacred than his vow of secrecy. He will not discuss his faith with anyone.

All of these sects and the dozens more that together make up the Shiites are still just a small minority, although a very aggressive minority, within Islam. By far the greatest number of Muslims, over 85 percent, adhere to the faith known formally as *Ahl al-Sunna wa'l-Hadith.* The *Sunna* is the "path" laid down in the Koran, while the *Hadith* is made up of the sayings and acts of Muhammad as collected after his death. Thus they have two guidebooks for their faith, much as the Jews have both the Talmud and the Torah. This is the substantial majority of Muslims known as the *Sunni.* The Shiites and the Sunnis do occasionally work together in the face of a common enemy or to achieve a common Islamic purpose, but the animosities are as strong as they are ancient in their origins and not likely to disappear. In the course of my research for this work, I talked to a devout Sunni Muslim. When I asked several questions about the Shiites he said, "Why do you want to know about Shiites? They believe in a false God!"

It was that incessant animosity between the Shiites, who controlled Egypt, and the Sunnis, who controlled Syria, that made the successes of the First Crusade possible, especially in that the Sunni Syrians also had to contend with Shiite enemies to the other side of them in Persia. At the time of that Crusade, the Sunni caliph was based in Baghdad, while the Shiite caliph was resident in Cairo. It became the focal point of Christian diplomacy to play off one side against the other, until the time came that all of the Middle East was united under one dynamic leader who was given the honorary title of *Salah-ed-Din,* or Saladin.

Within the context of the Crusades, the Christian leaders had to learn with whom they were dealing. They had to learn that the leader of their enemies, the spiritual successor of Muhammad, was the *khalifa,* the caliph. He was the ruler, because Islam began with no separation of church and state. The secular administrative duties were usually assigned by the caliph to a chief executive officer, called the *wazir,* or vizier. A military general or governor of a city-state was frequently known as *amir* or emir. A male descendant of Muhammad's bloodline was honored with the title of *sharif.* Hussein of Jordan has a title much more important to certain of his followers than that of king, in that he is also the hereditary sharif of Mecca. Since he is of the clan named after the Prophet's great-grandfather Hashim, the official name of his domain is The Hashimite Kingdom of Jordan, just as the Egyptian empire was called "Fatamid" because Caliph Ali had been married to Muhammad's daughter Fatima.

There are still both Shiite and Sunni states that believe they must conform to Shari'a, the Koranic law, as administered by a judge called a *qadi,* or kadi. At the time of the Crusades the punishments called for under Koranic law were, if anything, less brutal than those levied upon Christians in medieval Europe and in the Holy Land. Today, however, many people, including some Muslims, cannot accept that someone guilty of adultery should be stoned to death, although there are probably those who would approve the law that says if a man accuses a woman of adultery and cannot prove it with witnesses, he should be punished with eighty "stripes" of a whip on his bare back. Sura IV of the Koran sets forth the rights of women, but Verse 34 would give trouble in many places today because it permits a husband to beat his wife for disobedience. It says in part, "Men are in charge of women, because Allah hath made one of them to excel the other, and because they spend their property [in the support of their women]. So good women are the obedient...as for those from whom ye fear rebellion, admonish them and ban them to beds apart, and scourge them."

Perhaps the best known punishment is that set forth in Sura V, Verse 38: "As for the thief, both male and female, cut off their hands. It is the reward of their own deeds, an exemplary punishment from Allah." In practice, the punishment was reserved for a third offense and meant the loss of the right hand only, for social reasons. Eating in any family or other group was from one large communal bowl, with the selected bits removed with the right hand only, because the left hand was used for wiping after a visit to the toilet. The loss of his right hand made the thief a social outcast, never for the rest of his life permitted access to the communal food pot, into which he could only dip his contaminated left hand. He had to eat alone as best he could for the rest of his days. One might be tempted to believe that the enforcement of Koranic law will steadily decline, but the evidence suggests that it will be a slow process. The government of the Sudan announced the reinstatement of the Koranic code in January of 1991. Seven months later, Pakistan announced a return to the death penalty for anyone who defames the Prophet Muhammad. At the time of the Crusades, Koranic law was universal to all Islam and strictly enforced.

This was the new world the Templar order had to learn, a world different in religion, law, custom, tradition, and language. They would learn to deal with the leaders of Islam, often as enemies, frequently as allies. They would have Muslim tenants on their grazing lands, farms, and sugar plantations, and in their factories. They would meet Muslims in death struggles, but also in trade, and even in banking. Some Templars would master the Arabic tongue and be selected by Christian kings as their envoys to Muslim courts. They would come to rely on Muslim craftsmen and employ Muslim servants. The Templars, after all, were not involved in a crusading pilgrimage that would find them returning home in six months to a year's time. They had signed up for the duration, not the duration of a war, but the duration of their lives. They were in the Holy Land to fight for their God, and so were their adversaries. Many a Templar would die on the battlefield, where the last words he might hear would be the battle cry of his enemy: *Allahu Akbar!* "God is great!"

PART TWO

At War in the Holy Land

5

St. Bernard's Crusade

1126 to 1148

$\mathcal{A}$S THE NEWLY RECRUITED Knights Templar arrived in the Holy Land, most of them were assigned to Jerusalem, where there was more than enough room for all the men and horses at the base in the al-Aqsa Mosque on the Temple Mount. It was only natural for the Templars to acquire houses and stables in the other Christian cities, too, so they would have bases at both ends of the pilgrim roads they were dedicated to protecting. The major routes from the coast to Jerusalem, then on to the Jordan River and to the towns of Nazareth and Bethlehem, stretched for many miles through threatening countryside, but to the king of Jerusalem road protection was just a side issue, a service that did not address the sovereign's dire need for military units that could take the field in war.

After his coronation as king of Jerusalem, Baldwin II had assigned his county of Edessa to his cousin and loyal vassal, Joscelin of Courtenay. As king, Baldwin had presumed that the Christian lords of Edessa, Antioch, and Tripoli would naturally come together in cooperative efforts against Muslim incursions, based on their common Christianity. He was disappointed, as it grew obvious that the nobles' individual determination to increase their own lands and power was much stronger than their love for Christ.

As Grand Master de Payens had prepared to seek papal approval in Rome for his Templar order, Baldwin II had urged him to plead with the monarchs and nobles of Europe to take the cross. Without them, the Latin kingdom probably could not survive. Many knights did take the Crusader vow but, as it turned out, not nearly enough. A strong new Muslim leader, Zengi, was on the rise. Zengi was positioned for power when the Seljuk sultan named him to be the *atabeg* (deputy) for the Kurdish city of Mosul. Zengi made a separate treaty of peace for Edessa with Joscelin of Courtenay, then proceeeded to take over the Syrian city-states of Aleppo, Shaizar, and Homs, adding their fighting forces to his own.

The heir to Bohemond, the original ruler of Antioch, came of age and sailed from Italy to the Holy Land to assume power as Prince Bohemond II. He soon took Alice, a daughter of Baldwin II, as his princess. For a couple of years Bohemond looked with avarice on some nearby lands in Armenia, and finally in the year 1130 he set out with an army to add those lands to his principality of Antioch.

He did not know that the king of Armenia, many of whose followers lived in Antioch, was aware of Bohemond's plans and had prepared to meet the threat through an alliance with the Turks. As the inexperienced Bohemond marched confidently into Armenian territory, he was suddenly slammed by hordes of Turkish cavalry roaring at him from all sides. When the brief battle was over, the grossly outnumbered army of Antioch was sprawled dead on the field, since not even the wounded or the captives were allowed to live. Bohemond's head was brought to the Turkish leader, who had it cleaned and pickled, then sent as a gift to the Sunni caliph at Baghdad.

The heiress to the throne of Antioch was Bohemond's two-year-old infant daughter, named Constance. The child's mother, Princess Alice, decided that she would put the child in a convent and rule the land herself. The nobles of Antioch were not happy with Alice's moves to take control and sent for her father, King Baldwin II. In response, Alice dispatched an envoy to the Muslim *atabeg* Zengi. Incredibly, she offered that the Christian principality of Antioch would do homage to the Muslim ruler, if he would just confirm her power and protect her from the wrath of her father.

Unfortunately for her, Baldwin's men intercepted Alice's envoy to Zengi, learned of his mission, and hanged him without further ado. At the city walls, Baldwin found Antioch barred to him, but no fight was necessary as loyal nobles inside overpowered the guards and opened the gates. Alice feared for her life, but was merely exiled to nearby Lattakieh. Baldwin II made himself the regent of Antioch and went home to Jerusalem, where he began to suffer from increasing health problems, until his end appeared near. In midsummer of 1131 Baldwin assembled his court to tell them he was dying. He asked that all recognize the succession of his oldest daughter Melisende and her husband Fulk, and of their infant son, also named Baldwin. He said good-bye and abandoned his royal robes for the simple garb of a monk. He went through the ceremony to become a canon of the Holy Sepulcher and died about a week later.

The rulers of Antioch and Jerusalem were dead, and Joscelin of Courtenay, count of Edessa, would not survive them long. As Baldwin lay dying, Joscelin was besieging a castle in Syria. His engineers had dug a tunnel, apparently without proper concern for roof support. Joscelin was standing above the tunnel when it caved in, plunging him into a deep hole where he was crushed by falling rock. He was dug out still alive, but died a few weeks later.

One of King Fulk's first problems was that, with Baldwin II dead, Count Pons of Tripoli, Princess Alice of Antioch, and young Joscelin II of Edessa all asserted their independence, recognizing no authority above their own. Fulk had to take an army to Tripoli and Antioch to bring them back into his kingdom.

Count Hugh of Jaffa went so far as to conspire against Jerusalem with agents of Egypt, to the point that one of his own stepsons publicly accused him of treason and challenged him to let God judge the issue in a trial by combat, a perfectly legal procedure of the day. Armed and mounted, Hugh's stepson waited on the field at the appointed time, but for whatever reason, Hugh didn't show up. A royal council declared him guilty by default. His punishment was a three-year exile. The punishment was unusually light, but there was a reason for that. King Fulk's beautiful wife was totally in love with Hugh and not with Fulk, whom she had been ordered to marry by her father. Fulk was eager for her love, and so careful not to offend her.

As Hugh waited for the ship that was to take him into exile, passing the time in a dice game, a French knight came up behind him and stabbed him several times. The knight, obviously guilty, was captured immediately, but a rumor spread swiftly that King Fulk had instigated the attack. The knight confessed that the attack had been his own idea, and that he had hoped that the murder of the king's enemy would win him some royal reward. Fulk's actions as he attempted to clear his name with his subjects and with his wife must stand as extraordinarily barbarous, even in those barbarous times.

The guilty knight was taken to a public square. After confessing his own guilt and the king's innocence, he was tied down so an executioner could chop off one of his legs with an ax. Assistants standing by quickly applied boiling pitch to the gaping wound, adding to the pain but preserving his life. With the first sign that the mutilated man had somewhat recovered, the other leg was struck off, with the same agonizing first aid. After a while, an arm was hacked off, then the other arm. When fully revived, the limbless trunk was propped up and prodded with hot irons to force the knight to scream out the king's innocence. Then the last merciful stroke cut off his head.

Zengi's Syrian vassals made several raids to take portions of Edessa and Antioch, but there was no outbreak yet of total war. As often happened, the threat from Egypt was temporarily relieved by the special brand of lunacy that thrived at the court in Cairo. The latest event was the reign of the vizier Hasan, the favorite son of the Shiite caliph. The young man's blood-crazed defense of his own power led to frequent executions at all levels, resulting in open revolt after he had beheaded over forty emirs of the empire. Those that were left took up arms while there was still time. The caliph saved himself by murdering his own son and delivering the body to the angry emirs.

Fulk had no fears of the Egyptians to the southwest—the court was too disparate and disorganized to plan an attack on the Christians—but Zengi's raids on the Crusader lands and those of his Syrian vassals kept him constantly in the field. Every Christian casualty in his tiny army was a serious loss. It was about this time that the new master of the Hospitallers, a French nobleman, decided that his order should emulate the Knights Templar, and take in knights that would fight for the Holy Land, but it would be a while before they had recruited enough men to make an army that could help the king.

Reviving a political problem that Fulk didn't need, Princess Alice came back to Antioch and reasserted her right to rule. The answer was to find a husband for the rightful heir, the nine-year-old Princess Constance, so Fulk arranged her betrothal to Raymond, a younger son of the duke of Aquitaine. Since the arrival from Europe of such a lofty noble could not be kept secret, Princess Alice was told that Raymond had come to Antioch to press his suit with her. As she dressed for the occasion and sat with her assembled ladies to receive Raymond at her palace, he was in the cathedral being married to her daughter Constance. Raymond became the lawful prince of Antioch.

What Raymond found as he surveyed his new principality was an eastern frontier lost to Zengi, a castle lost to the sect of Assassins, and several towns taken by Prince Leo of Armenia. Raymond took to the field to recover some of these lands, expecting help from Joscelin, count of Edessa, against Leo of Armenia. Shocked and bewildered, he was beaten back by both Leo and Joscelin, who was Leo's nephew. Joint efforts by Latin Christians were still out of the question.

Nor were the Muslims as yet unified. Zengi had added to his growing kingdom the city of Homs, which was the dowry of his new wife, the mother of the young ruler of Damascus. Perhaps the young man's behavior became wilder as a result of his mother's absence, but about a year after her departure he apparently had a set-to with three boys, sexual playthings officially known at court as "pages." The three pages teamed up one night and murdered their master in his sleep, for which they were all publicly crucified.

Under King Fulk, the Knights Templar began turning away from their original purpose of protecting the routes of Christian pilgrims and started participating in Christian battles, but their first recorded engagement brought them no glory. They had evidently not yet learned the favorite Turkish battlefield move, the feigned retreat, employed to induce the enemy to give chase and be drawn into a trap. A company of inexperienced Templar knights was induced to chase after a band of "retreating" Muslim cavalry that led them straight into an ambush. They all died in a very important lesson learned the hard way.

Fulk was not a brilliant king, but he was holding his kingdom together with very limited resources, and he was succeeding only because of the constant wars between rival Muslim factions. Then, on a beautiful fall day in 1143, he decided to take a break from all the turmoil and spend a day of recreation in the country with his wife and children. Riding across a field, the party flushed a rabbit, and the king and his men galloped after it in a joyful chase. Fulk's horse stepped in a hole and went down, taking the king with it. He died a few days later from the head wounds he sustained in the fall. Now the kingdom of Jerusalem would be ruled jointly by Queen Melisende and her thirteen-year-old son Baldwin. It was a great opportunity for Zengi, who over the next few months would deliver the most severe blows the Crusader states had yet taken.

Zengi had some of his troops make a feint at a vassal of Joscelin, which soon saw Joscelin leading the bulk of his army out of Edessa on a rescue mission. The way was open for Zengi to bring his main army up to the walls of Edessa. Behind the walls, Joscelin's small army would have put up a strong defense, but in the open field they were well outnumbered by Zengi's forces. Joscelin appealed to Raymond of Antioch to come help him save his capital city, but he was ignored. An appeal to Queen Melisende was more successful, but she took too long to assemble a relieving army.

With Joscelin and the leading soldiers outside the walls, leadership of the defense fell on the archbishop of Edessa, who had no military experience. Zengi had siege machines and miners, which the civilians in Edessa did not know how to combat. It took just four weeks for the Muslims to take down a section of the city wall, and the citizens inside could do nothing to stop the Syrians,

Kurds, and Turks who came at them over the rubble of the breach. The Christians ran across the city to the protection of the citadel, but for some insane reason the archbishop had ordered the doors of the castle to be barred. The civilians, crowded together on the square in front of the citadel, were easy to kill, and by the time Zengi arrived to take personal control thousands had died, including the archbishop. Zengi had the remaining population sorted out, leaving alone the Armenian and Greek Christians. The Roman Christians were further sorted into two groups, the men separated from the women and children. The men were killed, while the women and children were spared for the slave market. Zengi re-formed his army, then set about capturing every city and town in the county of Edessa east of the Euphrates River. Joscelin was left with the smaller remnant on the west side of the river. The Muslims had taken back a substantial portion of the lands won by the Christians in the First Crusade.

Zengi moved his armies toward the south to take Damascus, but he never got there. On the campaign, he assailed a eunuch he had caught drinking from Zengi's own glass. The furious eunuch waited until his master retired for the night, then murdered him in his sleep. Zengi's oldest son galloped off to Mosul to take control there, while his younger son, Nur ed-Din, took over the Syrian lands, supported by his brilliant Kurdish general, Shirkuh, whose nephew would become the most memorable Muslim leader of the Middle Ages.

The county of Edessa had been a great shield for the kingdom of Jerusalem against the militant Turks and Persians to the north and east. Its loss threatened the continued existence of the Crusader states and the Christian control of the Holy Places of Jesus Christ.

In 1145, Queen Melisende of Jerusalem sent the bishop of Jabala to the new pope, Eugenius III, with a frantic appeal for help. The bishop was shocked to find the pope not at Rome but in exile at Viterbo. Angry at the government of the Church, a committee of powerful Roman citizens had driven the papal curia out of Rome, so Pope Eugenius had pressing problems of his own. He decided that he would call for a Crusade to save the Holy Land, but the call would have political considerations.

Conrad of Hohenstauffen, king of Germany, would not go, for he was the pope's hope of retaking Rome and restoring it to papal control. Conrad would also be asked to hold back aggressive moves against papal authority coming from Roger II of Sicily. Roger, who had gained control of the Norman lands in Sicily and Italy, had challenged the authority of the Church when he had crowned himself king without seeking either the blessings or annointment of the Holy See.

Eugenius decided to turn to King Louis VII of France, who had already managed to alienate the papacy and was anxious to make amends. In armed conflict with the count of Champagne, he had attacked the castle at Vitry-sur-Marne, where his troops had set the castle ablaze, but so carelessly that the entire village caught fire. The frightened villagers crowded into their central church, which was soon also swept up in the blaze. The screaming occupants could not escape, and those who did not die from smoke inhalation met their end when the great roof crashed down on top of them. Louis VII had burned down a house of God, killing thirteen hundred Christians who had sought refuge there. The pope placed him under interdict, but that was not as threatening to the young king as the angry letters that reached him from the most influential man in France, if not in all of Europe. Louis VII had aroused the fury of Bernard of Clairvaux.

Bernard's influence and reputation had grown since he had acted as sponsor for the order of the Knights Templar back in 1128. His every speech, his every letter, was taken as the voice of authority. Pope Eugenius III had started as a lowly member of Bernard's Cistercian order and still looked to his former abbot for advice, which Bernard didn't hesitate to offer. Louis VII, at risk of making an enemy of the most important churchman in Europe, made the sensible choice. He yielded to Bernard's criticism and asked for guidance. His new guide was the most Crusade-oriented churchman of his time, so it is not surprising that Bernard suggested that Louis VII expunge his grievous sin by taking an army to the Holy Land.

Louis's response was to call a meeting of his leading nobles at Bourges at the end of 1145. He told them of his decision to take the cross and to lead a French army to Jerusalem, then called on his vassals to take the Crusader vow with him. He got little response, and it appeared that there would be no Crusade. It was a situation that called for all the fire and organizing ability of a Bernard of Clairvaux. His friends the Templars, under the command of their French preceptor, Everard de Barres, were already recruiting and equipping men for the Crusade that Bernard had promised them. Bernard went to work on the French.

First, he caused a bull to be issued by Pope Eugenius, addressed primarily to the king and barons of France, exhorting them to take the cross. Next, a great assembly was called, to take place on Palm Sunday of the following spring at Vézelay. The principal speaker was to be Bernard of Clairvaux. Ample time was allowed for the bull's distribution and for travel plans for those who would cover great distances to hear the famous speaker.

The assembly was well planned. As with the Council of Clermont that had called the First Crusade, the anticipated crowd would not fit in the cathedral, so a high platform was erected outside, from which Bernard would deliver his address. He was so confident that he could arouse men to take the Crusader vow that hundreds of red cloth crosses were sewn in advance to be distributed to those who would take the sacred oath.

As expected, the Palm Sunday gathering at the Vézélay was vast, and the crowds were not disappointed. Bernard was at his most eloquent, as he promised the favor of God, total absolution from sin, and an eternity of heavenly bliss for those who would risk their lives for Christ. The response was more than even Bernard had hoped for. When the ready-made supply of crosses ran out, he took off his own red cloak and ordered that it be cut into strips to make more on the spot. The Second Crusade was assured. It would leave for the Holy Land the following year.

Bernard himself was caught up in the frenzy he had created and was not modest about his achievement. To Pope Eugenius III he wrote, "I opened my mouth, I spoke, and at once the Crusaders have multiplied to infinity. Villages and towns are now deserted. You will scarcely find one man for every seven women. Everywhere you see widows whose husbands are still alive." But he must have been aware of his gross exaggeration. Far from an "infinity" of Crusaders, there were nowhere near enough to make up an effective army, so he went on the road to make his boast a reality.

He preached his way successfully through Burgundy and Lorraine and into Flanders, where a message from the archbishop of Cologne caught up with him. A monastic fanatic named Rudolph was reported to be preaching his own maniacal answer to the call to Crusade, inciting the people to massacre the Jews living in their communities. Bloody mass murders had taken place in the archbishop's own city of Cologne and in Strasburg, Worms, and Mainz. Since Rudolph was a member of Bernard's own Cistercian order, the archbishop's message begged the abbot of Clairvaux to stop the senseless slaughter.

Bernard hurried to Germany, where the situation quickly confirmed the truth of what he had been told. The anti-Semite Rudolph was ordered to return to his monastery and to stay there with his mouth shut. That put an end to the problem Bernard had come to solve, but since he was already in Germany, he decided to take this opportunity to exhort the German nobles to participate in the coming Crusade.

There was no enthusiasm for a Crusade among the German barons, who felt that they had their own crusade at home. For generations they had been fighting incessant wars against the pagan tribes on their eastern borders. They didn't need to travel over a thousand miles to prove their love for Christ on foreign soil: Weren't they already forcibly converting the heathens they subdued, and killing those who refused to accept Christ? Nor was King Conrad any more enthusiastic. Conrad had made a deal with Pope Eugenius in which he had agreed to drive the dissidents out of Rome, to return it to the papacy, and to keep Roger II in his place. In return, Eugenius would anoint Conrad as Holy Roman Emperor, placing him on a level higher than all the kings of Christendom. Conrad wanted nothing to interfere with that arrangement. Bernard found that out when he met with Conrad, who was unmoved by the abbot's pleas for German help for the Second Crusade. But Bernard had a driving will and a reputation to uphold. Even though he had to ask the German bishops to provide interpreters, he made a preaching tour throughout Conrad's lands. He met with enough success, especially among the commoners, that Conrad agreed to meet with him again at the end of the year. Bernard selected Christmas Day as the time to deliver his impassioned petition for Crusader support, but he got no response from the German king. In a fit of frustration, Bernard appeared at Conrad's court again two days later. This time his sermon was angry. He turned on Conrad, describing the great benefits that had been bestowed on him by a generous God. Finally, Bernard had a question directly from Christ to put to the German king. "Man," he thundered, "what ought I to have done for you that I have not done?" Conrad's resistance collapsed, and the victory went to Bernard of Clairvaux. Now there would be a German army as part of this great Crusade.

Pope Eugenius had not received the news about Conrad by the time he left Viterbo for France in January of 1147. He still perceived the coming Crusade as a French operation, especially because of his own experience in trying to go back to Rome. He had gone there hoping to receive a warm welcome, but after a few days he had been forced to run for his life. He was still counting on Conrad to help restore the ancient papal seat, but arriving in Lyons in March, the pope got the news of what he considered to be Conrad's defection. His plans to regain Rome were shattered by the German king's decision to go to Jerusalem. When messengers from Conrad met him a few weeks later with Conrad's request for a personal meeting, Eugenius flatly refused to meet with the German king who had betrayed him.

Proceeding toward the goal of his visit, the pope joined King Louis VII during Easter week at St. Denis. It was an event of great ceremony and pageantry, which included a force of three hundred Knights Templar in orderly ranks, most of them recently recruited, clad in their pure white robes and commanded by the French master who would lead them in the coming campaign. Abbot Suger, who was to act as regent of France during the Second Crusade, presented Louis VII with a magnificent scarlet and gold banner, the oriflamme of St. Denis, to be carried before the French host. Pope Eugenius III had a special presentation for his private army of Knights Templar.

This was a time when heraldry was taking hold, and nobles and kings were proud to display symbols of their rank and power. Monks, of course, did not require or even merit such devices, but the Knights Templar were different. They were all of knightly lineage, mixing in the secular world. As warriors for Christ, they had a right to be recognized at any time by any Christian, and a need to quickly recognize one another on the field of battle. The pope decreed that from this day forward the Knights Templar, and only the Knights Templar, would wear a special red cross with blunt wedge-shaped arms called the cross *patée* on the left breasts of their white robes. In addition, in what may have been the creation of the very first military shoulder patch, Eugenius decreed that a smaller version of the distinctive red cross would be worn on the Templars' left shoulders.

For the young Templar recruits, the event strongly reinforced their decision to join the holy order. They had never expected to see a pope in their lifetime, yet here they were in the presence of the Holy Father, receiving his personal blessing. Not only had he prayed for them, but he had honored them with their own distinctive badge. In the days ahead, as each man had the red crosses added to his white robe, he would be infused with a new pride in his Templar vows.

He already had a difficult image to live up to, not an image as yet earned on the battlefield, but one fantasized by St. Bernard. Grand Master de Payens had several times asked Bernard for a definitive treatise on the aims and merits of the Templars that could be used for soliciting gifts and attracting recruits. Bernard had responded, "to brandish my pen at the foe in place of the lance I may not wield," with *De laude novae militae,* a document that struggled to find more and more ways to praise the Templars, while working just as hard to level every demeaning accusation at the secular knights. It assumed a level of virtue, bravery, skill, and devotion that no man could live up to, but it did help to keep rich gifts flowing to the order.

Nor was the time wasted while the Templars waited for the long march to begin. The recruits had to learn attitudes totally new to them, like instant response to orders with no questions asked. They learned to inspect their horses and equipment on a daily basis, with punishments for those who didn't. They learned to move and fight together. They went to bed when they were told and got up when they were told. The rewards of that discipline and training would become obvious to everyone on the journey ahead.

Conrad grew tired of waiting for the French Crusaders. In May of 1147 he began an independent march eastward with an army of about twenty thousand men. He was joined by the kings of Bohemia and Poland and by his heir, Duke Frederick of Swabia, together with a battery of German nobles and bishops. Jealousies and disagreements among the leadership were to build up along the way, although there was little trouble during their passage across Hungary, because the long trek was just beginning. They had food supplies, with plenty of money to acquire more. As they advanced into the territory of the emperor of Byzantium, however, both food and money were running low.

Men desperate with hunger often don't much care who owns the food, or what price is put on it. The German soldiers roamed the countryside, and wherever they found food they took it. Peasants and merchants who objected to being robbed were frequently killed for their recalcitrant attitudes. The Greeks also found it prudent to hide their women from an army that acted increasingly like uncontrollable rabble.

Once the Germans had stolen the food they wanted at the town of Philippopolis and seemed to have calmed down, a local juggler ventured to earn a few pennies by showing off his extraordinary skills to the visiting Crusaders. The Germans, who had never seen anything like it, superstitiously decided that what the juggler was showing them was beyond human ability. They grabbed him, accusing him of sorcery. The commotion triggered a riot in which the houses outside the walls were burned to the ground, while the local citizens ran for the protection of the city walls.

Emperor Manuel sent Byzantine troops to keep the Crusader army in line, but they were not effective against the aggressive Germans. Stragglers became almost certain victims of Byzantine revenge. However, when a German noble developed a sickness and dropped behind the army, only to be murdered and robbed by marauding Greeks, Frederick of Swabia took a personal hand in the punishment. He burned down a nearby Greek Orthodox monastery, after killing every monk inside it. The Germans arrived at Constantinople in September, but were no more welcome there than they had been in the countryside. The emperor Manuel tried, without success, to get them to cross over immediately into Anatolia.

Louis VII had started out about a month after Conrad with an army of about fifteen thousand. He was accompanied by his wife, Eleanor of Aquitaine, whose uncle was Prince Raymond of Antioch. The wives of several French nobles went along, as did a horde of camp followers. The French preceptor, Everard de Barres, took his place at the head of his regiment of Knights Templar. Like Conrad, the French had little trouble crossing Hungary, but once they entered the Byzantine lands they too suffered food shortages, as well as the antagonism caused by the Germans who had preceded them. Fortunately, the French commanders were able to keep better control of their men, and the disciplined Templars were a strong force for order. Louis VII finally appointed the Templar master to go ahead to Constantinople as his ambassador to Emperor Manuel.

As to that monarch, he wanted no part of either army, other than to see them on their way. He had been at war with the encroaching Turks during the prior year and had personally led his armies into the field. He was angry that he had been forced to cut short his campaign upon the news of the approaching Crusaders, afraid to be away from his capital when they arrived. To be able to leave the battlefield, he had reluctantly made truces and peace treaties with the rulers of several Turkish city-states. The truces with the infidel aroused the suspicions of the Crusaders when they learned of them. Furthermore, Manuel had reason to believe that Roger II of Sicily was about to go to war with Byzantium at any time, as indeed he did before the summer was out. The emperor's greatest fear was that the Turkish nobility, whom he had bribed, tricked, and encouraged in every way to be at each other's throats, would now be drawn together by the common threat of a Latin invasion.

Manuel was relieved to get Conrad and his Germans across the Bosphorus just before Louis VII arrived. He advised the Germans to travel the longer road along the coast, where the lands were in Byzantine hands, and to avoid the shorter inland roads through Turkish mountains, where they would be constantly in danger. In spite of the warning, Conrad elected to take the shorter route across Turkish territory. Manuel reluctantly accepted Conrad's decision and provided the Germans with a party of guides.

At Nicaea, Conrad decided to follow Manuel's advice in part. He put Otto of Freisingen in charge of a body of soldiers who were to escort the noncombatant pilgrims and camp followers along the longer but safer coastal road, while he would lead the larger part of the army on the short-cut across the interior. Conrad moved the army on October 25, and the soldiers soon found out what it meant to be away from any opportunity to forage for food and discovered the agony of being without sufficient water. They were also about to learn the penalty for failing to maintain flanking forces and outriders. After ten days on the march they were happy to come to the river Bathys, near Dorylaeum. It was little more than a creek, but the thirsty Germans had never known a more welcome stream. The knights quickly dismounted to water their horses and themselves, and soon the whole German army was spread out along both banks, dismounted and relaxed, happy to have this chance to rest their bodies and slake their thirst.

The Seljuk army had been following them, well out of sight, waiting for the right moment to strike. This was it, and soon the unwary Germans experienced the spasmodic shocks of wave after wave of Turkish light cavalry. Each wave of mounted bowmen loosed flights of arrows into men and horses, and there seemed to be no end to them. It was impossible to assemble the strung-out German forces, and most died where they stood. The Turkish bowmen were followed by sweeps of cavalry with razor-sharp swords, as the battle went on hour after hour. By evening, Conrad's guard was able to get him out of the valley on the road to Nicaea, along with a few of his knights who had managed to mount their horses to act as the king's bodyguard. Four out of five German Crusaders were left on the field, as was everything they had brought with them. The wounded were slaughtered by the victorious Turks, and the loot they took was so extensive that it went to markets as far away as Persia for its disposal. As the survivors struggled to get back to Nicaea, Turkish riders galloped off to report their great victory. All Islam could take heart from this fresh proof that the armored Franks were not invincible.

As the army of Louis VII left Constantinople and marched into Anatolia, short of water and supplies, the men became difficult to control. Only the Knights Templar observed any kind of discipline, so the king asked the Templar master to send Templar officers to each division of the army, with orders that all should heed their advice and follow their commands. For the first time, the Templars enjoyed a role new to European armies, that of military police. They had also moved away from their original role of highway patrol and were now functioning as a military unit.

At Nicaea the French met Conrad with the remnants of his army. The emperor told them of his great catastrophe at Dorylaeum, which Conrad believed was the result of his betrayal to the Turks by the emperor Manuel.

The two kings decided to go on to the Holy Land together, but this time they followed the safer coastal road, where they could maintain contact with a Byzantine fleet. At Ephesus, Conrad fell ill and couldn't go on, so he was taken by ship back to Constantinople. What was left of his army continued with Louis VII.

Discipline and obedience are difficult to impose on the high and mighty, and the lack of it almost led to the French army suffering a defeat similar to the Germans' downfall a few weeks earlier. Two days out of Laodicea the French had to follow the only road through the mountains, which climbed over a high pass. The king's uncle, Amadeus of Savoy, commanded the vanguard of the French army. His orders were to camp at the top of the pass for the night, staying within clear sight of the main army at the bottom of the north slope. With plenty of daylight remaining, Amadeus decided to ignore his orders and marched his men over the pass to the bottom of the south slope of the narrow pass. Now the French army was split and vulnerable to the Turks who had positioned themselves among the rocks above the Crusader divisions camped at opposite ends of the canyon, out of sight of each other. It was another opportune moment for Islamic arms, and the Muslims struck hard. Rocks and tree trunks rained down on the Crusaders, dispersing them in panic. Archers above them could pick their targets at will. The king saved himself by scrambling up to shelter among the rocks. As the Crusader army appeared totally undone, the Turks climbed down to the road to finish them off. One unit, however, had not panicked: Everard de Barres had his Templars in tight control, and he had grasped the situation immediately. His men jumped to obey his orders, and the disciplined Templars on their massive war-horses easily beat off the dismounted Turks.

After that near-fatal experience, Louis VII placed the entire army under the direct command of the Templar master, who had his now much-respected Templar knights to enforce his orders. The French king was loud in his praise of the Templars, and his opinion was reinforced when the order made a substantial loan to him to re-plenish his depleted treasury.

The king and his court moved on to Antioch by sea, leaving his army and the Templars to follow on land. The prince of Antioch was delighted to see Louis because he wanted the French to join him in a campaign to seize Aleppo, the principal city of the new Muslim leader Nur ed-Din. Joscelin of Edessa wanted the new armies to recapture his lost lands: After all, the loss of Edessa had brought on this whole crusade. Louis VII declined. He would not participate in further military action with his battered forces until he had kept his Crusader vow by completing the pilgrimage to Jerusalem. Conrad, who had recovered from his illness, had traveled directly to Jerusalem by sea from Constantinople and was waiting for Louis in the Holy City.

Once there, they found that Queen Melisende, acting as regent for her young son Baldwin III, also had private military ambitions.

She asked Conrad and Louis to join her in the conquest of Damascus. The great walled city of Damacus was the key to Syria and, as a major trading hub, it was incredibly rich. Louis and Conrad agreed. Joined by the Templars and Hospitallers, the combined crusading armies of France and Germany set out with the local barons to add Damascus to the Christian kingdom of Jerusalem. It was a great mistake.

The emir Unur of Damascus had maintained the friendliest relations with his Christian neighbors. He could scarcely believe that the largest Christian army ever assembled in the Holy Land had his domains as its target. Messengers on swift Arabian horses were dispatched to all parts of his realm to summon every fighting man to Damascus. The emir was even worried enough to seek help from Nur ed-Din, knowing full well the risk to himself once that ambitious fighter had his troops inside the walls of Unur's capital city.

On Saturday, July 24, 1148, the Christian army, which had summarily taken the smaller towns in its path, arrived at the lush gardens and orchards for which Damascus was famous. They felled many of the valuable trees to build a palisade facing the city's south wall. Inside, the city panicked, and barricades were constructed in the streets to slow down the Christian horde that was fully expected to erupt over the wall. But the next morning, before the Christians made their move, Muslim reinforcements began to march into the city through the gates on the northern side. Unur's confidence grew as his numbers increased. He launched his own attacks on the Crusaders, as Muslim archers functioning as snipers penetrated the gardens around the Christian camp, where the thick growth of trees and bushes rendered the mounted knights almost useless. Encouraged by success, Unur launched mounted raids again and again, while the men infiltrating the gardens took an ever-increasing toll with their bows.

Louis, Conrad, and young Baldwin of Jerusalem made a joint decision. They would move the entire Christian army from the fertile overgrown fields of the south to the barren plain of the east. No Muslim guerillas could sneak up on them there.

Common sense should have told them that the southern fields were lush with growth because they had plenty of water, while the bleak eastern plain was barren because it had no water for plants, nor for thirsty soldiers, but common sense played little part in this campaign. To prove it, the leadership began bickering over who would own the realm of Damascus once it was taken. As thousands of men grew dehydrated from the severe water shortages, the quarreling among their leaders grew heated. Louis and Conrad favored the position of County Thierry of Flanders, who wanted to rule

Damascus himself as an independent Crusader state. The local barons declared that they had committed their lives and fortunes to this campaign only because they expected Damascus to be added to the kingdom of Jerusalem. Their enthusiasm for the war declined visibly, and ugly rumors started.

It was whispered throughout the army that Unur had paid fantastic bribes to get the leaders to move their armies to the waterless plain in front of the stronger eastern wall. The local barons were rumored to be getting rich from their betrayal of the cause. Even the dedicated Templars became a target of slander. A chronicler of Würzburg, attempting to absolve the German king of any blame, wrote, "King Baldwin would have fulfilled his desire of Damascus, had not the greed, trickery and envy of the Templars got in his way. For they accepted a huge bribe from the Philistines [the Damascenes] to give secret aid to the besieged inhabitants. When they could not free the city by this means, they deserted the camp, the king and their companions, at night. Conrad III was enraged by this and, in hatred of the Templars' deceit, relinquished the siege and left the city, saying that he would never again come to the aid of Jerusalem, neither himself nor any of his people."

Archbishop William of Tyre, who never flinched from openly attacking the Templar order, didn't agree with that account, which was totally untrue, but he did believe that the incredibly stupid moves of the leadership must have involved treachery. He wrote that the leaders of Damascus "...came up with the intention of storming with money the souls of those whose bodies they could not overcome by fighting...bringing a countless quantity of money, to persuade some of our leaders to play the part of the traitor Judas." The truth is that the decision to drop the siege was brought on by greed, jealousy, and the simple fact that, quite predictably, the besieging army had run out of food and water.

As the Christian host turned away from Damascus and back toward Galilee, Unur proved that he had no allies among them. His light cavalry harassed the Christians all the way. Men died every hour of the journey from Muslim swords and arrows, and more fell from exhaustion, thirst, and heatstroke. With mounted Muslims all around them, to drop was to die, and no other unit had the Templar dedication and discipline that refused to leave any fallen brother to die on the roadside. The Second Crusade called by the holy St. Bernard was over, and it was in every way a miserable failure.

Conrad immediately took ship to Constantinople, where he made an alliance with the emperor Manuel against Roger of Sicily. Louis stayed in Jerusalem until spring, to attend the Easter services at the Church of the Holy Sepulcher. Returning home on a Sicilian ship, he paused at the Italian port of Calabria to make a pact with Roger against Conrad. Europe was getting back to normal.

It was normal, too, to find someone to blame for the utter failure of the divinely ordained campaign. Roger of Sicily saw great potential advantage for himself and accused the emperor Manuel of betraying the Christians to the Turks. He urged a Crusade against Byzantium. Louis agreed, as did many among the Church hierarchy, and especially Bernard of Clairvaux. The Second Crusade had been his brainchild. With his own powers of persuasion he had put the Crusade together and had been waiting to be acclaimed as the savior of the Holy Land. Now he needed a scapegoat, and he eagerly pounced on the emperor Manuel as the guilty party. Of course, for a Crusade against Byzantium to succeed, Conrad would have to abandon his alliance with Manuel and fight against him. Conrad declined. Bernard stormed at him, but Conrad wouldn't budge. He had had enough of the advice of Bernard of Clairvaux to last a lifetime, and the fiery preaching could no longer move him. The thought of a Roman Christian attack on the Greek Orthodox city of Constantinople was appealing to many, and it would happen, but its time was not yet at hand.

Bernard probably found it small consolation, but the abbot's protégés, the Knights Templar, had won the complete approval of Louis of France. In the king's opinion they were the best body of fighting men in all Christendom. The Templars would, of course, agree with him totally, but their increasingly arrogant confidence in their own ability could be costly, as their next campaign was to prove.

If anything, the Muslims came out of the Second Crusade stronger, because they had completely wiped away the myth of the invincibility of the armored Christian knights, even when led by their kings, and had proven their own fighting ability. There was a resurgence of pride throughout all Islam. Surely no man could doubt now that Allah was the one true God.

6

The Breach at Ascalon
1149 to 1162

EVERARD DE BARRES, who had been elected grand master of the Templar order in 1149, returned to Europe to raise additional funds and recruits. A visit to his old friend and sponsor, Bernard of Clairvaux, was mandatory, but it was not a happy occasion. At the start of the Second Crusade, which Bernard regarded as his very own, they had both felt invincible, optimistic, and glorious. Now all they had to discuss was humiliation and ignominious failure.

The exact course of their conversation is not known, but its outcome was that Everard resigned from the power and wealth that he had enjoyed as grand master of the Knights Templar. Following the Templar rule that any brother leaving the order must enter a stricter order, Everard became a monk of Clairvaux, probably in a spirit of mortification and atonement for the failure of the divine mission.

The grand chapter of the Templars elected as their new grand master Bernard de Tremelai. André de Montbard, one of the original nine founders of the Templar order and an uncle of St. Bernard, was chosen to act as the seneschal of the Temple. The new officers were appointed just in time.

With the Crusader armies of Louis and Conrad gone from the Holy Land, Nur ed-Din renewed his encroachments on the holdings of Prince Raymond of Antioch. Raymond could find no allies among his fellow Christians, but he did manage to negotiate an alliance with the Kurdish leader of the Shiite Assassins, who hated Nur ed-Din on religious grounds. The war went back and forth until June 1149, when Raymond, with his entire army of four thousand horse and a thousand infantry, was camped for the night in a low plain near the Fountain of Murad, about forty miles south of Antioch.

All through the night Nur ed-Din placed his superior numbers around the oasis, so that Raymond awoke to find his army completely surrounded. A wind had sprung up, and Nur ed-Din wisely chose to attack downhill with the wind at his back. As Raymond's men rode up the long dry slope to meet him, the wind beat the dust and sand into their eyes.

It was total slaughter. Raymond's head was struck off, and later boiled and cleaned, so that his gleaming skull could be encased in a beautiful silver mounting to be sent to the caliph of Baghdad as a trophy of Muslim supremacy. Joscelin of Edessa, who had avoided an alliance with Raymond in order to protect his own remaining lands in Edessa, was the next Muslim target. Joscelin wanted desperately to recover his lost lands, but he had no substantial army with which to do it.

A few months after Raymond's death, Joscelin was in the north in the small walled town of Marash. When news arrived of the approach of a large army of Seljuk Turks, Joscelin simply left the town and took a few of his followers with him. The men left behind had to choose between death and surrender, and they chose the latter course when the Seljuk sultan Mas'ud promised that if they would lay down their arms, they could leave in peace. Led by their priests, they marched unarmed out of the town and down the road to Antioch. Relieved to have been spared, they were totally unable to defend themselves when the Turks rode them down and slaughtered every man in a treacherous act of betrayal.

In April 1150, still looking for allies, Joscelin was riding toward Antioch. At a pause in the journey, he left his men and went off into the brush to answer a call of nature. He was quickly seized by a band of Turkish adventurers who had been following Joscelin's party in hopes of robbing some straggler. Now they had a great prize. They demanded a substantial ransom for the safe return of the Christian noble.

Nur ed-Din, who had his own plan, had no intention of allowing Joscelin to be ransomed by his Christian friends. When he received word of Joscelin's capture, he immediately dispatched a troop of cavalry to take the prisoner by force and to bring him to the fortress city of Aleppo. There he was chained, publicly blinded, and thrown into a dungeon.

Joscelin made an effective example for Nur ed-Din to display to visiting Muslim nobles. As they congratulated Nur ed-Din on the capture of this troublesome Christian, they also learned an important lesson. Looking at the emaciated, blind prisoner, covered in rags and and festooned with heavy chains, they could see for themselves the penalty for being regarded by Nur ed-Din as an enemy.

It helped them to decide that it was best to accept his leadership. It also provided a reason for keeping Joscelin alive, which his jailers managed to do for nine more years.

With Prince Raymond of Antioch dead, Nur ed-Din began to take the outlying castles and towns of the Christian principality, working his way toward the goal of the great city itself. Fortunately for its inhabitants, the mantle of leadership in Antioch was assumed by the energetic patriarch Aimery. He immediately looked to the city's defenses, and he dispatched messengers to Jerusalem to seek the help of young Baldwin III. He held off Nur ed-Din by promising that Antioch would be surrendered to him if Baldwin failed to answer the call for help.

Baldwin saw the urgency in Aimery's request, but it would take days and weeks to summon his vassals to Jerusalem to make up a relieving army. He turned to the only standing army available to him.

The king's messenger had only to go next door to see the Templar grand master, where his plea for help was very welcome. This was the kind of magic moment the order lived for. Orders were shouted in the halls, stables, and supply rooms. Knights ran to get their chain mail hauberks, as their attendants ran to help them don their armor. Horses were saddled in the stable, supplies not already on the wagons were doled out for packing. Men-at-arms were named to go along, then rushed to get their own armor and weapons. Spare horses were designated, men were assembled and then inspected to make certain they had all the proper weapons. The Knights Templar were ready to go to war. As Baldwin marched north, most of the men with him were under the personal leadership of the grand master of the Temple, well reinforced by the Templars who had come out with Louis of France. Their arrival at Antioch persuaded Nur ed-Din that a truce was the proper course for a prudent man to follow.

As for the nineteen-year-old Baldwin III, he could easily see that he would not have been hailed as the savior of Antioch without the swift, unquestioning support of the Knights Templar. He needed to give every support to such a force, if he was to achieve any success in his plans to rescue and reinforce the borders of his shrinking kingdom of Jerusalem.

A matter to be addressed immediately concerned the government of the principality of Antioch. Raymond's heir, Prince Bohemond III, was just five years old, so a male regent would be required for years to come. The patriarch Aimery had assumed that role upon Raymond's death, but the barons of Antioch did not want a priest as their liege lord. Besides, they said, Aimery's loose morals made him an unsuitable guardian for a young boy. The expedient answer was for Raymond's widow, Princess Constance, to remarry. Baldwin suggested three candidates among the Christian nobility, but Constance rejected them all.

In the meantime, an unexpected problem presented itself to King Baldwin. Count Raymond of Tripoli was insanely jealous of his wife, the countess Hodernia, and attempted to keep her in a state of seclusion similar to that practiced by Muslim potentates. Hodernia, who loved the gay, open life of the Christian court, would not tolerate such isolation and announced that she wanted to end her marriage. It was a problem for Baldwin because Hodernia was his mother's sister. Now he and his mother, Queen Melisende, must go to Tripoli to deal with what was at the same time a political and a family matter.

Trying to solve two problems at once, Baldwin sent for Constance of Antioch to come to Tripoli. Melisende and Hodernia berated Constance for rejecting the king's candidates for marriage, but Constance remained unmoved. Making no commitments, she returned to Antioch.

Baldwin and his mother had better luck with Hodernia and Raymond. The couple agreed to try to preserve their marriage but also agreed that they would both benefit from Hodernia taking a holiday in Jerusalem with her sister Melisende. Count Raymond and two companions escorted the royal sisters for a short distance on their journey to the Holy City. As the count and his men turned back and passed through the great south gate into Tripoli, they were set upon by a band of knife-wielding Assassins, who pulled them from their horses and stabbed them all to death.

In response to their cries the castle garrison rushed outside to learn that their count had been murdered. They ran through the streets, killing every Muslim they met, but none of those killed belonged to the group of successful Assassins, who seemed to have just faded away.

When the news of Raymond's murder reached Nur ed-Din, he immediately began to raid the outlying lands of Tripoli. A small band of his men went all the way to the coast and succeeded in taking possession of the castle of Tortosa, between Tripoli and Antioch. Their number was too small, however, and they were driven out.

Now Baldwin had two Crusader states without leadership, Tripoli and Antioch, and Nur ed-Din was on the move. He could not afford to let the Muslim leader drive a wedge to the sea between the two, which meant that he must strengthen the great castle of Tortosa. To achieve this, and with the approval of Countess Hodernia of Tripoli, he appealed to his friends, the Knights Templar. Grand Master de Tremelai accepted the responsibility and dispatched a body of Templars to take possession of what would be the Templars' strongest fortress.

The Christians were actually in no immediate danger from Nur ed-Din. His central ambition was the conquest of all Syria, especially its rich capital city of Damascus. The emir Unur, who had held off the armies of the Second Crusade, had died in August 1149, and now Damascus was ruled by the emir Mujir ed-Din, who didn't hesitate to seek an alliance with the Christian kingdom of Jerusalem. The Christians agreed, because they had a common enemy in Nur ed-Din.

Raymond of Antioch had been criticized for his alliance with the fanatical Shiite sect of Assassins, but now the entire Christian kingdom was the ally of a Muslim state. The crusading concept had changed since the warrior pilgrims launched the First Crusade based on deeply religious motives. Now religion took a back seat. The governing motivation was the desire to preserve landholdings and power and, if possible, to expand them. Greed was triumphing over God, not for the first or the last time.

In 1151 Nur ed-Din moved his armies up to Damascus, only to have his plans thwarted by the timely arrival of Christian support for the city. It worked both ways. In 1152 a small Turcoman army asked Mujir ed-Din to join with them for a joint attack on Jerusalem. The emir declined to march against his Christian allies.

The Turcoman leader decided to try it alone and made a wide cavalry sweep across the Jordan River. The Christian leaders of Jerusalem were away at a council in Nablus together with their army, so the Muslims were able to set up camp on the Mount of Olives, overlooking the city. The benefits of a resident standing army were demonstrated again as the garrisons of Knights Templar and Hospitallers, together with the few knights left in the city, immediately attacked and drove the Muslims off the Mount. Not expecting such a vigorous defense, the Muslims retreated back to the Jordan, where Baldwin's returning army caught and destroyed them completely.

With Nur ed-Din effectively held in check to the north by the Muslim-Christian alliance, Baldwin III had turned his attention toward Egypt. The government, under the Shiite caliphs, had been a continuing bloodbath for the past generation, with constant rivalry between the caliphs, who were the religious leaders, and the viziers, who were the secular heads of state. The caliph al-Amir had been murdered in 1129. His successor, Caliph al-Hafiz, tried to end the rivalry by naming his own son Hassan as vizier. It worked for a while, but when a revolt broke out in 1135, as we have seen, he felt no compunction in saving his own life by ordering that his son be put to death. When al-Hafiz died in 1140, his son al-Zafir became caliph, but before he could name his vizier, a war broke out between two of his generals who were contenders for that position. Amir ibn-Sallah won the fight and was appointed vizier, but his murder in 1152 cut short his exercise of the power he had craved.

To Baldwin III, this turmoil in Egypt spelled opportunity, so he began to strengthen and supply the southern fortress city of Gaza. It was obvious to the Egyptians that these were preparations for an attack on Ascalon, the southernmost Muslim city on the coast of Palestine. An ambassador was sent from Egypt to Nur ed-Din, asking him to attack Galilee to divert the Christian army while the Egyptian fleet would attack the Christian seaports. To Nur ed-Din, the prospect of the Christians concentrating their forces in the southwest, away from his own target of Damascus to the northeast, was very appealing. He would do nothing to disrupt the Christians' plans.

In January 1153 the Christian army arrived before the city of Ascalon, its high wall scribing a great semicircle with the sea as its base. This was the city that had offered to surrender voluntarily during the First Crusade but would only yield to the person of Raymond of Toulouse. Godfrey de Bouillon, incensed at the concept of a surrender to anyone but himself, had rejected the offer. Now many Christians would pay with their lives for that arrogance.

Baldwin had brought every available siege engine with him, and to solicit divine favor he had the patriarch of Jerusalem bring the relic of the True Cross to the battlefield. The military orders were there with all the men they could muster, under the personal command of the grand masters of the Hospitallers and the Knights of the Temple. The grand master of the Templars, Bernard de Tremelai, was to lose his life in the battle ahead through an incredible act so devoid of reason that it still puzzles historians today, unable to fathom a sensible motive for his rash actions.

As the Christian forces settled down to what promised to be a long siege, Baldwin III had a visitor. Princess Constance of Antioch had finally found a man she wanted to marry, and he had traveled to the battlefield to ask the king for his approval.

The suitor was called Reynald of Chatillon, a name that would become one of the blackest in the history of the Crusades. He had come out with Louis VII of France to seek his fortune, because as a younger son there were no lands or titles for him at home. When the French army went home with its king, Reynald stayed behind, offering his services to the kingdom of Jerusalem. He had been one of those knights who had joined Baldwin and the Knights Templar when they had hastened to the rescue of Antioch. It was apparently during that mission that Constance had first noticed him.

Many in the king's entourage objected to the marriage. Reynald had no title of his own and was from a family considered to be very much on the lower levels of the nobility. In no way was he a fitting candidate to be the prince of Antioch. The Templars held a different view. Some of them had come to know Reynald during their march from France and on the journey to Antioch. They saw a man skilled with arms, always aggressive, eager to join in battle. He was handsome, dashing, and daring. They spoke in his favor to their friend Baldwin III.

Reynald's petition came at the right time. Baldwin was totally occupied with the capture of Ascalon; the marriage of his cousin Constance, which he had sought for so long, was now simply a distraction. Anxious to return to his main objective, the king finally approved the marriage. A very happy Reynald of Chatillon, who had achieved more wealth and power with this alliance than he had ever dared to fantasize, hastily thanked the Templars for their support, then hurried back to Antioch with his good news. Baldwin had made a great mistake.

Facing his main concern once more, Baldwin had his siege engines pound the city walls day after day, but he could effect no breach. A fleet of Egyptian supply ships managed to unload supplies for the besieged city, making the chances of starving out the Fatimid defenders extremely remote.

Months after the siege began, the Christians built a wooden tower higher than the city wall. After taking severe losses as they filled in a portion of the protective ditch, they managed to roll the tower close to the wall. Now their archers had targets they could see, and stones and fire could be aimed at the rooftops of the city.

This was a threat the Egyptians were compelled to combat. One night in July a party from the garrison was able to fight through to the tower, douse the lower timbers with naphtha, and set it on fire. Made entirely of timbers and virtually hollow inside, it became a roaring, flaming chimney. As the base weakened, the strong night wind pushed the structure against the wall, where its searing flames licked the stones the Christians had been hammering for months. At first the stones expanded in the intense heat, then they began to disintegrate. The Knights Templar, who had been assigned that part of the wall as their sector, watched in mounting excitement as the stones of the wall began to dislodge and drop.

By morning there was a breach in the wall, and Grand Master de Tremelai drew his sword to personally lead his Templars into the city. Now occurred the incredible event for which no explanation seems possible. After leading a party of forty Knights Templar over the breach, the grand master ordered the remaining Templars to turn their backs to the city, to defend the breach against any of their fellow Christians who tried to follow him into the city. Apparently he had decided that the capture of Ascalon should be a purely Templar victory, if one can believe that he really thought forty Templars could defeat thousands of well-armed Egyptian soldiers.

By now, the Templars had a well-earned reputation for ferocity. When the soldiers and citizens of Ascalon nearest the breach saw those bearded fanatics clambering over the rubble, coming at them with fierce battle cries, they ran. But no more followed. Suddenly the Muslims realized that the entire enemy they had to deal with was this little group of dismounted knights. The Egyptian soldiers turned on the Templars, and in a matter of minutes killed, wounded, or captured every one of them. In the meantime, others drove the remaining Templars out of the breach and hastily filled it with loose stones and timbers.

Later that day, cries and cheers from the top of the wall attracted the attention of the frustrated Christian army. As the men peered up at the screaming mob of Muslims along the wall, they made out the figures of one after another of the forty Templars, now all dead, dangling naked at the ends of ropes dropped down the walls. The Templars had lost their grand master and other important officers. They had also lost much of their hard-won reputation. And the men hanging on the wall had lost their heads, which had been lopped off and sent to the Shiite caliph in Cairo.

Aghast and depressed by the day's events, King Baldwin called a council of his nobles. In the presence of the True Cross he discussed the possibility of abandoning the siege of Ascalon. The patriarch of Jerusalem and the grand master of the Hospitallers were strongly in favor of continuing the siege. While what had happened might be disastrous for the Templars, it had brought no harmful effect on the rest of the Christian army. There were now twenty Christian galleys offshore to keep away Egyptian supply ships. This was no time to quit. Gradually, their persuasive arguments won others to their side. Seeing the level of determination to take this city, Baldwin made his decision to continue the siege.

It was the right decision. Supplies in the city were getting very low and seven months of bombardment had taken their toll. Less than a month later, word came from the city that the inhabitants were prepared to surrender. In exchange, they asked that their lives be spared and that they be allowed to leave the city with all of the personal possessions they could carry. Baldwin quickly agreed to their terms. A few left by sea, but most had to take to the road, unarmed, with their belongings on their backs. Baldwin kept his word as the column was allowed to wend its way down the road to Egypt, but the refugees did not fare so well at the hands of their Muslim brothers. The marauding Bedouins attacked them all along the way in a profitable orgy of blood and booty.

The naked Templar bodies were taken from the city wall to a Christian burial, that of Grand Master de Tremelai among them. As his successor, the Templars chose the most experienced Templar of them all, the elderly André de Montbard. As the uncle of Bernard of Clairvaux, André had been a key figure in the great outburst of support that the original band of poor knights had elicited from the abbot. Whatever André's influence may have been, however, it passed away a few days later when his saintly nephew, ill and despondent, died at his abbey at Clairvaux.

The mountain of plunder taken at Ascalon was divided among the Christian leaders, and the rule of the city was given to Amalric, Baldwin's younger brother and heir to the throne.

The emir Mujir of Damascus was so impressed by the Christian victory that he not only sought the friendship of the kingdom of Jerusalem, but agreed to pay an annual tribute in gold. Such wallowing at the feet of the Christians had the reverse effect on his Muslim followers, who began to look more favorably on Nur ed-Din at Aleppo.

To assist in his proposed conquest of Damascus, Nur ed-Din turned to two Kurdish brothers who had served him faithfully. One brother, Shirkuh, was a man of great military skill who had risen to become a general in Nur ed-Din's army. The other brother, Ayub, drew on a natural talent for administration and had been made the emir of Baalbek. Ayub had a young son, Yusuf, who had yet to make his mark, but who one day would become the greatest Muslim hero of the crusading period. In those days to come Yusuf's followers would call him "The Prosperity of the Faith," or, in Arabic, *Salah ed-Din*. The Christians would call him Saladin.

Ayub sent secret agents into Damascus to spread rumors and to turn the people against Mujir. They played on Mujir's rejection of Muslims in favor of the hated Christians, and they stirred resentment against Mujir's payments in gold to the king of Jerusalem. At the same time, Nur ed-Din raised suspicions in Mujir's mind about the loyalty of his nobles. Mujir turned on them with false allegations, which he now believed, and that understandably aroused their anger.

With both nobles and commoners at odds with the ruler of Damascus, Nur ed-Din sent Shirkuh to Damascus as his ambassador, backed by a military escort. Mujir was too frightened to let Shirkuh into Damascus and turned him away. Nur ed-Din used this insult as an excuse to bring an army to Damascus, but no fight was necessary. Ayub had done his part very well. A woman opened the gate of the Jewish quarter to a party of Nur ed-Din's soldiers, who were joined by citizens inside. They opened the eastern gate to allow Nur ed-Din's army to hurry into the city. Mujir fled to the citadel, but surrendered within a matter of hours. He was sent to Baghdad in exile.

Whatever triumph the Christians felt over their victory at Ascalon was now overshadowed by Nur ed-Din's triumph at Damascus. He was now the most powerful ruler the region had seen for generations. He was content, for the moment, with his successes, and happy to confirm the peace treaty between Damascus and the kingdom of Jerusalem, but he refused to pay any tribute.

While all this was happening, Reynald of Chatillon was itching to do something. In exchange for spending a few minutes before a priest taking marriage vows, Reynald had been elevated from a landless knight without prospects to the lordly prince of Antioch, replete with vassal barons and knights at his command. He was anxious to flex his newly acquired muscles, and the opportunity was provided by the emperor Manuel of Byzantium. Technically, Manuel had rights over Antioch and should have been consulted about the marriage, but there was little that he could do to enforce his rights now, since he was totally occupied by a war with the Seljuk Turks.

Manuel's inviting message to Reynald was that he would formally recognize the new prince if Antioch would attack the Armenians. Success would also mean a gift of money. The prospect suited Reynald, because there were lands on his border with Armenia that he coveted for his own principality. Reynald successfully sought the assistance of his new friends, the Knights of the Temple, and went to war. They quickly drove the Armenians out of the area around Alexandretta, and Reynald made a proposal to the Knights Templar. In order to have the security of their presence on his new northern border, he offered to turn Alexandretta over to the Templars if they would garrison the castle. They would also have the surrounding lands and villages to provide income. The Templars were more than willing. They moved men into Alexandretta and dipped into their treasury to rebuild the nearby castles of Baghras and Gastun, which controlled the great pass known as the Syrian Gates.

Reynald followed the Templars' advice and made a truce with Thoros of Armenia. Indicating how little he cared about Manuel's approval, he decided that much more loot would be his if he could conquer the Byzantine island of Cyprus.

For such an expedition, Reynald needed money for men and ships and supplies. The richest man in Antioch was the patriarch Aimery, but Reynald, by his marriage to Constance, had taken away the secular power that Aimery had loved so much. He wouldn't part with a penny for any of Reynald's schemes. Reynald's frustration gave way to an outburst of temper in which he ordered the patriarch to be arrested and taken to a dungeon in the citadel of Antioch.

With the patriarch in chains, Reynald demanded the money again. Aimery's every refusal earned him vicious blows to his head, which was soon covered with blood, but the patriarch just would not have his money beaten out of him. In the morning, Reynald ordered him taken to a tower, where his head wounds were smeared with honey. He was chained in the blistering summer sun, which with the mixed blood and honey had the effect Reynald had expected. Soon the patriarch's head was covered with a swarming mass of insects that crawled into his mouth, nose, and ears. At the end of the day, Reynald offered him a choice: Part with the money, or endure another day in the sun. Aimery chose to pay.

When the news of the patriarch's torture reached Baldwin, he immediately dispatched the chancellor of the kingdom and the bishop of Acre to deliver the king's order to release the patriarch. By the time they arrived, Reynald had the money and had no further use for the aging priest. Aimery returned with the king's envoys to Jerusalem, where he vowed that he would not go back to his Church post at Antioch so long as it was ruled by the madman Reynald.

Ignoring the criticism and censure of his fellow nobles, Reynald teamed up with his new ally, Thoros of Armenia. Together, they invaded Cyprus in the spring of 1156. The governor of Cyprus, John Comnenus, nephew of the emperor Manuel, never dreamed that any Christian would dare to invade the rich Byzantine island, but it was no dream when he found himself Reynald's prisoner. The Cypriot militia was weak and few in number. Reynald had the island to do with as he wished, and what he wished was a slice of hell. The women were raped, including the nuns. All of the captive citizens were drived down to the coastal towns for export to the slave markets, except those too young or too old to walk, who had their throats cut. Churches and convents were seized and emptied of their gold and silver, and every Orthodox priest had his nose cut off. The loot was being loaded onto their ships when word arrived of an approaching Byzantine fleet. Reynald decided to leave without the general population, but he took with him every leading merchant or noble who might earn a ransom payment.

The deed was done, and there was no one to punish Reynald for his brutal invasion of the peaceful island. His friends the Templars did not abandon him, probably because, in their position as a private army of the Roman pope, they bore no affection for the Byzantine Greeks. Their grand master, André de Montbard, died that year of 1156. As one of the original founders of the order, and especially as the uncle of Bernard of Clairvaux, André had done much to turn a poor band of nine knights into the powerful order he was leaving behind. In grand chapter, the Templars elected to succeed him as grand master Bertrand de Blanquefort, who was soon to lead his Templars into battle.

Early in the following year, Baldwin III was brought news of vast herds of sheep and horses that had been brought south for winter pasturage near Banyas, at the northern edge of Galilee. Thinking more like Reynald of Chatillon than like a king, he decided that the easy profit was too good to pass up. He took a mounted troop north, killed or ran off the shepherds, then drove home thousands of animals to be sold in the Christian markets.

The Syrians looked to Nur ed-Din, who could not overlook the bold raid that had robbed his subjects. His response was to lead an army to Banyas to lay siege to the town and its castle. The town fell easily, but the castle up on the mountain was much more of a problem. Enough time passed to allow Baldwin to come north with a relieving army, which included about four hundred Knights Templar under Grand Master de Blanquefort. Nur ed-Din wanted the criminals, not the castle, so he set the town on fire and drew back into the mountains to let Baldwin ride in uncontested.

After fighting fires and repairing walls, Baldwin led his army back toward Jerusalem, which was what Nur ed-Din had been waiting for. His scouts watched the Christian army take the road down to the valley of the Jordan. With Baldwin committed to a route home, Nur ed-Din was able to select his ground in advance of the Christian column, and to position his troops out of sight for a massive ambush. The Christians marched right into the Muslim trap.

The great kettledrums sounded the signal and the Christians found themselves surrounded, attacked from all sides by superior numbers. Baldwin and his bodyguards fought their way out to safety, but the Knights Templar were not given the necessary order to permit them to retreat. By the time the battle ended, over three hundred lay dead or wounded on the bloody field. About eighty more, including Grand Master de Blanquefort, were taken prisoner. They were paraded through the streets of Damascus to the jeers and cheers of the jubilant Muslims, who mocked their red crosses.

Once again the Templars at Jerusalem were driven to contact their preceptories in Europe with urgent pleas for replacements.

The Christians and Muslims kept men in the field who fenced with each other but managed to avoid a decisive battle. Fortunately for Baldwin, the Seljuk Turks to the north were too busy facing the troops of the Byzantine emperor to attack the Latin Christians. Baldwin was not certain what level of help, if any, he could expect from the emperor Manuel, who reportedly was still enraged by Reynald's rapacious butchery on the emperor's island of Cyprus.

Prudence suggested a firm alliance between the Greek and Roman Christians, so Baldwin sent ambassadors to Constantinople, asking that Manuel provide him with a bride from the Greek royal family. Manuel agreed, and selected his niece Theodora to become the queen of Jerusalem. To seal the pact, he offered a dowry of one hundred thousand pieces of gold, and ten thousand more to cover the costs of a sumptuous royal wedding. When Baldwin had confirmed all the negotiated terms, in September 1158, Theodora was sent in full state to her new husband. She was only thirteen years old, but she possessed the features and full figure of a classic Greek goddess. Baldwin was almost as thrilled with her as he was with the enormous treasure that came with her.

As for Manuel, he had decided to visit his new kinsman in person and to demonstrate along the way the power of his empire. He meant to assert his ancient rights over Antioch and to seek personal vengeance against Prince Reynald. The emperor led a huge army overland and swept the Armenian rulers out of Cilicia. Prince Thoros, Reynald's ally on the Cyprus raid, fled into the mountains.

Reynald, who now feared for his own life, sent word to the emperor that he was prepared to turn over the citadel of Antioch to a Byzantine garrison. His fears increased to panic when the emperor replied that the surrender of the city was insufficient penance for Reynald's savage insults to the empire. But Reynald was an opportunist, an adventurer. Unburdened by scruples and with a total disregard for the opinions of others, he could adapt to anything. When on top, he could growl. On the bottom, he could grovel.

When Manuel, joined by King Baldwin, camped with his army near Antioch, Reynald was ready to throw himself in the dirt, literally. He hurried to Manuel's camp, barefoot and clothed in the sackcloth of a penitent pilgrim. Manuel gathered his guests around him, including embassies from Nur ed-Din and from the caliph of Baghdad. Reynald walked alone through the crowd, his head bowed, trudging in abject humility to Manuel's throne. His Templar friends watched as he threw himself down in front of the throne and ground his face into the dirt.

Manuel kept him that way for a while, then pronounced the terms on which Reynald of Chatillon would be permitted to live: The citadel of Antioch was to be turned over to the Greeks whenever they asked for it; Reynald must provide troops and supplies for the emperor's army; a Greek patriarch, not Roman, would govern the religious life of Antioch. Reynald, in a great wave of relief that his life was to be spared, readily agreed. Some weeks later, when the emperor entered Antioch in state on Easter Sunday, 1159, Reynald was with him, on foot and leading the emperor's horse, so that the entire population could grasp quite clearly who was in supreme command.

From Antioch, Manuel took his army east toward the Muslim states. The Latin Christians were elated, thinking that the emperor was going to win their war for them, but they were disappointed. Manuel had goals that were more important to him for the protection of his own capital of Constantinople. He made an alliance with Nur ed-Din. In exchange for Manuel's agreement not to proceed against him, Nur ed-Din agreed to mount a campaign against Byzantium's most active Muslim enemies, the Seljuk Turks. In addition, he agreed to release six thousand Christian captives crowding his prisons, most of them German Crusaders taken during the Second Crusade.

Manuel was acting in his own best interests. He knew that the Latin Christians were friendly to the Greeks only when their help was needed. The emperor did not want them secure and strong, with no enemies to worry about. The Crusaders did reap some benefits, because with Nur ed-Din campaigning against the Turks, some of the pressure would be diverted from the kingdom of Jerusalem. And among the captives released as part of the treaty were Grand Master de Blanquefort and his eighty Knights Templar.

When the emperor Manuel left to return to Constantinople, Reynald's contrition and humility left as well, as he shrugged off all traces of his recent mortification to become his old self again. He knew that every autumn the Muslim herdsmen moved their animals from the mountains to winter in the great valley of the Euphrates. Here was vast loot for the snatching, because herdsmen could never prevail against professional soldiers: King Baldwin himself had proven that. In the fall of 1160, Reynald took his cavalry to the valley and scooped up one herd after another.

Well pleased with his efforts, he turned to go home with thousands of horses, sheep, and cattle. Anyone less self-absorbed would have guessed that somebody would surely ride for help, but Reynald was taken totally by surprise by an army of Muslim cavalry that had been hastily sent to the rescue by Nur ed-Din's vassal, the emir of Aleppo.

Reynald was taken alive and thrown into prison. There he met Joscelin of Courtenay, whose father, the count of Edessa, had been blinded and imprisoned years before. The two men became friends, and much later they would ally themselves with the Knights Templar to control the destiny of the kingdom of Jerusalem. In the meantime, it took all of Reynald's strength of will and skill at adapting to stay alive for the sixteen years he would spend chained in his Muslim dungeon.

With Manuel's truce in place, a feeling of peace came to the Holy Land. At Antioch, Constance announced that since Reynald had ruled only because of his marriage to her, his imprisonment meant that she would now assert her personal right to command. Her daughter, the extraordinarily beautiful Princess Maria, had caught Manuel's eye during his visit to Antioch, and now the bonds with the Greek empire were made stronger as he took Maria as his empress.

The Knights Templar used this time to recruit and train replacements for their brothers who had fallen in the recent campaigns and to strengthen their growing number of fortifications.

Baldwin had emerged a successful monarch. At the age of thirty-three he had consolidated and even expanded his domains. But there were unseen enemies in the Middle East that didn't hesitate to strike down healthy, successful young men, and against whom there was no known defense. One of the mysterious local diseases put Baldwin in his bed, and no treatment worked. He died on February 10, 1162.

Baldwin III had no children to succeed him, so the crown of Jerusalem went to his brother Amalric, who had already been given the city of Ascalon after the victory over the forces of Egypt. Amalric had ambitions of his own, while off to the north, in Syria, the ambitions of Nur ed-Din were stirring again. Before too long, the Latin Christians would find themselves fighting for their lives again. The Knights Templar would need all the men who had been released from prison, and more.

7

The Coming of Saladin
1163 to 1174

AFTER THE LOSS OF Ascalon, the turmoil and savagery of the Egyptian court grew worse. The vizier Abbas had kept his post in spite of the disaster, but only because his handsome son Nasr had become the caliph's favorite lover. They became so involved that the caliph actually tried to persuade the young man to perform a political service by killing his own father. Nasr told his father what the caliph wanted him to do, and in response, Nasr was persuaded by his father that his own interests, and those of his family, would be better served if he murdered the caliph instead.

Careful plans were made to control reactions to the proposed murder. When they were ready, Nasr invited the caliph to his house for a midnight homosexual orgy. The caliph dressed and perfumed himself for a night of erotic adventure, but as soon as he had arrived and relaxed, Nasr stabbed him to death.

When Vizier Abbas got the message that the deed was done, he immediately took a waiting body of troops to the caliph's palace. He accused the caliph's brothers of the murder and had their heads struck off. A wide-eyed witness to the beheadings was the murdered caliph's five-year-old son, al-Fa'iz. Abbas put the boy on the throne as the new caliph, but the butchery the boy had been forced to watch took its toll. He suffered from nightmares and convulsions for the rest of his brief life.

To reward himself for his new-found power, the vizier had his men carry away all of the caliph's treasure, in the expectation that he could now sit back and enjoy his success. Unfortunately, his well-laid schemes were spoiled by the dead caliph's sister and daughters, who had expected to share in that treasure. They sent an appeal for help to the emir Ibn Ruzzik, whom the caliph had made governor of Upper Egypt.

Ibn Ruzzik, seeing a chance for his own advancement, marched on Cairo. Abbas learned of the approaching army and was told that his own officers were defecting to Ibn Ruzzik. Abbas gathered up his son Nasr and the dead caliph's treasure, then fled for the safety of Damascus, making a wide sweep through the Sinai Desert. A Syrian visitor to the Egyptian court went with them. He was Usama, son of the emir of Shaizar, who joined the fleeing party as a means to get home. As they came out of the desert south of the Dead Sea, tired and thirsty, they were pounced upon by a Christian patrol from the nearby castle of Montreal. In the brief battle that ensued Abbas was killed, while both Nasr and Usama were taken prisoner. The victors kept the treasure, but turned Nasr and Usama over to the Knights Templar.

Before the Templars could do him any harm, Nasr pleaded his intense desire to become a Christian. Taking him at his word, the Templars made him comfortable and arranged for him to be instructed in the life and teachings of Jesus Christ.

Word got back to Cairo of the fate of Abbas and Nasr. An emissary from the court of the caliph interrupted Nasr's Christian education by offering the Templars sixty thousand gold dinars for the return of the caliph's murderer. It was an easy decision for the Templars, who promptly draped Nasr in chains and sent him back to Cairo.

Criticism of the Templars' action came from all sides. The Templars had condemned a Christian to death. They had put gold before God. They had followed the example of Judas. The Templars' answer was that Nasr's only interest in Christianity was as a means to save his skin, not his soul. They claimed that he had no real love for Christ (and they might have added that any fool should know there is a world of difference between thirty pieces of silver and sixty thousand pieces of gold).

The Templars would also have been criticized by many for their treatment of Usama of Shaizar, but for a totally different reason. Usama was welcome at the Templar headquarters on the Temple Mount as a house guest, because he and the Templars were old friends. The criticism would have stemmed from the Templars' insistence on religious tolerance, which went so far as to establish a part of their property as a place for their Muslim guests to say their daily prayers facing south to Mecca. Usama recorded in his diary:

"When I was in Jerusalem I would go to the Mosque al-Aqsa, beside which there is a small oratory which the Franks have made into a church. Whenever I went into the mosque, which was in the hands of the Knights Templar, who were friends of mine, they would put the little oratory at my disposal so that I could say my prayers there. One day I had gone in, said the *Allahu Akbar* and risen to begin my prayers, when a Frank threw himself on me from behind, lifted me up and turned me so that I was facing east. 'That's the way to pray,' he said. Some Templars at once intervened, seized the man and took him out of my way. But the moment they stopped watching him he seized me again and forced me to face east, repeating that this was the way to pray. Again the Templars intervened and took him away. They apologized to me and said: 'He is a foreigner who has just arrived today, and he has never seen anyone pray facing any direction other than east.' 'I have finished my prayers,' I said, and left, stupefied by the fanatic.''

There was no tolerance of any kind waiting for Nasr, as he arrived in chains at Cairo, where chief among the mourners were the dead caliph's four wives. As a result of Nasr's murder of their husband, they had gone from their privileged positions in the palace to the somber lives of widows, and Nasr's crime had deprived them of their expected share of the caliph's treasure. They asked for, and got, the chance to work off their sorrow on their late husband's homosexual lover. Mindful of their instructions not to kill him, they took knives in hand to wreak their vengeance. The wives cut and sliced at his naked body, and did not forget to hack away the offending sex organ. When they were finished, Nasr's bleeding body was taken to be hanged at the Zawila Gate to the city, for all the world to see his punishment and learn by his example.

Ibn Ruzzik had rescued the caliphate, so had no trouble in having himself named vizier to the young caliph, who lived until his health gave out in 1160. His place was taken by a cousin, al-Adid, who at the age of ten was forced to marry Ibn Ruzzik's daughter.

A sister of the murdered caliph al-Zafir, who was one of the women who had sent for Ibn Ruzzik, now realized that her family was as unsafe as ever. She persuaded a few of her friends to pounce on the vizier as he walked down a palace corridor, where he was stabbed repeatedly. Ibn Ruzzik was carried to his bed, his life slipping away with his blood. His last act was to have the guards drag the guilty princess to his bedside, where a knife was put into his hand as he summoned up enough strength to kill her himself.

During the year before the murder of Ibn Ruzzik, King Baldwin III of Jerusalem had decided that the time was right for an invasion of Egypt, but he had abandoned the expedition on the Egyptian promise of a payment of one hundred and sixty thousand gold dinars. Now that Baldwin was dead, his brother Amalric decided that the failure to pay the tribute was a legal excuse for him to mount his own Egyptian invasion.

Before he could do anything, however, Amalric had to get the nobles of Jerusalem to agree to his coronation. Legally, the king of Jerusalem was to be elected by the barons, but the tradition of granting titles by inheritance was strong, and there were no other claimants to the throne. The only objections to Amalric's assuming the throne were based on his marriage.

His wife was Agnes of Courtenay, sister of Joscelin of Courtenay who was languishing in the dungeons of Aleppo with Reynald of Chatillon. Their marriage had not been blessed by the patriarch because Agnes was Amalric's third cousin, a relationship that the Church considered close enough to be condemned as incestuous. The nobles and the patriarch agreed that they would readily confirm Amalric's kingship if he would consent to the annulment of his marriage.

That demand gave Amalric no problem. The marriage had been arranged on political grounds. Agnes was much older than her husband and a constant source of embarrassment because she was essentially devoid of morals, famous for the number of men who had experienced the comforts of her bedchamber. Amalric happily agreed to the annulment, asking only that his two children, Baldwin and Sibylla, be recognized as legitimate for the purposes of inheritance.

Agnes of Courtenay didn't get to be the queen of Jerusalem, but she didn't disappear from history, either. As the mother of a future king, she would one day join with Reynald, Joscelin, and the Knights Templar to set the kingdom of Jerusalem on a disastrous course.

For now, Amalric, with the crown of Jerusalem firmly on his head, turned his thoughts to his great ambition, the conquest of Egypt. As he assembled the army of Jerusalem for the invasion, the government of Egypt went through another series of kaleidoscopic changes. Vizier Ibn Ruzzik's son al-Adil had become vizier upon the murder of his father. He had lasted for fifteen months before he in turn was murdered by the emir Shawar, who had replaced his father as the governor of Upper Egypt. Shawar made himself vizier. He had held the office for just eight months when he was deposed, but amazingly not killed, by his chamberlain, Dirgham, just one month before Amalric set out for Egypt. In the meantime, acutely conscious of the fates of his predecessors, declaring himself as the new vizier, Dirgham made up a hit list of every leader who might be considered a threat to his own life, then had them all killed. As a result, Amalric was moving against an Egyptian army that had been stripped of many of its top officers.

In September of 1163 King Amalric led his army, including a contingent of Knights Templar, into Egyptian territory. Meeting no resistance, he crossed the Isthmus of Suez to the Mediterranean coast to position his troops around the delta city of Pelusium, which found itself besieged for the first time ever by a Christian army.

Unfortunately for Amalric, his timing was bad. The level of the Nile was up in its annual flood, and Dirgham didn't need his army, with or without top officers. All that was necessary was to issue the order to break the dikes near the city. As torrents of water were unleashed onto the plain, the Christian forces had to strike camp immediately and back off fast, to keep from drowning.

Far behind him in Syria, Amalric's venture into Egypt had loosed a different kind of flood, one of Muslim soldiers. With the Christian king and most of his available troops off in the opposite direction, Nur ed-Din saw a chance too good to pass up. He took an army toward Tripoli and entered the plain of Buqaia to lay siege to its great castle of Krak (which soon would become the Hospitaller stronghold of Krak des Chevaliers).

This time, good fortune was on the side of the Christians. A group of nobles, with their retainers, was just crossing Tripoli on its way back from a pilgrimage to Jerusalem. The nobles hastened to support Count Raymond of Tripoli, while fast gallopers rode off for more help. Prince Bohemond III of Antioch answered their call, as did a contingent of Byzantine troops from the north. Together they attacked the Muslim camp, forcing Nur ed-Din to retreat and team up with the Muslim reinforcements who were on their way to join him. Concerned that any attack on the Byzantine troops might affect his truce with Emperor Manuel, Nur ed-Din decided to abandon the raid and led his forces back behind the walls of Damascus.

It was in his capital that he received Shawar, who just a few weeks earlier had been deposed as vizier of Egypt. Shawar proposed that if Nur ed-Din would attack Egypt and restore him to his former power, he would see to it that Nur ed-Din would be reimbursed for the entire cost of the campaign, plus an annual tribute equal to one-third of all the tax revenues of Egypt. Nur ed-Din, dubious about a lengthy march through Christian territory, would not commit himself. Ultimately turning to God for guidance, and mixing a bit of magic with his religion, he opened the Koran at random and put his finger on the page that fell open. The verse that lay under his finger was interpreted as proof that Allah would favor the Egyptian invasion. The decision was made.

Nur ed-Din's plan was to feign an attack on the castle at Banyas to draw the Christians to the north. With the Christians distracted, his favorite general, the Kurd Shirkuh, would lead a large body of cavalry in a swing south across the desert into Egypt, taking Shawar with him. Setting unforeseeable but momentous events in motion,

Nur ed-Din ordered that Shirkuh's young nephew, Saladin, accompany the expedition.

The plan worked well, and by the time Dirgham learned of the approaching force, Shirkuh had crossed the Suez. Rushing to meet him with all the troops he could muster in a hurry, Dirgham's brother met Shirkuh near Pelusium. The Egyptian army was defeated quickly and completely, allowing Shirkuh to continue his march on Cairo, where Dirgham found his own forces falling away. He looked to the caliph for support, but got none. His own bodyguard of five hundred picked soldiers began to desert. As British historian Stanley Lane-Poole recounts his end, ''...the guard itself gradually dispersed, till only thirty troopers were left. Suddenly a warning cry reached him: 'Look to thyself and save thy life!' - and lo! Shawar's trumpets and drums were heard entering from the Gate of the Bridge. Then at last the deserted leader rode out through the Zawila gate. The fickle folk hacked off his head and bore it in triumph through the streets; his body they left to be worried by the dogs.'' Shawar was once again the grand vizier of Egypt.

The whole adventure had been a total success for Shawar, and the arrogance of power soon took possession of his senses. He totally rejected his promises to Nur ed-Din and told Shirkuh that his job in Egypt was finished. He should return to his Sunni master at Damascus; Shawar did not need any help to rule his Shiite empire. Shirkuh, angry at the ungrateful man he had served so well, refused to leave. He backed off about forty miles from Cairo to seize the city of Bilbeis, which would serve as a base for his army until he could get instructions from Nur ed-Din.

Shawar appealed for help to King Amalric of Jerusalem, with the unusual incentive that he would give his allies one thousand gold dinars for each day of the twenty-seven-day journey from Jerusalem. Amalric had no desire for the militant Nur ed-Din to control the rich Egyptian empire, which he had designs on for himself, so he hurriedly put together an army and set off to join up with Shawar and his Egyptian troops in a siege of Bilbeis.

Three months later neither side had gained the advantage, but Shirkuh was running low on food. He did not object when Amalric suggested ending the deadlock with an agreement that both armies should abandon the war and go home. Amalric was certain of his own ultimate victory in Egypt, but the acquisition of new foreign territory was by no means as important as saving what he already possessed. Word had reached him that Nur ed-Din had assembled a substantial army and was moving on Antioch. Amalric had to get home.

Shirkuh saw no reason to stay in Egypt, because his orders had been carried out. Soon both armies were on a westward route out of Egypt. The only one happy with the situation was Shawar, who now personally controlled the entire Egyptian empire, having shrewdly tricked others into fighting his war for him.

(It's interesting to speculate that the Templar contingent riding back to Jerusalem may have carried with them loot from their foray into Egypt. It may have been on this campaign that they acquired the figurine of the cat that was sacred to the Egyptian goddess Isis. Generations later they were to be accused of worshiping just such a statue.)

The entire Christian kingdom was shocked by the Muslim invasion of Antioch. Nur ed-Din had stopped to put his army into camp around the Christian frontier fortress of Harenc, and the drawn-out siege gave Prince Bohemond III the valuable time he needed to send for help and assemble a defending army. His call was answered by Count Raymond of Tripoli, Prince Thoros of Armenia, and a detachment of troops from the Byzantine army. Once gathered, the Christian army took to the field in August 1164. At the approach of a larger Christian army than he had expected, Nur ed-Din abandoned the siege, reassembled his army, and moved back toward Damascus.

The Christian leaders, in pursuit of a decisive victory, took six hundred knights and chased after the Muslims. Bohemond ignored the warning that they were greatly outnumbered, and even when he caught up with the Muslim army, he was not impressed with what he saw. He ordered an immediate attack. The Muslims broke into a run, which Bohemond perceived as a full retreat. What he could not see was that, up ahead, reserves of Muslim light cavalry were waiting for him, stationed in the hills to both right and left.

As they rode down the valley in wild pursuit of the "retreating" Muslims, waves of Muslim cavalry suddenly came at the Christian knights from both sides. As they turned to meet these new enemies, the retreating force in front of them did a sharp about-face and charged back into them. The long lines of flanking Muslim cavalry came together behind them, and suddenly the Christians found themselves completely surrounded by overwhelming numbers. Prince Thoros and a small party of Armenians managed to ride out of the trap, but the rest of the Christians were either killed, wounded, or captured. As usual, the wounded had their throats cut wherever they were found, while the prisoners were bound and marched off to the dungeons of Aleppo. Among them were Prince Bohemond, Count Raymond of Tripoli, Hugh of Lusignan, and Constantine Coloman, the commander of the Greek forces.

Nur ed-Din had not anticipated Greek involvement and had no

desire for war with Byzantium, so he rejected the desire of his emirs to march on the city of Antioch. He quickly agreed to release the Byzantine general Constantine Coloman in exchange for the unusual ransom payment of one hundred and fifty robes of silk.

He was not so generous about his other prisoners. He negotiated the release of his high-born Christian captives for substantial ransoms in gold, but would enter into no discussions about the release of Raymond of Tripoli. Emperor Manuel paid part of the ransom for Bohemond, but only on condition that Bohemond permit the patriarch of Antioch to be Greek Orthodox. Bohemond agreed, and the Roman Catholic patriarch Aimery was sent away into exile.

In October Nur ed-Din attacked again and took the castle of Banyas, but he abandoned any further incursions, for the moment, in exchange for a large cash payment from the local barons.

King Amalric was becoming concerned. Every raid, skirmish, and battle depleted his limited number of knights and men-at-arms, and they were not being replaced by fresh Crusaders from Europe. He decided to follow his brother Baldwin's example and try to find help closer to home, through an alliance with the emperor Manuel at Constantinople. Now unmarried, he would seek a bride from the imperial family. As his ambassador to the Byzantine court to arrange the royal marriage, he selected a Knight of the Temple.

Amalric had become impressed with the abilities of a Knight Templar named Odo de St. Amand. He had asked the grand master to allow Odo to run his household as the royal butler. The Templar grand master, always happy to have a pair of friendly ears at any court, readily agreed. Amalric was pleased with Odo's conduct as a member of his personal staff and now asked permission to send him to Constantinople, which was freely given. The archbishop of Caesarea went with him. Their instructions were to arrange the marriage of Amalric to a Byzantine princess and to secure an alliance with Manuel for the next Christian attempt at the conquest of Egypt. Though the mission was ultimately successful, it resulted in no immediate help because Manuel kept the archbishop and the Templar officer bogged down in frustrating negotiations for the next two years.

Meanwhile, Nur ed-Din continued his raiding probes of the Christian defenses. A Muslim army sent into Oultrejourdain under Shirkuh managed to capture and then destroy a small castle that the Knights Templar had built in the mouth of a great grotto south of Amman (Jordan). Shirkuh had lost none of his high standing with Nur ed-Din, and he constantly urged his lord to let him go back to Egypt. He had not forgotten the treachery of the vizier Shawar, a crime that cried out for punishment.

Shirkuh tipped the scales in his own favor when he succeeded in getting the Sunni caliph at Baghdad to agree that a Sunni invasion of Shiite Egypt would be a *jihad*, a holy war for Allah. At that pronouncement, Nur ed-Din's deep religious convictions made the decision inevitable. He gave his full support to Shirkuh in both men and money, for a war against Egypt. His nephew Saladin had conducted himself so well before that Shirkuh awarded him a post of command. The invading Sunni army, now fighting for Allah with the assurance of eternal rewards for those who would fall, left Damascus in January of 1167.

The Christians could not afford to have one ruler in control of the Muslim forces in Syria and Egypt, on both sides of them. They agreed that they should attack Shirkuh to rescue the Egyptian vizier who was his primary target. All the Christian nobles were ordered to assemble with their retainers. Any baron who ignored the summons would suffer a fine of 10 percent of his annual revenues.

Grand Master de Blanquefort called in all the Templars who could be spared from their castles, including a Templar named Geoffrey, who had a fluent command of Arabic. The Christians had a much shorter march to Egypt from Jerusalem than the Muslims had marching down from Damascus, so the first move was to intercept Shirkuh before he could reach the Egyptian border.

They were not in time. Shirkuh reached the Nile first, about forty miles above Cairo, then crossed the river and moved down to establish his base at Giza, across the river from Cairo. Shirkuh suggested to Shawar that they join forces against the approaching Christians, but Shawar knew very well what it had meant when the Sunni caliph had called a holy *jihad* against his Shiite empire. He sent emissaries to ask the Christians to come to the walls of Cairo, across from Shirkuh on the other side of the wide river. The emissaries told Amalric that Vizier Shawar would pay him four hundred thousand gold bezants in exchange for a Christian agreement not to leave so long as Shirkuh remained on Egyptian soil. Amalric sent Hugh of Caesarea and the Arabic-speaking Templar brother Geoffrey ahead to Cairo to set the final terms for a formal treaty. They were successful, and the Christians marched to Cairo.

During the month that the two armies sat staring at each other across the Nile, Amalric had the Egyptians assemble a flotilla of hundreds of river boats a few miles below the city, out of sight of Shirkuh's camp. In the dark of night they loaded thousands of men and the war-horses of the Christian knights to take a combined Christian/Egyptian army to Shirkuh's side of the river. Once disembarked and in ranks, they moved through night to attack one of Shirkuh's outlying camps. Shirkuh was totally exposed and outnumbered. He ordered his army into full retreat south, up the river. Now victory seemed certain, as Amalric and Shawar led their armies after him to drive the Sunni Muslims out of Egypt. Their combined force was so large that Amalric left most of his own army behind to guard Cairo.

They found Shirkuh camped among ancient ruins, far up the Nile. Shirkuh's advisors pointed out that the Syrians were greatly outnumbered and advised an immediate retreat. Shirkuh overruled them, confident that his thousands of cavalry could hold their own against an Egyptian army all on foot and backed by only a few hundred Christian knights. He stood his ground.

Amalric's decision was made for him. He reported that St. Bernard of Clairvaux had appeared to him in a dream. Apparently as warlike in dreams as he had been in life, Bernard chastised Amalric for holding back. He ordered Amalric to attack the foes of Jesus Christ and His Holy Church without delay. Amalric was convinced that he had experienced a divine vision, so the next morning, in obedience to the militant saint, he ordered the attack.

By now Shirkuh's tactics should have been predictable, but once again they worked. His center collapsed and his men ran as though in panic, with the excited Egyptians and Christians racing after them. Shirkuh's flanks let them pass, then closed in on both sides, while Shirkuh's reserves closed the circle behind them. Amalric and Shawar, with an army made up almost entirely of men on foot, found themselves completely surrounded by a mounted enemy who began to loose thousands of arrows into the massed infantry. Both leaders had personal bodyguards who fought their way out of the trap, but much of their army was left dead or dying on the field. Next, Shirkuh made a surprise move, heading northwest all the way to the Mediterranean and the great walled seaport of Alexandria. Preferring Shirkuh to the hated vizier Shawar, the officials of Alexandria opened their gates and let him ride in with his army.

The city of Alexandria was rich and well fortified, and it was Egypt's major seacoast trading center. It simply could not be left to Shirkuh without a fight. Amalric and Shawar, whose combined armies still greatly outnumbered the Syrians, moved up to lay siege to Alexandria. Ships were called in to prevent Shirkuh from receiving supplies by sea.

After a month of doing nothing, Shirkuh grew restless. He was a man of action and loath to be bottled up, no matter how rich the city or how thick its walls. One night he had his men mount up in columns before the gates.

He entrusted Saladin with one thousand men, his first independent command, and gave him orders to hold the city and the attention of the enemy for as long as possible. Then he ordered that the gates be opened, and he rode his light cavalry out at the gallop, circling Amalric's camp. At first it appeared to be a night attack, but Shirkuh's cavalry rode right through the Egyptians and kept on going.

Shirkuh went along the Nile to upper Egypt, where he could raid the smaller towns at will. None of them came close to the value of Alexandria, however, so the armies of Amalric and Shawar stayed put, determined to starve out Saladin and his meager forces. Shirkuh was on the loose, but he couldn't win the war. He would always be outnumbered in the field, and Cairo was too well equipped with men and supplies to be in any danger.

This time it was Shirkuh who suggested a plan to break the deadlock, the same plan that Amalric had proposed to him the last time they had confronted each other in Egypt. He proposed that both he and Amalric leave Egypt and call off the war. Worried about reports he was receiving about raids back home, Amalric was moved to agree. After all, Amalric's treaty with Shawar stipulated that he would not leave Egypt as long as Shirkuh was there, so he would be fulfilling those terms. There could be no good reason for the Egyptians to forego the payments the treaty had promised. For good measure, Vizier Shawar was forced to sign another treaty that required him to pay an annual tribute to the kingdom of Jerusalem of one hundred thousand gold pieces. The treaty would also allow the Christian knights to stay behind in control of the city gates of Cairo.

The Christian army headed home, arriving at Ascalon on August 4, 1167. A few days later Amalric learned of the success of the mission he had sent to the emperor Manuel two years before. The archbishop of Caesarea and the Templar Odo de St. Amand had landed at Tyre with Amalric's bride-to-be. She was Maria Comnenus, Manuel's niece. Amalric hurried to Tyre and found that his future queen was every bit as beautiful as he had been told. He didn't wait to get back to his capital at Jerusalem, but married Maria in the cathedral at Tyre on August 29. As the emperor's son-in-law, he could deal from strength with the emissaries who had come with the princess to negotiate the proposed alliance against Egypt.

It was to be over a year before that alliance was agreed upon, and there were some things for which Amalric couldn't wait. He was very concerned for the security of his realm and had come to realize that, with the selfish ambitions and rivalries of his nobles, only the Knights Templar and the Hospitallers could be relied upon. The county of Tripoli was an immediate concern, because its count was still in Nur ed-Din's prison. The great northern castle of Tortosa had been given into the care of the Knights Templar, along with much of the surrounding countryside to help support it.

Now the Hospitallers were given the castle of Belvoir, by the fords of the Jordan. They also received control of the lands to the south of their great castle Krak des Chevaliers in the Buqaia. In Antioch the Hospitallers got lands at the south end of the principality, while up on its northern border the Templars acquired extensive holdings around their castle of Baghras, giving them effective control of the whole northern end of the Christian territories. The military orders were occupying more and more of the great Crusader fortresses, becoming in the process two of the greatest landholders in the Holy Land.

What the Templars and the Hospitallers provided in exchange was protection for everyone's property, for the people, for the nobles, and for the king. With the self-serving greed of the feudal system in full swing, they had the only disciplined armies across the entire sweep of the Holy Land. King Amalric thought that the military orders, in exchange for the great properties he had given them, would give him complete support for his own military ambitions. In the case of the Knights Templar, he was wrong.

Toward the end of summer in 1168 a body of crusading knights and men-at-arms arrived from France, led by the count of Nevers. As with all new arrivals, they were eager for combat with the infidel. For Amalric their arrival and their eagerness to fight made possible a fresh invasion of Egypt. Emperor Manuel still had not agreed to a military alliance against Egypt, and many of the Christian leaders were tired of waiting. To settle the matter, Amalric called a council at Jerusalem.

The strongest voice for an Egyptian campaign was Gilbert de Assailly, the grand master of the Hospitallers. Calling for immediate action, Gilbert got the support of the count of Nevers and the majority of the Christian nobles. The assembly was shocked when the Templar delegates announced that their order would have nothing to do with any campaign into Egypt. They gave as their reason the treaty that King Amalric had signed with the vizier Shawar. The Knights of the Temple would not flagrantly cast aside a solemn agreement.

The Templars' detractors claimed that this moral position was fraudulent. The Templars would oppose the expedition just because the Hospitallers were enthusiastically in favor of it. The Templars, they claimed, were extending banking services to the Muslims. The Templars financed Italian traders, whose commerce with Egypt provided their biggest source of income. The Templars did not answer their critics, but would not budge: Any invasion of Egypt would have to be carried out without the Knights of the Temple. Their position did not change the mind of anyone else, so the departure of the Christian army was scheduled for October. Unfortunately, the count of Nevers died of fever before they started, and although his men were eager to go, they now lacked any strong leadership.

Shawar panicked when he received word in Cairo that a Christian army had marched out of Ascalon on October 20. The vizier had made no backup plans for a Christian violation of their treaty, so he sent emissaries rushing to meet Amalric, to attempt to block the invasion through diplomacy. Amalric offered various reasons for breaking the treaty, including the weak excuse that a recently arrived band of Crusaders was determined to invade Egypt, and he himself had come along to hold them in check. He added that he just might induce the Christians to turn back if the vizier would deliver up two million pieces of gold. That ended the diplomatic efforts.

Ten days out of Ascalon, Amalric arrived before the walled city of Bilbeis. It was commanded by the vizier's son Taiy, who tried to put up a fight, but within three days the city fell.

What happened when the gates of Bilbeis were opened to the Christian army was a repeat of the bloody massacre at Jerusalem during the First Crusade. The butchery began as soon as the invaders were inside. Victorious Latins charged through the streets, hacking away at men, women, and little children. Many of the citizens were Coptic Christians, but their religion didn't save their lives. They were dressed like Muslims, so they died like Muslims. Houses and shops were broken into, and soon the crusading army was a raving, rioting mob, completely out of control. It took days for Amalric to restore any kind of order. He personally bought prisoners from the Christian victors, including Shawar's son, but the damage was done. Shawar had been intensely disliked and feared by many Egyptians, who would have preferred to be governed by the Christians, but as the news of the Christian conduct at Bilbeis spread, the entire Egyptian population rejected the idea of assisting these butchers.

When the Crusader army moved on to the walled town of Fostat just outside Cairo, Shawar didn't even attempt to defend it. Instead he set it on fire. Now his emissary appeared before Amalric to state that Cairo, too, would be burned before it would be surrendered. Amalric, always willing to trade conquest for cash, suggested that the wiser course would be for the vizier to pay him to leave. They quickly agreed upon a ransom of one hundred thousand dinars for

Shawar's son, but stalled on making more payments in gold. Word reached Amalric that his ships had been stopped by barricades in the river, so the support he had expected to sail up the Nile to meet him would not be coming. To be on the safe side, Amalric moved his army down the river, away from the burned-out town, to wait for negotiations to be completed.

It was there that unwelcome news arrived: Once again the Kurdish general Shirkuh was on his way to Egypt with an army of horsemen. The sixteen-year-old al-Adid, the Shiite caliph, had ignored Vizier Shawar and sent a message to Nur ed-Din on his own initiative, offering a rich reward for the rescue of the Fatimid empire from the rapacious Christians. He knew well the dangers inherent in an alliance with a Sunni government that believed him to be the chief Muslim heretic of the world, but in the face of a blood-crazed Christian army, al-Adid felt he had scant choice. He offered Nur ed-Din one-third of the land surface of Egypt, plus separate grants of lands for his generals.

Nur ed-Din was quick to respond, and Shirkuh was always ready to attack Shawar. Nur ed-Din gave him eight thousand light cavalry and a budget of two hundred thousand dinars to finance the campaign. Saladin, with no particular love for war, declined to go with his uncle to Egypt, but he received direct orders from Nur ed-Din to accompany Shirkuh as a member of his staff.

Shawar warned Amalric of Shirkuh's approach, hoping that his two enemies would cut each other to pieces. Amalric took his army to the frontier, hoping to catch Shirkuh as he came out of the desert, but it was not difficult for Shirkuh to ride right around the slower-moving Christian army and head straight for Cairo.

The Crusader campaign had been a complete failure to this point, with the promised ransom not paid, and now the time had come for Amalric to admit it. He sent word down the river for his fleet to go home and pulled the Christian garrison back from Bilbeis. On January 2, 1169, the Christians began their retreat.

One week later Shirkuh arrived at Cairo, where he, too, ignored Shawar and went straight to the palace of the caliph. He was received with lavish ceremony. How Egypt was to be divided up with Nur ed-Din had never been conclusively defined, and now the negotiations dragged on day after day, apparently because of Shawar's behind-the-scenes interference. Saladin rapidly lost patience with the lack of action, and on the tenth day he invited vizier Shawar to accompany him on a religious pilgrimage to the tomb of a Muslim holy man. Once they were away from the city, in a surprising act for this peaceful young man, Saladin and his companions dragged Shawar off his horse and made him their prisoner. To keep things legal, Saladin petitioned the caliph for an official order for Shawar's execution as a traitor. The caliph promptly provided the order, and before the day was over the head of Shawar was respectfully placed at the feet of the caliph.

Shirkuh took over the lands that had been seized by Shawar for himself and his family, then distributed some of them as rewards to his emirs, in keeping with the caliph's promise. Then he declared himself to be the vizier and assumed the new title of king of Egypt. His victory was as complete as Amalric's failure had been, but he did not have the good fortune to enjoy his power for long. He died from severe stomach trouble (suspected to have been induced by poison) on March 23, 1169.

Back in the kingdom of Jerusalem, Amalric had to work to calm down his barons, who were trying hard to fix the blame for the Egyptian fiasco. Many blamed Amalric's seneschal, Miles de Plancy, who always encouraged Amalric to seek gold and avoid battle. The followers of the count of Nevers were universally condemned, but the fiercest accusations of responsibility were leveled at Gilbert de Assailly, the grand master of the Hospitallers who had urged them all to take part in the doomed invasion. He was attacked with such brutal criticism that he resigned his high office of grand master and returned to Europe. Some might have wanted to blame the grand master of the Knights Templar, Bertrand de Blanquefort, for refusing to participate, but he had died just a few days after Amalric's return.

The only winner was Saladin. With the full approval of the caliph al-Adid, he assumed his uncle's titles and was now the secular ruler of Egypt. The caliph's advisors had opposed the appointment because Saladin had absolutely no experience in government. That, however, was precisely why al-Adid had selected him. His inexperience would require that Saladin lean heavily on the knowledgeable Egyptian officials. Besides, Saladin had an aggressive, efficient army with him, making him a man not to be shunted aside.

Unable to resist intrigue, al-Adid had his chief eunuch, a high court official, write a secret letter to Amalric, promising full cooperation should the Christians decide to mount another invasion of Egypt to oust Saladin.

This was cheering news for the Christians, but the letter didn't remain a secret for long. It was to be circulated among the local barons in an attempt to reverse their negative attitude toward another Egyptian campaign, and one of Saladin's secret agents in Jerusalem was alert enough to notice that one of the shoes worn by a royal messenger appeared misshapen. He managed to get the shoe while the messenger was sleeping and slit it open to discover the letter, which was copied and then sewn back in the shoe. When Saladin received the copy at Cairo, he decided to do nothing about it for the moment, but it was far from forgotten.

Amalric decided to go, and the emperor Manuel surprised everyone by moving before Amalric could gather his forces. He launched a great fleet in July 1169, part headed for Cyprus and part for Acre, ready to support the new invasion of Egypt. Amalric still had problems with his recalcitrant barons, and the Hospitallers had suffered serious losses in the previous Egyptian war. Amalric again approached the Knights of the Temple to ask for their support, but the Templars would not budge from their previous stand. No Knights Templar would accompany Amalric to Egypt.

The Templars had functioned without a grand master since the death of Bertrand de Blanquefort in January, but finally they chose his successor in August 1169. Politics appear to have been heavily involved in the choice. Apparently in hopes of healing the breach with King Amalric, they elected their Templar brother Philip de Milly, a widower and former lord of Oultrejourdain, to lead their holy order. Philip had an excellent reputation both as an administrator and as a fighter, but most important, he was a close friend of Amalric. There was one point, apparently, on which the grand chapter of the Knights Templar got de Milly's approval before he was offered the post: Even after he assumed command, the Templars still refused to support the Egyptian campaign. They would, however, perform the valuable service of protecting the Christian kingdom while the king was away.

While the Templars were putting their house in order in Jerusalem, Saladin was doing exactly the same in Cairo. Having carefully made his plans, he had his men seize the chief eunuch who had written the secret letter to Amalric. That bit of penmanship cost the eunuch his head, and with the court in a state of shock, all of the Egyptian officials who were judged to be loyal primarily to the caliph were summarily dismissed, to be replaced immediately by men already identified as loyal to Saladin. Any comfort that al-Adid had drawn from Saladin's inexperience was gone.

Guard regiments for the palace were traditionally recruited from all parts of the Egyptian empire, and now the caliph and the discharged officials incited the Nubian guard to rebel against Saladin. As they attacked his palace, Saladin sent men to set fires behind them in the Nubian quarters. When the news reached the Nubians, they turned and ran, thinking now only of saving their wives and children. Saladin's men, waiting for them in the side streets, poured out of the darkness and killed them all. The fire also took the quarters of the Armenian guard, who were burned to death in their homes. Caliph al-Adid's response was to deliver a hasty message to Saladin, assuring him of the caliph's love and loyalty.

Amalric was getting his army together, but it was taking too much time. Saladin had regular reports of his progress and took advantage of the delay to move into Bilbeis on the frontier, expecting the Christians to follow their previous line of march.

This time, however, the campaign was to be a combined land and sea operation, so the inland city was not a Christian objective. A better strike would be against a port city on the Mediterranean, where a victory would be more significant politically and, in consideration of the potential for rich plunder, economically. The Greeks had enough ships to carry the Latin army by sea, but they chose to march overland, a journey that would postpone their strike by a couple of weeks.

The expedition began on October 16, 1169, under the command of a very nervous Byzantine admiral. Expecting a fast attack by land and sea, the Greeks had loaded supplies for just ninety days, but that time had run out. Their forces were already subject to strict rationing, and the war hadn't even begun.

The objective the Christians had agreed upon was the strongly fortified river city of Damietta, which commanded the main channel of the Nile through the great delta. A run straight up the river to Cairo could have meant an early victory for the Christians, but they found a massive chain strung across the river, blocking their ships. They had no means to break the chain, unless they first took Damietta.

Although the news of an attack from the sea was a surprise to Saladin in his capital at Cairo, he wasted no time in getting more troops and supplies to the threatened city. The relief operation had no problems, since the journey was made with the current, traveling straight down the Nile from Cairo to Damietta by barge. The winds were also downriver, so no sailing ship could expect to be able to sail up to interfere with the mission.

The Greek admiral wanted an immediate attack because his supplies were almost gone, but Amalric doubted his army's ability to storm the great walls. He set his men to building siege engines, while the Greeks had to face near-starvation. The Latins had hardly had time to dip into their own supplies and had plenty on hand, but they refused, insanely, to share with their Greek allies. To make things worse, the Egyptians loaded a ship with combustibles and naphtha, set it on fire, and let the strong Nile current carry it right into the midst of the closely moored Greek ships, causing considerable damage. Then the winter rains began, turning the low Christian camp into an ocean of thick, sticky mud.

News that a supporting Muslim army was on its way overland from Syria was the final straw. Food not already ruined by the rains was almost gone. Men were dejected, and the inevitable diseases were beginning to take a heavy toll. The Muslim enemy behind the great walls of Damietta was high and dry and well supplied. The Christians had made no attempt to study the defenses of Damietta in advance, which could easily have been done, and now they had run out of ideas, and out of hope. They gave up.

The siege engines were burned on December 13, as the Christian army began its dreary march home, having accomplished absolutely nothing. The men arrived at Ascalon on Christmas Eve, but the advent of Christ's birthday festival found in them no feelings of self-reproach, as once again they cast about to find someone to blame for their failure. The most popular target among the Latin Christians, of course, was the Byzantines. Some might be critical of the Knights Templar for not having fought with them, but good sense could not permit any valid criticism of the Templars' military judgment. In the face of such a disaster, however, some felt justified in hating the Knights Templar for having been right.

At least the Latins had managed to get home, which was not true of most the the Greek navy. Devastating winter storms had caught them on the return passage. Ships beyond control capsized and their crews drowned. Ships that did survive the storms were blown far off course. It took some Greek sailors many grueling weeks to get home, but they were still better off than the hundreds of their companions whose bloated bodies came bobbing to shore all along the coast of the Holy Land.

Saladin, on the other hand, had gained much. He had defended his new subjects against two great enemies and had saved Egypt with no cost to his own people. His popularity soared. It soared, that is, except with his lord and master, Nur ed-Din. Nur ed-Din's gold had financed the Egyptian campaign, and his Turkish cavalry had kept Saladin on his new throne. Now the young man who had been reluctant to accompmany his uncle to Egypt was the grand vizier of that empire and called himself the king of Egypt. He personally controlled vast lands, including farms enriched by the legendary fertile soil of the Nile valley. He personally controlled the great trade routes from East Africa and from the Indies through the Red Sea. He controlled rich seaports and the only substantial Muslim navy in the Middle East. Had he claimed these riches and this power for himself, or for his lord? Saladin was paying limited lip service to Nur ed-Din, but the overlord in Damascus was far from confident of the loyalty of his suddenly successful vassal. To put his own mind at rest, Nur ed-Din sent Saladin's father, Najm ed-Din Ayub, to join

Saladin at Cairo. Ayub's loyalty was unquestioned, and perhaps he could hold his son's ambitions in check.

In the meantime, Nur ed-Din had acquired a strange ally, a renegade Knight Templar. Two years earlier Prince Thoros of Armenia had died, having named as heir his little son Prince Roupen II, and having named a regent to rule until the child came of age. Thoros's brother, Mleh, felt that the throne, or at least the regency, should have been his. Mleh was a wild-minded adventurer whose conduct was totally unpredictable. After disagreements with his brother, Prince Thoros, he had abandoned his Armenian Orthodox faith and embraced Roman Catholicism in order to take the vows required to become a Knight Templar. Still angry, he was discovered later at the center of a plot to assassinate his brother. His Templar membership provided no protection from the punishment for that crime, so he fled the Templar castle at which he was stationed. Days later he presented himself at the court of Nur ed-Din, offering his services and declaring his desire to become a Muslim.

Finally convincing Nur ed-Din of his grand plan to take the Armenian principality of Cilicia and to change it from a Byzantine holding to a part of the Islamic empire, Mleh was given command of an army of Turkish cavalry. His invasion was a complete surprise and a complete success. He took his little nephew off the throne and easily captured the fortified towns of Tarsus, Adana, and Mamistra. Not satisfied, Mleh then turned his troops south into the principality of Antioch and attacked his former brothers, as he laid siege to the Templar castle of Baghras.

Amalric responded quickly to the joint appeals from his friend, the new master of the Templars, and from Prince Bohemond of Antioch. He hurried north with a relieving army, but no battle was joined. Mleh wanted loot, not land, and since he had plundered the country he simply backed off and let Amalric retake Cilicia. Mleh had not given up, but he waited a year before coming back again.

With his northern boundaries secure, Amalric got bad news from the south. Toward the end of the year Saladin had appeared with an army before Daron, south of Gaza. Daron was the Christian fortress closest to the border with Egypt, but by no means one of the strongest in the Christian kingdom. Amalric had to move swiftly again, and this time the Knights Templar, grateful for Amalric's rescue of their castle at Baghras, went with him. He drove straight to Ascalon, then turned to the great Templar castle at Gaza. All of the Knights Templar who could be spared from Gaza went with King Amalric, who left his seneschal, Miles de Plancy, in charge of the town in front of the castle walls.

Amalric's heavily armored column broke through Saladin's light cavalry and entered the fortress of Daron. Saladin responded by gathering his cavalry and moving off to attack Gaza. The town was taken easily, and Saladin made no attempt to control his men as they slaughtered the people in the streets and in their homes. He had no siege engines and was not prepared to pay the price of trying to scale the lofty walls of the Templar castle, so he had his people gather up whatever loot they could carry and led then back to Egypt.

The Christians were relieved to learn that this time Saladin's foray was just a raid and not a full-scale invasion, but the threat was always present. Then, too, there was always the chance that Saladin would approach from Egypt in the southwest at the same time that Nur ed-Din attacked from Syria in the northeast. The conquest of Egypt was vital for the survival of the kingdom of Jerusalem, and for that goal to be achieved the Christians still needed the naval support of the Byzantine empire. In the spring of 1170 Amalric decided to go personally to make another military alliance against Egypt with the emperor Manuel.

Now the Knights Templar learned the true loyalties of their new leader. Philip de Milly, who had been elected grand master because of his close friendship with King Amalric, showed just how close that relationship really was. He resigned as grand master of the Knights Templar to serve Amalric as his permanent ambassador to Byzantium. The vow he had taken to obey the Templar Rule demanded that upon leaving the Templars he must join a stricter monastic order, but Philip simply ignored that part of his vows. The king he now served followed him to Constantinople.

The king had cost the Templars a grand master, and now the grand chapter would deprive Amalric of one of his own court officials. They elected Odo de St. Amand, who promptly resigned his post as the king's butler. Unlike Philip de Milly, Grand Master de St. Amand was firmly on the side of his order. He would go to any lengths to protect the power and preserve the privileges of the Knights Templar. That attitude angered some of his fellow Catholics, notably William, archdeacon of Tyre. The Templars, however, were well pleased with their choice.

Archdeacon William not only consistently chronicled his dislike of the new master of the Temple, but about the same time he recorded an incident involving the king's young son, one which held dire portent for the future. William was acting as tutor to the nine-year-old Prince Baldwin and several of his friends. He watched his young students one day as they played one of their rough boyish games. They were digging their nails into each other's bare arms, to see how much pain they could stand. Prince Baldwin appeared to be the champion, because he was able to stand any amount of pain without flinching or crying out. But in a shock of discovery, the archdeacon realized that Prince Baldwin's insensitivity to pain was not evidence of his bravery. It was leprosy. It appeared reasonable to assume that the boy would not live long enough to ever take his seat on the throne of Jerusalem, so to assure the succession a husband must be found for his sister Sibylla.

In Cairo another boy ruler died. When he got the news that the Shiite caliph al-Adid had died in his sleep, Saladin gathered up all of al-Adid's relatives and confined them to their palaces under close guard, in what must have been the most luxurious prisons in the world. He permitted no successor to al-Adid. The Shiite Fatimid caliphate was dead.

Relishing his new power, Saladin launched a new raid into Christian territory, this time to lay siege to the castle of Montreal, south of the Dead Sea in Oultrejourdain. His father went with him. Just when it seemed that he would have the victory, Saladin was told that Nur ed-Din was close at hand and riding in. Nur ed-Din, who had not been consulted about Saladin's actions, was furious. Saladin immediately ordered his forces to pack and mount up for their return to Egypt. Some of Saladin's followers urged him to assert himself, because he was now mightier than Nur ed-Din. His father, however, drew him aside and convinced him of the dangers inherent in flouting Nur ed-Din's authority. He advised Saladin to apologize and vow total submission to his lord. Saladin took Ayub's advice, and Nur ed-Din appeared satisfied for the moment, but the incident put a great strain on their relationship.

The following year was one of negotiation, not war, and Amalric's most significant achievement may have been arranging for the ransom of Count Raymond of Tripoli. Nur ed-Din set a price of eighty thousand dinars, with fifty thousand to be paid at once, the balance later. It was left to King Amalric and the Hospitallers alone to come up with the money, because the Knights Templar declined to contribute. Count Raymond was released, and in the years to follow he would not forget his friends, nor the order he now considered his enemy. Nor did that attitude of the Knights Templar do anything to soothe Amalric's animosity toward them.

In the meantime, the relationship between Nur ed-Din and his vassal Saladin was growing ever more strained. It was clear to Nur ed-Din that Saladin saw himself as an independent sovereign ruler and needed to be disciplined. Only his close friendship with Saladin's father held him back. When Nur ed-Din learned in August that Saladin's father had died, he announced to his court in Damascus that he would personally lead an army into

Egypt the following spring to put Saladin in his place.

A few weeks later King Amalric got a surprising, but welcome, visit from the new leader of the Syrian Assassins. They had established an independent state in the Nosairi mountains of Syria and the Assassin leader in Persia had sent one of their number, Sheikh Rashid ed-Din Sinan, to rule over the new territory. Sheikh Rashid was a wily and ruthless leader whom the Crusaders came to refer to as the Old Man of the Mountain. He was a fanatical fundamentalist Shiite, as were most of his followers, and he loathed Nur ed-Din and his followers as hell-bound Sunni heretics. He considered them to be much lower than the Christians, with whom he was willing to ally his people in order to punish the Sunnis for the destruction of the Shiite caliphate at Cairo.

Amalric welcomed the alliance because the Assassins were fierce, relentless fighters with the best intelligence network in Syria, but he was not taken in by their broad hints that they might all convert to Christianity. He had no trouble at all in granting their request that the annual tribute demanded of their people living in the Templar lands near Tortosa be immediately discontinued.

Grand Master de St. Amand did not agree with Amalric's cavalier disregard for Templar revenues, nor did he care for decisions regarding the Knights Templar being made without consulting him. As the Assassin emissaries left to take the road north to their mountains, a party of Knights Templar, commanded by a one-eyed knight, Gautier de Mesnil, was ahead of them. The unprepared Assassins rode right into a Templar ambush. Within a matter of minutes all of their heads were separated from their bodies.

Amalric couldn't believe the news. Had the Knights Templar actually put a few pieces of gold ahead of his royal promise? Did they believe that the king of Jerusalem could be ignored, insulted, degraded? In a rage, he sent a message to Odo de St. Amand at Sidon demanding that the Templar Gautier be surrendered to him for judgment and punishment. The grand master's reply only served to add to the king's fury. He was told that even though he was the king, he had no authority to judge, much less punish, a Knight of the Temple. On the other hand, if the king so desired, the grand master would send Brother Gautier for judgment to the pope in Rome, the only person on earth other than the grand master himself who held such authority.

The king's answer was to appear at the gates of Sidon with a body of troops. He forced his way into the Templars' house and took Gautier as his prisoner. Word was sent to Sheikh Rashid that justice would be done, and the Assassins appeared satisfied with the king's actions. Amalric, however, was not satisfied with the punishment of just one Templar. He asked Archdeacon William of Tyre to prepare a papal petition for his signature and seal. He intended to demand of the pope that the order be disbanded, since the Knights Templar were no longer welcome in the kingdom of Jerusalem. But he couldn't get up nerve enough to execute his Templar prisoner.

In the fateful year of 1174, disease, as it often did, changed the course of history. As Nur ed-Din consulted with his emirs abut the army being assembled to crush Saladin, he fell sick with a severe inflammation of the throat. Within days he was dead.

King Amalric was happy to get the news, but not happy about his own health. A strong young man just thirty-eight years old, he had begun to suffer from frequent and increasingly severe bouts of dysentery. Within a few weeks he was confined to his bed, where his suffering grew worse. His court doctors could do almost nothing to alleviate his pain, driving Amalric to prescribe for himself, demanding that his veins be opened for bleeding and his aching bowels be completely purged. The Greek and Arab physicians flatly refused, telling the king that his weakened body could not be expected to survive such brutal treatment. His Frankish doctor disagreed and carried out the kill-or-cure treatment as the king had ordered. Two days later, Amalric was dead. There would be no petition to the pope to dissolve the order of the Knights Templar, who during the next reign would rashly contribute to the success of their enemy Saladin, now the uncontested ruler of Egypt. The Christian kingdom would be ruled in its time of greatest peril by a teenaged leper who was strong of mind and gallant of spirit, but too physically ravaged to control those around him.

8

The Horns of Hattin
1174 to 1187

UPON THE DEATH OF King Amalric in 1174, the crown of Jerusalem went to Baldwin IV, the thirteen-year-old leper whom no one had thought would live long enough to gain the throne. After some political infighting, Count Raymond of Tripoli, the man whom the Templars had refused to help ransom, became regent until the king would come of age at sixteen. Miles de Plancy, who had been Raymond's most aggressive competitor for that powerful position, was murdered in the streets a few weeks later.

The new regent had to contend with two distinct political factions, each trying to persuade the young monarch to its point of view. One group, based on the "old guard" establishment of resident barons, with the support of the Knights Hospitaller, favored negotiations that would lead to a peaceful coexistence with their Muslim neighbors. The other party was in favor of militant aggression against the infidel. This faction, partially based on more recent arrivals among the barony, included the ever-hawkish Knights Templar and had the support of the king's mother and of the patriarch of Jerusalem.

Raymond of Tripoli had a built-in enemy within the Templar order. A couple of years earlier a Flemish knight, Gerard de Ridfort, had taken service under Count Raymond with the understanding that he would be granted the hand of the next available heiress. Accordingly, Gerard expected to wed Lucia, daughter of the lord of Botrun, upon the death of her wealthy father. Instead, Raymond gave Lucia in marriage to an Italian merchant, whose offer to Raymond of the lady's weight in gold took precedence over an unprofitable promise, especially since Lucia was a plump little lady whose weight was recorded as ten stone, or one hundred and forty pounds. Lucia went on the scale, the gold went into Raymond's treasury, and the bitterly angry Gerard de Ridfort went into the Order of the Temple. He rose quickly within the hierarchy, but no level of personal success did anything to cool his craving for revenge.

One of Baldwin IV's few mistakes may have been his insistence that his mother, the Lady Agnes, countess of Courtenay, be restored to her position at court, which had been lost when she and Baldwin's father, Amalric, had been divorced by papal annulment. Agnes had an excessive desire for money and an equally insatiable desire for men. One of her many lovers was an extremely handsome young priest, and even though he was semiliterate at best, Agnes campaigned for and obtained his appointment as archbishop of Caesarea. She was also delighted to receive good news about her brother, Joscelin of Courtenay, who had been languishing for years in a Muslim dungeon at Aleppo with Reynald of Chatillon.

What had happened was that Saladin had been hesitant to react to the death of Nur ed-Din in May 1174, because any attempt on his part to take Damascus might have triggered an alliance between the Syrians and the Kingdom of Jerusalem. With the death of the aggressive King Amalric two months later, and with the Christian crown placed on the head of a thirteen-year-old leper, it appeared that Allah was smiling at the sultan of Egypt. Beha ed-Din, a chronicler who knew how to please his sovereign, wrote: ''The Sultan, having assured himself of the death of Nur ed-Din, and knowing that the son of that prince was a young man unequal to the cares and responsibilities of sovereignty and of the task of driving the enemies of god [the Christians] from the land, made preparations for an expedition to Syria.''

Within a month of the coronation of Baldwin IV, Saladin led an army out of Egypt for the conquest of Damascus and its new ruler, as-Saleh Imail, the eleven-year-old son of Nur ed-Din. When it was clear that Saladin was coming, the young ruler was rushed to the fortress city of Aleppo, ruled by Emir Gumushtekin, who was also the prince of the Kurdish capital city of Mosul. Saladin walked right into Damascus, then turned his army to the cities in the north. He easily took the city at Homs, but the castle garrison mounted a fierce defense. Leaving part of his army to finish the capture of the castle, Saladin moved off to take Aleppo and the young prince as-Saleh. Emir Gumushtekin sent envoys to Count Raymond, as the regent of the Christian kingdom, to plead for help against Saladin.

In response, Raymond called his people to arms and led a relief column into Syria. They did not move to Aleppo to confront Saladin, but marched to the smaller Muslim army still trying to take the castle at Homs. Raymond attacked Saladin's men from the outside of the city, while the relieved castle garrison happily attacked from the inside. Saladin's army was caught in the middle. When the news came to Saladin, he abandoned the siege of Aleppo to hurry south to rescue his army at Homs. When he got close, Raymond simply drew back his Christian forces. For the moment, at least, Aleppo and Prince as-Saleh were safe, although the temporary setback did not prevent Saladin from adding to his titles by declaring himself to be the king of Syria. To express his profound gratitude for the rescue of his city, Gumushtekin released all of the Christian prisoners at Aleppo, including Joscelin of Courtenay and Reynald of Chatillon. Had he bothered to ask in advance, he would have learned that Raymond would have much preferred a simple thank-you note. He had no liking and no use for either Reynald or Joscelin.

As Lady Agnes's brother and the uncle of King Baldwin IV, Joscelin was welcomed at the royal court. At his mother's urging, Baldwin appointed Joscelin of Courtenay as the seneschal of the kingdom, making him the chief administrative officer of the court, with knights, soldiers, and servants at his command.

Reynald of Chatillon, after seventeen years in a Muslim dungeon, found his own welcome at the headquarters of his old friends, the Knights Templar. Eager for news, he learned that Count Philip de Milly, the lord of Oultrejourdain, had years earlier abandoned his secular life upon the death of his wife to finish out his days as a Knight Templar. He had risen to the post of grand master, but had resigned the order in 1171 to go to Constantinople as the ambassador of King Amalric.

Reynald learned that there was no lord of Oultrejourdain at the moment. Philip de Milly's daughter Stephanie was widowed when her husband, Miles de Plancy, had been the victim of a midnight murder, apparently because he was Raymond of Tripoli's chief rival to be the regent for the young king. Stephanie now hated Raymond. She was convinced that he had killed her husband. Whoever married Stephanie would be the lord of Oultrejourdain, with its lofty castles of Montreal and Kerak.

We can see Reynald smiling. Life was so simple. He was never so charming as in his courtship of Stephanie de Milly, and never stronger in his condemnations of Raymond of Tripoli. Stephanie, impressed by this strong, vibrant man, agreed to the marriage. His Templar friends congratulated him on such a profitable wedding and congratulated themselves for gaining another powerful ally.

In 1177 King Baldwin turned sixteen and the regency ended. One of Baldwin's first acts with his full royal authority was to look to the succession of the throne. His leprosy was advancing, so it was vitally important to his plan for the succession that a husband be found quickly for his seventeen-year-old sister Sibylla, who under the law could not rule as queen without a king beside her. The choice fell on William of Montferrat. The couple seemed happy with each other, but within two years William was dead of malaria. A few months later Sibylla gave birth to their son, so the crown did have its male heir. It was obvious, however, that the leper king could not live much longer, so without a husband for the future queen, a child-king and a regency were assured. A second husband had to be found for the princess Sibylla. But as important as that political measure was, it was not as pressing as the new military threat.

In November of that year Saladin left Egypt for a campaign against the Christians. When news of Saladin's invasion reached the Templars, they called in knights from other castles to defend their fortress of Gaza, while Baldwin IV quickly gathered about five hundred of his own knights and moved behind the walls of Ascalon, which stood between Saladin and Jerusalem. Undeterred, Saladin left a small siege force to keep the king bottled up in Ascalon and took his main army on toward Jerusalem.

The king somehow managed to get a message through the besieging Muslims to the Templars, asking them to abandon Gaza to join him at Ascalon. Eager for a fight, the Templars responded immediately and the king moved out of the city to meet them. Their combined forces quickly shrugged off the token force Saladin had left behind and set off in pursuit of the main Egyptian army. That army was moving casually toward Jerusalem, with no thought of possible danger to the rear. They were pillaging and foraging, maintaining no kind of order of march, and as they were crossing a broad ravine the combined royal and Templar armies struck. It was a total surprise and a total rout. Those Muslims who were not killed dropped their loot and even their weapons to make an unencumbered flight back to Egypt. Jerusalem had been saved.

Early in the year 1179, William, now advanced from archdeacon to archbishop of Tyre, responded to an invitation from Pope Alexander III to attend the Third Lateran Council in Rome. It would deal with matters important to the Church, and the archbishop was anxious to bring before it his own anger and disgust at the conduct of the military orders, especially the Templar grand master Odo de St. Amand. His complaint was that the grand master put the selfish interests of the Templars above all other other things, even above the rights and privileges of the bishops. If a bishop excommunicated a man, the Templars would shelter him or even take him into their order. If an excommunicate died in that condition, so that he was not allowed a Christian burial, the Templars would bury him in their own cemetery with full religious rites, always in exchange for a gift to their order.

If a bishop put an entire community under interdict to let it feel the heavy hand of ecclesiastic censure, so that its church would be closed to holy communion, baptism, marriage, or Christian burial, the orders might send their own priests to open the church. They would perform all of those services, based on the erroneous idea that since the orders and their members were exempt from interdict or excommunication, they could pass those privileges on to others. They made the bishops look foolish by flouting their authority and diverted important sources of church revenues by accepting "alms" for their services. Cemeteries were important sources of income, and William wanted them to be prohibited to the military orders. As William of Tyre voiced his complaints to the Council, other bishops from all over Europe supported him with reports of similar experiences.

The Council lasted from March 5 to March 19, finding time to chastise the military orders: "Now we have learned from the strong complaints of our brothers and fellow bishops that the Templars and Hospitallers... going beyond the privileges granted to them by the apostolic see, have often disregarded episcopal authority, causing scandal to the people of God, and grave danger to souls. We are informed...they admit those under excommunication and interdict to the sacraments of the church and to Christian burial." William of Tyre could not have been happy that Grand Master de St. Amand was let off the hook with conciliatory language: "...the faults arise not so much with the knowledge or permission of the superiors as from the indiscretion of some of their subjects." And finally, to make the Church position clear: "We declare that those who are excommunicated or interdicted by name, must be avoided by them [the military orders] and all others according to the sentence of the bishops."

No punishment was meted out beyond that "cease and desist" decree. The pope was not prepared to drive a wedge between himself and the military orders that answered only to him. The bishops may have been disappointed that the pope hadn't been stronger against the Templars and Hospitallers, but they must have been even more distressed that the pope took the time to put some constraints on the bishops themselves. The lower clergy and the religious orders had complained to the Holy See that a formal visit from a bishop or archbishop could be financially ruinous. The bishops came calling with droves of clerics and attendants, sometimes with hundreds of horses to be fed. As for a bishop's visiting party, it expected every meal to be a lavish feast. The limitations set by the Council gave hints to the style in which the bishops moved in regal pageantry to inspect their dioceses.

As the pope put it: "...some of our brethren and fellow bishops place such burdens on their subjects in the accommodations demanded that sometimes, for that reason, subjects are forced to sell church ornaments, and a single hour consumes the food of many days. Therefore, we decree that archbishops on their visits to their dioceses are not to take more than forty or fifty horses...bishops are never to exceed twenty or thirty.... They should not set out with hunting dogs and birds, but they should travel in such a way that they are to be seen seeking not things of the world, but things of Jesus Christ. Let them not seek rich banquets, but let them receive with thanksgiving whatever is duly and suitably provided to them."

Nor was it just the higher clergy that was ordered to make a change in lifestyle: "...clerics in holy orders, who in flagrant concubinage keep their mistresses in their houses, should either cast them out and live continently or be deprived of ecclesiastical office and benefice." On the question of living and working with Jews: "Jews are not allowed to have Christian servants in their houses.... Let those Christians be excommunicated who choose to live with them. We declare that the evidence of Christians is to prevail against that of Jews in every case..."

One final decree of the Council was to have a direct bearing on the future of the Crusades and specifically on the future of the Knights Templar: The pope gave secular authorities the right to use the force of arms against heretics, in this case a growing sect in the Languedoc region of southern France. They were called Cathars, and their greatest crime was that they denied that there was any scriptural justification for the existence of a pope. Decreed the pope, "...the loathsome heresies of those called the Cathars...has become so strong that they no longer practice their wickedness in secret, as do others, but proclaim their error publicly, attracting the simple and weak to join with them, we declare that they and their supporters and those who receive them are under anathema...." The foundations for Crusades against other Christians are laid here: "...on all the faithful we demand, for the remission of their sins, that they oppose this scourge with all their power and by force of arms protect the Christian people against them. Their goods are to be confiscated and princes are free to condemn them to slavery. Those who in true contrition for their sins die in such a conflict should have no doubt that they will receive forgiveness for those sins and the prize of an eternal reward." And to make the impending crusading connection even more clear: "Meanwhile, we take under the protection of the church, as we do those who visit the sepulchre of our Lord, those who fired by their faith have assumed the task of driving out these heretics...."

It would be almost thirty years before Crusaders would be diverted to a full Crusade against the Cathar heretics in France, but the stage was set here in Rome in 1179. What the Third Lateran Council had *not* addressed was the need for more Crusaders to protect the Holy City. While the bishops had been discussing issues important to them, Saladin had invaded the kingdom of Jerusalem, and Baldwin IV had led out the Christian army to stop him.

On April 10, 1179, Saladin sent a small army under the command of his nephew to reconnoiter ahead of the Muslim invasion. The nephew came upon the royal army in a valley in the forest of Banyas and immediately attacked. This time it was the Christians who were taken completely by surprise, and the result was a thorough defeat, although Baldwin was able to escape, due to the alert rear-guard action of his bodyguard. Saladin followed up this success with sweeps through Galilee and Lebanon to destroy the crops and gather whatever loot he could find.

King Baldwin rallied his forces, sent out his scouts, and then took to the field again when he learned that a large raiding party under Saladin's nephew was on its way back from the coast, loaded down with plunder. What the king did not know was that Saladin's spies kept the sultan informed of the movements of the Christian army, so that the pursuers were also the pursued. On June 10 Baldwin took part of the Christian army to attack the Egyptian raiding party in a valley between the Litani and upper Jordan rivers. The other part of the Crusader army, led by the Knights Templar, traveled ahead toward the Jordan River.

At the entrance to the river valley, the Templars sighted Saladin's main force. The most rudimentary military judgment would have called for falling back to join Baldwin's army or holding until the kings' forces came up. At bare minimum, Baldwin should have been informed immediately, because he was close at hand. Unfortunately, such prudence frequently stood contrary to the Templar quest for action and glory. Grand Master de St. Amand was personally in command and summarily ordered his Templars to charge into overwhelmingly superior numbers. It was very difficult for armored knights on heavy horses to regroup after the initial impact of their charge, and Saladin's massive counterattack easily turned the dispersed Templars, sending them into flight back toward Baldwin's troops, who had not yet regrouped after their battle with the Egyptian raiders. Soon the entire Christian army was in retreat. Some of the defeated Crusaders, along with Baldwin, were able to cross the Litani River to safety. Those who could not make their escape were killed or taken prisoner, and among those prisoners was Odo de St. Amand, the Templar grand master, whose impulsiveness had brought on the disaster.

Other important prisoners were ransomed for money, but Saladin knew of the Templar Rule that forbade any payments for ransom. In exchange for the grand master, he asked for his nephew, who was being held captive by the Christians. Odo de St. Amand rejected the exchange, his pride refusing to acknowledge that there could be any one Muslim of equal value to the grand master of the Temple. The trade would be demeaning. The exchange was called off, and an angry Saladin ordered Odo into a deliberately miserable Damascus dungeon, where he died in his chains the following year.

One of the most important prisoners ransomed after that battle was Baldwin of Ibelin. The widowed Princess Sibylla had fallen in love with Baldwin, but he had gone off to war before the formal betrothal could be arranged. Perhaps this information, which would have told Saladin that he was holding the future king of Jerusalem, influenced him in his excessive demands. The ransom set for Baldwin of Ibelin was the release of one thousand Muslim prisoners plus one hundred fifty thousand gold dinars. The young man of such great prospects was paroled upon his promise to deliver the ransom payments.

Upon his release, Baldwin learned that his true love had a practical side tempering her devotion. Sibylla was not going to marry a man who was one hundred fifty thousand dinars in debt. Baldwin turned to the only place he knew of to procure such an enormous sum, and with success. The Byzantine emperor Manuel was happy to pay the ransom to put the next king of Jerusalem in his debt. Emperor and knight, however, were both disappointed, because when Baldwin reached Jerusalem bearing the good news, the princess was already betrothed to the handsome but frivolous Guy of Lusignan.

Lady Agnes had been busy cooking up a plot of her own. She did not like the Ibelins and had disapproved of one of them marrying the heiress to the throne of Jerusalem. On the other hand, she was very fond of Amalric, a son of the count of Lusignan, who had risen to the post of constable of the kingdom of Jerusalem. He also had risen to the post of lover to the king's mother. Together they plotted to bring to Palestine Amalric's younger brother Guy, a young man reputed to be of extraordinary beauty and courtly charm. While Baldwin of Ibelin was traveling to Constantinople to see the emperor, Amalric was off to France to get his handsome young brother.

Princess Sibylla found that Guy was everything she had been

told and quickly announced that this was the only man in the world she would marry. King Baldwin objected. This foppish young Frenchman, who had no experience in military leadership or administration, nor in anything else that mattered, was in no way suited to become the next king of Jerusalem. Sibylla and Lady Agnes pleaded Guy's case incessantly, but then the king discovered that Guy and Sibylla were already lovers. He wanted to have Guy executed for his violation of a royal princess, but the Templar officers sided with the young couple so strongly that the physically feeble king relented and permitted the marriage to go forward. As befitted his new station, Guy was named count of Ascalon and Jaffa, and he began his career in friendly relations with the Knights Templar who had so strongly supported him.

In an effort to restore peace to his kingdom, Baldwin IV decided to propose a truce, and Saladin agreed. Both sides had suffered the effects of a drought that threatened them all with famine, and there would be no food supplies to keep armies in the field. A treaty was signed in May 1180 that declared a two-year truce. Food and other supplies had to be imported during the shortage, so the treaty also established that Christian and Muslim merchants would be allowed to cross each other's territory in complete security. Within the year, Reynald of Chatillon would break that treaty.

At home there remained the arrangement of marriage for the king's half-sister Isabella, second in line for the throne. In October of 1180 the king betrothed Isabella to the extraordinarily handsome Humphrey of Toron, a scholar and an expert in both spoken and written Arabic. For the sake of propriety the wedding was put off for three years until 1183, when the bride would be eleven years old. Although he was to become a trusted advisor to the king and a frequent royal emissary because of his command of Arabic, Humphrey was intensely disliked by the warrior barons of the court. To them he was an effeminate bookworm and not a fitting prospect to be second in line for the crown of Jerusalem.

In October of 1180, the same month that Isabella was betrothed, the king's mother scored another political victory. The patriarch of Jerusalem had died. Within two weeks, Lady Agnes had succeeded in having one of her lovers, Heraclius, whom she had already maneuvered into the post of archbishop of Caesarea, named patriarch of Jerusalem. It hadn't been easy, because William, archbishop of Tyre, had come to the court for the express purpose of stopping the elevation of Heraclius. In a sense he succeeded, because the electors picked Heraclius as their second choice, not the first. Undaunted, Lady Agnes had persuaded the king to give the appointment to Heraclius, regardless of the constituted elections.

With their own patriarch in place, one political faction was now firmly in control. Its principal leaders were the Lusignans, the Courtenays (led by the king's mother), Count Reynald of Chatillon, and the Knights Templar. Reynald was a dangerous ally, both for the Templars and the kingdom. In the summer of 1181 he deliberately broke the two-year truce agreed upon a year earlier. He could not resist the temptation of rich but poorly guarded merchants passing so near to his massive inland castle at Kerak, and one day he swooped down on a Muslim caravan on its way from Damascus to Mecca, helping himself to the people, the animals, and the trade goods. Saladin demanded compensation, and King Baldwin agreed with both the fairness and the legality of that demand, but Reynald rejected any thought of returning or paying for the illicit booty. His faction at court, including the Knights Templar, supported his position.

The archbishop of Tyre did not relent in his outrage at the machinations of the ruling political faction behind the throne. He reported them directly to the pope, along with specific tirades against Heraclius and the Templars. In retaliation, he was excommunicated by the patriarch Heraclius. Unable to persuade or coerce Heraclius to retract the excommunication, William went to Rome in 1183 to plead his case before the papal court. Before he could present that case he was murdered by poison, reputedly by the hand of an agent sent to Rome for that purpose by the patriarch.

By the summer of 1183, Saladin had completed his campaigns against fellow Muslim rulers and had emerged with all of the Islamic lands from modern Libya to Iraq under his effective control. He was now the most powerful Muslim potentate of the past two centuries. Having established his capital at Damascus, Saladin could now set about his last great task for the benefit of Islam and his own personal power, the matter of pushing the hated Latin Christians into the sea, and one Christian in particular, Reynald of Chatillon.

While Saladin had been occupied with his efforts to consolidate his empire, Reynald had decided upon a sea campaign that could be expected to yield successive prizes of rich plunder. He marched his men to the Red Sea with long teams of horses dragging galleys made inland. They raided up and down the Red Sea, taking one port town after another, including ports serving Mecca and Medina. They captured merchant ships at sea and even stripped a huge caravan on land. In what was perhaps the worst crime to the faithful, they sank a shipload of Muslims on pilgrimage to Mecca. The Christians stayed too long, however, permitting time for an Egyptian fleet to come against them. Reynald's ships were taken, and almost all of his men were captured and promptly condemned to public beheadings, some of them as part of a spectacle staged in the court-yard of the great Mosque at Mecca. Reynald contrived his own escape, but he had incurred Saladin's unforgiving rage and his deter-mination that this Christian, above all others, must be punished.

The Christian world was in no condition to repel an invader. Princess Sibylla, the patriarch, and the king's mother had success-fully badgered the weakening king into making the effete Guy of Lusiganan the regent of the kingdom. By 1183 Baldwin IV was moving into the advanced stages of leprosy. He had lost the use of his arms and legs, as they began to rot away. His sight was almost gone. The king knew that he had to make someone the adminis-trative head of the realm, and he finally agreed to make Guy regent for all of the kingdom except the city of Jerusalem, which he wished to keep for himself.

In September of that year Saladin moved his army across the Jordan River near the Sea of Galilee, so Guy of Lusignan assembled an army and went out to confront him. The two armies met and camped on opposite sides of a tributary of the Jordan River. Some of the more aggressive Christian knights, goaded by the Templars, wanted to attack, while others wanted to stay on the defensive and let Saladin attack them. They looked to their leader and found no leadership. Guy of Lusignan, regent of the kingdom of Jerusalem, just could not make a decision. As he procrastinated, supplies began to run out. Saladin tried to provoke the Christians into a fight, but finally gave up and moved his army from the west bank back across the Jordan into Syria. As the Christians went home from the battle that never happened, they were convinced that Guy of Lusignan had been proven a coward.

Back in Jerusalem, Baldwin IV did not criticize Guy but did ask a favor of him. In the belief that the air of the coastal city of Tyre would be more healthful for him, the king asked Guy to accept Jerusalem in exchange for Tyre. Guy's answer was both negative and insulting. In his anger, the king removed Guy from the regency. The king himself, even though by this stage unable to walk, to read a document, or even to sign his name, took personal control of the kingdom. His early death assured by the the increasing ravages of his leprosy, he named as successor to the throne of Jerusalem the six-year-old Baldwin, son of Princess Sibylla by her first husband. Guy's answer to all this was to retire to his own counties of Ascalon and Jaffa and to forswear any further allegiance to Baldwin IV.

Sick as he was, Baldwin IV could not tolerate Guy's disobedience. He had himself carried on a litter to Ascalon, where Guy denied him admittance. The king then turned to Guy's other city of Jaffa, which readily admitted him. He declared Jaffa forfeit to the crown and appointed a governor, but even this move could not bring Guy out of Ascalon. Arnold de Toroga, elected grand master of the Temple after the death of Odo de St. Amand, together with his friend the patriarch Heraclius, tried to intercede for Guy, which so angered Baldwin that he banished both of them from his court. They reached a kind of truce when the king asked them to return to Europe to mount a new Crusade to help him against Saladin.

Toward the end of 1184, in response to Baldwin's urgings, the grand masters of the Templars and the Hospitallers returned to Europe with the patriarch Heraclius. The emperor Frederick, Louis of France, and Henry of England all received the delegation royally and expressed sympathy for their plea for a new Crusade. In practice, however, not much materialized from their efforts except for some scattered recruiting for the two military orders.

Templar Grand Master Arnold de Toroga had died along the way at Verona, so the English master had to stand in for him as he joined the patriarch and the Hospitaller grand master in their appeals to Henry II at the Grand Priory of the Hospitallers in London. The king listened to them graciously, but it became clear that he had no taste for a war a thousand miles from home. His twenty-eight-year-old second son Richard was of a different stripe: Richard, who had a taste for war any time, anywhere, absorbed every word. These armed monks were his kind of people. He had grown up with them all about him and had heard their stories of combat in Outremer. They couldn't have him now, but in just three years he would be king of England, and then he would waste no time setting about the adventures in the Holy Land that would earn him a prominent place in crusading history. For now he had to hold his peace.

The mission in England became one of recruiting for the military orders. As part of his penance for the murder of Thomas à Becket, archbishop of Canterbury, Henry II had been required to give to the Templars and to the Hospitallers the funds needed to keep two hundred knights in the field for a year. Now they needed to recruit those knights.

The Templars had been building a new church in London with stone brought from Normandy for the purpose. Designed in their typical circular style, it was to be the principal Templar church in Britain, standing on their property between Fleet Street and the Thames. The patriarch Heraclius was happy to personally dedicate and consecrate this new church for his friends the Templars.

With the two grand masters and the patriarch away in Europe, Baldwin IV had proceeded to lock in the succession to the throne of Jerusalem during the few weeks of life left to him. He called a council of his nobles early in 1185 and announced his decisions, to be incorporated into his will, which all present were asked to swear to uphold. The throne was to go to his sickly seven-year-old-nephew, also named Baldwin. The boy's stepfather, Guy of Lusignan, was specifically excluded from the regency, which was to go to the king's cousin, Count Raymond of Tripoli. Raymond would have the city of Beirut as payment for his services. The personal guardianship of the child-king would be entrusted to the king's uncle, Joscelin of Courtenay. It was provided that if the boy should die before he reached the age of ten, the succession to the throne would be decided by four powers: the pope, the Holy Roman Emperor, the king of France, and the king of England. Until their decision was reached, Raymond of Tripoli would continue as regent of the realm.

The patriarch Heraclius and the Hospitaller grand master Roger de les Moulins, who had returned during the council, joined the barons in swearing to uphold the king's will. Meanwhile, the Templar grand chapter, in a heated session, elected Count Raymond's bitter enemy, Gerard de Ridfort, as grand master of the Templar order. He, too, took the oath to support the king's will and testament.

As expected, Baldwin IV died a few weeks later, at the age of twenty-four, and his mutilated body was laid to rest in the Church of the Holy Sepulcher. As regent, Raymond of Tripoli was now the ruler of the kingdom of Jerusalem. He suggested to the barons that since the mission to Europe to bring a crusading army to their assistance had failed, and since the deficiency of winter rains promised a severe food shortage ahead, they should seek a four-year truce with Saladin. The barons agreed, as did Saladin himself. The sultan was having problems with restive Muslim vassals who were beginning to flout his authority, and they could be dealt with best if there was no Christian war to dilute his forces.

The truce enabled land and sea trade to go forward without danger and encouraged the return of Christian pilgrims, who were a major source of revenue. The kingdom began to prosper, and all seemed to be moving smoothly toward a peaceful coexistence of Muslim and Christian. Then, in August 1186, the eight-year-old King Baldwin V died at Acre, and since he had not achieved ten years of age, his death triggered the provisions of Baldwin IV's will relating to the succession.

Giving some evidence that the arrangements had been well thought through in advance of the boy's death, his guardian, Joscelin of Courtenay, immediately suggested that Raymond call a meeting of the barons at his own city of Tiberias in Galilee. There, well away from the possible interference of the patriarch and the Templar grand master, he could proceed to carry out the instructions of the king's will. Joscelin, for his part, would take the boy's body to the Church of the Holy Sepulcher in Jerusalem for burial. The suggestions made good sense to Raymond, who set off for Tiberias.

As soon as Raymond was out of sight, Joscelin broke into a frenzy of activity. He got the Knights Templar to take the body to Jerusalem, then sent his own troops to secure Tyre and Beirut. Word was rushed to Princess Sibylla and her husband, Guy, to proceed in all haste to Jerusalem, ostensibly to attend the royal funeral. A messenger summoned Reynald of Chatillon from his castle at Kerak to join the others in the Holy City. Joscelin then sent out a proclamation declaring Sibylla to be queen. While the doves were being called to Tiberias, the hawks were gathering at Jerusalem, where the patriarch and Grand Master de Ridfort were waiting for them.

When the news of the proclamation reached Raymond of Tripoli, he angrily summoned a council of the High Court of the kingdom. As the barons debated their course of action, an invitation arrived for all of them to attend the coronation of Sibylla at Jerusalem, where they were expected to pledge their fealty to their new queen. Their response was to dispatch two Cistercian monks to Jerusalem to remind everyone there of the sacred oath sworn to Baldwin IV and to caution them to do nothing until the High Court reached a decision.

The Cistercians were ignored. Besides the royal household guard at Jerusalem commanded by Joscelin of Courtenay, Sibylla was backed by the military forces of Guy's brother Amalric, who was the constable of the kingdom, and the troops that Reynald of Chatillon had brought with him from Kerak. To round out her military support, there were all of the Knights Templar in the realm under the total control of Gerard de Ridfort, who would do anything to thwart the ambitions of his sworn enemy Raymond of Tripoli. For his part, the patriarch Heraclius gave Sibylla the full support of the Church. She would be difficult to uproot.

There was one man in Jerusalem who was strongly opposed to the support for Sibylla, and that man was Roger de les Moulins, grand master of the Hospitallers. His position was not just political; it was based on the fact that they had all sworn a sacred vow, which was now being broken. He, for one, would not forswear his oath, nor would he have anything to do with those who did.

Ignoring his objections, plans for the coronation of Sibylla went forward, but there was a problem. The coronation regalia was kept in a chest with three different locks. The three keys had been entrusted to the patriarch and the grand masters of the two orders. The Hospitaller master would not give up his key to break his oath or to help others to break theirs. Nor would he allow any Hospitaller knight to participate in or even to attend what he considered to be an illegal coronation. Badgered to a fit of anger by de Ridfort and the patriarch, he threw his key out of the window. It was easily found in the courtyard below, and the chest was opened.

The coronation now took a twist because of the unpopularity of the new queen's husband, Guy of Lusignan. The patriarch would crown only the queen. Then he placed another crown beside her and told her that she should place it herself on the head of the man who would reign beside her as king. Sibylla summoned Guy to the throne, where he knelt before her as she placed on his head the crown of Jerusalem. As the coronation party processed out of the church, Gerard de Ridfort could hold back no longer. He shouted out loud that this crown repaid Raymond of Tripoli for the broken promise of marriage to Lucia of Botrun.

Raymond of Tripoli proposed that the opposition barons crown the princess Isabella as their queen of Jerusalem and her husband, Humphrey of Toron, as their king, then march on Jerusalem. The plan was ruined by the timid Humphrey, who was terrified at the prospect of becoming the focal point of a civil war. He secretly hurried off to Jerusalem and swore fealty to Sibylla and Guy. That left his supporters with no cause to fight for. Raymond of Tripoli stayed in his wife's lands in Galilee, declaring that he would never follow the cowardly Guy of Lusignan, while privately nursing his true feeling that only he himself was fit to be the king of Jerusalem.

With the succession settled, albeit bitterly, Palestine settled down to enjoy its progress under the four-year truce with Saladin, but not for long. Predictably, Reynald of Chatillon found it increasingly difficult to resist the temptation of the great Muslim caravans passing across his lands. Truce or no truce, the sight of so much plunder was maddening. His restraint finally gave way one day toward the end of 1186, when he was informed that an extraordinarily large caravan was on the move. It was traveling up from Cairo on the road to Damascus, lightly guarded by just a handful of soldiers, because the only raiders the Egyptian merchants expected were occasional bands of marauding Bedouins. Gathering his forces, Reynald fell on the caravan with a surprise attack that was over in minutes. All of the Egyptian soldiers who were not killed in the brief skirmish were executed as soon as it was over, and all of the merchants, their families, and their servants were rounded up to be sold as slaves. Together with all of their goods and animals, they were taken back to Reynald's massive castle of Kerak. Reynald was ecstatic. It was plunder far beyond the value of any he had ever taken before.

Saladin was furious, not only because the truce had been broken but also because it had been broken by the man who had consistently broken truces before, the man he despised most in all Christendom. Although outraged, he chose to adhere to the treaty that he had signed. Instead of an army, he sent envoys to Kerak to demand of Reynald that he free his Muslim prisoners and return their possessions. Reynald would not even talk to men on such a ridiculous errand. The envoys proceeded to Jerusalem to lay their case before King Guy, who agreed with their position and demanded that Reynald comply with Saladin's request. Reynald ignored him, confident that Guy was in his debt and, in any event, could not enforce the order.

The only answer now was war, but it was not to be a war that had the sympathy of all of the Christian rulers. Prince Bohemond of Antioch and Saladin agreed that the truce between them was still in full force. Raymond of Tripoli reasserted the truce with Saladin for his own county of Tripoli and for his wife's territory of Galilee, even though they both were held in fealty to the king, and so owed him support in war. In the negotiations he also revealed his true ambitions, as he solicited and received Saladin's support for Raymond's intention to have himself declared king of Jerusalem after the impending conflict.

Grand Master de Ridfort, who still had capacity for revenge, could not let any infraction by Count Raymond go unpunished. He convinced King Guy to assemble his forces and march to bring Galilee and its capital city Tiberias back into submission to the crown before the war could begin. While in camp on their way to attack Tiberias, they were joined by Balian of Ibelin, who tried to turn them from a course that could only mean civil war, making all of them easy prey for the Muslims. He urged a parley with Raymond to meet the more constructive goal of a united Christian front against the enemy, and finally Guy had to agree with the wisdom of his arguments. The king decided to send a group to negotiate with Raymond, which would include Balian of Ibelin, the archbishop of Tyre, and the grand master of the Hospitallers. An essential member of the mission, they all agreed, would have to be Gerard de Ridfort, because the strong enmity between the Templar grand master and Count Raymond was well known. Unity would require that the two of them put aside their anger toward each other, at least for the duration of the war that was now inevitable. Ten Hospitallers would accompany them as escort.

They set out for their meeting with Raymond on April 29, 1187. The following day Balian dropped out to attend to some urgent business of his own, promising to catch up with the group later.

It was an innocent event, but it deprived the others of Balian's sober counsel, which they could have used to offset de Ridfort's disastrous actions in the hours ahead.

On April 30, while the delegation was riding toward Tiberias, Raymond was visited by an envoy from Saladin's son al-Afdal. His father had ordered him to reconnoiter through Galilee for one day, and in keeping with Saladin's agreement with Raymond, al-Afdal was asking the count for permission to cross his territory. As uncomfortable as the request may have been for him, Raymond had little choice under their agreement and gave permission. Within hours, an army of Muslim cavalry came on a path that would intersect the road being followed by the delegation from Jerusalem. Having just that day learned of their approach, Raymond immediately sent a galloper to inform the Christians of the Muslim reconnaissance, so there would be no trouble between the two groups.

Raymond's message arrived on that same afternoon, and the Hospitaller grand master was in favor of Raymond's suggestion that they not move for that day to avoid any confrontation. De Ridfort of the the Temple held just the opposite view. Here was a God-sent opportunity to attack the enemy. He called in James de Mailly, grand marshal of the Temple, who was in a castle a few miles away with ninety Templar knights. Thus reinforced, the little group moved up to Nazareth, where they were able to encourage about forty local knights and a group of foot soldiers to join them. The archbishop of Tyre, who was not a fighting man, prudently chose to stay in Nazareth as the group marched out. As they moved through the town, de Ridfort shouted to the people that there was about to be a great Christian victory. They were invited to come out to the battlefield to gather the plunder from the fallen infidel.

As the pitifully small troop of fewer than two hundred Christian knights reached the crest of a hill beyond Nazareth, they found themselves looking down on seven thousand Muslim cavalry in the valley beneath them, watering their horses at the Springs of Cresson. James de Mailly, as marshal, was the principal military leader of the Templars, but still subject to the supreme authority of the grand master. His military judgment, as well as plain common sense, said that they should get out of the area as quickly as possible. The grand master of the Hospitallers agreed completely. Gerard de Ridfort exploded. He accused them both of cowardice and chastised his marshal for being afraid to die for the Cross. They finally broke down under Gerard's insults and the order was given to attack, but what resulted was not so much a battle as it was a slaughter. The marshal of the Temple died in a matter of minutes, as did the grand master of the Hospitallers. Of the Templars only Gerard de Ridfort and two others, all three wounded, managed to stay on their horses and get out of the valley. Citizens of Nazareth, who had believed the overconfident Templar master and gone out to pick up loot from the field, were rounded up by the Muslims and marched off to a lifetime of slavery.

Watching from his castle wall, Raymond saw the Muslims riding back as promised from their one-day reconnaissance. There was something strange about the lances of the men in the vanguard. As they came closer he could see that on their lance points were heads with beards that hung down below their severed necks, heads of Knights of the Temple.

Raymond was in shock over the results of his private treaty with Saladin, and was ready to assuage his guilt when Balian and the archbishop arrived to complete their mission. He canceled his agreement with Saladin and traveled to Jerusalem to swear fealty to Guy. The king welcomed him with all honor, and the objective of Christian unity appeared to be achieved. It was just in time. Saladin was calling troops from all parts of his empire, until east of the Jordan he had about thirty thousand men, the largest single army he had ever assembled.

To the west side, King Guy ordered all fighting men in his kingdom to gather at Acre. The Templars and Hospitallers left only skeleton forces at their castles, sending every possible man to the army. To help finance the war, the Templars contributed some of the money that had been sent to them as part of the penance of King Henry II of England for the murder of the archbishop of Canterbury. Even Prince Bohemond of Antioch relented from his side agreement with Saladin and agreed to contribute troops to the coming campaign. The patriarch Heraclius was asked to bring the relic of the True Cross to lead the Christian army, but he wisely declined on the grounds of poor health, sending instead the bishop of Acre to carry the sacred relic into battle.

On July 1 Saladin crossed the Jordan at the southern end of the Sea of Galilee. He sent half his forces into the hills nearby, while the other half moved north to attack Raymond's city of Tiberias. Count Raymond was off with the king's army, so his wife, the countess Eschiva, took charge. The town fell quickly and the countess withdrew with her troops into the castle, prepared for a long siege.

At the council at Acre Count Raymond gave sound advice. In the fierce summer heat the advantage would lie with a defensive position based on an ample supply of grazing and water. No commander could maintain an army in that bleak, water-poor countryside, and sooner or later Saladin would have to retreat. That would be the time to attack, when the Muslim men and horses would be exhausted, sapped of energy by the unrelenting heat and their craving for water. Muslim discipline under those conditions would be weak, and the fresh Christian army turning from comfortable defense to swift attack would gain the victory. In addition, a defensive posture would give time for the promised reinforcements from Antioch to arrive. It all made good sense, except to Grand Master de Ridfort. Perhaps he was simply incapable of approving any advice from Raymond of Tripoli. Whatever the reason, he accused his rival of cowardice and of having sold out to Saladin. He berated them all for entertaining any plan other than immediate aggressive action against the enemy. Once again, insults prevailed over wisdom, as the king gave way to de Ridfort and ordered his army to march to meet the Saracens at Tiberias.

The Christian army headed southeast and on July 2 made camp at Sephoria, less than twenty miles west of Tiberias. There was an abundance of water and plenty of vital pasture for the horses. The location offered an ideal base from which to operate against Saladin. Militarily, it was a place to dig in and wait. Unfortunately, a messenger arrived from the besieged Countess Eschiva, holding out with her small garrison in the castle of Tiberias. Her sons stood up and begged the others to save their mother, then Count Raymond rose to address the council once more. It was his wife they proposed to rescue and his city, but all that he told them before was still true. The army should not march over the barren ground in the oppressive heat. It would sap the strength of men and horses, and there was no water along the way. If the heat didn't kill them, thirst would. As a Christian he vowed that he would rather lose his city and all of his friends and loved ones in it than lose the Holy Kingdom of Jerusalem. His words sobered the council. The army would stay entrenched at Sephoria.

After all had retired for the night, Gerard de Ridfort went back to the king's tent. He used every argument he could muster to persuade the king to move. Raymond of Tripoli was a traitor and the secret ally of Saladin. He had tried to stop the king's coronation. He had been responsible for the massacre at the Springs of Cresson. How could they live with themselves knowing that they had deliberately sacrificed the principal city of Galilee and the gallant woman defending it? The Templars could not stand the shame. They would rather lose their order than turn their backs on this chance to avenge their fallen brothers. De Ridfort and his Templars had supported Guy during his entire time in the Holy Land. He was a proven and trusted friend. At last King Guy gave in to the forceful arguments of the grand master and sent out his orders that the army would march at dawn.

It would have been better if they had marched at night. July 3 was a day of fierce sun, with not a trace of breeze. The road they had chosen wound up and down through bleak hills, with no trees for shade. Saladin had moved his army, setting up camp to block the road just before it reached the Sea of Galilee above Tiberias, around the village of Hattin, a location that provided all the water his men could possibly need. Now he put heat and thirst to work for him as he sought to slow down the Christian host. All day long bands of mounted Muslim archers hit the Christian column like swarms of hornets, especially the Templar contingent that served as the rear guard. They rode in, shot their arrows into men and horses at short range, then galloped off unharmed, frustrating the Templars, who had been ordered not to break ranks to follow them. And always there was the scorching, unbearable heat, causing men soaked in sweat and trapped inside their ovenlike armor to begin to dehydrate.

That afternoon they reached the barren shelf above the village of Hattin. Ahead of them was a rock structure that rose into two summits, known locally as the Horns of Hattin. Beyond it, the road dropped to the Sea of Galilee, but Saladin's army was across the road. Gerard sent word to King Guy that his harassed Templars could go no further that day and that the Christians should make camp where they were. Most of the barons, including Raymond of Tripoli, wanted to press on immediately and fight their way through to the life-giving waters of the great lake. The army just could not go on for more hours without water. Once again the Templar grand master won out, and the king ordered the army to make camp. Some of the men struggled to the slope of the Horns of Hattin, where they had been told they would find a well. They found it, but it was dry. No form of discipline could keep reins on men crazed with thirst, and several groups broke away to search for water. They were easily killed off by the Muslim outposts.

Knowing that the Christians were already overcome with heat and thirst, Saladin decided to add to that discomfort by depriving them of sleep. The nobles had tents, but the whole army chose to sleep in the open to enjoy the cooling breeze. The Muslims set fire to the dry brush that covered the hills. Soon the breeze carried the hot acrid smoke into the Christian camp, making it difficult to breathe. Using the cover of the smoke and the darkness, Saladin positioned his troops throughout the night, so that when dawn broke, the army of Jerusalem found itself completely surrounded.

A whole night after a whole day without water was driving men mad with thirst, made worse by the dawn reflecting off the waters of the fabled lake below them. Some suddenly started to run for the water, and as the momentum built, thousands of foot soldiers rushed down the hill, not to fight, but to drink. Those who were not chopped down by the Muslim cavalry as they ran were herded together and taken prisoner. Raymond of Tripoli led a charge against the Muslims, but they simply opened their ranks and let his party gallop through, then closed ranks behind him. Once outside, there was no way Raymond's party could rejoin their comrades, so eventually they rode off the battlefield and back to Tripoli. Some of those left behind were convinced that they had witnessed an act of treachery.

The remaining knights fought to their limits, making charge after charge and repelling the cavalry sweeps of the Muslims, but they were steadily driven back up the hill.

Saladin's son al-Afdal remembered: "When I saw them retreating with the Muslims in pursuit, I cried out in joy, 'We have beaten them!' The sultan pointed to the bright red royal tent of King Guy at the top of the hill and said, 'Be silent. We shall not defeat them until that tent falls.' As he spoke, the tent fell.''

The Christians were beaten as much by sheer exhaustion as by numbers. When the victorious Muslims broke through to the center of the Crusader defense they found knights and barons, including the king himself, prostrate on the ground with no strength left to lift their arms, much less their weapons. The leading nobles were all made prisoner and taken to a regal pavilion set up for Saladin on the battlefield. There the sultan greeted them with courtesy, inviting King Guy to sit by his side. Knowing that his royal guest was suffering from severe thirst, Saladin handed him a cup of cool water. Guy gratefully took a long drink, then handed the cup to Reynald of Chatillon. Saladin immediately asked Guy to remember that it was he, not the sultan, who had passed the cup to Reynald. That should have told them what the sultan had on his mind. Saladin was telling them that what would happen next did not violate the Muslim laws of hospitality that protected a man who was given food or drink by his host.

Saladin then turned to Reynald of Chatillon, whose crimes he began to recite angrily, cataloging Reynald's lies, his betrayals of trust, his breaking of one truce after another. Made even angrier by Reynald's arrogant reply, Saladin grabbed up a sword and struck off his head. He quickly assured the shocked Christian nobles that they were not condemned to share Reynald's fate. They would be ransomed or exchanged.

Such mercy did not extend to the Knights of the Temple and the Hospitallers who had been taken in the battle. They were to be the star performers in a bizarre and brutal drama. Saladin was being visited by a group of Muslim Sufis from Egypt. Although fanatic Muslims, the ascetic Sufis were students of the Koran, not warriors. Saladin announced that they would have the honor of cutting off the heads of hundreds of captured knights of the military orders. Afraid to deny the great sultan, they took the proffered swords in hand as Grand Master de Ridfort was forced to watch. When a lucky stroke cleanly severed a neck, a cheer went up from the watching Muslim soldiers, while taunts and shouted suggestions went to those who hacked away at their victims six, seven, or eight times to get the head separated from the body. It was a grotesque carnival of blood, and one can only speculate on de Ridfort's thoughts as he watched the horror for which he was principally responsible, knowing as well that he was the only captured warrior monk who was to be spared this death by amateur executioners.

Saladin took time for one other piece of business. The bishop of Acre had been killed in the fight, and the Muslims had taken the holy relic of the True Cross. Saladin expressed his intention to have it taken to Damascus to be placed under the doorstep of the principal mosque of the city, so that each time one of the faithful entered the mosque he would trample on the Christian relic. It was the ultimate humiliation. It was not, however, the ultimate victory. The Christians still held the holy city of Jerusalem.

9

The Fall of Jerusalem
1187

$\mathcal{A}$ S HE LOOKED out over the bodies of fallen Christians on the slopes of the Horns of Hattin, while his men carried the headless bodies of military monks away from his camp, Saladin could not envision any obstacles to his total conquest of the Holy Land. Most of the leading Christian nobles were his prisoners, including the king. Even if they had been free, they could do little to stop him, since he had just destroyed their army. The fanatical military orders were shattered as well, with the Hospitaller master dead on the field and the grand master of the Knights Templar in captivity. The rest should come easily. It certainly appeared so, as the countess of Tripoli surrendered Tiberias to him the very next day, July 5, 1187.

Three days later, as the next step in his plan of conquest, Saladin took his army toward the city of Acre and camped before its walls. Its commander, Joscelin of Courtenay, had no way to fight off the Muslims and could see his own death as a likely result of resistance. He sent an emissary to Saladin on July 8 to offer the surrender of the city in exchange for the lives of the inhabitants. Saladin agreed, and kept his word. On July 10, with his banners flying and kettle-drums booming out his victory, he marched his army through the gates of Acre. The loot was so extensive that it easily recovered Saladin's expenses for the entire campaign.

With the port city as his base, Saladin sent his emirs to accept the submission of castles and towns between the coast and the Sea of Galilee. Nablus and Toron were his within a few days. When his brother al-Adil arrived from Cairo with reinforcements, Saladin sent him to take the port city of Jaffa. The undermanned garrison and the civilians would not surrender, so al-Adil ordered his men to storm the walls. The town fell easily, and although he had been prepared to spare its inhabitants in exchange for voluntary surrender, they had chosen to resist, so must be punished. Every man, woman, and child who could walk was turned over to the slave dealers. Those who could not walk to the markets because of age or handicap did not live out the day.

Saladin moved his army north on the coast road to Tyre. The city did not offer immediate surrender, so he tried an assault with scaling ladders. The attack failed to get the Muslims over the high walls. He could take the city easily with siege engines, but siege warfare took time. Other, easier, Christian targets were available more readily. Saladin decided to move on and come back to deal with Tyre later.

The Knights Templar, who had thought of themselves as the major force for the protection of Jerusalem, could do little now. Knights had been called in from all the Templar castles to go with King Guy to the Sea of Galilee, along with sergeant brothers, men-at-arms, Turcopoles, and bowmen, but they had lost ninety of the knights at the Springs of Cresson and over two hundred at the Horns of Hattin. Those battles had taken away almost half the Templar knights in the Holy Land. There was now not a single Templar castle with a full garrison.

Brother Terricus, the Templar preceptor of Jerusalem, had assumed command of the order, with no more important task than imploring the Templar preceptors in Europe to move quickly to provide the men and money necessary to keep the order alive. His letter to them was full of despair:

"From Brother Terricus and the brotherhood—that brotherhood, alas!, all but annihilated—to all preceptors and brethren of the Temple to whom these presents shall come, greeting.

"Neither by our words nor by our tears can we hope to make you understand the many and great calamities with which, because of our sins, the anger of God has permitted us to be visited. The infidels assembled an immense multitude of their people and fiercely invaded the Christian territories. Uniting the forces of our country, we accordingly attacked them, directing our march toward Tiberias, which had been taken by storm. After repulsing us among some dangerous rocks, they attacked us with such fierceness that they captured the holy cross and our king. A multitude was slain and two hundred and thirty of our brethren, as we believe, taken and beheaded.... After this, the pagans, drunk with the blood of the Christians, went tempestuously with their hosts to the city of Acre and, taking it by storm, spread themselves throughout all the land, only Jerusalem, Tyre, Ascalon, and Beirut now being left to us and Christendom. These cities too, since almost all the citizens have been slain, we shall be unable to hold unless we speedily receive divine assistance and are given your aid. At the present time [the Muslims] are besieging Tyre and cease not to assault it either by day or night. So vast are their numbers that, like swarms of ants, they have covered the whole face of the land from Tyre to Jerusalem and Gaza. We beg you, therefore, at once to grant succour to us and to Christianity, which is all but ruined in the East, so that by the aid of God and with the support of your arms, we may save the rest of these cities.''

Saladin was indeed having things his own way. The city of Sidon gave up without a fight on July 20. A week later Beirut surrendered to him. Then Saladin's forces turned south, taking King Guy and the Templar grand master with them, appropriately draped in chains. A few days later Saladin arrived at Ascalon. Guy had been offered his freedom if he could effect the surrender of Ascalon without a battle, and he accepted. Saladin had the Christian king escorted to the wall by the main gate, where he pleaded with the besieged citizens to surrender their city. Grand Master de Ridfort added his pleas to the king's, but they were both greeted with shouted insults for their cowardice. Ascalon chose to fight, but since the resident knights and soldiers had largely been stripped away for the recent expedition, it was not much of a battle. The defense was so feeble that upon the city's surrender Saladin allowed the citizens to leave. King Guy had failed, and remained a prisoner.

The deal Saladin had made with de Ridfort was much easier to deliver, because of Templar discipline. The grand master was to have his freedom in exchange for the bloodless surrender of the Templar castle at Gaza. The Templar Rule forbade ransom for money, but it did not specifically prohibit the grand master from paying his own ransom in the form of land, fortifications, and fellow Christians. What it did state clearly was the vow of unquestioning obedience of every Knight Templar to the grand master. When de Ridfort appeared before Gaza and ordered his Templars to surrender the castle, they had no choice. They laid down their arms and marched out. True to his word, Saladin freed de Ridfort on the spot, although one must wonder, under the circumstances, just how glad the Templars were to have their grand master back, as he led them northward to the city of Tyre.

The citizens of Tyre had certainly been willing to surrender, and had been waiting for Saladin to come to take their city, but something important had happened. Conrad of Montferrat had been in Constantinople, and after being suspected of taking part in a murder, had decided to leave for a while. Taking a group of retainers with him, Conrad had set sail for the Holy Land, not yet having heard of the disaster at the Horns of Hattin. As his ship approached Acre, its captain expressed surprise at the absence of the bells. He explained to Conrad that there were great bells in the tower at the harbor that were rung to signal the approach of every ship. This was the first time he had ever known the bells to be silent.

Conrad wisely advised that they drop anchor until the mystery could be explained. A Muslim port official came to them in a small sailing vessel to invite them into the city. Conrad, pretending to be a seagoing merchant, asked—as any trader would ask—for the latest news. The Muslim official proudly informed them that Allah had delivered Acre to the great Saladin just four days before. The official cleared them to land and headed back to the port. As soon as he was far enough away from their ship, Conrad ordered the captain to set sail for Tyre.

Once inside the walls of Tyre, Conrad heard nothing but bad news. Men who had escaped from Hattin were straggling into the city with tales of catastrophe and woe. The True Cross was gone. The army was gone. The king was a prisoner. Even Conrad's own father, the marquis of Montferrat, had been taken prisoner. The whole city was in a state of depression and defeat.

Conrad shared none of it. He berated the citizens for not seeing to their defenses and manning the walls. Impressed by his energy and optimism, the people of Tyre asked Conrad to lead them. They agreed that if he would become their military commander, they would recognize him as the ruler of the city. That was something Conrad could understand, so exuding confidence, he put his natural talents for organization to work. Only his presence and his leadership were responsible for the city's defiance of Saladin's initial approach. Some of the more devout citizens decided that God had sent their new leader to them.

It had been a mistake on Saladin's part to pass the city by after just one assault, because Tyre had been at its weakest point at that time. As Saladin had moved on to other conquests, the refugees from every Christian town and castle he took fled to Tyre. Even the Christian ships from Sidon and Beirut sought the safety of Tyre, so Conrad soon had an army, a navy, and a source of supplies.

That buildup of Tyre was not uppermost in Saladin's mind. His top priority was the emotional center of his invasion, the capture and cleansing of Jerusalem, sacred to his faith and that of every man in his army. It was with great excitement that the sultan's men obeyed his orders to march to the Holy City. They camped before its walls on September 20.

Jerusalem was now under the command of Balian of Ibelin, who had gone there from Tyre to fetch his wife and children. He had been pressed into command by the Christian citizens, all of whose leaders had fallen at the Horns of Hattin and who, largely as a result of the reported conduct of their grand master at Ascalon and Gaza, would not accept the leadership of the Knights Templar among them. The city was jammed with refugees from the surrounding area. They were of no value in a fight but constituted a tremendous drain on existing food supplies. Balian sent out foraging parties to bring in all the food they could find. With only two knights left in the entire city, he knighted sixty sons of knights and burgesses for no reason other than that they had reached the age of sixteen. Conferring the honor, however, did not confer the military experience.

A few days after the Muslim army arrived, they began mining operations, tunneling under the wall at approximately the point at which Godfrey de Bouillon had gone over it eighty-eight years before. By September 29 Saladin's sappers had effected a breach in the wall. The Christians tried to fill and defend as best they could, although by now both sides knew that it was just a matter of time. The Greek Orthodox Christians in the city got word out to Saladin that they would open the gates to him, in exchange for his mercy. They had come to bitterly resent the arrogant Roman clergy who had forced them to attend church services alien to their traditions, conducted in a language they did not understand. They would welcome a return to the religious tolerance they had enjoyed under Muslim rule.

As it turned out, their help was not necessary. The day after the wall was breached, Balian went out to negotiate with Saladin for the surrender of Jerusalem. Baliam conceded that Saladin could now take the city whenever he wished, but at the price of the execution of all of the Muslims in the city and the complete destruction of the sacred Islamic buildings in the Temple area, the al-Aqsa Mosque and the mosque of Omar called the Dome of the Rock. Saladin reminded him of the brutality of the Crusaders when they had taken the city from the Egyptians, but they finally came to terms. A ransom was set of ten dinars for a man, five for a woman, and one for a child. Balian pointed out that there were over twenty thousand refugees in the city who had no money, and it was finally agreed that for a lump sum payment of thirty thousand dinars, seven thousand Christians would be free to go. The deal was struck, but Saladin delayed his entry into the city for two days, for a reason that would find favor with all the Muslims in the world.

In the Muslim calendar October 2 was the twenty-seventh day of the month of Rajab, the anniversary of that glorious night when the beautiful winged animal called Buraq had flown through the night sky, carrying the Prophet Muhammad from the Kaaba in Mecca to the *Haram es-Sharif*, the Temple Mount in Jerusalem. It was that journey, which had found Muhammad entertained by all of the prophets of old and had permitted him to ascend the celestial ladder to the very throne of Allah, that made Jerusalem the third holiest location in the Muslim faith.

As the army of the faithful marched into the Holy City on that sacred anniversary, no man among them could doubt that this great victory was the will of Allah, effected by his most zealous servant, Saladin.

Perhaps it was the religious timing of the occupation that held the Muslims in check, in dramatic contrast to the Christians when they had taken the city during the First Crusade. Now not a building was broken into, not a single citizen slaughtered. Balian emptied the treasury of the kingdom to raise the thirty thousand dinars of bulk ransom for seven thousand of the inhabitants, but there were still thousands who would be sold to the slave dealers if their ransoms could not be raised. Appeals to the wealth of the Church, the Templars, and Hospitallers were not welcome, although the military monks did not hesitate to violate their rules against ransom payments to purchase their own freedom. The patriarch Heraclius paid the ten-dinar ransoms for himself and a few servants, then left the city with a small caravan carrying a fortune in rare carpets and silver plate, riding without emotion past columns of the poor being marched into slavery. Saladin's brother, by contrast, was so moved by the pitiful sight that he asked for the right to free a thousand Christian captives as compensation for his services in the campaign, a request that was promptly granted. Saladin himself decided to free all of the aged, both men and women. For the women who had been ransomed or freed, he promised to release any husband or father who was being held captive.

As an indication that Saladin's anger against the Crusaders was perhaps more political and personal than religious, he invited the Jews and Orthodox Christians of Jerusalem to stay in the city. When news of the treatment of the Greek clergy reached the Byzantine emperor Isaac Angelus, he dispatched envoys to the sultan to congratulate him on his victory and to request that the places sacred to the Christians be returned to the care of the Orthodox Church. Saladin agreed.

The Temple area was completely cleansed of all evidence of Christian occupation. The Templar headquarters was scrubbed, scented with rose water brought from Damascus, and reconsecrated as the al-Aqsa Mosque, to which Saladin went with his officers on the Muslim Sabbath, Friday, October 9, to give thanks to God. The Christians still held the north, but Palestine belonged completely to the followers of Muhammad.

The Templar preceptor Terricus wrote an eyewitness account to King Henry II of England: "Jerusalem, alas, has fallen. Saladin ordered the cross to be cast down from the Temple of the Lord [the mosque of the Dome of the Rock], and for two days to be carried about the city and beaten with sticks. After this he ordered the Temple of the Lord to be washed with rosewater, inside and out and from top to bottom."

The Knights Templar left the city that had been their headquarters since their founding. They acted as escorts and guards for one of the three columns of refugees. A second was protected by the Hospitallers, and the third by Balian of Ibelin with his group of newly made young knights. The protection was necessary, because the refugees had been given the right to carry their possessions with them, and refugees have always been fair game for banditry. In this case, it was not just the Arabs who robbed them but their fellow Christians as well, eager to profit from the helpless condition of thousands of dejected families hoping to find refuge somewhere.

They were only partly successful in finding refuge at Tyre. Conrad would admit only fighting men. He had no intention of wasting his valuable food supplies on useless civilians, so soon a great refugee camp grew outside the city. The Templar knights and men-at-arms from Jerusalem were welcomed and joined their brother Templars already in the city with their grand master.

In November, with Jerusalem secure, Saladin turned his energies to the unfinished business of the conquest of Tyre. His spies had reported the steady arrival of reinforcements, including the Knights Templar from Gaza and Jerusalem. Ships had arrived with more supplies, so any siege would be a long one. Saladin was certain that appeals would have been sent back to Europe, and he wanted to take this important city before fresh Crusader help could arrive.

He was right about the pleas for help. Conrad had sent back Josias, archbishop of Tyre, to make direct appeals to Pope Urban III and the Christian kings. The Templars and Hospitallers wrote frequently to their preceptors in Europe, repeatedly asking for funds and more recruits.

Tyre was in an unusually strong position, surrounded by the sea, with just a narrow neck of land connecting it to the shore. Even that had a massive wall protecting it, so Saladin ordered a complete siege train for his assault on the city. The Christian refugees who had been barred from the city fled to the protection of the hills as Saladin arrived with stone-throwing mangonels to batter down the defenses. The distance from the mainland out to the city walls was too great for his catapults to be effective, nor could he use his miners, because they would have to tunnel under the sea. In an attempt to cut off Tyre's supply ships he ordered ten Egyptian fighting ships up from Acre, but the Christian ships captured five of them and destroyed the others.

Frustrated by the military problems at hand, Saladin welcomed the intelligence that Conrad of Montferrat was the new ruler and military commander of Tyre. That knowledge opened up the possibility that the city could be taken with no further struggle. The sultan ordered that the aging marquis of Montferrat, who had been captured at the Horns of Hattin, be taken from his prison and brought to Tyre. Conrad, who had wondered at the lull in the fighting, got his answer when his father was paraded up and down in front of the wall. Saladin got word to Conrad that he had a choice: Surrender the city or watch his father die from slow torture. Conrad replied that his duty to God was more important to him than his duty to his family. That was an answer that Saladin could understand and respect. Complimenting the marquis on the conduct of his son, Saladin spared the old man's life and ordered him taken back to his prison in Damascus.

Facing up to the fact that the siege of the city of Tyre could go on for a year or more, and angry with himself for not taking the city when it was much weaker, Saladin again made the decision to retire. His army had been in the field for many months, and his men were tired. Saladin let half of his men return to their homes, planning to finish the conquest of the remaining Christians in the spring. As the year of 1187 ended, Saladin could look back on a great string of victories, highlighted by the retaking of the Holy City of Jerusalem after almost a century of Christian occupation. His conquest thus far, while not complete, was very satisfying to his people. But inside the walls of Tyre, Conrad of Montferrat was a great hero.

10

Frederick Barbarossa
1187 to 1190

EACH PIECE OF NEWS that arrived in Europe from the Holy Land inspired new waves of despair that passed through all levels of society. The Christian army was destroyed at the Horns of Hattin. Galilee had fallen. Muslims held the city of Christ's birth. Jerusalem had been taken, and the church that held the Holy Sepulcher was desecrated. The True Cross, the most sacred relic ever held in Christian hands, was being defiled by the Antichrist. The king of the Christian kingdom of Jerusalem was in a Muslim dungeon.

Many great nobles were missing. Those known to be dead were mourned for a time, but heirs were there to take their places. The source of greatest concern was those who might have been taken captive. The ransoms asked for their release could mean that all of the people on their lands might be taxed to the point of starvation. The news that had come was bad, but for those on the vast estates of the missing nobles, the news that had not yet arrived might be worse.

The fears of ransoms did not bother the Templars, whose Rule forbade them, but they did have the additional strain of having to scrape together all possible funds, and to put forth extra efforts in recruiting, just to assure the continued existence of their order. As for the highest secular and church authorities, they did not know what might be expected of them, nor could they make plans, because all they had was unconfirmed rumors, not official reports.

The rumors were turned into fact by the arrival of Archbishop Josias of Tyre at the Sicilian court in the summer of 1187. Now that King William II had authoritative reports on the full extent of the disaster, he was thunderstruck. Along with the catastrophe to the Holy Land he could see a more personal catastrophe coming for his own kingdom. If the Muslims were to gain control of all the port cities at the eastern end of the Mediterranean, they would cause nothing but trouble for an island kingdom in that sea. William put on the sackcloth garment of a penitent and went into a secluded retreat for four days of prayer. On the fifth day he began sending letters to all the courts of Europe to urge their participation in a Crusade of rescue, to which he would contribute troops and a fleet of ships. He recalled Sicilian fighting ships engaged in an expedition against the Greek islands, ordering that they be refitted and supplied, then sail to help save what was left of the Holy Land.

Archbishop Josias proceeded to Rome to inform the pope, to find that the bad news had just been delivered by messengers from Genoa. The frail, elderly Pope Urban III, already a sick man, was in no condition to withstand such a shock. Traumatized into the blackest depression, he died on October 20. His successor, who took the papal name of Gregory VIII, sent a call to Crusade to every Christian monarch, reminding them that the loss of Jerusalem and of the True Cross was the direct result of their having ignored the papal entreaties of the past, preferring their petty wars at home to a war for God and the Savior. Now they could make up for those past sins by taking up the Cross to go on Crusade. The total remission of sins and the eternal bliss of God's heaven would be the reward for every Crusader. The pope declared a day of total fasting on every Friday for the next five years, with no meat to be eaten on Wednesdays or Saturdays. To emphasize the dedication of the leaders of the Church, he added that he and all of the cardinals, and all of their relatives, would also fast every Monday.

Gregory VIII never knew the results of his efforts, because he died after only two months on the Throne of Peter. Perhaps because of the panic at the loss of Jerusalem, it took less than forty-eight hours to elect a successor, who chose the papal name of Clement III. Taking a more personal and direct approach than his predecessor, Clement III sent Archbishop Josias of Tyre to preach the Crusade to Henry II of England and to Philip Augustus of France, while the pope himself undertook a direct appeal to Frederick I, the Holy Roman Emperor, known familiarly as Frederick Barbarossa.

Josias of Tyre found the English and French kings at one of those rare times when they were together, this time discussing truce terms at Gisors. The fall of Jerusalem had already been recounted to them in detail in letters from the patriarch of Antioch, and Henry's son Richard, count of Poitou, had already taken the Crusader vow. Both kings agreed to join in the Crusade personally, with plans that even included such details as their agreement that the English would wear white crosses, the French crosses would be red, with green for the Flemish.

Henry II of England imposed a "Saladin Tithe" of 10 percent on all of his subjects. The Knights Templar, experienced tax gatherers, were asked to aid in the collection of the crusading tithe, but they were angered and embarrassed when their Templar brother Gilbert of Hoxton was caught generously helping himself to the collected funds. Henry apparently didn't hold that individual crime against the whole Templar order, because he ignored a complaint against the Knights Templar brought to him by the archbishop of Canterbury.

The archbishop had received a letter from an angry Conrad of Montferrat at Tyre. It seems that the Templars still had some of the money given to them by Henry of England as part of his penance for the murder of the archbishop's predecessor, Thomas à Becket. Conrad had demanded that those funds be turned over to him to be used for the defense of Tyre, but Grand Master de Ridfort had refused to part with a penny, and would not budge. Conrad wanted the archbishop of Canterbury and King Henry to order the Templars to give him that money. Henry declined to interfere, perhaps because de Ridfort's reaction was exactly what his own would have been.

Plans for a Crusade from England seemed to be moving ahead, but Prince Richard's personality slowed things down. He hated defiance of his position, and Crusade or no Crusade, he felt compelled to punish some of the fractious subjects in his county of Poitou who were challenging his authority. Then, with his own subjects beaten into a contrite state, he decided to go on a punitive expedition against the count of Toulouse. That angered Philip Augustus, who attacked King Henry's territory at Berry. That action provoked Henry, who attacked the French territory of King Philip Augustus. Richard, whose qualities did not include even a shred of love or respect for his father, didn't hesitate to enter into an alliance with Philip Augustus against King Henry. The enthralling religious brotherhood invoked by the archbishop of Tyre at Gisors had dissolved into internecine warfare.

Frederick I took the Crusader vow in March 1188 and agreed to put together the largest Christian army ever to go to the Holy Land, but such a tremendous effort would take time, and time was what the citizens of the beleaguered cities of Tyre, Tripoli, and Antioch were afraid they did not have.

Saladin had kept his promise to renew his war against the Christians. While Frederick I was on his knees making his sacred vow of Crusade, Saladin embarked upon another invasion of the Holy Land. He made a move at the Hospitallers' strongest castle at Krak des Chevaliers, then decided to pass it by. He repeated that decision after an unsuccessful assault on the Templars' strongest castle at Tortosa, choosing instead to gather up easier locations first, taking the coastal cities of Jabala and Lattakieh, between Tyre and Antioch.

In July, in response to an appeal from Queen Sibylla, the sultan decided to release King Guy, probably for political reasons. The Christians appeared united behind Conrad at Tyre, and Saladin now knew that the divisions in leadership fomented by Guy of Lusignan and Grand Master de Ridfort had contributed substantially to the events leading to his victory at the Horns of Hattin. Sending the Christian monarch back might split the Christians again. King Guy willingly took an oath to never again take up arms against any Muslim, and to sail across the sea away from the Holy Land. Saladin agreed to free ten additional nobles with him, including Guy's brother Amalric, who was the constable of the kingdom. Once free, they ran for Tripoli, where Queen Sibylla had found shelter with young Count Bohemond, who had inherited the title upon the recent death of Guy's old enemy, Count Raymond of Tripoli. Grand Master de Ridfort came up from Tyre to meet with King Guy, and while there decided to go further north to inspect the Templar castles at Tortosa and on the little offshore island of Ruad. King Guy, probably for want of something to occupy his time, went with him. On the journey, they had lots of time to discuss how to reestablish Guy's rule of the kingdom in the face of the arrogant stance of Conrad at Tyre, whose followers encouraged him to conduct himself as the head of a sovereign state.

They were not, however, able to make any effective plans to stop Saladin, who was now helping himself to the tattered remains of the Christian kingdom. All of the castles of the military orders were seriously undermanned and now were major objectives. Saladin took the Hospitaller castle at Sahyun, then moved all the way north to capture the Templar castles of Baghras and Darbsaq, which had guarded the passage through the Armanus mountains between Armenia and Antioch. Moving south, he took the castle of Safed, which the Templars had thought was impregnable.

He did not forget an objective that was almost as emotional to Saladin as Jerusalem itself, the castle of the hated Reynald of Chatillon across the Jordan at Kerak. The knights and soldiers there had assisted Reynald in all of his illicit raids on Muslims, and it was to Kerak that Reynald had brought his Muslim prisoners to sell to slave dealers. For his own personal satisfaction Kerak must fall, so Saladin sent his brother al-Adil with a Muslim army to lay siege to the massive castle, perched on a high mountain shelf.

Catapults were impractical for Kerak, so the plan was to starve the Christians out. It took months, but it worked. As the Christians began to run out of food, they ate all of their horses, and then consumed all the birds, dogs, and cats in the city. Some of them pushed their women and children out of the gates to avoid having to feed them, not caring that the Arabs in the mountains would gather them up for sale into slavery. Some of the captive women told stories of cannibalism in the castle. When the Christians finally surrendered toward the end of 1188, the conquering Muslims could not find the tiniest scrap of food in the extensive fortress. When they took the nearby castle of Montreal a few weeks later, all of the land on both sides of the Jordan River belonged to Saladin.

Back in Tripoli, Saladin's political scheme seemed to be working. The party of Lusignan was rebuilding. Joscelin of Courtenay decided to leave Tyre to join King Guy, accompanied by his own followers. Others of the local knights, offended by the ever-increasing arrogance of Conrad of Montferrat, decided to join their king. The young count of Tripoli was happy to have the experienced fighters in his city and welcomed them all. Grand Master de Ridfort assured the king that when the time came for him to make his move, he would have the full support of the Knights Templar. That time was near, but first King Guy had to be formally released from his oath. It was no problem to find a priest who agreed that an oath to an infidel, given under duress, was not valid. Guy also added, perhaps with a smile, that he had fulfilled his oath when he had traveled "over the sea" with Grand Master de Ridfort to the Templar castle two miles offshore on the island of Ruad.

Guy assembled his growing band of knights and men-at-arms and led them to Tyre, but Conrad would not let them into the city. He informed Guy that he should no longer consider himself to be the king of Jerusalem. Who would rule the Holy Land would be decided according to the stated wish of Baldwin IV, who had specified in his will that the king should be picked by the pope and by the rulers of England, France, and Germany. There was nothing he could do, so Guy led his disappointed friends back to Tripoli.

When news came to Tripoli in March 1189 that Saladin had moved back to his new capital at Damascus, Guy decided to try again and led a larger group of followers on a second march to Tyre. As they moved down the road, a Pisan fleet of fifty-two ships arrived at Tyre in response to the pope's call to Crusade. The Pisan leader, Archbishop Ubaldo, went into Tyre to visit Conrad and was offended at his reception by the man who insisted upon being obeyed as the ruler of the Holy Land. As the Pisans discussed what course to take, King Guy provided a solution by showing up at Tyre.

The archbishop was much happier with his respectful reception by King Guy, who suddenly had a sizable fleet to assist in his plans, although as yet he didn't have a plan. The ships and soldiers sent by King William II of Sicily arrived, and it seemed to them to be the proper thing to do to report to the king. Guy now had troops and a strong navy. His power was growing, but he had no desire to lay siege to the Christian city of Tyre.

By August 1189 he had made up his mind. He ordered all of his followers, and the fleets of Pisa and Sicily, to follow him to Acre. He would besiege a Muslim city and start to rebuild the Christian kingdom. It was an audacious move, probably foolish, and the only time in all the two centuries of the Crusades that a besieging army was less than half the size of the army inside the city, but it was exactly the kind of bold move that was called for. Conrad had established a fine reputation for leadership, but had shown no inclination to do anything more than hold on to Tyre. Now King Guy had given the Christians a rallying point. When the news got back to Europe, Guy's reputation, which was lying in tatters in the dirt, would begin to rise again. We don't know how he might have been encouraged in his decision by Grand Master de Ridfort, who was a champion of daring and foolish actions, but we do know that de Ridfort kept his promise of full support. He proudly led a large body of his Knights Templar to the siege of Acre.

Conrad of Montferrat did not like what happened over the next few weeks. Independent groups of Crusaders were arriving from Europe. They had come to fight, not to sit, and went right to King Guy on the field before Acre, not to the inert city of Tyre. A Danish fleet arrived, then a group of French and Flemish knights commanded by the highest lords of the nobility. Louis of Thuringia, who had decided not to take the slow landward march with Frederick I, brought a group of Germans. The archbishop of Ravenna brought a contingent of Italians. King Guy's army was growing fast, and no one was paying much attention to Conrad of Montferrat. Finally, in fear that some major event might occur of which he would not be a part, Conrad took troops of his own to join the siege of Acre. He made it clear that he was *not* under the command of Guy of Lusignan, but he was seething inside that all of the newly arrived Crusaders were looking for guidance to King Guy of Jerusalem, and not to the hero who had preserved the kingdom.

Saladin could not ignore this Christian buildup. He sent an army to make the first Muslim attack on the besieging Christians in September, but by now the Christian force was strong enough to hold them off. Three weeks later, excessively proud of their accomplishment in having held back a small Muslim army, the

Crusaders decided to attack the Muslims, but by now Saladin himself had arrived with substantial reinforcements. The Knights Templar under Grand Master de Ridfort took their position in the Christian left wing. The fight went back and forth, but was essentially a draw. The Christians ultimately decided to fall back to the safety of their own defenses, except for one man.

The Templar grand master, with his growing madness now in full flower, refused to leave the battlefield until there was a complete Christian victory. All alone, he brandished his sword and shouted out his challenge to the entire Muslim army. The Muslims watched him for a few minutes in amazed amusement, then easily made him their prisoner. Saladin didn't waste his time on conversation or even on comment. He simply ordered the grand master's immediate execution. There are those who feel that the death of Gerard de Ridfort made a significant contribution to the turnaround in the Christian fortunes, and especially in the conduct of the king, who for the first time in his entire reign was without the advice of his wild-eyed counselor.

Historically, the importance of Gerard de Ridfort is that his actions gave a tarnish to the Knights Templar that they could never polish away and inspired the accusation that they had been responsible for the loss of the Holy City. This taint was preserved in the annals of other religious orders, and over a hundred years later would be used as evidence against them.

For now, King Guy had held against the Muslims and was the beneficiary of constant reinforcements from Europe. Word had reached Conrad that his cousin Frederick Barbarossa was on his way with an army of a hundred thousand men. Frederick would want to fight, so he would probably back King Guy in his siege of Acre. It appeared obvious that Guy was not going to go away, so prudence suggested the wisdom of making a deal. Conrad agreed to recognize King Guy as the rightful king of Jerusalem. In exchange, Guy agreed to Conrad's right to hold Tyre as well as Sidon and Beirut, once they were retaken from Saladin by the German Crusade.

Through the coming year of 1190, new Crusaders continued to arrive at Acre. The most important was the dashing young Count Henry of Champagne. He was a grandson of Eleanor of Aquitaine, which made him the kinsman of both Richard of England and Philip Augustus of France. He was to play a leading role in the unfolding events in the Holy Land. A month after Count Henry came Duke Frederick of Swabia, son of Frederick Barbarossa, leading a ragged remnant of the mighty army his father had called together for his own German Crusade. The tale he had to tell was full of tragedy.

In May 1189, three months before King Guy made his move at

Acre, Frederick Barbarossa had set out on his own Crusade. He decided not to wait for Henry of England or Philip of France, nor to seek any alliance with them. He had no need for an alliance with anyone, because he alone commanded the largest army ever to go on Crusade. His hundred thousand followers comprised a larger army than Henry and Philip together could muster. On the march, the army was strung out for miles and took days to pass a given point.

The size of the army created logistical problems beyond any that the German leaders had ever experienced. Even limiting the troops to just two meals a day would require a million and a half meals each week, for week after week. It was impossible to carry such enormous supplies, so Frederick had sent envoys ahead to arrange to purchase food in Hungary and Byzantium. The march across Hungary was in good order and disciplined, as a result of the cooperation of King Bela. The food supplies were waiting at prearranged locations and were paid for promptly out of the closely guarded treasure that Frederick was taking with him to cover his crusading expenses.

The emperor was pleased with the uneventful six-week march across Hungary, but his mood changed when his army crossed the Danube River. Riding day after day deeper into Byzantine territory, he had plenty of time to reminisce about the events that had given him a lifelong suspicion of the Greeks at Constantinople.

Over forty years earlier, in 1147, as the duke of Swabia, Frederick had answered St. Bernard's call to Crusade and had ridden east with his uncle, King Conrad. He remembered their problems at the Byzantine court, but no memory was as vivid as that of the humiliating massacre of 80 percent of the German army when they had stopped to relieve their burning thirst at the little Bathys River. He was one of the few who had managed to break out and ride back to Nicaea with King Conrad. He had gone with his uncle to Jerusalem and then had taken part in the Christian shame in the retreat from the unsuccessful siege of Damascus. He was one who was totally dedicated to Bernard's position that the German disaster had resulted from Byzantine treachery.

Now the flaming color of his hair that had caused the Italians to call him *Barba rossa*, or Red Beard, was mostly gray. He was much older and, he hoped, much wiser. He had political reasons, too, to be wary of the Greeks, for Frederick's son Henry had married Constance, the heiress to William II and his kingdom of Sicily. Ever since the Norman Robert Guiscard had taken Sicily from the Greeks just before the First Crusade, there had been incessant hostility between the Sicilian monarchy and the Byzantines. Even now their ships were attacking each other in the Greek islands. When Constance came into her inheritance, the island kingdom would be governed by her husband Henry, who would also become the next German emperor. Frederick could not predict whether he would be received at Constantinople as a crusading knight or as an enemy.

The Byzantine emperor Isaac Angelus certainly did not feel good about a German army in his empire. He had enough problems with his own people and didn't need outsiders stirring things up. A relative, Isaac Comnenus, had led a successful revolution on Cyprus, taking away that wealthy colony. The Serbs and Bulgarians, always resentful at having lost their independence to the Greeks, were in open revolt, and the Germans were marching right through lands being held by the rebellious Serbians. As the Serbs picked off the German stragglers, Frederick decided that they had been bribed to do so by the Greeks. He met with the Serbian leaders, explained his mission, and gave them rich gifts to permit a peaceful passage of his army. When Isaac Angelus heard that news, he decided that the Germans were supporting his own rebellious subjects.

The conflict came out in the open when Frederick sent a party of envoys to Constantinople to purchase food and to arrange for ships to take the army across to Asia. Isaac Angelus seized the envoys as his prisoners and put them in chains, informing Frederick that they were now hostages to guarantee his compliant behavior. Frederick had not held his throne for thirty-five years without learning how to deal with threats. He seized a Greek city and informed Isaac Angelus that the Germans now held the entire population of the town as hostages. He also told him that dispatches had gone to Henry in Germany asking him to assemble a Sicilian fleet to attack Constantinople from the sea. The choice for the Byzantine emperor was simple: Release his German prisoners and provide transportation for Frederick's army, or go to war.

The prospect of fighting a hundred thousand well-armed, fully equipped German soldiers on one side and a fleet of warships on the other was not very appealing. The Byzantine emperor counseled, raged, fumed, threatened, and boasted for a few weeks, and then collapsed. The German envoys were released, transportation was provided across the Dardanelles, and a supply of food was sold to the Germans. Now Frederick Barbarossa could get on with his Crusade, but the year was drawing on and he decided to winter his weary army on the Greek side. This kept the Byzantines in a nervous state, hoping the conflict between the two emperors would not break out again.

Frederick's winter of delay brought even more nervousness to King Guy and the Christians camped before Acre. They all anticipated the arrival of the great German army coming to their rescue, and would have preferred that Frederick keep moving. The news that he had parked his army for the winter was disheartening, because by now the Egyptian navy had managed to break the Christian blockade and was bringing supplies to the city. The Christians did not have the power to take Acre by storm, and Saladin could call on his whole Muslim empire for reinforcements. They had no idea how long they could hold out, even with the occasional boost of small parties of Christians arriving from Europe. The Knights Templar were being reinforced with men recruited by their preceptories in Europe, but they had not yet agreed on a successor to their fallen Grand Master de Ridfort. In the interim, they sent for Gilbert Erail, the Templar officer who had narrowly lost the grand master election to Gerard de Ridfort. It was with a great feeling of relief that Guy welcomed the news brought by a Christian ship in March 1190 that at last the Germans were crossing into Anatolia.

Saladin had received the same news. He responded by sending letters to the Muslim potentates in the north, urging them to make every effort to impede the march of the German Crusade and to remove or destroy all of the food supplies ahead of them. Saladin knew that every day lost by the German army would mean the fast dwindling of their stocks of food.

As Frederick entered the territory of the Seljuk Turks his army was in totally hostile country. The Turks hung around the German column as it moved. Stragglers were killed, and foraging parties sent out to look for food were wiped out. Any German who wandered away from the main column, for whatever reason, was a dead man. It was now the month of May, and the heat and the water shortage were beginning to claim their victims. Finding the occasional spring might be helpful, but couldn't do much for tens of thousands of thirsty men and horses. By June they reached the bleak Taurus mountains and crossed the high passes into Armenia, heading for the coastal plain and the city of Seleucia, just off the coast on the Calycadnus River. Coming out of the mountains, Frederic decided to lead the way with knights of his personal bodyguard.

History remembers what happened then, but not how it happened. With no enemy in view on the plain, Frederick left his bodyguard for a few minutes to go to the river. We do not know if the emperor slipped, or if his horse slipped. We don't know if he cried out. All we know is that when his bodyguard reached the water, the emperor was on the river bottom, held there by his heavy armor. By the time his men could drag him out to the riverbank, Frederick Barbarossa was dead.

The news flew back along the German column. For many of

these men, Frederick had been their ruler for their entire lives. They couldn't imagine life under another emperor. Many of them, including barons and princes, went to Armenian ports and arranged for ships to take them home. They were not here because of any religious zeal, but because the venerable *Kaiser Friedrich* had ordered them to follow him. His second son, Duke Frederick of Swabia, took command of the disintegrating army. Remembering his father's desire to be buried next to Christ's own tomb at the Church of the Holy Sepulcher in Jerusalem, the duke had his father's body preserved in a cask of vinegar to carry along with his dejected troops.

The emperor's death, coupled with the heat and thirst and hunger, demoralized the army to the point that any enforcement of discipline was hopeless. Wandering off to search for food and water, the men were easy prey for the swarms of mounted Turkish archers. Losses grew greater as they passed through the Amanus mountains to the territory of Antioch. Most of them hung together in self-protection, but once within the secure walls of Antioch the last shreds of discipline and organization in the shrunken army disappeared. The chroniclers do not tell us how they felt about song, but do recount that they went crazy over wine and women. What was left of the proud, disciplined army of Emperor Frederick I decomposed into a drunken rabble that kept every prostitute in the city working overtime.

No one had awaited their coming with more eagerness than Conrad of Montferrat, who was a cousin of Frederick and so of the Duke of Swabia. He hurried to Antioch to urge that the German Crusade come quickly to his city of Tyre. The duke was willing, but not his army. Many of them simply refused to go any farther, and no threats could budge them. As the duke's army came apart, so did his father's body, as attendants reported that the vinegar wasn't working. The emperor's body was rotting into pieces. Duke Frederick ordered that the remains be buried in the Cathedral of Antioch, but had some of the bones wrapped to take along, so that at least a relic of Frederick Barbarossa could rest by the Holy Sepulcher, assuming of course that Jerusalem could be retaken from Saladin. If that could actually happen, it was now clear that it would not be accomplished by the pitiful remnant of the German Crusade.

Duke Frederick led his bedraggled force to Acre, which they reached in October, now reduced to just five thousand of the hundred thousand soldiers who had started out. Later in the month an English contingent arrived, led by the archbishop of Canterbury. His troops were welcome, but not as welcome as his news of the progress of Richard of England and his Crusade. Richard's help had been promised to King Guy over a year ago, when Henry II had died and Richard had become the king of England. The delay had been maddening to the Christians before Acre, but now they learned that Richard and Philip Augustus had gathered their crusading armies and at last were on their way. The Knights Templar were delighted to learn that Richard was also bringing a contingent of English Templars with him.

Unfortunately for King Guy, there was an unwelcome visitor that fall, in the form of an epidemic. Among its victims were all of Guy's royal family, including his wife, Queen Sibylla, and their two daughters. Guy was king of Jerusalem only on the basis of his marriage to Queen Sibylla. Now there was a question as to whether he had any authority at all. No one put forth more effort to make certain that everyone understood Guy's precarious position than Conrad of Montferrat, whose hopes of becoming the king of Jerusalem were suddenly alive again. The rightful rulers were now Queen Sibylla's younger sister Isabella and her husband, Humphrey of Toron. Only Guy's friends the Knights Templar stood with him, and they made certain that everyone understood that Conrad had no legal right to the throne of Jerusalem.

They were right, of course, but Conrad had a plan to solve that problem. If Isabella's marriage to Humphrey of Toron was annulled, she could marry Conrad. Then Conrad would have an undisputable legal right to the crown. The local barons favored the plan because they didn't like Humphrey of Toron. They had not forgotten how he had left them hanging to run to Jerusalem and kneel before King Guy. In their opinion, he was too pretty to be a real man, and his well-known homosexual proclivities meant that he was not likely to produce an heir.

Humphrey hated anything resembling a confrontation. He quickly promised the warrior barons who called on him that he would not interfere with their plan. Isabella flatly refused. Homosexual he might be, but Humphrey was always kind to her, with a completely courteous and generous nature. Also, he was nearer her own age. She had no desire to be mated with a domineering, pompous man easily old enough to be her father. The barons turned to Isabella's mother, who wanted very much to be the mother-in-law of a king. She testified before the church leaders that Isabella had had no choice in this marriage. After all, she had been only eleven years old at the time of her marriage. Knowing Humphrey's sexual preferences, she stated that the marriage had probably never been consummated, even though several years had gone by. The archbishop of Canterbury was asked to declare the annulment and perform the marriage, but he objected on the grounds that Conrad already had a wife in Constantinople. He would not extend the blessings of the Church to a clearly bigamous, adulterous union.

Undismayed, Conrad and his supporters approached the archbishop of Pisa. The religious arguments presented to him were that Conrad would be so grateful to the archbishop and to Pisa that he would grant very important trading privileges to the Pisan merchants. That would enhance the archbishop's standing at home because rich profits would flow to those merchants, whose numbers included members of the archbishop's own family. The archbishop decided that God wanted Conrad to be king of Jerusalem and agreed to effect the annulment. The wedding was arranged for a couple of weeks later, and upon the announcement the archbishop of Canterbury thundered out his condemnation and excommunication of Conrad and his supporters. That didn't bother anyone, because the current epidemic claimed the life of the English archbishop a few days later. King Guy vented his own anger by flinging down his gauntlet to challenge Conrad to trial by combat to let God decide the issue. Conrad, who had clearly emerged victorious, saw no reason to risk that victory and ignored the challenge. The marriage went forward.

Now Guy of Lusignan, who had no solid support except the Knights Templar and the tiny contingent of English Crusaders, was down to his last shred of hope. His family, the le Bruns of Lusignan, were important vassals and good friends of King Richard of England. He could only hold his peace and pray for the safe arrival of the man who would prove to be the most colorful and most legendary Crusader of them all.

11

The Lion Heart
1190 to 1191

RICHARD OF ENGLAND and Philip of France were unlikely partners. Richard was a tall, powerful man with long red-gold hair and a glint of fire in his eyes. Philip, at the age of twenty-five, was eight years younger than Richard, shorter in stature, with unruly hair and one blind eye. Richard was dramatic, flamboyant, skilled in the arts of war, and eager for hand-to-hand combat. Philip leaned more toward politics and diplomacy than to war, with the style of an unemotional man of quiet cunning. Their one common trait was their mistrust of each other, which meant that they had to leave on Crusade together. Neither would take his army away and leave his European lands at the mercy of the other. Whatever love or lust had brought them together in a homosexual affair years earlier was gone now.

Richard sent his fleet to Marseilles and marched his land army to join up with Philip at Vézelay, where Bernard had called the Second Crusade almost fifty years earlier. With him went a contingent of Templar knights, a few with experience, but most newly recruited in response to the urgent pleas of the remnants of the order in the Holy Land. Another volunteer who insisted upon going with him was Richard's extraordinary mother, Eleanor of Aquitaine, whose second husband was Henry of England. After a religious ceremony in the beautiful cathedral, the two armies set out together on July 4, 1190. Apparently the joint launching of their Crusade was just to give each king the assurance that the other was definitely going, for the armies parted company south of Lyons. Philip continued southward to Nice, then eastward along the coast to meet his ships at Genoa. The French and English fleets were to rally off Sicily, then make the long voyage across the Mediterranean together.

The stop was not essential to the Crusade, but Richard wanted to look in on his favorite sister, Joanna, who had married King William II of Sicily. William had died the previous November, and with no children, Joanna was left with only her dower rights and her inheritance from William, whatever that might be.

The succession to the throne of Sicily and Naples, too, was a problem. William's closest heir was his aunt, who was married to Prince Henry of Hohenstauffen. As the eldest son of Frederick Barbarossa, Henry was also the heir to the Holy Roman Empire. Pope Clement III had no intention of letting the rulers of Germany rule Sicily and southern Italy as well, which would have locked the papal territories in a German vise, squeezing them from both north and south. With pressure from the Holy See, the papal party ignored the Hohenstauffen claims and put on the throne of Sicily Count Tancred of Lecae, a bastard cousin of King William. The new king promptly recalled the ships and men that William had sent to the Holy Land, to help him to put down the revolts that quickly sprang up in Sicily and on the mainland of Italy. That act weakened the Crusader forces in Palestine at the exact time they were fighting for their very survival.

Once Richard reached Marseilles, he yielded to his dread of seasickness and ordered the army to go on to Sicily by ship, leaving him with a small escort to continue by land. He proceeded along the coast to Genoa, from which Philip and his army had already set sail, then turned south beyond Naples to Salerno, where he waited until news arrived assuring him that his fleet had successfully made port at Messina. After sending his escort by ship to Messina to prepare for his ceremonious arrival, he continued his march south with just one companion.

Passing a house in Calabria, Richard was attracted to a hunting hawk in the yard. He decided to take it for himself without asking or paying, as was his custom in his own lands. At home, no one would have dared to touch him, but here he was a stranger and a common thief, as he learned when he was beaten senseless by the enraged Calabrians. Even the thought that peasants would raise their hands to him would have infuriated Richard, but the actual beating put him in a black mood that still enveloped him as he reached and crossed the Straits of Messina.

Philip had arrived quietly at the Sicilian port city of Messina, disembarking like any common traveler. In contrast and by prearrangement, Richard was welcomed and paraded by his men with great ceremony. Although staged at his orders, the regal reception did nothing to help his mood. Nor did the fact that his fears about King Tancred had been well founded. His sister, the dowager queen

Joanna, was being held in confinement for fear that she might serve as a rallying point for Tancred's enemies. To their numbers Richard could now be added, since Tancred had decided to keep for himself the wealthy dower that was rightfully Joanna's. More alarming to Richard, Tancred had also decided to ignore that part of King William's will that had bequeathed a fortune in gold, ships, and crusading supplies to his father-in-law, Henry II of England. As Henry's son and heir, Richard should have been the beneficiary of a fortune Tancred now chose to claim for himself.

Tancred had been warned of Richard's temper, so he assigned to him a palace that was well outside the walls of Messina, hoping to placate him by permitting his sister Joanna to lodge with him. Richard's response was to send some of his troops to the Italian mainland to occupy the coastal town of Bagnara, to which he moved his sister to get her out of the path of trouble. Then he took a small island just offshore from Messina and had the resident monks driven out of their monastery, which he turned over to his troops. His fleet moved to threaten the harbor at Messina.

Tancred was dazed by Richard's explosive reaction to the treatment he and his sister had received at Tancred's hands. He ordered the gates of the city secured and the walls manned by every available Sicilian soldier. The whole crusading effort was at an impasse. When Tancred was drawn miles away by other business in Catania, Philip of France decided to assume the role of peacemaker. He called for a meeting at Richard's headquarters outside the walls and marched out to meet him, accompanied by Tancred's chief admiral, the local archbishop, and a group of Sicilian nobles. The procession made a colorful medieval spectacle, and the townspeople left the city to follow it. They gathered around the meeting place, heedless of the fact that no one had bothered to close the massive gates behind them.

At the conference, Richard took offense at what he said were personal insults and erupted in another fit of temper, although this one seems to have been planned in advance. He shouted for his troops to attack the city, and they were on the move within minutes. The relaxed Sicilians were completely unprepared for the attack. English troops ran through the open gates into the city, and the result was a complete rout of the local garrison. Richard rewarded his men by turning them loose to plunder the city at will, excluding the quarter occupied by his French allies. He sent men to the harbor to burn the Sicilian fleet anchored there. By the end of the day his personal banner had been placed on the highest tower to crack in the coastal breeze. Richard was in total control of Messina.

To Philip, it seemed the ideal time and circumstance to negotiate a private alliance with the Mediterranean kingdom. He dispatched one of his noblest vassals, the duke of Burgundy, to Catania to make terms with Tancred, offering Philip's help against Richard. The proposal held little appeal for Tancred: The talker was offering to help him against the fighter. Besides, both Philip and Richard would be leaving soon to fulfill their crusading vows, leaving Tancred alone to deal with Henry of Hohenstauffen. Henry was bound to resort to war to establish his right to the Sicilian throne, and Philip of France was known to be friendly with Henry. On the other hand, Richard of England was antagonistic toward Henry. More important, Richard was a man of action and a winner. All that told Tancred that diplomatic wisdom lay in the direction of an alliance with Richard.

Tancred set the stage by informing Richard of Philip's overtures, then made the kind of offer that could always be guaranteed to get the English king's attention: Twenty thousand ounces of gold to settle the claims of his sister Joanna, and twenty thousand ounces of gold for Richard himself, to satisfy his claims to his father's inheritance from King William. Richard accepted without argument, showing his good will toward his new ally with the proposal that his own heir be betrothed to one of Tancred's daughters. The treaty was drawn and sent to the pope for his blessing. It was quickly given, because Clement III would favor any alliance that served to keep his Hohenstauffen enemies away from the throne of Sicily.

Resigning himself to the surprising new friendship between Tancred and Richard, Philip suggested to Richard that they get on with what was supposed to be their principal objective, the rescue of the Holy Land. He did demand, and Richard agreed, that any future gains should be shared between them equally.

Philip, however, would not agree to waive the arrangements already made with Richard's father, Henry II, by which Richard was pledged to marry Philip's sister, Princess Alice of France. During the negotiations to get Richard's agreement to the union, Alice had stayed with Henry, who had decided to take it upon himself to introduce his future daughter-in-law to the joys of sexual congress. Her husband's behavior was taken by Queen Eleanor as an unforgivable affront, both to herself and to her favorite son. She set about arranging a bride for Richard more to her liking. Now, with Henry dead and Richard on the English throne, there was no barrier to Eleanor's plans except the previous pledge to France. Richard simply dismissed the arrangement as having been canceled by Princess Alice's promiscuous behavior. There was no way for Philip to force Richard to honor their bargain, so in his frustration he decided to leave without Richard and continue the journey to the Holy Land alone. Richard elected to winter in Sicily and instructed his mother to bring to him her choice as the future queen of England, a princess of Navarre with the romantic name of Berengaria.

A storm at sea drove Philip's fleet back to Sicily, where he could only watch in annoyance when Richard and Tancred met in state to effect a formal treaty of alliance in November 1190. Then, just after Christmas, news came that Queen Eleanor and Princess Berengaria had arrived at Naples. Richard sent word to them to remain in Italy with their large escort, because Messina was already overcrowded. Philip now must either agree to release Richard from his betrothal to Princess Alice or force him to honor his pledge. He chose the more practical course and reluctantly released Richard from the betrothal agreement, which Richard himself no longer regarded as binding, pledge or not. Philip's decision restored the good will between the monarchs, and on March 30, 1191, Philip sailed off to the Holy Land with his French army.

Philip reached the Christian army besieging Acre three weeks later. His reinforcements were most welcome, as was the reassuring report that Richard of England was right behind him. Philip was embraced by his cousin, Conrad of Montferrat, who expected to use Philip's support in his own quest to be named king of Jerusalem.

Richard, however, was in no hurry. His mother had finally brought Princess Berengaria to him in Messina, where his sister Joanna took over the duties of chaperone to the queen-to-be. Richard set sail on April 10, accompanied by Joanna and Berengaria, after making arrangements with the resident Knights Templar to look after his interests in Sicily. His English Templar knights went with him. None of them were aware that on the very day of their departure Tancred's sponsor, Pope Clement III, had died in Rome. Propitiously, Henry of Hohenstauffen was in Rome at the time and seems to have exerted some influence, such as gold, over the election of Clement's successor. Almost the first act of the new pontiff, Pope Celestine III, was to officiate at the coronation of Henry, making him the Church-anointed emperor of the Holy Roman Empire.

Fierce winds at sea split up Richard's fleet. As a raging storm howled around them, Richard's ship battled its way into port at the island of Rhodes, far off course, on April 22. Richard rested there for ten days, even after the storm abated, to recover from his violent seasickness and to await news of the fate of the ship carrying his sister and his future queen. The women's vessel was one of three that had been swept all the way around to the southern coast of Cyprus. The other two ships broke up on the rocks, but the one bearing the royal party managed to drop anchor safely near the harbor at Limassol. Their reception changed the course of history in the Middle East for the next two centuries.

Isaac Ducas Comnenus was a Byzantine nobleman who, five years before, had taken advantage of the state of turmoil at the eastern court to seize Cyprus for himself. The thirty-five-hundred-square-mile island supported a population dedicated to agriculture, mining, and crafts, and was strategically placed at the eastern end of the Mediteranean, just south of the Armenian kingdom in Cilicia and due west of the Holy Land. Isaac Comnenus, the self-styled emperor of Cyprus, now made the grave mistake of mortally offending Richard of England.

When Isaac learned of the appearance of the three English ships off his southern shore, he hurried there with a detachment of his local army. As the surviving sailors made their way to the beach, Isaac summarily captured the exhausted Anglo-Norman mariners and put them in chains. He confiscated for himself all of their cargoes that could be salvaged. Learning from his prisoners of the important passengers on the ship at anchor, he sent an emissary by boat to invite the dowager queen Joanna and Princess Berengaria to come ashore to be his honored guests. Joanna had learned her politics in a hard school and realized that she and Berengaria would make valuable hostages, for whom Isaac could demand exorbitant ransoms. Feeling certain that her brother would come for her and his betrothed sooner or later, she gracefully declined Isaac's invitation, but did ask permission for a party to come ashore for fresh drinking water. Isaac flatly refused.

Instead, he turned his men and their prisoners to building hasty earthworks around the area to ward off all possible attempts at landing by any rescue party. That party did indeed come within the week, on May 8, in a small fleet headed by Richard himself. When he learned of Isaac's imprisonment of his followers and the treatment of his royal sister and fiancée, Richard's fury was unleashed. He quickly moved his ships just far enough away for his troops to land unopposed, then led them in a swift attack on Isaac at Limassol. Startled by this unexpected aggression, Isaac hastily retreated from the area. Richard made camp, but not before sending one of his ships to Acre to advise the Latin Crusaders that he had arrived at Cyprus.

Isaac and Richard both learned quickly that the Cypriots bore no love for Isaac and his burdensome taxes. They were inclined to regard the Crusaders as their liberators. Isaac decided to negotiate, placate Richard, and send the Crusaders on their way. At Isaac's request, Richard readily agreed to a meeting, with a guarantee of safe passage for Isaac to and from the English camp.

Isaac offered friendly terms. He would free all of Richard's imprisoned followers and pay full compensation for all of the salvaged cargo he had confiscated. The English could purchase all the provisions they needed, free of any duties or taxes. As a further gesture of his good will, he would even place one hundred men under Richard's command for the duration of his Crusade, and to guarantee his performance he would provide his daughter as a hostage.

Richard accepted the terms, but once back at his own base, Isaac had second thoughts. Richard's armed force was much smaller than Isaac had expected it would be, and to his mind it was no match for the army Isaac could pull together quickly. There was no way he would make costly reparations to an enemy he could beat. He declared as much in a message to the English king, ordering him to leave the island at once, or suffer the consequences. It was a terrible piece of timing.

As Isaac was composing his ultimatum, more ships began to arrive at Limassol. The leaders of the parties that had been shunted aside by Conrad of Montferrat, now supported by his cousin Philip of France, had decided not to wait for Richard's arrival at Acre. They came to Limassol to enlist his support and accept his leadership. The group included King Guy of Jerusalem, his brother, the count of Lusignan, Prince Bohemond of Antioch, Prince Leo of Roupenia, and Humphrey of Toron, all with armed retainers, as befitted their station. Best of all, considering the immediate crisis, the group included the battle-wise officers of the Knights Templar, with a contingent of experienced knights to add to the Templar force already with the English king. They all greeted Richard as their savior, and he relished the role.

They desperately needed Richard's support at Acre but were well aware of the strategic importance of Cyprus. They unanimously pledged their arms and their lives to Richard's idea that, with their combined forces, they could easily conquer the whole kingdom of Cyprus, especially if they waited for the arrival of the rest of Richard's fleet. While waiting, with the illustrious local nobility on hand, resplendent in their semi-oriental costumes and joined by the enlarged force of Knights Templar, Richard and Berengaria were married in a magnificent ceremony at the church of St. George in Limassol. The honeymoon that followed was to be short, however, because the balance of Richard's fleet arrived the very next morning.

Once the news of the English reinforcements reached Isaac, he withdrew to the walled city of Famagusta on the eastern shore of the island, opposite the Holy Land. Richard sent part of his forces overland and part by sea to bottle Isaac up in Famagusta. Isaac's reaction to their approach was to flee that city for his inland capital of Nicosia. The Crusaders simply walked into the walled port city of Famagusta and took over.

Encouraged by reinforcements that arrived at his capital, Isaac took his army on the road back to Famagusta, after first sending his wife and daughter to safety at his castle of Kyrenia, on the northern coast. Richard marched out to meet him and defeated Isaac in a battle that was little more than a skirmish, although the Crusaders were incensed that the Cypriots were apparently using poisoned arrows. Isaac, having managed to flee the battlefield, sought refuge to the northeast at his castle of Kantara.

Richard entered the capital city of Nicosia as a conqueror, but almost immediately fell ill. Isaac could now hope that the Latins, deprived of their leader and under pressure to return to the conflict with Saladin, would depart for the Holy Land and leave him alone. But King Guy, filled with the new resolve that had manifested itself in his decision to besiege Acre after the fall of Jerusalem, now took charge, with the counsel of his Templar friends. They and the English army headed swiftly for the north coast to secure the castle at Kyrenia, taking the empress and her daughter as their prisoners. Then, in cooperation with the fleet, they blockaded Isaac's northern castles of St. Hilarion and Buffarento. Isaac was beaten.

Richard, by now recovered from his illness and delighted with the conduct of his new ally and friend, King Guy of Jerusalem, was in a very good mood. When Isaac finally offered unconditional surrender, asking only that he not be put into iron chains like a common criminal, Richard readily agreed, probably smiling to himself. When Isaac left his castle to surrender, Richard was waiting for him with heavy chains made of pure silver.

The English fleet headed due east out of Famagusta into Mediterranean waters on June 5, 1191. With Richard on his flagship were his admiral, Robert de Sablé, his prisoner Isaac, and the Templar officers. Their first sight of land was easily recognized by the Templars as the Hospitaller castle of Marqab, far to the north of Acre. As the fleet turned south to follow the coastline, Richard made arrangements with the Templars to take Isaac off his hands until his fate could be decided. They dropped anchor offshore from the Templar castle of Tortosa, where a party of Knights Templar took Isaac, still draped in his silver chains, to the castle commander. Happy to cooperate with his Templar brothers, the commander had Isaac taken to his new home in a dungeon in the depths of the castle fortress.

Continuing south, Richard had the fleet anchor off Tyre. He received something of a shock when, instead of the royal welcome he had expected, he was refused admission to the city of Tyre on the direct orders of Conrad and Philip. Not eager to begin his Crusade with a pitched battle against his allies, Richard swallowed his pride for the moment and ordered his fleet farther south. On June 8 he joined the Crusader forces that were besieging Acre, where his welcome was much more to his liking. Loud cheers and the blasts of military trumpets pierced the air, creating a festive atmosphere against a backdrop of great bonfires.

The Christians needed Richard. Siege warfare was very acceptable to Philip, who enjoyed the planning, the meetings, the administration of the camp. He had ordered the construction of stone-throwing machines to support the efforts of the two great catapults owned by the Hospitallers and the Knights of the Temple. It may have been a satisfactory way to conduct a military campaign for an administrator, but not for a warrior. Richard wanted action.

The basic problem was that the Christians faced two enemies at the same time: the garrison at Acre and the army of Saladin circling them inland. Whichever way they turned they would have an enemy at their backs. They had to find a way to defeat one force or the other, and their best chance was the city. Saladin had his whole empire at his back to keep him supplied with provisions and a steady flow of reinforcements. The city, on the other hand, could get no help by land, with the Latins camped on all sides, and now the king of England had brought twenty-five galleys to abolish any hope they had of continuing to be supplied by sea. Saladin had several times sent crack troops to break through to the city, but every such raid had failed. The Crusaders had no more luck in their own attempts to force a breach in the city walls.

The waiting was not easy. Disease was rife in both armies. The patriarch of Jerusalem had died. Both Philip and Richard suffered from a strange malady that the locals called "arnaldia," which produced a high fever and frequently the loss of hair and nails. Saladin, a generation older than both of them, was covered with hideous boils from the waist down. The people of Acre were starving to death, subject to every evil brought on by malnutrition.

Politics was a killing disease, too. Richard was now the leader of the party behind King Guy, supported by the Knights Templar. Philip was just as firmly behind Conrad, and the commitment of the Templars to Richard and Guy had brought the Hospitallers into Philip's camp. The Pisans sided with Richard, so it was only natural that Genoa decided to support Philip. The quest for the crown was threatening to kill the quest for the cross.

The Templar commitment to Richard grew stronger as the result of a suggestion Richard made to the Templar leadership. Grand Master de Ridfort had been dead for over a year, and the leaders had not yet met to elect a successor. Richard suggested his friend, Robert de Sablé, who was of good family and distantly related to Richard. His wife was dead, his son was dead, his daughters were married and gone from his house. Although a wealthy man, he had little reason to return home. He was also a good administrator and an experienced fighting man. More important to the Knights Templar, Robert de Sablé as grand master would assure them of Richard's strong support. Just as important, de Sablé could serve them locally better than any of their own, for he could not possibly be accused of any of the actions that had led to the disaster at the Horns of Hattin and the fall of Jerusalem. He was an eminently suitable candidate, so the Templars dispensed with the usual ritual of initiation, and Robert de Sablé became the eleventh grand master of the Temple.

The Crusaders' attention was abruptly drawn back to their primary purpose on July 4, when emissaries of Acre came to Richard's camp with complex proposals for the surrender of the city. Richard rejected their plan as totally self-serving and unacceptable. The siege would continue.

The garrison of Acre despaired of help ever coming from Saladin, because they could not hope to get a courier through the Crusader lines to report their desperate plight to their sultan. Finally, an unknown Muslim hero, who must have been a magnificent swimmer, undertook to get a message to Saladin by sea. Slipping into the harbor on the night of July 6, he swam a couple of miles down the coast beyond the Crusader lines, then came ashore to make his way to the sultan to report. People were dying in Acre every day. Their food was gone. Without Saladin's immediate help, the beleaguered garrison had to choice but to sue for peace on any terms it could get.

With both the French and English armies now on the scene, it was impossible for Saladin to break through the Christian lines to get supplies into Acre and prevent a surrender. On July 12 the city offered to yield on terms that Richard found acceptable. Everything in Acre, even the ships and their cargoes in the harbor, would go to the Crusaders, plus two hundred thousand pieces of gold. The fragment of the True Cross in Saladin's possession would be returned. The emirs also agreed that fifteen hundred Latin prisoners would be set free, and of these the Christians could specify one hundred men of knightly rank by name. The Crusaders, who were holding about twenty-seven hundred Muslim prisoners, plus their families, agreed that these captives would go free when all of the surrender terms had been met. In the meantime, their wives and children would not be separated from them.

There had been no way for the leaders at Acre to confirm these terms with Saladin, who would need to ratify them and guarantee them. When the terms were disclosed to him, Saladin was stunned.

There was no way that he would agree to such conditions, but as he was denouncing the action from his hilltop position, he saw the Christian banners being raised on the towers of Acre. It was too late: The Christians were inside. As a man of honor, he would do his best to live up to the commitments made to the enemy by his emirs, although the conditions could not be easily fulfilled and might take time. Negotiations began as to how the terms would be met, and those negotiations fell primarily to Richard because Philip of France wanted to go home.

Philip had been ill almost every day throughout the campaign, but he had done what he could to support his cousin Conrad. At a conference chaired by the papal legate, Bishop Adelard of Verona, agreement had been reached that Guy would keep the crown of Jerusalem until his death, when it would pass to Conrad. In compromise, Conrad would be lord of Beirut, Sidon, and Tyre, and share in the royal revenues.

More important, perhaps, was Philip's unhappiness with the way the conquest of Acre had worked out. As soon as the city was taken, Richard had moved into the former royal palace, so Philip had taken second best and moved his court into the Templar headquarters, on the seaward side of the city. Grand Master de Sablé led a delegation of Knights Templar to their friend Richard, asking his support in evicting the French king. They had not exhausted their resources and shed their blood to capture this city, only to have their property stolen from them. Richard agreed with them completely, as did King Guy, so Philip, too weak from illness to stand up against the combined assault, had moved out of the Temple to lesser quarters. It was all too demeaning. True, his banner flew alongside Richard's above the city, but when Leopold of Austria had raised his banner beside the others, to give credit to the contributions of the remnants of Frederick Barbarossa's German Crusade, Richard's men had torn it down and thrown it into the ditch. Leopold would get his revenge later, but for now the prospects for a multinational Crusade totally dominated by the king of England, as unpredictable as he was skillful, did not bode well for the reconquest of Jerusalem. Besides, Philip's future did not lie here. He had fulfilled his Crusader vow, and now he wanted to get back to the business of running his own country.

Richard had a kingdom at home, too, and wanted Philip where he could keep an eye on him, but Philip swore that he would not attack Richard's lands in his absence. He further assured Richard that most of the French army would stay behind under the command of the duke of Burgundy. His mind made up, Philip left on July 31 for Tyre, where he would take a ship for France. Conrad, who had no desire to remain in Richard's presence without the support of his royal kinsman, went back to Tyre with Philip, on the excuse that urgent matters required his attention. Richard was now in firm, autocratic control.

Two days later, on August 2, Richard sent word to Saladin that the sultan's schedule of payments of the sums agreed upon at Acre was acceptable. The cash payments would be made and the Christian prisoners returned in three equal monthly installments. Richard would free the twenty-seven hundred Muslim prisoners when he received the first cash installment and the first group of Christian prisoners from Saladin.

Saladin didn't know Richard well enough to trust him completely, so he sent an agent to the Knights Templar. He hated the Templars but nevertheless trusted them, and he asked if they would undertake to guarantee Richard's compliance with the agreement. The Templar officers, who by now knew Richard quite well, declined to accept the risk of guaranteeing his behavior. Their flat refusal must have caused Saladin some misgiving, but in the absence of any reasonable alternative he determined to keep his part of the bargain.

On August 11, Saladin made the first cash payment and released five hundred Christian prisoners. In keeping with their agreement, he now demanded that Richard release the twenty-seven hundred Muslim captives and their families. Richard's emissaries went to Saladin to report that the money count was correct and acceptable, as was the count of five hundred prisoners. However, those prisoners did not include any of the one hundred prisoners of noble rank who had been designated by name in accordance with the original agreement. For this reason Richard could not release the Muslim prisoners being held by the Christians. Saladin protested that it would take more time to locate the named prisoners who might be in prisons anywhere in Egypt or Syria. Richard's ambassadors were adamant. Saladin, concerned about the safety of his imprisoned followers, asked that the Christians accept hostages as a pledge that the noble prisoners would be released, or leave Christian hostages with him to guarantee the safety of his imprisoned officers and men. Both alternatives were rejected. As far as Richard was concerned, Saladin had violated the agreement.

Now the Egyptian sultan would see an aspect of Richard's character that he had never suspected and that popular history has quite forgotten. Richard had picked up a fortune in gold and a large share of the loot of Acre. Now, ready to march to Jerusalem, he was not going to be burdened by thousands of prisoners who would have to be guarded and fed. The orders he issued led to what may have been the blackest day in all of the two hundred years of the Christian Crusades.

On August 20, a bright, clear day, the Muslims watching from the surrounding hills saw a gate open and files of Anglo-French troops proceed to surround a low hill called Ayyadieh. Then came a great crowd of men in chains, with women and children clinging to them, as all were driven with whips and clubs to the top of the hill. These were the Muslim prisoners whose safety had so concerned Saladin.

A few emirs with ransom potential and a handful of muscular men slated for hard slave labor had been left behind, but most of the Muslim prisoners were here, confused and frightened. As the Muslims nearby watched in disbelief, Richard's men began to carry out his orders to kill them all. Swords, spears, knives, axes all flashed in the sun as they rose and fell. This time the children were not saved for the slave markets, but were butchered with their fathers and mothers. Even babies in their mothers's arms felt the knives of the blood-drenched Christians. Horrified, the watching Muslims gave way to anguished rage and raced for the hill, but in their scattered ranks could not penetrate the thicket of English spears and the storm of crossbow bolts that met them.

The killing completed, Richard's army started back to the city, while on the top of the hill a few loot-crazed butchers lurched from one body to another with their bloody knives, hastily disemboweling corpses to recover any gold pieces that might have been swallowed for concealment.

Saladin's chronicler Beha ed-Din recorded, "The following morning our people went out to see what had happened, and found all the Muslims who had been martyred for their faith stretched out on the ground.... Various motives have been assigned for this massacre. According to some, the prisoners were killed to avenge the death of those slain previously by the Muslims. Others say the king of England, having made up his mind to try to take Ascalon, did not think it prudent to leave so many prisoners behind in Acre. God knows what his reason really was." Well said.

Fortunately for his memory and legend, Richard was called *Coeur de Lion*, the Lion Heart, but history might just as well have remembered him as "The Butcher of Ayyadieh." Nor were the prisoners and their families the only deaths he was responsible for that day. As news of the slaughter spread throughout Saladin's empire, Christian prisoners everywhere were tortured and murdered in reprisal for the infamy. But now, with the annoyance and expense of his Muslim prisoners out of the way, Richard felt free to march on Jerusalem.

12

Impasse

1191 to 1192

S ALADIN DIVIDED HIS ARMY to block Richard's expected march inland, placing one body of troops across the road to Jerusalem through Tiberias on the Sea of Galilee, and another across the road that led to Jerusalem through Nazareth. Richard frustrated the Muslim leader by selecting a third alternative. He decided to move south down the coastal road to Ascalon, then turn inland to Jerusalem from a base on the sea that could be kept supplied by his fleet. On the march south along the shore, he could only be attacked from the landward side. His fleet would follow him offshore to keep his army supplied with food and to fend off any Egyptian fleet.

The Christian column of combined armies was almost two miles long. First came the Knights Templar with their own scouts ahead of them and on their flanks. Behind them marched the French Crusaders, followed by King Guy with the local barons and Richard's knights from his county of Poitou. Next came the English and Norman Crusaders, who had built a tower "as high as a minaret" on a great wagon, topped with a pole flying a huge banner with a cross. The Hospitallers made up the rear guard, on the watch for stragglers and deserters. When the ground permitted, the supply train and the herds of thousands of spare horses moved parallel with the army between the road and the sea, under the protection of Henry of Champagne, who resented the mundane role now assigned to him, but who would soon rise to royal heights of glory.

When Saladin became aware of Richard's chosen route, he sent engineers and laborers ahead of the Crusader army to dismantle the defenses of Caesarea, Jaffa and Ascalon, to prevent them being used as Christian fortifications. He moved his main army to a position on the slopes of Mt. Carmel. From there Saladin dispatched groups of mounted bowmen to harass the Christian column, and sent light cavalry units to follow the Crusaders and pick up stragglers. Those they could avoid killing were taken to Saladin's camp, where they paid the price for Richard's savagery at Ayyadieh. They were tortured to reveal whatever they might know of Richard's plans, then publicly executed.

An Arab chronicler cited examples to show that this had become a war of vengeance: "...they brought two Franks to the Sultan who had been made prisoners by the advance guard. He had them beheaded on the spot, and the soldiers cut their bodies to pieces." Then, "Two other Frank prisoners were brought before the Sultan.... They were put to death in a most cruel manner, for the Sultan was terribly wroth at the massacre of the prisoners from Acre." The Muslims usually took women for the slave market, but when the Muslim raiders captured a group of fifteen Christian men and women, including a young woman of the nobility who would normally have been held for a substantial ransom, Saladin had them all beheaded in a public ceremony. Any mercy for Christians in this campaign was out of the question.

After a week on their march to the south, the Crusaders were getting closer to the Muslim army. Raids and sporadic fighting became commonplace, but the Christians kept their discipline and did not break their column. Richard usually rode in the van with the Knights Templar, but he occasionally rode back down the line, hearing stories of armored men already defeated by the burning sun, fainting and even dying from sunstroke in the summer heat. Those who dropped had to be picked up and carried along, because anyone left behind would most certainly be tortured and killed by the Muslim raiders.

Two Bedouin Arabs had come to King Richard to inform him that the Muslim army was very small. Deciding to test the good news for himself, he sent a detachment to reconnoiter. The scouting party was hit hard by a Muslim division, and more Christian knights had to rush into the battle to rescue their companions from an ever-increasing horde of Muslim cavalry. After fighting their way back to the protection of the main army, the Crusaders tallied almost a thousand men killed or wounded. Richard sent for the two Bedouin informers, who were waiting to receive a rich reward for their information. Instead, they were forced to their knees and had their heads cut off.

Saladin had the advantage of picking the ground for the coming battle and chose a plain just north of the coastal town of Arsuf, where he could maneuver the thousands of light cavalry that were his main strength. Richard's scouts brought word of the Muslim army's battle position, so on September 5, 1191, eighteen days out of Acre, Richard placed his men for battle by turning the Christian column to face inland, with the sea at their backs.

The Templars in the van became the Christian extreme right wing, the Hospitallers at the rear turned to become the left. Richard took up his place in the center, with the main army of secular knights. A line of crossbowmen and spearmen with shields was placed out in front of the knights to hold the Muslim bowmen out of range of the Crusaders' horses.

In a decision that must have been difficult for a man of his temperament, Richard decided to stay on the defensive, holding his ground as the Muslims hammered steadily on the Christian left, where the Hospitallers bore the brunt of wave after wave of swift charges by mounted Muslim archers and swordsmen. Christians fell in every attack. Finally the grand master of the Hospitallers reported to Richard that his sector would collapse if not relieved soon, but Richard was not ready. Like the Templars, the Hospitallers had a firm rule ordering severe punishment for any knight who broke ranks without orders, but under the incessant Muslim attacks, the Hospitaller knights were writhing with frustration.

Just minutes before Richard had planned to order to attack, a Hospitaller and a secular knight gave in to their desperation. Shouting their battle cries, they charged toward the Muslims. Their companions immediately surged forward after them, followed by the Flemish knights next to them. Soon a great wave undulated down the whole Christian line, as every Christian knight joined in the charge, including the entire Templar contingent. Richard, momentarily shocked by the move, quickly dug in his spurs and galloped to the center of the battle. The Muslim horsemen, who had had it all their own way to that point, now saw coming at them thousands of armored knights, astride their massive horses, wielding lances, swords, and battle-axes. Some of the lightly armed Muslim horsemen came forward to give battle, but most broke and ran.

In the end it was their reputation, not their valor, that saved Saladin's army. Richard had been told, as had the other recently arrived Crusaders, of the favorite battle tactic of the Muslims. They would pretend to be retreating in a desperate rout, flying from the battlefield in a maneuver that usually brought their triumphant enemies in fast pursuit into a carefully prepared trap. Caution had been emphasized repeatedly, so now, when the Muslims were truly in a flight for their lives, there was no pursuit. The Christian horsemen stayed on the field in commendable discipline, while the surviving Muslims thankfully rode into the hills to safety.

Although Richard had not ordered the charge, his personal

actions throughout the combat drew praise from all who had seen him, and he got all the credit. This was the first Christian victory in open war since the Horns of Hattin, and spirits soared. Richard was a hero and Crusader morale was at a peak.

Saladin suffered the opposite reaction. First he had been stopped at Tyre. Then there was the loss of Acre, and now this humiliating defeat in the field. Rumors spread throughout his troops that Saladin's health was working against him. In addition to the agony of his hideous boils, he was now suffering repeated attacks of malaria. The rumors were true, but Saladin was far from finished. Richard had won the Battle of Arsuf, but by no means had he won the war. The sultan's army was still intact, and he ordered it now to Ramleh, to block the road from the coast to Jerusalem. He had already sent out messengers to his vassals throughout his empire, ordering that more men and supplies be sent to him.

Saladin was correct in his perception of Richard's ultimate target, but Richard was in no hurry. He took his army to the port city of Jaffa, which he decided would be his base for seaborne supplies to support the coming inland campaign. He set his troops to rebuilding the fortifications that Saladin's engineers had torn down.

As if the military and political problems of the Holy Land were not enough, Richard received news of problems in the lands he had left behind. Richard had been concerned that he could never effectively administer the government of Cyprus from Europe, and now he learned that of the two vassal barons he had left in charge of Cyprus, one was dead and the other was fighting back against a revolt of the local population. The other bad news, that his brother John was usurping power and stirring up the great barons of England, meant that Richard must return home soon. He decided to solve the problem of Cyprus and build his war chest at the same time by selling off Cyprus to the Knights Templar, an idea that probably came from the Templar grand master de Sablé. The Templars agreed to buy the island kingdom for one hundred thousand gold bezants, paying forty thousand down with the balance to be paid from the considerable revenues of the island. Cyprus was the largest and by far the richest property the Templars would ever own. It was an ideal trading center, with ports facing Egypt to the south, Syria to the east, and Byzantium to the north. It had productive copper mines and fertile farms, with extensive orchards of citrus fruits that were always in demand.

Unfortunately, the Knights Templar, totally committed to an active military campaign, could spare few men to govern Cyprus. Only fourteen men were sent, under the command of Templar brother Armand Bouchart. Even more unfortunate, these were rough fighting men, not administrators of the type that might have been called in from the Templar preceptories in Europe, had time permitted.

With an increasingly urgent need to get back to Europe, Richard tried negotiation, even suggesting that his sister, the widowed Queen Joanna, should marry Saladin's brother al-Adil. From their capital in Jerusalem the royal couple would rule all of Palestine—except for the lost properties of the Knights Templar and the Hospitallers, which would be restored to them—in a combined Christian/Muslim rule. No one liked that strange idea, least of all the prospective bride and groom, both of whom vehemently rejected Richard's proposal.

While Richard's mind was giving vent to fantasy, Conrad of Montferrat was conducting his own negotiations with Saladin, with much more practical proposals. In exchange for Sidon and Beirut, Conrad would break away from the other Crusaders to form an independent state. His emissaries hinted that he might even discuss the return of Acre to Saladin. The negotiations were put on hold when Saladin suggested that Conrad's proposal would only be acceptable if Conrad would agree to join the Muslims on the battlefield in their war against Richard. That move would make Conrad an outcast to every Latin Christian in the world.

Saladin did encourage the continuation of talks with Richard, with the clear knowledge that the flamboyant king, sooner or later, would leave Palestine for his homeland. Conrad, on the other hand, whose military and administrative skills the Muslims respected, would be staying behind to assert the rights he had acquired upon his marriage to Princess Isabella of Jerusalem.

The talks back and forth with Richard went on for so many weeks that the whole campaign was dampened by the beginning of the winter rains. Warfare was traditionally abandoned during the winter months. Saladin sent half of his men home to rest, while moving his court and part of his troops behind the walls of Jerusalem. The balance of his army, reinforced by fresh forces called up from Egypt, camped in the protection of the nearby hills.

Rain or no rain, Richard decided that it was a good time to take action. He ignored the warnings of the resident Templars and the local barons that the gentle rains would inevitably turn into torrential rains driven by fierce winds.

In mid-November 1191, Richard took his army up the Jerusalem road to the site of the fortress of Ramleh, which the Saracens had torn down. He sat there for six weeks while the rains grew steadily heavier and the winds fiercer. On December 28, he went on the march toward Jerusalem, with his whole army wallowing in a great sea of mud. It took them five days to reach the fortress of Beit-Nuba, only twelve miles from the Holy City.

As Richard planned his grand assault on Jerusalem, the Knights Templar, the Hospitallers, and even his own barons tried to get him to face reality. The wind was so strong that the men couldn't even put up their tents. With no protection, the entire army was soaked to the skin. Their bread was a soggy mass and the rest of the food was ruined. No one could possibly assemble siege engines under these weather conditions, and even if they did manage to set up a siege around the city perimeter, no part of that strung-out Christian army would be safe from attacks on their rear by the Egyptian army waiting in the hills. They were simply inviting disaster. Slowly, reluctantly, Richard gave in to the power of common sense and ordered the retreat back to Ramleh. After a few days of rest there, he took the army all the way back to the coast at Ascalon, where his men spent the next four months rebuilding the walls that Saladin's engineers had leveled to the ground. Ascalon was the gateway to Egypt, and as he watched from Jerusalem, Saladin became concerned that Richard might have decided to invade Egypt, which he could easily reach before Saladin could catch up with him.

Conrad was still sending emissaries for talks with Saladin, but the sultan wanted an agreement with Richard first. On March 20, 1192, Saladin's brother al-Adil called on Richard personally to propose a treaty. The Christians could keep all of the lands and cities they had taken and could even have the city of Beirut if its walls were dismantled. The relic of the True Cross would be returned, and all Christians would be free to practice their religion and make pilgrimages into Jerusalem to the Church of the Holy Sepulcher. The Roman Church would be permitted to have priests in attendance.

To Richard, it was an effective compromise. With that agreement reached, he could answer the pleas of the prior of Hereford, who had arrived from England to report to Richard that things had grown worse at home and that his brother John was ruthlessly taking personal control of Richard's kingdom. There was just one more important issue to settle before returning to England, and that was the matter of who would occupy the throne of Jerusalem. Richard called a council of the high nobility of the Holy Land to put the matter to rest.

In assembly, the barons were offered the choice of Conrad of Montferrat or Guy of Lusignan. Opinions were expressed that Guy had been king only because of his marriage to Princess Sibylla. Any rights he had to the crown of Jerusalem had died with her. Princess Isabella was the legal heiress, and as her husband, Conrad of Montferrat had a legal right to the throne of Jerusalem. Besides, by his leadership at Tyre Conrad had saved the Holy Land from the disaster worked upon it by Guy of Lusignan at the Horns of Hattin. When the discussion died, Richard realized that not one man had spoken in Guy's favor, so the choice was clear. Guy had supported Richard in every way since his arrival, and the two had become friends, but Guy of Lusignan could not be the king of Jerusalem.

Richard's nephew, Count Henry of Champagne, was sent to Tyre to deliver the good news to Conrad. When the announcement was made public, the whole city went wild with joy. Conrad agreed that his coronation would take place in the cathedral at Acre a couple of weeks later, to allow Richard and his barons time to attend. A great medieval pageant could be expected, and at Conrad's request Count Henry went off to Acre to make the arrangements.

Before that regal event could take place, a shock came that reverberated across the Holy Land. The man who set it in motion was Sheikh Sinan, the Old Man of the Mountain, the ruler of the Shiite sect of Assassins.

The Assassins had taken no part in the conflicts of recent months, content to watch two enemies killing each other off. As Ismaili Shiites they hated the Sunni Kurd Saladin. They would have been happy to see a Christian victory, but during the prior year Conrad had aroused their anger by seizing a fully loaded merchant ship that belonged to the Assassin sect. He had stolen the cargo and the ship for himself and had the crew thrown overboard to drown. Such an act cried out for vengeance, and if there was one special skill that had been mastered by the Assassins, it was vengeance.

Sinan sent two carefully coached Assassins into Tyre. They were educated, well dressed, and provided with ample funds, all calculated to convey the outward image of impeccable members of the Muslim aristocracy. Once in Tyre, they professed a desire to embrace Christianity and so came to the attention of Conrad, who actually acted as their sponsor at their baptism into the Roman Catholic faith. They became a familiar sight around Tyre and even at Conrad's court.

Just one week after receiving the joyous news of his choice as king of Jerusalem, Conrad strolled out to visit his good friend the bishop of Beauvais. As he walked home, Conrad was completely relaxed, graciously accepting the greetings of homage from the people he passed in the street. The two familiar Muslim converts approached him, saying that they had a letter for him. As Conrad reached for the letter, one of the men grabbed his sword hand while the other plunged a dagger deep into Conrad's body.

One of the Assassins was killed immediately by men in the street, but the other was taken alive. While the dying Conrad was being carried to his palace, the captured murderer was dragged to the torture chamber. He was fully prepared for death, but not for the horrible agonies that were inflicted upon him now. Finally, just to hasten the death that he knew would come as soon as the torture stopped, he confessed that he was an Assassin sent by Sheikh Sinan to murder the future king. The confession satisfied his questioners that he had told everything he knew and earned him the swift death he had hoped for.

Henry of Champagne hurried back to Tyre when he got the news. To the local citizens, the handsome young count appeared to provide the ideal solution to the problem of finding a new husband for Isabella, a man who would then be eligible to reign as king of Jerusalem. Princess Isabella, a beautiful young woman twenty-one years of age, had not had much success at marriage. She had been married first to the handsome but homosexual Humphrey of Toron, and then to the stern, middle-aged Conrad of Montferrat, by whom she had an infant daughter. Perhaps a third marriage, with this dashing, wealthy, popular man, would be the answer. She agreed to the marriage with Henry.

King Richard, who had also hastened to reach Tyre upon learning of Conrad's murder, enthusiastically supported his nephew as the next ruler of Jerusalem. Normally, the Church required one year of mourning before a widow could remarry, but this was an emergency. As for Isabella, one week seemed more than enough time to mourn the passing of the domineering Conrad of Montferrat. The wedding took place just seven days after Conrad's death, and Henry of Troyes, count of Champagne, became King Henry of Jerusalem. He established his capital at Acre.

As for Guy of Lusignan, he may well have pondered regaining the throne by marrying his dead wife's sister, but the Church held that marriage to an in-law was as much an act of incest as marriage to a close blood relative. Guy seemed to be completely left out in the cold, but then destiny gave him a reward much more valuable than the remnants of the kingdom of Jerusalem.

The Knights Templar had failed miserably in their attempts to govern the island of Cyprus. Their arrogance in taking whatever they wanted, and their insulting treatment of the local barons and people, had generated increasing animosity that finally broke out into an open revolt. Brother Bouchart had been driven back to seek the safety of a Templar castle and ordered all the Templar knights and sergeants on the island to come to him. When fully assembled, they stormed out of the castle in a fierce attack on the local population. The results were bloody enough to submerge the revolt for the moment, but Bouchart could only report to Grand Master de Sablé that a much greater rebellion could break out at any minute, which his handful of Templars could not hope to repel.

The grand master discussed the problems of Cyprus with his friend Richard, suggesting that the Knights Templar would like to sell Cyprus back to him. Instead, Richard used the Templar dilemma to solve his own problem of how to provide for Guy of Lusignan, who had supported him so faithfully and who had been responsible for saving Cyprus for Richard during his illness on the island. He talked Guy into buying Cyprus from the Templars. The Italian merchants were eager to advance Guy the money for the down payment, to be repaid out of the island's revenues, because they well knew the advantages that Cyprus held for trade. They negotiated concessions because they knew that ports and trading centers in Cyprus were much safer and easier to defend than their counterparts on the mainland. Agreeing that the Templars would keep their castles and lands on the island, Guy sailed off to become king of Cyprus, a kingdom that would be ruled by his family for the next three hundred years, and for long after the Christians had been driven out of the Holy Land.

Richard was pleased that the affairs of the Christian kingdom were being sorted out so well, but he was not at all pleased that Saladin had shelved the final arrangements for the treaty between them. The sultan had personally taken an army to Mesopotamia (now Iraq) to put down a rebellion led by one of his own nephews. While waiting for his return Richard was growing impatient and, typically, craving some action.

Saladin's absence gave Richard a chance that he decided not to pass up: He would take the walled city of Daron on the border between Egypt and Palestine. Taking part of his army and a contingent of Knights Templar, Richard moved south on Daron by land and sea. Five days later the city was his, and the castle garrison had surrendered. Some of the Muslim soldiers were taken prisoner, but many were killed where they were found in the citadel. One group was reserved for a senseless theater of death that perhaps was staged to provoke a response from Saladin, or perhaps just to provide a show for Richard's troops outside the city, as part of their victory celebration. Richard had the Muslim prisoners taken to the top of the high wall, from which they were ceremoniously flung to their deaths, one at a time, in full view of his cheering army of triumphant Christians.

Now joined at Ascalon by King Henry and exhilarated by their latest victory, the Crusaders clamored for a march on Jerusalem, to which Richard readily agreed. On June 7, 1192, the Crusader army marched inland to attack the Holy City. Once again, they set up camp at Beit-Nuba, twelve miles from Jerusalem and a two-day march through the hills. Saladin waited in Jerusalem, welcoming the reinforcements that were coming to him from Egypt and Syria. He was convinced that Richard would not besiege the city, because his spies had told him that the Christians did not have the supplies necessary to stay in the field more than a few weeks.

Richard's spies were busy, too. A group of Bedouin Arabs he had hired reported to him that the largest caravan any of them had ever seen was near the foothills of Hebron, moving toward the Holy City. It was a long-awaited supply train coming to the sultan's army from Egypt. Saladin's own chronicler Beha ed-Din tells the story, which is worth recounting in detail, because it shows why Richard was so highly regarded as a soldier and field commander:

"When [Richard] received certain information that the caravan was close at hand...a thousand horsemen set out, each of whom took a foot soldier [on his horse] in front of him....The Sultan, who had received intelligence of the enemy's movements, sent word to the caravan. The officers sent by Saladin were given instructions to take the caravan through the desert, and to avoid the neighborhood of the Franks, for an encounter was to be dreaded above all things."

The Muslim officers disregarded their orders, deciding that since they had seen no Christians on their way to the caravan, the same route should provide safe travel on the way back. The leader had been advised to have the caravan continue by night, to get out of the area as soon as possible, but he disregarded that advice, too, afraid that the caravan might get scattered on a night march. He halted at an oasis about ten miles north of Beersheba, where the caravan settled down for a night's sleep, within easy reach of the Christians who had been moving in that direction. Richard's Arab spies hurried to give him the good news.

"...When this was reported to the King of England he did not believe it, but mounted and set out with a small escort. When he came up to the caravan, he disguised himself as an Arab, and went all around it. When he saw that quiet reigned in their camp, and that everyone was fast asleep, he returned, and ordered his troops into the saddle. At daybreak, he took the great caravan unawares, falling on it with his infantry and cavalry.... This was a most disgraceful event: It was long since Islam had sustained so serious a disaster."

How serious? Three thousand camels, three thousand horses, five hundred prisoners, and a mountain of food and military supplies. "Never was the Sultan more grieved or rendered more anxious." And no longer could Saladin take comfort from the thought that Richard was running low on supplies.

Richard's good fortune at being resupplied by his enemy indicated the probability of an early attack on Jerusalem. Saladin ordered out men to block up or contaminate every well between Beit-Nuba and the Holy City. The Crusaders might have an abundant supply of food, but they would not be able to survive for very long without water. Saladin also had to police his own forces, because age-old hatreds had erupted into violence between his Turkish troops and the mountain fighters from Kurdistan.

Saladin was right. Men and animals needed water. Without it, thirst brought them to their knees in days, not weeks. Christians began to drop, then to die. Richard was forced to order a retreat to the coast, much to the anger of many of the leading barons (who probably had commandeered what little water there was). Richard apparently felt no better about losing his dream of glory than his soldiers did: There is a legend that while scouting in the nearby hills, he caught a glimpse of the sun reflecting off the gleaming roof-tops of Jerusalem. He quickly pulled his shield in front of his face, because he had no right to look on the Holy City that he had failed to conquer for Christendom.

Once again, Richard turned to negotiation with Saladin. He went to Acre with Grand Master de Sablé, who had established the new headquarters of the Knights Templar in that city. Richard's plan was to return to England to deal with his pressing problems there, without waiting for a formal treaty with Saladin to be finalized, but in his absence Saladin seized the opportunity to lead his forces in an attack on Jaffa. With no opposition to face from the army that Richard had taken away with him, the Muslims had no trouble breaking into the town. The Turks and Kurds gave up attacking each other to turn their anger against the resident Christians, and they ran through the streets competing in the killing and looting, totally out of control. The Christian garrison in the citadel had indicated a desire to negotiate terms of surrender, but Saladin sent word that they should stay in the citadel until he could bring his troops under control. It was the only way to assure their safety.

A fast rider had been sent off to Acre as soon as Saladin's army had been sighted, and Richard leaped to the rescue, so quickly that he didn't even take the time to put on his boots. He sent his army to Jaffa overland, but took eighty knights and four hundred crossbowmen with him on ships of Pisa and Genoa.

Saladin had brought his troops back under his control and had marched the main body away from the city. The knights of Jaffa were just beginning to march out of the citadel to surrender when the Muslim lookouts shouted out the sighting of Richard's fleet. The Christian knights immediately drew their swords, fought their way back into the citadel, and barred the great door. A Latin priest threw off his robe and swam out to tell Richard that the citadel had not fallen. To save time, Richard had the ships ram the sandy beach in front of the citadel like landing craft, so that he and his men could go over the sides and wade ashore. Caught up in the heady fever of battle, about two thousand Italian sailors and marines grabbed weapons and followed him onto the beach.

The unprepared Saracens, dispersed throughout the streets and houses, had no time to muster a unified defense. They collapsed under the ferocious Christian attack, which was reinforced by the garrison that now streamed out of the citadel. Within minutes the Muslims were in flight from the city.

Saladin's main army was about five miles inland, but the sultan ordered it back to the coast when he learned that Richard had only about two thousand men, who were camped outside Jaffa in an unprotected position. His scouts had already reported to him that Richard's main army was marching down from Acre, so he had decided to attack the English king in his weak condition before his army could arrive. He ordered the assault for dawn of the following day.

Saladin's arrival would have been a complete surprise to the Christians if not for the good fortune of a restless Genoese sailor who was up early, taking a stroll outside the camp. As the sun rose, he began to see flickering points of reflected sunlight in the distance, reflections off the Muslim weapons. He ran to rouse the camp, and Richard put the remaining time to extraordinarily good use.

First, a low picket of tent pegs was fixed in the ground to confuse and trip the Muslim horses. Well behind them, Richard set his line of spearmen, packed close together. Each man planted the bottom of his shield in the soft ground, then knelt with the butt of his spear in the earth, with the point angled to impale any horse that tried to crash the line. Behind the shield wall Richard placed half of his four hundred crossbowmen. The other half were placed directly behind them. The crossbow was slow to draw, so Richard had decided on a shorter front, with half his archers firing twice as fast. As the marksman in front picked his target, the man behind loaded for him. The Muslim cavalry had never experienced such rapid crossbow fire, and Richard had once again proven his superior skills in battle as the shield wall withstood seven charges, with each succeeding charge slowed down and confused by the growing number of fallen Muslim men and horses in front of the Christian lines.

When Richard felt that the Muslim horses were exhausted, he mounted one of the ten horses in the Christian camp and led his spearmen out in a charge of infantry against cavalry. He was in the thick of the fight, which Saladin from a nearby rise watched with grudging admiration. When Richard's horse fell under him, Saladin, who had hated the English king since the Massacre of Ayyadieh, gave in to an awed respect for this gold-bearded war god and sent two fresh horses to him in the middle of the fight, then recalled his army and left Jaffa to Richard.

His victories should have given Richard the advantage in the ensuing peace negotiations, but his position was compromised by his public declaration that, as soon as possible, he was going back to England. Had he stayed, he might have fought Saladin's condition that the Christians abandon Ascalon, but finally he gave in, agreeing to abandon the city his own men had rebuilt.

On September 2, 1192, Saladin signed a treaty of peace for five years and swore to uphold its terms. Richard agreed to the treaty but would take no oath to defend its terms, because he would be a thousand miles away. Instead, Saladin consented to the oaths being sworn by King Henry of Jerusalem, Grand Master de Sablé of the Knights Templar, and the grand master of the Hospitallers.

The Third Crusade had checked the Muslim advance and had regained lost territories, but it had not accomplished the recapture of the Holy City of Jerusalem. The Knights Templar had not regained their original headquarters in the al-Aqsa Mosque on the Temple Mount. For the next hundred years they would have to live with the embarrassing truth that they could lay no claim to the building that stood on the site of the Temple of Solomon, the ancient shrine to God from which they had taken their name.

Lacking the wisdom of hindsight, the Knights Templar would never understand that the great tragedy for their order in the Third Crusade lay in their sale of Cyprus. With its riches, they could easily have converted the Templar order to a sovereign state, as the Hospitallers were to do in the capture of the much smaller island of Rhodes, and later through their acquisition of the island of Malta. Cyprus generated more revenues than all of the Templars' European properties combined. With it as their base they could never have been suppressed and disbanded as they would be in the reign of Pope Clement V.

All that was in the future, but for the present the Templars could perform one more service for their friend Richard of England. He hated sea voyages, but after his actions at Cyprus he did not want to risk travel through Byzantine territory. He would go by ship only to the head of the Adriatic near Venice and continue overland from there. There was some risk in having to cross the lands of Duke Leopold of Austria, whose banner Richard's men had desecrated, so Richard hit upon a plan to travel in disguise. Grand Master de

Sablé provided Richard with the costume and equipment of a Templar Knight and appointed several Templar brothers to accompany him. The party set sail in October 1192.

The king and his companions succeeded in reaching the Adriatic Sea undetected, but a storm wrecked their ship on the northern coast of Yugoslavia. The Templar party proceeded on land almost to Vienna, but Richard was totally incapable of playing the role of a monastic knight. His imperious bearing and loud arrogance attracted attention and led to his capture. Duke Leopold was delighted to have in his power the man who had humiliated him by pulling the banner of Austria from the wall of Acre and hurling it into the ditch, and to surrender him to the German emperor. Richard was finally ransomed, but his people were taxed into a state of near-destitution to raise the money.

Within six months after Richard had left the Holy Land, fate rang down the final curtain on the most memorable and romanticized Muslim leader of them all. Saladin fell seriously ill and died on March 3, 1192. It had taken Saladin many years to fuse a mighty empire. It took his family just a few weeks to tear it apart.

13

The Sons of Saladin

1193 to 1199

SALADIN, WHO HAD TAKEN advantage of the Prophet's permission to have multiple wives, left seventeen sons behind him, all of whom had to be provided for. The oldest, al-Afdal, who was twenty-two years old, got off to a bad start by calling Muslim nobles together to demand their sworn allegiance to him. They resented his requirement that they swear to divorce their wives and disinherit their children as a penalty for breaking their oaths of allegiance. His unbounded arrogance put them off.

His young brother al-Aziz was in Cairo, where he declared himself to be the sultan of Egypt. Another brother, az-Sahir, held the city of Aleppo, the former capital, and declared himself a sovereign ruler. The sons of Saladin regarded each other only with suspicion, which was well justified in the case of al-Aziz. He went so far as to take an Egyptian army to the very walls of Damascus, from which he withdrew only when al-Afdal agreed that al-Aziz could add Judea to his Egyptian empire. Of Saladin's two surviving brothers, Toghtekin held Yemen and al-Adil controlled the recently conquered Christian county of Oultrejourdain. The Muslim lands that Saladin had welded into a single state were totally disintegrated, awaiting another leader strong enough to pull them together. Al-Afdal finally proved equal to the task, but it took him eight years to do it.

The turmoil in Islam should have meant an opportunity for the Crusader states to regain some of their lost territories, but the Christian leaders were just as divided as the Muslims.

At the end of the first year of his reign as king of Jerusalem, Henry discovered that the merchant colony of Pisa in the city of Tyre was plotting to seize the city and turn it over to Guy of Lusignan. They had loaned Guy funds with which to buy Cyprus, and he had been generous to them in trading concessions. Henry, on the other hand, had favored the merchants of Genoa. As for King Guy, he would be happy to have back any part of his old kingdom.

Henry's response to the plot was to imprison the Pisan leaders and to eject the Pisan merchants from Tyre. Their answer was to raid the coastal settlements between Tyre and Acre, so Henry ejected the Pisans from Acre as well. Amalric of Lusignan, who many years before had schemed with Lady Agnes of Courtenay to bring his younger brother Guy from France, was still constable of the kingdom. He pleaded with Henry on behalf of the Pisans. That so angered Henry that he decided that if Amalric liked the Pisans so much, perhaps he would like to share their dungeon with them, and put him in chains.

The Knights Templar, who had been the political allies of the Lusignan family for a generation, now petitioned Henry for the release of their friend. Henry may have resented the Templars' interference with the affairs of the kingdom, but he desperately needed the support of the military orders. When the Hospitallers joined in the plea, Henry had no choice, and he reluctantly let Amalric go free.

Once out of Henry's prison, Amalric decided to get as far away from Henry as he could. He moved his family south to Jaffa. There he would be safe, because King Richard had made Amalric's brother Geoffrey the governor of the city. When Geoffrey decided to go back to France, Amalric of Lusignan became lord of Jaffa.

While Henry was facing his problems in Acre and Tyre, there were more problems to the north in the principality of Antioch, where Prince Leo of Armenia had been encroaching. Two years earlier, during his march into Antioch, Saladin had captured the lofty castle of the Knights Templar at Baghras. Since he could not hold it, he had ordered his engineers to take it down. When Saladin's engineers left, Prince Leo moved in with an army of workmen. Saladin's men had dismantled the castle, but the foundations and the stones were still there. Leo had his people rebuild the castle, then took possession of it for himself, along with a sizable piece of the frontier lands of Antioch.

Prince Bohemond demanded that Baghras be returned to the Knights Templar. Armenians in that castle meant a threat to him personally, but Knights Templar in the castle would mean security, the same security he felt with the Templar control of the castle of Tortosa on the northern coast. The Knights Templar wanted the castle back as much as Prince Bohemond wanted them to have it, even to the point of discussing retaking it by force.

Such thoughts were put off by the sudden illness and death of

Grand Master de Sablé in September 1193. Perhaps it was that event, which left the Knights Templar temporarily without a supreme commander, that prompted Prince Leo a month later to invite Prince Bohemond to Baghras to settle the matter of the ownership of the castle. Prince Behomond traveled in state, accompanied by his wife Sibylla. As soon as Bohemond and his party were inside the gate of Baghras, they were surrounded and made Leo's prisoners. His price for their release was that Bohemond must recognize Leo as his feudal lord, giving Leo the ultimate authority over Antioch. Bohemond's life was at stake, so he felt he had no choice but to agree.

Prince Leo immediately dispatched Armenian troops to take possession of the capital. The citizens of Antioch offered no resistance, because the Armenians were there with the approval of their ruler, Prince Bohemond. On religious grounds alone, though, the Armenians were not easy to accept. The Greeks in Antioch regarded the Separated Armenian Church as heretical since it had broken away from their own Greek Orthodox faith. The Latin Christians had been taught that their new Armenian over-lords were heretics because they would not recognize the pope in Rome. The Knights Templar and the Hospitallers owed their allegiance to the pope alone and had never functioned outside Roman Catholic lands except in battle. The Italian merchants seldom had religious problems, but they were uncertain about what was going to happen to their lucrative trade concessions under Armenian domination.

It was religious animosity that triggered the solution. Saint Hilary was the patron saint of the palace chapel, which was served by a chapter of French monks. One day in a gathering at the palace an Armenian officer made such insulting remarks about the French saint that one of the French monks abandoned his benign humility to begin throwing stones at him. Armenian soldiers grabbed the monk, and in turn were jumped upon by Latin Christians. The fight quickly spread from the chapel into the rest of the palace as pent-up hatreds broke loose. The riot spilled from the palace into the streets, where hundreds more antagonists enthusiastically entered the battle.

The small band of Armenians was no match for the entire popula-tion of Antioch, so they were easily ejected from the city. As the Armenians fled back to the safety of Baghras, the leaders of Antioch gathered in St. Peter's Cathedral. They elected a governing commune of prominent citizens, who convened to swear their allegiance to Prince Bohemond's son Raymond for as long as his father was held captive by the Armenians. Letters were dispatched to Raymond's brother Count Bohemond of Tripoli, as well as to King Henry of Jerusalem, asking their help to save the city from the ambitious Armenian ruler.

It was a time of great political stress, but the Knights Templar still had not met to elect a new grand master. Now the grand chapter felt the need to act. They decided to give the leadership to a man whose entire adult life had been one of service to the order. He had served as preceptor of Jerusalem, master of the Templars of Spain and Provence, and deputy grand master of the order. Passed over twice in the elections of Gerard de Ridfort and Robert de Sablé, his time had come. Gilbert Erail became the twelfth grand master.

Another election took place that year that would impact the Knights Templar and all other Christians in the Holy Land, but even had they known of it they would have denied that it could ever affect them. It was too far away, thousands of miles off to the east. In this year of 1194 a twenty-seven-year-old chieftain named Temujin was chosen as the *khan*, the "lord," of all the Mongol clans. He was given the name *Genghis*, the "powerful." No one gave him the name "Scourge of God." He would earn that for himself.

In the spring of that year King Henry of Jerusalem decided that he must settle the threat of conflict between Antioch and Armenia. He proceeded north with a large armed escort and was met along the way by ambassadors of the new chief of the Assassins. With Sheikh Sinan dead, the new leader of the sect wanted to effect an alliance with the Latin Christians, who were less threatening to his followers than the Sunni sons of Saladin. Henry agreed to a meeting and was led to the principal Assassin castle, perched on a crag in the nearby Nosairi mountains. There he was entertained regally and found himself the recipient of many lavish gifts. Then came an "entertainment" that stunned him with disbelief.

The Assassin leader, holding forth on how valuable his friendship could be because of the extraordinary loyalty and obedience of his followers, pointed up to a group of young men gathered on the highest tower of the castle. At his signal, one of them climbed up on the parapet and flung himself to certain death on the rocks below. Moments later, another man followed him over the wall. Apparently they were all prepared to die just to help their leader demonstrate his point, but Henry pleaded with him to stop. Henry was now anxious to leave these crazy people, but not before the chief made one more gracious gesture to bind their new alliance. He offered to prove his good will toward Henry by arranging the murders of any of his opponents the Christian king would care to designate. Henry counted himself lucky to get out of the Assassin castle alive.

Continuing his northward march, Henry entered Armenian territory and went to Leo's capital at Sis. He found Leo with no desire for open warfare and anxious to negotiate. Leo agreed to release Prince Bohemond from captivity and to abandon his claim to the overlordship of Antioch. In exchange, Henry agreed that Leo could keep Baghras and the lands around it, which would henceforth be recognized as Armenian territory. To bind the treaty and to some-day combine Armenia and Antioch under a single ruler, it was agreed that Leo's heiress and niece, the princess Alice, would marry Prince Bohemond's son Raymond. An impediment to the plan was that Alice was already married to an Armenian noble named Hethoum. Henry had no way to eliminate that barrier to the alliance, but the problem went away a few days later when Hethoum was murdered. Henry may have thought that his new Assassin allies were already at work for his benefit, but he chose not to investigate.

Henry returned to Acre to receive the praises of his subjects for achieving the peace, but he received none from the Knights Templar. Henry had traded away their claim to the castle of Baghras to achieve a political goal of his own, and the Templars were angry. Henry also had to be aware that the Templars had developed tighter bonds with their old ally Guy of Lusignan and had been rewarded with more lands on Cyprus. The same was true of many of Henry's former vassals, the landless barons who went to Cyprus to serve King Guy in exchange for lands to replace those they had lost to Saladin. Henry had regarded Guy of Lusignan as his most dangerous rival, but Guy stopped being a threat when he died in May of that year, 1194. Henry felt that as the king of Jerusalem he should have a strong say in the choice of a successor, but the barons of Cyprus disagreed with him. They wanted someone who would put the interests of Cyprus first. The barons sent to Jaffa for Guy's older brother, Amalric. He quickly agreed to be their king, and now there was no question that Henry would have to swallow a little pride and seek a spirit of friendly cooperation with a man he had once imprisoned. The Knights Templar were pleased, because Amalric had been their friend and ally since the days before the fall of Jerusalem.

Henry and Amalric met, and the solution they worked out to resolve the destructive rivalry of their two kingdoms was the same solution Henry had used to settle the differences between Armenia and Antioch: They would set their thrones on a path that would someday combine them in a single heir. Amalric's three young sons would be betrothed to Isabella's daughters Maria, fathered by Conrad of Montferrat, and Philippa and Alice, daughters of Henry of Champagne.

For now, Amalric was concerned about confirmation of his kingship and a formal coronation. To a Latin Christian such confirmation could only come from a pope or an emperor. He certainly could not turn to the emperor of Byzantium, who considered the kingdom of Cyprus to be property stolen from him. He was afraid of the pope, who might decree that he could only be king if he would agree to be subservient to the kingdom of Jerusalem. That left the German emperor, Henry. In 1195 Amalric sent an ambassador to the emperor to plead his case.

As it happened, the emperor was in a receptive frame of mind because he was still disturbed by the pathetic contribution of the Germans to the Third Crusade. It could be said that their failure resulted from the untimely death of his father, Frederick Barbarossa, but Emperor Henry felt a residue of personal humiliation. He was considering another Crusade, to be led by himself, and a vassal state in the Middle East could be of great value. He agreed to bestow the crown of Cyprus on Amalric and sent him a royal scepter as a pledge of the coming coronation.

Emperor Henry's brother, Philip of Swabia, was eager to go on Crusade with him. Philip, married to a daughter of the Byzantine emperor, Isaac Angelus, had received word that his father-in-law had been deposed. Isaac Angelus was known everywhere for having built the most opulent personal lifestyle in all the world, and perhaps in the whole history of the world. It took twenty thousand personal servants—eunuchs, slaves, and domestics—to operate his household. It was said to cost four million gold bezants a year to cover Isaac's personal expenses, a statistic no Greek citizen would question, as ever-increasing taxes were forced on them to maintain the constantly escalating living standard of the money-mad emperor.

It had to stop somewhere, and Isaac's brother Alexius decided to do the stopping. He sent his personal guards to arrest Isaac, who had just enough warning to get away. Alexius's men pursued Isaac for fifty miles into the mountains before they caught up with him and sent him back in chains. Alexius was deaf to his brother's pleas and ordered him into a tower dungeon. There the royal executioner was ordered to blind Isaac by piercing his eyeballs with a red-hot silver awl. No one could predict the impact of that cruel act on the entire future of the crusading concept.

Isaac's twelve-year-old son, also named Alexius, was made a prisoner but spared the brutality inflicted on his father. He was held in a kind of house arrest, from which he would ultimately escape to act as a pawn in one of the greatest crimes of rape and murder in Christian history.

Leo of Armenia learned of Amalric's petition to Emperor Henry to legitimize his crown, and Leo decided to do the same. He wanted the security of being a vassal of the greatest monarch in Europe, but he got no answer beyond the point that the emperor would consider the request when he got to the Holy Land. Leo then turned to the pope in Rome. Well aware that it was pure fantasy to imagine that the Roman pope would authorize the coronation of a king who did not recognize papal supremacy, Leo hinted that he might bring the whole Armenian people into the Roman fold. That approach accelerated a decision from Emperor Henry, who sent a message that he would grant a crown to Leo in exchange for the recognition of the Holy Roman Emperor as the overlord of Armenia. Henry wanted no expansion of papal power anywhere.

In August 1197 the first of Emperor Henry's German Crusaders reached the Holy Land. The troops came to Acre, but the imperial chancellor Conrad of Hildesheim, with the papal legate Archbishop of Mainz and the German nobles, put in first at Cyprus, following the orders of Emperor Henry to officially crown King Amalric and receive his homage.

The German troops assembling at Acre without their leaders didn't know and didn't care about the intricacies of local politics. They had come to fight the infidel and were ready to march into battle. Nor did any of them care that Henry of Champagne was opposed to any acts of war at this time. Henry had successfully maneuvered Saladin's sons into antagonistic positions against each other and wanted no war to force them to come together in common defense.

The Germans ignored him and marched off into Galilee to show the infidel the might of German arms. As King Henry had feared, al-Adil responded with a call to all Muslim potentates to cast aside their differences and unite against this fresh wave of unbelievers. Without waiting for the others, al-Adil took to the field and led out his mounted army, which showed its vast numbers to the Christian invaders from the hillcrests around them. With no real plan and no real leadership, surprised to find themselves so disastrously outnumbered, the Germans did not know how to react. No one gave the order, but the Germans suddenly broke to flee back to Acre. The foot soldiers marched as fast as they could, but they could not keep up with the mounted knights and sergeants galloping off ahead of them. The infantry was suddenly stranded alone and confused in the desert.

When King Henry got the news he hastily assembled his own knights and rode out to take charge of the leaderless German infantry. He placed them in line of battle and prepared to receive the cavalry of al-Adil.

The Muslim troops were ready to fight, but al-Adil had no intention of wasting them on a meaningless encounter in the open field. More constructively, he took his army on a wide sweep to the south and appeared on the coast before the walls of Jaffa.

In September, while on Cyprus Amalric was busy receiving his crown and scepter from the imperial chancellor, Henry in Acre was frantically assembling forces for the relief of Jaffa. He had made peace with the merchants of Pisa and now asked them to provide troops and ships to combat al-Adil. While waiting to welcome a Pisan delegation in a high room in his palace, Henry stood on the sill of a large window, watching his own troops being assembled in the courtyard below. He turned when the Pisan leaders entered the room. Still standing on the windowsill, Henry put one foot behind him to assume the posture of a courtly bow, but the foot went down on open air. As Henry started to fall backward his jester, a dwarf named Scarlet, grabbed his master to save him. The big man pulled the little one out the window with him, and they both crashed to their deaths on the stone pavement of the courtyard.

Henry's sudden death was understandably a shock. There was an active Muslim army in the field, and even with the help of a growing force of German Crusaders the kingdom of Jerusalem could not be allowed to remain leaderless for long. The obvious answer was the earliest possible wedding for Queen Isabella, who, still in her twenties, was now facing the prospect of a fourth husband being selected for her by men who wouldn't dream of asking her opinion.

Count Hugh of Tiberias suggested his younger brother Ralph, but the Knights Templar and the Hospitallers voiced their strong objections. Ralph could bring nothing to the throne. His family's lands in Galilee, along with their capital city of Tiberias, had been lost to Saladin after the battle at the Horns of Hattin. Now they had nothing but their titles and their proud lineage. Ralph would act as king not to serve the people, but to replenish the lost fortunes of his own family.

The Knights Templar were much happier with the suggestion from the papal legate, who had just come from the coronation of Amalric. Knowing that the pope would much prefer a united Christian government, he suggested that Queen Isabella marry the widowed King Amalric of Cyprus. The Templars immediately threw their support behind the papal legate's recommendation, because in Amalric they would have an old friend and ally ruling both kingdoms.

The Germans gave their support because Amalric had just given homage to Emperor Henry VI. If Amalric also ruled the mainland kingdom, it could only increase the influence of the German emperor, whose personal Crusade was just beginning. Only Isabella resisted. She had fallen in love with Henry of Champagne after their marriage and now was truly in mourning. She was pressured to put her duty ahead of her personal feelings, and the papal legate freely gave his dispensation from the one year of mourning required by the Church.

Amalric didn't wait for the marriage vows to set his own policies in motion. The new capital city of Acre was separated from the Christian county of Tripoli by the port cities of Sidon and Beirut, still in Muslim hands. In October 1197 Amalric turned to the Germans to solve that problem. With al-Adil occupied before Jaffa to the south, he encouraged the duke of Brabant to lead a German army north to take the coast between Acre and Tripoli. The troops found the city of Sidon still in a state of ruin, with no defenses, and simply walked in. The Muslims scurried out to seek refuge in the suburbs and surrounding small towns, where no one bothered them.

Beirut had been occupied by a Muslim pirate, who used it as a base from which to attack Christian ships. He was the real target of the expedition. Saladin's men had torn down the walls of Beirut, and the pirate chief did not have the manpower to rebuild them. As the Germans approached, he loaded his men and his treasure on his ships and sailed away. The coast had been restored to Christians and the Crusader lands were united again. For the Germans, there had been loot and victory with practically no fighting, so they were eager to do more. Led by their archbishop, the German Crusaders decided that they were ready to retake Jerusalem. Within a month of the conquest of Beirut they marched into Galilee again, this time to lay siege to the town and castle of Toron.

In January of 1198 Prince Leo of Armenia finally got his crown, and he was overwhelmed by the importance of the visitors who came to witness his coronation. It appeared that everyone wanted his friendship. An envoy from the emperor of Byzantium sent Leo a golden crown. The emperor Henry had sent a royal scepter. The religious rite of the coronation was performed by an Orthodox archbishop, a Roman archbishop, and the Jacobite Christian patriarch. Even Muslims were there, with gifts from the caliph of Baghdad. Now it appeared that the Knights Templar could never expect to recover their castle of Baghras.

During the same month another great pageant celebrated the marriage of Queen Isabella to King Amalric of Cyprus. Those who thought that there would be just one Christian kingdom in the Middle East were disappointed when Amalric made it very clear that the two kingdoms would be ruled separately, and that no one should expect that the revenues of Cyprus would ever be used for the defense of the mainland. The crown of Cyprus was his by personal right, and the crown of Jerusalem only by reason of his marriage to Isabella. Amalric wanted no future problems with the succession of his own domain.

With the Germans still engaged in the siege of Toron, the Knights Templar finally got some encouraging news. Upon the death of Pope Clement III, Cardinal Lothair, a close personal friend of Grand Master Gilbert Erail, had been elected to the Throne of Peter and had taken the papal name of Pope Innocent III.

In their besieging camps before the walls of Toron the German Crusaders got the news of the death of their emperor Henry VI. Problems of imperial succession could have a heavy impact on the future of any noble house, so the leaders discussed the wisdom of going home. Then the flames of fear were fanned by news that civil war had broken out in Germany. That information had far more impact on the German barons than the news that a Muslim army was coming at them from Egypt. As the army of al-Aziz approached Toron, word ran through the tents of the German knights and soldiers besieging the city that the imperial chancellor and the great lords were gone.

The response to that news was panic, as the leaderless Germans decamped in haste and didn't stop moving until they were back in Tyre. If their leaders had gone home, they would go home, too, and for weeks every available ship left the Holy Land loaded with Germans who had abandoned the Crusade.

A few landless German knights decided to stay, only because there was nothing for them at home. They tended to gather around a German hostelry that had been established in Acre during the previous German Crusade, and they decided that here they had the beginnings of a separate military order for Germans. Calling themselves the Teutonic Knights, they petitioned the new pope for official recognition, which was granted later that year. They patterned their Rule after that of the Knights Templar, and they angered the Templars by copying their distinctive white robe. They also took the distinctive Templar cross, changing only its color. Instead of the brilliant red of the Templars, the Teutonic cross would be black. Later, after they had conquered pagan tribes in northeast Europe and turned their lands into the state of Prussia, their cross lived on into modern times as the German military Iron Cross. Their group was small at its founding, and it was permitted to occupy quarters at Acre in the tower at the Gate of St. Nicholas, on the opposite side of the city from the castle fortress of the Templars.

With the aggressive Germans out of the way, Amalric and al-Adil, neither of whom had wanted a war, now had no trouble arriving at a six-year treaty. Amalric agreed that the Muslims could have Jaffa, and al-Adil ceded Beirut and Sidon to the Christians. Al-Adil was still trying to regain his father's empire and needed no Christian enemies at his back while he faced the aggressively independent members of his own family. As for Amalric, he was especially happy to have the treaty in place when the antagonistic al-Aziz died later that year and the much more tractable al-Adil moved in quickly to take control of Egypt.

The Knights Templar were having no success with their petitions to the pope asking him to demand the return of Baghras. Grand Master Erail sent one letter after another to his friend Innocent III, seemingly unable to grasp the pope's point of view. The pope already had total control of the Knights Templar, with no fear of losing their allegiance. Leo of Armenia, on the other hand, had still not been able to deliver the submission of the Armenian people to the supremacy of the Roman pontiff. Innocent III did drop hints to Leo about Baghras, but in the turmoil of the struggle for the succession of the rule of Antioch, he refused to make an issue of it. To soothe the feelings of the group he saw as his own private army, he did reaffirm the Templars' rights and privileges as outlined in the prior bull *Omne Datum Optimum*, and he even sent a gift of gold for the Templars' use. He wanted them to remain loyal, but the whole nation of Lesser Armenia was more important to him than one Templar castle.

In all other matters he did support the Templars, and there came a time in 1199 when they needed that support. A prior bishop of Tiberias had deposited thirteen hundred bezants with the Templars for safekeeping, and now the present bishop wanted the money returned. Perhaps the records had been lost during the disastrous wars with Saladin, but for whatever reason, the Templars did not return the money. It was decided to put the matter to the bishop of Sidon for arbitration.

The bishop's idea of arbitration was not to patiently hear both sides of the issue, but rather to summarily demand that the payment be made to his fellow bishop within three days, or he would excommunicate the entire order of the Knights Templar. Though they had no fear of the bishop actually carrying out that illegal threat, the Templars made good on the deposit and returned the money.

It could only have been with complete disbelief that the Templars learned that the bishop of Sidon, in spite of the payment, had formally and publicly decreed the excommunication of every member of the Templar order. Grand Master Erail dispatched messengers to the pope in Rome to declare that if the Knights Templar were excommunicated, their vows were wiped out, and every man would be free to do as he wished.

The pope exploded at the idea that a lowly bishop in an obscure diocese would take it upon himself to disband the pope's private army. The bishop of Sidon was relieved of his bishopric, and all clerics everywhere were warned that the same disciplinary measure awaited any man who dared to interfere with a holy order responsible to the pope alone. The pope's fast action in their defense confirmed the Templars' power and privilege, but widened the substantial gap that already existed between them and the Latin clergy.

The last decade of the century had seen the rescue of the Holy Land and the preservation of the crusading ideals. The first decade of the new century would witness those crusading ideals corrupted and desecrated in a great blood orgy that put greed for gold before the glory of God on a scale never seen before.

14

A Crusade Against Christians

1200 to 1204

DEATH AND RIVALRY had disorganized the leadership of Europe at the beginning of the thirteenth century, creating a situation that was full of opportunity for the fanatically ambitious new pope, Innocent III. In 1199 Richard of England had been killed in battle by a random arrow. His deplorable brother John claimed the throne but was opposed by Richard's nephew Arthur, who had the support of King Philip Augustus of France. The conflict could well lead to an English civil war, which was all right with Philip.

The thirty-two-year-old Emperor Henry VI had died at his Sicilian port of Messina, and the great Crusade he was planning to launch from that city died with him. His widow Constance, heiress to the kingdom of Sicily, entrusted the care of their little son to Innocent III and entrusted her island kingdom to him as well. There was civil war in Germany, where Henry's brother, Philip of Swabia, claimed the right to be the new emperor. Innocent III disagreed and gave the imperial crown to Otto of Brunswick, who was more likely to do what he was told. Within the year, Otto refused to obey orders from the pope and was excommunicated from the Church and deposed from his throne.

Pope Innocent III was emerging as the strong man of Europe, which was very much in line with his dedication to establish papal supremacy over the secular world once and for all. He was pleased when the count of Champagne wrote to him expressing his desire to organize a new Crusade. Innocent was very much in favor, so long as it was a Crusade not led by a king or emperor. Then it could be a papal Crusade, commanded by a legate or noble who would take his orders directly from the pope.

Innocent's principal agent to promote the French Crusade was the fiery priest Fulk of Neuilly, renowned for his oratorical powers and his fearlessness. In his sermons he did not flinch before the highest nobility, as he had proven when he had thundered a demand to Richard that he give up his "daughters": Pride, Greed, and Lust. (Fulk could only seethe with anger at the way the English king agreed to give them up. Richard suggested that he would marry off his Pride to the Knights Templar, his Greed to the Cistercians, and his Lust to the bishops. They would all be perfect matches.)

An impressive array of nobles took the crusading vow: Geoffrey de Villehardouin, marshal of Champagne and the chronicler of the coming Crusade; Simon de Montfort, who would one day lead a bloody Crusade against heretics in France; and Boniface of Montferrat, brother of that Conrad who had been murdered just before he was to have been crowned king of Jerusalem. The acknowledged military commander of the Crusade, with full papal approval, was Tibald, count of Champagne and Brie.

The leaders met to plan their strategy. They were reminded that King Richard, as well as others who had been to the Holy Land, had declared that Egypt was the soft underbelly of the Muslim empire. It was good logistically because the vital roles of transportation and supply could be filled by Christian ships, with little or no overland travel. It was unanimously agreed that Egypt would be the opening target. A party of six nobles under Geoffrey de Villehardouin was sent to negotiate with the Venetian Republic, the only possible source for sufficient ships to carry the multinational army that would leave the following year.

Before the arrangements could be made, Count Tibald died. The nobles decided that his successor as commander of the Crusade should be Boniface of Montferrat, not only because of his experience at war, but also because he was the uncle of Princess Maria of Montferrat, the heiress to the crown of Jerusalem. That status should guarantee a good working relationship for him with the resident barons of the Holy Land. A month after Tibald's death in April 1201, the Crusaders reached agreement with Venice.

The Grand Council of Venice agreed that by the end of June 1202 they would provide transportation for forty-five hundred knights, nine thousand esquires and sergeants, twenty thousand foot soldiers, and twenty thousand horses. They would provide them all with food enough for one year. In addition, Venice would supply fifty war galleys, manned with Venetian troops, to protect the fleet and to fight alongside the Crusaders in Egypt. In payment, they would receive eighty-five thousand silver marks and 50 percent of all loot and land taken. The word went out to all who had taken the Crusader vow to gather at Venice by June of the following year.

Fate sent Boniface of Montferrat to spend the winter with his friend Philip of Swabia in Germany. The conversation turned frequently to Constantinople, because Philip's wife was the Byzantine princess Irene Angelina. The deposed emperor Isaac Angelus, living with burned-out eyes in a dank dungeon, was her father. She had had little news of her younger brother Alexius, only that he was not imprisoned but living under house arrest with his uncle, Alexius III, who had seized the throne for himself.

It was a happy reunion when her brother Alexius actually came to Irene Angelina in Germany. Friends had helped the boy to stow away in a ship which had brought him to Sicily, and from there more friends had helped him get to his sister. With the heir to the imperial throne of Byzantium as their house guest and a great army assembling to go to the east, Philip and Boniface began to get ideas. They both hated the Greeks, and this was an opportunity too good to pass up. They began to put together a plan.

The Venetians were busy with intrigues of their own, an activity at which they were acknowledged experts. By no means did they want a Crusade against Egypt, which would cut off their lucrative trading centers there. If it is strange to think of a government that could contract to deliver an army to a country, then assure that country's rulers that the army would never arrive, something must be understood about Venice. It was all business.

From the days centuries earlier when they had been driven to seek the protection of the islands and lagoons of the Adriatic Sea, the Venetians had looked more to the sea than to the land. Their economy was not based on farming and serfs, like the feudal economy that prevailed at the time, but on trading. Ultimately their government was made up entirely of the heads of great merchant families, who formed the Grand Council. The Council elected a duke (called a *doge* in the Venetian tongue) to serve for life, but not as an autocrat: The Venetians feared nothing more than one man trying to take over their city-state. They appointed a Council of Three to watch the doge. He could not receive an ambassador or even a messenger while he was alone, nor could he write or receive a letter privately. Discipline was fierce, and bronze heads of lions were placed throughout the city, into the open mouths of which anonymous accusations could be dropped in the black of night by any citizen who had any transgression to report. A galley hulk used to train those sentenced to be chained to the oars was moved to the Grand Canal right in front of the ducal palace, so that the whole world could see and be warned of the price of breaking the laws set by the Grand Council.

The council had one consistent goal in its lawmaking: to promote, protect, and expand trade. In the beginning the Venetians had produced little in the way of trade goods, counting primarily on selling dried fish and other products of the sea. Then they learned of the demand for healthy slaves. The first great surge in their economy came with raids on the Dalmatian coast, across the Adriatic, for prisoners to sell as slaves in North Africa. There they could buy products to bring home on their ships, to be traded overland into the continent of Europe. So many thousands of Slavs were taken for the slave trade that the word *slav* created the word "slave."

The other Italian trading centers of Pisa, Genoa, and Amalfi, on the western side of Italy, tended in the beginning to trade in the western Mediterranean, so the Venetians concentrated on the opposite end of the sea, where goods came in all the way from an unknown world in the east. There wasn't much in Europe that the easterners wanted, so Venice turned to the manufacture of trade goods, especially glass. When that led to the discovery of how to silver the glass to make a mirror, they had a valuable monopoly and passed laws to protect it. Had the United States existed then and made the discovery, it would have published the formulas and provided scholarships and transportation costs so that foreign students could come to learn how to make mirrors, but the Venetians had a different view of proprietary technology. They passed a law decreeing that death would be the fate of anyone who told an unauthorized person the secret of how to make a silvered mirror. Legend says that at one point a family of mirror-makers decided to leave to make a greater fortune elsewhere. The council sent agents, who followed them all the way to the Atlantic coast, to kill them where they were found.

The Venetian attitude toward religion was equally pragmatic. When the Venetians felt that they had outgrown their obscure patron saint, St. Theodore, they decided that in their power and glory they deserved no saint less than an apostle. They mounted a commando-style raid on Alexandria and stole the remains of St. Mark. Now that Venice possessed his bones, no one could doubt that St. Mark, *San Marco*, was the city's patron saint. They built the magnificent San Marco cathedral to hold the saint's tomb, the majestic square in front of it became the Piazza San Marco, and the Lion of St. Mark became the symbol of Venetian power.

The business of Venice came before the business of God, an attitude perhaps best summed up in the words of a doge on trial. It was the custom in Venice to conduct formal impeachment proceedings against any doge who lost a military campaign or a major battle. When one of the Grimani doges found himself in that situation, he pleaded in his own defense, "Does not my son, Cardinal Grimani, pass on to us all of the secrets of the Holy See so that we can look to our own best interests?"

That was the government that the Fourth Crusade planned to reply upon. The French nobles didn't event suspect that while they were negotiating the transport of their army to Egypt, Venetian envoys were in Cairo negotiating more favorable trade concessions for themselves. The Crusade agreement was signed in April 1202, just two months before the Crusaders were to launch their Egyptian campaign, and only after the Venetians had assured the emissaries of Sultan al-Adil that Venice would participate in no aggression against Egypt.

In June the Crusaders were assembled, but not their money. Each man was to pay his own share, but many had spent all their funds getting to Venice. Appeals were made to the wealthier barons, some of whom contributed additional funds and even gold and silver objects to be melted down, but they could scrape together no more than fifty thousand marks. The Venetians had built the ships and accumulated the food stores, but would part with nothing until they were paid in full. The payment was still thirty-five thousand marks short.

For the three months the Crusaders camped on an island in the Venetian lagoon, hard pressed to come up with money with which to buy their daily food from their Venetian hosts. The Crusader nobles negotiated with the elderly doge Enrico Dandolo, who was especially interested in the thoughts of Boniface of Montferrat. The doge disliked the Greeks as much as Boniface did. He had suffered a face wound in a street fight in the Byzantine capital that had almost totally deprived him of his sight. Alexius III had taken a hard line with the Venetian traders, who depended upon their Greek trading stations to get furs from Russia and silk from the caravans that came overland from China. And now Boniface was playing host to the rightful heir, whose father had been deposed and blinded by Alexius III. Interesting.

In September 1202 the doge revealed the first part of his plan. The Venetians had lost the fortified city of Zara in their war with the king of Hungary over control of the Dalmatian coast of Yugoslavia. If the Crusaders would recover Zara for Venice, the Venetians would postpone the collection of the thirty-five thousand marks due them until it could be paid from the loot of future conquests. The Crusaders argued bitterly over this proposed attack on fellow Christians but decided that they had no choice. In November the Crusader flotilla embarked on the two-day cruise down the Adriatic to Zara. The city resisted but finally surrendered after five days of fierce fighting. Because Zara had resisted and had caused Crusader casualties, the crusading army and the Venetian navy felt free to help themselves to anything of value. The battle was a decided economic success.

It was not regarded as a success in Rome, where the pope bellowed in rage that his crusading army had attacked a Christian city. He excommunicated everyone involved, but he released the Crusaders when he learned how they had been pressured into the attack by the Venetians. The doge paid no attention to the pope's condemnation. Venice had profited.

As the expedition settled down in Zara for the winter, the master plan unfolded. Boniface received a message from young Alexius and Philip of Swabia that contained a formal offer.

If the Crusade would go to Constantinople to help Alexius regain the throne, the young prince would assure the success of the invasion of Egypt. First, he would pay the Crusader debt to Venice. Then he would fortify the Crusader army with ten thousand Byzantine soldiers. Once the war was won, he would maintain five hundred mounted men in the Holy Land to help the Christians to hold on to their gains. Most important of all, he would guarantee that the Greek Church would universally accept the primacy of the Roman Church, in full recognition of the supremacy of the pope. Some of the Crusaders objected to attacking Christians, but the Venetians were unanimous in their support of the plan, probably because it had been worked out with their doge in advance.

At first the pope was confused, but finally the end won out over the means. His personal control over the Orthodox Church of the Byzantine empire was too great a prize to be cast aside.

In the Holy Land, the news of the embarkation of the great Crusade had excited the local barons and the military orders, who prepared for its coming. Gilbert Erail, the Templar grand master, had died in 1201, and a career Templar, Philip de Plessiez, had been elected the thirteenth grand master. His priorities had quickly changed when a series of strong earthquakes hit Syria and the Holy Land. Men and funds that had been gathered by the Templars for the coming war in Egypt now had to be used to rebuild collapsed buildings and fallen walls and towers. Fortunately, the Muslims had the same problems, so that the rebuilding necessitated an unwritten truce.

Young Alexius arrived at Zara at the end of April 1203, and the crusading fleet sailed for Constantinople. With supply stops along the way, the fleet arrived before the Byzantine capital two months later. The Crusaders were awed by the magnificent walls and towers of the largest city they had ever seen. It had never been conquered by an enemy, but the Crusade had arrived at a good time. Alexius III had been so occupied with the politics of his palace revolution that he had neglected the defenses of the city. Almost all of the soldiers inside were mercenaries fighting for money, not in defense of their homes.

After skirmishes at nearby towns, the Venetians managed to break the chain that barred the harbor, and the fleet sailed in. Alexius III didn't know what would happen next and didn't wait to find out. He scooped up all of the precious gems and gold he could quickly lay his hands on and fled the city.

The officers of the court took the sightless Isaac Angelus from his filthy dungeon, bathed him, draped him in jeweled imperial robes, and sat him on the throne. They sent word to the Crusaders that Isaac's crown had been restored, so there was no longer any need for war. The problem was that the Crusaders' contract was with the young prince, not with his father the emperor. The Crusaders proposed that Isaac agree to the arrangement made with Alexius and, further, that Alexius be crowned a co-emperor with his blind father. It was an extraordinary suggestion, but acceptable if it prevented all-out war. Alexius IV was made co-emperor of Byzantium in a ceremony in the lofty cathedral of St. Sophia on August 1.

Now came the time for Alexius IV to keep his promises, which he found impossible to do. The Greek patriarchs and the people had no intention of recognizing the supremacy of the pope in Rome. To try to force them could easily lead to civil war. The political turmoil before and after the overthrow of Isaac Angelus had led to the rape of the imperial treasury, so there was not enough money to make the promised cash payments. None of his subjects liked the solutions Alexius came up with, as he forced new taxes on the people and sent parties of soldiers to seize gold and silver objects from the churches. These were not just the wealth of the Church, but religious symbols important to the popular devotions.

For the rest of the year Alexius IV struggled to raise the money he needed, while crusading soldiers wandered through the city drinking, whoring, and brawling. A band of French soldiers set fire to a mosque that was used by the local Muslims, and the fire spread to wipe out one whole section of the city.

In Byzantium it was only natural that antigovernment plots would be formed, and the strongest of them was led by Alexius Marzuphlus, son-in-law of the deposed Alexius III. He organized a riot against the Crusaders in January 1204. A few weeks later an embassy of the Crusaders was attacked by the crowd as they left the imperial palace.

A mob of Byzantine citizens crowded into St. Sophia to declare that Alexius IV was deposed. As their new emperor they proclaimed a Greek nobleman named Nicholas Canabus. Marzuphlus had no intention of letting someone else get the rewards of the revolt he had set in motion, so he gathered a band of armed followers and stormed into the imperial palace. Nicholas Canabus was dragged off to prison. So was young Alexius IV, although to a different fate. An executioner was sent to his dungeon to strangle the young co-emperor to death with a bowstring. His father, the blind Isaac Angelus, was savagely beaten and thrown into another dungeon, where he died a few days later. The city gates were closed and barred.

The Crusaders camped outside the city now knew that they had no choice but to storm the walls of Constantinople. As their anger grew, so did their confidence, and they called a council to choose their own Catholic emperor to rule when the city would be theirs. The Venetians had just one condition: If the emperor was to be a Frankish Crusader, the patriarch of the Roman Church must be a Venetian. Then they got down to the serious business of dividing up the anticipated spoils. The imperial palace, of course, must go to the new emperor, who would also have 25 percent of the capital city and the nation. The other 75 percent of the empire would be divided equally between the Crusaders and the Venetians. No mention was made of any Crusade to Egypt or the Holy Land.

The attack began on April 6, 1204, and lasted for just six days, with final victory coming from a unique Venetian invention and a fire that many historians believe was set by Venetian agents in the city. The Crusaders had made the land attack, while the Venetians took their ships to a point where the outer wall of the city came right to the water. Using spars, they built narrow bridges. One end of a bridge was raised to the top of a ship's mast, then the other was raised and swung to the top of the wall. Knights on foot climbed ladders up the masts, then moved over the bridges, while cross-bowmen tried to reduce the Greek resistance on the wall in front of them. Once the Venetians had control of a small section of the wall, other men rushed over the narrow bridges to join them, to widen their position on the outer wall. The defenders fell back to the inner wall, but someone behind them set the nearby buildings on fire. Caught between the Venetians and the fire the defenders fled, and soon gates were opened to the Crusader army. The city was theirs.

All seemed in reasonably good order that night as the Venetian doge and the Crusader nobles gathered in the imperial palace. Then the explosive announcement was made that as a reward for its hardships and its victory, the army would have three days to do as it wished with the city. What the soldiers wished was drunkenness, desecration, thievery, rape, and murder.

Constantinople was the richest city in the world. It had an accumulation of nine hundred years of art treasures, built on a base of art and craftsmanship from the ancient Greeks and Romans. The Venetians, knowing this, organized an orderly plunder of items they could take back to glorify their city. The army, with no such motivation, treated art like trash, smashing statues, slashing paintings, and breaking exquisite icons. Books beyond counting were destroyed, and priceless illustrated manuscripts found an unintended use as toilet paper. No palace, church, business, or house was left untouched. The wine was drunk, the women were raped. Convents were treated as cost-free houses of prostitution. Any nun who fought back, or any nun who was too old to interest even drunken soldiers, was killed and her body thrown out into the street. The butchery was universal: Those who did not resist were killed as quickly as those who did. If a soldier found a mother clutching her child, it was simply a matter of deciding which one to kill first.

The monumental cathedral of St. Sophia was an architectural wonder, the largest house of God in the world. Now it became the largest tavern in the world. Everything of value was stolen or destroyed, and the wine flowed like a river. One drunken prostitute, holding a sacred chalice filled with wine, sat on the patriarch's throne to be cheered by the French soldiers as she sang them a bawdy song in their own language.

After the three-day debauchery the army was brought to a reasonable state of control, although many resisted the order that all loot taken should be delivered to collection points at three designated churches. Greek citizens were routinely tortured into revealing the treasure they had hidden while the city was under attack. Greed replaced lust, and a French count hanged one of his own knights who was found to be hiding some of the loot he had taken.

The first payment made from the plunder was the money still owed to Venice, then the rest of the treasure was divided equally with the Venetians. A distribution was made to the army on the basis of one share for a foot soldier, two shares for a mounted sergeant, and four shares for a knight. Not surprisingly, a noble's share was many times that of a knight. After all that distribution of treasure, the balance remaining was four hundred thousand marks, which one chronicler noted was about seven times the annual royal revenue for the entire kingdom of England.

The Venetians carefully packed and stowed the art treasures to be taken home for the glorification of their city. Today, tourists to Venice, admiring the four magnificent bronze horses above the entrance to St. Mark's Cathedral or the two great marble columns near the Grand Canal beside the ducal palace, are looking at a tiny part of the loot of Constantinople.

Next came the division of land. With the whole empire to hand out, there was more than enough. Commander Boniface of Montferrat received broad territories, including the island of Crete. The Venetians were happy to use part of their share of the loot to buy it from him, and it became an important Venetian trading center.

On May 16, 1204, in the restored cathedral of St. Sophia, the imperial crown of Byzantium was placed on the head of Count Baldwin of Flanders and Hainault. The Knights Templar sent a delegation to the coronation from the Holy Land, not so much to attend the ceremony as to make a fervent appeal for the original purposes of the Crusade. The delegation was disappointed and had to give up when the papal legate issued a formal decree that relieved every member of the Crusade from his vow to go to the Holy Land, so that each might stay in Byzantium to consolidate the great Catholic victory.

The loss of this crusading army wasn't the only blow to the Knights Templar and the other leaders of the Holy Land. Local knights and barons from the Holy Land, learning that Greek lands were available for not much more than the asking, were departing in increasing numbers. Salvation could wait: This incredible opportunity for instant riches must be grasped now. The same attitude motivated fresh Crusaders leaving Europe, who changed their destinations from Acre to Constantinople. The new Latin emperor needed all the help he could buy and had plenty of land to buy it with. He welcomed the defectors with enthusiasm. Only the men recruited for the Knights Templar and the other military orders ever saw Outremer. The burden on the orders to protect the Holy Land was stronger than ever.

It did no good for the Templars to complain to the pope, because Innocent III saw the victory as one that spread his own authority. The entire Greek Church was now under his control. He would learn in time that he had temporarily gained the Greeks' obedience, but would never own their hearts. Some of the Greeks ran to Nicaea in Turkey and set up a government-in-exile there. That, plus the growing power of the Turks, shut the door forever on the overland Crusader route from Constantinople to the Holy Land.

Other Greeks allied themselves with the Bulgarian tribes and made war on Byzantium. The following year they faced a Latin army led by the usurper emperor Baldwin, captured him, and led him off to die in a Bulgarian dungeon.

The Fourth Crusade did nothing to recoup the Holy Places of

Jesus Christ. Although the pope for the moment was happy with the results, the Crusade had converted the rivalry of the Greek Orthodox Church to irreconcilable, seething hatred. The Turks benefited by having their strongest Christian enemy shattered for them by other Christians. The only winners were the Venetians, who had almost instantly become the strongest and richest naval power in the Christian world.

Most important, the Crusaders' ideal had been corrupted from one of expanding the territories of God to extending the power of the pope. From this beginning, Innocent III would corrupt the crusading vision still further into a bloody instrument of papal power. And he would order the Knights Templar to help.

15

The Albigensian Crusade
1205 to 1214

THE CRUSADERS IN Constantinople were not at all concerned with affairs in the Holy Land, so they scarcely noticed the death of King Amalric in 1205. To his vassals, however, his passing meant that the two Crusader kingdoms of Jerusalem and Cyprus were divided once more. The crown of Cyprus went to Amalric's six-year-old son Hugh. Jerusalem went back to Queen Isabella, for whom still another husband must be found; but before that could happen Isabella, too, passed away. Her thirteen-year-old daughter by Conrad of Montferrat became Queen Maria of Jerusalem, but couldn't rule without a husband.

Maria was old enough to marry, but the distraction of the conquest of Constantinople had lessened the interest of any great noble in committing himself to a lifetime in the Holy Land. It would take time to find a king, and in the meantime Isabella's half-brother, John of Ibelin, the lord of Beirut, took charge as regent. Fortunately, during the year before his death, Amalric had signed a six-year peace treaty with al-Adil. There was no indication that the sultan was going to take advantage of the king's death to break the truce. He was having more threatening problems with his Turkish neighbors to the north.

To replace the reward-seeking knights and barons who had gone to cash in on the great land distribution in Byzantium, the Templars and the Hospitallers had to bring renewed pressures on their European brothers for more recruits and more money. They were the only knights totally committed to the Holy Land, so they were among the very few buyers for properties offered for sale by owners who took reduced prices to abandon their holdings to move to Greece. The purchases used up their funds, and every new holding called for additional manpower.

The Knights Templar appealed to Pope Innocent III, but the pope had plans of his own. Putting down a challenge to his own supremacy was higher on his list of priorities than regaining the home of Jesus Christ. He was calling a great Crusade to be fought in France. All of the spiritual rewards promised to Crusaders—total remission of their sins and an assured place in Heaven—were now available to men who didn't have to mortgage their lands and journey across the seas to earn them. As for the Knights Templar in France, they were ordered to join in this new Crusade against Christians. Local heretics, not Muslims, were now the important enemy.

The group targeted for death was the Cathars, who followed a religious pathway totally apart from that of the Roman Church. They made up about half the population of a beautiful region in the southeast of France known as Languedoc. The Cathars believed that Jehovah, the God of the Old Testament, was an evil god who had created material things. The God of the New Testament, Jesus Christ, had created only spiritual things. Material was bad, Spiritual was good. Bodies were material, so bodies were the repositories of sin. Therefore the joining of two bodies in sexual congress was sinful, whether or not the parties were married. The Cathars did not harass or molest the sinners, whom they agreed vastly outnumbered the righteous. Still they strove in their worship toward a spiritual ideal, as exemplified in Jesus Christ, who they believed was only divine and had never had an earthly body like other men. The few among their number reckoned to have achieved their goal, called *perfecti*, had no possessions and abandoned all sexual pleasures. What they possessed in great measure was the total respect of their fellow believers. When a man decided that he could not attain the status of the *perfecti* but still wanted to renounce all things material, he could avail himself of a universally accepted and respected rite of suicide, called the *endura*. Implacably opposed to the veneration of material images, the Cathars condemned many things dear to the Roman Church, such as the ornate vestments, the holy relics, the lavish altars, even the bread and wine and the cross itself.

The cult had spread and induced a favorable reaction when compared with the blatant corruption of the Church in the region, which Innocent III himself had recognized, as had Bernard of Clairvaux. However, there was one great crime of the Cathars, in the Church's eyes, that could not be tolerated: They saw no scriptural justification for a pope. They recognized no papal authority and were even known to condemn the materialistic popes of Rome as the Antichrist. Innocent III had been ruthless in his demands for the total supremacy of the papacy throughout the western world, using his considerable powers to achieve domination over both men and things. One chronicler recorded a comment that summed it up: "It now appears safer to question the power of God than to question the power of the pope."

The repression started gently enough in 1205, when a priest named Dominic Guzman, who had been sent to convert the heretics by his preaching, had given up. Frustrated by the unyielding Cathars, he could only recommend force. Another cleric, Peter of Castelnau, was sent to the area with greater authority as the papal legate. Peter ordered the greatest Catholic lord of Languedoc, Count Raymond of Toulouse, to stamp out the Cathar heresy. The task was virtually impossible, but no excuse was accepted. Peter of Castlenau excommunicated the count of Toulouse and added to his condemnation, "He who strikes you dead will earn a blessing from God." His curse did not result in Raymond's death, but in his own. The very next day, one of Raymond's knights rode at Peter and drove his lance through his body. The blood-soaked white robe of the Cistercian monk was carried to Innocent III with the news of the crime.

A Roman Catholic knight had killed Peter of Castelnau, but that was not the way the murder was reported to the world. Innocent III blamed the Cathar heretics. In March of 1208 the pope issued a bull of anathema against the Cathars, condemning them all to death. At the same time he declared Peter of Castelnau to be a saint of the Catholic Church.

A call to Crusade went out, promising identical spiritual rewards for going to southern France as previous Crusaders had been promised for going to the Holy Land. The bloody robe of St. Peter of Castelnau was taken from one town to another to rouse the people to join in the war of extermination.

The murder of a Cistercian had been used to trigger the call to Crusade, and now Innocent III appointed another Cistercian as papal legate to lead it. He was Arnald-Amalric, the Cistercian general. Forty days was all the military service he required for any knight or commoner to earn the Crusader's special place in heaven, although as it turned out it took years to accomplish the maniacal slaughter throughout such an extended area.

The Crusade began with the public confession and humiliation of the count of Toulouse, who swore to obey the Church in all things and pledged himself and his vassals to eliminating the Cathars. He took his knights from Toulouse to join the growing Crusader army at Montpellier.

Their first target was the walled city of Béziers, whose citizens, sympathetic to the gentle Cathars among them, would not open their gates. It was well known that the Cathars constituted only a small minority of the population of Béziers, and they looked exactly like their Catholic neighbors. How were the Crusaders to know which ones to kill? They put the question to Arnald-Amalric. The papal legate's reply ranks as one of the most memorable quotations in military and religious history. "Kill them all," he said. "God will recognize his own."

The men of Béziers were on the walls when the crusading army broke through the defenses. The Catholic women, their children, and the elderly were gathered in their churches for sanctuary and prayer. Seven thousand of them had crowded into the great church of St. Mary Magdalene. On their knees, they could hear just two sounds: In front of them, two Catholic priests were celebrating mass; behind them Crusaders were hacking through the barred door with axes. When the doors came crashing down, the papal legate's orders were followed to the letter.

Swords and axes rose and fell as the butchers forced their way to the sanctuary, leaving a lake of blood behind them. Finally, they reached the altar and the two Catholic priests. One held a crucifix above his head, the other the chalice holding the wine that had become the blood of the Savior. They were both killed where they stood.

After the slaughter the looting began. When some order was restored, the leaders announced that all loot taken must be surrendered to contribute to the expenses of the Crusade. The blood-drenched soldiers were outraged. If they couldn't have the loot they felt they were entitled to, no one would have it. They set the city on fire.

At the end of the victorious day, the papal legate took up his pen to make his report to Pope Innocent III. "Today, your Highness, twenty thousand citizens were put to the sword, regardless of age or sex." It is difficult to grasp, at this distance in time, that the report was written in a spirit of pride and accomplishment, in the confident expectation of eliciting praise, which it did. Twenty thousand human beings had been killed in one day, and all but a few hundred of them were devout Roman Catholics. This was the birth of an insane principle that would guide future inquisitors, a principle that declared it was better to burn a hundred innocent people than to allow one heretic to go unpunished.

If anything, the madness got worse. The papal legate appointed Simon de Montfort as commander of the army, the same Norman leader who had played an enthusiastic role in the rape of Constantinople. With full Church approval, de Montfort simply burned to death everyone he could identify, or even suspect, as a Cathar. When he captured the castle of Bram, however, he changed the fate of several hundred prisoners to use them in a fully approved act of psychological warfare. After they were bound, he ordered that all prisoners should have their noses sliced off, their upper lips cut away, and their eyes gouged out. Only one man was permitted to keep one eye, in order to act as guide. Then the blinded prisoners were lined up behind him, each man with his hand on the shoulder of the man in front. In agony from their untreated bleeding wounds, they were set on the road to the town of Cabaret. Their arrival achieved its objectives, striking fear into the hearts of the defenders and placing a severe drain on their supplies because they now had to feed hundreds of helpless men. Historian Zoé Oldenbourg summed up the leadership of Simon de Montfort by writing, "...one is forced to admit that the soldiers of Christ could hardly have chosen a commander less worthy to be called a Christian."

One of the Cathar cities that put up strong defenses was Albi, whose residents were called Albigensians. As their story spread, they appeared to personify the Cathar resistance. They gave their name to the sanctimonious savagery remembered as the Albigensian Crusade.

The Spanish priest Dominic Guzman was active throughout the period and famed for his preaching against the heresies. When he sought approval for the establishment of a new order of preaching friars to be dedicated to the salvation of souls, he met with a favorable response. His Order of Preachers, commonly known as the Dominicans, was founded in 1215.

In April 1223 Pope Gregory IX promulgated a fateful bull that established the Holy Roman and Universal Inquisition. The Inquisition would root out heresy wherever it could be found, even in the Church; since the mendicant orders were outside the control of local bishops, they appeared best able to administer it. The first two inquisitors were the Dominican brothers Peter Seila and William Arnold, and as its activities expanded, the Inquisition became effectively the province of the Dominican order. The inquisitors were provided with scribes, jailers, torturers, and armed bodyguards. Their authority as the protectors and purifiers of the faith was not subject to control or even influence by the existing secular or religious systems of justice, which wiped out generations of the efforts of conscientious men to introduce the rudiments of legal rights for accused parties awaiting judgment. The suspected heretics, or even those thought to have knowledge of heretics, were arrested with no authority beyond that of the inquisitors themselves. They were questioned in private. They had no right to know by whom they were accused, or the names of witnesses against them. They had no right to legal counsel. In short, they had no rights at all. The concerns for the purity of the faith and the primacy of the pope had taken justice back to the Dark Ages.

A key factor was that the faith to be kept pure was not simply that set forth in holy scripture, but included all the teachings of the Church, a growing body of complex conclusions and decrees that was almost impossible for the average person to be aware of, much less understand. There was no shortage of objections from peasants, nobles, and the Catholic clergy, but many of them chose to remain silent, realizing that they were attempting to combat a system that had terror as its most effective defense. Those who objected to the Inquisition could easily become its victims, as could any innocent party. A man who did not know of any heretic could easily be persuaded by the pressure of excruciating pain to accuse anyone he could think of, just to stop the pain. And it behooved everyone to seek advice on personal habits and behavior that might arouse ecclesiastic suspicion. One woman was arrested because she was known to bathe every Saturday, a habit not in keeping with Christian custom. Another was taken because she did not care for pork, surely ample proof that she was a secret Jew.

The success and longevity of the Inquisition was unquestionably due in large measure to the enthusiasm of those who administered it. The Dominicans saw themselves as blessed with a divine mission and took great pride in the papal ceremony in the spring of 1235 that bestowed sainthood on their founder, Dominic Guzman. Oldenbourg recounts an incredible tale of an event that took place in Toulouse on St. Dominic's first feast day, later that year. Word came to the celebrants that an elderly woman of the local nobility, on her deathbed, had confessed her adherence to the Cathar faith. A party of Dominicans, accompanied by a local bishop, hurried to her bedside to urge her to save her soul by confessing her sin, rejecting her demonic faith, and embracing the Holy Roman Church. The old lady remained firm, and as recorded by Dominican brother Pelhisson, who was there, "persevered with increasing stubbornness in her heretical allegiance."

Her confession was clear, uttered before witnesses, so she was judged to be guilty of heresy. Since she could not walk, her bed was carried out of her house to an open field, where it was placed on a pile of faggots and tied to a stake. As the holy men clustered about her and raised their prayers to heaven, she was burned alive. The Dominican Pelhisson rounded out his narrative with, "This done, the Bishop, together with the monks and their attendants, returned to the refectory, and after giving thanks to God and St. Dominic, fell cheerfully upon the food set before them." The prior of the Dominicans followed the banquet with a public sermon in which he wallowed in the miraculous coincidence that this blessed burning had occurred on the very feast day of their saintly founder.

The significance of all this in a history of the Knights Templar is that the Templars would one day become the victims of this unholy institution, as the Inquisition would turn its maniacal ministrations on them to extract confessions of heresy within the Templar order. Perhaps the Dominicans were unhappy that the Knights Templar in southern France had not joined in the antiheretical Crusade, but the simple fact was that they couldn't. All of their preceptors in France had been hit again and again by letters from the Middle East urging that every Templar who could be spared should be sent to the Holy Land.

The Templar burdens of protecting the Christian states were steadily increasing as the flow of Crusader-pilgrims dried up. Why should any knight drain his treasury and leave his lands and his family to spend a year or more fighting for the True Cross, when the same spiritual rewards were available with just forty days' service in the south of France? Nor could the Holy Land compete for the services of the more adventurous landless knights, who could easily find land and wealth in the conquered Byzantine empire. There is no record that the Templars disagreed with the Albigensian Crusade, or even that they took a position of neutrality. The truth is that they had no one to send. That's why they were happy to take in new recruits, even of Cathar knights and those suspected of heresy. For these recruits, membership in the order protected them by giving clear evidence of their allegiance to the Roman Church, and their lifetime vow earned them the total remission of all their sins, even the sin of heresy.

There was one surprising instance of Templar participation in the Albigensian Crusade, surprising because it was on the other side. The kings of Aragon had extensive lands on the French side of the Pyrenees Mountains, which were being encroached upon by the crusading forces of Simon de Montfort. In 1213 King Pedro II took a Spanish army across the Pyrenees to join up with his French vassals and friends to attack de Montfort. Pedro had left a Muslim enemy behind him, counting on his men on the frontier to hold them in check while he went to France. The major factor in that frontier defense was the men and castles of the Knights Templar. Pedro did have a small contingent of Templars at his court, who went with him to France, where he met his death in September at the Battle of Muret, ending the Aragonese effort. To us, the interesting point is that the pope had called the Albigensian Crusade, and here were Knights Templar, even if only a handful, fighting on the other side. There is no record of any papal criticism of their behavior, which appears to support the concept that the Iberian Templars had gradually given their principal allegiance to the kings. Their warfare was not a Crusade, but simply an ongoing struggle to expand the lands of the Christian kingdoms by pushing out the Muslims, who had been on the Iberian Peninsula for over five centuries, since their original landing at Gibraltar.

The possibility of relief for the Holy Land by a French Crusade was slowed by the setback of still another Crusade against Christians, called by Innocent III as part of his constant battle to achieve universal recognition of the primacy of his papal throne. His target this time was King John of England.

Richard the Lion Heart had been a terrible king, spending less than ten months of his reign in England and taxing the people to finance his wars, but even so he was immeasurably better than his brother John. Apparently possessed of no morals whatever, John indulged himself with lying, cheating, and adultery. He tortured wealthy Jews to extort money from them. He sought out the mistresses of priests, not to enforce clerical chastity, but to force the priests to pay a "sin tax" of two pounds per year in order to keep their concubines.

John went too far for Innocent when he taxed Church property and clerics without papal approval. Then, when the see of Canterbury became vacant, John nominated his own archbishop. Innocent named the official Church candidate, Stephen Langton, but King John would not let him assume his rights and duties. The pope gave John three months to accept Archbishop Langton, and when the time ran out placed all of England under interdict. With the removal of God's grace there could be no baptisms, no marriages, no Christian burials. Such a severe punishment could well foment revolution, which is exactly what Innocent had in mind. King John's response was to announce that if any English bishop enforced the papal order, John would send every priest and monk in England to Rome with his nostrils slit and his eyes put out. Ignoring the barbaric threat, the local clerics read the order of interdict in the churches of England on Palm Sunday in 1208, and all eight thousand churches were closed.

After eighteen months, the papal sanctions had not produced the desired result, so the pope excommunicated King John and called upon King Philip of France to lead a Crusade against England. Once again, those who participated would receive the same indulgences and rewards as those earned by Crusaders to the Holy Land. Philip was promised the English throne as a further reward, and he began to assemble his forces. The Knights Templar in France and England were to take part in King John's downfall.

With nowhere to turn for support, the English king sent word to Rome that he was prepared to negotiate. Innocent sent Cardinal

Pandulf to England, and in his anxiety John traveled to meet the cardinal as he landed at the port of Dover, rather than wait for him at Westminster. The king swore to return all the land and treasure he had taken from the Church. Further, he signed a document that gave all of England "to God and to our Lord Pope Innocent and his Catholic successors." England had become a papal state. John and his successors could rule the country only as secular administrators, subject to papal orders and upon payment to Rome of one thousand marks each year. It was strictly a business arrangement, as the Christians in England learned that they were to be denied spiritual comforts for another year, until the payment to the pope was made in full. Only then were the churches opened so the English could become practicing Christians once more.

The French king was furious when he learned that England had become papal property. He had wasted a fortune assembling the Crusade against England at the command of Innocent III. His followers had been promised land on a scale not seen since William the Conqueror had divided England among his followers in 1066. The French disbanded and went home in disgust. They wanted to hear no more pleadings or exhortations about the glories of going on any Crusade.

The Knights Templar in England, on the other hand, could enjoy a sense of relief. It had been a confusing period for them. John's brother Richard had been their good friend, and they had grown accustomed to serving the royal house. The problems that had risen between John and the pope had placed them in an uncomfortable position. Now, with England a papal state and King John a vassal of their lord the pope, the Templar brothers' loyalties were clear again.

As for John's conduct, once his attitudes toward the Church in Rome were under papal control, the Holy See did not care how he treated his secular vassals. His continued violations of feudal agreements caused his barons to organize a resistance that eventually produced a landmark document defining and confirming baronial rights and the Common Law, a charter remembered in history as the Magna Carta. To John it seemed that everyone was against him, even Stephen Langton, now installed as archbishop of Canterbury. Of the leaders, John could count on one. The English master of the Knights Templar stood by his side as he reluctantly put his seal on the momentous document that was the first small step toward constitutional law.

When Innocent III learned of the Magna Carta he was enraged. He called it "contrary to moral law." The king was not subject to the people, he was subject only to the pope. The people didn't make laws and pass them up to the kings. Popes made the rules and passed them down to the secular throne to enforce. He published a formal bull condemning the Magna Carta and forbade the English king to obey it. Anyone trying to enforce the charter's provisions was to be excommunicated. Archbishop Langton refused to publish the threat of excommunication in England and was removed from his post.

Pope Innocent III had turned the crusading ideal from an army dedicated to achieving Christian possession of the Holy Places of Jesus Christ to an army raised to achieve the goals of the papacy. The religious zeal that marked the First Crusade had fallen so low that it was even difficult to find a noble of high rank willing to reign as king of Jerusalem. Queen Maria had reached the age of seventeen, an age when most women were married and bearing children, yet no husband had been found for her. It was decided to appeal to King Philip of France to produce a suitable bridegroom.

It took Philip almost two years to select a king for Jerusalem, and the chosen candidate was not very exciting, either as a king or as a bridegroom for the young queen. He was sixty-year-old John of Brienne, whose career of military service to France had taken him from his start as a landless young knight to a position of command in Philip's army. It appears that the reason for the choice was that Philip wanted John out of France, to break up a scandalous affair he was having with Countess Blanche of Champagne. To endow him with something closer to the stature a royal candidate would be expected to have, Philip provided John with a dower of forty thousand pounds of silver, which Pope Innocent III matched with a further forty thousand.

In July 1210, before John of Brienne arrived in Jerusalem, Amalric's six-year truce with al-Adil expired, but the sultan expressed his desire to extend it. The regent John of Ibelin called a council to approve the extension. The masters of the Hospitallers and the Teutonic Knights agreed, but Philip de Plessiez, grand master of the Knights Templar, disagreed strongly. He argued that a new king, who would arrive in just a few weeks, should not be bound by long-term agreements on which he had not even been consulted. The common sense of the Templar master's approach swayed the bishops and nobles to his point of view. It was also a shrewd move to establish a good starting relationship with John of Brienne, who appreciated the grand master delaying an important decision until he could be there to exercise his leadership. He arrived on September 13, 1210, and was married to Queen Maria just twenty-four hours after she first set eyes on a bridegroom old enough to be her grandfather.

In that same year, the Templars met to replace Grand Master de

Plessiez, who had succumbed to illness. They chose William de Chartres to serve as their fourteenth grand master. John of Brienne was very cooperative with the Knights Templar, and during the following summer he permitted some of his vassals to join in a Templar raid on the Egyptian coast. In 1212 he agreed to a long-term military treaty with Sultan al-Adil, but he listened to the military orders when they recommended that the five-year period be used to promote a new Crusade. John wrote to the pope asking that a new Crusade be timed to coincide with the expiration of the new truce in 1217.

In the second year of John's reign, Queen Maria gave birth to a daughter, called Yolanda. The complications of the birth took the life of the queen, so that legally the little baby was now the ruler of Jerusalem, since John ruled only by reason of his marriage to her mother. Remembering the difficulty they had experienced in finding a king, the nobles of Jerusalem readily agreed to John's continued rule. Technically, he was simply the regent, but in practice he continued to be addressed and regarded as King John. In 1214 he married Princess Stephanie, the daughter of Leo II of Armenia.

The struggle of Leo of Armenia to take control of Antioch had turned into a power game that made a mockery of morality. Leaders switched loyalties, switched religions, made alliances with traditional enemies, and readily resorted to murder. The rivalry of the Knights Templar and the Hospitallers, who were politically and emotionally on opposite sides, grew intense enough to find their knights fighting each other in the streets, sometimes to the death.

To solicit the backing of Pope Innocent III, Leo had asked that the Armenian Separated Church be placed under the control of the Church in Rome. Innocent favored the plan, as had popes before him; it would extend his own power still further. After the papal legate Peter de Saint Martel had presided over the coronation of Baldwin of Flanders as the Latin emperor of Byzantium, Innocent ordered him to Armenia. Leo thought all would go smoothly, but he flatly refused one papal condition. The Knights Templar had obeyed their lord pope in every way, and Innocent had reconsidered permitting a wedge to be driven between himself and the Templars that might affect that loyalty. His major condition, urged upon him by Bohemond of Antioch, was that the castle of Baghras be returned to the Knights Templar. That return was not subject to negotiation. Baghras was Leo's strongest threat against Antioch, and he refused to give it up until Antioch was his. In the meantime, he would rather get along without the pope in Rome than be without the castle of Baghras.

A revolt of some of his vassals in Tripoli pulled part of Prince

Bohemond's army away from Antioch, which inspired Leo to attack the city. Emir az-Zahir of Aleppo, who hated Leo more than he did Bohemond, sent a mounted army to thwart Leo's attempt on Antioch. Leo had no desire to engage in open war against a Muslim force that outnumbered him and drew back to Armenia.

Peter, the Roman patriarch of Antioch, berated Bohemond for interfering with the pope's plans for the Armenians, and Bohemond, exasperated, finally deposed Peter. In his place he appointed a Greek Orthodox patriarch. The commune of leaders of Antioch fully agreed. They hated the Armenians and wanted no one who favored them, nor did they want an Armenian alliance with the pope.

The patriarch Peter had a spiritual weapon available to him, so—with full papal approval—he formally excommunicated Bohemond and all of the members of the commune. Confident that the Latins in the city would not follow excommunicated leaders, Peter then organized a few knights loyal to him and proceeded to try to take over the city by force. To his surprise, the garrison of the citadel of Antioch chose to obey their prince, not the patriarch, and quickly subdued the revolt.

The patriarch Peter was taken prisoner, formally tried for treason against Antioch, and found guilty. He was confined to a dungeon, where it was apparently Bohemond's intention to let him starve to death. With no food or drink whatever, Peter was driven to near insanity by hunger and thirst. In desperation, he drank all of the contaminated oil in his lamp, with the result that he died writhing on the dungeon floor in a spasm of agonizing convulsions.

The pope charged the patriarch of Jerusalem with the responsibility of settling the matter of the Armenians, but by now that matter was a diplomatic mess. The Hospitallers had raided the territory of Bohemond's Muslim allies, evoking the response of a Muslim raid into Tripoli. Leo again took advantage of the distraction to begin his own military incursions into the territory of Antioch. Bohemond created a distraction of his own by arranging attacks on the other side of Armenia by the Seljuk Turks. He also threatened the Hospitallers for the damage they had caused him. Albert, the patriarch of Jerusalem, did his best to bring some sense to the situation, but he leaned in the direction of his very good friends the Knights Templar. He repeated to Leo that he absolutely must return the castle of Baghras to the Templar order. He persuaded Bohemond, as a move toward peace, to remove the Greek patriarch and replace him with a Roman.

Leo of Armenia, who was growing weary of trying to effect an alliance with the pope in Rome, abandoned that concept and instead made an alliance with the exiled Greek court that had moved from Constantinople to Nicaea with loyal factions of the Byzantine army.

Bohemond's antagonism toward the Hospitallers brought him a cruel blow. In 1213 Bohemond's eldest son Raymond was visiting the Knights Templar at Tortosa. As he attended a religious service in the cathedral, Raymond was attacked and stabbed to death by several Assassins. The patriarch of Jerusalem bitterly accused the Hospitallers of having arranged the murder. The confirmation came soon, as a band of Assassins murdered the patriarch.

Bohemond had lost a son and the Templars had lost a powerful friend. Joining forces, they mounted an attack of vengeance on the Assassin stronghold of Khawali. Now the Shiite Assassins appealed to the Sunni emir of Aleppo. The emir, perhaps because he had no desire to earn priority listing on an Assassin hit list, demanded that Bohemond back off. The emir had already saved Bohemond from Leo on a previous occasion, and Bohemond could not afford to lose his Muslim ally. He backed off.

With a new patriarch of Jerusalem in place who was not so dedicated to restoring the property of the Knights Templar, Leo of Armenia decided to make another attempt to secure an alliance with Rome, and this time he succeeded. The pope, who had different plans now, assured Leo of papal support if the Armenians would participate in the Crusade Innocent was planning to call. Innocent ordered the new patriarch to cooperate with Leo, who was no longer required to return the Templar castle at Baghras.

That cooperation probably cost Bohemond his principality. While he was away in Tripoli, Leo, now confident of the support of the patriarch of Jerusalem, smuggled a substantial number of Armenian troops into Antioch. When they revealed themselves, Bohemond's forces in the citadel yielded without a fight.

Probably to reward the patriarch, who should be able to make a favorable report to the pope, Leo announced that since he now possessed the city of Antioch, he no longer needed the castle of Baghras. He gave it back to the Knights Templar. Now the Templars could repel any Arab or Turkish invasion of Leo's territory of Antioch with their own forces, and at their own expense.

Leo of Armenia was a happy man. He was lord of Armenia and lord of Antioch. He had married off his daughter Stephanie to John of Brienne, thus acquiring an influential position in the kingdom of Jerusalem, and that influence would be greatly enhanced if Stephanie could manage to have a son. Leo considered himself to be well on the path toward total control of all the Latin Christian lands in the Middle East.

There remained only the matter of another great Christian Crusade from Europe. The Roman popes, starting with the Holy Land, had extended their influence to the conquered Byzantine territories, and now to Armenia. Pope Innocent III was not the kind of man to let that extended power slip away. He was able to assure the Templar grand master that another Crusade was coming, and soon.

16

A Cardinal Sin

1215 to 1229

$\mathcal{J}$NNOCENT III HAD planned to have a Crusade in place by the time he called the Lateran Council of 1215 to deal with a variety of Church matters. There were items as difficult as a plan for the consolidation of the Greek Orthodox Church and as simple as bestowing honors and praises upon Simon de Montfort for his religious zeal in leading the Albigensian Crusade. The council would have to deal with the problems of a new Crusade to the Holy Land as well, because the lack of response to the pope's appeals had been discouraging.

The pope was firm in his conviction that the time for a great Christian victory was at hand. The Book of Revelation had described how a great beast would work against God and ravage the earth. The prophecy said, "Let him that hath understanding count the number of the beast: for it is the number of a man; and his number is six hundred, three score and six." Pope Innocent III, certain that he possessed the requisite understanding, was equally certain that the beast of the great prophecy could only be God's greatest enemy, the Prophet Muhammad. Muhammad had been born in the year A.D. 570, and his 666 years of abominations were about to run out.

The patriarch of Jerusalem was invited to the council to add his own ideas to those of the Holy See. The council quickly confirmed the absolutions and indulgences to be granted the Crusaders, and gradually the bishops caught some of the pope's enthusiasm. They returned home to preach the Crusade and to prepare for the reception of the special preachers to be dispatched from Rome.

The preceptors of the European bases of the Knights Templar reported to the grand master in Acre that it appeared a new Crusade would be starting out in the summer of 1217. In response, and as they expected, they were ordered to step up their own efforts at recruiting and fund-raising.

Innocent III did not get to see the launching of the Crusade he had worked so hard to bring about. Illness claimed him in July 1216, and death took him a few days later. It took only forty-eight hours to elect a successor; the elderly Cardinal Savelli ascended the Throne of Peter as Pope Honorius III. His commitment to the Crusade was just as strong as Innocent's had been. He imposed a 5 percent Crusade tax on all the revenues of the Church and ordered that this tax be collected by the treasurer of the Knights Templar in Paris.

The plans to spend those funds, unfortunately, were poorly drawn. The absolute need for transportation was grossly neglected. The leadership was divided, because the monarch who was expected to lead the Crusade found a succession of reasons to delay his departure. He was Frederick II, king of Germany and Sicily. Frederick didn't want to leave for the Crusade until he had the imperial crown, but his coronation as Holy Roman Emperor had been held off because the Church wanted him to voluntarily reduce his power by making his young son Henry the king of Sicily. As king and pope maneuvered and manipulated, smaller contingents of the crusading force began to leave without their leader.

In the summer of 1217 a French army reached Italy, but no ships had been provided for them. King Andrew of Hungary led an army to his own Dalmatian coast of Yugoslavia, where he was joined by Duke Leopold VI with the Austrian army, but there were no ships for them, either. The pope sent orders that they should proceed immediately to the Holy Land but offered no suggestions as to how they might get there.

By September, Duke Leopold had arranged for only one ship, so he decided to go on ahead with just a personal bodyguard. During the following month, King Andrew managed to get his hands on two ships and followed Leopold, but the bulk of their armies was left behind. Concerned that during his absence the greedy Venetians across the Adriatic Sea might move against his western provinces, King Andrew named Brother Pons de la Croix, master of the Knights Templar in Hungary, to watch over Dalmatia and Croatia until the king's return. In October, part of a Frisian fleet put in south of Naples, reporting that the rest of their force had decided to winter in Portugal. The ships just arrived would winter in Italy.

As the Austrian and Hungarian leaders arrived at Acre and Tyre, King Hugh of Cyprus joined them with an army of his own. The total army assembled was not a massive one, but it was sizeable enough to score some victories, so King John of Jerusalem urged an immediate campaign. The Knights Templar and the Hospitallers agreed to join them, and in November 1218 the Crusaders left Acre for their eastward march. The Muslims moved into defensive positions before Damascus and Jerusalem, but no threat to those cities ever came.

With no central authority, there could be no universal discipline. The Hungarians listened only to their king, Andrew. The local barons recognized King John. The Cypriots took their orders only from King Hugh. As for the military orders, the Knights Templar and the Hospitallers obeyed no one but their own grand masters. The disparate Christian forces moved across the Jordan, northward around the Sea of Galilee, then back west toward Acre. Muslim scouts watched them over every foot of ground they covered, but saw no decisive moves to report to the waiting Muslim armies. A few small Arab towns were overrun, but none of any real significance. As the Crusader army returned to camp outside Acre, the men could only reflect on a long, tiring hike through Palestine with nothing accomplished.

The only leader who felt successful was King Andrew of Hungary. With his passion for religious relics, he perhaps thought that taking sacred objects back to Hungary would appease his people for the taxes forced out of them to pay for the Crusade. Now he had treasures of incalculable value to lay before them. The local dealers in relics must have offered up their own private prayers of thanksgiving to God for sending them this royal pigeon, who had exhausted his funds to purchase their wares. He was convinced that he would be going home with the head of St. Stephen, the head of St. Margaret, the right hand of St. Thomas, the right hand of St. Bartholomew, one of the jugs that had held the water Jesus turned into wine at the wedding at Cana, and a piece of the staff of Aaron.

King John of Jerusalem was frustrated by the rejection of his leadership by the Austrian-Hungarian Crusaders. He decided to launch an attack without them on a stone fortress that al-Adil had built on Mount Tabor, just south of Nazareth. He dashed out of Acre with his own men to make the first attack on December 3, 1217, but the fortress held. Two days later he was joined by contingents of the Knights Templar and the Hospitallers, but a second attack by the combined forces was equally unsuccessful. Reluctantly bowing to the reality that men on horses could not scale or shatter high stone walls, John ordered his army back to Acre.

In the meantime, King Andrew and Duke Leopold, with King Hugh of Cyprus, traveled north to Tripoli to pay a social call on

Bohemond IV. While there, King Hugh was struck down by an illness that resulted in his death a few days later. The crown of Cyprus went to his son, Henry, an eight-month-old baby. Henry's mother, Alice of Jerusalem, became the ruler of Cyprus as regent for her infant son.

As soon as he returned to Acre, King Andrew announced his decision to go home. The patriarch of Jerusalem thundered at him, but Andrew was unmoved. He had kept his promise to the pope. He felt he had fulfilled his sacred Crusader vow. Besides, he was eager to show his people his wonderful collection of divine relics. Having accomplished absolutely nothing, he sailed back to Hungary.

King John had mixed feelings. Andrew had been the major factor in depriving John of the command of the Crusader forces, so on that basis his departure was beneficial. Unfortunately, he had taken his army with him, and it would be missed.

That problem began to solve itself as Crusader forces delayed in Europe began to pour into the Holy Land. Both sections of the Frisian fleet arrived, which guaranteed Christian control at sea. It appeared that a major Crusade was at last a reality, and since no king had arrived, King John could plan that Crusade with the assurance that he would be in command.

The Knights Templar, meanwhile, were not paying much attention to the Crusader activities. They had finally begun a project that they had been planning for a long time. Those plans had required the gradual accumulation of over a million gold bezants, which would now be spent to build the most extensive Templar fortification of them all.

For years the Templars had contemplated the natural defenses of a rocky promontory called Athlit. It jutted a third of a mile out to sea a few miles south of Haifa. They had maintained a coastal watchtower there called Destroit, but felt that the location called for a much stronger and more important fortification. With three sides protected by the sea, it should be possible to build an impregnable fortress. What they built was more like a whole fortified town.

The entire area was surrounded by walls, with the landward wall the most massive in the Middle East. It was ninety feet high and sixteen feet thick at its base. The gate was actually a seventy-foot tunnel, angled in such a way that no invader could properly employ a battering ram against the inside door. A deep *fosse*, or ditch, was dug in front of the wall, deliberately excavated below sea level so that it could be flooded. Any Muslim miners who tried to get under the wall could easily be drowned in their tunnel as soon as they reached the deep moat.

Inside the walls were quarters for up to four thousand people.

There was a freshwater spring flowing to a fish pond. There were gardens and orchards and even grazing lots to support the herds of horses, cattle, and sheep that would be driven inside in the event of an impending siege. With food and water inside and more supplies readily and indefinitely available by sea, the fortification should be able to hold out forever against a besieging army. It was the Knights Templar's crowning achievement in castle-building. Mindful of the original purpose of their order, the Templars called their new base *Chastel Pelerin*, or in English, Castle Pilgrim.

Castle Pilgrim was used as a supply stop for the Crusader fleet that had finally assembled and was being led to Egypt by King John. With their superiority at sea the Crusaders felt they had a much greater chance of success on the Nile than in the mountains of Syria. The first target would be the fortified river city of Damietta on the main branch of the Nile. As the first Crusaders reached the mouth of the Nile on May 29, 1218, King John took his place in undisputed supreme command, supported by Duke Leopold of Austria. The Knights Templar, Hospitallers, and Teutonic Knights were as usual under the command of their own grand masters.

The city of Damietta was upriver, guarding the broad Nile flowing down from Cairo. Damietta itself was fortified with high, thick walls, but in order to reach it, the Crusaders had to deal first with an island fortress called the Tower of Chains that guarded the approach. Its name derived from strong chains that were stretched out from both sides of the fortress to the eastern and western shores. When Sultan al-Adil received word of the invasion, he immediately reinforced the garrison of the Tower of Chains, but he had little concern about its walls being assaulted or scaled from the water. The first Christian attempt on the walls in June was easily repulsed, which seemed to indicate that al-Adil's confidence was well placed.

Skirmishes were continuous, on both land and water. At one point, Muslim ships managed to come at a Templar galley from both sides at once. Hordes of Egyptian slave-soldiers called Mamelukes climbed or jumped from their own ships onto the deck of the Templar galley and soon crammed the upper deck, shouting out their victory. Several Templars who were below, knowing that their time had come, decided to take the Muslim boarders with them. With their battle-axes they chopped a hole in the bottom of their ship, triumphant as the water rushed in. A hundred and forty knights, sergeants, and mariners of the Temple went down with their ship, but they were victorious in death as they sent almost fifteen hundred Muslims, all weighted down with chain mail, to the paradise promised to them in this holy war.

The stalemate was broken when the Christian engineers built

a new type of siege engine. They erected a scaling tower on a base of two galleys lashed together, covered with just-butchered green hides to resist fire. At the top, the floating tower had a long, narrow bridge, like a movable boom, to be lowered to the top of the wall.

The tower was ready by late August and was rowed to the fortress wall. A bitter fight went on for a whole day, with dead and wounded Christians falling into the sea, but at last a band of Crusaders established a bridgehead on the wall. As other men followed them over the bridge, they fought their way left and right, clearing a space at the top of the wall. That permitted scaling ladders to be put from the deck to the wall to get more men into the fight. As their number grew, the hand-to-hand fighting flowed off the wall and into the streets, until the garrison surrendered. The great chains were cut loose and allowed to fall to the bottom of the river. Now the Crusader ships had a clear passage to Damietta. Before advancing, they took the time to build a pontoon bridge to the shore to carry off the tremendous amount of plunder found in the river fortress. The new Crusade was off to a glorious start, gratifying to both piety and purse.

When the bad news reached Cairo, the initial success of the invasion proved too much for Sultan al-Adil. Now almost seventy-five years old and ill, he plunged into a pit of depression and died within the week.

As the Christian army prepared for the move up the Nile, French and English Crusaders arrived on ships of Genoa paid for by Pope Honorius, who had used Church funds to provide transportation for the Crusaders who had been gathering at Brindisi on the Adriatic. Unfortunately, any benefit to the Crusade from the pope's help was more than offset by his choice of a papal legate, who sailed with the armies to Egypt. The legate was a Spanish cardinal by the name of Pelagius of Santa Lucia, an arrogant, opinionated, totally self-righteous prelate with no military experience whatever.

Cardinal Pelagius lost no time in announcing to the Crusade leaders that, as the official representative of His Holiness, Pope Honorius III, he alone was now in supreme command, and that his command was military as well as spiritual. He rejected King John totally, pointing out that John's role as king of Jerusalem existed only because of his marriage, and since his wife was now dead, John of Brienne was no longer entitled to style himself king of anything. Since Cardinal Pelagius came armed with documentation setting forth the papal authority for his claims, the grand masters of the three military orders felt compelled to support him. Pelagius reveled in his new supreme power. Not only did he wear the red cape and red hat that were the badges of his position as a prince

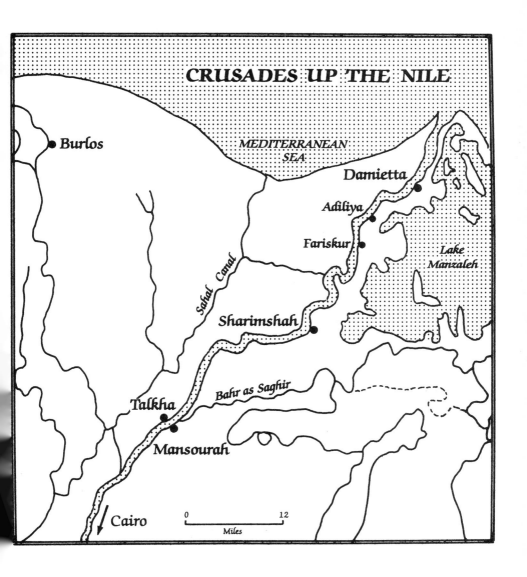

Exterior of the Church of the Holy Sepulchre from David Roberts's descriptions of the Holy Land in the nineteenth century. Roberts found it strangely disappointing despite it being so sacred a place

158

VRBANVS II.
12. Martij an.1088.
dies 18. Obijt die
Vac. Sed. dies 14.

Gallus, creatus die
Sedit an. ii. mens 4.
29. Iulij ann. 1099.

Odo de Lagéry, Pope Urban II

A Saracen warrior

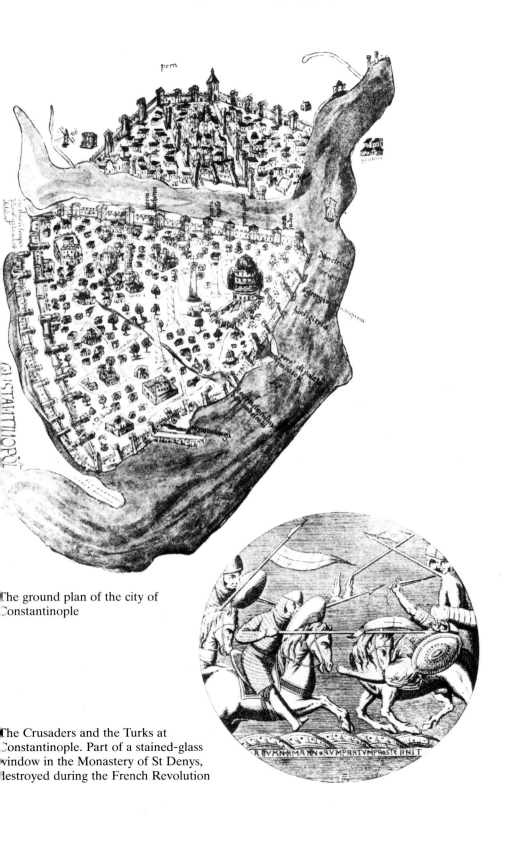

The ground plan of the city of
Constantinople

The Crusaders and the Turks at
Constantinople. Part of a stained-glass
window in the Monastery of St Denys,
destroyed during the French Revolution

Seljuks in flight from Crusaders, from the Abbey of St Denys

An Eastern Knight, from the Apocalypse of St Severo

Antioch, surrounded by mountains, was a strong defensive position behind its great walls

Siege towers were constructed some distance from the city walls

Saracens parley with Crusaders in their camp, from *Chroniques de St Denis*

The Iron Gate in the walls of Antioch

The Tower of David in Jerusalem

The Holy Sepulchre

of the Church, but he also enriched his riding apparel with custom-made red saddlecloths, along with bright red covers for his saddle, bridle, and stirrups.

Upriver in Cairo, al-Adil's eldest son al-Kamil had inherited his father's title as sultan of Egypt. His younger brother al-Mu'azzam disregarded that authority and proclaimed himself the sovereign ruler of Syria. The Muslim empire was split once more. His brother could be dealt with later, but the Christian invaders were at his doorstep, so Sultan al-Kamil turned his attention to an attack by boat on the Crusaders' camp. King John led the troops and the Templars to beat off the Muslims without waiting for Cardinal Pelagius to issue the order to do so.

For weeks the two armies picked and probed at each other without joining in serious battle. Then at the end of November a fierce gale drove the waters over the Christian camp, which was almost at sea level. Men and horses drowned, and much of their food supply was ruined. Cardinal Pelagius ordered a dike to be built around the camp, but it was too late to do any good. With everyone short of food, soaked to the skin, and living in a sea of mud, the welcome mat was out for disease. An epidemic struck: men came down with a high fever and their skin turned black before they died. The majority survived, but by the time the epidemic died down, one out of six Christians was dead.

The sultan based the Muslim army at the smaller walled town of al-Adiliya, on the Nile about two miles upriver from Damietta, and waited. The sick and miserable Christian army rested for a couple of months until Cardinal Pelagius decided that they should get things moving again. Pelagius rallied the army for an attack on the Egyptian camp in early February, but unfortunately, he didn't understand the rainy season of the Nile delta, nor would he listen to those who did. A great rainstorm broke on the marching Crusaders, who had to beat their way through deep sucking mud to get back to camp.

Then came the surprising news that the Egyptians were abandoning al-Adiliya. The Christians didn't know it yet, but al-Kamil needed his troops in Cairo, where an assassination plot had been uncovered: the sultan was to be killed and replaced by a younger brother, al-Faiz. As the price for taking part in the plot, the young prince was strangled to a bloodless death with a bowstring, but while al-Kamil was busy saving his throne and his life, the Christians marched into al-Adiliya. Now they held the fortresses both north and south of Damietta. They could block any attempt to reinforce Damietta from Cairo, but when the sultan moved an army up close to them, they decided to postpone their drive up the Nile for an all-out assault on Damietta. Off in Damascus, al-Mu'azzam decided to take steps to protect his own lands, just in case the Christians succeeded in conquering Egypt. He ordered the walls of Jerusalem taken down, then dismantled the fortresses in Galilee.

Summer came, the ground dried, and the Christians began bombarding the walls of Damietta with huge stones that had to be brought by ship, while the defenders shot back pots of Greek fire and naphtha to destroy the siege engines. Occasional fighting went on between the opposing armies outside the walls, with no clear victories. The Templar grand master de Chartres was a good administrator, but he considered it a grand master's first duty to lead his knights in battle, in spite of his failing health. In a defensive action in August 1219 he took a wound serious enough to cause him to announce his resignation, so that a healthy grand master could take his place in the field. He died a few days later. His followers could not be certain whether he had died of his wound or from the encroaching disease that had brought gangrene to his gums and weakness to his legs.

Duke Leopold of Austria, who had been on Crusade for two years and had seen enough death and disease to last a lifetime, decided to go home.

As the French King John argued strategy with the Spaniard Pelagius, the Italian soldiers decided to act on their own. Not in disciplined ranks, but as a disorganized mob, they ran at the Egyptian army. Following almost automatically their traditional battlefield maneuver, the Muslims pretended to retreat until the Italians chasing them were strung out, then turned to form ranks for an orderly attack. The Italians panicked. Cardinal Pelagius, who had followed them out, tried to rally the fleeing Italians, who ignored the red-draped figure high up on his horse, screaming at them to go back to the fight. King John led out a group of French and English knights. Together with parties of Knights Templar and Hospitallers who were already in the saddle, he managed to stop the Muslim charge and save the Christian camp. The cardinal could take no credit for anything on that day.

The obvious answer to the unrest was to take Damietta, but the high walls and fierce resistance thwarted every attempt. In one effort to scale the walls with ladders on August 21, 1219, the Knights Templar lost fifty men, while the Hospitallers lost thirty-two. That was not many out of any army of tens of thousands, but these were serious losses to the military orders, whose role in maintaining order was growing every day.

The bishop of Acre, strong in his praise of the conduct of the Knights Templar, wrote, "The Templars were filled with the spirit of Gideon, and their example was an inspiration to the other Christians." A German poet went even further, taking the Templars into the world of fantasy. The minnesinger Wolfram von Eschenbach, who had come to the Crusade with a group of German soldiers, was awed by the zeal and dedication of the military orders, especially the Knights Templar. In his epic "Parsifal" he made the Templars the equals of the Knights of the Holy Grail, which led to their role in the legends of the Round Table as the guardians of the Grail Castle. Perhaps his spiritual interpretations of the bloody, disease-ridden pageant before him were partially inspired by an even more notable visitor who had come to take a hand in the Christian struggle.

Men could hardly believe the startling news that shot through the Crusader camp. They came running and crowded around to get a glimpse of the famous holy brother, Francis of Assisi, who had just come among them. Francis had decided to come to the war front because, in spite of all the evidence to the contrary (continuing to this day), he held the saintly belief that peace could easily be effected in the Middle East if men of good will from both sides would sit together to talk things out. He was an unwelcome guest to Cardinal Pelagius, who saw the veneration of Francis as a possible threat to his own authority, but there was no way he could withhold his permission for Francis to visit Sultan al-Kamil under a flag of truce.

The sultan had been advised that the visitor was a very holy man (a "Christian dervish") and much honored by men of his own faith, but he was shocked by the man presented to him. Francis still clung to his vow of abject poverty, so he presented himself to the sultan with bare feet and tousled hair, in a ragged robe, and most shocking to al-Kamil, filthy dirty. The sultan nevertheless gave Francis a place of honor and listened to him patiently. He was offered refreshment and, at the end of his visit, was presented with rich gifts, which his vow of poverty required that he decline. Francis was pleased that he had been treated with such obvious respect, but it was not the respect due a man who would be made a saint of his Church. Rather, it was the respect that the sultan's culture required be shown to anyone whom Allah had touched with madness. Neither man understood the other at all.

Reports were coming to al-Kamil that disease was taking its toll on the Muslim garrison isolated inside Damietta: They could not be expected to hold on much longer. Reports from the northeast indicated the probability of war in Syria, because a Kwarismian shah from central Asia had succeeded in taking much of modern-day Iran and Iraq and was holding the Sunni caliph of Baghdad as his prisoner. Under those circumstances, the sultan's brother al-Mu'azzam in Damascus could not be expected to release any of his forces to assist in Egypt.

Al-Kamil's answer was to free a captive Latin knight with a message for the Crusaders. Al-Kamil suggested a brief truce, during which he was willing to negotiate the ownership of Jerusalem. The Christian leaders accepted the truce but rejected any negotiations. Both sides used the truce period to strengthen their defenses. The Knights Templar used the time to call secret grand chapter meetings in the field to elect a battle-wise brother, Pedro de Montaigu, to serve as their fifteenth grand master. It was unusual for the essentially French order to select a Spanish Templar as its leader, but the knights probably felt that it would be easier for a Spaniard to work with the Spanish cardinal Pelagius.

Now al-Kamil had a wonderful shock for the Crusaders. This time he released two Latin prisoners, probably so that there would be a corroborative witness to his startling offer. If the Crusaders would just leave Egypt, he would give them Jerusalem, central Palestine with Nazareth and Bethlehem, and the territory of Galilee. The Muslims would keep only the castles of Oultrejourdain. To seal the bargain, he would return the relic of the True Cross. Here was a total victory for Christ. The European nobles urged the immediate acceptance of the offer, as did King John, who could expect to rule over all of the lands being returned.

Cardinal Pelagius was totally opposed to the sultan's offer. He wanted a complete, unconditional victory over the infidel in which he alone would dictate the terms of surrender. The officers of the Knights Templar and the Hospitallers also objected, but for more practical reasons. First, Jerusalem and the lands around it had been claimed by the sultan's brother, al-Mu'azzam of Damascus. How could al-Kamil give them properties that he did not control? Second, when the treaty was made the European pilgrim-Crusaders would go home, leaving the defense of the regained territories to the military orders. But with the walls of Jerusalem torn down and the fortresses of Galilee destroyed, the Muslims could attack whenever they wished, then dash back over the river Jordan to the castles they were keeping in Oultrejourdain. The Knights Templar were anxious to reestablish their headquarters in the al-Aqsa Mosque on the site of the Temple of Solomon, but not on such a precarious basis. The only practical solution was that al-Kamil must agree to include in his offer the return of the fortresses of Oultrejourdain.

The Italian merchant city-states were so angered by the sultan's proposal that they exploded into a bloody riot that saw a Templar knight killed trying to restore order. The Italians' problem was that they could see no profits coming from the territories of central Palestine and Galilee. Damietta, on the other hand, was the small end of a geographic funnel for the trade of central and east Africa and the spices of the Indies. There was money to be made by pursuing the battle on the Nile. They supported the position of Cardinal Pelagius, who resolutely rejected al-Kamil's offer.

Jacques de Vitry, the recently arrived bishop of Acre, covered for his cardinal and for himself when he reported to Rome: "Many of our pilgrims judged those offers important and proper...but those who knew by experience the fraud of these [Egyptians] who change unceasingly...the Templars, the Hospitallers, the Teutonic Knights, the legate, the Patriarch, the archbishops, the bishops... made nothing of their false words, thinking that the Saracens had no other intention than, under the veil of a simulated peace, to disperse the army of Christ...." Nice reading for the pope, but the bishop and the cardinal had absolutely no previous "experience" with the Egyptians, although they would have plenty by the time they got home.

With his peace offer rejected, the sultan was frustrated because he could not get reinforcements or food supplies into Damietta. All the reports coming to him said that the city was on the brink of starvation and being ravaged by an infectious disease. The dead, they said, were lying in the street, because the living were too weak to dig their graves.

The Christians learned of the problem a few days later, when it was noticed that there were no defenders on the outer wall of Damietta. The Crusaders approached the wall cautiously, alert to possible trickery, and placed their scaling ladders. Climbing slowly, half-expecting a surprise attack from the wall, they got to the top to find the entire outer wall abandoned. Moving to the inner wall, they found almost the same situation. The feeble defense there was no more than a scuffle. The gate was opened with little opposition, and the puzzled Crusader army walked unopposed into the city.

There was no wholesale slaughter of the Muslim defenders this time, because the people they found were mostly already dead or too miserable to kill. All left alive were taken prisoner without protest or defense. In spite of the inevitable private looting, a substantial treasure was assembled for distribution to the army. As usual, the share allocated to the knights and sergeants of the Knights Templar, Hospitallers, and Teutonic Knights went to their treasurers.

Cardinal Pelagius declared that the conquered city was now Church property under his sole command, but no one agreed with him, not even the military orders that had supported him in every other decision. When King John threatened to leave with all the local barons and their troops, Pelagius compromised. He agreed that John could act as governor of the city, but only until the arrival of the emperor Frederick who, he was convinced, would be showing up at any moment. The cardinal was dreaming. Frederick was not going to leave Italy until his position as Holy Roman Emperor was officially sanctioned by the Church, with an imperial coronation presided over by the pope himself. Frederick would lead no German army to support the Crusade in Egypt, but he did send a few knights and soldiers to keep up the pope's confidence in the emperor's ultimate adherence to his crusading vows.

King John went over Cardinal Pelagius's head to ask Pope Honorius for permission to leave the Crusade in order to respond to events in Armenia. King Leo II had died, naming his four-year-old daughter as his heiress. John felt that his wife Stephanie, Leo's oldest daughter, had a better claim to the Armenian throne, especially since they had a male heir in their infant son. He wanted to go to Armenia to press their claim and the pope agreed. Unfortunately, knowing that John would be away, the pope also reconfirmed that his legate, Cardinal Pelagius, would be in supreme command of the Christian army in Egypt.

When John arrived at his home in Acre, he discovered that his wife had been abusing his little daughter by his first marriage. In his fury, John beat his wife so severely that she died from her injuries. When a fatal illness took their baby son a few days later, John had no further claim to the throne of Armenia.

He did not go back to Egypt right away, because al-Mu'azzam of Damascus, apparently to take the pressure off his brother al-Kamil in Egypt, had moved an army into Palestine. He attacked Caesarea, then moved northward up the coast to camp in front of the massive landward wall of the Templars' Castle Pilgrim. When word came to the grand master at Damietta that the castle was under siege, he took a group of Templars on their own galleys from Egypt to enter the castle from the sea and aid in the defense. King John waited at Acre to see if the Templars would need his help, but Castle Pilgrim was in no danger of being taken by a force made up mostly of light cavalry.

News from the far north was ominous, but as yet no one understood its significance. The great Mongol hordes had moved westward almost five thousand miles from the birthplace of Genghis Khan and had met their first Christian enemy. As the Mongols approached the Turkish province of Azerbaijan, the king of Georgia had led his mountain fighters out to stop them. The Georgians were famous warriors, but never had they faced such a disciplined force in such overwhelming numbers. The Georgians were mangled on the field and virtually destroyed as an independent military power.

In Egypt, al-Kamil was putting the months of stalemate to good use. Although the Christians controlled the eastern branch of the Nile that flowed past Damietta, the totally unguarded western branch entered the Mediterranean Sea at the port city of Rosetta, near Alexandria. Al-Kamil rebuilt his navy and in the summer of 1220 sent the new fleet down the west branch and out to sea, sailing right around the Christian invaders. The Egyptian fleet moved north to the island of Cyprus, where they spotted a Christian fleet anchored off the port of Limassol. It was a squadron of fresh Crusaders, revictualing at Cyprus before making the final run to join the crusading army at Damietta. The Egyptian fleet sailed in among the Christian ships, which were totally unprepared to defend themselves in what they had thought were safe waters. Every Crusader ship was sunk or captured. Thousands of men were taken prisoner and in the weeks to come found themselves sold as slaves to Muslim masters.

When the news reached the Crusader headquarters, all eyes turned to Cardinal Pelagius. It was well known that spies had consistently reported the buildup of the Egyptian navy, and that the Egyptians could easily have been kept bottled up in the western branch of the Nile. Unfortunately, Pelagius, deciding that the news was of no significance, had done nothing about it. The military genius who had ordered a dike to be built only after the flood had engulfed the camp now ordered the Pisans and Venetians to patrol the mouth of the western branch of the Nile after the Egyptian fleet had already escaped.

At the end of the year the news Pelagius had been waiting for finally arrived. In November Frederick had come to Rome, where from the hands of Honorius III he had received the imperial crown as Holy Roman Emperor. In return, he had sworn to fulfill his sacred Crusader vow, announcing that he would lead an army to Egypt the following spring. In passing this exciting news to the legate, the pope cautioned the cardinal that no peace treaties should be accepted or rejected without papal approval. Honorius had no desire to anger the newly crowned emperor.

Frederick didn't go to Egypt in the spring of 1221, as promised, but he did send troops. In March, two of Frederick's envoys arrived with a small German army. At about the same time he dispatched another army from Italy under the command of the duke of Bavaria. In July, eight galleys arrived in Egypt with troops under the count of Apulia. A strong Christian army was growing on the lower Nile. The new arrivals were eager for action, as was Cardinal

Pelagius, but their leader, the emperor Frederick, still had not arrived. The men agreed to move but insisted that a seasoned military commander was vital to the war. They demanded that the cardinal send for King John of Jerusalem. Pelagius was furious but had to break the stalemate. He reluctantly sent for King John.

John came back to Egypt in July, as did Grand Master de Montaigu and a contingent of his Knights Templar. John had learned, as had the Templars, that al-Mu'azzam was assembling an army in Syria, so this was not a good time for them to be away from home. The Nile floods were coming, making it a singularly inopportune time for launching a campaign in the delta. King John urged the leaders to wait, but when Cardinal Pelagius accused him of cowardice in the presence of the others, pride took precedence over common sense. John agreed to lead the offensive.

The long period of inactivity had given al-Kamil plenty of time to get ready, so when the Crusaders began their march up the Nile on July 12, a great Muslim army set out to meet them. The Christians had by now assembled an army of almost fifty thousand men, of whom about five thousand were mounted knights, with an incredible flotilla of over six hundred Christian ships moving up the Nile to support the army. As impressive as the Crusader totals were, the Muslims, who had also been busy assembling an army and navy, now outnumbered the Christians in both men and ships. More important for the days ahead, they knew their own country and the annual behavior patterns of what was then recognized as the mightiest river in the world.

The Christians moved up the Nile to the walled town of Sharimshah, which surrendered to them on July 20. King John wanted to wait there, because he knew that the annual Nile flood was due at any time. He had heard that it brought an unbelievable amount of water, fed by the torrential rains running off thousands of square miles to the south. Cardinal Pelagius rejected that cowardly suggestion: He was certain that he knew all about floods.

The Nile delta is a spiderweb of waterways. One branch, called the Bahr as-Saghir, flowed out from the east bank of the river, ahead of the Crusaders. One Muslim army camped on its own side of the shallow branch, while another crossed it well out of sight to the east, to be on the Christian side. The Muslims circled around the Crusaders and took up hidden positions behind them, between the Crusaders and their base at Damietta.

On the western side of the Nile, another branch left the river and traveled all the way to the sea. Below the captured town of Sharimshah, and behind the Christian fleet, a canal connected the branch back to the river. When the Christians had passed by that canal a few days earlier, they had mistakenly ignored it as an unimportant shallow drainage ditch.

The Muslim timing was all based on flood levels and the speed with which the waters rose. They were not disappointed. Soon the water in both the east and west branches was too high to be marched across. As the western branch rose swiftly, it fed the shallow canal below Sharimshah, turning it into a navigable river. An Egyptian fleet sailed down the west branch, turned into the canal, and entered the Nile, cutting off the Christian fleet from Damietta and the sea.

As the patrols and scouts came in to report, Cardinal Pelagius had to face up to the unnerving evidence that before anyone could strike a single blow, his Christian force had been totally surrounded, outnumbered, and outmaneuvered. The Christians were practially in a state of siege, a not inapt description because an inventory revealed that the army had less than a three-week supply of food. The Crusaders could not move forward across the raging Nile or the greatly swollen Bahr as-Saghir, so their only hope lay in an orderly retreat. The cardinal had never expected to give such an order, but he finally got a grip on his pride and passed the word for the Crusade to fall back immediately. Since the men must travel too quickly to be slowed down by wagons, any supplies they could not carry were to be destroyed.

To waste their precious casks of wine was a form of sacrilege to the common soldiers, so they decided to drink it up before the move. When the retreat started on August 26, much of the army was staggering, not marching. Even so, they might have gained a head start, had not the Teutonic Knights made a mistake. Rather than take the time and energy involved in opening and dumping supplies, they chose to take the lazy way and set them on fire. The billowing smoke signaled the Muslims that the Christian army was on the move.

The level terrain of the delta over which the Crusaders retreated was now lower than the river, as they discovered when the Muslims ran to the dikes to open the sluice gates. Water gushed out to flood the low plain, and soon men and horses were floundering knee-deep in water, on a base of silt that thousands of marching feet and pounding hooves soon churned into a shifting, muddy morass. With every floundering step they were cut down by flights of arrows and harassed by Turkish cavalry and black Nubian infantry. Only King John and his barons turned to hold the cavalry in check, while the Templars and Hospitallers dealt with the foot soldiers. Everyone else ran.

Thousands of Christians died in the retreat, and thousands more were wounded. Unfortunately for the latter, Cardinal Pelagius had used his supreme authority to effect a quick escape. He had hurried to the river and commandeered a large ship that carried him on the rushing Nile current right through the Egyptian fleet and on to safety. His brilliant escape saved the cardinal's own life, but there is no way to know how many other Christians were killed by it, since the ship he had taken held all of the army's medical supplies. Most of the Christian ships that tried to follow the cardinal downriver were sunk or captured.

Grand Master de Montaigu sent a letter to the master of the Temple at London that summed up the current situation:

"Our provisions were lost, many men were swept into the water, and we could make no progress. The water continued to rise, and we lost our horses and our saddles and our baggage and everything that we had. We could neither advance nor retreat and we did not know where to turn. We had no food, and being like fish caught in a net, we could do nothing but plead for peace."

The grand master was correct in his assessment. The Christians would be starved into submission in a matter of days, and the cardinal realized that he had no choice but to negotiate a peace. The sultan's concept of negotiations at this point was to make an offer that the Christians could either accept and live, or reject and die. They accepted.

First, Damietta must be surrendered. Then all the Crusaders must leave Egypt. A truce would be signed for a period of eight years. The True Cross would be returned. To assure the orderly takeover of Damietta, al-Kamil insisted upon an exchange of hostages, to be freed only when the city was firmly in Egyptian hands again. He specifically asked for Cardinal Pelagius, King John, the grand master of the Knights Templar, and a number of Christian nobles. In exchange, the sultan offered hostages to guarantee his own performance, including one of his sons, one of his brothers, and a group of Egyptian emirs.

Before he surrendered himself to hostage status, Cardinal Pelagius sent delegations of Knights Templar and Teutonic Knights under their grand masters into Damietta to tell the Christian garrison of the agreement to surrender the city. Perhaps he didn't go himself because he knew very well that anger brought on by catastrophe is often turned on the messengers who bring the bad news. A furious mob attacked the Templars and Teutonic Knights, who barricaded themselves in the buildings housing their headquarters.

The sultan entertained his hostages at a great banquet while the terms of the surrender were being carried out. Glancing at King John, he expressed his surprise at seeing tears running down the cheeks of such a famous warrior. John replied that the tears were the overflow of his feelings of guilt. Here he sat with all he could eat of the most magnificent dishes, while at the Christian camp the men he had led here were starving to death. The sultan clapped his hands, summoning his stewards, and gave his orders. A few hours later, pack animals and carts loaded down with food were driven into the Crusader camp. Now the Christians could ponder how these swarthy turbaned men, whom they had been taught all their lives were the very essence of evil and the instruments of Satan, could also be these angels of mercy bringing life-saving provisions.

This irony was a fitting note on which to end the Fifth Crusade, which was a momentous military and religious disaster. It might remotely have been considered something of a religious victory at the last moment, but when the time came to deliver up the True Cross, Sultan al-Kamil could only apologize. That hallowed symbol of the crucified Christ was of no importance to anyone at the Muslim court, and sometime during the recent war it had been misplaced. The sultan had ordered a thorough search, but the True Cross was lost. Some of the Crusaders decided God probably did not want them to have it.

17

The Emperor Frederick
1221 to 1229

KING JOHN OF JERUSALEM used the period of peace after the disaster in Egypt to rebuild trade with the Muslims, which was vital to the economy of his little country. To the north, however, there would be no peace until the matter of the succession to the throne of Armenia could be settled, and along with it, the rule of Antioch. The struggles for power turned bloody, with the Knights Templar and the Hospitallers deeply involved in the intrigue, still on opposite sides, in spite of their recent cooperation on the Crusade up the Nile.

Upon the death of King John's wife and son, the legitimate heirs to the Armenian kingdom, Prince Raymond-Roupen of Antioch asserted his own right to claim the throne. He had the support of both the pope and the Knights Hospitaller, to whom he entrusted the citadel of Antioch. He also made an agreement with the Hospitallers that if they could retake Jabala from the Muslims, it would be theirs, including the surrounding lands.

Bohemond of Tripoli wanted Antioch back and had the full support of the Knights Templar. His chance came when the Armenian nobles rejected the claim of Raymond-Roupen and chose instead to pledge their allegiance to the young Princess Isabella, as their dead king had ordered them to do. They were not Roman Catholics and resented the pope trying to interfere in the government of their country, which they strongly felt was none of his business. They chose an Armenian noble named Adam of Baghras to act as regent, to rule in the princess's place until a husband could be found. A few weeks later a bag of gold changed hands as the Hospitallers arranged to have Adam murdered by the Assassins. Bohemond took advantage of the resulting confusion to attack Antioch, assisted by the Templars, and easily overwhelmed the city, although the Hospitallers still held the citadel. Bohemond bottled them up there to squeeze them into surrender.

As the replacement for the murdered regent Adam of Baghras, the Armenian nobles selected one of their own number, an ambitious soldier named Constantine, head of the house of Hethoum. Constantine immediately assembled an army from among his supporters and went after the rival claimant, Prince Raymond-Roupen, who with Antioch gone had little military backing against the Armenian army. After a brief clash, the prince was taken prisoner and, to no one's surprise, died in his cell a few weeks later. Now Isabella was the unquestioned ruler of Armenia, but she would have a regent running the country for her as long as she remained unmarried.

In Antioch, Bohemond's isolation of the citadel was successful. As their food ran out, the Hospitallers abandoned the fortress. Most of them left the city, to the delight of the Templars. They were even happier when Bohemond disavowed Raymond-Roupen's promise that the Hospitallers could have the rights to Jabala and assigned those rights to the Knights Templar. The papal legate calmed the growing tension between the orders, removing a very real threat of battle between the Templars and the Hospitallers by getting them to agree to share equally the rights to the as yet unconquered Jabala.

Bohemond responded to the papal legate's interference by seizing all of the Hospitaller property in Antioch. The legate countered by excommunicating Bohemond. Then, angered by the Templar's continued alliance with the man he had excommunicated, the legate complained to the pope, who confirmed the excommunication and ordered the Knights Templar to abandon their friendship with Bohemond. They had no choice but to obey, or at least to appear to obey. The pope offered no warning or advice to the Hospitallers about their alliance with the Muslim Assassins.

Politics now suggested that the best way to guarantee peace between Antioch and Armenia would be for one of Bohemond's sons to marry Queen Isabella of Antioch. A few months earlier the Armenian demands would have precluded such a marriage, but Bohemond, now excommunicated, had no qualms about agreeing to the Armenian insistence that Bohemond's son Philip, selected as the bridegroom, must renounce his Roman Catholic faith and join the Separated Armenian Church.

The ex-regent Constantine predictably refused to relinquish his power to the new young king from Antioch. One night Philip was kidnapped and thrown into a dungeon in the castle at the Armenian capital of Sis, which Constantine had under his control.

Queen Isabella, frightened for her life, fled for protection to the

Hospitallers. It was a grave mistake. When Constantine demanded that the young queen be turned over to him, the Hospitallers, who recognized that Constantine would now be the enemy of their own enemy Bohemond, delivered the terrified girl to him. Constantine sent his executioners to murder Philip in his dungeon, then forced Queen Isabella to marry his own son.

Bohemond's act of vengeance for the murder of his son was to inform the Seljuk Turks that they could raid into Armenia with full assurance that Bohemond would not interfere. For his part, Constantine made essentially the same proposal to the Sunni emir of Aleppo, suggesting that the emir should feel free to attack Antioch. Neither Muslim group could be incited to attack, happy to have the Christians at each other's throats, and for the time being the bitterly angry stalemate lent some stability to the rule of the two northern principalities.

To the south King John had concerns about his own succession. He needed to find a suitable husband for his daughter Yolanda. He could see no likely candidate in the Holy Land, so in 1222 he decided to travel to France. He would seek the help of the king who had been responsible for the marriage arrangements that had made him the king of Jerusalem. King Philip would find a husband for his eleven-year-old daughter.

John's plans changed when he stopped off in Rome to visit the pope. Hermann von Salza, the grand master of the Teutonic Knights, was there and offered an intriguing suggestion. His idea was that Yolanda should be betrothed to his good friend the Holy Roman Emperor Frederick II. The emperor, whose wife had died just four months before, was still in his twenties; surely there could be no better match in all the world. The pope was delighted. If Frederick were to become king of Jerusalem, he would be moved to act on the vow he had made back in 1215 to lead a Crusade. As for John, the marriage would mean that he would be the father-in-law of the Holy Roman Emperor and perhaps the grandfather of the next emperor. But as he reflected, he became increasingly concerned about his own position in the Holy Land once the royal marriage was consummated. Grand Master de Salza reassured him: John would rule as regent for the rest of his life.

For Frederick II the prospect of a new opportunity to extend his personal power was always welcome. It was from the Holy Roman Emperor that King Amalric of Cyprus had received his crown some twenty-five years earlier, so Frederick as the present emperor had suzerainty over the island kingdom. Since the present king, Henry I, was only eleven years old, Frederick should have no problem asserting his authority there. Once married to Queen Yolanda, he would be king of Jerusalem. All together, events seemed to indicate that he should be able to bring all of the Crusader states under his autocratic rule, the only kind of rule Frederick understood.

The only objection might come from King Philip of France, who had expected to be the one to nominate a husband for the little queen, but Philip was in ill health. He died in July 1223, but he did not forget the Holy Land. He left substantial bequests of gold for the support of the Knights Templar, the Hospitallers, and the kingdom of Jerusalem. The portion for Jerusalem was turned over to King John.

As pleased as Frederick was with the general plan, he took his time with the arrangements, and it was not until August of 1225 that the archbishop of Capua arrived at Acre to act as proxy for Frederick in a marriage ceremony without the bridegroom. Having reached the legal age of fourteen, Yolanda could now be crowned queen of Jerusalem, and the coronation ceremonies following the marriage-by-proxy took place in the cathedral at Tyre, with the military orders in full attendance, along with the local barons.

Yolanda was brought to Frederick in Italy, where a second wedding took place in the cathedral at Brindisi. Frederick was now king of Jerusalem, although John still labored under the impression that he remained regent for his daughter.

The truth emerged a few days after the wedding, when John visited his daughter to find her weeping uncontrollably. It seemed that Frederick had already seduced one of Yolanda's cousins who had traveled with her to Italy. When John went to Frederick to deliver an outraged father's reprimand, his remonstrances were totally ignored. Instead, a cold, imperious son-in-law informed John that he was finished. The promise that John would retain his role as regent had not been made by Frederick personally, and no such promise would be honored. The emperor demanded that the gold John had received from the estate of King Philip of France be turned over to him as the legal ruler of Jerusalem. He then ordered John from his court, telling him not to come back. John seethed in furious frustration, but even his friend the pope had to agree that the legalities were on Frederick's side. Yolanda had a worse shock of her own when Frederick ordered that the queen be taken to the harem he maintained in Sicily, guarded by Muslim eunuchs.

No one who knew Frederick well would have been surprised by any of these actions. He was a brilliant man, educated beyond his years, but he obeyed no moral code whatsoever, fully convinced that whatever he chose to do was automatically right. He was the most powerful ruler in Europe and recognized no higher authority than himself, especially not that of the Church. He had no interest in the spiritual rewards the Church claimed to be able to bestow, because his mind was concentrated on the rewards he could have here and now. Similarly, he had no personal fear of the spiritual weapons of the Church, although he was well aware of the horror his Christian subjects felt at threats of interdict and excommunication. As a safety measure, therefore, he drew upon the substantial Muslim population of his lands in Sicily and southern Italy to maintain regiments of Islamic soldiers, loyal only to him and contemptuous of the Catholic notion that the pope alone was the director of admissions to paradise.

No one questioned that the most powerful monarch in Europe was also the best educated, with an impressive grasp of mathematics, navigation, astronomy, and philosophy. Frederick possessed a natural talent for languages, which he mastered easily. He learned German from his father's people, Italian from his mother's, and Latin from his ecclesiastic tutors. He was fluent in French, and through mixing with the conquered peoples of Sicily where he grew up, he became completely at ease in Greek and Arabic. He was fascinated, but not captivated, by the various religions around him and studied each of them. Yet with that deep knowledge of the world's great moral and spiritual teachings, he forged a way of life that paid no regard to the moral principles of any of them. He was intrigued by all he heard of a variety of sexual practices and tried them all. He maintained a harem at Palermo, established on the Islamic model, and it was to that alien atmosphere that he had condemned his teenage queen Yolanda. She died there at the age of sixteen, giving birth to Frederick's heir, Conrad II. She had exercised the only right she was allowed as a married woman, the right to have a baby.

Frederick had put his intimate knowledge of Middle Eastern affairs to work and for several years had been exchanging envoys with Sultan al-Kamil of Egypt. Saladin's empire had by now achieved a measure of stability in its division into three parts, ruled by three brothers who were nephews of Saladin. Mesopotamia (Iraq) was ruled by al-Ashraf. Damascus was under al-Mu'azzam, and Egypt was ruled by Sultan al-Kamil, who was technically over his brothers, on a legal basis of inheritance that al-Kamil could not enforce. A bitter dispute had broken out between al-Kamil of Egypt and al-Mu'azzam, whose Syrian holdings included the Christian Holy Places of Jerusalem, Nazareth, and Bethlehem. When al-Mu'azzam sought an alliance with Jelal ad-Din and his Kwarismian hordes, who had been driven from their Central Asian homeland by Genghis Khan, the Egyptian sultan turned to Frederick II. He preferred the idea of Christian allies from Europe because they came, fought, and then went away. Muslim allies were more likely to take lands and keep them.

To test the water, Frederick sent two envoys to al-Kamil with a special gift, a magnificent horse with a saddle covered in gold and set with precious stones. The sultan responded by housing the envoys in the sumptuous splendor of the palace of the former vizier. He loaded them down with valuable gifts to take back to Frederick, along with his assurances of friendship and cooperation.

Following instructions, one of Frederick's envoys then went to Damascus, bearing gifts for al-Mu'azzam. The reception was cold, the accommodations mean. When the envoy left, al-Mu'azzam told him to convey the message to Frederick that the only gift the emir of Damascus had for the German emperor was the sharp edge of his scimitar. It didn't take a brilliant mind to get the message and choose between the two rulers.

Al-Kamil and Frederick reached a satisfactory agreement with ease. In exchange for military assistance against his brother al-Mu'az-zam, the sultan would give to Frederick the Holy City of Jerusalem, along with the lands and towns around it. Frederick had bartered his way into a successful Crusade without even leaving home.

Before embarking on that Crusade, however, Frederick was most anxious to establish his rule over the Lombard states in northern Italy. His kingdom of Sicily extended farther than the Mediterrean island itself, including as it did all of Italy south of Rome. With Lombardy he would rule all of Italy except the maritime city-states on the coasts and the Papal territory in the middle. Pope Honorius fully realized the danger to the papal domains, but he never gave up on the idea that Frederick could be swayed by compromise and conciliation. That optimistic attitude died with him in March 1227.

The bishops of the Church, concerned about Frederick's threat to their properties and privileges, wasted no time in electing a successor who would fight for the rights of the Holy Mother Church. The very day after the death of Honorius III they named the cardinal bishop of Ostia to ascend the papal throne. The cardinal took the title of Pope Gregory IX. Gregory held little respect for compromise as a constructive tool in establishing Church supremacy. He intended to reestablish the traditional vassalage of the kingdom of Sicily. He also wanted Frederick to lose his struggle for control of Lombardy. In fact, he wanted Frederick out of Italy. The simplest method to achieve that goal was to demand that the emperor abandon his everlasting procrastination and go on Crusade.

Under constant pressure from the new pope, in August of 1227 Frederick finally sent an advance army of several thousand knights and soldiers to the Holy Land under the command of Duke Henry of Limburg, accompanied by Hermann von Salza, grand master of the Teutonic Knights. Together they mounted a drive on Sidon as soon as their army arrived at Acre. By treaty, Sidon had been divided between Muslims and Christians, but now the Muslims were driven out. Preparing for Frederick's arrival, troops were sent south to reinforce Jaffa and Caesarea. Duke Henry joined with de Salza in the capture of the castle fortress of Montfort, which was turned over to the Teutonic Knights. Later, with its name changed from the French Montfort to the Germanic Starkenburg, it became the headquarters of the Teutonic order.

Frederick was amassing a crusading army at Brindisi on the Adriatic coast, and he was pleased when his army was joined by one of his favorite vassals, Louis of Thuringia, with several hundred mounted followers. Frederick's fleet left on September 8, 1227, a few weeks after Duke Henry's departure, and Frederick took his friend Louis of Thuringia with him on the flagship. Louis was struck down by a severe illness just a few days out, so Frederick ordered the ship to make port at Otranto. Louis died there, unmourned, remembered in history for a single act of meanness, while his wife by that same act became the object of adoration by millions from that day to this. The story is that in a time of famine, his wife was deeply concerned for the people in the village below their castle. Although the castle was more than amply supplied with provisions, Louis was exasperated by his wife's constant appeals to share what they had with the starving villagers. He flatly refused to part with any of the stocks of food in the castle. In frustration and compassion, she decided to thwart his authority. One night she filled her apron with fresh loaves from the castle bakery and slipped out the postern gate, intending to smuggle the bread to the starving peasants.

Louis had been watching her and confronted her on the road, demanding to know what she was holding in her apron. Frightened by the thought of the punishment that would inevitably fall on her, his wife answered that her apron was full of roses. Fortunately, the Holy Virgin had also been watching her, touched by her concern for the poor. When Louis pulled the apron down to expose the evidence of his wife's crime, beautiful, radiant roses tumbled out. The compassionate wife was saved by the intervention and protection of the Holy Mother. Louis's life is long forgotten, but his wife is remembered every day as St. Elizabeth of Hungary.

When Frederick reported the death of Louis to Pope Gregory, he added that he, too, had succumbed to the same sickness and was off to restore his health at the spa of Pozzuoli before resuming the Crusade. The prospect of the emperor wallowing in luxury at a spa when he should be fighting for the True Cross was the last straw. Gregory immediately issued a formal proclamation excommunicating the Holy Roman Emperor. Now Frederick couldn't go on Crusade even if he wanted to, or so the pope thought. Frederick felt otherwise. He dispatched letters to all the monarchs of Europe justifying his own actions and deploring a politically ambitious, avaricious papacy. Ignoring the pope's warning that as an excommunicate he could not participate in a Crusade, Frederick organized a fresh band of followers and left for the Holy Land in June 1228. Now, however, his arrival was not met with the welcome he had expected.

Al-Mu'azzam of Damascus had died in November of the previous year and had been succeeded by his ineffective son an-Nasir Dawud. Sultan al-Kamil no longer felt the danger that had troubled him before al-Mu'azzam's death, and he certainly didn't need Frederick's help to dominate his young nephew. In addition, Queen Yolanda had died, and with her Frederick's right to the title of king of Jerusalem. At most, he might assert his right to act as regent for his infant son Conrad, the rightful heir, but under the laws of Jerusalem that position still needed ratification by the High Court of Jerusalem. Frederick, typically, decided to bully his way to control and to begin with the island kingdom of Cyprus.

King Henry I of Cyprus was just eleven years old, and his mother, Alice of Jerusalem, was his regent. With Queen Alice's consent, the High Court of Jerusalem had invited the boy king's nearest male relative to act as *bailli*, or governor, of Cyprus. He was the aging John of Ibelin, the lord of Beirut and the most respected nobleman in the Holy Land. John was on hand to greet Frederick as he landed at Limassol to offer him the use of the royal palace. The emperor announced that he would stage a banquet, to which he asked John of Ibelin to bring his own sons as well as the young king, so that he could get to know them all better. Although friends warned him of the treacherous nature of his host, John could see no basis on which he could refuse. He led the invited guests to the great feast.

As the dishes were set before them, Frederick's soldiers took control of all the doors leading out of the palace. Then some of them moved idly around the great hall until there was a man with a drawn sword behind every guest. As soon as they were in position, Frederick dropped his mask of hospitality and revealed his true character and purpose. Backed by the imminent threat of cold steel, he demanded that John immediately surrender the mainland city of Beirut to him, and further, that he be given all of the Cypriot revenues that had been collected during the boy king's reign.

If Frederick had expected John of Ibelin to cave in to the imperial commands, he was disappointed. The old soldier stood up and looked Frederick in the eye. He stated his position clearly. He had been entrusted with Beirut by his sister, Queen Isabella of Jerusalem. It had not been so much a gift as a responsibility. He had rebuilt the walls of the city that the Muslims had torn down. He had fortified the city, provided it with a garrison, and given it a Christian government according to the laws of the kingdom of Jerusalem. Since the death of Queen Yolanda, Frederick was not the king of Jerusalem and could not take the city away. John would defend his rights to Beirut before the High Court of Jerusalem. As to the revenues of Cyprus, John was offended that any man would impugn his honor by questioning his administration. As quickly as the revenues had been collected, in accordance with the law and in keeping with his fiduciary responsibility, they had been turned over to the regent, Queen Alice. Threats of death did not change the facts, and they certainly would not change the law of the land.

As the two stared each other down, the man of great personal honor and the man with no honor, they both knew that Frederick had only brought about three thousand soldiers with him to Cyprus, far too few to risk in outright warfare. The autocrat switched from imperious dictator to man of reason. Did not the Holy Roman Emperor have rights of suzerainty over Cyprus? The High Court of Jerusalem had no legal right whatever to name the *bailli* of Cyprus. As to John's city of Beirut, the High Court certainly had jurisdiction there and the matter would be put to them. It was agreed that John would step aside for a *bailli* for Cyprus to be named by Frederick.

The guests got away from the banquet alive, but when the nobles of Cyprus learned what had happened, they were all in favor of assassinating Frederick while he was still in Cyprus. John persuaded them that only war could result from that rash act, and the Germans could call up the largest army in Christendom.

Frederick had also sent for Prince Bohemond of Antioch and Tripoli to come to him on Cyprus. Bohemond answered the call and took up quarters in Limassol, prepared to meet the emperor. Totally relaxed, he was shocked out of his complacency by the story told him of the emperor's style of entertainment. He had himself carried to his ship on a pallet, while a messenger was sent to report to Frederick that Bohemond had been struck with a sudden severe illness and was being taken home to die. Once out to sea, Bohemond experienced a miraculous recovery and counted himself fortunate to have so narrowly escaped the clutches of the predatory monarch.

In spite of the stories that might have reached the mainland about his conduct on Cyprus, upon his arrival in Acre in September 1228 Frederick was greeted as a savior. One chronicler reported that Knights Templar prostrated themselves before him, and that some wrapped their arms around his knees. It appears, though, that their adoration may have been more political than passionate. Great favor was being shown to the Teutonic Knights, with gifts of gold and land, and it is likely that the Templars were anxious not to be left out of the imperial largesse.

In Rome, Pope Gregory was furious to learn that Frederick had ignored the papal order not to go on Crusade and excommunicated him again for this latest transgression. Letters arrived at Acre instructing the patriarch of Jerusalem to forbid Frederick's entrance into any church or participation in any religious services. Specific letters to the Knights Templar and the Hospitallers instructed them to have nothing to do with the excommunicated emperor, who had come among them in a state of grievous sin. For his own part, the pope busied himself with attempts on Frederick's authority in Lombardy and in the kingdom of Sicily, which led to the use of papal funds to assemble an army. The dispossessed John of Brienne, ex-king of Jerusalem, was delighted to accept the military command to fight on the side of the Church against his enemy Frederick.

Sultan al-Kamil had not waited for Frederick. With his brother al-Mu'azzam dead, replaced by his inexperienced young son an-Nasir Dawud, al-Kamil had decided to take over Syria. He marched into the Holy Land and seized all the lands between Egypt and the Jordan, including Jerusalem. An-Nasir begged his other uncle, al-Ashraf, to bring an army from Mesopotamia to rescue him from al-Kamil. Al-Ashraf came, but not to rescue an-Nasir. He publicly announced that he had brought an army to hold back the new Christian invaders, the same claim announced to the Muslim world by al-Kamil. But when the two brothers met privately near Gaza they dropped their propaganda effort and got down to business. They readily agreed to divide young an-Nasir's lands between them. The terrified young man, who had just learned an important lesson about family ties among the mighty, shut himself up in Damascus, which was under siege a few days later. Now the presence of Frederick and his army were an annoyance to al-Kamil. The sultan could not concentrate his forces at Damascus because he could not predict what Frederick's reaction would be when he learned that Jerusalem was not going to be handed over to him in accordance with their previous agreement. An Egyptian army had to be kept in reserve in case Frederick opted for war.

Once the emperor had a tally made of all the available Christian forces, he had to be realistic. The total came to about eight hundred knights and ten thousand soldiers, but many of them were not likely to follow him. He had alienated the French nobles of Cyprus, so their loyalty was doubtful. The seasoned forces of the Knights Templar and the Hospitallers had been specifically ordered by the pope to separate themselves from him. And there was no good way to evaluate the number of Italian soldiers who had been swayed by the thundering sermons of the patriarch, who lost no opportunity to point out the perils to the soul of any Christian who would follow a man who had been excommunicated by the Holy Father himself. The emperor decided that he must advance on Jerusalem, but with such a small army, wisdom dictated that he simultaneously try diplomacy. He dispatched envoys to al-Kamil and set his army on the road leading south along the coast.

Pedro de Montaigu, grand master of the Knights Templar, had an important decision to make. He obviously could not ignore a direct order from the pope, but he knew that the army marching out from Acre knew neither the country nor the enemy. Could the Templars live with themselves if they allowed Christians to be butchered while they simply stood by? And what if Frederick, either through battle or bargaining, could actually regain the Holy City? If Jerusalem was to be taken, the Knights Templar wanted to be there, especially to make certain that they would regain their lost headquarters on the Temple Mount. De Montaigu couldn't take orders from Frederick, but neither would he let him go alone. As a result, while Frederick's army moved on ahead, the grand master and his Knights Templar followed the Christian army one full day behind. The Hospitallers found that to be a working solution for them as well and followed just behind the Templars. In obedience to the pope, neither order would obey any directives of the excommunicated emperor.

On the march, Frederick turned his diplomatic skills loose on the military orders behind him. He promised the grand masters that his name would not appear on any orders. All official military directives would be issued only in the names of God and the Lord Jesus Christ, whom they all served. The grand masters and their officers decided to accept that bit of religious reasoning, and soon the Templars and the Hospitallers were riding with Frederick's—or rather, God's—army. They marched down to Arsuf, where Richard of England had done battle with Saladin, then on to Jaffa.

While Frederick set his men to work strengthening the defenses of Jaffa, his envoys were making good progress with al-Kamil. The emperor knew that the Muslim leadership set great store by the need to save face, and it was on that basis that his plans were presented to the sultan. Frederick had come here at al-Kamil's invitation. To keep his word to the sultan he had suffered a serious break with the leader of his own Catholic faith. Jerusalem was a miserable place now. Its walls had been torn down, and most of the residents were gone. It could be of no real importance to al-Kamil or Islam but was vital to Frederick, because with its possession he could return home with honor and restore his relationship with his religious leaders. To al-Kamil, all that talk simply meant that in return for one defenseless inland city Frederick would go home, leaving the sultan to pursue his goal to take the much richer city of Damascus.

Al-Kamil agreed to give Jerusalem to Frederick, but only on certain rigid terms. The emperor was not concerned about terms: He had received word that the pope had managed to assemble an army to invade Frederick's lands in Italy, led by John of Brienne, who was enthusiastic about this blessed opportunity to take his revenge on his former father-in-law. Frederick was much more anxious to leave Palestine than al-Kamil realized.

The terms were spelled out. Frederick was to have Jerusalem, but it was to remain undefended. He would also have Bethlehem and Nazareth, but the Muslims would keep Hebron. The Holy Places of Islam must be respected, so the Christians could not have the Temple Mount, the *Haram es-Sharif*, with its two great mosques, the Dome of the Rock and the al-Aqsa. Frederick agreed.

The Knights Templar were furious. Grand Master de Montaigu announced that his order would not participate in such an agreement. For Christianity as a whole the most important building in Jerusalem was the Church of the Holy Sepulcher, but for the Knights Templar it was the al-Aqsa Mosque, the building that had been given to the founding knights by Baldwin II on the site that had given them their name. The Templars would have nothing to do with Frederick's occupation of the Holy City, especially since the emperor's treaty would bind them in a truce with the Muslims for the next ten years, for long after Frederick would have gone home.

The patriarch of Jerusalem, equally incensed, agreed with the Templars, especially angry that Frederick had actually agreed that the Muslims could have guards on the Temple Mount (the same situation that infuriates Orthodox Jews today). The patriarch placed the entire city of Jerusalem under interdict.

Any man who could ignore the pope would have no trouble ignoring a patriarch, so Frederick entered Jerusalem on March 17, 1229. He immediately set about currying favor with the Muslims of the city, eager to show off his knowledge of their faith, thus losing support among many of the Christians around him. Upon rising on his first morning in the city, Frederick asked why he had not heard the muezzins calling the faithful to prayer. The reply was that the calls to prayer had been silenced out of respect for the Christian emperor. Frederick assured the Muslims that he enjoyed hearing the muezzins praising God from their minarets and asked that the calls to prayer go forward in the customary way. When he saw a Catholic priest stroll into the al-Aqsa Mosque with the Christian bible in his hands, Frederick had the priest ejected and dressed him down in the presence of both Christian and Muslim onlookers. He told the priest to pass the word to his clerical colleagues that any such profanation of a holy mosque in the future would earn the penalty of death. He praised Islam and mocked Christianity to such a degree that he produced the opposite effect to the one he desired. The Muslims could understand and respect any man's veneration of his own religion, even his willingness to die for it, but they felt suspicious of a man who would mock his own religion while praising another's.

Frederick had one remaining task to fulfill before leaving the Holy City. He intended to be crowned king of Jerusalem in the Church of the Holy Sepulcher. The patriarch, the Knights Templar, and the Hospitallers refused to attend. With Frederick still under a proclamation of excommunication and the city of Jerusalem under interdict, there was no member of the clergy who would officiate. The closest Frederick could come to Church participation was the Teutonic Knights, who on this campaign had discovered that they were Germans first and Roman Catholics second.

The crown was placed on the altar in what turned out to be a purely secular ceremony. The emperor picked up the crown and put it on his head. Then his friend Hermann von Salza, grand master of the Teutonic Knights, read a eulogy on the self-crowned king which Frederick had prepared for him. It recited Frederick's faithfulness to his crusading vow. It extolled his success regaining the Holy City, in spite of the unreasonable opposition of others who called themselves Christians, by which he meant the Templars, the Hospitallers, and the patriarch of Jerusalem. Surely, von Salza said, the time had come to set aside the excommunication of this devout son of the Church. Frederick rewarded the Teutonic Knights for their loyalty by giving them some of the newly acquired lands near Jerusalem, which added to the growing anger of the Knights Templar.

Another group was unhappy with the manner in which Frederick had obtained Jerusalem from Sultan al-Kamil, because legally the city was not al-Kamil's to give. Palestine belonged to Damascus, and the people of that city were not pleased that the Egyptian sultan had given their property to the Christians, especially since that property was sacred to the memory of the Prophet and his nocturnal journey to the throne of Allah. They closed the gates of Damascus to Christians as well as Egyptians.

Now it was the turn of the local barons and the Italian traders to be angry with Frederick. A profitable trade had grown up between the inland caravan terminal of Damascus and the Christian ports that sent their goods on to Europe. Now Frederick had caused those profits to be shut off. They were merchants, not mystics, and Jerusalem meant little or nothing to them. They wanted Frederick out of their country, and out of their hair.

That gave popular backing to the patriarch, as well as to the Knights Templar who supported the patriarch's every word and action against the German emperor. Frederick decided to punish the Templars in a way that would hurt. He would capture their great stronghold of Castle Pilgrim at Athlit and give it to the Teutonic Knights. Some of those German knights had seen Castle Pilgrim and urged Frederick to abandon the idea. The huge fortress had been built to be impregnable. It had supplies enough for years of siege and could be constantly reinforced by sea. It had its own freshwater spring. Many men would die trying to take Castle Pilgrim away from the Knights Templar in a siege that might well go on for years. Frederick had no desire for a long stay in the Holy Land, so he abandoned the idea to take the castle, but he had another plan to punish the Templars that he set in motion upon his return to Acre.

His plan was to kidnap the Templar grand master and take him back to Italy as a hostage, to keep the order under his personal control. To that end he had his soldiers block all of the streets leading to the Templar fortress in the southwest corner of the city. The problem was that whenever the grand master went out, he had a body of battle-hardened Knights Templar before him, behind him, and alongside him in full battle armor, with their hands on their swords. The German soldiers were prepared to obey their emperor, but these bearded fanatics were ready to die for their grand master, and their hostile glances seemed to be inviting a fight. For the Germans, politics required that they scowl ferociously back at the Templars, but prudence dictated that they keep their hands off their swords. After a few days the kidnap plan was abandoned.

Frederick's popularity, or lack of it, was dramatically demonstrated during the final minutes of his stay. He was anxious to defend his lands from the papal army at home and had arranged for his departure on May 1, 1229. His problem was that to get to the harbor he had to pass through the Street of the Butchers. Had Frederick been riding out on this May Day in his own land, he would have been pelted with fragrant flowers and festooned with garlands of spring blossoms, but as he proceeded down the narrow passage between the slaughterhouses, he was pelted with dripping organs and festooned with the bloody intestines of slaughtered animals. His procession continued on its way, but one must give in to the vision of bearded Knights Templar grinning at Frederick's discomfiture as they watched him peel away fetid strings of offal from his imperial robes while struggling to maintain a dignified, stately progress to the royal ship.

18

The Disorder of the Temple
1229 to 1239

FREDERICK HAD NO INTENTION of abandoning his claims to the crown of Jerusalem, as he would soon prove. First, however, he had to deal with the problems that had brought him home. His forces held the papal armies at bay in Italy, permitting him to seize Church property in Sicily, including the properties of the Knights Templar. He easily proved his military superiority, but the stigma of his excommunication was giving him problems with his people, which was exactly its purpose. He proposed reconciliation to the pope and they finally reached mutually acceptable terms in 1230.

The essence of their agreement was that the emperor bought off his excommunication. Frederick agreed that the Church in Sicily and southern Italy would be returned to papal control. No longer would he subject the clergy there to his secular laws, nor would he interfere in the granting of benefices or the appointment of bishops. He reluctantly agreed to return to the Knights Templar the lands he had seized as punishment for their disdainful treatment of him during his Crusade. The final arrangements were made at a private dinner to which, with Gregory's approval, Frederick invited his friend Hermann von Salza. The grand master of the Teutonic Knights had stood firmly behind the emperor during the time when he was under excommunication, and Frederick wanted to make certain that the German military order would not be punished by the Church.

The pope, of course, had not excommunicated the emperor to effect the eternal damnation of his soul, but as a weapon in their duel for supremacy. In exchange for Frederick's concessions and payments, the pope happily reversed his excommunication, content that he was getting real property and hard cash in exchange for spiritual currency, of which the Church had an inexhaustible supply. At Frederick's request, the pope also ordered the patriarch of Jerusalem to lift the interdict he had laid on the city of Jerusalem.

Now Frederick could get on with his plans for Jerusalem and Cyprus. Upon his departure from the Holy Land, Frederick had appointed *baillis* to rule in his place. He had given the joint governorship of the mainland kingdom of Jerusalem to Balian of Sidon and a German nobleman named Garnier. They made no demands on the local barons or on the military orders, so they had no trouble. On Cyprus it was a different story.

Frederick had actually decided to place the rule of the island in the hands of not one man, but five. He had given the baillis firm instructions to eject all members of the Ibelin family of John of Ibelin and all of his followers. To recoup some of the expenses of his expedition to the Holy Land, Frederick ordered them to collect for him the sum of ten thousand marks. To raise that money they levied new taxes on all the people of Cyprus and began confiscating any property that belonged to relatives or friends of John of Ibelin.

An appeal was made to John to come to Cyprus to halt the impoverishment of men whose only crime was that they were known to be his friends. Using his influence and wealth, John assembled an army and sailed to Cyprus, then marched inland to the capital of Nicosia to give battle to the army assembled by Frederick's five *baillis*. Joined by his friends on the island, John's army prevailed and drove Frederick's barons to the safety of the three different castles. John's men took the weakest of the three, then settled down to a long siege of the other two. The fortresses held out for almost a year, but finally both castles surrendered to John of Ibelin in July of the year 1230, three months after Frederick had made his peace with the pope. John assumed the governorship of Cyprus, which he planned to hold until King Henry reached the legal age of fifteen, in two years time.

When the news reached Frederick, he was outraged at the affront to his authority. He put together a small army of about forty-five hundred men, including six hundred knights and a hundred mounted sergeants. He gave command of the army to his imperial marshal, an Italian named Richard Filangieri, who as Frederick's legate was to take control of the kingdoms of Cyprus and Jerusalem. Filangieri took with him to the east his brother Lothair and another Italian noble, Count Walter of Manupello. A fleet of thirty-two galleys was assembled to carry this imperial disciplinary force to the Middle East.

John of Ibelin, having received advance word of the approach of Frederick's punitive expedition, guessed correctly that Filangieri would approach Cyprus first. Collecting all of his men at Beirut except for a token force to guard the citadel, John hurried to Cyprus. When Filangieri arrived offshore, he learned that John had an armed force in place protecting King Henry. He dispatched an envoy to the young king, demanding in the emperor's name that John and all other members of the Ibelin clan be exiled from Cyprus, and that all their lands be forfeit to the crown. Since John was obviously in control, Filangieri was not surprised at the rejection of his demand, but he was delighted with the rumors that John had emptied Beirut of fighting men to make this stand. He could easily beat John to Beirut because his men were already standing by their ships, and the galley slaves were ready at the oars. Those slaves were strained to their limits in response to Filangieri's order to proceed to Beirut at top speed.

As expected, he found Beirut undefended and took it without so much as a scuffle. He assigned men to keep the tiny garrison cooped up in the citadel and dispatched troops to occupy Sidon and Tyre. Stunned by the sudden and successful onslaught of the imperial army, the local barons responded to Filangieri's demand for an assembly of the High Court of Jerusalem. He showed his formal letter of appointment as Frederick's *bailli* for the Christian states, which no one contested. The Templars still detested the emperor Frederick, but could no longer take a stand based upon his excommunication.

Filled up with his newfound power, Filangieri then announced that he was seizing all lands of the Ibelins, which would henceforth be the property of his imperial majesty Frederick II. Now the local barons grew vocal. What was proposed for the Ibelins could also happen to them. They pointed out that under their system of law only the High Court could confiscate land, and then only after the owner of that property had the opportunity to formally defend himself. Filangieri made it clear that he had come to enforce the laws of the emperor, not those of Jerusalem. The effect was to draw almost all the local barons into a single party opposed to the imperial usurpation.

On his side, Filangieri had his own army, the Teutonic Knights, and the merchants of Pisa. The strongest uncommitted faction was the Knights Templar. The revocation of Frederick's excommunication made their cooperation with him possible, and Frederick certainly now had the backing of their master, the pope, but the Templars had a lot to remember. Frederick had plotted to take their stronghold at Athlit. He had embarked upon an unsuccessful attempt to kidnap their grand master. He had confiscated Templar property in Sicily. The Knights Templar, with no reason to like the Holy

Roman Emperor, had no desire to help him establish his autocratic rule over the Holy Land. Whether they would actually take steps to oppose him remained to be seen. For now, they stood aside to watch the events unfold. The patriarch of Jerusalem and the Hospitallers also decided to stay uncommitted.

When John of Ibelin got word of Filangieri's occupation of his city, he left Cyprus with his own troops, reinforced by an armed force of sympathetic Cypriots. Landing near Beirut, which did not expect any attack, John's men went over the wall at night and opened the gates. With sympathizers in the city, they fought their way through the streets and took the citadel. Filangieri called for help from the local barons, but only a few chose to join him. Hoping to prevent an all-out war of one Christian party against another, the patriarch of Jerusalem went to Filangieri with the grand masters of both the Knights Templar and the Hospitallers, but Filangieri refused to negotiate. The emperor had told him to oust the Ibelins and take their lands. There could be no compromise with direct orders from the mightiest potentate in the Christian world.

John was in the citadel at Beirut, ready for a fight, with leading Cypriot nobles beside him. Young King Henry had been sent to Acre for his safety. The opportunity was too good for Filangieri to pass up. He loaded a major part of his army into his galleys, with orders to make all speed to Cyprus, which was sitting there undefended and ripe for plucking.

Now there would be all-out war, as John of Ibelin commandeered all of the ships at Acre to take a relieving army to Cyprus. King Henry offered land in exchange for service to any knight who would enlist against Filangieri. He needed money for supplies and equipment, so two nobles of the Ibelin clan offered to sell properties in Caesarea and Acre to provide the necessary funds. With such an uncertain state of affairs, there were only two prospective buyers who were confident of their own future positions, the Knights Templar and the Hospitallers, both always willing to acquire additional holdings, and both with cash on hand. Between them, the military orders made purchases amounting to over thirty thousand gold bezants, not caring that Filangieri might see their actions as giving aid to the emperor's enemies. The money was turned over to the combined Cypriot/Ibelin army.

The Genoese merchants, well aware of the trading advantages of Cyprus, had been increasingly concerned about the political turmoil on the mainland. They decided to cast their lot with King Henry. They agreed to provide ships and soldiers in exchange for exclusive quarters in port cities on Cyprus with freedom from tolls and tariffs. Although they both had castles in Cyprus, the Knights

Templar and the Hospitallers decided to remain neutral in the conflict, but the coming battle would force the Templars to make a decision. On May 30, 1232, the Ibelin army set sail for the Cypriot port of Famagusta, on the eastern side of the island.

Filangieri was off in the north besieging the castle of Dieu d'Amour, where King Henry's sisters had been taken for safety, but he had left an army of over two thousand mounted men in Famagusta. They could easily have held the walled city and probably would have if Filangieri had been with them. Instead, the Ibelin army came ashore below the city at night, then sent boats into the harbor with their men shouting battle cries and making great clanging noises with their weapons and shields in the darkness. The surprise attack was a complete success, without striking a single blow. The leaderless Italians were convinced that a great army had come against them and fled the city, taking the road to the inland capital of Nicosia.

As soon as daylight came, the invading army moved out in pursuit of the Italians. At Nicosia they took the north road toward the castle of Kyrenia, close by the castle that Filangieri had under siege. The last stage of the journey would take them over a high pass in the hills, and it was there that Filangieri decided to stop them. He assembled his army at the top of the pass, looking down the slope at the approaching force. Filangieri, who had been told that a great army had landed at Famagusta, was delighted to learn the truth as he watched the small force starting up the slope to the pass. Confident of a quick victory, he ordered the attack.

Count Walter of Manupello was put in command of the first detachment of Italian horse, which would break the ranks of the small army. They galloped into the Ibelin flank, but the line of spears held them off. The momentum of the charging horses carried them downhill, right around the Ibelin army. As they regrouped below, Count Walter decided that with their horses gasping for breath he could not effect a charge back up the hill, so he decided to lead his men off the field. They took the road that led toward the Knights Templar's castle of Gastria, where they expected to be given shelter and support.

The Ibelin army moved into the rocks flanking the road, where the knights dismounted to fight on foot. When Filangieri's second charge of heavy horse came at them, the Italians found the rock-strewn ground to be impossible footing. Most of them were thrown from their horses onto the rocks where, bruised and loaded with armor, many couldn't even manage to stand up.

Filangieri, watching from the top of the pass with his reserves, saw his superior forces being beaten by the outnumbered Ibelins.

But before those reserves could be sent into the battle, he got another surprise. Balian of Ibelin, John's son, had led a party of knights up a goat track that Filangieri didn't even know existed. Balian suddenly charged the Italians at the top of the pass. Nothing was going the way he had planned, and to save himself Filangieri had his remaining knights cover his own dash down the opposite slope, away from the battle and toward the sheltering walls of the north coast castle of Kyrenia. The day belonged completely to young King Henry and John of Ibelin, who sent a party to chase down Count Walter of Manupello.

Walter did reach his destination at the Templar castle of Gastria, but now the Templars had to make a decision. If they let him in and sheltered him from Ibelin's forces, they would be taking sides with the hated emperor Frederick against the local barons and the king of Cyprus. If they shut him out and left him exposed to the Ibelins, their actions would most certainly anger the emperor. They decided that the latter position could be defended on the basis of their complete neutrality. The gate was kept barred and Count Walter's shouted pleas were ignored. The next morning he was found by an Ibelin patrol, trying to hide in the great ditch in front of the Templar castle. He was taken prisoner and put with the other Italians taken at the battle below the pass.

Kyrenia was a strong sea-side fortress, and well-supplied. It held out for almost a year, but long before its surrender Filangieri had slipped away on one of his own ships. He tried without success to get help from the kingdom of Armenia, then went to the city of Tyre. The local barons were now his enemies and the Templars and Hospitallers ignored him, so in frustration he went back to Italy to consult with Emperor Frederick. He had not a shred of good news to report to the imperial court. The outcome of his visit was that he was permitted to govern the city of Tyre and act as the emperor's guardian for Jerusalem, but he was removed as Frederick's *bailli* for the kingdom of Jerusalem.

As the new *bailli* of the Crusader kingdom Frederick named a young local baron who he did not know, but of whom he had received glowing reports in the past from Filangieri. He was Philip of Maugastel, by no means a popular choice. His unpopularity stemmed from his homosexual relationship with Filangieri, which had inspired those glowing reports. When Philip summoned the local barons to swear allegiance to him in accordance with the orders of the emperor, the result was a riot. The frightened young noble ran for his life to Filangieri's city of Tyre, and John of Ibelin was elected mayor of the commune of Acre. Based on no more authority than almost universal respect, he effectively governed Christian territories until his death in 1236. Had he lived he might have been able to prevent an action of the Knights Templar that was motivated only by the desire for profit and that triggered new hostilities with their Muslim neighbors.

A great band of Muslim nomads had settled down in a valley on the eastern side of the lake of Antioch, peacefully watching their flocks and herds. The Templars at nearby Baghras could not resist all that easy plunder and rode out to attack the defenseless civilians. It was not a battle, but simply an act of robbery. The Templars helped themselves to everything of value and triumphantly drove the captured animals back to their castle.

Muslim victims had hurried to Aleppo to plead for protection, and soon the victorious Templars at Baghras found themselves surrounded by a besieging army. Now it was the Templars' turn to send for help, a call that was answered by a relieving force under the personal command of Prince Bohemond of Antioch. The Muslims retired, agreeing to a truce negotiated between Bohemond and the emir of Aleppo. The Templars did not like the terms, but Bohemond made it clear that the acceptance of the truce was the price of his support. The Templars gave in and signed the agreement.

To William of Montferrat, preceptor of the Knights Templar at Antioch, the truce had brought disgrace on his order. It was just the latest in a string of humiliations. Although the Templars had remained substantially neutral in the recent conflicts between Frederick II and the local barons, they had several times turned the swords toward their Muslim neighbors, without success. In 1230, in one of those rare periods of cooperation with the Hospitallers, based upon their mutual dislike of Frederick, the Knights Templar of Tortosa had joined a contingent of Knights of the Hospital for an attack on the Muslim town of Hama. The Muslims had advance word of their approach and carefully prepared an ambush. The knights rode right into the trap to be thoroughly mauled and cut up by the enemy. The few knights who managed to escape counted themselves lucky to be alive.

During the following year, mindful of the arrangement that the two military orders could jointly own Jabala if it could be retaken, the Templars and Hospitallers joined forces again. In a swift attack they managed to occupy Jabala but were driven out by a Muslim army just a few weeks later.

Now the Templars' castle at Baghras had had to be rescued by outside help. The Templars had little to be proud of in recent years and had no good answers for the critics who mocked them. William of Montferrat decided to restore the Templar pride, and no truce was going to stand in his way.

The preceptor ordered the Knights Templar of Antioch to arms and persuaded a few local knights to join them. The objective was the Muslim stronghold of Darbsaq, to the north of Baghras. The Templars had no siege engines with them, so when they arrived at Darbsaq they had the choice of a long siege or the difficult task of assaulting the high walls with scaling ladders, a dilemma the preceptor should have realized before they started out.

As the Templars settled down to ponder how they might take the castle, they should also have realized that upon the first warning of their approach, fast gallopers would have been sent to the emir of Aleppo. As the Templars set up their tents before the walls of Darbsaq, all of the available cavalry at Aleppo was in the saddle and on its way.

As the great horde of Muslim horsemen thundered down at them, the small Christian force could see that it was grossly outnumbered. The knights fought valiantly, but there was no way to prevent a complete rout. Most of the Templars were captured, but among the dead left on the field was the vengeful Templar preceptor who had brought this disaster on his brothers.

The Muslim victors well knew that the Rule of the order absolutely forbade the use of their funds to ransom captive Templars, so once a ransom figure was agreed upon, the Muslims set a time to raise the money, before the Templar prisoners would be executed. If the money was paid, they would also agree to maintain the truce signed with Prince Bohemond.

The Templars appealed to the pope, who was not at all pleased with their conduct. The order was still important to the defense of the Holy Land, but the pope had more important matters at home on which to spend the funds of the Church. In the end, he provided funds for the ransoms, but with the money he sent a direct order that the Knights Templar should avoid independent action in the future and must honor the truce.

In all the confusion and strife of recent years, anyone might wonder why the Muslims had not taken advantage of the disorder to make a concerted move against the Christians. The answer was that while the Christian factions were chasing each other across the hills of Cyprus and killing each other for control of the Holy Land, the Muslims had been doing the same thing, attacking each other and adding the finishing touches to the disintegration of the empire of Saladin. Their blood feuds set the stage for the mixed success of a new Crusade that was being preached by Pope Gregory—a crusade that was denied complete success by the inability of the Christians to set aside their own rivalries and to follow a single leader.

19

Tibald of Champagne
1239 to 1240

BACK IN JUNE 1229, as Frederick II was arriving back in Italy, the Muslim prince al-Ashraf, nephew of Saladin, succeeded in deposing his own nephew an-Nasir as ruler of Damascus. As a member of the family, an-Nasir was given lands in the valley of the Jordan, with the town and castle of Kerak as his capital, but he was now a vassal subject to the ultimate rule of his uncle, Sultan al-Kamil of Egypt.

Al-Ashraf had barely settled down in his new capital of Damascus when word came to him that the huge horde of Kwarismian horsemen uprooted by Genghis Khan had reached his lands and had already taken one of his frontier castles. The homeless invading army, under its ambitious ruler, Jelal ad-Din, had then turned to attack the Seljuk Turks. Traditionally, the Seljuks and the Syrians were bitter enemies, but since they were now both in danger of being destroyed by the barbaric invaders, al-Ashraf sent envoys to the sultan of the Seljuks to effect an alliance against Jelal ad-Din. The Seljuks agreed, and al-Ashraf personally led his army into the field to join with them against the Kwarismians.

The combined armies outnumbered Jelal ad-Din, as neither would have done alone, and drove him from the field. Now Jelal ad-Din was caught in the middle. He could not move forward, nor could he lead his people back the way they had come, because the all-conquering Mongols were right behind them. He didn't have that or any other problem for long, however, because a Kurdish soldier took advantage of the confusion of the retreat to satisfy a point of personal and family honor. Jelal ad-Din had killed his brother, so now the Kurd, as required by the rules of the blood feud, murdered the man who had murdered his brother. Kurdish honor was satisfied, but with Jelal ad-Din dead the Kwarismians not only had nowhere to go, they also had no one to lead them. They broke up into rapacious marauding bands. There were many thousands of them, eager to fight, eager to find a new home. They would be ideal mercenaries if properly controlled and motivated, because they had their own horses and weapons and knew how to use them, but for now they were simply huge bands of thieves and murderers.

A few months later, death claimed Templar Grand Master de Montaigu, who had not shown any great ability to control the actions of his men. The new grand master was an abler man, who would die not in bed, but in battle. His name was Armand de Perigord.

Drastic changes in the Muslim states were brought on by a series of deaths. When al-Ashraf died in August 1237, his younger brother Ismail immediately took control of Damascus, but his uncle al-Kamil of Egypt was not going to let him keep it. The sultan took an army out of Egypt to Kerak, where he was joined by an army of his nephew, an-Nasir. Together they marched on Damascus and displaced Ismail, compensating him with the lordship of Baalbek, in modern Lebanon. Then, a few weeks later, Sultan al-Kamil died at Damascus.

Al-Kamil's older son Ayub, heir to the sultanate of Egypt, was with a small army in the field when he got the news. He immediately marched on Damascus to assert his rule. Concerned that his own force might not be large enough to back his claim, he paid a band of Kwarismian cavalry to assist him. He took Damascus, but he was angry at the news that his most valuable inheritance, the empire of Egypt, had been given in his absence to his younger brother al-Adil. The Egyptian nobles did not want Ayub, although he was the older brother, because his mother was a black Sudanese slave. Rather than follow a half-black sultan, they had put al-Adil on the throne. They regretted the move quickly, as they learned that al-Adil was under the strong influence of a homosexual lover, an unusually handsome young black. Al-Adil worshipped him so completely that he actually turned the government of Egypt over to his lover.

Ayub was determined to push his brother al-Adil off the throne of Egypt, but before he could lead his army out of Damascus, he was himself deposed by a palace plot that had been engineered by his uncle Ismail, who now took Damascus back for himself. Ayub fled to Kerak and pleaded with his cousin an-Nasir to help him regain his patrimony of Egypt. An-Nasir agreed, but before they could start out, a message came that the nobles of Egypt had thrown out al-Adil and his black lover. They now invited Ayub to take the throne as sultan. Ayub hastened to take up his new power, which he immediately used to reward his loyal cousin, an-Nasir, with the government of all the Muslim lands in Palestine.

In summary, the Muslim Middle East was now ruled by the young sultan Ayub of Egypt in bitter rivalry with his uncle Ismail, who ruled Syria from his capital at Damascus. Between them geographically, Ayub's vassal cousin an-Nasir held Palestine and Oultrejourdain. Ayub was secure in Egypt, but Ismail felt anything but secure in Damascus. Bands of mounted Kwarismian freebooters were spreading terror throughtout northern Syria and eastern Armenia. The Seljuk Turks of Anatolia were encroaching upon Ismail's lands in Syria whenever they got the chance. To the east and north the juggernaut of the Mongol horde was inexorably moving on all of them. The Muslim rulers had little time to concern themselves with a small Christian element strung out in a few port cities, controlling a narrow strip of coastal land that at no point was more than a few miles wide, except for the area around the Holy City.

As for those Christians, Prince Bohemond VI held Antioch and Tripoli, Richard Filangieri held Tyre, while a commune of citizens ran the city of Acre. Vassals of the kingdom of Jerusalem held the southern ports. The Holy City of Jerusalem belonged not to the kingdom, but to the emperor Frederick. The military orders were by far the strongest military force and by now the greatest land-owners. The titular king of Jerusalem was the underage Conrad, who had never set foot in his kingdom and was still living in Italy under the guardianship of his father, Frederick.

Pope Gregory IX called for a new Crusade in the summer of 1239, in anticipation of the expiration of the treaty that had been signed ten years before by the emperor Frederick and Sultan al-Kamil. The pope did not want his enemy Frederick involved in this Crusade, so he sent his preachers into France and England to rally the rulers and the people to take the oath for the Cross.

The response was good, especially in France. By mid-year of 1239 an impressive group of nobles had taken the Crusader vow, including the duke of Burgundy, Count Peter of Brittany, Count Henry of Bar, and the count of Nevers, all to be led by Tibald of Champagne, who was also king of Navarre. A thousand knights would take part in the French Crusade, plus squires, attendants, and men-at-arms.

Frederick II had fresh reasons to be angry with the pope. He considered the Holy Land to be his personal property. His young son Conrad was the rightful heir to the throne, and as Conrad's guardian, Frederick thought of himself as king of Jerusalem. Even the Holy City of Jerusalem, which he had regained for Christianity, had been given into his personal care. He felt that if the pope had wanted a Crusade, it should have been called only through Frederick II. The other cause for dissension was that this new crusading force was French, as were almost all of the barons of Outremer. Except for the Teutonic Knights, even the military orders were substantially French. Based on cultural and linguistic ties, the locals would be far more likely to cooperate with a French Crusade than they had been with Frederick's Germans and Italians. There was a real danger that they would all team up against the German emperor to reject his claims in the Middle East.

The treaty with Sultan al-Kamil expired in August 1239. Tibald of Champagne arrived at Acre on September 1. A council was called to coordinate the crusading effort, and this time the Knights Templar, who still held their animosity toward Frederick, were happy to participate. Grand Master de Perigord and his Templar officers explained to the new arrivals the complex maneuvers that had divided the Muslims and the opportunity provided by that division. They recommended that the campaign be directed against Egypt, but many of the European Crusaders present thought that Damascus should be their first objective. The local barons objected because Damascus was still the major trading hub feeding their port cities with commerce. The Templars, who had put surplus funds to work in merchant banking transactions, had a number of Muslim clients in the Syrian capital.

Tibald settled the dispute by agreeing to take both Cairo and Damascus, and he finally decided on a plan to retake Ascalon and Gaza, the Palestinian gateways to Egypt, to be followed by a move against Syria. After a month of discussion and planning, the crusading army headed south toward the Egyptian border and their first target of Gaza. With them went contingents of Knights Templar and Hospitallers, each led by its grand master.

Tibald of Champagne was nominally in charge, but he was not totally in command of the lofty nobles, who looked upon themselves as independent sovereigns. Near Jaffa, Count Peter of Brittany got word of a rich caravan of Muslim merchants nearby. He saw no need to ask permission from anyone and decided to act entirely on his own initiative.

The caravan, following the trade route from Arabia to Damascus, was now in the valley of the Jordan River, in the territory of an-Nasir of Kerak. Hastily assembling a force of two hundred knights eager to go with him, Peter of Brittany was guided to the Jordan ahead of the caravan and prepared an ambush. The caravan was well guarded by light cavalry, who put up a brisk defense, but the heavily armored knights ultimately won the day. They triumphantly drove the flocks and herds back to the crusading army. Fresh food is always welcome to an army on the move, and the expedition had drawn the first enemy blood in a Christian victory. The heroes were very pleased with the loud praises for their deeds.

Off in Kerak, where the gates had been opened to receive the wounded and beaten Muslims, the outraged an-Nasir assembled his emirs and officers to plan a suitable act of vengeance for this bloody incursion into his domain.

The Egyptians, who had been getting good information every step of the way, knew that Gaza was the Crusader objective, and they dispatched an army to meet the Christians there. Unfortunately, the Crusader intelligence was based more on hearsay than on fact, and the Christians accepted the very mistaken report that the Egyptian army was made up of no more than one thousand men. Count Henry of Bar, envious of all the praise heaped on Count Peter of Brittany, decided to take independent action against the Egyptian force, which he thought he could overwhelm with superior numbers. He talked to his friends, all of whom were eager for the fight, and quickly got the cooperation of the duke of Burgundy, the local count Walter of Jaffa, and even one of the Ibelin family, John of Arsuf. As they tallied their followers, they could count on about five hundred knights and mounted sergeants, plus about a thousand infantry, more than enough to soundly defeat an army of a thousand Egyptians.

The news reached Tibald, who hurriedly assembled a small group of supporters and went to plead with Count Henry, who was already marching out of the camp. With Tibald was Grand Master de Perigord of the Knights Templar, who had become one of Tibald's closest counselors, and Count Peter of Brittany. They begged Count Henry to abandon this expedition in favor of a concerted action by the whole Crusader force. They pointed out that he was taking needless risks. In response, Count Henry accused them all of cowardice and denied that Tibald or anyone else could issue orders to himself or his companions. They were using their best judgment in the circumstances, and that judgment dictated that they should march out to meet the Egyptians. Henry's friends, true Crusaders, had come to the Holy Land to fight, not to talk. Nothing Tibald or the Templar grand master said could change their minds, and Henry resumed his march into the night.

By dawn, Count Henry's force came upon a great fold in the sand dunes along the shore near Gaza. He ordered his men to take cover there and rest for the coming battle. After marching all night, most of the Christians gratefully took the opportunity to stretch out and make up the sleep that they had lost in the all-night march. The Christians posted no sentries and sent out no scouts, in the tragic belief that they were resting out of sight of the enemy.

The Egyptian commander was delighted and could hardly believe his good fortune. Not only was his army five times larger than the Christians thought it was, but they had actually exhausted themselves by marching all night to face him, only to relax with no defenses of any kind. They hadn't even posted sentries. He dispatched archers with orders to crawl around the dunes out of sight to completely encircle the Crusaders. The circle was almost closed when a wakeful Walter of Jaffa suddenly realized what was happening. Knowing the perils of deep, soft sand from years of experience, Walter hastily warned Henry that neither man nor horse could possibly maneuver while staggering ankle deep through shifting ground. He urgently advised an immediate retreat to escape the Egyptian entrapment. That made sense to the other nobles, and when Walter rode out of the huge bowl of sand, they followed him—all except Count Henry, who would not abandon the infantry he had brought to this place, nor the few friends who elected to stay with him. The noble, foolhardy enterprise cost him his life. First came the deadly arrow flights, followed by a fast, hectic battle. The sand soaked up the blood of almost a thousand Christians; they gave their lives discovering the difference between the grassy turf of home and the treacherous, almost liquid ebb and flow of the dry sands in which they now floundered helplessly. About five hundred prisoners were draped in chains and sent marching back to the dungeons of Cairo. The Egyptian casualties were hardly worth counting. For the small crusading army the losses were so severe that the survivors reluctantly abandoned the expedition to Gaza and limped back to Acre.

Now it was an-Nasir's turn. He decided to punish the Christians for the caravan raid by hitting them where it would hurt the most. He marched on Jerusalem. Frederick had turned its care over to Richard Filangieri, who had been charged with the responsibility of rebuilding the walls, but in his constant angling for power Filangieri had neglected his duties. Most of the wall was still down, so an-Nasir's army simply rode into the city unchallenged. The citadel called the Tower of David had been repaired, but it was grossly undermanned. An-Nasir chose not to try to storm the citadel, but rather to starve out the garrison. There had been more neglect in providing provisions for the fort, and in less than thirty days the starving garrison surrendered in exchange for an-Nasir's agreement that they would be allowed to go free. By the end of the year the rebuilt sections of the wall were torn down again, and the Tower of David was completely dismantled.

To the new sultan of Egypt, the Christians appeared to be more a tiresome annoyance than a threat. His serious enemy was his uncle Ismail in Damascus. The Egyptian army, organized for a drive against Syria, would be joined along the way by the Jordanian army of an-Nasir. Ismail considered his options and decided that his best protection was an alliance with the Christians, who had recently moved their army into Galilee. He sent envoys to Tibald's camp, and now the Knights Templar came into their own.

The Templars had agents in Damascus and had had active banking services there. They knew the politics of the Muslim court and had already provided good counsel and assistance to Tibald of Champagne. Now they were given the responsibility to negotiate a treaty of alliance with Ismail of Damascus. The local barons were eager for a Templar success because they had no desire for a war that would cut off their primary Muslim trading center. The Templars had their own reasons for wanting the alliance: to avoid the prospects of debts they could never collect if their order had to go to war against Syria.

Whatever the motivations, the negotiations were successful. The Christian army would move to the frontier where Palestine joined Egypt to block any aggressive move by the sultan of Egypt. The Christians would also provide a quantity of military provisions to Ismail. In exchange, Ismail agreed to turn over two great castle fortresses: Beaufort, northeast of Tyre, and Safed, a few miles west of Acre. Beaufort went to Balian of Sidon, whose family had owned it before its capture by the Muslims, and as a reward for their valuable services, the Knights Templar got the castle of Safed. The local barons and the Italian merchants were lavish in their praise of the Templars for preserving their important Damascus connection.

Many of Ismail's followers were angry that he had summarily given away two important Muslim strongholds to the unbelievers, but not nearly as angry as the Knights Hospitaller upon learning that the very strategic castle of Safed and the lands around it were to go to the Knights of the Temple. They would not sign the treaty with Ismail, claiming that for their order the treaty had no validity. The smoldering intensity of their fury drove them to a decision to conduct their own negotiations. If the Templars sided with Ismail of Damascus, the Hospitallers would seek an alliance with Ayub of Egypt. The sultan, delighted to have the opportunity to destroy the Christian alliance with Ismail, made the Hospitallers an extraordinary offer. If the Christians would maintain a position of uninvolved neutrality in the Muslim conflict, he would release all of the prisoners taken at Gaza and give the Christians the city of Ascalon. The grand master of the Hospitallers signed the agreement and led his Hospitallers into Ascalon, but the treaty needed more than the Hospitaller seal to make it valid. The Christian leaders had to ratify it.

The barons of the Holy Land were incensed, both on the moral grounds of flagrant violation of the treaty with Damascus and on the economic grounds of the estrangement of their Syrian trade sources. Tibald of Champagne cared nothing for their trade, nor did the other nobles he had brought with him, but they all had friends, even relatives, languishing in the dungeons of Cairo. This treaty would set them free. It meant breaking their word and their treaty with Damascus, but they rationalized away their quandary by assuring each other that breaking a treaty with the infidel was no sin.

It was more than a sin to the resident nobles: It ruined their major source of revenue. They were loud in their condemnation of Tibald, who had so much abuse heaped upon him, day after day, that he decided to return home. He made a fast visit to Jerusalem to fulfill his Crusader vow, then left the Holy Land in September 1240. Some who had come with him decided to remain in the Holy Land a while longer, mostly because they felt that the job they came to do had not been completed. At least one man stayed in anticipation of acquiring the material rewards he had come for and not yet found. The fortune seeker was the young count Ralph of Soissons, who managed to catch the eye of the wealthy and influential dowager queen Alice of Cyprus. Alice was so wealthy that Ralph found himself quite able to overlook the fact that the queen was more than old enough to be his mother, and they were married a few months later. The count of Nevers stayed because he was ashamed of the behavior of his colleagues. He moved in with the Knights Templar, still hoping to fight for the True Cross.

Tibald could return home with some claims of success. His leadership had been a military failure, since the only battle was the disaster at Gaza and the Holy City had been lost, but it could be counted as something of a diplomatic success because the castles of Beaufort and Safed and the city of Ascalon had been restored to the Holy Land. That success was limited, however, because he had left rivalry and disunity behind him. The Hospitallers now based in Ascalon and Walter of Jaffa were dedicated to maintaining the agreement with the sultan of Egypt. The other faction, led by the Knights Templar and the other resident barons, camped north of Ascalon, determined to preserve the treaty and the friendship of Ismail of Damascus. The Christians, who had benefited from the conflict between the Muslim states, could no longer exploit that split in the enemy ranks because of the split in their own.

Other greater crusading leaders would come to the Holy Land, but while we wait for their ships to arrive we should take a look at a growing military phenomenon in Egypt that would soon have a disastrous impact on the Christian barons, and on the Knights of the Temple.

20

Triumph and Tragedy
1241 to 1247

$\mathcal{F}$OR SEVERAL CENTURIES Muslim rulers had hired Turkish mercenaries from the steppes of Asia because of their military skills. They were especially effective at shooting their short, powerful bows while on horseback, even at the gallop. Since archery required the use of both hands, they had developed a mastery of horsemanship, guiding animals with their legs alone to leave both hands free.

The problem with hiring such men was that, at best, they came temporarily, fully intending to go home when their short-term service contracts had been fulfilled. At worst, since they were usually hired in large groups, they frequently became impressed by their own power, which might be turned against their employers, even to the point of assassination, in their determination to gather loot to take home with them.

Out of that dilemma grew an unusual practice in Egypt, the purchase of young boys to be trained for a lifetime of military service. That approach became so popular that some merchants became specialists in the military slave trade. They would visit the nomads of the steppes and the Caucasus not to steal slaves or to buy captives, as the Arab merchants did in Africa, but to buy boys from their own families. Thus it became the boys' sworn duty to fight for their employers; to return home would have meant disgrace to their families.

Nomadic life was hard. A herd of animals of a given size would support just so many people, and if the family or clan outgrew the herd, the result was poverty. The sale of the boys relieved that problem and brought in welcome cash or trade goods, such as weapons, cloth, and salt. They became easier to buy as the nomads learned that the boys, usually ten to twelve years of age, would not be taken into lives of brutal labor but would ride and hunt and fight, all admired activities. They would have good horses, colorful clothing, and fine weapons. They might even rise to positions of wealth and power, because their slave status was not permanent.

During his early years the boy would live with his owner, who, though stern in the need to teach military discipline, would also be like a foster father. He would see to the boy's proper care, would clothe him and feed him, look to his religious training as a devout Muslim, and watch his training in the use of the bow, the crossbow, the sword, the lance, and the battle-ax. When the young man came of age, his owner would provide him with horses and weapons, then formally set him free to take service with the army of the ruler, as his owner's contribution to the defense of the realm. Tradition required that the former owner continue to be treated with the deference and respect due to a foster-father.

This superbly trained soldier was called a *Mameluke*, ''one who was owned.'' A tribute to both of the military groups regarded as the best soldiers on their respective sides was given by an Arab chronicler who wrote, ''The Mamelukes are the Templars of Egypt.'' Arranging for the purchase of boys to become Mamelukes had become easier in recent years, because of the tribes that had been driven from their homes and left destitute by the Mongols. The Kipchaks, who had inhabited the land between the Don and Volga rivers, were an especially rich source of supply.

One boy, acquired from the Kipchaks by the Egyptian emir Aydekin el-Bunduqdar, was chosen because he was large for his age and was obviously intelligent. The blue-eyed boy was given the name of Rukn ad-Din Baibars Bunduqdari. His promise of size was kept as he grew into a huge young man, and both his intelligence and his flair for leadership were evidenced so often that at an early age he was promoted to the rank of *emir*, or general, in the army of the sultan Ayub. No one appeared to have noticed yet that the young Baibars was completely ruthless and seemingly unfettered by any code of morality. Soon every Christian in the Holy Land would learn to dread his name, as a result of events set in motion by the intense Christian rivalries that existed in spite of the conciliatory efforts of the next Crusader-pilgrim leader. He arrived just after the departure of Tibald of Champagne in October 1240.

The new leader was Richard, earl of Cornwall, brother to King Henry III of England and brother-in-law to the emperor Frederick. His pilgrimage had the full blessing of Frederick, who delegated to Richard all of his own imperial authority over the kingdom of Jerusalem. Richard brought with him another brother-in-law, the intensely ambitious Simon de Montfort, earl of Leicester. De Montfort had taken the cross to earn remission of the sins incurred by his marrying the beautiful and wealthy sister of Richard, then consummating that marriage in spite of the fact that she had taken a sacred vow of chastity before the archbishop of Canterbury.

The deep divisions in the Christian ranks that had led to the two political factions led by the Knights Templar and the Hospitallers were a complete surprise to Richard of Cornwall. He could scarcely believe the reports coming to him of the Templars and Hospitallers fighting each other in the streets of Acre. The emperor's man, Filangieri, had kept himself and his city of Tyre apart from the dispute, but he was actively being courted by the Hospitallers. The Teutonic Knights, whose primary loyalty was still to the German emperor, had turned their backs on the quarrels and on the kingdom of Jerusalem to dedicate themselves to an alliance with Hethoum of Armenia. Somehow, Richard had to bring order and unity to this special part of Christ's earthly kingdom.

Believing that he was acting in the best interests of all, Richard went to Ascalon to meet with envoys of the Egyptian sultan. The envoys wanted Richard to confirm the Egyptian truce with the Hospitallers, but he would approve it only on condition that the sultan would respect the agreements made between the Knights Templar and Ismail of Damascus. As a gesture of Muslim sincerity, Richard also asked that Sultan Ayub part with the entire province of Galilee, which would mean surrendering to the Christians the town and castle of Tiberias, the capital of Galilee, along with the castles of Mount Tabor and Belvoir, properties then held by the sultan's vassal nephew, an-Nasir. With a fresh Christian army at hand, the sultan agreed.

Richard was well pleased with his accomplishments, which he felt satisfied both the Templar and Hospitaller parties and came close to restoring the original Christian borders of Palestine. He was not happy about the absence of a strong central ruler, a role that his brother-in-law Simon de Montfort was eager to assume. Richard sent a formal petition to Emperor Frederick requesting the appointment of de Montfort as Frederick's *bailli* for the kingdom. The emperor didn't say no, he just ignored the petition. When it became obvious that de Montfort would not rule the Holy Land, he took his intense ambitions home, where they would one day find him leading a civil war in an attempt to gain the throne of England, an adventure that would cost him his life. Richard of Cornwall could do no more, and he returned to England in May of 1241.

Richard thought that his arrangements with Sultan Ayub had been fair. Apparently he was not aware that political rivals want supremacy, not fairness. The Knights Templar refused to recognize any agreements with the Egyptian sultan and saw no barrier to attacking an-Nasir's city of Hebron on the frontier just south of Bethlehem. An-Nasir, who was growing much more sure of himself, responded by positioning his forces to control the road from the coast to Jerusalem.

As Frederick had spread the news throughout Europe that he had regained Jerusalem for Christianity, the flow of pilgrims had started again. Now those pilgrims were forced to pay a heavy toll to an-Nasir for the right to approach the Holy City. Perhaps remembering their original purpose of protecting the pilgrim roads, the Knights Templar decided to teach an-Nasir a lesson. In October 1241 they moved on Nablus, a Muslim city northeast of Jaffa, on the road to Damascus. By the end of the month they had taken the town, swarming inside bellowing out their battle cry, while the terror-stricken citizens scrambled for places to hide. The Templars sought out soldiers and citizens alike from every part of the city and killed them all. After they had gathered up all the plunder they could find, they set fire to the great mosque in the center of the city. The Templars had advised no one of their plan and saw no reason to seek anyone's permission. All three mililtary orders, in the absence of central authority, continued to think of themselves as sovereign powers.

Richard Filangieri, who still held Tyre, decided to have one more try at establishing his own supremacy over the Holy Land. He solicited the cooperation of the Hospitallers, who were still smarting over the favored relationship the Templars enjoyed with the local barons. They would begin by jointly seizing the capital city of Acre. Early in 1243, Filangieri, with a group of his soldiers, secretly entered Acre to join the Hospitallers and put their takeover plan into effect. News of his presence leaked out, the alarm bells were sounded, and soon a fully armed mob was in front of the Hospitaller headquarters demanding Filangieri's head, only to learn that he had run from the city as soon as the alarm was sounded. He had galloped at full speed back to the safety of Tyre, and the Hospitallers had fallen still further from local favor.

In April of the same year, the rightful heir to the throne of Jerusalem, Queen Yolanda's son Conrad, reached the legal age of fifteen years, so could rule in his own name as king of Jerusalem. Now it might be expected that a strong central government would at last be reestablished—except that the local barons would not take oaths of allegiance to a king who had chosen never to even visit his kingdom. Although young King Conrad sent an Italian nobleman, Thomas of Acerra, to act as his personal representative, the barons decided that until Conrad came himself, they would need to agree upon a regent to rule in his stead. At a great parliament attended by the barons, the leaders of the Church, the Italian merchant colonies, and the military orders, the assembly elected Conrad's aunt, the dowager queen Alice of Cyprus. All of the local nobles present swore their allegiance to the new regent.

One noble not at the council was Richard Filangieri. Upon the appointment of Thomas of Acerra as deputy for King Conrad, Filangieri had been recalled to Italy. When he finally arrived, Frederick made very clear his feelings about Filangieri's accomplishments by having him thrown into prison.

Ralph of Soissons, the follower of Tibald of Champagne who had stayed behind in order to marry the aging but wealthy Queen Alice, now regarded himself, not the queen, as the regent and ruler. With Filangieri gone, Tyre had reverted to the crown, so Ralph now demanded that Tyre be turned over to him personally. His claim was firmly rejected. In his fury at the realization that after the long wait, after his marriage to a woman twice his age, he was not going to win the prize of supreme power, Ralph of Soissons abandoned his wife and the Holy Land and went back to Europe. No one tried to talk him out of it.

The Knights Templar were riding the crest of political influence in the kingdom, partly because of their good working relationship with Ismail of Damascus. When word was received at Acre that an-Nasir of Kerak had quarreled with his uncle, Ayub of Egypt, and had now allied himself with his uncle Ismail at Damascus, the Christians saw an opportunity for even closer ties with Damascus. Because of their good relations with the emir, the Templars were asked to lead the talks. As a result of the Templars' efforts Ismail and an-Nasir agreed to recall the Muslim clerics from the mosques on the Temple Mount in Jerusalem. The Islamic priests would leave the sacred mosque of the Dome of the Rock and the equally sacred al-Aqsa Mosque, the original headquarters of the Knights Templar. The Templars were overjoyed. They went so far as to seek approval of the new arrangement from Sultan Ayub. Jerusalem was not a key military base, and Ayub had no desire to drive the Christians deeper into the arms of Ismail, so he gave his blessings to the agreement.

Now Jerusalem was a Christian city once more. With Filangieri gone there was no one to assert that it rightfully belonged to Frederick. Once again the Holy City would be the center of the kingdom of Jerusalem. The Knights Templar volunteered that their order would see to the rebuilding of the walls and the citadel of the Tower of David. Toward the end of 1243, as the word spread through the courts of Europe, the Templars enjoyed a great wave of popularity and drew lavish praise from the pope, to whom they had brought much honor. The euphoria did not last for long.

It was just a few months later that open war broke out between Ayub of Egypt and Ismail of Damascus. The Templars had no difficulty in persuading the local barons to declare the Christian kingdom on the side of Ismail and to back that declaration with full military support. Another of Ismail's allies, al-Mansur Ibrahim, prince of Homs, came to Acre to negotiate the terms of the military alliance, where he was welcomed as the house guest of the Knights Templar.

The terms agreed upon held potentially rich rewards for the Christians in the Holy Land. After the allies had succeeded in their joint conquest of Egypt, the Christians would be given a fair share of Egyptian territory, which would expand their holdings to a total area larger than they had ever known. This would be the most profitable campaign since the First Crusade a century and a half earlier.

Sultan Ayub, who knew all about their plans and agreements, countered with a much more direct plan of his own. He sent envoys north beyond Damascus to strike a bargain with the chiefs of the Kwarismians, who were still men without a country, totally prepared to kill for a price. Ayub's envoys delivered enough gold to engage the services of ten thousand mounted Kwarismian Turks, and gave them their assignment. As a bonus, any plunder they might take would be their own.

In June 1244 the Kwarismian horde burst into Syria in a fast frenzy of killing, looting, and burning. They destroyed farms, villages, and even sizable towns. They swept around Damascus itself and poured into Galilee. They took the capital of Tiberias in a great rampage of rape and murder, then moved south in the direction of the Holy City.

The grand master of the Knights Templar, with the Hospitaller grand master and the patriarch of Jerusalem, hurried to the city with additional men and supplies. The Templars had completed the walls and now reinforced the garrison. The patriarch and the grand masters left Jerusalem for their own safety, leaving their followers and the civilian population to their uncertain fate.

A few days later those keeping watch on the wall saw a flood of horsemen thundering toward the city from all directions, streaming down the valleys and cresting the hills. There seemed no end to them. The garrison was far too small to defend all of the city's two miles of perimeter wall, and soon Kwarismian Turks were dropping inside those walls to cut down the men who were guarding the gates.

Triumphant tribesmen screaming for blood rode in through the gates and into the streets. The attempts to hold them back were valiant but futile. The preceptor of the Hospitallers was killed in the hand-to-hand combat that drove the knights and soldiers back into the citadel. At the Armenian convent the nuns were raped and the monks were slaughtered. Most of the civilians shut themselves up in their houses and prayed.

Their prayers were answered, but not by Christian rescuers. Someone had managed to get a message through to an-Nasir of Kerak, who now came to Jerusalem with an army at his back that outnumbered the invaders. The Kwarismians had been hired as mercenary forces to go against the enemies of Egypt, which included an-Nasir, so his proper conduct would have been to attack the mercenaries, but he apparently had not yet totally committed himself. He called for a parley.

The terms arrived at were simple. The Kwarismian chiefs agreed to let the garrison and the civilians leave the city of Jerusalem without harm. An-Nasir, who would add the city to his own domains, would take his army and go home. The Kwarismians would keep their loot. There would be no battle.

The various contingents of the garrison—Templars, Hospitallers, and local knights—marched out of the citadel and out of the city, led by their officers. The leaderless civilian population waited several days in confusion and finally streamed out of the city on August 23. As they wound across the plain and onto higher ground, some of them looked back and shouted in excitement. There were Christian banners flying from the towers of Jerusalem! The city must have been retaken by the Christian armies! Praise be to God, they could go home again. As the word spread among the fugitive throng, they turned back toward the city.

The truth was that the Kwarismian Turks were half-wild tribesmen. They didn't hold with heraldry and such trappings as flags and banners. The Christian banners were above the towers of Jerusalem, snapping in the wind, because the Turks simply hadn't bothered to take them down. They didn't understand why the people of Jerusalem were coming back down the road, and they didn't care. An-Nasir had led his army away from the city, so now the Turks could deal with the returning Christians any way they liked.

As the joyful civilians approached the city they walked blindly into an ambush, and the slaughter began. Those in the front of the column were butchered in the road, while those in the rear broke to scatter in all directions. Two thousand innocent people died before the walls of Jerusalem, but more than that died at the hands of professional bandits and Bedouin marauders as they tried to find their way to the coast. Of the six thousand men, women, and children who had marched out of Jerusalem, only about three hundred reached safety behind the walls of Jaffa.

The victorious Kwarismians now had a city that they didn't want. Street after street was searched, every house and shop, for whatever loot they could yield. The Muslim tribesmen were offended by the Christian churches, so as soon as the buildings were emptied of valuables they were set on fire. At the Church of the Holy Sepulcher the Kwarismians were startled to discover priests of the various Christian denominations still there, having decided that God would want them to stay on the sacred ground. They were killed on the spot, including the priests who were at the high altar saying mass. Gold and silver items were plucked from the altars, then the tombs of the kings of Jerusalem were broken open for whatever gold and jewels had been buried with them. Once the possibilities for plunder had been exhausted, the holiest church in Christendom was set ablaze.

The city of Jerusalem was now totally desecrated in this year 1244. No Christian army would pass through its gates for many centuries to come. For now, the Kwarismians bundled up their loot and proceeded on their westward march to join the Egyptian army.

About a month later the Christian army was ready to give battle. The local barons provided about six hundred horsemen. There were three hundred Knights Templar, led by their grand master Armand de Perigord. The Hospitaller grand master led a similar number of his own knights, and there was a smaller troop provided by the Teutonic Knights. Ismail of Damascus had sent a small army, as had the prince of Homs. An-Nasir was there in personal command of his own forces, which included a contingent of Bedouin cavalry. There were fully armored knights, mounted men-at-arms, Muslim light cavalry and infantry. They all set out, in October of 1244, to confront the army of five thousand Egyptians and ten thousand Kwarismian mercenaries combined under the command of the young Mameluke emir, Rukn ad-Din Baibars. His name would be used by Christian parents for generations to come to frighten their children.

The two armies met on the plain near the town of La Forbie, northeast of Gaza. The prince of Homs cited his knowledge of the Kwarismians as the basis for his strong recommendation that they stay in place and work night and day to surround their camp with impregnable fortifications. He explained that the Kwarismians, an impatient people, would soon insist upon an attack, but they seemed to balk at storming any strongly fortified position. A powerful defensive posture would therefore be to the advantage of Christians and their allies.

Many of the Christian nobles, led by Count Walter of Jaffa, strongly disagreed. They were convinced that they could beat the army before them on the field, particularly the poorly disciplined Kwarismians. They pushed for an immediate attack, and their argument prevailed. The combined forces took up battle formation with an-Nasir on the left, the troops of Homs and Damascus in the center, and the Christians on the right. As Baibars placed his men to receive them, he decided that his own highly trained Mamelukes were the best troops to meet the armored Christian knights. He set the Kwarismians to attack the Muslim center and left. It was Baibars's plan to hold the Christians in check, hoping that one or more of the Muslim sections would give way, so that the mounted Kwarismians could break though and move around to hit the flank or come up behind the Christians. He got his wish.

The skilled Mamelukes, well mounted and protected by chain mail, held their own against the Christians and stopped their advance. The men of Homs held firm, but next to them the troops of Damascus finally broke and ran, rapidly joined in their fight by the forces of an-Nasir. The troops from Homs had no trouble fighting their way free, because the Kwarismians were ignoring the disorganized Muslims to carry out their orders to swing around behind the Christian army. The maneuver was a total success. Caught between the two armies, grossly outnumbered without their Muslim allies, the Christians were doomed.

The battle raged fiercely in hundreds of hand-to-hand encounters, but the Christians could not hope to prevail over the superior numbers of their enemies, who simultaneously attacked individual knights at their fronts, backs, and sides. When the battle ended, over five thousand Christians lay dead on the field, including the Templar marshal and Grand Master Armand de Perigord. The Hospitaller grand master was taken prisoner by the Egyptians, while the Kwarismians succeeded in capturing Count Walter of Jaffa. A few survivors managed to make their way to Jaffa, including just thirty-three Knights Templar out of the original force of three hundred. They had suffered almost 90 percent casualties. It would be a dejected grand chapter that would have to meet to elect a grand master to replace the leader they had lost at La Forbie.

After the battle, the Egyptian army divided. The Mamelukes made an unsuccessful attack on Ascalon, which was too strong to take without siege engines. The Kwarismians took Count Walter up to the walls of his city of Jaffa, where they tied him to a crude cross made from the fork of a tree and threatened to kill him in full view of his subjects unless the city was surrendered to them. The count, to his credit, shouted to his men to hold firm and not to trade a Christian city for a single life. The Kwarismians gave up, and out of respect for Count Walter's courage they spared his life, which would later be lost to the dismal conditions of an Egyptian dungeon.

In Cairo, Baibars was feted as a hero for his destruction of the sultan's enemies and rewarded with rich gifts and additional power. The homeless Kwarismians had also expected to be rewarded, especially with lands of their own, which they desperately craved. The sultan, however, considered them much too dangerous to have in his own country. He went so far as to post troops along the frontier to keep them out. In response, the Kwarismians turned and conducted another great raid of destruction through Palestine, then turned north for a sweep up to the walls of the Christian capital of Acre. No one came out to stop them.

For the moment, the Christians had lost any desire for war. There was no Christian family that was not mourning men who had died at La Forbie. The military orders had been shattered and now faced the pressing need to call on their European preceptors for more recruits and more funds. All were acting in an atmosphere of shock and depression. Such a short time before they had been so proud of all the lands they had regained, and especially of the total recovery of Jerusalem. They had basked in the praises of the whole Christian world. Now all of those gains, and more, had been lost in a matter of weeks.

Had Sultan Ayub chosen to act now, he could have pushed every Christian out of the Holy Land. But Ayub knew that for his own personal safety the first priority was not the defeat of Christians, but of his own brother Ismail. He sent a besieging army to Damascus that marched across Palestine, then up the west bank of the Jordan, taking possession of the lands of an-Nasir. The army arrived at Damascus in April of 1245. The aimless Kwarismians, with no clear goals of their own, decided to join the Egyptians there, in hopes of a share of the loot of the wealthy city.

Ismail held out for six months but finally came to terms, surrendering Damascus for a personal fief based on the city of Baalbek. The Kwarismians were turned loose again. Since Sultan Ayub had no further need of them, they had no problem in offering their slay-for-pay services to Ismail, who looked on them as a God-sent opportunity to recover Damascus. Gathering his own followers to join the Turks, he immediately set out to lay siege to the city. He thought his Muslim allies would join him, but they had not forgotten their humiliation on the plain of La Forbie, nor their friends and relatives who had been cut down by these same Kwarismians. They were much more sympathetic to the envoys of Sultan Ayub, who offered them a chance for revenge against the Turkish tribesmen. Ismail's former allies now joined the sultan of Egypt and moved toward Damascus.

Ismail and the Kwarismians, turning around to meet them, found an emotionally charged enemy that fought like devils. The Kwarismians were almost totally destroyed. Their few survivors rode out of the area forever, while their leader's head was paraded through the streets of Aleppo impaled on the point of a lance. The Kwarismians were never again a factor in Syria. Ismail was chastised and sent back to Baalbek to brood on his failure.

With his new Muslim allies, Sultan Ayub concentrated on taking back from the weakened Christians the towns and castles they had negotiated away from Ismail. Tiberias, the capital of Galilee, was occupied. Belvoir fell, and then Mount Tabor, south of Nazareth. Galilee was totally restored to Muslim rule.

The last city to be recovered was Ascalon. It had been given up by Ayub himself in his negotiations with the Hospitallers, but now the time had come to take it back. Ascalon was strategically important for the Christians and a constant threat to Egypt. Help was organized for its protection as Ayub put his besieging army in place before the city. A Christian fleet was launched from Acre with reinforcements, which included a hundred knights from Cyprus, along with a large supply of food. An Egyptian fleet of war galleys moved to stop the Christian flotilla but was struck by a fierce storm that wrecked the Egyptian ships on the rocky shore. The Christian reinforcements landed safely.

The Muslims had no siege engines with them, and there was no suitable timber available until a Muslim engineer had an idea to turn disaster into opportunity. Men were sent along the shore to gather the timbers from the wrecked ships to build the siege weapons needed to breach Ascalon's walls. They bound timbers together to make a powerful battering ram, then built a "cat," a long, low shed used to protect the men operating the ram. The location selected for hammering was a section of wall that was part of the structure of the citadel of the city.

The garrison inside felt no great danger from the constant day-and-night pounding, in the belief that the mighty wall could withstand any degree of shock, but they were mistaken. They were caught totally unprepared as a section of the castle wall fell away. Suddenly the muffled pounding was replaced by cries of "Allahu Akbar" as fiery-eyed Mamelukes poured through the breach into the castle. They took a handful of prisoners, but the majority of the defenders, who were mostly Hospitallers, were killed. Those who were merely wounded quickly bled to death after their throats were slashed.

Ayub had no intention of garrisoning Ascalon, so he ordered the citadel and the city walls taken to the ground. He moved up to

Damascus and held court there, where all the Syrian nobles came to swear allegiance to him. It had taken many years, but Ayub at last had overcome his greatest enemies, his own family, to reestablish the empire of his uncle Saladin. With all of the Muslim states united under his sole control, he could now address the problem of the Christians.

The sultan did not know as yet that another great crusading army was on its way from France to challenge his ambitions. The Knights Templar met in grand chapter to elect a new grand master. Richard de Bures, who had served since Grand Master de Perigord was slain at La Forbie, had died of illness. To lead them during a great Crusade they required a fighting man. The Templars selected one of their best, brother William de Sonnac. He would die fighting in the Nile delta for the only Crusader ever to be elevated to sainthood.

21

The Man Who Would Be Saint

1244 to 1250

King louis ix of France had been ill with malaria to the brink of death in 1244, and he had promised God that in exchange for his life he would lead a Crusade to rescue the Holy Land. With the king restored to health, it was clear that God had kept his part of the bargain, so now it was up to Louis to deliver on his. His family, his vassals, and the leading churchmen of France tried to talk him out of it. The political rivalries in Europe made it dangerous for their king and his army to be away from his kingdom. The bishop of Paris pleaded with him:

"My lord king, remember that when you took the cross, making such a vow hurriedly and without advice, you were ill, and to tell the truth, your mind was wandering. Blood had rushed to your brain so that you were not of sound mind, and the words you then uttered lacked the weight of truth and authority. The lord pope will be good enough to grant a dispensation, knowing the critical state of the kingdom's affairs and your bodily weakness. On the one side, the power of Frederick...is to be feared; on the other the plots of the king of the English, who has plenty of money...Germany is disturbed, Italy restless; access to the Holy Land is difficult, your reception there uncertain...."

Seeing the bishop getting nowhere, the king's mother, Blanche of Castile, tried a different tack: "Dearest son! Instead of resisting your own prudence, hear and pay attention to the advice of your discerning friends. Bear in mind what a virtue it is, and how pleasing to God, to obey and fall in with the wishes of a mother. Stay here, and the Holy Land will suffer no detriment...God neither plays tricks nor does he quibble. You, my son, are sufficiently excused by what happened during your illness: the deprivation of your reason, the dulling of your senses, the oncome of death itself, or the alienation of the mind.''

The English monk Matthew Paris relates that the day came when Louis IX had had enough of everyone around him trying to get him to abandon his Crusader vow on the basis that he had made that vow when out of his mind with a seemingly terminal illness. Gathering his major critics, the king said: ''You claim that the change in my senses was the cause of my assuming the cross. There now, as you wish and have argued, I shall lay down the cross, handing it over to you.'' The king grasped the red cloth cross that had been loosely sewn on the left breast of his robe and tore it off. He put the cross into the hand of the startled but pleased bishop of Paris. But the bishop misunderstood what the king had in mind. If his prior vow was invalid because it had been made when he was ill, he would take that vow again, when there could be no doubt that he was in full possession of his mental faculties. ''My friends, certainly I am not now deprived of my reason or senses, nor am I powerless or infirm. Now I demand back my cross.'' He let them know that he would suffer the self-imposed penalty of death by fasting should he fail to make a new crusading vow. ''He who ignores nothing knows that nothing edible will enter my mouth until I have again signed myself with it.'' His opponents gave up.

This story not only shows a man dedicated to his God, but reveals as well a man who is dedicated to having his own way in the face of any advice or opposition. Not a day passed without an expression of his devotion to God, but he also believed that God had selected him to be the king of France. He was militantly religious, expressing all manner of humility and austerity, but also militant in his administration of his duties and the protection of his authority. He was a stern disciplinarian to his people and could treat non-Christians with a furious brutality. He managed to achieve sainthood with no personal commitment to poverty, obedience, or chastity. To add to his domains, he married Margaret of Provence, known as a high-spirited, happy girl with a twinkle in her eyes. It took just a few years of marriage to Louis to reduce her to an austere, joyless queen.

Louis's strong mind did not live in a strong body. He was tall, slender, and frail. He was frequently ill and suffered all his life from anemia. He put his body through the demands imposed upon it by sheer strength of will.

One familiar at his court who was delighted with the king's determination to go on the Crusade was the preceptor of the Knights Templar for France, Renaud de Vichiers. He assured Louis that a company of Templars would join the French Crusade, which de Vichiers would lead personally. He assisted the king in the collection and safe deposit of funds and was appointed by Louis to arrange sea transportation for the crusading army. The preceptor negotiated the charter of thirty-eight Genoese ships, which would be ready to make sail when needed. As it turned out, they weren't needed until 1248, after three years of preparation.

Louis called upon his subjects, especially the higher nobility who controlled the supply of armored knights, to follow him. Two of his brothers took the cross, both arrogant men who would have decisive effects on the future of the Holy Land: Robert, count of Artois, who would make disastrous decisions in the coming Crusade, and Charles, count of Anjou, who to further his personal ambitions would shake up the political future of both Europe and the Christian states in the Middle East. The flower of French nobility followed them: the duke of Burgundy, Count Peter of Brittany, Count Hugh of La Marche, Count William of Flanders, and a host of others. With them was a man worthy of special note, Jean of Joinville, seneschal of Champagne. He was an ardent diarist, and although his chronicles are often one-sided to avoid any possible criticism of his king, they provide the most complete record available of the disastrous events ahead.

This was a Crusade definitely not desired by Pope Innocent IV. In the summer of 1245 the pope had been driven out of Rome by the forces of the emperor Frederick and was now in exile at Lyons. The Crusade he wanted Louis to mount was against the German emperor, not the sultan of Egypt. He tried, but not even the dignity and the spiritual power of the supreme pontiff would sway the decision of Louis of France, who had his own direct line to God.

Louis did not want the Germans on his Crusade, but he favored English participation, hoping to divert as many English knights as possible to the Holy Land and away from any temptation to attack French lands in the king's absence. For precisely that reason, Henry III of England wanted no part of the Crusade that would take Louis and his army away from France. In spite of his efforts, some English knights decided to flout the king's will and to take the cross, at least partly because of a wave of religious fervor that swept England in October 1247.

It was probably staged as part of an effort by the new Templar grand master to heal an old wound with Henry III and to get his favor for the new Crusade. When Grand Master William de Sonnac was the master for England he had gravely offended Henry III. The king had become increasingly impatient with the pride and haughty demeanor of the Templars in his kingdom. He reminded the Templar master that the properties he guarded so jealously could be taken away as easily as they had been given. Far from the reaction of submission Henry had expected, the master replied that the king had best watch his tongue or he might suddenly find himself without a throne, certainly proof that the arrogant Templar pride that so angered Henry was actually there, and in full measure.

Now came an act of reconciliation that could not be ignored. It was so powerful in its impact that Henry summoned the highest clergy and nobility in the land to hear the good news. Matthew Paris relates the story. With the lords and bishops assembled, the announcement was made that "...the masters of the Templars and Hospitallers with the testimony of a good many seals, namely those of the patriarch of Jerusalem and the archbishops and bishops, abbots and other prelates, and magnates of the Holy Land, had sent some of the blood of our Lord, which he had shed on the cross for the salvation of the world, in a most beautiful crystal container, in the care of a certain well-known brother of the Templars."

The next day a colorful pageant unfolded in the streets as the king went on foot, carrying the real blood of Christ before him with both hands. The procession went from St. Paul's to Westminster Abbey, then to the palace of the bishop of Durham and back to Westminster. It was so drawn out that men had to be assigned to walk alongside the king to support Henry's arms, lest his tired muscles allow the crystal decanter to fall into the road. The bishop of Norwich celebrated the mass that day and followed it with a stirring sermon to emphasize the importance of this invaluable gift. "Of all things held sacred among men," he said, "the most sacred is the blood of Christ, for...its effusion was the salvation of the human race."

Now the people of England need no longer be envious of the French because their king owned a relic of the True Cross. "True, the cross is a most holy thing, but only because of the shedding on it of Christ's blood; nor is the blood holy because of the cross." The English had a holy relic even more holy than the relic of the cross, and the bishop added (perhaps because Henry III was in the audience) that only the sanctity of Henry made it possible. "It was mainly because of the reverence and holiness of the lord king of the English, who was recognized as the most Christian of all Christian princes, that this incomparable treasure had been sent..." In the wave of Christian ecstasy that gripped England it was impossible for Henry to discourage all of his subjects from the crusading vow, nor would it be prudent for him to punish those who took the cross. A small English army assembled to assist the French effort, headed by William, earl of Salisbury.

The French fleet set sail on August 25, 1248, after a great feast to which the Templar preceptor de Vichiers was invited in recognition of his services to the Crusade: He had arranged for the fleet of ships that were now loaded with men, horses, and supplies, including those of the contingent of Knights Templar, together with the household goods and wardrobes of the French queen and the ladies of her court.

Louis decided to make Cyprus the assembly point for all of the forces joining in his Crusade, and he put in to the port of Limassol on September 17. King Henry of Cyprus extended a sincere welcome, promising to send his own knights on the campaign. Many of the local barons came to the king from the Holy Land, as did the Templar grand master de Sonnac and the acting grand master of the Hospitallers. They all agreed that Egypt should be the initial objective, but they disagreed about the timing of the invasion. Louis was all for starting immediately, to achieve what he naively thought would be a surprise attack, but the local barons, and especially the Templar grand master, tried to dissuade him with descriptions of what the winter storms would do to the Christian fleet. The dangers were clear enough for Grand Master de Sonnac to win his point, but he was somewhat set back by Louis's order that the Templars must stop all private negotiations with the sultan or the Syrian Muslims. From this date forward, all approaches to any infidel would be only with the approval of Louis of France. Legally, he had no authority over the Templars, but this was no time to alienate the French king. His orders were acknowledged.

The king's problem now was to restock and transport his armies. The Genoese ships had contracted to bring them out but had long since gone home. The French Crusaders ate up all their food supplies during a whole winter of waiting. The local merchants were asked to find more supplies, which they did happily, but the purchases took a serious bite from Louis's treasury, as did the search for ships. He had expected the Italian maritime states to supply them, but Venice, which had established profitable trading activities with the Egyptians, was opposed to this Crusade and refused to aid the French in any way. Genoa and Pisa had no such problems, but some ships had to be brought from far away. The Templars, of course, had their own, as did many of the local barons. Count John of Jaffa brought his magnificent galley, which required three hundred men at the oars.

The effort took longer than expected, so the Crusaders were not ready to sail for Egypt until mid-May of 1249, nine months after they had sailed from France. The long period of waiting had given the Egyptians ample time to prepare to receive them. One hundred and twenty ships had been secured for the crossing, and it took weeks to get them all loaded and out to sea. Then a storm scattered them before they had time to assemble offshore. The group that Louis led to the coast near the mouth of the eastern branch of the Nile was only about a quarter of his total force. They reached the beach on June 4.

Sultan Ayub, the half-black sultan who had experienced difficulty in getting his throne, had held on to it for a long time. He was an elderly man now, reported to be suffering seriously from asthma, ulcers, or tuberculosis; he was so ill and in such pain that he may well have suffered from all three. But he was well enough to order an army to Damietta, about ten miles up the Nile from the sea—the same river city that had been taken then lost in the Crusade led by Cardinal Pelagius. The command was given to the emir Fakr ad-Din, on whose staff was the huge young Mameluke Rukn ad-Din Baibars. As word came to him of the sighting of the Crusaders' ships offshore, the emir ordered his army to move to the coast to repel a landing.

To the French, the concept of establishing a beachhead was new; coastal attacks were more the province of the Scandinavian or Italian naval powers. Nevertheless, they appear to have had correct instincts, or at least to have followed the example of sensible leaders. John of Jaffa had his rowing master increase the oar speed to the maximum during the last few yards and rammed his galley into the soft sand of the beach. The men in the bow dropped onto dry sand while the men behind them dropped into the shallow water and waded ashore. Other galleys followed suit and soon knights and soldiers on foot collected on the beach. The Egyptian army, watching from beyond bow-range, delayed too long before making its charge.

This was a situation the Crusaders knew how to handle, and the Templars were eager to join in. The pointed shields were dug into the sands, while the butts of spears and lances were braced in the sands with the points lowered to impale the approaching horses. Archers and crossbowmen took their stations behind the shields, while behind them the crews hurried to unload the horses. As Joinville described the successful defense, "We, when we saw them coming, fixed the points of our shields into the sand and the handles of our lances in the sand with the points turned toward them. But when they were so near that they saw the lances about to enter into their bellies, they turned around and fled." The Muslims rode close enough to fire their arrows, which did little damage. The Christian beachhead continued to grow with every new Crusader ship that landed.

In the course of several futile runs at the shield wall by the Muslim cavalry, more and more fully saddled war-horses were brought to shore so that the armored knights could mount counterattacks. The Egyptian response was to ride off the field, back to safety behind the high walls of Damietta. To the nomadic Bedouin cavalry that made up a large part of the Egyptian force, the fully armored men on the biggest horses they had ever seen were a totally new enemy. Many of the nomads didn't even stop at Damietta but kept riding away from the field.

Messages were sent by carrier pigeon from Damietta to the sultan at Cairo to let him know that the Crusaders had landed. When no answer came, the false rumor flew through the Egyptian ranks that the elderly sultan was dead. Anything could happen now, including civil war, so many of them started to desert. The people of the city, gripped by panic, also began to flee, and Fakr ad-Din, seeing his forces shrinking and all morale shattered, decided to abandon Damietta by night. He ordered that when all were out of the city, the rear guard should destroy the bridge of boats from the shore to the island fortress-city. In the haste to get away his orders were ignored.

The next morning a party of Egyptian Coptic Christians came to tell the Crusaders that Damietta was totally undefended. With the bridge intact, the army of Christ trooped through the gate of the city in total triumph. A surprise was waiting for them. The sultan had spent months transporting food and war supplies into Damietta to reinforce it for a prolonged siege, and all that wealth had been abandoned.

Louis ordered his entire army to thank God for this early victory, but with the Nile in flood he did not follow it up. He would wait for the waters to fall, which would take several months. The Crusader army would not fit inside the city walls, so most of them had to camp in the open, as did the reinforcements that arrived under Louis's third brother Alfonso, count of Poitiers. The waiting time was used to clean out the principal mosque of Damietta and consecrate it as a cathedral, and to divide the loot among the principal barons and the military orders. Louis sent to Cyprus for his queen, who came with her ladies.

Up the river at Cairo, Sultan Ayub, too, was busy with administrative affairs. The abandonment of Damietta had aroused his fury, so now the leaders of the defecting Bedouin Arabs were beheaded, as was any man who could be identified as having deserted the city. He humiliated the Mamelukes to the point of rebellion, and his swift actions in quelling that budding revolt were probably all that saved the life of Emir Fakr ad-Din, who had ordered the defenders away from Damietta. Since his army appeared to be in tatters, the sultan followed the example of his predecessor during the Fifth Crusade, offering to trade Jerusalem and the lands around it for the return of his city of Damietta. Louis, who believed that God would not want him to bargain with unbelievers, rejected the offer as soon as he heard it. The Crusaders would take Cairo and conquer all Egypt, then dictate the terms.

After the Christians had sat at Damietta for five months, the waters of the Nile were down, but so were their food supplies. The summer heat had taken hold, as had some diseases they could not even identify. Joinville lamented that the Christians, in the way of bored soldiers with nothing to do, turned to drunkenness and prostitution. The court at Cairo had offered a cash payment for every Christian head taken, and every morning in the camp revealed headless bodies, the midnight victims of Muslim bounty hunters.

Count Peter of Brittany had plenty of support for his plan to take the port city of Alexandria. Then the Egyptians would be cut off from the sea, and Cairo could be attacked by water up both branches of the Nile. It was a sensible plan, but it was completely opposed by the king's brother, the count of Artois, who persuaded Louis that the only proper course of action was to move straight up the Nile to Cairo. The only real barrier to such a plan was the walled city of Mansourah, built specifically as a fortress-city to defend the capital, but surely it would be easily taken by this glorious Christian army. Louis issued his orders and the Crusaders prepared for the march. Leaving a strong garrison at Damietta to protect his queen, Louis led his army up the road along the Nile on November 20, 1249.

As the march began, the Egyptian commander sent a unit of light cavalry to harass the Crusaders and slow down their march. Louis ordered that such harassment should be ignored and that no Christian should leave the column. Joinville recorded an example of Templar disobedience:

"...the King ordered us to make ready to ride forward, while at the same time forbidding anyone to be so bold as to attack the enemy around us. It happened, however, that when the army began to move forward and the Turks realized that no attack on them was contemplated (for their spies had told them that the King had forbidden it), they grew bolder and flung themselves on the Templars, who formed the van. One of the Turks bore a Knight Templar to the ground, right in front of the hoofs of the horse on which brother Renaud de Vichiers, at that time the Marshal of the Temple, was mounted. On seeing this, the Marshal cried to his brother Templars: 'For God's sake, let's get at them! I can't stand this any longer!' He struck his spurs into his horse, and all of the army followed. Now our men's horses were fresh, and those of the Turks already weary; and so, as I have heard, not one of the enemy escaped, but all perished." There is no record that the king chastised his friend de Vichiers for the rash, but successful, insubordination.

The Crusader king didn't know it yet, but just three days after his march began the Egyptian sultan had died. His own subjects didn't know it either, as a bizarre drama unfolded at Cairo. Sultan Ayub's favorite wife, the Armenian Shajar ad-Durr ("Spray of Pearls"), knew very well the confusion and conflict usually triggered by the death of an eastern potentate, which could be fatal in the face of any enemy invasion. With the cooperation of the chief eunuch, she concealed the sultan's death and would allow no one to enter his apartments. The conspirators practiced forging the dead sultan's signature, then put his name on a decree that appointed Emir Fakr ad-Din as commander-in-chief of the armies and the sultan's viceroy until he recovered from his illness. The document confirmed that the sultan's son Turanshah was the legitimate heir to the throne. Turanshah was far away on the Euphrates, so secret gallopers were sent off to tell him of his father's death and to urge him to make haste to Cairo. A dead body can't be kept around for long, and the news of the sultan's death did leak out, but by then Fakr ad-Din and Shajar ad-Durr had a firm grip on the government, and Turanshah was on his way.

The forty-mile road from Damietta to Mansourah was on the eastern side of the Nile, but intersected by dozens of canals of various sizes. The largest of these, the Bahr as-Saghir, guarded the approach to Mansourah. Fakr ad-Din camped the major part of his army behind that broad flow of water, but he sent small units of cavalry to harass the Christians as they crossed the smaller, fordable streams. The Knights Templar, who had insisted on their right to be in the vanguard, engaged in one mounted skirmish after another, easily pushing aside the Muslim horsemen.

On December 7, the Christian army had to cross a larger-than-usual canal and were hit by a larger force of Egyptian cavalry. The usual skirmish turned into a battle. The Crusaders won the day, but the Templars were so exhilarated by their pursuit of the retreating Egyptians that they rode too far. They found themselves surrounded and had to fight their way back to rejoin the Christian army. The king was only mildly critical of these devoted knights who were fighting for him so fiercely.

Two weeks later the Crusaders reached the broad expanse of the Bahr as-Saghir. The opposing armies lined the banks and stared at each other, with occasional shouts of defiance. For six weeks they did little more than stare and shout. A party of Egyptian horsemen did manage at one point to cross the Nile in boats and come up behind the Christian army, but it was quickly beaten off by Charles of Anjou.

After consulting with his engineers, Louis decided to build a dam across the wide canal. Timbers were scarce, but enough were gathered to build a protective shed for the workmen. The Egyptian answer was to catapult barrels of flaming naphtha and Greek fire onto the wooden shelters. Some of the Christian soldiers, including those ordered to put out the fires, were burned horribly, but the king insisted that the work go forward. Then the Egyptians came up with an even better idea. As the Crusaders struggled to build their dam inch by inch, a horde of Muslim workmen dug away at the bank on the opposite side, maintaining the width of the canal. "Thus it happened that in one day they undid all that we had done with three weeks labor, for as fast as we dammed up the stream on our side, they broadened the stream by the holes they made on theirs." In the face of such frustration, it was futile to continue the back-breaking labor, so the project was abandoned during the week before Christmas.

Joinville recorded an event that happened in the Christian camp a few days later, worth recounting because it illustrates the discipline and the readiness of the Knights Templar in the camp:

"On Christmas Day, I and my knights were dining with Pierre d'Avallon. While we were at table the Saracens came spurring hotly up to our camp and killed several poor fellows who had gone for a stroll in the fields. We all went off to arm ourselves but, quick as we were, we did not return in time to join our host, for he was already outside the camp, and had gone to fight the Saracens. We spurred after him and rescued him from the enemy, who had thrown him to the ground. Then we brought him back to camp with his brother, the Lord de Val. The Templars, who had come upon hearing the alarm, covered our retreat well and valiantly."

The stalemate was broken by a local Coptic Christian, who offered to show the Crusaders a ford across the Bahr as-Saghir for a payment of five hundred gold bezants. He led them to a place well to the east and out of sight of the Muslim camp. The plan was that an advance party would cross the canal by moonlight and defend the position, while the Christian engineers would build a pontoon bridge for the main army to cross over. The advance party consisted of the knights of the count of Artois and the English contingent under Earl William of Salisbury, all preceded by a vanguard of about three hundred Knights Templar under Grand Master de Sonnac. As the king's brother, the count of Artois was placed in command of the entire force.

The water was fairly deep and the footing was treacherous, but they did manage to slowly pick their way across. Fortunately, they were at an isolated stretch of the canal and encountered no resistance. Their very emphatic orders were to fan out and protect the crossing of the Crusader army, and under no circumstances to launch an attack without the specific orders of the king. The count of Artois rejected his brother's orders and called for an instant surprise attack on the Egyptian camp. Grand Master de Sonnac reminded him of his orders, and the earl of Salisbury joined the grand master in urging their leader to wait for the rest of the army. His answer was to accuse the English commander of hiding behind the natural cowardice of his race, and to berate the grand master for his timidity. They reluctantly but angrily agreed to follow him.

In the first phase of their independent action, it appeared that the count of Artois had been right: The Egyptians were just rubbing the sleep from their eyes, ready for another dull day of waiting, and were totally unprepared for the Crusader attack. Men were cut down as they tried to struggle into their armor or running to get to their horses. The emir Fakr ad-Din had just gotten out of his bath and was having his gray beard dyed red-brown with henna when he heard the clamor of the attack. He ran to his horse, with no armor, and galloped right into a cluster of Knights Templar. They hacked him down having no idea that they had just killed the Egyptian commander-in-chief.

Those Egyptians who could ran off the field, many in the direction of the fortified city of Mansourah, just two miles away. It was the only major fortress between the Crusaders and Cairo, and Robert of Artois was determined to take it. The Egyptian army was scattered, and the count could win the war here and now. Once again Salisbury and the grand master urged their leader to wait for the main army. A walled city was not a tent camp in the open fields. Men on horseback could not scale walls fifty feet high. As before, their advice brought on insults and accusations of cowardice. Robert had touched the pride of the aging grand master, who looked him in the eye and replied, "The Templars are unaccustomed to fear. We will go with you, but know you well that none of us will come back." It appeared at the last moment that reason might prevail, as a dozen knights who had crossed the ford rode up with the king's direct orders that no further advance be made, but Robert of Artois was experiencing an overwhelming self-assertion in his victory over the camp. King or no king, he would ride to the conquest of Mansourah.

What none of them knew was that the Mameluke Baibars had taken charge at Mansourah. He had sent his men to gather in the fleeing Egyptians to the walled city. He correctly assumed that the Crusaders would next come to Mansourah, and he made the city a trap. He ordered that the gates be left open to entice the Crusaders to ride in. The streets of the city were narrow, built for pack animals, not wagons. The main street from the gate to the citadel was left invitingly clear. Baibars kept a cavalry contingent just out of sight to block the far end of the main street, and he set Muslim foot soldiers and cavalry to block the side streets. The civilians were ordered to carry timbers, stones, and heavy furniture to the roof-tops along the streets where the Christians would be bottled up.

It was as though Baibars had a crystal ball. Everything unfolded as he had expected and planned for. The Crusaders riding up to the city could not resist the magnetic appeal of the open gates. They spurred their horses to a dash through the gates before someone in the city would think to close them. They galloped down the main street and suddenly hit a solid wall of Muslim resistance. The Chris-tians stacked up on each other, crowded in a narrow passage that rendered lances useless. They could use their swords and axes, but there was no one to use them on. Those ducking down side streets to get out of the press found themselves bottled up there.

Then came the rain of missiles from above, with no way for the Crusaders to get at the people dropping heavy stones and massive beams on their heads. Then came the arrows and crossbow bolts from the archers stationed on the rooftops. Horses fell, taking their riders down with them to be trampled by the panicked horses around them. The Crusaders were caught like cattle in the chutes of a slaughterhouse.

As more and more Christians fell, Baibars turned his foot soldiers loose on them. Robert of Artois and a group of followers broke down a door to barricade themselves in a house, but they were easily killed by Muslims coming at them through doors and windows. William of Salisbury died in the street. Of two hundred and ninety Knights Templar who had ridden into Mansourah, only five managed to cut their way out. One of them was Grand Master de Sonnac, his face and beard dripping blood from a deep wound that had taken out one of his eyes. A few Christian knights managed to escape on foot and ran to the Nile. In their frantic desire to swim to safety they forgot, or didn't have time, to remove their heavy coats of chain mail. As they leaped into the river they sank right to the bottom and drowned. Count Peter of Brittany was able to fight his way through, at the cost of a serious head wound, and was able to stay on his horse long enough to ride to the king with the news of the massacre at Mansourah.

Louis had most of his army across the ford and deployed them to receive the attack he was certain would come from Mansourah.

His entire corps of crossbowmen was on the other side of the canal, to guard the rear. They were told to stay there to cover the engineers, who were now ordered to complete the pontoon bridge across the ford. The boats for the bridge had already been built.

As the planking of the bridge went forward, the Christians heard the trumpet blasts and booming kettledrums that heralded the attack of the Egyptian army. The Christians retreated to a defensive posture behind a shield wall as the Muslim cavalry rode close to loose thousands of arrows. A body of mounted knights was standing by and rode out in a countercharge when the Christian leaders decided that the Muslim archers had exhausted their supply of arrows. The Muslims fell back for more ammunition, then came again. The day was probably saved by the completion of the pontoon bridge, which allowed the three hundred Christian crossbowmen to trot across the bridge and take up positions behind the shield wall. Now the mounted Muslim archers dared not come too close. They were ordered back into Mansourah.

Three days later, the Egyptians came again. Although still suffering from the head wound taken at Mansourah and the loss of an eye, Grand Master de Sonnac insisted on taking personal command of the surviving Knights Templar, who were assigned a place in the Christian right wing. The Muslim cavalry came in wide sweeps, sending thousands of arrows into the Christian army. After a period which the Crusaders hoped had exhausted the Muslim horses, Louis ordered a counterattack by the entire Christian army. As the two armies met, the battle broke into thousands of ferocious hand-to-hand combats. By a freakish coincidence of war, Grand Master de Sonnac took a cut on the other side of his face, which took his remaining eye.

After hours of fighting, the Egyptians retired again behind the walls of Mansourah. Thousands of dead and wounded lay on the field. The few Templars left searched the ground for their fallen grand master and found him, but he died a few hours later, in anguishing pain and totally blind. Perhaps he welcomed the death that provided the only relief he could expect. Joinville made a simple but sincere entry in his diary: "May God bless him."

During the next eight weeks, as the Christians sat battered in their camp, uncertain as to what to do next, the young sultan Turan-shah arrived at Cairo, then came down the Nile to join his army.

The sultan ordered a fleet of light boats to be built, then carried down the western road on the opposite side of the Nile and past the Christians, each boat between two pack-camels. They were put into the water between the Christian camp and Damietta to intercept the boats bringing food supplies to the Crusader army. They swarmed out onto the river, loaded with archers and swordsmen, to surround and board each Crusader vessel that tried to get through. Every Christian crew member was killed, the food was taken to feed the Muslim army at Mansourah, and the Christian ships were added to the Muslim fleet. The operation was so successful that it completely dried up the Crusaders' food supplies. Starvation would be a real possibility within a week, and with it came a strange malady. Joinville wrote, "...a disease spread through the army, of such a sort that the flesh on our legs dried up, and the skin became covered with black spots and turned a brown earthy color like an old boot. With those who had this disease the flesh on the gums became gangrened, and no one who fell a victim to it could hope to recover, but was sure to die. An infallible sign of death was bleeding from the nose."

Joinville speculated that this horrible malady, quickly spreading throughout the entire Christian army, was caused by the "unhealthy Egyptian climate," or from eating the flesh of eels that fed on the drowned corpses in the river. The real cause was the lack of vitamin C. Giving a man the juice of a single orange would have arrested the course of the illness, which was scurvy. (Centuries would pass before the British learned that scurvy could be ended in their navy by the simple expedient of giving every man a few ounces of lime juice every day, a scientific achievement that earned for them the derisive sobriquet of "Limeys.")

When dysentery and typhoid also arrived, it was decided that rather than have everyone die in this camp, including the king, the army would go back across the Bahr as-Saghir and move down the Nile closer to Damietta, where the soldiers should be able to find food. As they decamped and waited their turns to cross the boat-bridge, the harassment by the Muslim archers was incessant, and Egyptian cavalry moved all around them, alert for stragglers. The crossing was not easy, because many of the Christians were by now too weak to walk. Thinking it an act of mercy, Louis said that those who could walk or ride should march down the road, while the wounded and seriously ill should be sent down the Nile by boat. They were easy prey for the waiting Muslim fleet, so most of them didn't survive the river journey. The king himself was obviously moving by sheer will alone; he suffered not only from scurvy, but also from the complication of advanced dysentery. The lower part of his drawers was cut away because the attacks came so swiftly that he didn't have time to drop his pants. He was closely attended, to catch him as he fainted several times in the course of each day.

If it had been an act of Egyptian stupidity to neglect to destroy the pontoon bridge at Damietta, it was easily matched by the Crusaders who neglected to destroy the pontoon bridge they had built over the Bahr as-Saghir. The morning after the Christian army had crossed over, the Muslim cavalry was surprised to find the bridge intact. Healthy and well-fed themselves and mounted on well-fed horses, they joyfully trooped across the bridge to pursue the army of sluggish invalids ahead of them.

In spite of the constant hammering on all sides, the Crusader army made it about halfway back to Damietta, by which time the king could not sit on his horse and had to be carried along. Diplomacy was tried, remembering the offer of the dead sultan Ayub to exchange Damietta for Jerusalem, but the offer was, not surprisingly, rejected by Turanshah, who had no need to bargain now. All manner of rumors were running through the army about the condition of the king.

Then occurred an event that will probably never be clearly understood. A French sergeant named Marcel, either gone mad or swayed by treasonous bribery, rode through the French army like a herald. "Surrender, all you knights," he shouted, "for the king commands it, and do not let his Majesty be slain!" Perhaps because the bogus order made sense to them, the French knights and soldiers dropped their weapons and surrendered to the Muslims surrounding them, all without the permission, or even the knowledge, of the bedridden king. By the time Louis got the news, almost his entire army had surrendered. There was no one to protect the king from that same fate. He was found by the victorious Egyptians and symbolically put in chains, even though he could hardly move. The king was fortunate in his royal rank, because all other Christians who were so disabled by wounds or disease that they could not walk to their prisons were killed where they lay. As they made the long journey to their prisons at Cairo, every man who dropped was killed. As they stopped at the end of each day's march, three hundred Christian prisoners were ceremoniously beheaded.

One blessing of imprisonment for the Christians was that no matter how miserable the food provided by their Muslim jailers, it was much better than no food at all. Many began to regain their health. King Louis got royal treatment, not out of respect for his titles, but in view of the ransom that he was expected to bring, a project which required that Louis be alive and well. Louis insisted that any ransom must be for all of the thousands of French prisoners, many of whom were from the first families of France. He would have endless problems at home if he left them in Egyptian prisons while buying his own freedom.

The price was high. First, the peaceful surrender of Damietta, which was still strongly garrisoned. Next, the cash payment of one million bezants, which in Louis's own money meant five hundred thousand *livres tournois* (the French pounds minted at Tours). It was indeed a king's ransom, but Louis agreed. It was arranged that Louis and his highest-ranking vassals would be taken to Damietta to preside over the surrender of the city on April 30.

As Louis waited, violence once again overturned the government of Egypt, threatening the arrangements that had just been made. Delighted with such a resounding victory so soon after taking the Egyptian throne, Sultan Turanshah held a feast of celebration in his pavilion by the Nile. He invited all his close friends who had come to Cairo with him. They had been rewarded by being given all the major administrative posts of the empire, while all the previous Mameluke officials were stripped of their posts. The Mamelukes were already angry when they received a letter from Turanshah's mother, Shajar ad-Durr, who had saved the throne for him. The young sultan had demanded from her all of the property that she had received from her husband, Turanshah's father. Her letter was an appeal to the Mamelukes to help her. She had successfully conspired with them before, and she found success again.

As Turanshah's banquet came to a close, a party of Mamelukes broke into the pavilion with their swords drawn, led by the towering figure of Rukn ad-Din Baibars. The agile young sultan took a cut on his hand but leaped away from the slashing swords to run out to the safety of a wooden watchtower that had been built on the edge of the Nile. When the Mamelukes set the tower on fire the sultan leaped into the river. Standing waist-deep, he begged for mercy, dodging arrows shot at him from the bank. When no arrow found its mark, Baibars waded into the stream and killed the sultan with his sword. The principal Mameluke emir, Izz ad-Din Aibek, became the supreme military commander, but he quickly married Shajar ad-Durr and styled himself Sultan Aibek.

The captive Christians were terrified of the bloodthirsty Mamelukes and thought that their agreements would now be set aside, but they soon learned that the Mamelukes loved money as much as they loved blood. They did not increase the ransom, but rather made it a bit more palatable by reducing the total ransom from five hundred thousand to four hundred thousand *livres*. They also demanded that half the sum be paid at Damietta to purchase the freedom of the king and his leading barons. The other Christian prisoners, including the king's brother Alfonso, would be released only upon payment of the full amount.

Just three days after the king's capture, his queen at Damietta had given birth to a son and a few days later had been taken to Acre.

Some of the members of the retreating Christian army, including a number of wounded, had managed to make their way to the safety of Damietta. Now, as Louis prepared to surrender the city, he asked for assurance that his wounded followers would be properly fed and cared for. He was assured that they would be looked after by skilled Muslim physicians. The Mamelukes also agreed to Louis's request that his catapults and trebuchets be protected, along with the substantial stores of salted meat in the city, all of which he would send for later. On the other hand, the Mamelukes asked that Louis assume a penalty for failure to pay the second half of the ransom. They requested that Louis swear that if the full payment was not made, the king would renounce Christ, a horrifying suggestion that Louis would not even consider.

Inside Damietta, Louis had his reserve treasure counted out. It came to just one hundred and seventy thousand *livres*. The king was thirty thousand *livres* short, and he welcomed suggestions as to where to turn for the balance. Joinville told the king that there was much more than that on board the Knights Templar's flagship galley. He was correct. The largest galley held not only the Templars' own funds to finance their part in the Crusade, but also the funds of a number of French nobles that had been entrusted to them for safe deposit. Not deterred by such details, the king sent for the ship's commander, Etienne d'Otricourt, and the Templar marshal Renaud de Vichiers. Joinville informed them of the king's order that they deliver up thirty thousand *livres* in gold. Joinville recorded, "...brother Etienne d'Otricourt, the commander of the Temple, gave me their reply. 'My lord Joinville,' he said, 'this advice you have given the king is neither good nor reasonable. For you know that all money placed in our charge is left with us on condition of our swearing never to hand it over except to those who entrusted it to us.' On this many hard and insulting words passed between us."

Templar marshal de Vichiers had enjoyed the king's favor since he had helped to plan this Crusade back in Paris, and he stepped in now to give the king what he wanted. In veiled language he indicated that although the Templars could never voluntarily surrender money entrusted to them, they could not defend themselves or the money if it was seized by force, since they would not raise their weapons to a king's officer. Besides, they had more than thirty thousand of the king's money at Acre and could easily replace it there.

His suggestion led to the acting out of a charade in the hold of the Templar galley the next morning. Sent to collect the money, Joinville demanded the keys to the treasure chests. The Templars firmly refused. Then Joinville snatched up a hatchet that was conveniently located in the area and threatened to break open a chest,

"…and told him I would make it serve as his Majesty's key." That was the moment which de Vichiers called other Templars to witness. "…the Marshal seized hold of me by the wrist and said to me: 'Since you evidently intend to use force against us, we will let you have the keys.' " The Templar sense of trust had been honored, and Louis got his thirty thousand pieces of gold.

The Muslims occupied Damietta on May 6, 1250. The two hundred thousand *livres*, payment of half the ransom, was turned over and the chains of the prisoners to be freed were struck off. As he embarked for Acre, Louis was happy to learn that the Mameluke sultan had decided to free Louis's brother, the count Alfonso. As the Christian ships sailed away, the Mameluke commander at Damietta issued his orders. No Muslim was going to guard a warehouse full of pork, so the barrels of salted meat were ordered to be burned. To get the fire going, he ordered his engineers to dismantle the French king's siege machines and to stack up the timbers. The roaring fire would also provide a convenient way to get rid of dead bodies, which they soon had in abundance. The order was given to cut the throats of the Christian wounded, the final abomination of the Sixth Crusade.

At Acre, no one could have been very sympathetic when Louis ignored the rivers of blood shed by the men who had died, and the thousands of men in miserable prisons because of his leadership, to state that the great disaster was, incredibly, a sign of God's favor to him. He appeared to actually believe that God had deliberately engineered all that human misery just to bestow on the saintly king of France a divine lesson in humility.

22

King-of-the-Hill

1250 to 1261

$\mathbf{J}$F LOUIS IX had returned to France immediately, he would have done so under a dark cloak of humiliation and disgrace. His Crusade had been a total failure. The money forced from his people in heavy taxation had been wasted. There was hardly a noble family in France that did not have an honored member dead from wounds or disease, or being held a prisoner in the dungeons of Cairo. The fighting force of the Christian residents of the Holy Land, always meager, had been decimated. The military orders had lost men and money and had to call once again on their preceptories in Europe to replenish both. And the saintly king of France bore the major responsibility for all this misery.

Louis needed to raise the rest of his promised ransom money to buy the freedom of the thousands of his followers still captive in Egypt. To desert them now would be an additional disgrace too difficult to bear. He announced his intention to stay in the Holy Land and pleaded with his vassals to stay with him, but they had had enough. They had fulfilled their feudal obligations as well as their crusading vows, and most had run out of money. They had taken part in a great catastrophe, had nothing to be proud of, and just wanted to get home. Louis was reduced to negotiating payments and subsistence to those who would stay. As his army sailed away, he found himself with fewer than fifteen hundred followers.

With no great army to back him and with no legal grounds whatever, he simply asserted his total authority over the Holy Land, and none of the battle-weary local barons chose to argue with him. Louis did see one opportunity to bolster his power, and that was in the leaderless Knights of the Temple, who had not yet elected a grand master to replace the fallen William de Sonnac. Louis had in mind his friend Renaud de Vichiers. Renaud had proved his loyalty to the king when, as the Templar preceptor in France, he had made the transportation and supply arrangements with Genoa. As marshal of the order he had assisted Louis in getting the final portion of the first half of his ransom money from the Templar treasury. If Louis could get Renaud de Vichiers elected grand master of the Knights Templar, he could exercise effective control over the military order.

Louis had no problems with the electors of the Templar grand chapter. The Templars were a French-speaking order, most of their properties were in France, and their Temple in Paris was their most important base in Europe. Most of the Templars had relatives who were the subjects of the French king. It appeared to be an intelligent move to have as their grand master a friend of the monarch, with whom the new master could exert influence to the benefit of the Temple. They happily elected Renaud de Vichiers as the nineteenth grand master of the Knights Templar, never suspecting that he would bring a great humiliation down upon them, as de Vichiers would put his loyalty to Louis ahead of his loyalty to the military order he now commanded.

Jean of Joinville, the seneschal of Champagne, very early felt the benefits of the relationship between the king and the grand master. Joinville was one of those persuaded to stay in the Holy Land, in return for cash subsidies for his household. Cash kept at home was always a risk, unless there were soldiers available to guard it around the clock. The Knights Templar, with their carefully guarded vaults, provided the only safe alternative, so when Joinville received four hundred *livres* in gold from King Louis, he held back forty for current expenses and entrusted the balance to the Templars.

When his ready cash ran low and Joinville sought to withdraw some of his funds from the Templars, the commander of the Templar citadel at Acre told him that there was no record of funds being held in his name. Perhaps the commander remembered Joinville's treatment of the Templars on their treasure ship at Egypt and had decided to teach him a lesson.

Joinville complained to the new grand master de Vichiers, "whom the king...had helped make Master of the Temple," asking for justice for an officer of Louis of France. Four days later de Vichiers came to him with the news that the commander at Acre had been demoted and sent off to the little village of Sephouri. The new commander had orders to make Joinville's funds available to him on demand.

The local barons watched all this with some interest, but the

Templar connections of the French king were not their major concern, which was simple survival. With a good part of their fighting force in graves or in chains, it appeared that the Mameluke sultan Aibek could walk right over the Christian states whenever he wished. They wanted Louis to exert his influence to defend them from the inevitable Muslim invasion.

It appeared to be an impossible task, until word came that the Muslim empire was divided again. The Syrian city-states were still loyal to the Ayubbid line founded by Saladin. They rejected the authority of the Mameluke revolt in Cairo. In July 1250, when the prince of Aleppo, Saladin's great-grandson an-Nasir Yusuf, was told of the murder of his cousin Turanshah, he gathered an army and occupied Damascus. Now Sultan Aibek had a much more serious problem than the meager Christian territories along the coast.

As the political maneuvering got under way, both Muslim factions sought the cooperation of the Christian knights. Louis leaned in the direction of an alliance with the sultan of Egypt, to whom he still owed two hundred thousand *livres*, and who was still holding his Frankish prisoners. The local barons favored an alliance with Damascus, with which they had a history of cooperation. They did not trust the Mamelukes, whose sole reason for existence was war. They watched with keen interest as a Muslim army moved out of Damascus, then across Palestine, for an invasion of Egypt. The Syrians moved across the Isthmus of Suez to the upper delta. The Mameluke army, commanded by Sultan Aibek, met them in February 1251 on a field about twelve miles from the river town of Zagazig.

The Syrians were done in by an act of treachery that had probably been planned in advance. The regiment of Mamelukes in the Syrian army understandably favored the Mameluke revolt in Egypt, but they had kept that information to themselves. Their loyalty was unquestioned until a critical moment in the heat of battle, when the Syrian Mamelukes suddenly turned on the army of Damascus. It was the shock of the betrayal as much as anything else that demoralized the Syrians, who fled the field and didn't stop until they were back at Damascus.

Although there was no reason to expect that the treachery that lost the battle with Egypt would ever occur again, an-Nasir Yusuf wanted to strengthen his hand. Envoys were sent from Damascus to King Louis suggesting that in exchange for a military alliance, Jerusalem might be returned to the Christians. This was a proposal that could quicken Louis's blood. If he could occupy Jerusalem, he could return to Europe as a great hero in spite of his defeat in Egypt, because the primary goal of the Crusade was the rescue of the Holy Places. What stood in the way of that accomplishment was the thousands of French prisoners in Egypt. The local barons had assured Louis that if they went to war against Sultan Aibek, all of the Christian prisoners in Egypt would be killed. Louis's recovery of Jerusalem had to come from a treaty with Egypt, not Damascus, in order to free the prisoners.

As he kept an-Nasir Yusuf dangling with no definite answer, Louis sent an envoy to Sultan Aibek. The mission was a great success: Aibek, to show his good faith, released three thousand Christian captives. These men added greatly to the fighting force, restored to health since even on their simple prison diet they at least got enough vitamins to overcome the malnutrition that had laid them low in the delta.

Encouraged by this success and bolstered by the praise that came from all sides, Louis decided to ask for more. He sent his envoys back to Cairo, this time to demand the release of all the rest of the Christian prisoners and cancellaton of the two hundred thousand *livres* of ransom still due. Sultan Aibek knew that the Christians were in active negotiations with Damascus and that Jerusalem was part of the bargaining. He countered with the proposal that in the event of a decisive military victory, the Christians would have all of the former kingdom of Jerusalem, bounded to the east by the Jordan River.

In the midst of those negotiations, Grand Master de Vichiers came to Louis with a report that enraged the king. It seems that the Templars, as was their custom in recent years, had been negotiating their own affairs with an-Nasir Yusuf in Damascus. The ownership of a large tract of land was in dispute, and Templar envoys had arrived at an agreement to divide the land. Louis was stunned that any Christian would dare to treat with any Muslim ruler without his permission. He sent for Hugh de Jouy, the Templar marshal who had negotiated for the Temple, and the emir who had come to sign for an-Nasir Yusuf.

The king demanded a great ceremony of apology that would not have been tolerated by any grand master except de Vichiers, who now proved conclusively that his loyalties were to his king, not his order. The entire Christian army was invited to watch the pageant, and three sides of the king's pavilion were raised so that all could see. The grand master and all of the Knights Templar in the area, dressed in their white monastic robes but with their feet bare, marched through the gathered ranks of Christians to kneel before the king's throne. The king ordered the grand master and the Muslim envoy to sit on the ground at his feet.

"Master," shouted the king, so that all could hear, "you will tell the sultan's envoy that you regret having made any treaty with his lord without first speaking to me. You will add that since you did not consult me you must hold the sultan released from the agreement he had made with you, and hand all relevant documents back to him." The grand master obediently took the treaty document out of his robe and handed it to the envoy, saying, "I give you back the contract that I have wrongly entered into, and express my regret for what I did."

Then the grand master got to his knees and formally surrendered to King Louis everything that the Order of the Temple owned in the Holy Land and in Europe, so that he might help himself to all or any part of it as punishment for the order's grievous affront to his royal authority. Louis did not take the Templar property, which he must have known the pope and the order would not permit, but did declare that Brother Hugh, the Templar marshal who had negotiated the agreement, must be banished for life from the Holy Land.

The Templars kneeling before the king must have been seething with anger toward the king and their grand master. Everything had been wrong about this humiliation. Louis had no authority whatever over the Templar order, which was responsible only to the pope. The grand master had no right to offer to surrender any property of the order. The king had no right to banish any Templar officer. If the Templars had resisted, Louis would not have been able to force them, but they were sworn to obey their grand master. His must be the responsibility for the basest act of degradation to which the order had ever been subjected, and all just to satisfy the royal ego and to assert to all the world the supreme authority of Louis of France. Templar morale was shattered.

That didn't bother Louis, who took his army south to meet the Egyptian sultan and consummate the treaty that would make Louis a hero in Europe. Before they could join up, an-Nasir Yusuf sent an army to Gaza to keep them apart. They all sat there for almost a year, with no one anxious to start the war. Louis used the time to strengthen the defense of Jaffa, while an-Nasir Yusuf used the time to call upon the caliph of Baghdad to make peace between the Muslim factions. The caliph accepted the charge with enthusiasm. He managed to convince Sultan Aibek that he should be content to be the uncontested ruler of Egypt, with Palestine thrown in for good measure. The Jordan River would be the boundary to the east, the Sea of Galilee to the north. Beyond that would be the domain of the Syrian ruler an-Nasir Yusuf, who had agreed to the boundaries. With that treaty signed, there was no role for the Christians, and no reward. In his dejection, there was nothing for Louis to do but march from Gaza back to Acre.

An-Nasir Yusuf also went home, but he made his joyous journey a fast raid through the Christian territory. Villages fell, prisoners were taken, flocks and herds were driven before them. It was an army on horseback, so sieges didn't fit in, but the Muslims did raid the town of Sidon, helping themselves to property and people and ignoring the garrison in the castle, who were not numerous enough to come out to do battle.

Frustrated by the resolution of the Muslim treaty, Louis was in a receptive mood when he was called upon by ambassadors of the Ismaili order of the Assassins. He had heard enough about them to be concerned, as any monarch should be when faced with thousands of fanatics whose ruler traveled with a herald in front of him holding a battle-ax bound with knives, shouting, "Turn out of the way for him who bears in his hands the death of kings!"

The envoys stated that they had come to ask why their master had not received from Louis the gift of gold that he traditionally received from kings. And if Louis did not feel inclined to pay such a tribute, their master would be satisfied if Louis would arrange that the Assassin sect could stop paying tribute to the Knights Templar and the Hospitallers, so that the military orders would not harass the members of the sect who lived on or near the lands controlled by them. They explained to Louis that although they had ample means and sufficient suicide-prone adherents to kill any enemy, it would do no good to kill a grand master. His order would simply elect another master of equal ability, and the Assassin sacrifice would have been for nothing.

Louis listened, then invited the envoys to meet with him later in the day. When they returned, they found the grand masters of the Templars and Hospitallers seated with the king. The Assassin envoys were ordered to repeat their demands, which they did reluctantly. Then they were ordered to meet on the following day with the two grand masters alone, without the king. At that meeting the grand masters pointed out that it was not the place of the Assassins to make demands for rich gifts from the French king; the proper conduct was the other way round. They should think of what rich gifts they would give, not what they would get. The grand masters emphasized that only their respect for the French monarch kept them from killing the Assassin envoys now, nor would they fear any reprisal. Much shaken, the envoys returned to their leader.

A couple of weeks later the envoys returned, bearing their ruler's shirt and ring as evidence of the symbolic wedding of the rulers of France and of the Assassin sect. With these, they also brought caskets filled with rich gifts of carved crystal, amber, and gold. Louis responded with rich gifts of jewels and gold to the Assassin leader. No military aid resulted, but the Templars and Hospitallers continued to receive their tributes, and Louis could go about his business without fear of assassination.

Still in search of allies, Louis turned to the Mongols, about whom he knew almost nothing. When Louis was told that Sartaq Khan, a great-grandson of Genghis Khan, had become a Christian, he sent two Dominican preachers to suggest a Christian alliance with the young khan. Sartaq had no authority to effect such an important agreement. Besides, he was not really familiar with the concept of an "alliance." Rulers submitted to the Mongols, paid annual tribute, then governed their people as Mongol vassals, or they did not submit and were killed. It was really quite simple. The message the good friars brought back to Louis was along those lines: Submit, and send a yearly tribute. Otherwise, Louis would be destroyed, as so many kings had been before him.

Before Louis could make any further effort to find friends and allies, a report from France told him that his mother had died. She was a strong woman and had looked after Louis's interests in his absence. Her death had been the signal for the king of England to renew his encroachments into French lands, and Louis's own vassals were beginning to assert independence, since their king had been away for almost five years. Louis had no choice if he was to protect his kingdom. He sailed away from the Holy Land, leaving just a token military force behind.

Before leaving, Louis had committed to a two-and-a-half-year treaty with Damascus and a ten-year treaty with Egypt, but the treaties were observed only for purposes of diplomacy. Raids and counter-raids began almost immediately. As the year 1256 opened, Christians plundered a great Muslim caravan. A few weeks later, the governor of Jerusalem led a raid of vengeance on Christian territory and was killed in a decisive Christian victory. Still the actions did not provoke total war, which neither side wanted.

The real problems of the Holy Land were internal. Emperor Frederick's son, King Conrad of Jerusalem who never laid eyes on his kingdom, had died in May of 1254. The legitimate heir to the throne of Jerusalem was his infant son Conradin. Ignoring the rights of the baby-king off in Italy, Louis had named Geoffrey of Sargina as seneschal of the kingdom of Jerusalem, and Count John of Jaffa was recognized by the local lords as *bailli*. In 1253 King Hugh of Cyprus died, leaving the crown to his son, Hugh II, who was less than a year old. The baby's mother, Queen Plaisance, claimed the regency of both Cyprus and Jerusalem, but the barons of the kingdom of Jerusalem rejected her claim. Now each of the two Christian kingdoms was ruled by a baby, with no strong central authority exercised on his behalf.

Such authority would have been useful in putting an early end to a senseless squabble in Acre that exploded into open warfare. The walls of Acre embraced many acres of land, including the sections assigned to the merchant states of Venice and Genoa, which were separated by a hill. On top of that hill sat the ancient and peaceful monastery of San Sabas. Both the Genoese and the Venetians claimed ownership of the monastery, apparently without regard for the opinions of the resident monks. The arguments grew increasingly more heated and bitter, as both sides retained lawyers to prepare cases to set before the Commune of Acre.

Confucius had stated that the man who strikes the first blow shows that he has run out of ideas, and that is what may have happened to the men of Genoa. At dawn on a day in the late winter of 1256, an armed party of Genoese crept up the hill and occupied the monastery. After some light resistance, the Venetians inside the monastery were driven back down the other side of the hill into their own quarter. The Genoese found no Venetian force there strong enough to stop them, and the hilltop raid turned into a brief battle that then gave way to a frenzy of looting. An argument over a small piece of Church real estate—which was not a source of profit or protection for either side—had turned into a forced seizure, then into a battle, which in turn degenerated into the plundering and killing of civilians and the seizure of ships, and so to an open act of war between Genoa and Venice, all in the course of a single morning. As soon as the Genoese retired, one of the remaining Venetian galleys was dispatched to Venice to inform the doge and the Grand Council.

The local barons should have stepped in speedily to restore peace, but some saw instead an opportunity to achieve personal profit from the situation. Philip, the lord of Tyre, seized his chance and pushed the Venetian traders out of the one-third of the city of Tyre that legally belonged to them. He took it for himself, seeking cover behind an alliance with Genoa.

While this new internal struggle threatened to shatter the Holy Land, the Knights Templar met in grand chapter to elect a new grand master. There is no record whatever as to what had happened to Grand Master de Vichiers, who had led the Templars to such humiliation at the feet of his friend, King Louis IX. He may simply have died in office, or he may have resigned and gone home with the king of France, or he may possibly have been impeached by his angry brothers-in-arms. We know only that early in 1256 the Templars elected Thomas Berard their twentieth grand master. Had de Vichiers still been in command of the Templar order, he undoubtedly would have asked Louis of France to tell him how the order should react to the Genoese aggression. With de Vichiers gone, the new English grand master wouldn't care what King Louis wanted, one way or the other—a strong reason for his election.

Now, as the resident Crusaders and merchants took sides in a conflict that looked ugly enough to break out beyond the two Italian city-states into full-scale civil war, the Knights Templar did not hesitate to side with their ancient Venetian allies. The Hospitallers, to no one's surprise, chose to support the Genoese. Henry of Jebail sent troops to aid the men of Genoa, so his suzerain and rival, Bohemond VI of Antioch and Tripoli, responded by sending troops to fight for Venice.

Nor were the Venetians looking solely to allies to fight their battle. Always quick to defend their commercial interests, the Grand Council of Venice had responded to the news of the struggle by dispatching every available war galley, each with a complement of fighting men. The Genoese had taken the harbor at Acre and had stretched a chain across to keep out rival ships. When the Venetian fleet arrived, the experienced seamen rammed and broke the chain. The galleys landed their troops, who pushed back the men of Genoa in brutal hand-to-hand street fighting, until the harbor area was clear and the Venetians had occupied the hilltop monastery of San Sabas, where the fighting had started.

The ancient monastic buildings of San Sabas had never been a military objective. They were simply the fuse that set off the explosion of greedy commercial rivalries that had been growing to the point where almost any conflict would have been taken as justification for open war. The fighting went on, with no king and no local noble strong enough to stop it.

In 1258 Queen Plaisance saw the internal conflicts as an opportunity to assert the claims of her son King Hugh II of Cyprus, now five years old, who was next in line for the throne of Jerusalem after the German Conradin. She took her son to Antioch to get the support of her brother, Prince Bohemond. Backing that support with a military escort, Bohemond took her to Acre, where he called for a meeting of the High Court of Jerusalem. He asked that the assembly acknowledge that King Hugh II should have all of the royal power in Conradin's absence, and that the child's mother, Queen Plaisance, should serve as regent.

The majority of the nobles of the High Court agreed, subject to the rights of Conradin, should he ever make an appearance. The Knights Templar, probably influenced by the pope's hatred of the Hohenstauffen dynasty, of which Conradin was a member, gave their full support to the decision. The Knights of the Hospital were quick to assert their objections, stating that they would recognize only Conradin as king. Venice agreed with the High Court. Genoa naturally disagreed. The High Court prevailed, at least legally, and the establishment of a central authority should have put an end to the conflict. Instead, that authority merely furnished more fuel for the fires of civil war.

In that same year of 1258, Conradin had been deprived of the Sicilian crown by his uncle Manfred, an illegitimate son of Emperor Frederick II. That loss did not alter the child's claim to the throne of Jerusalem, but it had stripped his Sicilian supporters of a military power base from which to operate. It was unlikely that the six-year-old king could make any strong move to occupy the throne of Jerusalem for many years to come, if ever.

Genoa sent a fleet to the Holy Land in an attempt to end the civil war with a decisive Genoese victory. All of the Genoese ships in the Middle East were assembled to join the new fleet at Tyre, for a total of forty-eight Genoese galleys. They easily outnumbered the thirty-eight galleys of Venice and Pisa that lay off Acre.

It was to be a combined land and sea attack, with the land forces moving down the coast to Acre under the Genoese ally Philip of Montfort, lord of Tyre. The land forces of Acre, together with all of the Knights Templar that Grand Master Berard could pull in from nearby Templar castles, prepared to march north to intercept Philip of Montfort before he could approach the walls of Acre.

The Venetians were outnumbered, but they were not out-fought. They had generations of experience to draw upon in the approaching battle with their traditional enemies. Cannon were far in the future, so galley warfare usually led to direct contact. Apart, but close enough, the ships could attack each other with flights of arrows or try to hit each other with stones and pots of fire, not easily aimed when both target and artillery base were moving in a choppy sea. More certain victory came from hand-to-hand combat on bloody decks or from a successful ramming.

Fixed to the bow of every galley was a metal-capped battering ram at the waterline, designed to smash a hole in the enemy ship too large to be plugged up in time to keep the sea from rushing in. Sometimes the ram locked the two ships together, and then the sailors and marines of the sinking ship would try to save their lives by climbing or jumping over the side onto the deck of the ramming ship, to take it in hand-to-hand battle. The galley slaves in a successful ram were doomed. Compassion might suggest that as their ship began to sink they should be relieved of the chains that kept them fastened to their benches, but practical wisdom had to consider that, once free, their built-up muscles might combine with their pent-up anger in an attack on their captors. They usually went to the bottom with the ship.

The rowers, of course, were vital to success at sea. Victory with galleys went to the masters of maneuver, and in battle the galley slaves were the sole means of propulsion. They might be called upon to effect a sudden turn or put on an extra burst of speed. It was agonizing work, and the miserable men at the oars could become so completely exhausted that even the brutal whips laid on their bare backs could coax no more energy from them. The Venetians had the advantage because they had preserved that energy. By the time the Genoese arrived to give battle, their rowers had been straining their muscles for hours, while the Venetians had sat waiting for them.

Naval battles usually had high casualty rates, and the great clash off Acre was no exception. The Genoese lost twenty-four of their forty-eight ships and almost two thousand men. The casualties on land were lighter, but the victory was just as decisive. The Knights Templar and the forces of Acre completely routed the army of Philip of Montfort, who beat a fast retreat back to Tyre. Now the division became geographical as well as political. The Genoese fled Acre and made their base at Tyre, while all the Venetians who had been in Tyre joined their countrymen at Acre.

The papal peacemaker arrived early in the summer of 1260. He was the newly appointed patriarch of Jerusalem, James Pantaleon, who had no way of knowing that he would soon be selected to reign over the Church from the Throne of Peter. He listened to the accounts of the Mongol incursions into nearby lands and of the creation of a military Mameluke sultanate in Egypt. He listened to the background of the Christian civil war that he had walked into, and although he favored the Venetians and the Knights Templar, he could see that the very survival of the Crusader states depended upon all of the Roman Christians working in common cause.

He worked every day to bring them together, and his efforts led to a peace-seeking assembly of the High Court of Jerusalem in January of 1261. The meeting was attended by its regular members, the local barons, but was extended to also include representatives of the warring Italian states and the grand masters of the Knights Templar and the Hospitallers. The court confirmed that the Genoese would have their trading base at Tyre, while the Venetians and Pisans would operate from Acre. The local barons agreed to live and work together. The Knights Templar and the Hospitallers went through the motions of agreeing that their differences were now laid to rest. The Italians kept their word as it applied to conflict on land, but the rivalry and hate were still there, as evidenced by their incessant attacks on each other at sea.

In spite of the conflict, Venice definitely had the upper hand in the eastern trade, which flowed through three important channels. In the first channel, goods traveled by ships from the Indies up into the Arabian (Persian) Gulf, then overland to the Mediterranean. This was the trade that came to Acre, Tyre, and the other ports of the Palestine-Lebanese coast, largely through the merchants of Damascus. In the second route, ships came up through the Red Sea to the Isthmus of Suez, joining the flow of trade from central and eastern Africa. The Venetians were there, too, because they willingly supplied the Egyptians with important military and naval stores such as long, straight timbers and ingots of iron. The third trade route, the overland road from Central Asia, India, and even China, was growing fast. The Mongol leaders encouraged it, and they provided absolute safety to those caravans that dutifully paid their proper tolls and taxes. As a result of their role in the Fourth Crusade, the Venetians held a large quarter in Constantinople, the major terminus for the overland trade, and they held trading privileges throughout what had been the Byzantine empire.

The Genoese, who saw huge profits going to their rivals, matched their frustration with determination to come up with a plan. The success of the plan would be a great blow to Roman Catholic Christianity in the Middle East, but it would bring a golden flow of profits to Genoa, and that, to an Italian merchant, was what life was all about.

The plan was simple: Do what Venice had done for the Latin Christians, but do it for the Greeks. The original Byzantine empire as conquered by the Crusaders was being chipped away in successful wars of independence by the Serbs and Bulgarians. The Seljuk Turks grabbed off pieces of Anatolia wherever they could, but the displaced Greek royal family still held on to an independent state around Nicaea under its emperor, Michael Paleologus. Michael had had some success at recovering bits of his lost empire, but he simply did not have the naval force necessary to retake Constantinople. This was the basis of the Genoese plan.

Genoa's proposal was very welcome to Emperor Michael, and in March of 1261 he signed an agreement of alliance that would give the Genoese a clear position of trading supremacy in exchange for their naval support of an attack to retake the greatest city in the Middle East. Four months later the triumphant Greek army entered Constantinople to a background of cheers from the happy citizens who lined the streets. The Genoese replaced the Venetians, the Greek Orthodox Church replaced the Roman Catholic, and the flow of landless Latin knights from Outremer to Byzantium was now reversed. Unfortunately for them, the shrunken Holy Land had no lands to give them.

Later that same year Patriarch Pantaleon received delegates from Rome who informed him that he had been elected to rule the Roman Church. He took the papal name Urban IV, and although he was intensely aware of the need for a new Crusade in the face of the twin threats of Mongol and Mameluke, he had to look first to the priorities of his Church. He had been urged by the local barons and his friends in the Templar order to use his new power to call that Crusade, but for now the papacy had need of a Crusade of its own.

The Genoese had helped to change the rule of Byzantium, and now the Church wanted to change the rule of Sicily and Naples. There was a new ruler in Persia, and soon a new ruler would come to power in Egypt. The Holy Land would struggle to survive the impact of all these changing sovereignties, most of which they understood, but to have a good grasp of the political and military upheavals that would soon burst forth, we need to take a brief diversion to understand the newest player, the Scourge of God who had come west out of Mongolia.

23

The Khan of Khans
1167 to 1260

BACK IN 1167, while the Crusaders were besieging Saladin at Alexandria, a baby boy was born thousands of miles away in the Lake Baikal region of Mongolia. Legend says that as he emerged from his mother's womb he was clutching a blood clot in his tiny hand, a hand that would spill more blood than any before or since. He was named Temujin.

When his father died, Temujin became the chief of a nomadic tribe weakened by war. For protection, he pledged himself as vassal to the more powerful khan (lord) of the Nestorian Christian tribe of Kerait. With their help, he successfully conquered the hereditary enemies of his murdered father, bringing them under his rule. In 1203 Temujin asserted his supremacy over the Keraits as well. Combining all his forces, he defeated the Naimans, until then the dominant tribe of western Mongolia. In 1206 he called a great Kuriltai, or legislative assembly, of all the tribes to declare himself the Khagan, the Khan of Khans, the King of Kings. A man with extraordinary skills in organization, a true military genius and totally ruthless, Temujin was ready now to embark upon his great ambition to conquer the world under his new royal name, Genghis Khan.

Great waves of horsemen had come to Europe from the east over the centuries. First came the Huns, who had pushed the Goths out of the Russian steppes and into the heart of the Roman Empire. The Bulgars had spread into eastern Europe, then the Magyars into Hungary, followed by a series of Turkish tribes. None, however, had come with the numbers, the furious energy, or the insatiable brutality of the hordes of Genghis Khan.

He began his conquests by moving his army into northern China, taking the great walled city of Peking (Beijing) in 1215. Storming westward into Central Asia, he subdued the land of Kara Khitai (Turkestan). The Kwarismian empire, the dominant power in Central Asia, which included the walled cities of Khiva and Bokhara and the legendary Samarkand, became his next target in 1219. Genghis assembled a mounted army of two hundred thousand men, undeterred by the fact that the Kwarismian ruler, Muhammad-Shah, could muster more than twice that number. The first of the major cities to be overwhelmed was Bokhara. The civilians who surrendered were spared, but the garrison, which had tried to hold out, was butchered to a man, along with the Muslim holy men who had ordered them to stand and fight. At the city of Samarkand the Turkish soldiers not only surrendered without a fight but offered to join the Khan's army. Genghis detested their disloyalty to their rightful ruler and ordered immediate execution for all of them.

The Khan's enemies were learning how to be spared his wrath. The people of the city of Balkh gave up without a fight and were permitted to live. The people of Bamian chose to fight, in a battle that unfortunately for them brought the death of Genghis Khan's grandson. When the city was in Mongol hands, every human being in it was put to the sword. Genghis's son-in-law died in the attack on Nishapur, so after the city had fallen, his widow was allowed her personal revenge by presiding over the systematic mass beheadings. The heads were separated as to men, women, and children, then stacked in great pyramids. There was even a pyramid of heads of cats and dogs, for the Khan's orders had called for the death of "every living creature" in the city.

The greatest resistance to the Mongol horde was mounted by the Kwarismian prince Jelal ad-Din, the son of Muhammad-Shah. After a bitter, losing fight, he took his army on an orderly retreat into Afghanistan. A Mongol army was sent after him, and Jelal ad-Din prepared to receive it at Parvan, a dozen miles north of Kabul. The Mongols had expected him to be on the run and were not fully prepared for the Battle of Parvan, where for the first time in the Kwarismian war a Mongol army was soundly defeated.

Such a humiliation could not go unanswered, so Genghis himself led a fresh army against Jelal ad-Din. Ad-Din fell back with his army to the Indus River, where the Mongols caught him in November of 1221. His army was shattered, but Jelal ad-Din escaped by spurring his horse into the river, fighting the strong current to reach the safety of the far shore. The family that he had left behind was taken captive to await the judgment of the great Khan. When that judgment was delivered, every male child in the family was butchered in full view of his mother and sisters.

A false hope sprang up in the city of Herat when news of the

Mongol defeat at Parvan reached them. The city, a magnificent metropolis with a population of over three hundred thousand, had submitted peacefully to the Mongols, but on the news from Parvan it rose in jubilant revolt, ejecting or killing its handful of Mongol overlords. Now the people of Herat must be punished for their misguided rebellion. The Mongols had no machinery, so the siege took months, but they finally broke into the city in June 1222. Genghis Khan's judgment called for the death of every human being in the city. Even for an army of men who were by now masters of the techniques of massacre, the mass murder took more than a week to complete.

An army under two of the Mongols' best generals, Subotai and Jebe, was sent after Jelal's father, Muhammad-Shah, who had fled west in the opposite direction. The generals, in no hurry to catch their fugitive, paused long enough to destroy cities along their westward march across Persia. They captured the holy city of Qum (which would centuries later be the seat of the Ayatollah Khomeini), then killed every person in it. Continuing northwest, they approached the Turkish emirate of Azerbaijan, where they accepted a huge payment in gold to pass by the capital city of Tabriz, sweeping on instead toward the kingdom of Georgia and their first encounter with a Christian enemy. King George IV personally led his fierce fighters in an attempt to halt the Mongol invasion, but he was severely beaten, at the same time that the Crusade under Cardinal Pelagius was meeting its own defeat in Egypt. Meanwhile Muhammad-Shah, in his panic to avoid falling into the hands of the blood-crazed Mongols, had finally found refuge on a tiny island in the Caspian Sea, where he died from exhaustion, stress, and despair.

Free to move wherever they wished, the Mongols decided to raid north beyond the Caspian, easily crushing the Caucasian tribesmen who were unlucky enough to find themselves in their path. The Kipchak Turks offered alliance and gold to the Russian princes, urging that they agree to join forces to stop this human plague. The princes of Kiev, Smolensk, Chernigov, and Galich answered the call, taking their combined armies to meet the Mongols near the Sea of Azov. Those armies were destroyed in the onslaught, and the Russian soldiers who were wounded or taken captive were executed. The four Russian princes were taken alive, to be bound and stretched out on the ground. A wood floor was placed on top of them, and then the Mongols feasted and danced on the floor. To no one's surprise, when the party was over the Russian princes were found crushed to death beneath the floor. Then the Mongol army, whose mission was to raid, not to occupy, stormed through the Crimea, where they met their first Roman Catholic Christians as they looted a Genoese trading post. Swinging back eastward to rejoin Genghis Khan, they left behind them a wide swath of farms, villages, and whole cities now populated only by rotting corpses.

Both Muslims and Christians, themselves quite capable of barbarous atrocities, were nonetheless unable to comprehend such wanton destruction and wholesale butchery. The Mongols were demons from hell, described in letters as "surprisingly ugly" and "incredibly stinking." Fortunately, they had come and gone, like a raging storm or an earthquake that devastates and then dies out. There seemed to be no realization that they had been the victims of an exploratory raid and not an all-out war, or that the Mongols would return. A Russian chronicler wrote, "...we know not whence they came, nor where they hid themselves again. God knows whence He fetched them against us for our sins."

In 1227, while Emperor Frederick II was assembling his crusading army in Italy, Genghis Khan, now sixty years old, died leading the conquest of Tibet. All of the princes of the royal house were called to a Kuriltai at their capital at Karakorum. After the burial of the great Khan in a secret tomb that has not yet been discovered, his son Ogodai was elected Khan of Khans.

In accordance with Mongol custom, Ogodai's youngest brother Tului was assigned the administration of the homeland. His brother Batu was assigned the task of subduing the lands to the west that had been raided by the Mongol general Subotai, who was assigned to go with him.

During the lull in the Mongol wars, the Kwarismian prince Jelal ad-Din broke out of his safe haven at the court of Delhi in India. Gathering the remnants of his Kwarismian cavalry, Jelal set out to establish a new kingdom in the west. Raiding across Iran into Iraq and the lands around Baghdad, he moved northwest to conquer Azerbaijan and then down into Syria and to the lands of the Seljuk Turks. Jelal presented a much greater threat to Sultan al-Kamil of Egypt and Prince al-Ashraf of Damascus than the red-faced Emperor Frederick II, who was strutting through his negotiations for the occupation of Jerusalem. The Christians could be dealt with later, but Jelal ad-Din must be stopped now.

Al-Ashraf's suggestion of a military alliance with his traditional enemies, the Seljuk Turks, was most welcome. Together, they met Jelal ad-Din in a mounted pincer movement with Turks at his front and Syrians attacking from the rear. The Kwarismians were decisively beaten, but thousands of them managed to gallop away from the battlefield. In the following year, 1231, the armies clashed again. Jelal ad-Din experienced another defeat and was murdered in its aftermath. The leaderless Kwarismian horsemen became roving bandits, their services available to anyone willing to pay their price. These were the mercenaries who were hired to invade Palestine and retake Jerusalem from the Christian Crusaders.

In 1237, as the Christian concerns were directed toward the expiration of the ten-year truce that Frederick II had arranged with the sultan of Egypt, Batu and Subotai launched a devasting western invasion. They sent word to the Russian princes that to avoid total destruction they must become vassals of the Mongol Khan. They should signal their submission by paying a 10 percent tax on everything they held—men, treasure, horses, everything of value. The princes refused, which was tantamount to an act of mass suicide. One Russian city after another fell to the Mongol horde, including the relatively unimportant river town of Moscow, and as each city fell its inhabitants were slaughtered. It has been estimated that the killings took 80 percent of the people in the lands through which the Mongols passed, more than the deaths caused by the worst of the plagues. The Franciscan friar John of Plano Carpini, passing through that countryside about ten years later as a papal envoy, reported to the pope, "In this country...we came across many skulls and bones of dead men lying on the ground like dung."

The Roman Christians of Europe were peacefully ignorant of the renewed Mongol invasion until the following year, when a strange delegation visited the courts of France and England. It was a party of envoys from the grand master of the sect of Assassins. The Mongols had appeared in their homeland of Persia, and they feared for their continued existence. They had come to urge a grand alliance of Christians and Muslims against the murdering Mongols. They had no success.

Matthew Paris provides clear indication that the European Christians were untroubled by stories of Mongol terrors. He recorded that when Henry III of England expressed to the bishop of Winchester his concerns about the Assassin envoys' report, the good bishop replied with ecclesiastic arrogance, "Let these dogs destroy one another and be utterly exterminated, and then we shall see the universal Catholic Church founded on their ruins and there will be but one fold and one shepherd."

That arrogance was lowered a few notches when, after destroying the Russian city of Kiev in 1240, the Mongols split into two armies. The larger force, commanded by Batu and Subotai, headed toward Moravia and Hungary. The other wing swept through Galicia and into Poland, where it easily beat a combined Polish and German army at Liegnitz on April 9, 1241. Two days later the main Mongol army defeated the Magyar forces near Buda (across the river from Pest). The king of Hungary fled the field for his territory of

Dalmatia, on the western side of modern Yugoslavia. A Mongol detachment chased him tenaciously all the way to the shores of the Adriatic, sending shock waves through the Republic of Venice, on the other side of the narrow sea. Another Mongol contingent raided deep into Austria.

Now the European Christians had good reason to be gripped with dread. Nor was the ever-faithful companion to calamity forgotten, as pulpits began to resound with sermons heralding Armageddon, the last great battle, the end of the world. God's ultimate punishment for the sins of man was at hand.

Just as real panic was beginning to take hold, news began to arrive from Poland, Bulgaria, Hungary, Romania, and Austria. All along the eastern battle line the Mongols were reported to be in full retreat, disappearing back into the void from which Satan had vomited them forth. The Christians didn't know it yet, but word had come to the Mongol armies that Ogodai Khan was dead. The leaders had been summoned to a Kuriltai in Mongolia to elect his replacement. The armies, however, did not go all the way back with their leaders. They stayed in Russia, camped along the Volga, ready to move again at Batu's command.

Batu had ordered his best general, Baichu, to continue the pressure on the nearby Muslim states during his absence. In 1241 the Mongols rode against the Seljuk Turks. After a year of unsuccessful defense, the Seljuk sultan could see his own end coming and saved himself by accepting the suzerainty of the Mongol conquerors.

King Hethoum of Armenia had listened with great joy to the news of the Mongol victories over his Turkish enemy. He would have been glad to see the Seljuks completely destroyed, but he was stunned by the news of the Seljuk submission to the Mongols. There was no way that Armenia could survive a combined Turkish-Mongol invasion, so he sent a message to the Mongols that Armenia, too, recognized the overlordship of the Mongol Khan.

By 1245 Louis IX of France had made his vow to lead a new Crusade. It appeared to be just in time, as word arrived at Rome of the Christian defeat at Gaza a few months before. Baibars of Egypt had led an army of Mamelukes and Kwarismian mercenaries in a great battle that had killed thousands of Christians, including the grand master of the Knights Templar and most of his Templar companions. At home, the armies of Frederick II had driven the papal army out of Italy. The Church, too, was fighting for its life as Pope Innocent IV called a great council of the Church at Lyons. The council approved the crusading plans of Louis of France and dispatched Church prelates to support him by preaching the Crusade throughout France. In response to the concerns and confusion expressed at the council about the mysterious Mongols, the pope decided to send envoys to the great Khan, bearing two papal letters addressed to the Mongol leader.

The man selected to head the mission was a sixty-five-year-old, barefoot Franciscan friar, John of Plano Carpini. He was a brave and resourceful man. He had to be, because he was leading his party on a journey of thousands of miles to a destination totally unknown to him. He would need to pass through a dozen lands and languages of whose very existence he was as yet unaware.

Setting out from Lyons in 1245, John of Plano Carpini traveled first to Poland, where he spent the entire winter. In the spring his hosts pointed him in the direction of the Russian steppes. The Mongols were taught to have respect for official ambassadors, so the men in the Mongol outposts took him to their commander, who sent him to Prince Batu on the Volga River. Batu provided the party with relays of horses, a means of transportation strange to most Franciscans. The friar and his friends had ample opportunity to learn to ride: Their escort took them over three thousand miles to the east, a journey longer than a trip across America from the Atlantic to the Pacific.

The weary travelers arrived at the Mongol court in July of 1246, after thirteen months of travel, just in time for the coronation of Guyuk Khan. A few days later they were escorted to the royal pavilion. As their escort looked at the friar's bare feet, he warned the devout Franciscan that he had best cover his feet or risk losing them as punishment for appearing before the Great Khan in such an insulting condition.

There was really no hope for understanding between the Christian pope and the Mongol emperor. The Great Priest and the Great Khan were each convinced of his own right to personal supremacy over the whole world. Their customary means of communication was by giving orders. Friar John began by presenting the two letters from the pope to the khan. The first letter instructed the khan to become a Christian. The pope explained that he had sent the holy men to provide the necessary evangelical information, "so that following their salutory instructions you may acknowledge Jesus Christ the very Son of God and worship His glorious name by practicing the Christian religion."

The second letter was much stronger, as the pope recited the Mongol crimes: "...we are driven to express in strong terms our amazement that you...have invaded many countries belonging both to Christians and others and are laying them waste in a horrible desolation, and with a fury still unabated you do not cease from

stretching out your destroying hand to more distant lands and...
sparing neither age nor sex, you rage against all indiscriminately
with the sword of chastisement.''

Next the pope ordered that "for the future you desist entirely
from assaults of this kind and especially from the persecution of
Christians, and that after so many and such grievous offenses you
conciliate by a fitting penance the wrath of Divine Majesty, which
without doubt you have seriously aroused by such provocation.''

The papal letters made no sense whatever to the Mongol leader,
whose grandfather, Genghis Khan, had told his followers that
the greatest happiness a man could experience was to kill his
enemies and then watch the wretched weeping of their wives and
children. Guyuk Khan gave Brother John a letter to take to the pope,
expressing the only answer that made sense to a Mongol lord who
believed that all men should submit to the all-powerful Khagan:
"Thou, who art the great Pope, together with all the Princes, come
in person to serve us. At that time I shall make known all the
commands of the *Yasa* [the Mongol code of law].

"You have said that supplication and prayer have been offered
by you, that I might find a good entry into baptism. This prayer
of thine I have not understood. Other words which thou hast sent
me: 'I am surprised that thou hast seized the lands of Christians
and others. Tell us what their fault is.' These words of thine I have
also not understood. The eternal God has slain and destroyed these
lands and peoples because they have neither adhered to Genghis,
nor to the Khagan, both of whom have been sent to make known
God's command, nor have they adhered to this command of God.
Like thy words, they were impudent, they were proud, and they
slew our messenger emissaries. How could anybody seize or kill
by his own power contrary to the command of God?

"Though thou also sayest that I should become a trembling
Christian, worship God and be an ascetic. How knowest thou whom
God absolves, in truth to whom he shows mercy? How dost thou
know that such words as thou speakest are with God's sanction?
From the rising of the sun to its setting, all the lands have been
made subject to me. Who could do this contrary to the command
of God?

"Now you should say with a sincere heart, 'I will submit and
serve you.' Thou thyself, at the head of all the Princes, come at once
to serve and wait upon us! At that time I shall recognize your submission.''

Stalemate. And so much for the prospect of understanding between east and west. The visit of the papal envoys was no more than
an amusing interlude for the Mongols. They were preparing for more

war, but they were held in check by the untimely death of Guyuk Khan in 1248. Guyuk's widow wanted the supreme post for one of her three sons, but none of them was highly regarded, and their mother was too preoccupied by her fascination with sorcery to have gained the respect of the leaders. A strong opposition party was led by Prince Batu, who as the oldest living direct descendant of Genghis, even though illegitimate, enjoyed great prestige. He favored the sons of Genghis Khan's youngest son, Tului, whose wife was a devout Nestorian Christian. Their four extraordinary sons, Mongu, Kublai, Hulagu, and Ariqboga, were much admired.

In 1251, in spite of the scheming of Guyuk's widow, who even planned the assassinations of her opponents, Tului's son Mongu became the Khan of Khans. His brother Kublai was given the government of China and, as Kublai Khan, became the most famous of the four brothers, through the journal of Marco Polo. The youngest, Ariqboga, stayed home to administer the homeland. Hulagu was given the territory of Central Asia and Persia. Their uncle and sponsor, Prince Batu, was given the lands to the far west. His were the legions of Mongols remembered in history as the Golden Horde. As for Guyuk's scheming widow, she was tried, found guilty of attempted assassination, and sentenced to a bloodless royal death by drowning.

As soon as King Hethoum of Armenia learned about the new Khagan he made the long journey to Mongolia to offer his personal submission. An alliance with the Mongols made much more sense to him than an alliance with the shrinking Crusader states, which fought each other as often as they fought the Muslims. The current internal struggle was the war of San Sabas, which pitted the Venetians and the Knights Templar against the Genoese and the Hospitallers. The conflict offered an ideal opportunity for a Muslim war against the divided Christians, but turning their faces to the Crusader states would mean that the Muslims had to turn their backs on the Mongols, who were on the move again.

Hulagu, brother of the Great Khan and commander of the Mongols in Central Asia and Persia, had been given firm orders to move into Mesopotamia to take the city of Baghdad, where he was to destroy the religious power and leadership of the Sunni caliph. He also had a shock in store for the Shiites, in his total dedication to the destruction of the sect of Assassins. To the Mongols they were guilty of an unforgivable crime.

Years earlier, Genghis Khan's son Jagatai had ruled over part of Persia, the homeland of the Assassins. Certain Muslim practices required by the Koran were contrary to Mongol custom and so were outlawed. Jagatai would not permit the ritual ablutions before prayer and forbade the practice of *hallal*, the ritual throat-cutting by which the Prophet had decreed that food animals must be slaughtered. The Sunni Muslims were upset, but the Shiites were outraged. The most dedicated fundamentalists of them all, the Assassin sect of the Ismailis, decided that Allah wanted them to act according to their custom. The assassination of Jagatai was carefully planned and successfully executed.

To the Mongols the murder of an envoy or ambassador could only be punished by war. The murder of a son of the Great Khan was a crime infinitely more heinous than the murder of an ambassador, so something more punishing than mere conflict was required. Only one level of vengeance could match the enormity of the crime: Every member of the Assassin sect must die.

Supported by additional Mongol forces from the Golden Horde, together with contingents of Armenians and Georgians who were happy to kill fundamentalist Muslims, Hulagu launched his campaign. The Assassins controlled a wide area of mountains and valleys with a dozen strong fortresses, all of which Hulagu ordered to be taken. The mountain fortress-cities of Mazanderan and Meimundiz fell, and then the main Mongol army turned on the Assassin headquarters at the fortified city of Alamut. When it became obvious that the city would fall within a matter of days, the Assassin grand master Rukn ad-Din Khurshah came to Hulagu's pavilion to surrender, in the hope of saving his own life. He asked permission to go to Karakorum to negotiate peace terms directly with Mongu Khan, which Hulagu granted. Weeks later at Mongu's base, Khurshah was refused admission to the court. He was advised to return home to arrange the total submission of all Assassin fortresses before coming to the Khagan. On their way back to Persia, the Assassin grand master and his entire party were murdered.

Mongu also sent a message to Hulagu, criticizing his brother's negotiations with the Assassins. His orders had been clear: Kill them all. Hulagu complied with the command by overseeing the death of every human being in every Assassin city or town as it was taken. Many members of the sect lived outside the cities in villages or on farms, so word was sent out to all of them to come to a great census-taking. When the rural Assassin familes had assembled, Mongol horsemen with drawn swords rushed in among them and butchered them all. The only Assassins who escaped immediate death were the relatives of the grand master. They were bound and sent off to Jagatai's widow, so that she might have her personal vengeance by arranging their deaths in any manner that her anger suggested.

While the Mongols were exterminating the Persian Assassins and the Christians were occupied in a civil war, the Mameluke court of Egypt was having its own problems. The first Mameluke sultan, Aibek, had legitimized his rule by marriage to the widowed sultana Shajar ad-Durr; she was a heroine to all Egyptians because of her actions that had saved the country from defeat in the Crusade of Louis of France. She had ruled the country then and saw no reason not to continue to rule now. Aibek felt that he alone should rule and that Shajar ad-Durr should content herself with the traditional role of dutiful wife, a status that conflicted with Shajar ad-Durr's nature. She was also angrily jealous and had forced Aibek to divorce his first wife, who had borne him a son and heir. Their incessant quarreling increased in intensity until, during one argument, Aibek responded to a verbal attack with a suicidal reply.

He proposed to take another wife, the fourteen-year-old daughter of the emir of Mosul. Shajar objected. Why should he want another wife? "Because," he replied, "she is not only more beautiful than you, but she is much, much younger." The insult was more than Shajar was willing to take. She planned carefully for the murder of Sultan Aibek by her faithful eunuch slaves, who drowned the sultan in his bath.

Shajar tried to pass off the drowning as an accident, but under agonizing torture her slaves revealed the truth. Shajar was confined to the Red Tower in Cairo, where she spent her time hammering her jewels to powder, so that no other woman could ever wear them. At the end of three days she was led before Aibek's first wife, who then sat and watched as the women slaves of her household beat Shajar to death with hundreds of blows of their wooden clogs. They threw her half-naked body out of a tower window into the ditch below, where dogs were allowed to gnaw on the corpse for days, until someone gathered the remains for burial.

Because no crime was considered greater than the murder of the supreme ruler, the forty slave eunuchs involved in Sultan Aibek's murder were sentenced to a particularly horrible form of punishment. One by one, in full view of the rest, each man was dragged before the executioners, who stood waiting with sharp swords and axes. One by one, each slave took his turn at having his body slowly sliced at the waist and then chopped into two separate parts. While Hulagu was slaughtering the Shiite Assassins in Persia, the Egyptian court paid homage to the new sultan, Nur ad-Din Ali, the frivolous fifteen-year-old son of the murdered sultan Aibek.

Within a matter of weeks Hulagu had completed his extermination of the Persian Assassins and turned his attention to the conquest of Baghdad and the holy caliph. Following his instructions from Mongu, Hulagu first offered the caliph the chance to avoid war and death by total submission to the great Mongol Khan. Once again a leader spoke from a distorted view of his own supremacy. The caliph responded to Hulagu's demands with, "O young man, who have barely entered upon your career, and who, drunk with a ten day success, believe yourself superior to the whole world, do you not know that from the East to the Maghreb, all the worshippers of Allah, whether kings or beggars, are slaves to this court of mine, and that I can command them to take up arms?"

The defiant response was welcome. The waiting Mongol army desired death, not diplomacy, for the Muslim religious leaders. Hulagu's assault on Baghdad began in November 1257. In command of his left wing he placed his favorite general, Kitbuqa, a Nestorian Christian whom legend said was descended from one of the three Wise Men who had followed the star to Bethlehem. An attack on the far side of the city would be launched by the troops from the Golden Horde. The caliph sent a small army into the field outside the walls to halt the Mongol advance, but it was quickly hacked to pieces. By January 18 the Mongols had completely surrounded the city.

With the help of siege engines brought all the way from China, the outer wall was breached less than three weeks later. The people of the city surrendered, but the soldiers of the garrison attempted to escape. They were easily surrounded, captured, and bound. To spread the prize they were separated into groups and distributed to each segment of the Mongol army, so that all could share in their execution. The inhabitants were ordered to come outside the city to make their formal submission. Many obeyed, but once they had gathered, they were killed where they stood. They had been murdered outside the city to save the Mongols the bother of having to search them out house-by-house.

At the urging of his favorite wife, who was a devoted Christian, and in deference to his favorite general, the Christian Kitbuqa, Hulagu had permitted the Nestorians to deliver a message into the city, urging all Christians to go to their churches and stay there. These would be the only places where their safety could be guaranteed. Then orders went out to the army to spare only those in the houses of Christian worship.

Everyone else who had stayed in the city died in a massive orgy of looting, rape, and killing that went on for over two weeks, until almost a hundred thousand Muslim bodies covered the fields and streets. The caliph was led to believe that his life would be spared in exchange for revealing the hiding places of treasure that had been accumulating for five hundred years. When the greatest treasure he had ever seen was removed from the city, Hulagu ordered the death of the caliph, although as a mark of respect his death must be bloodless. The solution was to sew him up in a felt bag, which was then galloped over by succeeding troops of cavalry. Perhaps he was lucky enough to die of suffocation before his body was pounded to a pulp by the trampling blows of the Mongol horses.

The Christians were ordered out of the city, which the Mongols then set on fire, destroying what had been for centuries the center of the Sunni faith. The total devastation aroused wails of anguish throughout the Muslim world and brought fresh rays of hope to the Christians. The news indicated that the Mongols were bitter foes of Islam, and thus the saviors of Christianity. The Nestorians, Georgians, Armenians, and Greeks all gave thanks to God in their own services, and Hethoum of Armenia made approaches to Hulagu regarding the ultimate cession of Jerusalem to Christian care.

His request was timely, for now Hulagu proceeded with the next phase of his orders, the conquest of Syria and Egypt. He began with the siege of a city north of Syria (in modern Turkey) called Maiyafaqin, because its emir was proscribed for special punishment. He was al-Kamil Muhammad, a great-nephew of Saladin. His crime was his especially cruel treatment of a Jacobite priest who had been sent by Hulagu as a Mongol envoy. Brought before al-Kamil, the priest was used to demonstrate the young emir's attitude toward both Mongols and Christians: He was condemned to death by public crucifixion. It did not matter to Hulagu that the victim was a Christian, only that he was a Mongol ambassador.

The siege was conducted by a combined force of Mongols and Georgians, with a contingent of Armenians. Once the city was taken, a special punishment was meted out to al-Kamil. Small pieces of his flesh were cut away and toasted in front of his eyes. As more bits of his own flesh were crammed into his mouth, he had to swallow them to avoid choking. Gagging and bleeding profusely, he must have longed for his death, which was not long in coming.

From his new base in Azerbaijan, Hulagu ordered Hethoum to gather his whole Armenian army for the coming war in Syria, assuring him that when Palestine was taken, Jerusalem would be returned to the Christians. Bohemond VI, prince of Antioch and count of Tripoli, decided to follow Hethoum's example. He became a voluntary vassal of the Mongols and agreed to provide military support. In spite of their preoccupation with the Latin Christian civil war that had begun at San Sabas, the Knights Templar were following the events at the court of Hulagu closely. The grand master's secretary, remembered only as the Templar of Tyre, recorded, "Hethoum, King of Armenia, spoke to Hulagu on behalf of Bohemond his son-in-law, and thereafter Bohemond stood high in Hulagu's favor."

Hulagu began his advance in September 1259, accompanied by Christian forces from Georgia, Armenia, and Antioch. The first major objective was Aleppo, although they paused to destroy cities along the way. They moved more slowly than usual because Hulagu decided to take with him a large siege train of wagons bearing the parts for twenty-four stone-throwing catapults. As they marched, there was plenty of time for the news of the invasion to reach the Egyptian court at Cairo, where it brought about another change of leadership. The whole Muslim world was in grave danger of annihilation, but the teenage ruler of Egypt spent his happiest hours at cockfights and harem parties. He knew nothing of war.

A man who did, the Mameluke general Qutuz, who had served as principal deputy to Sultan Aibek, deposed the boy and took the throne for himself with no significant opposition. Qutuz justified his action with the sensible announcement, "We need a fighting king." He made no immediate military move to rescue Syria, but he sent agents to report back to him every step taken by Hulagu's invading army. They took carrier pigeons with them to assure fast, safe delivery of information to Qutuz.

What the sultan learned first was that the Mongol army had arrived before Aleppo in January 1260. Although the citadel held out for several weeks, the city itself had fallen within seven days. The ruler had been out of the city, so the defense was conducted by Prince Turanshah, an elderly descendant of Saladin. After the city was taken Hulagu spared the old man out of respect for his age and unquestioned bravery. No such mercy, however, was shown to any other Muslim in Aleppo. The Mongol army was rewarded for its victory by being turned loose for five days and nights to rape, kill, and loot, with no restraints or control of any kind.

The Christians in the city were spared, and the Christians with the Mongol army were rewarded. Hethoum received territory previously taken from the Armenians by their Muslim enemies. Prince Bohemond was given all the lands and towns that had ever been a part of the principality of Antioch, lands that had been lost to Saladin generations before. This very substantial restoration of his territories helped to offset the shock that Bohemond felt on learning that the pope in Rome had burdened him with the shame of excommunication. Bohemond's pope may have been unhappy with the prince's spiritual crimes, but his people were delighted with his earthly rewards.

The news from Aleppo reduced Damascus to a state of panic and despair. Sultan an-Nasir Yusuf, sparing no thought for the defense of his city or his people, fled with his family across Palestine to Gaza. Citizens anxious to follow his example bid against each other for the available pack animals, until the price of a single camel rose to seven hundred pieces of silver. Many who couldn't find animals took their most valuable portable possessions and fled on foot, becoming easy prey for the bandits who always spring up in the presence of affluent refugees. Calm was restored after a respected *kadi* (Koranic judge) went to Hulagu at Aleppo seeking mercy in exchange for surrender. He returned to Damascus with Hugalu's written declaration of amnesty for all if the gates of the city were opened to him. On March 1, 1260, the Mongol army under Kitbuqa passed unhindered through the gates to occupy Damascus.

As the victorious army moved through the streets, local Christians were relieved to see the Christian contingents from Georgia, Armenia, and Antioch holding crosses on high. The crosses gave the invaders the appearance of a new but quite acceptable form of Crusade. The Templar of Tyre, who would have received his information directly from Templar agents in Damascus, recorded that the Christians were permitted to convert a principal mosque to Christian worship. The Christian Mongol general Kitbuqa gave official sanction by attending the church services personally.

The military garrison of the citadel, which had declined to participate in the surrender, held out until April 6. A formal ceremony was held in which Kitbuqa carried out Hulagu's direct order that he should personally cut off the head of the governor of the castle. Sultan an-Nasir Yusuf lost his head as well, as a result of his attempt to flee from Gaza. He was captured and sent to Hulagu, who had no use for him.

Next on the Mongol agenda was the conquest of Egypt. Perhaps in the hope of repeating the easy victory at Damascus, Hulagu sent four ambassadors to the court of the sultan Qutuz. The letter, a cold, arrogant challenge, has been summarized by the English historian Sir John Glubb:

"From the King of Kings of the East and West, the Great Khan. Qutuz is a mameluke who fled to escape our swords.... You should think of what happened to other countries...and submit your fate to us. We are not moved by tears or touched by lamentations. We have conquered vast areas, massacring all the people. You cannot escape from the terror of our armies. Only those who beg our protection will be safe.

"Hasten your reply before the fire of war is kindled.... You will suffer the most terrible catastrophes, your countries will become deserts...and we will kill your children and your old men together."

Sultan Qutuz knew full well that to kill a Mongol envoy was to invite immediate war. He ordered the Mongol ambassadors to be cut in half at the waist. Then he had their heads cut off and be nailed to the great Zuwila Gate of Cairo. Now irrevocably committed, he prepared for war with the Mongols.

Once again the course of history was abruptly changed by the death of a Great Khan, which automatically required all princes to attend a Kuriltai to elect his successor. Hulagu answered the call by pulling his main army far back to the east. He left Kitbuqa in charge in Syria with an army of twenty thousand Mongols and orders to continue to press on to Egypt.

Kitbuqa sent a raiding party into Palestine first, cutting the usual Mongol path of rape and murder through Nablus all the way to Gaza, but he stopped short of Jerusalem. The Crusader states were now completely surrounded by the Mongol hordes, although they were in no danger from the Christian Kitbuqa, who apparently expected them to recognize the suzerainty of the Mongol Khan. And so they might have, had it not been for Count Julian of Sidon and Beaufort, whose rash conduct called to mind an earlier occasion and the reckless behavior of Reynald of Chatillon toward Saladin.

Julian was a big, handsome man who had the income of a lord but the personal tastes of an emperor. He was flamboyant in his dress, his equipment, and his entertainment, maintaining a lifestyle far beyond his means. As he ran out of cash he refused to reduce that lifestyle, preferring to turn to the Knights Templar for substantial loans. For collateral they took Julian's port city of Sidon and later, as his financial demands grew, his sizable castle at Beaufort.

To rebuild his fortune, Julian decided to take advantage of the Mongol-Muslim conflict to raid and loot some nearby Muslim towns and farms. Those Muslim lands were now under Mongol rule, and Kitbuqa took the position that, as administrator of the law, it was his duty to punish the lawbreaker. He sent a small punitive force under a favorite nephew to chastise the count. Julian called upon neighbors to join him, then set up an ambush in the hills. The Mongol police force was taken completely by surprise and scattered rapidly. Kitbuqa's nephew was killed in the process.

Now Julian's infraction of the law had become a serious crime. Kitbuqa sent an army this time, which moved all the way up to Sidon, where it plundered the town in wholesale massacre. The offshore Castle of the Sea was saved by reinforcements and supplies brought up from Tyre by a Genoese fleet. Julian had thoroughly ruined any prospect of an alliance between the Mongols and the Crusader states against their common Muslim enemy.

Banking, not battles, now added to the domains of the Knights Templar, as they called the loans against the destitute Julian, occupying the foreclosed properties at Sidon and Beaufort. The new acquisitions, however, hurt almost as much as they helped. The new fortresses meant that Templars had to be called in from already undermanned castles to garrison the new ones. Their available forces were being spread thin, since recruiting at the Templar preceptories throughout Europe had not completely filled the need for more members.

Meanwhile, all was not going well at the Mongol Kuriltai, where two rival factions among the princes were pitting Kublai Khan of China against his younger brother, Ariqboga. Hulagu backed Kublai Khan, but the khan of the nearby Golden Horde favored Ariqboga. Nor did the division stop there. Hulagu had leaned more and more in the direction of the Christians, while the Golden Horde looked favorably on the faith of Islam and did not hesitate to kill or persecute the Christians they encountered in the Caucasus. They disapproved of Hulagu's actions at Baghdad and in Syria. When war broke out in Mongolia between the followers of Kublai and Ariqboga, Hulagu had to take care that it didn't develop into a conflict between his own Mongol army and that of his cousins of the Golden Horde, camped to his north.

Sultan Qutuz of Egypt decided to make his move on the Mongols. With the major part of the Mongol army gone and the open conflict between the Mongols and the Christians at Sidon, it seemed to the sultan to be the time to strike.

On July 26, 1260, an Egyptian army began its march, with the Mameluke Baibars commanding the vanguard. His own military strength was sufficient to drive the small Mongol force out of Gaza without waiting for the main Egyptian army, and the war had begun. Kitbuqa, who had established his base to the north at Baalbek (in modern Lebanon), assembled his army and began a march to the south moving down the eastern side of the Sea of Galilee.

Qutuz, who wanted to travel north through the Crusader states to meet Kitbuqa, sent envoys to Acre to get official permission and, if possible, to arrange to purchase supplies along the way. The nobles of Acre were not in complete agreement on the Egyptian requests, nor on much else, for that matter, because their own internal strife was in full swing. They were very concerned about the Mongol raid on Sidon, but the Genoese who had backed Count Julian were not pleased that the Knights Templar had stepped in to repossess the city that Genoa had helped to save, at its own expense. After a long debate, part serious and part petty, the barons agreed to the requests of Qutuz, which they knew would make them open enemies of the Mongols.

Having reached agreement with the Latin Christians, Qutuz led his Egyptian army north to camp on the outskirts of Acre, where the merchants enjoyed a windfall of profits from the cash sale of huge stocks of food and supplies. It was while in camp there that Qutuz learned that the Mongols had circled the Sea of Galilee and were approaching the Jordan River, following the invasion route that Saladin had taken in 1183. Ordering his army to mount up, Qutuz rode southeast to meet them.

As Kitbuqa marched his army west across the Jordan and up the rising slope of the Plain of Esdraelon, Qutuz took his position at Ain Jalut, the "Spring of Goliath," where the plain narrowed to just three miles wide, with the steep slope of Mount Gilboa to the south and the hills of Galilee to the north. By now Qutuz was aware that he greatly outnumbered the Mongol invaders, so he hid substantial units of cavalry in the nearby hills. Kitbuqa, apparently believing that the army in front of him was the entire Egyptian force, immediately ordered the charge, which he led himself. Riding to meet him, the Egyptian vanguard was led by Baibars.

After a fierce clash that seemed to stop both sides, Baibars signaled his cavalry to make its prearranged retreat to the rolling hills. The Mongols rode triumphantly in pursuit and in a matter of minutes found themselves surrounded, outnumbered and defeated by the Egyptian cavalry reserves hidden in the hills. Brought before Qutuz, Kitbuqa was humiliated and insulted by the sultan's words to him. Unbowed and proud, the Mongol general replied, "Since I was born I have been the slave of my khan; I am not, like you, the murderer of my master!" Offended by such arrogance in a captive, Qutuz ordered that Kitbuqa's head be struck off. It was immediately dispatched to Cairo as evidence of the Egyptian victory.

The fleeing Mongols were pursued by the Mameluke cavalry to the west side of the Jordan River, near Beisan. There they decided to make a stand, but by now both men and horses were exhausted and on the verge of collapse. At the first Egyptian attack the Mongols broke and rode off, disorganized, in all directions, in a frantic haste to escape. The Egyptian victory was complete.

It is a rare history class in the west that hears even a mention of the Battle of Ain Jalut, yet it was one of the most significant events to influence the course of the history of the Western world. Had the Mongols succeeded in conquering Egypt, they would have had no problem in storming to victory across North Africa, through all of the modern states of Libya, Algeria, Tunisia, and Morocco. They would have clamped Christian Europe in a ring of iron all the way from Poland to the Straits of Gibraltar, capable of invading from so many different points that no European army could possibly have been positioned to hold them back. (In contrast, the Battle of Ain Jalut is an important event to the history classes in the Middle

East, where the name of the battle is also the name of a brigade in the Palestine Liberation army.)

After the victorious Egyptians had retaken Damascus, Aleppo, and the other major cities of Syria, accompanied by the vindictive slaughter of resident Christians, Baibars suggested that his services throughout the campaign entitled him to a special reward. He suggested that he should be given the emirate of Aleppo. Qutuz abruptly dismissed Baibars's petition, and it soon became obvious that he had no intention of dividing the conquests with any of his victorious generals.

As the conquering army returned to Egypt, it paused for a day of relaxation on the edge of the Nile delta. Qutuz went off on a hunt, taking Baibars and a few other Mameluke generals with him. During a lull in the action one of the generals approached the sultan as though to make a petition. Following the custom, he took the sultan's hand as though to kiss it, but as soon as he had taken the hand—the sultan's sword hand—he gripped it tightly. At that moment Baibars, who had come up behind Qutuz with his sword drawn, ran the curved blade through the sultan's body.

When the triumphant victory parade made its way through the massive gate, greeted by the cheering mob lining the main street of Cairo, the man leading the cavalcade was the new sultan of Egypt, Rukn ad-Din Baibars.

24

The Revenge of Baibars
1260 to 1274

KING MANFRED, who flatly rejected any papal claims to Sicily and the kingdom of Naples, had continued the Hohenstauffen tradition of suppressing the privileges and the income of the Church. Pope Urban IV decided to act on his conviction that King Manfred and the whole Hohenstauffen family must be driven out of Sicily and Italy.

As a French pope he naturally turned to the royal family of France to help the Holy See regain its rights—in exchange for substantial rewards, of course. He proposed to Louis IX of France that the king's younger brother, Count Charles of Anjou and Provence, make a bid for the crown of Sicily. Such a move would certainly mean war with King Manfred, but it would be a war with every means of spiritual and monetary support of which the Church was capable.

Charles of Anjou was excited at the prospect and agreed immediately. He was a very ambitious and ruthless man, unhappy that his principal identification was merely as the younger brother of a king. He wanted to be a king himself. He was an experienced military leader and had all the drive the task called for. His wife had three sisters who were queens, while she was just a countess. She was enthusiastically in favor of the proposed plan, which would put her on a social par with her arrogant siblings. King Louis not only approved the papal program for his brother, but levied a special tax in France to help build the war chest Charles would need to build and supply an army. Negotiations began to enlist the mercenaries who would make up the largest part of Charles's force. All this activity in Europe had little immediate impact on the Holy Land, but its ultimate result would be a blow from which Outremer would not recover.

For now the kingdom of Jerusalem seemed safe, as internal problems kept the Muslims at odds with one another. When Baibars proclaimed himself sultan of Egypt, Syrian nobles moved to assert their own independence in what they had assumed would be confusion at the court of Cairo. They did not know yet that Baibars was a man not easily confused. When a Mameluke emir seized Damascus for himself and a prince of the house of Saladin took over Kerak and Jordan, Baibars reacted quickly. He took an army to Damascus and drove out his political enemies. An easier victory was attained when he invited the prince of Kerak to a feast, giving him the false impression that the prince's sovereignty over Kerak was to be recognized there. With his guard down, the prince was murdered.

Baibars, far more than just a fiery-eyed fighting man, may have been the best diplomat of his time. He sent envoys to the emperor Michael at Constantinople, who was prepared to welcome any enemy of the Latin Christians and who created a favorable atmosphere by permitting the reconstruction of an ancient mosque in Constantinople that had been vandalized by the Crusaders.

The sultan sent envoys to the Golden Horde with rich gifts for the khan, with every expectation of a favorable reaction. Prince Batu had died several years before, and the present Mongol ruler Berke Khan had decided to embrace Islam. Berke's major rivalry was with the aging Hulagu, to whom Kublai Khan had given the title of Ilkhan of Persia, and who still favored the Christians. Baibars not only effected an alliance with Berke Khan, but sealed it by marrying the khan's daughter. Berke Khan was very pleased to learn that Baibars had ordered the khan's name to be included in the Friday prayers at every mosque in the Egyptian empire.

Baibars did not forget that the Christians of Armenia and Antioch had eagerly assisted in the Mongol invasion of Syria, and from a base in Aleppo he raided both territories on a regular basis, one time going so deep as to sack the Antiochene port city of St. Symeon. The Latin Christians in the Crusader states had felt secure because of their assistance to Sultan Qutuz in his expedition to Ain Jalut, but now they were getting nervous.

Count John of Jaffa was sent to the court of Baibars in 1263 on a peace mission that resulted in a truce and an agreement to exchange all Christian and Muslim prisoners, but that success was shattered by the military orders. The Knights Templar refused to participate in the prisoner exchange, for what they felt was a valid reason.

The Templars had years earlier established a policy regarding Muslim prisoners. Before being killed or sold to the slave merchants, the prisoners were interrogated as to their occupations. All craftsmen were held aside to become lifetime slaves of the order. There was a constant need for carpenters and stonemasons to maintain the Templar fortifications and a constant need for war materiel and equipment. It was simply not practical to import everything from Europe. At every Templar commandery there were craft shops turning out saddles, bridles, chain mail, and weapons. Supply wagons had to be built, and there were tents to be cut and sewn, horses in need of shoes, bread to be baked. The Muslim craftsmen became a vital part of the Templar war machine, and the Templars were not going to lose them and their products as the result of some arrangement made without even bothering to seek their approval. They would not budge from the grand master's decision to release no Muslim prisoners.

Baibars was furious that a treaty was broken almost as soon as it was made. In retaliation he dispatched an army to Nazareth, where the Christians were slaughtered, the city was sacked, and the central Church of the Virgin was demolished. Next he mounted a raid on Acre, not to try to breach the high walls, but to pillage and burn the suburbs and villages around the city.

Now no place in the kingdom of Jerusalem was safe from attack. The Knights Templar and the Hospitallers, whose stand on prisoner exchange had been the same as the Templars', at last decided to cooperate in an effort to hold the Mameluke army at bay. At the beginning of 1264 they rode south to take the small Muslim fortress that had been built on the site of the ancient town of Meggido, believed by many to have been the biblical Armageddon. Next they turned to a fast raid on the suburbs of Ascalon, near the Egyptian border.

That same year saw the death of Pope Urban IV. As the Christians in the Holy Land skirmished with the Muslims, the new French pope, Clement IV, continued the papal support of Charles of Anjou, who within the year led his army into Italy. He met and defeated the army of Sicily at Benevento, just east of Naples, where King Manfred was found dead on the battlefield. In the culmination of a great papal victory, the pope personally placed on the head of Charles of Anjou the crown of Sicily and Naples. No one paid any attention to the boy Conradin, who had been displaced by his uncle Manfred. Titular king of Jerusalem he might be, but in practical terms he was a young man without a country.

Back in the Middle East, Hulagu, ilkhan of Persia, died in February of 1265. Within three weeks Baibars had an army before the Christian city of Caesarea, located on the coast between Haifa and Jaffa. After a week of bombardment by the Egyptian stone-throwing catapults the walls were breached, and the Christians surrendered. Women and children were rounded up and marched off by the slave dealers who had come with the army, while the men were enslaved in labor battalions. Baibars sent an army north under the command of the Mameluke emir Kala'un with orders to attack Haifa. As soon as the Egyptian objective was clear, citizens and soldiers alike fought over places in the available ships and boats to make their escape from Haifa. The city was taken quickly, and those who had not managed to escape by sea were killed.

At the same time Baibars led his main army just south of Haifa to Athlit and Castle Pilgrim, the largest stronghold of the Knights Templar. He attacked for days, but the Templars were well organized for the defense, and well supplied. Baibars never liked to give up, but it was obvious that there might well have been some truth to the Templar claim of impregnability for this mighty fortress. In late March he abandoned his attack on Castle Pilgrim and went instead to the Hospitaller castle at Arsuf, well to the south near Jaffa. It took a few weeks, but the Egyptian catapults kept throwing their massive stones day after day and finally sections of wall began to crumble. Toward the end of April the Hospitaller commander agreed to surrender in exchange for Baibars's word that the garrison would all go free. Baibars gave his word willingly because he had no intention of keeping it. When the Hospitallers were in his hands, he had them put in chains.

Next on his list was the capital city of Acre, but before he could get there reinforcements arrived, brought to the mainland by King Hugh of Cyprus. Baibars decided that his expedition had accomplished enough and marched his army back to Egypt. Along the way he picked up the Christian prisoners from Caesarea and Arsuf, where defeat had been followed by back-breaking labor under the whips of Muslim overseers. The Christians had been put to the task of taking down the outer walls and the castles, stone by stone.

The captive Christians had one more role to fill for Baibars. After their grueling labor they were forced to walk all the way to Cairo, where they were organized for a triumphant parade. Broken crosses and crucifixes were hung around their necks, and they entered the city dragging their chains, with all their Christian banners held high before them, but upside down. As they moved through the streets they were pelted with anything that could be thrown, the more repulsive the better.

The following year Baibars came back to the Holy Land, this time with two separate armies. One he led himself, while the other was under his trusted friend the emir Kala'un. Baibars marched his army directly to Acre, which he found to be ready for him and well defended. He moved off to a feint before the Teutonic Knights' headquarters castle at Montfort (Starkenburg), then moved quickly to the Knights Templar's strong castle at Safed, which the Templars had acquired as a reward for their successful negotiations with Damascus twenty-five years earlier. It was a well-built, high-walled fortress that commanded the northern hills of Galilee, strategically located about twenty miles east of Acre and about the same distance north of Tiberias. It was strongly garrisoned by over two hundred Knights Templar and a much larger force of Templar Turcopoles, the light cavalry of mixed European and Syrian parentage. The garrison was well supplied and prepared for a long siege.

Baibars's first assault failed. His second assault failed. When his third assault achieved no better results, he decided to try a different approach. The sultan got word into the castle that Turcopoles who wanted to leave it could do so with no fear of harm. The Turcopoles wanted to accept the offer, but the Templar knights held them in strong discipline, which finally included physical beating. In response to that treatment the Turcopoles began to go over the walls at night, to be welcomed by Baibars. More and more deserted until the Templars were left almost alone, with not nearly enough men to defend the castle.

Baibars repeatedly offered terms, and after several weeks of undermanned defense the Knights Templar sent as their envoy a Syrian-born sergeant, Brother Leo. He returned with the good news that Baibars had pledged his word that in exchange for the peaceful surrender of the fortress the Knights Templar could leave the area unharmed, with safe escort all the way back to the Templar headquarters at Acre. They had apparently not heard of Baibars's failure to keep his word to the Hospitallers at Arsuf, so they agreed to the sultan's terms and opened the gate.

As soon as Baibars was in control, the Knights Templar found themselves his prisoners. The sultan told them they had a decision to sleep on. In the morning those of the Templars who abandoned Christianity to accept the true faith of Islam would live. Those who did not would die.

The next day the two hundred Templars, except for Brother Leo, were lined up in ranks outside the castle. Baibars demanded their answer, but before they could reply their commander called out to them to remain true to their God and the Virgin, to choose death rather than abandon the faith to which they had pledged their lives.

The Templar commander was pulled out of line, dragged in front of his men, and stripped naked. An executioner began to slice his skin into strips, which were pulled from his body with pincers, in response to the sultan's orders that he be skinned alive. The blood gushed from his raw, exposed flesh as screams tore from his mouth, but this bloodiest of deaths did not have the expected result. The watching Templars accepted their martyrdom, as each one chose death rather than give up the Holy Cross. In disgust, Baibars ordered that all of them be beheaded in their ranks. All, that is, except Brother Leo. The dead Templars never knew it, but their Templar brother, now converted to the Muslim faith, had betrayed them all to save his own life.

As Baibars consolidated his control at Galilee, including the capture of Philip de Montfort's castle at Toron, the Mameluke army under Emir Kala'un moved north. They took smaller towns and fortifications in the county of Tripoli, then, in the summer of 1266, turned to their primary objective. Armenia was invaded to inflict punishment for King Hethoum's alliance with the Mongols. The Knights Templar reinforced their castle of Baghras to block the invasion, but Kala'un simply circled far around the Templar stronghold, then moved to attack and capture one Armenian city after another, including Tarsus, the home of St. Paul. King Hethoum was away at the court of the ilkhan Abaga, who had succeeded his father Hulagu as ruler of Persia. Hethoum was seeking military support to help protect his kingdom, but he was too late. Two sons, Prince Thoros and Prince Leo, tried to take their father's place at the head of the Armenian army, but Thoros was killed in battle and Leo was taken prisoner. There was no effective barrier to Kala'un's destruction of the capital city of Sis.

The familiar pattern of Muslim conquest was repeated in the Armenian capital. Every occupant with market value as a slave was bound. Everyone else was killed. The entire city was plundered; everything of value was taken from the palace and from the cathedral, which was burned down as soon as it was emptied. It took hundreds of wagons and pack animals to take away the mountain of loot, and over forty thousand Christians were herded like cattle to the slave markets. Armenia was broken beyond recovery.

With the approach of autumn Baibars went back to Cairo, leaving a strong force based in the captured Templar castle of Safed. With Baibars gone, the Christians decided to recover some of their losses in Galilee. An army was assembled by the local barons, with contingents from the Knights Templar and the Hospitallers. As they took the field, they were attacked and routed by the Muslim forces from Safed, who turned out to be far more numerous than the Christians had expected them to be. The expedition was abandoned.

The military orders had lost castles, knights, horses, and supplies. New urgent pleas had to be made to their preceptories in Europe, with impassioned appeals for assistance from the Christian monarchs. The strongest appeals went to the pope; he alone could call upon all Latin Christianity for a new Crusade. The orders took heart from the information, largely unconfirmed, that King Louis IX of France was coming with all the nobles of France. With Charles of Anjou in his seat as king of Sicily, with the attendant tipping of the scales of power away from the Hohenstauffens of Germany to the advantage of the Church of Rome, perhaps a relieving Crusade was at last a real possibility. The Crusader states added the power of prayer to support their needs.

Baibars was on the move again in the spring of 1267. In May he approached Acre with a new bit of trickery. He had carefully preserved the battle banners captured from the Knights Templar and Hospitallers, which were now carried toward Acre in an attempt to get Muslim soldiers to the wall and even through the gate before the trick would be discovered. It almost worked, but the men on the walls realized the truth in time to bar the gate and call waiting defenders to the wall.

Baibars was ready to take Acre if his ruse had worked, but he had no desire to have his army pinned down in a lengthy siege. Instead, he set his forces to ravaging and plundering the towns in the surrounding area, hoping to draw the Christians out from behind their protective walls. Disregarding the provocation, they didn't budge from the city until Baibars was gone. Inspecting the damage around them, they found only what they had expected, with one exception. The thousands of bodies of dead Christians were without heads.

The Commune at Acre got word to Baibars that they wanted to send envoys to him to discuss a period of truce for the burial of the Christian dead. Baibars replied that he would receive the envoys only at his headquarters at Safed. Arriving before the castle, the Christian envoys found out, as they were supposed to, what had happened to the missing heads. They had been put with the heads of murdered prisoners and the skulls of the executed Templar martyrs in a great ring around the entire base of the castle. They created an eerie design element to identify a citadel of death. If it was done to strike terror into the hearts and minds of the Christians who saw it, it worked. Baibars, pleased to see their reaction, gave them the truce they requested, then returned to Egypt for the winter.

In March of the following year Baibars came again. His first target was the port city of Jaffa, the southernmost Christian holding. It was full of architectural beauty, the result of taxes and trade that had come to it for generations as a principal port for pilgrims to Jerusalem. John, count of Jaffa, had died two years earlier in 1266, leaving the city to a son who had not inherited his father's military skills. He was totally unprepared for the Egyptian assault, so twelve hours was all the time it took for the Mamelukes to take the city. When the initial killing died down, Baibars allowed the garrison to go free. His engineers supervised the dismantling of the castle and the careful removal of Jaffa's plentiful display of marble and carved timbers, which Baibars sent back to Cairo to be used in the construction of a magnificent new mosque.

The nearest Christian bases were the great Templar fortress of Castle Pilgrim at Athlit and the city of Acre, just north of it. They braced for the Egyptian attack, but Baibars took his army right around them, moving all the way up to the Templar castle of Beaufort, which overlooked the Litani River a few miles northeast of Tyre. The Templars had strengthened the castle over the twenty-five years since they had acquired it by foreclosing on Julian of Sidon. They were ready, but they had not anticipated that Baibars would drag catapults into the hills to use in the attack. A horde of Muslim stonemasons went to work quarrying and shaping the stones that would soon be hammering on the castle walls.

After ten days of constant pounding, the walls started to fall. The Templar commander surrendered on terms that would assure life, but not freedom, for the Knights of the Temple. The women and children were allowed to walk down the road to Tyre, because on this campaign Baibars could not be distracted by a large band of wailing slaves to slow him down. All of the men, including the Templars, were chained into labor gangs to work at restoring the castle's defenses.

Now Baibars turned his army northward again to the main purpose of this year's campaign. The prior year, it had been the punishment of Hethoum of Armenia. This year he would teach Bohemond, and the whole world, the price of alliance with the enemies of Islam. As the Muslim army approached Tripoli Baibars's spies reported that Prince Bohemond was in the city, but Baibars kept moving. He was out to destroy the principality of Antioch, which adjoined the already ravaged land of Armenia.

The Knights Templar had two castles between Tripoli and Antioch, Tortosa on the coast and Safita a few miles east in the hills. Before they put any Templars in the field against the Egyptians, the Templar officers sent envoys to Baibars to learn his intentions. Baibars had no desire to hold up his army with lengthy sieges or unrelated battles, so he made an agreement with the Templars that said essentially that if the Knights would stay out of the coming assault on Antioch, he would not attack Tortosa or Safita.

Arriving before Antioch on May 14, Baibars sent a small army to take the port of St. Symeon and block any support for Antioch that might come from the sea. He sent another to the north to prevent any interference by what was left of the army of Armenia. Antioch was the most extensive metropolis in Outremer, but since Bohemond had taken part of the troops of Antioch with him as an escort to Tripoli, it was not at full strength. That situation was made worse by a foolish act of the constable Bohemond had left in charge of the city.

Calling more on bravery than brains, the constable thought that a swift attack by a small troop of Christian cavalry could discourage an army that numbered in the tens of thousands. When his men were in the saddle, the constable ordered the gate opened. He led the charge personally, and as they watched this little group gallop out with lances lowered, screaming their battle cries, the Muslims could hardly believe their good fortune. Within just a few minutes a number of Christians were killed and the rest captured, including the foolhardy constable.

Now seriously undermanned, the garrison could do nothing to stop the blockbusting blows of the two-hundred-pound stones that came crashing into the city's walls. On the fourth day a breach in the wall appeared near the citadel. As men were called away from other parts of the wall to stop the flood of Muslims that was expected to come flowing through the breach, Baibars ordered an assault on all sections of the wall at once. Soon the Mamelukes were streaming over the walls and the city was lost.

Baibars was a man known for the savagery of his methods, but the treatment of Antioch went far beyond any levels of Muslim brutality that the men on either side had ever experienced. To start, he ordered all gates to the city barred and guarded so that not one Christian could escape his wrath. Everyone outside in the streets and squares was killed. Next came the systematic search of every home, factory, warehouse, and church. Any soldier, any civilian of either sex showing the slightest resistance, died on the spot. The very young, the very old, and the sick were slaughtered. The others were gathered together until there were thousands of stunned human beings for the slave dealers. The supply so exceeded the demand that a young girl could be purchased for a few pennies. Churchmen, generally regarded as poor slave material, were killed where they were found.

Antioch was not only the largest city in the Latin east, it was the richest in treasure, which had been accumulating for over a century and a half. There were gold and silver pieces from the altars, jeweled reliquaries, gold and silver coins, rich fabrics, jewelry, military stores, warehouses full of food, more plunder than Baibars or any of his emirs had ever seen.

After the captives were out of the city and the tons of plunder had been carried to safety, sections of the city were set on fire. Baibars's aim was destruction, not colonization. The city never regained its importance, and in time it became little more than a substantial village, overgrown with grass and weeds, surrounded by extensive ruins to give evidence of former greatness.

Baibars was a happy man. In his intense satisfaction at this act of vengeance he wrote a report on the capture of Antioch to Prince Bohemond in Tripoli, which read in part:

"Hadst thou but seen thy knights trodden under the hoofs of our horses! Thy palaces raided by plunderers and ransacked for booty! Thy treasures weighed out by the hundredweight! Thy ladies bought and sold with thine own treasure, at four for a single dinar! Hadst thou but seen thy churches demolished, thy crosses sawn in sunder, thy garbled gospels hawked about, the tombs of thy nobles cast to the ground, the monk and the priest and the deacon slaughtered on the altar, the rich abased to misery, princes of the royal blood reduced to slavery! Couldst thou but have seen the flames devouring the halls...the churches of Paul and Cosmas [Roman and Greek] rocking and going down—then thou wouldst have said 'Would God that I were dust!'

"This letter holds happy tidings for thee. It tells thee that God watches over thee to prolong thy days, inasmuch as thou wert not in Antioch. Hadst thou been there, now wouldst thou be slain or a prisoner, wounded or disabled. A live man rejoiceth in his safety when he looketh on a field of the slain.... As not a man hath escaped to tell the tale, we tell it to thee. As no soul got away to apprise thee that thou art safe, while all the rest have perished, we so apprise thee."

An English historian, commenting on this letter, gave the world a marvelous example of British understatement: "Baibars was a lion among men," he wrote, "but he was not a gentleman."

History does not tell us Bohemond's reaction to the demolition of Antioch, but we do know that it triggered meetings at the highest level for the Knights of the Temple. The Templars had long maintained two castles at a pass through the Armanus Mountains called the Syrian Gates, the principal route for Muslim invasions from northern Syria to the Mediterranean coast. These were the mighty castle of Baghras and a smaller but well-equipped castle called La Roche de Russole. Now those castles didn't guard anything, but were sandwiched between the hostile cities of Syria and what was now the Muslim territory of Antioch. They no longer had a sensible purpose.

The final decision was based in part on the needs of the Templar fortresses to the south. The Templars had lost men in the field and had lost both men and material at Safed and Beaufort. Their remaining castles were undermanned, as recruits from Europe were not coming in numbers sufficient to replace those who had fallen. The grand master decided to abandon the two frontier castles while the operation could be conducted in an orderly manner, and Baibars took no step to interfere. Now the military orders alone guarded the upper end of the Latin Christian states from their castles north of Tripoli. The Knights Templar's strongest castle in the area was Tortosa on the coast, with another strong castle called Safita in the hills a few miles inland. Two miles offshore from Tortosa they had a castle on the tiny island of Ruad. The Hospitallers had two major castles nearby: Marqab, on the coast just above Tortosa; and the strongest Hospitaller castle in the Holy Land, between Tortosa and the Syrian city of Homs, a magnificent fortress called Krak des Chevaliers, which was generally considered to be unconquerable.

Back in Europe events were stirring that would impact the very existence of the beleaguered Crusader states. A Hohenstauffen party had mounted a military campaign to oust Charles of Anjou, centered on the claims of Conradin, now a young man of sixteen, who was the rightful heir of Emperor Frederick II and in his own right the titular king of Jerusalem. The fierce battle took place in southern Italy, where King Conradin was captured. Charles had the boy taken to Naples, where a crowd was assembled in a public square to watch Conradin's head chopped off. The execution marked the end of Hohenstauffen claims to Sicily and the kingdom of Naples, and the end of Hohenstauffen claims to the crown of Jerusalem. It was a definitive victory for the papacy, dampened somewhat by the fact that there was no pope.

Pope Clement IV had died in that same year of 1268, but before his death he had extracted a promise from Louis of France that there would be a French Crusade to rescue the Holy Land from the fury of Sultan Baibars. Charles, who had especially enjoyed the influence and the treasury of the Church being used for his personal benefit, did not want that money and power diverted toward a Crusade that would interfere with his grand plan. He had made no secret of his ambition to conquer and rule Constantinople, and to that end he had opened diplomatic discussions with Sultan Baibars. Charles wanted to prevent any Egyptian interference that would require fighting two enemies at once, and a new Crusade would make any alliance with Baibars impossible. He would need to divert his brother Louis away from his crusading vow, but could not be certain how the next pope would react. His answer was to forestall the papal election by any means, including substantial bribes to cardinal-electors to delay the papal selection. By that means Charles managed to keep the Throne of Peter unoccupied for almost three years. The absence of a pope made the pleas for assistance more difficult for the kingdom of Jerusalem and the military orders, all of whom tried direct but unsuccessful approaches to the Christian monarchs of Europe.

Upon the execution of King Conradin by Charles of Anjou, Hugh of Cyprus, a great-grandson of Queen Isabella of Jerusalem, claimed the crown of Jerusalem for himself. Princess Maria of Antioch objected. Hugh was a great-grandson. She was a granddaughter and therefore one generation closer. The crown of Jerusalem should come to her. As always the political factions split up along predictable lines. The Knights Templar supported Maria's claim. The Hospitallers supported Hugh, as did their ally, Philip of Montfort, the lord of Tyre. The High Court went along with them, so King Hugh III was crowned in September 1269. Maria took her claim off to Rome, where she provided still another empire-building prospect for Charles of Anjou.

King Hugh III rewarded Philip of Montfort for his support by effecting a reconciliation between him and the Commune of Acre. The Templars were furious at the king. They had spilled Templar blood to protect Acre from Philip of Montfort and would have nothing to do with him now. Hugh did not succeed at all in reconciling the rivalry of the merchants of Genoa and Venice, who attacked each other in every way they could, whenever they could. This political chaos could only work to the advantage of Sultan Baibars, and the only hope now to bring order to the Holy Land was the coming Crusade under Louis of France. Louis did indeed mount a great Crusade, but thanks to the scheming of Charles of Anjou, it did not come to the Holy Land.

Charles had found the lever to divert the French Crusade. The African coast opposite Sicily and Italy was controlled by the emir of Tunis. The emir was not an aggressive enemy of Christianity and in fact had provided a safe haven for defeated Sicilian and Italian enemies of Charles. An alliance between Charles's own Christian enemies and the Muslims of North Africa could mean that they might one day come against Sicily, which was reason enough for him to stop them now.

Charles put his new plan to his brother King Louis and got the support of his allies at the French court. Charles told Louis that he was certain that the emir of Tunis and all of his people would convert to Christianity if they were not dominated by their Muslim neighbors. A Christian show of force there would provide the emir with the perfect excuse to bring his domains into the care of Holy

Mother Church and add tens of thousands of souls to the kingdom of Christ. Louis may have been saintly, but his mind apparently didn't spend full time in the real world. He accepted everything that his brother told him and agreed to take his crusading army to Tunis instead of Palestine.

Jean of Joinville, the seneschal of Champagne who had spent so many years on Crusade with Louis, declined to go and repeatedly begged the king to stay home. Louis was too weak from complicated illnesses to even go on a holiday, much less a military expedition. Joinville recorded the state of the king's health: "...he was physically so weak that he could neither bear to be drawn in a coach, nor to ride...so weak, in fact, that he let me carry him in my arms ...to the abbey of the Franciscans." Joinville was convinced that his king could not survive the proposed African Crusade and summed up his feelings: "I considered that all those who had advised the king to go on this expedition had committed mortal sin."

With Charles's prodding and the king's own fanatic determination to keep his sacred crusading vow, King Louis was on a course from which he would not retreat. He firmly held his nobles to the crusading vow they had taken with him, and the French Crusade sailed for North Africa on the first day of July in 1270. They arrived before Tunis on July 18 and were disappointed to find the emir ready for war, not for conversion to Christianity. The emir had called every fighting man he had into the walled city, and the envoys he sent to Baibars returned with assurances of the sultan's help, if it should be needed.

Past experience seemed to count for nothing, and the inadequate food stocks brought with the Christians began running low. In the fierce heat of a Mediterranean summer the men sweated profusely in their padded armor, with no way to replace the salt their bodies were losing. Severe shortages of drinking water guaranteed dehydration. That, coupled with malnutrition, created the perfect atmosphere for infectious diseases. It gradually came to the emir that there was not going to be a battle, as the whole French army was inert with sickness, with no one sicker than the king himself. When Charles of Anjou arrived with his Sicilian army on August 25, the first news delivered to him was that his brother Louis had died earlier that same day. The crime of the Eighth Crusade had played itself out.

Sultan Baibars was relieved that he would not have to send an army off in exactly the opposite direction from the faces of his Mongol enemies. He wanted no distractions from his plans for the Christians, either, and had already effected one more move while the French were camped before Tunis. He had a good working relationship with the Syrian Assassins because of the Egyptian defeat of the Mongols who had destroyed the Assassin sect in Persia and, closer to home, because his success against the principality of Antioch had enabled the Assassins to stop paying an annual tribute in gold to the military orders. They were happy to do their friend Baibars a favor.

An Assassin was sent to Tyre, where his careful training enabled him to pass himself off as a Christian. He attended the same church as the lord of the city, Philip of Montfort. On August 17, 1270, exactly one week before the death of Louis of France, the young Assassin had quietly entered the chapel of the cathedral, where Philip of Montfort and his son were on their knees in prayer, with their backs to the Shiite executioner. Too quickly for anyone to stop him, the Assassin took his dagger from his robe and thrust it into the unsuspecting Philip. The Assassin was captured, but he was content. Philip of Montfort was dead, and his murderer now had an assured place for all eternity on the highest level of paradise.

There was no pope in Rome and there would be no French Crusade. The most aggressive local baron had been murdered, so Baibars could see no barrier to his plans for the final destruction of the Holy Land. He now assembled his army for what he expected to be the last and totally victorious battle of Mamelukes against Christians.

25

The Pope of Good Intentions
1271 to 1274

THE KNIGHTS TEMPLAR in their castle at Safita began getting reports at the beginning of 1271 that Baibars was on the march again and heading in their direction. Soon the mountain passes were choked with thousands of Muslim cavalry and infantry, slowed down by trains of wagons carrying the components of siege machines. The Muslims passed by Krak des Chevaliers, the mighty fortress of the Hospitallers, and came straight at Safita.

The Templar castle, made of a light-colored stone that had given it the name of *Chastel Blanc*, the White Castle, was much, much smaller than Krak des Chevaliers, but it gained importance from its location between the strongest inland Hospitaller fortress and the strongest Templar castle at Tortosa on the coast. Though relatively small, Safita did have an outer wall eleven feet thick, a higher inner wall, and a central tower or "keep" from which archers could shoot down at the enemy.

On the negative side, it was seriously undermanned at the time and had more wall than it could possibly defend effectively if attacked from all sides. Once those attacks began, however, the small numbers were somewhat offset by the fierce defense put up by the Templars in the garrison, fierce enough that Baibars was willing to discuss terms with the defenders so he could turn around to his principal target at Krak des Chevaliers. He wanted Safita simply because he did not want the Templars at his back while he laid siege to the larger castle.

Thomas Berard was not having a very pleasant term as grand master of the Knights Templar, and once more he was called upon to make an unwelcome decision. The commander of the castle and the Knights Templar inside it were ready to fight to the death, and only the grand master could shift them from that resolve. Fortunately, Grand Master Berard realized that their deaths, however heroic, would do nothing for Christianity or for the order. He advised them to surrender on the best terms they could get. The sultan wasted no time in intricate negotiations, and quickly agreed that the Templar garrison would be free to walk back to their castle at Tortosa. This time he kept his word, and the handful of knights led their sergeants, archers, and servants away from the war, dejected in defeat but relieved to be alive.

The legend of the impregnability of Krak des Chevaliers had probably been born in the inability of the greatest of the Muslim conquerors, Sultan Saladin, to crack its defenses, but Baibars was not deterred by legend. As his siege train slowly made its way to join the Muslim army that he was marshalling into position around the great fortress, Baibars called in extra forces from his Syrian vassals, and his Assassin allies sent a contingent of their own blood-seeking mountain fighters.

With the siege engines in place, the Muslims concentrated the bombardment of huge stones on the tower that guarded the gate in the outer wall. After a few days of incessant pounding, the walls of the tower began to break up, and its defenders fell back to avoid the falling rock. Shrugging off the arrows and crossbow bolts that were too few to hold them back, the Muslim troops were able to get inside the tower to open the gate and climb the stone steps to the top of the wall, fighting their way in both directions to clear away the Christian defenders. Below them, more Muslims cleared the debris from the gate area to permit Baibars's army to enter the castle in force. All of the defenders who had not sought the safety of the central keep were doomed. The native-born soldiers and the servants were taken prisoner, but every Hospitaller knight taken, whether well or wounded, was beheaded in full view of his brothers watching from the citadel. The garrison of the keep held out for another ten days, then surrendered on Baibars's assurance that they would go free. Once again the sultan kept his word and saw them safely on the road to Tripoli, probably with the expectation that the reports of the defeated Hospitallers would demoralize the people in that city.

The sultan sent a smaller army south to take the Hospitaller castle at Akkar, and now he was ready for the final punishment of Bohemond with the complete destruction of Tripoli. All of the inland castles that for generations had sheltered the city from attacks from the Syrian Muslims were now in Muslim hands. As Bohemond prepared to receive the attack, envoys came with a message from Baibars. Bohemond expected to hear a demand for the surrender of the city, and he was shocked when the polite emirs stated instead the sultan's desire for a truce. Silently voicing his sincere thanks to God, Bohemond readily agreed.

The sudden change in Baibars's plan had resulted from the news that a new Crusader army from Europe was at hand. The sultan was not going to launch a long siege with no knowledge of the extent of the force coming against him and with no knowledge of the character or intentions of its leaders. He decided to bide his time and took his army back to Egypt. Along the way, he assaulted the headquarters castle of the Teutonic Knights at Montfort, the last inland castle of the Crusaders, strategically located midway between Acre and Tyre. The garrison surrendered after one week of bombardment. Now all three military orders had felt the wrath and the power of the Mameluke.

Baibars had reduced the Crusader states to a narrow string of coastal cities with lands that effectively extended no more than ten miles from the coast. All of the inland castles and towns belonged to him, and they had been taken from the hated Christian military orders. Those victories were good for the morale of his own men, who feared the religious knights more than any other of their Christian enemies. The military orders fought not for land or loot or glory, but for God, a concept the Muslims understood and respected. Now even Baibars would sing their praises, as victorious generals have always built up the reputations of their conquered enemies, as a means to emphasize the skill and glory of the victor.

Baibars would soon learn that the new Crusade was led by the English prince Edward, who would later prove to be one of England's most effective kings in his long reign as Edward I. He had come to the Holy Land at the encouragement of his father Henry III, supported by his friends the English Templars. His wife, Princess Eleanor of Castile, was eager to accompany him, but the English barons were not. Prince Edward was able to put together an army of only one thousand men, and even with another contingent brought by his brother a few weeks later, his army was not large enough to make a significant difference to the defense of the Holy Land. He had some help in the form of a small complement of soldiers from the continent, but their most important contribution was in the person of their leader. He was Tedaldo Visconti, the archbiship of Liege, who would soon ascend the papal throne as Pope Gregory X.

Edward had a natural ability for organization, a trait that showed in his careful plans, which were carried out with strong determination. All of his instincts of leadership were offended by the state of affairs he found in the Holy Land. He had expected the local barons, the religious leaders, the military orders, and the Italian merchant republics to draw upon their bond of Christianity to work together toward a common goal. Instead he found a disparate group of individual entities, each dedicated to its own selfish interests. He was especially incensed to learn that the Venetians had developed a profitable trade with the Egyptians in timber and iron, which the Egyptians used to produce siege engines, ships, and weapons to be used against the Christians. Edward had expected to add his own small forces to those already in place, arrange a military alliance with the Mongols against their common Muslim enemy, and then retake the lost lands of the kingdom of Jerusalem. A wonderful plan, but the prince soon discovered that it was not in keeping with the realities of the situation.

Edward went to the archbishop with his complaints against the Venetian trade with the infidel, but the archbishop had no power to stop it, although he would take a strong stand on that issue once he had assumed the papal crown.

Prince Edward, on his own initiative, did send envoys to arrange a military alliance with Ilkhan Abaga, who responded with a cavalry force of ten thousand Mongols who made a galloping raid through Syria to reach the Christian army, but when Baibars came against them with an army that easily outnumbered theirs, the Mongols retreated to the safety of Persia. Edward satisfied his own craving for action with some minor raids into Muslim territory, but he had neither the siege engines to take nor the men to hold any important Muslim fortification.

During these indecisive actions, Archbishop Visconti received three unusual visitors. They were a Venetian merchant, Nicolo Polo, his brother Maffeo, and his son Marco. The two older men had made a trading voyage to the Black Sea back in 1250. They had decided to travel inland on horseback to the court of the khan of the Golden Horde, and through a series of adventures had been passed eastward from one Mongol chief to another until they had finally found themselves at the court of the supreme lord of the Mongols, Kublai Khan. As the first of their race to reach that court, they were welcomed and plied with questions about their European world and their Christian faith.

After years of service to the great khan they had returned home, having been asked by Kublai to act as his ambassadors to the pope at Rome. They were to ask their pope to send learned men, well versed in religion and all of the arts, to share their faith and their knowledge with the Mongol court. Kublai had also asked for some of the sacred oil which he had been told was kept burning constantly over the Holy Sepulcher. The Venetians finally got back to Venice in 1269, where everyone had assumed that they were dead. The greatest surprise for Nicolo Polo was the discovery that his wife, now dead, had been pregnant when he left on his fabulous voyage. Now he was introduced to the son he had never seen before, the nineteen-year-old Marco Polo.

The Polos had arrived in Venice just at the time that Charles of Anjou was coercing and bribing the cardinals to postpone the election of a pope, so there was no way for the Polos to carry out their mission to Rome. After two years of waiting in vain for the cardinals to select a pope, they decided to return to Kublai Khan's court, taking young Marco with them. This was the story that they recounted to the archbishop of Liege at his palace in Acre. The archbishop helped them to secure the holy oil from Jerusalem and wrote a letter documenting its authenticity. He also complied with the travelers' request for a letter to Kublai Khan explaining why there was no pope.

The Polos proceeded on their journey northward through Armenia. A few days later the archbishop received letters from the cardinals at Rome telling him of his own election to the papal throne. Visconti did not want to miss the opportunity to establish an embassy at Kublai Khan's court, so he dispatched a letter to the king of Armenia, describing the Polos and asking that they be traced and sent back to Acre. The Polos were found, were delighted with the news, and rushed back to meet with the new pope. He gave them letters and gifts for Kublai Khan. He also assigned to their mission two Franciscan friars to preach the Christian doctrine and delegated to them the authority to establish churches and to ordain priests. Now the Polos, with the full blessing of the new pope, departed once more for Armenia and the east.

A few weeks later, the Knights Templar who were keeping watch from their castle at Tortosa were surprised to see a little party of Venetians approaching their gate, escorting two Franciscan friars. Taken to the castle commander, the weary travelers told their story to the Templars. Ever since the party had set out from Acre the Franciscans had listened to stories of bloody massacres inflicted on Christians by the Turks, the Mongols, and the Syrians. They were terrified by the urgent warnings that they must be prepared for the possibility of torture and death. As their fear grew greater than their faith, they had decided to risk the new pope's wrath and return home. To that end they had asked the Venetians to bring them here so that they could throw themselves on the mercy of the Knights Templar.

The Templar commander could not be expected to muster up much sympathy for the whining cowardice of his fellow religious, but, perhaps just to get the friars out of his sight, he arranged for their transportation back to the safety of Acre, where they were spared a papal rebuke because Tedaldo Visconti, now Pope Gregory X, was already on his way to Rome to try to rouse the faithful to an all-out Crusade.

The grand master was pleased, however, that Prince Edward had come to the Holy Land. As an Englishman, Thomas Berard had known Edward from earlier years. It was a relief to work with an English leader and to share with him what he knew of the situation in the Holy Land. Edward realized that there was little that he could accomplish in war and turned his attention to working out a treaty with Sultan Baibars. The sultan's major problem was not the string of port cities in the shrinking Christian kingdom, but the restless hordes of Mongols in Persia, Iraq, and the Turkish lands. He had received an arrogant, threatening letter from the ilkhan Abaga, demanding that Egypt bow down to the Mongol khan. Baibars decided to let Prince Edward have his peace treaty and agreed that the truce would last for ten years and ten months.

Perhaps the sultan signed the treaty because he had reason to believe that the English prince would not be alive to enforce it. The agreement was in effect for less than thirty days when a man that Edward thought was a Muslim converted to Christianity turned out to be an Assassin sent to murder the prince. His dagger did not enter Edward's body deep enough to bring death by itself, but the blade was covered with poison. Edward was painfully ill for several weeks, but did not die, probably because his princess had pushed the men aside to suck the poisoned blood from her husband's wound. A few of his knights chose to stay behind, but in September 1272, recovered from the wound that had brought him closer to his wife, the prince returned to England. Upon his arival Edward learned that his father had died, so that he was now King Edward I of England. He would have issues to address at home that were much more important to him than another Crusade.

In 1273 Thomas Berard died and the Templar grand chapter again faced the task of electing a new grand master. The current political situation, and especially the career and ambitions of Charles of Anjou, may have influenced them to elect one of their officers who was a cousin of Charles and of the king of France. William de Beaujeu became the twenty-first grand master of the Knights of the Temple, but before coming out to the Holy Land to take up his new duties, de Beaujeu spent months with Charles of Anjou in Sicily, then traveled with him to France to attend the Second Council of Lyons. The conclave had been called by Tedaldo Visconti, now Pope Gregory X, to deal with the matter of the Holy Land, as well as to address several problems of a Church that had been out of control during almost three years without a pope. To help prepare for the council, the pope had asked various members of the Church hierarchy to report to him on the prospects for a new Crusade. He didn't like anything he heard.

One report after another provided alarming evidence that three years without papal control had been tantamount to granting a three-year license for corruption. Not only barons, but bishops as well, took advantage of the inattention of their superiors to create little sovereign states of their own, stripping lands and revenues in their keeping to enrich themselves and their families. To avoid losing control of parish churches and their revenues, they were frequently assigned to men who were not ordained to the priesthood, to men who had no ecclesiastic training, and even to underage boys.

As to a Crusade, the people had lost their zeal for the dubious spiritual rewards that the Church promised them in return for spending their money, even mortgaging their properties, to travel to distant lands and risk their lives in a war that they were not at all certain God wanted. Weren't the Christian losses in the Holy Land concrete evidence that Christ did not favor their cause? The reward of eternal salvation lost its ethereal appeal in the face of reality. They had seen the very concept of Crusade, literally "for the cross," undergo a warped transformation into wars to assert the power of the papacy, as in the Albigensian Crusade in France and the papal "Crusade" against Frederick II in Italy.

Pope Gregory X was dedicated to the principle that while it was the duty of all Catholics to save the souls of men, it was the special duty of the pope to save the soul of Holy Mother Church. He, above all other men, had the responsibility to bring the Church back to those moral standards implicit in a sincere belief in the teachings of Jesus Christ. He alone held the authority to discipline the higher levels of the Church hierarchy. Church corruption, the profligate lifestyles that were supported by extortionate taxes forced upon the people, the diversion of funds, the immoral conduct of men who wore clerical dress had all caused the faithful to falter. They were losing their reverence for the sacraments and losing respect for sermons preached by men who were themselves immersed in sin. Gregory's main task was to correct those abuses by asserting and enforcing a strong moral papacy. The steps he took to accomplish that goal at the Second Council of Lyons in 1274 tells us much about the state of affairs in Europe toward the close of the thirteenth century, and the struggles for power that led to the ultimate loss of the Holy Land. Some of the issues addressed help to explain the disastrous events of the next quarter century. (One can only speculate on the course the council's deliberations might have taken had one of the greatest minds of the age lived long enough to attend, but St. Thomas Aquinas died on the journey to Lyons, just one year after releasing his landmark *Summa Theologica*.)

Gregory felt strongly that a new Crusade to save the kingdom of Jerusalem would help to pull the faithful together again. He knew full well that the more successful he was in attracting men to fight, the more money would be needed to transport them to the Holy Land and to sustain them in the field. The money would not be easy to come by, because it was well known that much of the gold collected for past Crusades had been diverted into the pockets of the higher clergy. It was used to support them in luxurious lifestyles that would be the envy of any prince—a rank to which the cardinals claimed full entitlement as "princes of the Church."

The pope knew from personal experience that the Italians were supplying the Egyptians with military supplies, and he had to stop that trade, no matter how profitable it might be. He knew that the ships of the Muslim maritime states on the African coast and of Muslim freebooters and pirates constantly preyed on Christian shipping, frequently selling their pilgrim prisoners into slavery. He had also learned that those predators were supported by Christian port towns whose merchants bought the pirates' captured cargoes and sold them the supplies they needed to put to sea again. That, too, had to be stopped.

Important visitors were coming to the council, and their petitions would need to be addressed. Maria of Antioch wanted the chance to present her claim to the throne of Jerusalem. Envoys of the ilkhan of Persia were seeking a Christian alliance against the Muslims. Ambassadors from Emperor Michael of Byzantium were attending to discuss the Greek recognition of the supremacy of the pope in Rome, in the hope that the emperor's submission to the pope would avert the threatened attack on Constantinople that was being readied by Charles of Anjou.

These were all matters of great weight, and therefore all the European monarchs were urged to attend the Second Council of Lyons in 1274. None did, with the exception of the aging king James I of Aragon, but he was unimpressed by what he found and soon went home. William de Beaujeu, the new grand master of the Knights Templar, was especially interested in the representatives from the Holy Land for what they could tell him of the current situation. Over the coming months he became friends with the bishop of Tripoli, who one day would be very grateful for that friendship. And always the grand master served as a listening post for his cousin, Charles of Anjou, who he supported in every way.

The constitutions resulting from the council are enlightening because they reflect a papacy using its authority not only to call for and fund a Crusade, but also to attempt to raise the level of morality both inside and outside the Church, an issue of scant concern to medieval monarchs. They begin with an overriding concern for a Crusade. Because of his term as patriarch of Jerusalem Gregory X could speak from personal experience.

"Alas! The very land in which the Lord deigned to work our salvation and which, in order to redeem humanity at the price of his death, he has consecrated by his own blood, has been boldly attacked and occupied over a long period by the impious enemies of Christianity, the blasphemous and faithless Saracens. They not only rashly retain their conquest, but lay it waste without fear. They savagely slaughter the Christian people there to the great offense of the Creator, to the outrage and sorrow of all who follow the Catholic faith. 'Where is the God of the Christians?' is the Saracens' constant question, as they taunt them. Such scandals, which neither mind can fully conceive nor tongue tell, inflamed our heart and inspired our courage so that we, who from our experience overseas have not only heard of those events, but *have looked with our eyes and touched with our hands*, might rise to avenge, as far as we can, the insult to the Crucified One. Our help will come from those on fire with zeal of faith and devotion. Because the liberation of the Holy Land should concern all who profess the Catholic faith, we convoked a council, so that after consultation with prelates, kings, princes, and other wise men we might decide and ordain in Christ the means for liberating the Holy Land."

Pope Gregory also declared that the council had been called to effect "...a reform of morals, which have become corrupt owing to the sins of both clergy and people."

To fund his Crusade Gregory X announced that he and all of the cardinals would contribute one-sixth of their revenues for a six-year period. He called on every bishop, every priest, every holy order to contribute 10 percent of their revenues for the same period. Fines imposed on all blasphemers were to be added to the crusading funds. Priests hearing confessions were to demand cash payments as penance before granting absolution, "...and to give the money to the Holy Land in full satisfaction of their sins." A box was to be placed in every church, and to ensure the ultimate use of the money, each box was to have three keys, "the first to be kept in the possession of the bishop, the second in the possession of the priest of the church, and the third in the hands of some conscientious lay person." The pope then ordered, "The faithful are to be instructed to place their alms, as the Lord inspires them, in this box for the remission of their sins.''

So that none should fail to make some contribution, the pope further ordered that all secular authorities should impose in their lands ''...a small tax of no burden to anyone, for the remission of sins...so that just as no one may excuse himself from compassion for the wretched state of the Holy Land, no one may be dismissed from contributing.'' With a view to preventing any repetition of past diversion of Crusade funds for personal gain, Gregory threatened the ultimate punishment of the Church. The ''anathema'' had originally meant a ban or curse, but by the time of the council had come to define the most serious form of excommunication, decreed with full ecclesiastic ceremonial. ''Lest these prudent arrangements concerning the Holy Land be hindered by anyone's fraud or malice, we excommunicate and anathematize one and all who knowingly offer hindrance, directly or indirectly, publicly or secretly to the payment of the tithes....''

Grand Master de Beaujeu listened with great interest to the recitation of methods of raising crusading funds, from all of which the Knights Templar were exempt. One of his primary reasons for coming to the Council of Lyons was to try for a share of those funds as a grant to his own order.

With the sources of funding defined and ordered, Gregory X turned his attention to those Christians dealing with both Muslim and Christian pirates: ''Since corsairs and pirates greatly impede pilgrims traveling to and from that [Holy] Land, by capturing and plundering them, we bind with excommunication them and their principal supporters and helpers. We forbid anyone, under threat of anathema, knowingly to communicate with them by agreeing to buy or sell.''

Addressing the problem of Christian sales of military supplies to the Muslims, which had so angered Edward of England, the pope condemned the guilty to poverty and slavery. Their excommunication made them exceptions to the rule that Christians should not make slaves of other Christians. ''We excommunicate and anathematize, moreover, those false and impious Christians who, in opposition to Christ and the Christian people, convey to the Saracens arms and iron, which they use to attack Christians, and timber for their galleys and other ships... [they] are to be punished with deprivation of their possessions and are to become the slaves of those who capture them.''

Now that funding had been set and war criminals dealt with, the Crusade needed men to take up the Cross and fight the fight. The first step, as the pope saw it, was to order the Christians in

Europe to stop fighting with each other, so that any man would be free to take his weapons and his military skills to the Holy Land. "We therefore ordain...that peace be generally kept in the whole world among Christians...to observe for six years a definitive agreement of peace, or a firm truce. Those who refuse to obey shall be most strictly compelled to do so by a sentence of excommunication against their persons and an interdict on their lands." The threat, and even the act, of excommunication had frequently failed to stop wars between Christian rulers in the past, so the pope warned that to punish those who "make light of the Church's censure," he might order secular war against them "as disturbers of the business of Him who was crucified."

His investigators had already told the pope that the promise of eternal salvation would no longer stir men to take the crusading vow, but Pope Gregory had no choice but to try, for there could be no Crusade without men. "We therefore, trusting in the mercy of Almighty God and in the authority of the blessed apostles Peter and Paul, do grant, by the power of binding and loosing that God has bestowed upon us, unto all those who undertake this work of crossing the sea to aid the Holy Land, in person and at their own expense, full pardon for their sins about which they are truly contrite and have spoken of in confession, and we promise them an increase of eternal life...." The same pathway to salvation was offered to those who could not go but would send "...suitable men at their own expense."

Based on the offer of the emperor Michael to submit the Greek Church to the authority of Rome, the union of the churches was enthusiastically approved, and the working arrangements for the union were carefully spelled out. The delegation from the ilkhan of Persia was given the opportunity to present its plea for a military alliance between the Mongols and the impending Crusade, with promises of the ultimate restoration of the Holy Land to Christian control. Maria of Antioch made her plea for the throne of Jerusalem.

One last matter had to be addressed on the agenda, the all-important issue of the election of a pope. Never again could the Church permit such a long interregnum in the papacy. From now on the election of the pope would be effected by the college of cardinals, with incentives to hasten their decision. The cardinals would have ten days from the time of the pope's death to assemble in conclave, all in one room with no partitions or curtains. The room would be sealed, with a window large enough to pass food through, but not large enough to permit a man to enter or leave. No messages were to be sent or received. If after three days they had not agreed to a pope, they would be reduced to two meals per day consisting of one dish only. If five days later they still had not chosen a successor, they would fast on bread and water until a pope was picked. During the election process, the cardinals were forbidden to receive any Church revenues of any kind. Gregory X intended that never again would it take years to elect a pope.

As much a change as the method to be used to select a pope was the exhortation to the cardinals to stop selling their votes or using them to make side deals to enrich themselves or their families. Rather they were to be guided only by what was best for the Church. "...we implore the cardinals...that they consider very carefully what they are doing. They are electing the vicar of Jesus Christ, the successor of Peter, the ruler of the universal church, the shepherd of the Lord's flock. They are...to be free from any bargain, agreement or pledge; they are not to consider any promise or understanding, to have no regard for their mutual advantage or that of their friends. They are not to look after their own interests or their individual convenience.... Their one aim is to provide, by their service and speedily, what is so useful and necessary for the whole world, a fitting spouse for the church. Those who act otherwise are subject to the divine retribution, their fault never to be pardoned except after severe penance. We invalidate all bargains, agreements, pledges, promises and understandings, whether confirmed by oath or any other bond; we nullify all these and decree that such have no force whatever." (Had this noble decree been embraced, rather than ignored, there might still be an official functioning order of Knights Templar in the world, but such was not to be.)

Addressing the petition of Maria of Antioch, Pope Gregory encouraged her to sell her claim to the crown of Jerusalem to Charles of Anjou for a cash down payment of ten thousand gold pounds, to be followed by a lifetime payment of four thousand pounds per year. The arrangement had the total approval of Grand Master de Beaujeu, Charles's cousin. The Templars had already pledged their support to Maria's claim, and now they would gladly transfer that support to Charles of Anjou so that he might add the crown of Jerusalem to the crowns of Sicily and Naples.

The union of the Greek and Roman churches never took place, because Emperor Michael was forced to back down when news of his proposed union kindled the wrath of his Greek subjects to the point of revolt. The Roman Church would not try to shelter Byzantium from the threat of conquest by Charles of Anjou. His strong alliance with Charles was the only immediate, tangible benefit that Grand Master de Beaujeu was able to report to the Templars on his return to the Holy Land, since by the time he had departed Europe the pope's call for a new Crusade had gone unanswered.

Although inclined toward unjustifiable optimism, Pope Gregory X was a good and sincere man, with a desperate desire to do what he felt was best for Christianity: He had sought a new Crusade to save the Holy Land; he had demanded a stop to the diversion of Crusader funds; he had ordered an end to deal-making as the central theme of papal elections; he had asked for military alliances between Mongols and Christians to hold back the Muslims; he had arranged for the crown of Jerusalem to pass to the Church's ally, Charles of Anjou; he had encouraged the submission of the Greek Church to the Church of Rome. He and the Church achieved not a single one of those objectives. Perhaps his posthumous beatification by the Church was intended to bring peace to his soul in Heaven to make up for the string of frustrating failures he had endured in his lifetime.

Having failed to achieve their mission at the council, the Mongol envoys stayed behind in Europe to visit some of the secular rulers and make direct appeals for alliances to fight the Muslims, but they finally returned home to report to the ilkhan that there would be no alliance with a Christian Crusade. There wasn't going to be any Crusade. The enthusiasm for dying for the Holy Land was itself dead. The pope was a man of formidable power, but he could no longer rally the faithful to leave their homes, their farms, and their families to risk death or mutilation in a war on distant battlefields in exchange for the remission of their sins, or even for the promised "increase in eternal life." The Mongols were on their own.

So were the Christians in the kingdom of Jerusalem.

26

A Kingdom Coming Apart
1275 to 1289

WHEN THE BISHOP OF Tripoli returned home from the unsuccessful Council of Lyons, he thought he was bringing bad news, but he found that many of the local barons were actually relieved. The counting house, not the Cross, had become the central feature of their lives. They had gradually developed luxurious semi-oriental lifestyles that would be out of the question for them back in Europe. The Muslim trade was the source of their flowing wealth, and they had no desire to see it cut off by a bunch of religious fanatics who would turn their lives upside down and then go home. They were willing to take their chances with their own abilities to negotiate with the Muslims, who they were convinced would never want to destroy the trading centers that were the Christian port cities of the Holy Land. Their fights were with each other, as almost everyone with power—or a craving for it—lied, cheated, and even killed to get a larger personal share of the ever-shrinking Christian territory.

The Knights Templar shared in the profits from the Muslim trade, though their profits came not from goods, but from gold. They had extended their banking activities to Cairo, Alexandria, Damascus, and other Muslim merchant centers. Those activities included the kind of clandestine intelligence network that almost always accompanies international banking. The system included well-placed and well-paid informants at the various Muslim courts. The information collected was screened and evaluated at their headquarters in Acre, then applied to further the Templars' own best interests.

When William de Beaujeu arrived at the Temple at Acre, it was his first appearance in the Holy Land since being elected grand master two years earlier. In grand chapter de Beaujeu explained his own diplomatic gains on behalf of the order, based primarily on his personal relationship with his cousin Charles of Anjou. He described the arrangement under which Charles was buying the claim to the throne of Jerusalem from Maria of Antioch, with the full blessing of Pope Gregory X. That meant Charles would soon be crowned king of Jerusalem, with the Templars high in his favor. He told them that Charles was in constant contact with Sultan Baibars of Egypt, who respected his accomplishments in the conquests of Sicily and Naples. Baibars had promised his full cooperation in Charles's plan to retake Constantinople, which had every expectation of success. From all of this, because of the Templars' firm support of Charles, the order could expect to reap a rich harvest of benefits in additional properties and power. In turn, the Templar officers were able to bring the grand master up to date on the events in the Holy Land during his absence, in particular the recent activities centered around the determination of King Hugh of Cyprus to have himself declared king of Jerusalem.

To start with, there was the strange situation in the Christian city of Beirut, where there was actually a guard detachment of Baibars's Mamelukes in the palace. When John of Ibelin had died, the city went to his widowed daughter, Isabella. The princess enjoyed her widowhood and wealth with zestful abandon, to the extent that when the pope learned of her bedroom behavior, he issued an encyclical ordering Isabella to remarry. She picked a handsome English knight named Hamo, who had stayed behind when Prince Edward left the Holy Land. The locals disparagingly called her new husband *L'estrange*, the Foreigner. When a terminal illness began to drain away his life, Hamo L'estrange appealed to Sultan Baibars to protect Isabella from King Hugh of Cyprus, whom Hamo felt certain would make every effort to take Beirut from her.

He was right. Soon after Hamo's death, King Hugh sent men to kidnap Isabella and bring her to Cyprus, where he intended to force her to marry one of his own people. Baibars immediately intervened and demanded that Isabella be released and sent home, which he had a right to do under his agreement with Hamo. The local barons supported the sultan, and Isabella was freed. Once Isabella was back in Beirut, Baibars provided her with a guard unit of Mamelukes for her security. It says something about the devious nature of Middle Eastern politics at that time, when a detachment of Muslim soldiers provided protection for a Christian noblewoman against the evil designs of a Christian king.

As to the Templars' long rivalry with the Knights Hospitaller, the grand chapter assured Grand Master de Beaujeu that this could now be dismissed. With the loss of their greatest fortress, Krak des

Chevaliers, the power and influence of the Hospitallers had declined sharply. Along with the other losses, the Hospitallers were reduced to just one important castle, which was far to the north at Marqab.

The Italian maritime states, Genoa and Venice, were still at each other's throats at every opportunity, so there was no change on that front. Genoa had a firm grip on the trade in Byzantium, a benefit earned by providing help to the emperor Michael, but the grand master pointed out that the situation could be expected to change once Charles of Anjou succeeded in his plan to capture Constantinople. The Templars' Venetian allies had good reason to support Charles and his claims with ships and men; in exchange, they expected to be returned to their former position as the dominant trading factor in the Byzantine territories.

Anxious to act before Charles of Anjou would complete his bargain with Maria of Antioch, King Hugh of Cyprus made plans to take control of the county of Tripoli. When Prince Bohemond VI died in 1275, Hugh rushed to Tripoli to announce that he would serve as regent until the fourteen-year-old heir came of age. Hugh was angered to learn that the boy's mother had anticipated just such a move. She had already asserted her own right to the regency and had sent her son off to the safekeeping of her brother, King Leo of Armenia, well beyond King Hugh's grasp. She had also turned the administration of Tripoli over to Bartholomew, the bishop of Tortosa, who had started a reign of terror in which the Knights Templar became involved.

By way of background, when the present prince's grandfather had died in 1252, his widow, Princess Lucienne de Segni, ruled as regent until their young son reached his majority. When the princess had come out to Tripoli from Rome, she had brought with her a large entourage of friends and relatives. One of those relatives, Paul de Segni, she had arranged to be made bishop of Tripoli. He was the same prelate who had won the friendship of Templar grand master William de Beaujeu at the Council of Lyons. The princess and the bishop had exerted their combined influence to have many of their Roman friends appointed to the most lucrative posts in Tripoli. Now the bishop of Tortosa wanted them all out, out of their jobs, out of the country.

It was not the bishop of Tortosa's style to request written resignations. He sent soldiers to the homes of some of the Romans to seize their property, then escort them and their families beyond the gates of the city, with orders never to return. Other Romans were not so lucky. They were taken from their houses, chained, and dragged off without explanation to the dungeons under the citadel. Then,

without even the slender benefit of a trial, Bishop Bartholomew
ordered their heads struck off and their properties forfeit. Bishop
de Segni knew that his turn would come soon, and in his panic
he could think of nowhere to turn except to the Templar grand
master. It was the right move.

William de Beaujeu, backed by a contingent of his armored
knights, hurried up from Acre to Tripoli to confront the bishop of
Tortosa. The grand master ordered the bishop to stop his attacks
on the Romans or on anyone else, admonishing him that to disobey
was to take the gravest possible risk. De Beaujeu spoke as the cousin
of the king of France, as kinsman of King Charles of Sicily and
Naples, as the commander of the strongest military force in the Holy
Land, and as the sole ruler of the city and castle of Bartholomew's
own bishopric of Tortosa. Bishop Bartholomew, now in fear for
his position, his property, and even his life, backed off, assuring
the angry grand master that his every word would be heeded. Paul
de Segni, bishop of Tripoli, walked the streets of the city again,
head high and totally secure. It paid to have friends in high places,
especially the ones with swords.

Watching these events, King Hugh decided to abandon any
attempt on Tripoli, choosing rather to direct his efforts at Acre. His
approach was not very realistic, since he knew that Acre was the
headquarters of the Knights Templar, who openly favored the claims
of Maria of Antioch and Charles of Anjou. It was also the headquarters of the Templars' Venetian allies, who had their own war
galleys and troops. He could expect no support from the patriarch,
who took his orders from the pope, and who also supported Charles
of Anjou. Nonetheless, Hugh ignored the facts and sailed to Acre to
declare himself king of Jerusalem. He was surprised and affronted
when no one in the city paid any attention to his royal claims. As
he left Acre to return to Cyprus, Hugh engaged in one more futile
gesture. He appointed his vassal Balian of Ibelin to rule in his absence
as his *bailli* and ordered that Balian be obeyed, on the preposterous
assumption that people who ignored King Hugh would gladly obey
his deputy.

During the following year of 1277 Charles of Anjou completed
his arrangements to purchase the crown of Jerusalem from Maria
of Antioch and sent his own *bailli*, Roger de San Severino, to rule
in his absence. Informed in advance of the new *bailli*'s arrival, the
Knights Templar and the Venetians met Roger's ship, saw him safely
disembarked, and took him into the city with a military escort.
The party confronted Balian of Ibelin with documents authen-
ticated by the signatures of Maria of Antioch and King Charles.
A letter from the pope gave the papal blessing to Charles as the

rightful king of Jerusalem. Balian had no choice but to step down.

By then, Bohemond VII had reached the legal age of fifteen and had assumed full control of Tripoli. Bohemond also retained the services of Bishop Bartholomew of Tortosa, who soon found a new way to enrich his own family. Young Bohemond had promised his cousin and vassal Guy of Jebail that Guy's brother John would have the hand in marriage of a very wealthy young heiress. Bishop Bartholomew persuaded the young count to break his word to Guy and give the affluent young lady's hand instead to the bishop's own nephew. Guy's response to Bohemond's betrayal of his promise was to kidnap the heiress in Tripoli, take her to his own city of Jebail, then marry her to his brother John as originally planned. Bohemond was angry with Guy, but Bishop Bartholomew was furious. He encouraged Bohemond to take a body of knights to arrest Guy and his brother and bring them back to Tripoli for punishment.

No doubt recalling how the bishop of Tripoli had saved himself from Bartholomew's vengeful wrath, Guy of Jebail fled to the protection of the Knights Templar, who readily took him in. In his frustration, Bohemond ordered the destruction of the Templar buildings in Tripoli. Grand Master de Beaujeu, himself an old hand at destruction, took a strong party of his Templars on a punitive raid through Bohemond's territory, looting and burning, topped off by burning Bohemond's castle of Botrun, between Tripoli and Jebail. Bohemond had no desire to confront the Templars in the field, but when word reached him that the grand master had led his Templars back to their headquarters at Acre, the king assembled his forces for an attack on Jebail. Apparently no one told him that the grand master had anticipated the attack and had provided for it. When Bohemond's troops confronted the forces of Jebail, they were surprised to find a detachment of Templars facing them, armed and eager. Bohemond was soundly beaten and driven back to Tripoli, having made an enemy of the strongest military commander in the Holy Land. Prudence suggested that Bohemond mend his fences with the bearded knights of the red cross. That course was supported by the disquieting news coming to him from the north.

Baibars had decided to raid into the Turkish lands of Anatolia. The Seljuk leader had died, and a four-year-old boy was the new Seljuk sultan. His government was in the hands of a greedy emir named Suleiman, who was helping himself more than his people and neglecting his defenses. To Baibars, it seemed like a good time to strike. The young sultan was now a vassal of the Mongol ilkhan Abaga, who kept a garrison of Mongol horsemen in Anatolia, a fact that did not arouse any fear in Baibars. He had beaten them before and could beat them again.

At the same time that Bohemond was stirring up internal conflict in the Holy Land, Baibars moved up from Syria and chased
the Mongols out of Anatolia. Suleiman made no attempt to rouse the
Seljuks to defend their land or to help the Mongols. Rather, he
demonstrated his dismal lack of courage by throwing himself at
the feet of Baibars, who he quickly acknowledged as the liege lord
of the Seljuk Turks.

When news of Baibars's success reached the ilkhan Abaga, he
ordered thousands of Mongols into the saddle and stormed out to
meet the enemy, leading the mounted army himself. Baibars, unprepared to challenge the overwhelming numbers of the whole Mongol
horde, simply moved out of Anatolia and back to the security of
Syria. There was no barrier to his reasserting his control of the Seljuk
territories at a later date. The spineless Suleiman was arrested by
the Mongols and taken back to Persia in chains. Legend has it that
at the Mongol victory banquet following the campaign, the featured
dish was a stew made of select portions of Suleiman's anatomy.

Baibars was annoyed at having been run out of Anatolia and
extremely resentful that a young Syrian prince was receiving far
more praise for his bravery during the recent action than was Baibars
himself. He was al-Qahir, who had succeeded his father an-Nasir
Dawud as prince of Kerak. The sudden popularity of the courageous
young descendant of Saladin represented a possible threat to
Baibars's rule, which meant the prince had to die. Baibars invited
the young man to a feast, where great quantities of *kumiss*, the
fermented mare's milk of the Mongols, were consumed. At one
point, the sultan took a vial from his robe and surreptitiously poured
a poison into the young prince's cup. Somehow in the drunken party
the cups got mixed up, so that Baibars drank the poison himself.
He died after a series of agonizing stomach convulsions on the night
of July 1, 1277. As brutal and ruthless as he was, Baibars was still
the best Muslim general, and as the best-organized sultan since
Saladin he had been an unending threat to the Christian states. News
of his death brought celebrations in the streets and prayers of
thanksgiving in the Christian churches.

Baibars's heir was Baraqa, the teenaged son of Baibars's Mongol wife. He and his companions, who depleted the national treasury
with the most luxurious lifestyle they could dream up, made a game
of finding ways to demonstrate Sultan Baraqa's autocratic power.
He imprisoned court officers who offended him or his friends in
the slightest ways, regardless of their rank. His response to a gentle
word of criticism from his elderly vizier was to order the old man
to be arrested and executed. After almost two years of such bloody
lunacy Baraqa, then at Damascus, was persuaded by his friends to

arrest two Mameluke generals, who were back in Egypt, one of whom was Baibars's favorite field commander, the emir Kala'un. Friends at court got word to the generals, who simply rode out of Cairo to join their armies, where no one would dare to come for them. The sultan refused to back off, and soon the generals announced that they were officially in a state of revolt and they rode back to Cairo with their armies behind them. The sultan assembled forces at Damascus to attack the rebellious emirs, but when the men of Damascus discovered the purpose of the expedition, they deserted and went home. Deprived of any type of military backing, Sultan Baraqa had no choice but to agree to live in exile in Kerak as the price of sparing his life.

Baibars's second son, a seven-year-old boy, followed his disgraced brother as sultan, with Kala'un as vizier and commander-in-chief of the armies of the Egyptian empire. After about ninety days of that charade, Kala'un yielded to the urging of his friends and to his own strong ambitions. The boy was set aside, and Kala'un declared himself to be the sultan of Egypt. A few months later the exiled Sultan Baraqa was dead. The official court announcement reported that he had been killed in a fall from a horse. The gossip in every marketplace in Egypt and Syria said that he had been poisoned at Kala'un's orders.

Later in that same year of 1279, Hugh of Cyprus decided to have another try at the city of Acre. Calling on the feudal obligations of his island vassals, he put together an armed force to stage what he intended to be open warfare, fully expecting that the mainland barons would join him. They didn't, choosing instead to remain neutral. The Templars were fully armed and ready for battle before Hugh could even get all of his men and horses off their ships, and they were backed by all the land and naval forces of Venice. Hugh chose not to fight, switching instead to diplomatic efforts. That didn't work either. After months of negotiating, threatening, and bargaining, the feudal contract put an end to the useless proceedings, because the vassals of Cyprus were sworn to a maximum of four months' military service away from their island. As the time ran out and their feudal obligations were satisfied, the king's vassals began to pack up and take ships for home. Hugh could do nothing but fume and follow them. He laid all the blame for his failure squarely at the door of the Knights Templar and, as punishment, seized all their properties in the kingdom of Cyprus. In answer to an appeal from the grand master, the pope wrote to King Hugh, ordering that for the good of his soul the Templar property should be returned. For the moment, however, Hugh of Cyprus elected to put retribution above redemption. He ignored the pontiff.

Nor was all going well with Tripoli. Bohemond had reached a one-year truce with the Templars, who were allowed to rebuild and staff their house in his city, but he still held twelve members taken prisoner in the past troubles. As the truce expired, there was another battle between about two hundred followers of Bohemond and about the same combined number of Templars and vassals of Guy of Jebail, in which Bohemond lost again, which led Bohemond to once again destroy the Templar property in Tripoli. The Templars attempted an attack from the sea, directing twelve of their own galleys to take the harbor at Tripoli, but the ships were dispersed by a sudden storm. Bohemond responded by sending a fleet of his own galleys against the Templar castle at Sidon, but understandably, the naval force alone could not take the high-walled fortress.

In the meantime the Mongol court, which had been relaxed by the news of the boy sultan of Egypt, was quick to respond to the much more ominous news that a Mameluke general had seized the sultanate. Ilkhan Abaga decided to move first. In the late summer of 1280 he sent a Mongol army into Syria, which took one town after another. By October the Mongols were in possession of the major city of Aleppo, where the Muslim inhabitants were slaughtered, warehouses pillaged, and mosques set on fire. The Hospitallers decided to take advantage of the prevailing turmoil and dispatched troops from their northern castle at Marqab to raid Muslim villages and towns in the interior. As they returned to Marqab after the raid, loaded down with loot, they were accosted by a troop of Muslim horsemen, which proved too small to stop them. Kala'un did not forget the insult of Marqab and marked the Hospitallers for special punishment.

The Mongol cavalry had successfully employed the speed and shock tactics for which they were universally feared and had seized Syrian territory, but in Egypt Kala'un could draw on the largest population base in all Islam. He assembled an army that would greatly outnumber the Mongols and set out to protect his kingdom. His cavalry and infantry made up the largest military force in the Middle East, and from sheer lack of numbers the Mongols were forced to retreat to Iraq. The Mongols needed to field a much larger army if they planned to take any part of Syria, Palestine, or Egypt away from the Mameluke sultan.

Sources of Mongol reinforcements were diminishing because the empire of Genghis Khan was breaking up, splitting into separate states under sons and grandsons of the Great Khan, each with his own leanings and ambitions. Kublai Khan, the strongest of them all, was gradually being absorbed into the ancient Chinese culture and was a devoted Buddhist. Much closer to home, the khan of the

Golden Horde—now called the Kipchak Mongols—leaned toward Islam, and before the year was out would formally declare himself and his family to be Muslims. As such, he not only would refuse to help the Persian Mongols against the Egyptian Mamelukes, but had to be considered a potential enemy himself. The Persian Mongols under Ilkhan Abaga were on their own, but they could call on their Christian vassal states of Armenia and Georgia and on elements of the Seljuk Turks. Bohemond of Tripoli had pledged fealty to Abaga, but had few troops to offer. The one substantial fighting force that might be sought as an ally was that of the Latin Christians of the Crusader states, including the military orders. Abaga sent ambassadors to Acre.

The Mongol envoys explained to the barons and grand masters that during the following year, 1281, the ilkhan Abaga planned to send all his forces, a mighty army of one hundred thousand men, into Syria with the final objective of the conquest of Egypt. In exchange for the assistance of the Crusaders with men and military supplies, Abaga would guarantee that their rewards would include all of the original kingdom of Jerusalem. Every object of the crusading desire would be fulfilled.

The Latin Christians still had no central authority and no central voice. They had been so splintered by their internal squabbles that they could not address the Mongol proposals. Roger de San Severino was under strict orders from Charles of Anjou to maintain friendly relations with Sultan Kala'un, so his response to the envoys' mission was to exert all the negative influence in his power. Abaga's ambassadors went back to him frustrated and confused, but quite certain that the ilkhan could expect no help from the Crusaders. Nor did Mongol envoys sent directly to the pope and the leading monarchs in Europe achieve any better results.

Fully informed by his own agents of the Mongol diplomatic initiative, Kala'un followed up the Mongol mission to Acre with envoys of his own, who proposed a ten-year truce which would include the Knights Templar and the Hospitallers. The proposal received full support from Roger de San Severino, who went so far as to appear to be acting as Kala'un's agent at the Christian gathering. In private, several of the Egyptian envoys advised the Crusaders not to rush into any arrangements with Kala'un because there was already a plot afoot to overthrow the sultan. They named names. Roger de San Severino rushed a warning to Kala'un, who was able to arrest and execute the conspirators in time to save his throne.

With Roger's assurances to William de Beaujeu that the proposed truce would please Charles of Anjou, the grand master signed for the Knights Templar in May 1281. The grand master of the Hospitallers signed for his order, followed by the signature of Bohemond a few weeks later. Kala'un was delighted that his diplomatic maneuvering had secured his western flank against any Christian threat in the coming Mongol war. While the negotiations were taking place, Kala'un had moved his army up from Egypt and established his own base at Damascus. He was ready.

By September the Mongol army was assembled and began its march into Syria. The alliance did not have the hundred thousand men Abaga had anticipated, but was nevertheless a very substantial military presence of fifty thousand Mongols, supplemented by thirty thousand Christians from Armenia and Georgia, who were positioned as the right wing of the Mongol army. They were surprised to be joined by a detachment of Hospitaller knights from Marqab, who had decided to ignore the truce signed by their grand master at Acre.

At the end of October 1281, Kala'un marched out to meet the Mongols near the city of Homs, about fifty miles from the coast between Tortosa and Tripoli, and took personal command of the Muslim center. Opposite him was Ilkhan Abaga's brother Mangu Timur, in supreme command of the Mongol force. As the two armies clashed, the armored Christians of the Mongol right shattered the Muslim left, whose horsemen finally broke and ran. The exultant Christians charged after the retreating enemy with so little attention to the distances they were covering that they completely lost touch with the main army. Regrouping their forces miles from the main battlefield, they settled down to rest, apparently in the false belief that their own success was being shared by the entire Mongol force. It might have been, but in the clash at the center of the line Mangu Timur suffered a serious wound that seems to have thrown him into a state of panic. He demanded to be taken from the field, ordering his own substantial guard to escort him away from the battle. When they were seen retreating, the same panic gripped the entire Mongol army, which soon was in full flight.

It is not hand-to-hand combat that inflicts the most damage to an army, but hand-to-back, as soldiers are struck down from behind trying to flee the field. The Muslims chased the enemy with spear, sword, and ax, leaving a trail of Mongol dead all the way to the Euphrates River. The relaxed and seemingly victorious Armenian and Georgian Christians found themselves trapped, alone. As the main Muslim army chased the Mongols off to the northeast, the Christians fought their way through to the northwest. Roger de San Severino made a personal gift-bearing visit to the court of Sultan Kala'un to express praise and gratitude for the decisive Egyptian victory, because that's what he thought his master Charles of Anjou would want. Roger couldn't foresee that in just a few months no one would any longer care what Charles of Anjou wanted.

The humiliating loss of the Battle of Homs was a great shock to the ilkhan Abaga, who sank into deep depression and died a few weeks later. His brother Tekudar took the throne, putting aside the claim of Abaga's son Argun. Although his mother had been a Nestorian Christian and his father a man of total religious tolerance, Tekudar had become profoundly impressed by the teachings of the Prophet Muhammad. He announced that he had decided to embrace Islam and to give up his Mongol title. On this day he ceased to be the ilkhan Tekudar and henceforth was to be addressed as the sultan Ahmed. He came to regret that his subjects did not quickly follow his lead in religious preference.

With the friendly Mongols defeated by their Mameluke enemy, there appeared to be a bit more effort among the resident Crusaders to settle their internal differences. Peace was effected between the Knights Templar and Tripoli, to the extent that the Templars were once again permitted to rebuild and garrison their quarters in that city. Perhaps that was why they were unsympathetic toward a new plan of Guy of Jebail, who had lost none of his hatred for Bohemond of Tripoli, a feeling that was enthusiastically reciprocated.

In January of 1282 Guy decided to resolve the conflict by seizing Bohemond at night in his own palace. With his two brothers and a party of friends, Guy got into the city under cover of darkness, and the conspirators gathered at the house of the Knights Templar, where they were not made welcome and were asked to leave. As they moved out through the city toward Bohemond's palace, an alarm was sounded. Guy and his group ran to the nearby head-quarters of the Hospitallers, where they were bottled up in a tower by Bohemond's guard. They could easily have been driven out over time by hunger and thirst, but the Hospitallers managed to extract terms from Bohemond under which Guy and his party would be set free in exchange for their surrender. Once his enemy was in his hands, however, Bohemond saw no barrier to breaking his word. Guy's followers were sent to the dungeons, where their eyes were put out, after which they were led back stumbling and bleeding to their families at Jebail. Guy, his two brothers, and a cousin were reserved for public punishment. They were taken to a ditch and buried up to their necks with their eyes turned toward the sun. They were left to a death of thirst and dehydration, no doubt hastened by an open invitation to the local citizens to pelt their exposed heads with anything handy.

Back in Sicily, an underground movement against the French had grown sufficiently confident to be ready to act. All winter long secret agents had moved throughout the island kingdom, evidencing all the elements of a strong covert organization among the lower nobility and prominent peasants. They agreed upon a date, based on signals that have never been revealed but that proved totally successful. On the evening of March 30, 1282, they rose in a unified front and murdered every member of the occupying French garrisons, their officers, and the administrative officials. This bloodbath was remembered in history as the Sicilian Vespers. (If certain Italian historians are correct in their assertion that the secret society behind the uprising evolved into the Sicilian Mafia, its medieval roots may help to explain how organized crime developed its completely feudal operational structure.)

The powerful alliance that had been so carefully and expensively built between Charles of Anjou and the papacy simply collapsed. That alliance had emptied the treasury of the Church in Rome, which now had nothing to show for it. When the news reached Spain, King Pedro III of Aragon rushed an army to take control of Sicily. The army in Italy that Charles had exhausted his funds to assemble for the invasion of Byzantium was now needed to attempt the reoccupation of the Sicilian kingdom. He lost his means to transport that army when the Aragonese navy defeated Charles's Sicilian fleet in the Straits of Messina, then moved north to destroy his Italian fleet in the Bay of Naples. Charles's nephew, Philip III of France, tried to stop the trouble at the source with an invasion of Aragon, but his troops took a severe beating from the forces of Pedro III. The pope wielded his mighty sword of ecclesiastic power by formally excommunicating King Pedro, which accomplished nothing at all. Genoa saw in Charles's fall a decline in the power of his Venetian allies and accelerated its war against the Adriatic republic.

In the east, the government and religious convictions of Byzantium were now beyond any threats of conquest as Charles fought to retain some remnant of his kingdom. Sultan Kala'un wrote him off as no help and no threat. Charles of Anjou could be ignored. When Grand Master de Beaujeu and his Templars learned of the fall of their powerful ally and patron, they were acutely aware that some of the power and influence of the Knights Templar had fallen with him. Charles now needed his trusted vassal Roger de San Severino to help him at home, so Roger returned to Italy, leaving his seneschal Odo Poilechien to act in his place. Poilechien was ready to be agreeable when Sultan Kala'un suggested a new peace treaty between the Muslim and Christian states.

The treaty essentially characterized the Christians as a source of commerce, not war. They agreed to refrain from expanding their defenses, and that included the Templars, the Hospitallers, and the Teutonic Knights, whose leaders the document called "the grand masters of Acre," and who were to act as agents of the sultan in the event of impending Crusades. Historian Amin Maalouf has quoted a portion of that treaty:

"If a Frankish king sets out from the west to attack the lands of the sultan or his son, the regent of the kingdom and the grand masters of Acre shall be obligated to inform the sultan of their action two months before their arrival. If the said king disembarks in the east after these two months have elapsed, the regent of the kingdom and the grand masters at Acre will be discharged of all responsibilty in the affair."

Any monarch contemplating a Crusade could hardly be happy that the Christian military orders were sworn to provide a Muslim sultan, the target of his crusading efforts, with two months' advance notice of the event, and therefore sixty days in which to make preparations to thwart his Christian purpose.

The treaty, to remain in effect for ten years, ten months, ten days, and ten hours, was signed in May 1283 by Odo Poilechien and the grand masters. It specifically excluded the Hospitallers of Marqab, whom the sultan would never forgive for joining the Mongol army against him.

Nor did he forget that the Christian king of Georgia had fought against him. Kala'un had paid informants at the Georgian court, and through them he learned that the king had decided to make a pilgrimage to the Church of the Holy Sepulcher at Jerusalem. The report could hardly have been improved upon by modern espionage technology, since it provided the Georgian king's complete description, including age, height, complexion, eye color, and visible scars, plus the route he would follow and the information that the king would be in disguise, with just one companion.

Kala'un's agents easily spotted the king at the frontier, then followed him for days, right through the gate into Jerusalem. Once inside, he was taken into custody and put in chains. On Kala'un's orders, he was then escorted to Egypt, where he was consigned to a royal dungeon deep inside the citadel at Cairo. The entire operation speaks eloquently to Kala'un's talent for organization.

In view of recent events, King Hugh of Cyprus, remarkably persistent, decided that the time might at last be right for him to establish his claim to the crown of Jerusalem. Once again he assembled an army of his feudal vassals and set out for Acre in July of 1283. This time a storm blew his fleet off course as far north as Beirut. When the winds died down, Hugh decided to proceed south by ship himself, but he ordered his troops to make the journey overland. Along the way, the Cypriots were severely cut up by Muslim raiders. When the news reached King Hugh at Tyre, he was seething with rage at the Knights Templar, who he was convinced were responsible for instigating the Muslim attacks.

He had a more concrete reason to be angry with the Templars when news of his latest claim to the crown of Jerusalem reached Acre. The Knights Templar were very happy with the total independence they enjoyed under the lackadaisical government of Odo Poilechien, as were both the Venetians and the Commune of Acre. The only way they would yield to Hugh's claim to the throne of Jerusalem would be through force of arms, which in the circumstances was not a very practical approach for King Hugh. Once again he fumed and argued while the four-month feudal obligation of his vassals ran out. This time the obsessed monarch did not go back to Cyprus with them, determined to stay in Acre until his claim was recognized. During the months that followed, fate dealt his ambition a terminal blow, when after many weeks of increasingly grave illness Hugh died at the beginning of March 1284.

The crown of Cyprus went to Hugh's son John, a very frail youth of seventeen years who did not have long to live. In spite of his condition, however, he was crowned king of Cyprus, then taken to Tyre, where he was crowned king of Jerusalem. That title and position was rejected by the Knights Templar, the Venetians, and the Commune of Acre, who pointedly ignored the sickly king.

Cyprus was not the only kingdom to change rulers that year. In Persia Argun, the son of the late ilkhan Abaga, had led an unsuccessful revolt to unseat his uncle Sultan Ahmed and was put in prison to await his fate. Fortunately for him, the Mongol garrison had not followed his uncle's example in converting to the Muslim faith. Argun, who still enjoyed the status almost instinctively rendered to a direct descendant of Genghis Khan, engaged the officers and men in conversation as often as possible. He constantly played on the point that all favor was now being shown to Muslims, that only Muslims could expect promotion. What was wrong with their own religion? Why would any true Mongol agree to cast aside the wise laws of Genghis Khan that had built the Mongol empire? Were they supposed to be ashamed of being Mongols? His reasoning and his appeals to their racial pride took root and spread. His guards finally released Argun, and the officers of the garrison pledged their support. They murdered Sultan Ahmed and put Argun on the throne. They were pleased when Argun announced that he would not give up his Mongol name and would use the Mongol title, styling himself the ilkhan Argun.

Not certain as to what Argun might do, Kala'un moved his court and a large part of his army up to Damascus. When it became apparent that Argun had no immediate military moves in mind, Kala'un decided to keep a promise he had made to himself, the punishment of the Hospitallers at Marqab. The closest help for Marqab would be the Knights Templar in their castle at Tortosa, a few miles to the south, but with his recent treaty Kala'un could be reasonably sure that the Templars would not interfere.

In April of 1285 Kala'un personally led a substantial army to the mountain castle of Marqab. His attack had been carefully planned and his army was well supplied. Tens of thousands of arrows had been made in advance, there was a supply of pitch and naphtha for fireballs, and seven massive catapults were assembled. The problem of the engineers in charge of the catapults was the height of the castle above the valley floor. Now it was not a matter of how far the machines could throw a heavy stone, but how high. They tried to find a solution by moving the catapults up the side of the mountain, but that made them easy prey for the Hospitallers, who had gravity on their side. All the knights had to do was to lob a stone over the wall with their own catapults, letting it fall down on the unlucky Muslims. Several Muslim catapults were lost that way, so Kala'un decided to switch to mining.

The Muslim miners and engineers managed to drive a tunnel under the north tower of Marqab and then carved out a large chamber under the foundations, which they supported with timbers. Using the pitch and naphtha they had brought with them, they soaked and coated the timbers, then set them on fire. As the wooden support of the foundation burned away, the tower came crashing down. The sultan sent word to the castle commander that a branch of that same tunnel went deep into the castle structure. He suggested that the Hospitallers choose surrender over certain death under falling rock and promised the safety of every Christian.

There seemed to be no choice, so the surrender was arranged. Not absolutely certain that Kala'un would keep his word, the Hospitallers were greatly relieved to learn that each officer would be allowed to keep one horse, his personal possessions, and even his weapons. All others in the castle would leave on foot with no possessions: What they were allowed to keep was their lives. They followed the coastal route south to the Templar castle at Tortosa, where the Knights Templar provided them with supplies and horses to get them back to join their brother Hospitallers at Tripoli.

On May 20, 1285, just three days before the fall of Marqab and scarcely more than a year after inheriting the throne of Cyprus, the frail eighteen-year-old King John died, to be succeeded by his healthy and vigorous fourteen-year-old brother Henry. Fortunately for the boy king, another death had occurred that smoothed his path to the crown of Jerusalem. Charles of Anjou had died and passed his titles to his own son, who would rule his southern Italian lands from Naples as King Charles II. King Henry sent an ambassador to Acre, asking that he be acknowledged as king of Jerusalem.

With Charles of Anjou dead, the Commune of Acre, the Hospitallers, and the Teutonic Knights had no objection. Venice decided not to resist the claim. After long discussions, Grand Master de Beaujeu and the Knights Templar bowed to the will of the majority and acquiesced. The sole objection came from an unexpected quarter. Seneschal Odo Poilechien, who had never lived so grandly or importantly in his entire life, refused to step aside. He barricaded the castle at Acre and garrisoned it with French soldiers, ready to do battle with the king of Cyprus, who arrived at Acre in June. Henry was patient and tried to be conciliatory, but the local barons soon tired of the fruitless conflict. The grand masters of the military orders sought an audience with Odo and warned him that he was alone in his resistance and endangering his own life. Under pressure, Odo was finally persuaded to turn the castle over to Henry. The young king of Cyprus was then universally acknowledged to be the rightful king of Jerusalem.

The royal family of Cyprus had fought long and hard to gain the throne of Jerusalem, and now must have wondered why. The kingdom hugged the coast from the Templar castle of Tortosa in the north to Castle Pilgrim in the south, and nowhere was it more than a few miles wide. Each major city was a separate fiefdom, with rulers who rarely cooperated with each other. The Teutonic Knights had lost their castle at Montfort, so could offer no real defense beyond a handful of knights. The Hospitallers had lost both Krak des Chevaliers and their mountain castle at Marqab, so were in an extremely weak position. The major defense of the kingdom, therefore, fell on the Knights Templar, who now held all of the frontier castles that were left. A new Crusade was desperately needed, and if the Christians couldn't have a Crusade, the only hope they had of holding their place in the Holy Land was an alliance with ilkhan Argun of the Persian Mongols.

That alliance was there, waiting for them. All they had to do was say "yes." The ilkhan could not have been more open about his desire for the Mongols and Christians to fight together. He had written a letter to Pope Honorius IV and could not understand why he had not received the courtesy of a reply. In 1287 the khan sent to Rome his personal ambasssador, a Nestorian Christian named Rabban Sauma, but by the time the ambassador arrived the pope was dead, and no successor had been named. He tried to explain the seriousness of the Middle Eastern situation to the assembled cardinals, but they insisted on turning every conversation into a probing inquisition into his Nestorian beliefs, then allowed themselves the scholastic satisfaction of pointing out the Catholic perception of the theological flaws in Rabban Sauma's replies. The Mongol ambassador was interested in what the Roman prelates felt about life after death, but his mission was to put off that death for as long as possible in the Middle East. He left for Genoa, where he was well received, but Genoa was busily engaged in its wars against the navies of Venice and Aragon.

Philip IV of France gave him a warm welcome in Paris, even promising to send a Crusade, but declined to pinpoint a date. Others told Rabban Sauma that Philip was preoccupied at the moment in his continental war with Edward I of England. The English king, who he found at Bordeaux, also welcomed the Mongol ambassador and reminisced with him about his own journey to the Holy Land as a Crusader in his younger days. Edward also talked agreeably about a Crusade, but he offered nothing concrete that Rabban Sauma could relate to his Mongol master.

In February 1288 Rabban Sauma received the news that Pope Nicholas IV had been elected to the papal throne. He dropped everything to get to Rome. Once more he was met with a warm welcome, weasel-words, and hollow, ill-defined assurances of interest. The papacy, too, was at war, trying to restore the Angevin rule in Sicily, in which it had such a substantial investment. A few weeks later Rabban Sauma returned home to Ilkhan Argun, dejected in spirit, unhappy to bear the bad news that there was absolutely no hope of a Mongol-Christian alliance and no hope of a new Crusade.

Argun tried again two years later with personal letters to the Christian monarchs in Europe. He proposed launching a campaign against the Muslims in January of 1291. In exchange for Christian support with men and military supplies, the Christians would have the entire Holy Land as their reward. He got nowhere, nor did he do any better with the Latin Christians of the Crusader states, whose very lives Argun felt were in grave danger. They wanted no part of him and no part of any war. They were leading comfortable, profitable lives off Muslim trade and had no desire to disrupt this state of affairs. They were convinced that trade was as important to the Muslims as it was to them and took complete comfort in their written treaty with Kala'un.

Then, early in 1289, Grand Master William de Beaujeu received a disturbing secret message from Emir al-Fakhri, an official at the Egyptian court in Cairo who was on the Templar payroll. Al-Fakhri's report said that Kala'un was sending a large army to Syria in preparation for an attack on Tripoli. The grand master immediately shared the information with the leaders of Tripoli. He advised them to inspect and repair their defenses and to gather men and supplies in readiness for a Muslim assault. No one believed him and nothing was done, but the grand master was so confident of his information that he dispatched a contingent of Knights Templar for what he was certain was an imminent attack. Only time, and precious little time, would tell if the Templar intelligence was accurate.

27

The Fall of Acre
1289 to 1291

THE TEMPLAR GRAND MASTER knew a great deal more about the situation than he had revealed to the citizens of Tripoli. He knew that Sultan Kala'un had actually been invited by a group of Christians to attack the city, in the culmination of a pathetic tangle of local politics.

Bohemond VII had died in October of 1287. The rightful heiress was his sister Lucia, who was living in Italy, but the local leaders wanted no part of absentee rule. They offered the county to the dowager princess Sibylla of Armenia. She accepted, and immediately tried to bring back the governor she had appointed during her prior term as regent. He was the thoroughly disliked Bishop Bartholomew of Tortosa, whose prior actions had called down the wrath of Templar grand master de Beaujeu. Lucia would not back down when the local barons and merchants objected. The local leaders responded by declaring that the royal line was deposed and that the government would henceforth rest in a Commune, as it did in Acre. They had the full support of the Templars, who detested the bishop. As mayor, they elected Bartholomew Embriaco. He could be counted on to show no sympathy for Bohemond's family, since his brother William was that cousin of Guy of Jebail who had been condemned to death and buried up to his neck in a ditch by Bohemond VII.

In 1288 the rightful heiress, Countess Lucia, arrived from Italy to assert her claim to Tripoli. The Commune didn't want to surrender its newfound power, so petitioned the doge of Genoa to accept Tripoli as a Genoese protectorate, with the Commune governing the city. The Genoese, who were delighted to get control of an important trading center, approved the petition, then dispatched five war galleys to help enforce it. Venice backed Countess Lucia, naturally opposing any move by Genoa. The Knights Templar asserted their support for the position of their Venetian allies.

A mysterious embassy of Christians soon arrived at the Egyptian court, begging Kala'un to intervene in Tripoli. The envoys made the point that if the Genoese controlled Tripoli, they would seriously impair Egyptian trading at Alexandria. The sultan was delighted with their request, because the invitation was an excellent excuse to violate the truce he had signed with Tripoli. The embassy was mysterious because there is no record of the names of the envoys or the parties they represented. The grand master's secretary, the Templar of Tyre, indicated that their names were known. The fact that neither he nor the grand master would reveal them probably means that they were Venetians, whom the Templars would shield from condemnation for triggering a war.

There was no question in Grand Master de Beaujeu's mind that such a war was coming, and soon, but he could get no one in Tripoli to believe him. The city's leaders had complete faith in their treaty of peace with Kala'un. Caught in an intrigue that he could not reverse, de Beaujeu could only warn the Commune and help with men and supplies. He even sent the Templar marshal, Brother Geoffrey de Vendac, to lead the Knights Templar in the defense of Tripoli.

Perhaps if he had shared all he knew, the grand master would have been believed. He gained full credibility, but too late, when men galloped into Tripoli from the frontier to announce that a great Muslim army was headed their way. As the news went out to the other Christian territories, Hugh of Cyprus sent a group of knights under his younger brother Amalric. French soldiers, no longer guarding the castle for Odo Poilechien, were sent up from Acre. Both the Venetians and the Genoese had galleys in the harbor, which were used to evacuate their own women and children to Cyprus.

In March 1289 tens of thousands of Muslims circled the city to the beats and blasts of hundreds of drums and trumpets. Wagons were unloaded, and soon nineteen stone-throwing catapults were assembled and ready to begin a steady bombardment of the walls. Fifteen hundred miners were on hand with all the tools of their trade, but as it turned out, they weren't needed. The catapults delivered all the blows necessary.

A corner tower fell first, and then a tower between it and the sea. The Venetians were the first to flee with their soldiers, but only after cramming their ships with all the trade goods they would hold. The Genoese soon followed, and the people left behind were now petrified with fear. The Italians had taken away most of the means of escape. When the news was brought to Kala'un that the

Italians were loading up and sailing away, he moved quickly. Tripoli was known to be full of goods that the sultan had expected to take. The city had grown famous for its luxurious silks and cloth of gold, produced by over four thousand household looms. Kala'un knew the Italian merchants well enough to know that their ships would be carrying silks, not souls, and determined to stop the flow of goods from the city. He ordered an immediate and general assault. Muslims met only scattered resistance as they came over the crumbled walls on all sides to open the gates to the rest of their army.

Amalric of Cyprus had come with four galleys, which he now loaded with his own knights and soldiers to flee the city, taking with him the Templar marshal de Vendac, the bishop of Tripoli, and the terror-stricken Countess Lucia. De Vendac left his Templar brother, Peter de Mocado, in charge of the Knights Templar. He was killed, along with other Christian knights, trying to hold back the Muslims in the streets. When the Muslims had killed every man they encountered in the streets, the house-to-house search began. The all-too-familiar aftermath took hold as the healthy children and healthy women suitable for slavery were bound and taken outside the walls, while every one else was slaughtered. A little island off-shore held a few houses surrounding the church of St. Thomas, to which some of the refugees had fled in small boats. The Muslims followed them, and the whole bloody process was repeated. The young emir Abu'l-Fida of Homs was there and recorded in his diary, "I myself rode out to the island on a boat after the carnage, but was unable to stay, so strong was the stench of the corpses."

After the tons of loot were taken outside, the sultan ordered the entire city and its walls taken down, stone by stone. Tripoli ceased to exist, which cannot be what the Venetian envoys had in mind when they asked Kala'un to get involved in the internal squabbles of the city. As for the Knights Templar, they had lost a body of experienced fighting men that they could ill afford to lose.

The Christians at Acre were numb with shock. They had found security in the totally false notion that their importance to Muslim trade was a great shield that would protect them from harm. What could they believe now? Were they about to lose their fortunes, their families, perhaps their own lives? Where could they turn? And so they went weak with relief when Kala'un volunteered to give the kingdoms of Cyprus and Jerusalem a pledge of peace for ten years.

King Hugh signed the truce along with everyone else, but it is to his credit that he had strong doubts about Kala'un's sincerity. Hugh sent ambassadors to the pope and to the major monarchs of Europe to stress the need for help if the Holy Land was to be saved. They were given polite and patient hearings, but had to report back that there was no realistic basis for expecting a new Crusade. The Holy Land, as it turned out, would have been better off without the only help that did come.

A mob of unemployed soldiers and peasants from northern Italy volunteered for service in the Holy Land. They were not the sort of military aid that was needed, but they were the only group that offered to go. The Venetians, who had a substantial stake in Acre, provided the ships to transport them. They were an ill-disciplined rabble and a source of trouble from the moment they arrived. They had come to kill Muslims, and the only Muslims they saw were walking the streets and hawking their wares in the marketplace, which angered the northern Italians. They had expected to be paid for their services, but no pay was forthcoming. As is almost always the way with unpaid soldiers, they drifted into thieving, drinking, and general debauchery. One day, for reasons long forgotten, a few of them got into a street fight with a group of Muslims. More and more men rushed to the aid of both sides, and soon a full-scale riot took over the streets. Fists gave way to clubs and knives. The Knights Templar and the Hospitallers both tried to rescue the outnumbered Muslims and to curb the fighting by arresting the apparent leaders, but it took a long time to get the bloodthirsty mob under control.

The families of the slain Muslims needed protection and longed for vengeance. Only one man could give them both, so a group of them made the long journey to Cairo. In the time set aside in every Muslim court for the petitions of the people, the group from Acre came forward, wailing for their dead and crying out for the blood of the murderers. One by one they laid the blood-soaked robes of their slaughtered relatives in front of Kala'un. The sultan, openly outraged, promised them that they would have the justice they sought. In private, he exulted that the stupid Christians had broken the truce, removing any barrier to their final destruction. He dispatched orders throughout Egypt and into Syria to see to the inspection of every siege engine in his kingdom. He ordered that the material be prepared to build scaling ladders and battering rams. To give all his acts the appearance of justice and the sanction of law in the face of a written treaty of peace, he went through the motions of a diplomatic solution, expecting and hoping that it would not work. He wrote to Christian leaders, demanding that the Italian offenders in their prison be turned over to him for trial and punishment.

The Venetians had brought the guilty soldiers to the Holy Land and felt that their surrender to Muslim justice would reflect poorly on Venice. They urged that the sultan's demand be rejected. For once, the Knights Templar took a position opposite to that of Venice. Grand Master de Beaujeu knew Kala'un's intentions and urged that the offenders be given to the Muslims. The penalty for refusal would be the destruction of Acre. He was shouted down with angry allegations: The grand master was a coward; the Knights Templar were more interested in their financial transactions with the Muslims than in the safety of Christians; the Templars had lost their love for Christ and the True Cross.

Some saw the grand master's wisdom, but more did not. The angry debate spread outside the hall to the people in the streets. Soon thousands of demonstrators were chanting and screaming their objections to the surrender of any Christian to any Muslim. In the end, a placid letter was dispatched to Kala'un, expressing regret for the unfortunate incident and hiding behind the point that the Venetians alone were responsible for the offending soldiers, not the kingdom of Jerusalem nor the Commune of Acre. Kala'un was pleased with the reply and with the time it had taken, because while the Christian leaders had been shouting at each other, the sultan had been preparing for war.

The Egyptian preparations in Syria were too obvious to be hidden, so the sultan hoped to put the Christians off their guard by announcing that he was planning an expedition up the Nile to punish the Sudanese and Nubians, who were delinquent in their annual tributes of black slaves and gold. The emir al-Fakhri, the Templar spy at the court of Kala'un, got a message to Grand Master de Beaujeu advising him to ignore all talk of a campaign into Africa. The real target was the city of Acre.

Once more the grand master shared his information with the leaders of the kingdom, and once more his intelligence was rejected. He had declined to side with the Venetians in the matter of the jailed murderers, so they declined to support him now. The Templar master knew that his information was accurate and that Acre was doomed. Failing to find any support, he decided to act on his own, sending Templar envoys to Kala'un to try to negotiate the Christians away from total destruction. Kala'un pointed out that he wanted the city, not the citizens, and agreed that every man, woman, and child could leave unmolested in exchange for a number of Venetian gold sequins (*zecchine*) equal to the total Christian population of Acre.

The sultan's demand was not impossible to meet, so de Beaujeu called for a meeting of the leaders of the city. He presented Kala'un's proposal and advised that they should accept. The response was an eruption of furious abuse. Insults were hurled at the grand master, along with accusations of treachery and cowardice. As he stomped from the hall, the shouted insults followed him out through the doors.

A few days later the news from Cairo brought another round of abuse to be heaped on William de Beaujeu: If the Commune of Acre had listened to the Templar grand master it would have been guilty of the crime of releasing Christian rioters to Muslim vengeance. If the grand master had had his own way, the citizens would have abandoned their mighty city and have paid good gold for the privilege. The grand master had wanted them to exhaust their resources preparing for war. The grand master had been shouting into the wind, because news had arrived that Sultan Kala'un was dead.

The news was true. As he had rested in camp ready to lead his army to Acre, the aging sultan had died in his tent. An old man for the times, well over seventy years old, his health had been failing for months. The smug leaders in Acre, however, should not have relaxed their guard. The Egyptian army was ready, and so was Kala'un's son, al-Ashraf Khalil, who assumed the sultanate. He picked up the reins of authority, saw to the ceremonial burial of his father, and told his emirs that he would keep his sacred vow to his father that the war against the Christians would go forward. It was welcome news to his army, but by now it was the middle of winter. The emirs advised that the campaign wait for spring and al-Ashraf Khalil agreed.

The leaders at Acre wanted a statement from al-Ashraf Khalil as to his intentions. The embassy they sent to Cairo was made up of the Templar knight Brother Bartholomew, a Hospitaller knight, an Arabic-speaking layman, and a secretary to handle any document preparation that might be required. The ambassadors never got to present themselves to the young sultan, who knew that they were coming and didn't care what they had to say. As soon as the envoys entered Cairo, they were arrested and taken to the dungeons. The only news about them that got back to Acre was that they were all dead. In a sense, it might be said that their mission was successful. There could hardly have been a clearer statement of the sultan's intentions than the murder of the Christian envoys before they had even had a chance to explain why they had come, but the point seems to have escaped the Commune of Acre, which did not prepare for the inevitable assault.

In March 1291 the Egyptian army was on the move, with orders to the Syrian army to meet them in front of Acre. Emir Abu'l-Fida went to Kerak to take charge of a huge catapult built for the siege. Called *al-Mansour,* "Victorious," it required a hundred wagons to carry its parts and supplies and took a whole month to travel a distance normally covered in a week.

The derision heaped on the Templar grand master now became

pleas to him to save the city. The Knights Templar did make up the largest body of knights in Acre, but the total Christian army was hopelessly inadequate to face the Muslim horde. Including the Templars, there were fewer than eight hundred knights and about fourteen thousand men-at-arms and foot soldiers, even counting the several thousand undisciplined troops from northern Italy. Against them was an army ten times their number, with sixty thousand cavalry and a hundred thousand foot soldiers.

As important as any other military factor, the huge Muslim army was under a single commander, while the Christians in Acre were made up of seventeen separate factions, each claiming some degree of sovereignty. The Templars and Hospitallers were ready, but the small body of Teutonic Knights was embarrassed that their grand master had resigned in the threat of attack, although they did manage to elect a successor before the Muslim army arrived. Pisa and Venice were prepared to defend their property, but the Genoese, seeing no profit in helping their rivals, loaded their goods and their people and sailed away. Knights and soldiers were sent by King Hugh of Cyprus, commanded by the king's brother Amalric. A party of English knights was commanded by Otto de Grandson, a Swiss officer in the service of King Edward I.

Acre was on a point of land bounded by the sea to the south and west. The landward side to the north and east was protected by double walls of stone, with the outer wall fortified by ten great towers. As imposing as they were, those towers offered only temporary protection, because al-Ashraf had brought with him enough engineers to provide a thousand miners for each of the ten towers, supported by a huge wagon train of tunnel supports and foundation timbers. Above ground, ninety-two Muslim catapults were set up facing the wall, supplied with huge stones to batter the walls and great clay pots of incendiaries to lob over those walls onto men and buildings. The mammoth catapult "Victorious" was positioned near the sea to batter the north wall, the sector defended by the Knights Templar. The bombardment started on April 6.

The Egyptians had not sent their fleet, so the Christians did have free use of the harbor to receive supplies. One Christian ship was fitted with a catapult and sailed along the shore east of the city causing considerable damage to the Muslim camp there. Unfortunately, the moving target the Muslims could not hit was the victim of natural disaster, as an offshore storm collapsed the catapult and broke up the ship.

The Knights Templar on the north wall were frustrated by simply standing and taking blows, with no opportunity to strike back. They decided to make a mounted sortie into the Muslim camp in front of them to set fire to the great catapult that was hammering their wall. Otto de Grandson asked to join them with his small group of English knights. On the night of April 15 mounted knights filled the street in front of the St. Lazarus gate. At the marshal's signal, the gates were opened to three hundred war-horses that broke into a thunderous gallop as soon as they were outside.

The knights cut their way through the outer guard but did not succeed in reaching the catapult, because they rode through the Muslim camp. In the darkness, their horses tripped on the maze of tent ropes. Every knight who was knocked from his horse was killed where he fell. The others counted themselves lucky to get out of the tangled web of ropes and back to the city. Abu'l-Fida, who was in that Muslim sector, remembered the raid:

"[One] night, a group of Franj made an unexpected sortie and advanced as far as our camp, but in the darkness some of them tripped on the tent cords. One knight fell into the latrine ditch and was killed. Our troops recovered and attacked the Franj from all sides, forcing them to withdraw to the city after leaving a number of dead on the field. The next morning my cousin, al-Malik al-Muzaffar, lord of Hama, had the heads of some dead Franj attached to the necks of the horses we had captured and presented them to the sultan."

Perhaps the Hospitallers meant to show the Templars how it should be done when they decided to mount their own midnight raid. Later that month they charged out through the St. Anthony gate in their own sector, but now the Muslims were ready with torches and brush piles. As the Hospitallers attacked, the fires were lit. In plain view, they were easily beaten off and they scurried back into the city. There were no more attempts at raids under cover of darkness.

The incessant pounding against the walls, the great bursts of fire day and night and the flights of thousands of arrows at a time demoralized the Christians, so it was with great joy that they received King Hugh of Cyprus on May 4. The king had used forty ships to bring two thousand soldiers to the beleaguered city, and he also brought the first semblance of a central command. Walls were beginning to crack, mines were being driven toward the towers, and the fields outside the city were covered by a sea of Muslim soldiers, so Hugh decided that diplomacy was at least worth a try. He dispatched an embassy of two knights to al-Ashraf, one of whom was the Arabic-speaking Knight Templar Guillaume de Cafran.

The sultan met them in front of his tent to ask if they had come to surrender the city. He reminded them that his father Kala'un had informed the Templar grand master months earlier that it was the

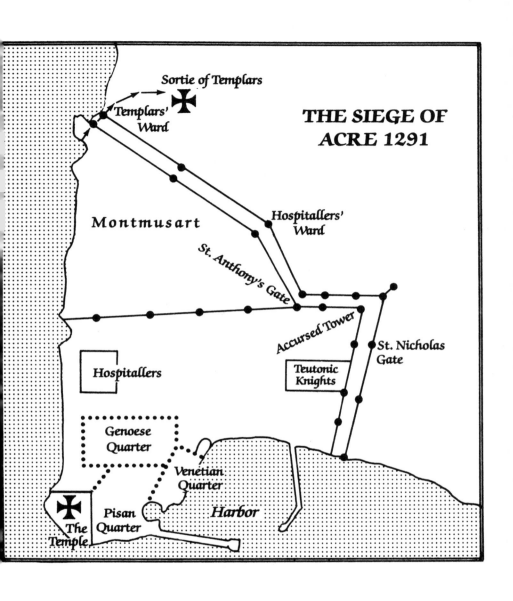

THE SIEGE OF
ACRE 1291

Sortie of Templars

'Templars'
Ward

Montmusart

Hospitallers'
Ward

St. Anthony's Gate

Accursed Tower

St. Nicholas
Gate

Hospitallers

Teutonic
Knights

Genoese
Quarter

Venetian
Quarter

Pisan
Quarter

Harbor

The
Temple

city of Acre he wanted, and not the people inside. They could leave unharmed if they would surrender the city. Before the envoys could reply, a huge stone from a Christian catapult landed just a few feet away, shaking the earth under their feet. Enraged, the sultan drew his sword to kill the Christians on the spot, but he was restrained by his emirs, who advised the two knights to leave quickly.

Within two weeks of King Hugh's arrival, Muslim miners reached the towers in the outer wall and set fire to the naphtha-soaked supporting timbers. As they burned away, one tower after another began to crack and crumble. On May 16 the Muslims forced their way into the ruined tower where the outer north wall met the eastern wall and fought their way along the top to force the Christians in that sector back to the inner wall.

On the morning of Friday, May 18, the sultan ordered all of the great kettledrums of the Muslim army brought to one place. Mounted on three hundred camels, their deafening message of doom carried to every corner of the city as they sent out the signal for a general assault on the walls. The Muslim attack was deliberately launched on every part of the wall to keep the Christian defenders spread out, but it was concentrated on the aptly named tower where the northern and eastern inner walls were joined: the Accursed Tower. The Muslims took it by the pressure of overwhelming numbers. Grand Master de Beaujeu led a party of his Templar knights to try to get it back.

His Muslim enemies might have called it *Kismet*, fate, and a Christian might have tried to find a reason to call it the will of God, but an incredible set of coincidences struck down the grand master. Muslim archers were launching thousands of arrows over the wall blindly, hoping that some would find Christian targets. As the Templar grand master raised his sword arm for a few seconds to strike an enemy, he exposed one small part of his body not protected by his chain mail. One of those randomly fired arrows found his momentarily exposed armpit and drove into his chest.

As Templar Knights took him away from the battle, a group of Crusader knights saw him leaving and begged him not to flee from the fight. Struggling to reply, the grand master said, "*Seigneurs, je ne plus, car je suys mort. Vees le coup.*" ("Gentlemen, I can do no more, I am dead. See the wound.") His followers got him back to the Temple across the city, where he died before the day was out.

Up on the inner wall, the Muslims fought their way south along the top to open the St. Nicholas gate in the Hospitaller sector. Then there poured through the gate an endless stream of turbaned swordsmen, pushing the battle line back into the narrow streets. In those crowded corridors a few men could slow down a larger force, but there were too many streets and too large a Muslim force to completely stop the advance. Such time as the Christian street fighters bought with their blood was used by others to escape.

The Hospitaller grand master took a wound and, protesting that he could still fight, was forcibly taken to the harbor by his knights, who put him on a ship. King Hugh and his brother Amalric gathered up their vassals, boarded their ships, and fled to Cyprus. Otto de Grandson commandeered Venetian galleys, filled them with his English soldiers, and then followed them on board. Civilians and soldiers fought over the rowboats and fishing craft in the harbor, hoping to reach the ships standing offshore. His friends found a small boat for the patriarch Nicolas de Hanape, but that good man invited so many Christians to share it with him that the boat sank, drowning them all. A Templar Knight, Roger Flor, oblivious to the heroism and sacrifice of his brothers, took the opportunity to amass a huge personal fortune as he commandeered a Templar galley moored dockside. His target was the wives of the nobles and wealthy merchants, now frantic with fear. They were told that the price of rescue was all of the gold and jewels that they had managed to carry from their homes. Hundreds of women and children who could not make it to the harbor found refuge in the Templar fortress.

As more and more of the Christian knights and soldiers left the fight to get away, those few who had chosen to stand firm could not hold the Muslims in check. Cutting down the Christians in front of them, the victorious Muslims swarmed through every street and every square, into homes, churches, warehouses, and factories. The first hours were spent killing every Christian man of every age, including those in the wailing mob in the harbor area that had not been able to get into boats. Plunder was next on their list. Following their traditional pattern, they took into slavery every female and every young boy who could walk. Older women and infants were slaughtered. When the butchery died away, the only Christian men left alive in the city were a group of about two hundred Knights Templar in their fortress headquarters. They chose to stay and fight rather than to abandon the women and children who had come to them for protection.

The Temple was at the extreme southwest corner of the city, with two sides facing the sea. It was possible to get additional supplies by boat, but no one thought to bring them. Following the tactic that had been successful against the city walls and towers, the sultan ordered his miners to start driving tunnels to the Temple foundations.

After five days al-Ashraf Khalil was growing impatient that his plans were being held up by just one building. He sent an envoy with a proposal to Templar Peter de Severy, who was in command of the castle. If the Templars would surrender the fortress, the lives of everyone inside would be spared. The Templars could keep their weapons, and they could take away with them anything they could carry. Many of the Templars wanted to fight on, but the safety of the women and children had to be the first consideration. De Severy agreed to the terms, and the gates were opened to receive an emir with a party of about a hundred Mamelukes who would monitor the surrender.

Once inside, the arrogant and overbearing posturing of the victorious Mamelukes finally gave way to raw lust, as they began to sexually abuse the women and the young boys. The Knights Templar exploded in outrage, drew the swords they had been allowed to keep, and killed every Mameluke who had been sent among them. The gate was barred and the sultan's flag was replaced by the banner of the Templars, as the knights shouted from the walls that the fight was now to the death. When darkness came, de Severy provided an escort for Tibald de Gaudin, the Templar treasurer, who took a boat moored at the sea-gate to the Temple. He loaded the Templar treasury, along with a few mothers and their children, then sailed north up the coast to the Castle of the Sea at Sidon.

A conciliatory embassy came from the sultan the next morning. Regrets were expressed, apologies were offered, and the sultan asked to have the privilege of receiving the Templar commander so that he might apologize in person. He would give his personal promise that the surrender terms would be observed in full, with all respect shown to the Christians in the Temple. Peter de Severy selected several Templars to accompany him. As soon as his party reached the Muslims waiting to take them to the sultan, the Knights Templar were seized, forced to their knees, and beheaded in full view of their brothers watching from the Temple.

On the surface it appeared to be a stalemate, but underground the sultan's miners had reached the Temple foundations. They widened their tunnels under the two landward sides of the great building, supporting the foundation with massive timbers as they drove forward. When all was ready the timbers were doused with naphtha and the miners pulled out, setting fire to the timbers as they moved back. On May 28 the foundation began to collapse as the walls above it tumbled down, now partially supported by charred and still blazing timbers. The sultan ordered a storming party of two thousand men across the breach and into the fortress, but their additional weight on the fallen stones completed the collapse of the foundation. The entire massive building came crashing down, crushing the life from everyone inside, Christian and Muslim alike.

When the walls of Acre were breached on May 18, al-Ashraf knew that the victory was his, although he didn't need and couldn't use his entire army. They were too numerous to be entirely accommodated in Acre, so he detached part of his forces and sent them northward to the city of Tyre. Tyre was ruled by the king's brother, Amalric of Cyprus, who had gone to Acre. He had assigned a Cypriot noble as its governor, who showed no heart for a fight and no desire to die away from home. As soon as the Muslim army was sighted, the governor of Tyre sailed back to Cyprus. No one made any effort to keep the Mamelukes from taking possession of the city, along with everything and everyone in it. The Muslim commander, Emir Shujai, sent messengers to the sultan to report another victory for Allah.

Proceeding northward, Shujai's army moved from Tyre to Sidon. Templar treasurer Tibald de Gaudin was there in the offshore Castle of the Sea, with the Templar treasure he had brought from Acre. It was there that he learned that the surviving Knights Templar had elected him their twenty-second grand master. Now he loaded the treasure on a Templar galley and sailed to Cyprus. He left behind his promise that he would return with reinforcements, but none ever came.

Standing on an outcropping of rock offshore, the castle was too far from the shore for catapults and impossible to mine, since any tunnel would be in constant danger of flooding. Instead, the Muslim engineers began to construct a broad causeway out to the castle. It would be used to get catapults closer to their target, or even to take troops with scaling ladders right up to the walls. As the causeway came closer every day, it became obvious that there was no hope for the castle or its garrison, so the Templar commander ordered his knights into their ships. They headed even farther northward to reinforce the Templar castle at Tortosa. The Mamelukes entered the Castle of the Sea on July 14, and Emir Shujai had another victory to report to al-Ashraf. He set his engineers to work, and soon the great stones that had taken months of backbreaking labor to shape and lift up to the high walls and towers were dropping into the sea.

Still moving north, Shujai took his army to the walled city of Beirut. Since a treaty between Beirut and Cairo was still in effect, the Christians of Beirut clung to the hope that they would not be dragged into this war. They leaped at the chance when an envoy from Emir Shujai invited the leaders to a feast at his pavilion as his honored guests. As soon as the Christians were all inside, dressed and scented for the banquet, they were made prisoners. Deprived of leadership, neither citizens nor soldiers knew how to react. They panicked. They grabbed what they could of the most valuable possessions, including the holy relics from the cathedral, and ran to the harbor, where they boarded anything that would float to get away from the ruthless Mamelukes.

Well content to have taken the city with no struggle at all, Shujai led his forces through the gates on July 31. It was well that the holy relics had been removed, because all Christian ornaments and decorations were stripped from the cathedral, which was consecrated as a mosque. The city walls were torn down.

As Shujai conducted the successful drive to the north, al-Ashraf led an army southward. His principal target was the port city of Haifa, which put up no real defense. On the day before Shujai entered Beirut, al-Ashraf had taken Haifa. His Islamic convictions were offended by the presence of a nearby Christian religious community, so he sent a troop of cavalry to the monastery at the top of Mount Carmel. Giving no quarter, the troops butchered every Christian monk, and after taking anything of value they burned down the monastery buildings.

Now all that was left of the entire crusading effort in the Holy Land were the two strongest castles of the Knights Templar: Tortosa, far to the north, and Castle Pilgrim at Athlit, to the south. As an order the Templars had been born to protect the Crusader states, but now there were no Crusader states. They had been born to protect the Christian pilgrims to the Holy Places, but now there were no pilgrims. The Templars were here and they could still fight, but for what? They were without purpose and without hope.

On August 4 the Templars at Tortosa loaded whatever they could get on their ships, and abandoned their castle to join the grand master on Cyprus. Ten days later the Templars at Athlit followed the same course. After they sailed away from Castle Pilgrim on that day, August 14, 1291, there was not a single Latin Christian in the Holy Land who was not in hiding or in chains.

The Templars kept their castle on the island of Ruad, about two miles off the coast near Tortosa, but it was of no value and difficult to supply. Even the drinking water had to be brought in by ship. After a few years it was simply abandoned to whomever might wish to move in.

The Arab historian Abu'l-Fida ended his summary of the situation with a prayer:

"With these conquests, all the lands of the coast were fully returned to the Muslims, a result undreamed of. Thus were the Franj ...expelled from all of Syria and the coastal zones. May God grant that they never set foot there again!"

He got his wish. The Crusades were over.

As for the Knights Templar, they were without a base in the Holy

Land for the first time since the order was founded in the aftermath of the First Crusade. For them, it appeared that life could not be darker, but that was because they could not foresee the tragedies and tortures that would be heaped upon them just a few years later by King Philip IV of France and Pope Clement V.

28

"Jesus Wept"
1292 to 1305

$\mathcal{A}$FTER GRAND MASTER Tibald de Gaudin had sailed away from Sidon to Cyprus, promising to return with supplies and reinforcements he had made no effort to keep his word. He had provided no leadership in the Templars' blackest hour, so no one missed him when he died the following year. It was a crucial time and called for a strong leader.

There were two principal candidates. First was Hugh de Peraud, the Templar treasurer and a consummate politician, who had developed a good personal relationship with King Philip IV of France, including loans to Philip from the Templar treasury. He was favored by the Templars from the south of France, who had grown to be the majority within the order. The northern French Templars were uncomfortable with their southern brothers; they had the easier style of their countrymen, with an interest in books and poetry, which had no place in the life of a fighting man. The northeners backed a Templar from the lower nobility of Burgundy who had been a Templar knight for all of his adult life. He had served well on the battlefield and just as well in administration during his term as the master of Templars in England. His name was Jacques de Molay.

The contest was close and grew so heated that the Templars sought the unusual recourse of asking the grand master of the Hospitallers to help them arrive at a rational settlement of their differences. With his help, grand chapter met again with the result that Jacques de Molay became the twenty-third and last grand master of the Knights of the Temple.

As the new grand master looked around him, there was not much good to see. With the Holy Land gone, the Templars were based at Cyprus, but they were not welcome in the island kingdom they had once had all to themselves. Had they hung onto it, they would now be the masters of this kingdom, but having sold away their rights to the Lusignans, they were simply unwelcome guests.

Just how unwelcome was made clear when King Henry of Cyprus informed de Molay that the king was the sole and supreme commander of all of the military forces in his kingdom, which most definitely included the Knights Templar. In response, the grand master informed the king that the Templar grand master was the sole and supreme commander of the Knights Templar, no matter where they were located, and that the Templar grand master took orders from no man on earth except the supreme pontiff in Rome, and that further the Knights Templar were not subject to the laws of Cyprus or any decrees of its monarch. A very high-level shouting match went on whenever they met, and their attitudes began to seep down to their followers. Finally, to avoid open clashes, it was agreed to put the dispute to Pope Boniface VIII. The pope ruled in favor of the grand master, admonishing King Henry that he should be grateful to have the valiant Templars in his island kingdom because of the added protection in the event of a Muslim invasion.

The grand master reveled in the papal decision and earned a begrudging measure of respect from some of the Templars who didn't like de Molay's style of leadership. The morale of the Templars was miserably low when de Molay took command, and he was of the military school that believes morale is directly tied to discipline. No wonder morale was so low, he told them, with their Rule subject to sloppy enforcement or none at all. He bombarded his men with corrective measures and saw to it that they were obeyed. Templars' effects were searched, and all written matter was seized, whether a letter from home or a page of scripture. Illiterate himself, de Molay had never found it necessary to read anything. If there were letters or orders or even papal decrees, there were brother clerics to read them out loud. If a knight received a letter, it was read to him in front of his commander and not given up to him. Items of non-official clothing or equipment were ordered to be disposed of. All religious duties were to be performed exactly as prescribed by the Rule. The dining hall rules were reinforced, and the laxity removed from the stables, the shops, and the training ground. De Molay was getting ready for the next Crusade.

Without another Crusade to recover the Holy Places, the Knights Templar had no purpose, no reason to continue to exist. They were dedicated and experienced, but too few to accomplish anything alone. That had become clear in the total failure of an attempt to retake the castle of Tortosa and an abortive expedition with local barons to try to capture Alexandria. The only answer was for the pope at Rome to call a full Crusade supported by all the Christian monarchs of Europe. The Knights Templar would take their honored place in the vanguard to lead the army of God to put the Holy Cross back on the Temple Mount in Jerusalem. The grand master spent all of his spare hours working on the grand plan, apparently with no knowledge or appreciation of the events back home that were working against his vision of renewed glory.

In the months following the loss of Acre and the Holy Land, Pope Nicholas IV had died, and the rivalry within the Curia had caused the cardinals to ignore the strict rules regarding the election of a new pope. Had they not, they would all have starved to death, because a year and a half later they were still debating and maneuvering. The problem was the Roman perception of the role of the pope. To the rest of the Christian world, he was the pope, first and last. To the Roman people, he was first the bishop of Rome. As the bishop of the diocese of the Blessed St. Peter, he was entitled, as the successor to Peter, to be the pope. Since he was their bishop, the Romans felt that they had the right to name the man to fill the seat, as people in other lands often picked their own bishops.

Over the years, power had gradually evolved into major factions led by two Roman families, the Colonna and the Orsini, each of which could claim great wealth, partially attributable to their constant presence as priests, bishops, cardinals and popes. The deceased pope had been of the Orsini clan, who did not want to relinquish their profitable power center. The Colonna were determined to regain that power for themselves. At the time, two of the nine cardinal-electors were Colonna.

After one more long and weary day of haggling, the dean, Cardinal Malabranca, told the others that he had received a letter from the holy hermit on Mount Morrone in the Abruzzi, prophesying severe divine vengeance on all of them if they delayed any longer in selecting a pope. Pietro of Morrone conjured up remembrances of the ancient hair-shirted, self-flagellating hermits of the Egyptian desert. He starved himself, whipped himself, and abandoned all human pleasures, and so was perceived as a very holy man. Pilgrims traveled to see him, and followers gathered to the point of establishing a new order around him dedicated to the Holy Spirit, whose members called themselves the Spirituals. It was an apt name because Pietro let them have no pleasures other than the spiritual. He wouldn't even let them laugh, pointing out that although Scripture said that "Jesus wept," it never said that He laughed. It was an easy rule to follow, because under Pietro's stern discipline they had almost nothing to laugh about. To get further from the world,

Pietro had moved his flock deeper and deeper into the mountains, until he now occupied a cell in a cave high up on Mount Morrone.

To the assembled cardinals, the most interesting thing about the ascetic hermit was that he was over eighty years of age. His frail, underfed body couldn't possibly hold out for much longer. They decided to do what cardinals had done before and would do again: They would postpone the solution to their political dilemma by naming a pope who had little time to live, no program of change of his own, and no allegiance to any faction. Cardinal Malabranca articulated their solution with, "In the name of the Father, the Son and the Holy Ghost, I nominate brother Pietro of Morrone." He was elected on the first ballot, much to the relief of Benedetto Gaetani, perhaps the most ambitious of all the cardinals, who had struggled for months to find a basis on which he could have the papal tiara, the object of all his yearnings. This election gave him time to plan better for the next election. He was twenty years younger than Pietro, so he was certain that his time would come.

The delegates who had to make the five-day journey south into the mountains to bring the new pope to Rome were surprised to find King Charles of Naples already there. Charles stated that he was there to personally salute a pope who was a subject of his southern kingdom. It didn't take the delegates long to learn the true purpose of the royal visit. After they finally talked down the old man's objections to being the pope and convinced him that he could not oppose God's will, they brought him down off the mountain expecting to take the new pope to Rome. Instead, King Charles took the new pontiff under his own protection as his entourage took the road home to Naples.

Pietro's coronation, at which he took the papal name of Celestine V, took place on August 29, 1294. About six weeks later he shocked the already confused hierarchy with the announcement that Naples, not Rome, would henceforth be the seat of the papacy. King Charles established him in the lofty Castello Nuovo ("New Castle") that still majestically guards the harbor at Naples. The pope's first order was that a small wooden cell be built for him inside the regal palace.

All of the Church administrators, politicians, and hangers-on hurried to Naples to reap the blessings of God conveyed by this senile old man who signed every document put in front of him, perhaps partly because he could not read the Latin language in which they were all written. Soon Church benefices, appointments, and lands were being dispersed among the greedy gathering. Some even offered for sale formal orders carrying the signature and the seal of the pope, with the top left blank for the purchaser of the document to fill in according to his own ambitions. The French king Charles of Naples was a bit more farsighted than most, and much more ambitious. He planned to get control of the Church away from the Italians permanently. He had Celestine V appoint thirteen new cardinals, of whom three were his own Neapolitan subjects and seven were French prelates selected with advice from his royal cousin, Philip IV of France. As the son of Charles of Anjou, he was eager to maintain a strong alliance with the French royal house from which he had sprung. Packing the college of cardinals was not done for the purpose of effecting an attack on the Knights Templar, but without it that attack might never have come.

There was just one document the pope could sign that would please Benedetto Gaetani, and that would have been his own abdication. Later, the Colonna would spread the story that Gaetani had made a small hole in the wall of Celestine's wooden cell, which he used at night to tell the aged pope, in a low, spooky voice, that this was the voice of an angel sent by God to inform Celestine that he must resign or face the fires of Hell. During the day the apparently kind, concerned Gaetani sympathized with the pope, who yearned for the peace and quiet of his isolated monastic home in the mountains. As a skilled lawyer, Gaetani was able to advise the pope on the various legal and traditional issues involved in contemplating the extraordinary prospect of papal abdication. During the time he spent away from the pope, Gaetani took every opportunity to ingratiate himself with King Charles.

The feast day of Santa Lucia on December 13 was a festive occasion for Neapolitans, who turned the nativity of their patron saint into a day of carnival. It was in the midst of that celebration that Celestine V called his last consistory of cardinals to announce his abdication. He had spent less than four months on the Throne of Peter.

The Orsini and the Colonna were as determined as ever to keep each other's candidates away from the papal throne, but now there was a larger faction, the French. The French cardinals were willing to elect an Italian pope, but only one approved by the French monarchs at Naples and Paris. Charles of Naples had been persuaded to favor Benedetto Gaetani, and since he was not a Colonna, the Orsini went along. The Colonna disagreed, but were defeated. The election process took just four days, after which Gaetani was crowned as Pope Boniface VIII. Within the month he had moved the papacy back to Rome. He had planned to take Celestine V back with him, but friends of the former pope advised him that his life was in danger, and William d'Estanard, the constable of Naples, secretly arranged his escape.

For five months the troops of the papacy and of Charles of Naples searched for the old man. They finally found him on the other side of Italy trying to escape across the Adriatic Sea. He was brought back to Rome in chains, where Boniface VIII ordered that he be confined in the papal prison of Fumone outside the city. The continued veneration of the imprisoned pope was a source of growing anger for Boniface VIII. More and more people were attracted to the principle that no man could simply resign from God's grand design. To them, Celestine V was still the true pope, and an imposter now sat on the Throne of Peter. On May 19, 1296, Boniface arranged to have that principle, and the aging pope, laid to rest. When the executioners came to his cell, the half-starved eighty-six-year-old martyr had no strength to resist. A cushion was pressed against his face until his breathing stopped forever.

The idea that Celestine V was the true pope did not die with him, evoking rage from Boniface, especially when the preservation and promulgation of that idea was traced to the House of Colonna. He attacked the Colonna cardinals, whose calm response was to demand that he step down from the throne that he had gained through fraud and trickery. To teach them who was in charge, Boniface stripped the two Colonna cardinals of all of their revenues and privileges as princes of the Church. They responded by publishing a list of the crimes of Boniface: fraudulent claim to the papacy, theft of Church funds, and a list of irregularities.

The charges of theft were true. Boniface was draining off incredible wealth to enrich his own family, acquiring such vast tracts of land and towns that the holdings of his own family soon rivaled those of the Orsini and Colonna. To him, the Church and its pope were one: What belonged to the Church belonged to the pope. No amount of criticisms or accusations could curtail the rape of the papal treasury.

One who decided to curtail it by himself was Stephen Colonna. He waited in ambush in the hills near Rome on May 3, 1297. The secret information that had brought him here with a group of Colonna mounted soldiers proved to be correct, as a well-protected caravan of mules came through the valley. They were loaded with Church gold being carried off to purchase more lands and towns for the pope's family. The Colonna cavalry rode to the attack, and a few minutes later left the field with the pope's gold.

Boniface's reaction was predictable. Even after Stephen's family pressured him to return the gold, Boniface demanded that the young man be delivered to him for personal punishment, but the Colonna refused. Boniface excommunicated them, with no effect. The common people and a handful of devout nobles might think that the excommunication by the pope would affect God's attitude toward them, but the growing sophistication of secular leaders had convinced them that the excommunication process was simply a papal weapon used to gain a point. More effective was a list of accusations against Boniface nailed to the door of every church in Rome. A copy was even delivered by some Colonna hero to the sacred precinct of the high altar at St. Peter's. The long list of crimes included the murder of Celestine V.

Off on Cyprus, the Templar grand master had been dictating one letter after another beseeching Boniface VIII to call a Crusade, and now the pope did just that. It was not, however, a Crusade against the infidel, but an official holy Crusade against the Colonna family. There was no need for anyone to spend the time and the money to go all the way to the east to earn the spiritual rewards of total remission of sins and an eternity in paradise, because they were available in Italy. And taking up arms in the service of God in this Crusade could well be profitable, since this saintly pope had announced that he wanted nothing for the papacy or the Church: All of the loot taken from the cities and palaces of the Colonna could be kept by the Crusaders who took it. They were free to kill members, friends, followers, or tenants of the Colonna family, regardless of age or sex, or to sell into slavery any of them who might be judged to be more valuable alive than dead. Those who could not come to the great slaughter could earn their own remission of sins by sending a suitable cash contribution to help defray the expenses of the war. And of course, since this was a formal Crusade called by the Holy Father himself, that august leader could now dip both hands into the treasure that had accumulated in Rome from gifts, fines, and penances to finance the next Crusade. As the nobles of Europe watched the pope mount a holy war against his political rivals, Boniface VIII dragged the very concept of the Crusade down into the sewers.

Philip of France stayed away from the pope's Italian Crusade, perhaps as part of the negotiations that had led to Boniface's agreement to the canonization of Philip's grandfather, the crusading King Louis IX. As the descendent of a saint of the Church, Philip had fresh support for his contention that God had chosen him to be king of France.

The rapacious, the ex-soldiers with no jobs, the freebooters, however, answered the call, led by the enthusiastic Orsini, who were delighted to take the lead in wiping out their ancient enemy. E.L. Chamberlain says that Boniface invited the Knights Templar to participate, but there appears to be no record that any of them ever did, nor were they needed. The predatory horde moved across the Colonna territories killing, raping, stealing, and earning their spiritual rewards, until the Colonna were cut down to one remaining property, their ancient city of Palestrina. The city was almost as old as Rome itself and filled with art and treasures from the old Roman empire. The heads of the family were gathered in their last outpost, led by the fierce general Giovanni Colonna, whose lifetime of aggression had earned him the nickname of *Sciarra*, "The Quarreler." He was prepared to fight to the death, but he lost the city to the most effective siege engine of all—treachery.

Boniface assured the Colonna that in exchange for their public apology and their public submission to the papal supremacy, their lives would be spared, as would their remaining property. A papal throne surrounded by all the palatial pageantry of the Church was set up outside the wall of the nearby town of Rieta, to which the Colonna walked as penitents, halters around their necks, to throw themselves at Boniface's feet, saying the words of submission in which they had been instructed. Now, with all of the leaders out of the city, the papal promise could be disregarded and Palestrina could be destroyed. Church historian Malachi Martin wrote that in October 1298, the result was to have "every man, woman, child and animal killed, and every building—except the cathedral—flattened in the town of Palestrina." One of the buildings taken down was the magnificent palace said to have been built by Julius Caesar.

The Colonna went into exile, which led in Sciarra's case to his being captured by Mediterranean pirates. Sciarra was surprised and pleased when his ransom was paid by Philip IV of France, who invited him to Paris. The events of recent years assured a warm welcome at the French court for any sworn enemy of Boniface VIII.

Popes would come and go, but one thing never changed for King Philip IV, called "the Fair" (for his beauty, not for his sense of justice). For all of his adult life Philip had been at war with King Edward I of England, a redoubtable, resourceful enemy with whom a stalemate might be counted as a victory. Edward's tenacious defense, and even extension, of his French lands on the continent cost Philip a never-ceasing outward flow of money. He taxed, borrowed, and confiscated every penny he could, but it was never enough. He even borrowed heavily from the Knights Templar. His envy of the Church in France turned to anger as he saw the bishops and abbots, who controlled a third of the land surface of his kingdom, constantly amassing revenues which they shipped off to Rome. In 1296 Philip decided that they should contribute to the defense of the kingdom off which they were living so well, so he imposed a 10 percent tax on all Church properties and revenues in France.

To Boniface, the tax was a blow to both his authority and to his purse, either one of which could stir up his wrath. He ordered the clergy of France to ignore the unauthorized tax. Philip responded by prohibiting any export of gold or silver from France without his specific written authority. The French clergy could continue to collect its revenues, but it couldn't send them to Rome. If the pope felt that he couldn't live with a 10 percent decrease in money from France, let him try to live without any of it. For once in his life Boniface had to compromise, but that didn't mean that he would forget the insult.

In that same year Philip completed arrangements for a peace treaty with Edward I, a treaty that the English king had sought with unusual vigor, because he had a problem of his own that until recently had had nothing to do with Philip. Although he, too, had spend a good part of his life at war with France, Edward also had a running battle with his northern neighbors in Scotland.

His latest campaign into Scotland had been a victory so complete that he had put the Scottish question out of his mind. He had forced every nobleman in Scotland to get on his knees and swear allegiance to the English crown, and to drive the point home he had taken away the sacred Stone of Scone, the ancient coronation stone of the Scottish kings that legend said had been a headrest for St. Columba. He had carpenters make a shelf under the seat of his own throne at Westminster, so now when he sat on the throne of England he was also sitting on the throne of Scotland. The battles to accomplish that end had been so brutal that not one single nobleman in Scotland would dare to raise his hand to Edward of England.

Now word had come that a young Scot from an obscure family, with no military experience whatsoever, had dared to defy the English rulers of his native country. His name was William Wallace.

Starting with two dozen friends behind him, Wallace's guerilla raids aroused the fervor of the common people, who came to him in droves. Soon he was a general in command of tens of thousands of angry Scots who exulted in every minute of their leader's campaign to drive out the hated English overlords. With incredible military genius, Wallace took one town and castle after the other, until even the reluctant nobility recognized his supreme leadership. This Scottish hero was the problem Edward had to deal with now, but he must first have an ironclad treaty with Philip the Fair before he could turn his back on France.

The agreement reached was that the widowed Edward would marry Philip's sister Margaret, while his son Edward, the first Prince of Wales, would marry Philip's daughter Isabella. One thing that stood in the way of the final agreement: the betrothal of Princess

Isabella to Prince Edward called for a substantial dowry payable in cash, and Philip didn't have the money. He turned to his friend Hugh de Peraud, the treasurer of the Knights Templar. Brother Hugh was happy to dip into his order's overflowing coffers to make another loan to Philip, under the very mistaken impression that only good things could come from having the king of France deeper in debt to the Knights of the Temple. He did not detect Philip's deep resentment that the French Templars had more cash than their king. His debts to the Templars were getting heavy, and Philip began to think through a plan whose success would mean that those debts need never be paid.

Traveling back to England, Edward I could be skeptical about the major thrust of his treaty with Philip. The idea behind the betrothal of the Prince of Wales to Isabella of France was that a son from that marriage could inherit both crowns to unite the kingdoms of England and France into one great invincible empire. The problem was that by now it was obvious that Prince Edward was an enthusiastic homosexual. Edward was not at all certain that his son could be encouraged to participate in the unwelcome activities necessary to produce an heir.

In London Edward sent for the master of the Knights Templar in England, Brian de Jay. He told the master of his plans to chastise the upstart William Wallace in Scotland and asked that the Templar Knights go with him to fight for England. The Templar master saw no barrier to committing his knights in a totally secular war that had nothing to do with religion or the True Cross. It had been years since the fighting men of the Temple had had anyone to fight. The calls for men and money no longer came from the headquarters in the East; they had no need for them. No monarch they knew in Europe was going to go on a Crusade, if even the pope should call it, which he wouldn't because the pope had something much more important on his mind. Boniface VIII had come up with a way to increase the papal treasury, a way that could come only once in a hundred years. The following year of 1299 marked the turn of a century, and Boniface would turn the usual secular celebration into a jubilee of joy for all Christians. Now there would be new pathways to the total remission of sins much easier than going off on Crusade. Full absolution was offered to any pilgrim who would come to Rome for fifteen days with his offering for the Church.

Even at his most optimistic, the pope had not foreseen the flood of pilgrims that would bring new prosperity to Rome. The local merchants and innkeepers were delighted with the business generated by almost two million pilgrims. Two priests stood all day and night behind the altar at the Church of St. Paul using rakes to drag away the steady stream of gold and silver offerings placed there by pilgrims who pushed their way through the mob to leave their gifts.

Boniface VIII was ecstatic. He remembered the words said to him as the papal crown had been placed on his head: "Take the tiara, and know that thou art the father of princes and kings, the ruler of the world, the vicar on earth of our Savior Jesus Christ." Now he indeed felt like the "ruler of the world" as he staged a regal pageant. He put on the dress and the insignia of the ancient Roman emperors and went out into the streets with two swords held high in front of him, indicating his supreme authority over both the secular and the spiritual worlds, with heralds crying out, "Behold! I am Caesar!"

With the Jubilee Year behind him, Boniface VIII turned to the problem of the proper discipline for Philip of France. Philip had offended God and the papacy by giving shelter to the excommunicate Colonna and by seizing Church lands and funds, so now Boniface called a council of clergy in Rome to deal with the insubordinate French king. Philip responded with a council of his own, which for the very first time included the third estate, the commoners. Heretofore the councils had included only the first and second estates, the clergy and the nobles, but Philip wanted to be certain of universal support in France. The nobles and commoners quickly asserted their support for the king's contention that he held his crown directly from God, and not from the pope, as Boniface claimed. They exhorted the French cardinals and bishops to rebuke the pope and to stand behind their king. The French clergy were in a terrible bind. They swore their loyalty to the king but pleaded that they also owed loyalty to the Holy Father and must obey his orders to attend his council. Philip absolutely forbade any French prelate to attend a council called to denigrate his king. To disobey would be to risk all his property in France.

The anger of Boniface VIII boiled over to produce one of the most famous and controversial papal bulls in the long course of Christian history. Against the advice of several of his cardinals, Boniface issued the bull *Unam sanctam*, the strongest claim of worldwide papal supremacy ever issued before or since. The bull expressed the pope's position of control over every king and emperor in the world and over every man, woman, and child on the face of the earth, emphasizing that "it is a condition of salvation that all human beings should be subject to the Pontiff of Rome." There could be no stronger statement of the control of one man over all others; it made him unquestionably "the ruler of the world," at least in his own mind.

There is a great difference, of course, between asserting authority and enforcing it. *Unam sanctam* caused many a monarch to raise his eyebrows, but none to drop to his knees. Philip of France stood by his assertion that his right to rule came directly from God and didn't pass through Rome. In response to threats of papal discipline, he called another council, prepared by an unusual man named William de Nogaret, a loyal servant to Philip as lawyer, agent, negotiator, and finally as chancellor. His parents had been burned at the stake as Cathar heretics during the Albigensian Crusade, and the orphaned boy had been turned over to the Church, which saw to his education. The priests who taught him probably thought that they were rescuing a soul for God, but to de Nogaret his religious education was a kind of Know-Your-Enemy course. He went all the way through university training in law, most of which was Church law. Any chance to strike back at the demons from Rome who had condemned his mother and father to the agonizing deaths of being burned alive would help to satisfy a lifelong craving for vengeance.

The eloquent de Nogaret, a master of oratory, stood up at the king's council and explained why Boniface VIII should be universally recognized as unfit to sit on the papal throne. He explained that the Church had been legally married to Pope Celestine V, so that Boniface had committed an unforgivable act of adultery by stealing away the bride of Celestine V while he still lived. The French council agreed. Thus encouraged, de Nogaret came back to them a few months later with twenty-nine charges against the pope, including blasphemy, sodomy, heresy, revealing the secrets of the confessional, stealing Church property, the murder of Celestine V, and even a charge to appeal to the commoner's fascination for sorcery and magic, the allegation that Boniface had secret sexual relations with a filthy demon that lived in his ring.

Dozens of scribes copied the list of charges for dissemination throughout all of Philip's kingdom and to the other Christian monarchs. It brought no response from outsiders, but it had the full support of the French people. It was not surprising that most of the nobility supported de Nogaret's call for papal impeachment, but it was very much a surprise that about twenty bishops agreed as well. Equally surprising was the stand of the Knights Templar of France. The English Templars had agreed to fight for one Christian king against another, but now the French Templars supported the call to impeach their papal commander.

Boniface reacted with his primary spiritual weapon, excommunication of the French king. To his intense frustration, the response in France was to stir up anger toward the pope and sympathy for their king. He then drew his next spiritual weapon, announcing that

on September 8, 1303, he intended to formally put the entire kingdom of France under interdict. That would mean the closing of
every church, no Holy Communion, no baptism, no marriage, no
Christian burial—an entire nation condemned to the fires of hell.
There was no way to predict the reaction of the people, but it was
not improbable that the ultimate effect could be outbreaks of
violence, perhaps even a revolution. Boniface had to be stopped,
and Philip had no better man for the job than William de Nogaret.
To recruit a partner who was as eager for revenge as he was himself,
de Nogaret invited Sciarra Colonna to join him, an invitation that
was met with gratitude and enthusiasm.

Boniface was to make the decree from the palace at his ancestral
home in Anagni. Colonna and de Nogaret hurried to Florence to
meet with enemies of the pope, including Colonna exiles and
sympathizers. Liberally dispersing the French gold that Philip had
given them for this mission, they assembled an armed force of
about fifteen hundred men and moved on Anagni. They found
the palace virtually undefended and simply walked in to take the
elderly pope as their prisoner. Sciarra Colonna took out his dagger
to end the old man's life, and it took all of de Nogaret's strength
and powers of persuasion to stop him. Instead, they held Boniface
for three days, degrading him and abusing him, even to the point,
as the pope claimed later, that Sciarra Colonna struck him in the
face several times with a fist covered in chain mail. While they
humiliated the pope, their little army looted and vandalized the
papal palace.

On the fourth day the people of Anagni finally got up their
courage to rescue their pope. He went back to Rome, thoroughly
shaken in mind and body. He died a few weeks later, some said in
an act of suicidal madness as he bit flesh off his arms and beat
his head against the stone wall of his room. Others reported that his
skull had been split open, with his brains on his shoulders and on
the floor, much too great a blow to be called suicide. Paintings, drawings, and wholesale excommunication preserved the Church's
memory of the face-bashing remembered as the Crime of Anagni,
but gave no official notice to the fact that a pope had had his brains
beaten out in the papal palace, undoubtedly because the crimes were
perpetrated by two different sets of criminals, one outside and
one inside.

The interdict was forgotten, the council to discipline Philip
of France didn't happen, and no Christian monarch voiced a
single criticism of Philip's actions. With a minimum of fanfare, the
cardinals took just ten days to elect a pro-French Italian, Niccolo
Boccasini, as Pope Benedict XI on October 22, 1303. He began

with a pleasant enough relationship with Philip IV, but he surprised the king when he firmly rejected the king's call for the posthumous impeachment of Boniface VIII. From his home in Perugia Benedict XI defended the papacy, formally condemned the Crime of Anagni, and ordered the excommunication of everyone associated with it. He was becoming a problem, but not for long.

In July 1304, after just nine months on the papal throne, Benedict XI was murdered in Perugia by means of a plate of poisoned figs. There were those who had no doubt that Philip of France, or his trusted agent, was responsible. Others said that the murder had been effected by agents of the Italian prelates at Rome, who would most certainly kill to return the papacy to the control of the Romans. Pope Benedict XI had fled to Perugia in fear of his life, and it had been that fear that had caused him to switch from friendly relations with France to the condemnation of the Crime of Anagni. Any French pope or any pope who favored France was in grave danger in Rome.

That was the situation that made it so difficult to select a new pope. The Italians, though dedicated to regaining the control of the Church, were not united. The Colonna, now restored to influence, were more embittered than ever against their ancient enemies of the house of Orsini, so that the Italian cardinals could not speak with one voice. Now established as a firm and powerful third faction, the French cardinals were not in the majority. The result was a deadlock that once more ignored the rules laid down for papal election set by the Second Lateran Council.

After a year of arguments and accusations, the French cardinals persuaded the Italians to agree to a unique concept. First, they should all agree to select a pope who was not a cardinal, so that no elector would be pushing for himself, but would look only to the best interests of the Church. Second, the French faction would take no more than forty days to select the pope from among three nominees to be chosen by the Italians.

The idea had come from Philip the Fair and was probably the brainchild of William de Nogaret. Philip totally controlled the French cardinals, all of whom had lands and revenues in France. The trick would be for Philip to identify a probable candidate of the Italians and to exchange the all-important final selection for a menu of promises the candidate would make to the French crown. The man they decided on was Bernard de Goth, the archbishop of Bordeaux. He was a likely candidate because he had sided with Boniface VIII against Philip and had been loud in his public condemnations of the French king. Also, de Goth owed no fealty to Philip because Bordeaux, although a part of France, was an English possession. Philip would not appear to have any political or economic power over him. He was attractive to Philip because if there was one great consuming fire burning in the belly of Bernard de Goth it was his intense desire to have the wealth, the honors, and the power that came with the papal tiara. He would do anything, agree to anything, to become the pope. Publicly, he continued to criticize the French king. Privately, he sat in secret meetings, cutting a deal.

An especially important reason for controlling the next pope was Philip's plan to get his hands on the wealth of the Knights Templar in France. The plan being worked out by de Nogaret promised several substantial benefits. The ease with which the Templars had produced the gold loaned to Philip for his daughter's dowry spoke to the probability of a substantial horde of wealth at the Templar commanderies, which would mean a very welcome prize of ready cash. Then there would be the relief of Philip's heavy debts to the Templar order. If charges of heresy could be established, the extensive Templar properties in France could be seized, then sold to raise cash or operated for future revenues. The Templars reported only to the pope and they existed on the basis of their charter from the Church, so charges of heresy would have to be brought before ecclesiastic tribunals. There was no body of evidence to back up the charges to be brought, so the answer would be to turn to the Inquisitors to apply their expert techniques to force confessions. Taken altogether, any plan to suppress the Knights Templar would require the approval and cooperation of the new pope.

Archbishop de Goth agreed that Philip would have the right to impose a tax on the clergy of France to the extent of 10 percent of its gross revenues for a period of five years. He agreed to remove all excommunications and other papal sanctions against the Colonna family and to restore their properties or compensate them for their losses (a side deal that assured Bernard de Goth would be named by the Colonna to be one of the three Italian nominees). He also agreed to cancel all the decrees and bulls of Boniface VIII against Philip of France, to call for a posthumous impeachment of the dead pope, and to remove all excommunications brought on by the Crime of Anagni, including those of William de Nogaret and Sciarra Colonna. (There is said to have been one more covenant, kept secret, that de Goth would cooperate in the suppression of the Knights Templar and in the confiscation of their treasury and property.)

Once Bernard de Goth was named as one of the three candidates from whom the pope would be selected, he could envision himself draped in the papal robes with the whole world at his feet. But he had to live with one final condition that summarized

Philip's feelings about the archbishop's trustworthiness. In addition to his sacred oath to keep his part of the bargain, Philip required that de Goth deliver up his brothers and two nephews, to put their lives on the line as hostages to guarantee the agreement. Archbishop de Goth agreed, and Philip delivered on his promise. On November 14, 1305, Bernard de Goth was unanimously elected to occupy the Throne of Peter, taking the papal name of Clement V.

Grand Master de Molay, waiting patiently for news of the election of a pope, was apparently unaware of the machinations that had led to that election. He had no idea of the plans being set for his order by Philip of France. He did not even suspect that the words being spoken as the papal tiara was placed on the head of Pope Clement V were the death knell of the Order of the Temple.

De Molay's only prayers about the papal election were to ask that God select a pope who would call a new Crusade to retake the Holy Land and so restore the lost glory of the Knights Templar. It could only have been with joy and excitement that he received the summons from Clement V to come to the papal court at Poitiers to discuss plans for a new Crusade. He was happily ignorant of the fact that waiting for him in France were whips, chains, and humiliations that would end only when he would be burned at the stake for defending the honor of his order.

PART THREE

Torture and Trial

29

Friday the Thirteenth
1306 to 1307

THE TEMPLAR GRAND MASTER had been summoned to Europe, probably at the instigation of Philip of France, but it took him a year to answer the call. Jacques de Molay wanted to arrive at the papal court fully prepared, with a carefully drafted plan for the reconquest of the Holy Land to lay before the pope, which should earn the gratitude of the pontiff and ensure a prominent role for the Knights Templar. Philip, who had already determined to get his hands on the Templar wealth, could hardly prevail with the Templar leader out of his reach, sitting on a Templar treasury that could be used to bribe allies and to hire thousands of mercenaries. Philip needed to have the Templar master where he could get his hands on him first.

What King Philip was planning was dangerous, and if improperly handled it could unleash forces that could easily turn on the French monarchy. Over a decade had passed since the Templars had decided to abandon their last castles in the Holy Land, and basic changes had taken place during that period. With no need for droves of recruits to be shipped off to the Crusades, the new knights taken into the order tended to stay where they were, and the order in Europe had taken on a posture approaching nationalization. The English master had taken his Templars to war against other Christians, fighting alongside Edward of England against the Scots. In the Spanish kingdoms, where the war against the Muslims was still raging, almost all of the Templars were Spanish. In Portugal, the Temple had agreed with the king that all of the Templars in his kingdom would be Portuguese. In Germany, the Knights Templar under Brother Hugo von Grumbach were almost all Germans. There was a chance that the Temple would split up along nationalistic lines, but if they all worked together under their grand master and pooled their men and revenues, as they had done in the Holy Land, they would constitute a major military force. They were experienced at hiring trained mercenaries, but they might not have to: There were a number of monarchs, not the least of whom was Edward I of England, who would happily ally themselves with the Templars against Philip to participate in carving up the corpse of the French monarchy. It was clear that Philip wanted only the Templar properties in France and wanted only his own debts to the Templars abrogated, but to achieve his goals in total security it would be necessary to suppress the entire order throughout the Christian world, so that it would be destroyed as a military force able to wreak revenge.

It was a risky prospect and would require skillful handling. Fortunately for Philip, he had some very skilled counselors, well versed in the law and adept at confusing that law.

Philip also had a firm grip on the French clergy, whose pulpits were a major avenue of communication with all the people in his kingdom, so the king was not concerned about his ability to get his people on his side. The problem was the rulers and the people of the other Christian kingdoms, who could best be reached and persuaded by the papacy. Just as Philip needed Jacques de Molay to come to France, he had to keep Clement V from leaving. In that he was aided by the fact that the pope was something of a physical coward, a trait that had helped attract him to Philip's attention in the first place. As a French pope, he must realize that his life would be in danger from the moment he set foot in Rome, but it wouldn't hurt to keep reminding him of that realistic danger. The Italians were still furious at having lost the papacy to the French, and they were mad enough to kill. The only real safety for the pope was to stay under the protection of his loyal son (and fellow schemer) King Philip the Fair.

The danger *was* real, of course, and would keep a long line of popes away from Rome in what would come to be called the Babylonish Captivity of the papacy, a seventy-five-year period in which not a single pope would run the risk of even a visit to Rome. Clement V would wander around France for a few years, never far from the armed forces of Philip, until in 1309 he would purchase Avignon in Provence from its owner, Joan of Naples, for eighty thousand gold florins. There the popes would build a magnificent papal palace and fortress from which to rule their spiritual kingdom.

Not that the pope's goals were strictly spiritual. Clement V evidenced an absolute genius for making money. Someone in years past had come up with the concept of the Treasury of the Church, sometimes called the Treasury of Merits. This was the limitless store of merits and blessings bestowed by God on Jesus Christ and his Holy Mother. Since their goodness was infinite, so was the supply of blessings, or merits. God had given the pope the sole control of that Treasury, and Clement V opened the doors for a great warehouse sale of those blessings. For sale were satisfaction of penances, partial or total remission of sins, reversals of decrees of excommunication, curtailment of years in purgatory for the already dead and the to-be dead, which included everyone. Papal honors went on the block, along with exemptions and annulments. Everything was for sale, and all was pure profit, since what was being sold cost nothing. Clement V invented "annates," fees of up to 100 percent of the gross revenues for every Church benefice granted to a new holder upon the death of the incumbent.

The money showed up in magnificent robes decorated with gold and jewels, luxurious furnishings, thousands of servants, solid gold table services, and elaborate ceremonies and pageantry. Clement V wallowed in his newfound wealth that was beyond anything he had ever dared fantasize.

For Philip of France, who desperately needed money for his own kingdom, watching the flow of treasure into the papacy could only renew his determination to satisfy his own needs. With de Nogaret and his other counselors, he laid a plan that was a kind of dress rehearsal for the arrest and suppression of the Templars. The target was the Jews of France, who would have few defenders. Secret orders were sent to all the seneschals of France in every corner of the country. They gave the command that every Jew in France was to be arrested and imprisoned at the same time on July 22, 1306. All of their records and their properties were seized to become the property of the crown; then the Jews were sent off into exile, destitute and homeless. Their property was inventoried and gathered for auction to the benefit of the crown, while the records were combed for debt instruments. All documents recording debts owed by the crown of France were destroyed. All other moneys owed to the Jews were now ordered to be payable to the king of France, who mounted an aggressive drive for their collection. As the king had expected, no one made any attempt to stop him.

Such a move against the Christian Templars was exactly what Philip had in mind, but it would be much more complicated because any Christian had legal protection not available to the Jews. In addition, the Templars were exempt from all secular law, responsible only to the pope. Their suppression would have to be based on offenses against God and against the canons and customs of the Church. The charge of heresy was a must, because it called for the confiscation of property. Other sins could be trotted out in order to thoroughly blacken the Templar name, as in the accusations of sodomy, blasphemy, and witchcraft hurled at Pope Boniface VIII, but heresy must play the major role.

Nor was it enough to prove the guilt of individual Templars. If found guilty of heresy, they had no personal property to confiscate. And if fifty individual Templars were found guilty of all manner of sins and crimes, they could be punished, even executed, without affecting the ongoing operations of the order. It was absolutely vital to a successful suppression and seizure of property that the order itself be found guilty of those sins and crimes. If an individual knight held heretical beliefs or engaged in any heretical practices, it must be shown that they were forced upon him by the Templar Rule or by his superior officers, so that the order itself was the guilty party and the individual Templar simply the victim of an evil organization.

Philip was encouraged by the fact that the one crime that allowed confiscation of property, the crime of heresy, might be the easiest to prove, regardless of guilt or innocence. The Church approved, and sometimes even insisted on, the use of torture to extract confessions of heresy. Concepts born during the Albigensian Crusade had been refined, defined, and well-organized during the years since the Holy Roman and Universal Inquisition had been established by Pope Gregory IX in 1229 during the suppression of the Cathars in southern France.

The Inquisition (from the Latin *inquirere*, "to look into") was largely based on the legal point that the most conclusive evidence possible was a confession. In the pursuit of the purification of the faith, it was reasoned that the use of torture was a legitimate means to extract such a confession, since God would enable the innocent to bear up under any amount of pain, even when induced by practiced experts at all the refinements of generating human agony. The next important legal point established was that a confession extracted under even the most hideous torture was valid and, extremely significant, nonretractable. Any person who confessed under torture and then retracted that confession when the torture stopped was labeled a "relapsed heretic." The relapsed heretic was conclusively and irretrievably guilty and was summarily handed over to the secular authorities, who had no choice but to burn the guilty party at the stake. The Knights Templar would learn all of those things firsthand during the coming months and years, and they would suffer under the frustration of yet another legal aspect of the Inquisition: that the accused had no right to know the identity of his accuser, nor of anyone who "witnessed" or gave evidence against him.

Since Philip's objective was to prove that the Templar order was guilty of heresy, the whole machinery of the Inquisition could be put to work for him. There was only one obstacle. As a religious order, the Knights Templar were exempt from the application of torture. A way around that exemption would have to be found. The best idea seemed to be to use the technique used so successfully against the Jews: Arrest the Templars in France all at one time. Then the torture could be applied immediately to extract some confessions of guilt before anyone could make a formal objection. The confessions would justify the action, but Philip would need the cooperation of the Inquisition. That wouldn't be too difficult to arrange: The grand inquisitor for France, Dominican brother Guillaume Imbert, was Philip's friend and personal confessor and had frequently benefited from the royal largesse.

In all of this, a factor in Philip's favor would be the Knights Templar's love of secrecy. All of their chapter meetings were conducted in total secrecy, usually at night, with Templar sentries outside the door with drawn swords. Their initiation ceremonies and rituals, whatever they might be, had always been cloaked in mystery. That enabled all manner of rumors to rise up from time to time, such as whispered reports that someone trying to eavesdrop on a Templar meeting had been killed, or that a Templar knight who revealed what happened at his own initiation had been murdered by his Templar brothers. The cloak of secrecy also covered the Rule of the order, which was revealed to the knight on a need-to-know basis, and he was sworn to reveal no part of the Rule known to him under the threat of severe disciplinary measures. It was thought that no more than a dozen or so of the highest officers of the order were familiar with the entire Rule. As always happens, their secrecy had aroused feelings from idle curiosity to envy and anger. It would work to Philip's benefit, because he could unleash a wide variety of accusations against the Knights Templar which no one outside the order could oppose on the basis of any personal knowledge.

Just what those accusations would be or what questions would be put to Templars on the rack were still undecided, but they took shape when an Italian criminal informer named Arnolfo Deghi, who had performed several special "missions" for William de Nogaret, introduced him to a renegade ex-Templar named Esquiu de Florian. Arnolfo Deghi had performed a valuable service for de Nogaret in 1300 when he presented accusations of sorcery and magic against the bishop of Troyes, so he had a fair idea of what de Nogaret was looking for to use against the Templars.

Esquiu de Florian had risen in the ranks of the Knights Templar to become the prior of the Templar preceptory of Montfaucon in the region of Périgueux, but for some lost reason he was removed from office and returned to the ranks. His attempts to get the provincial master to restore him to a position of authority were completely unsuccessful, so he let his anger drive him to punish the superior who could not be persuaded. Dagger drawn, he waited one night in the shadows and leaped out to stab the master to death. His own death would be the inevitable punishment, so he ran, apparently to Spain. A letter from de Florian to the king of Aragon was discovered generations later in the royal archives at Barcelona. It recites de Florian's attempt to provide information condemning the Templars in exchange for payment out of the property that would be confiscated from the order. The king of Aragon had not been convinced by de Florian's accusations against the Templars and declined to move against them, but as de Florian reminded the king in his letter, "You must remember, sir, that on my withdrawal from your chamber at Lerida, you promised me that if the affair of the Templars was discovered to be true, you would give me out of their property a thousand pounds [per year] in rents and three thousand pounds in money." The principal purpose of the letter was expressed as "...when the opportunity arises, deign to remember this."

There was no money coming from Aragon, so de Florian undoubtedly leaped at the chance to earn a reward from France. He would do whatever it took, and de Nogaret was too shrewd to rely simply on a public statement of accusations against the Templars that had no ring of authenticity. He decided to stage a drama, far from Paris, that would have the appearance of bringing the Templar crimes to King Philip's attention totally by accident. Deghi and de Florian were sent to occupy a cell together in the prison at Toulouse, de Nogaret's former home, where he had attended the university and still had many friends. Pretending a desire to confess their sins, the two prisoners by arrangement were denied the services of a priest, so taking advantage of the Church rule that permitted a Catholic with no access to a priest to confess to another Catholic layman, they heard each other's confessions. As a former Templar, de Florian unburdened himself of a battery of Templar sins based on greed, treachery, sorcery, homosexuality, and heresy. Deghi, confined under an assumed name, feigned shock and revulsion at the revelations and demanded that they be presented to the king. The prison officials, who had to have been in on the play-acting, arranged for the information to be passed to the royal court. Now de Nogaret had a document and a witness. He had a reason to arrest the Templars and a basis for questions they would be asked under torture. His authority could be drawn from the decrees of the Second Lateran Council, which had demanded that the secular authority root out and chastise heretics and that all secular princes cooperate in every way with the Holy Roman Inquisition. The stage was set. All that was needed now was the star player, the grand master of the Knights Templar.

After a year of Crusade planning, Grand Master Jacques de Molay was on his way to France. The grand master of the Hospitallers had also been commanded to appear, but he begged off on the grounds that his order was at war with the infidel, fighting to take the island of Rhodes, so that he could not be away at this time. That was fine with de Molay, who was just as happy to be the only grand master at the papal court to fight off another threat to the Templar order: a movement to combine the Templars and Hospitallers into a single order.

A few years earlier a priest and lawyer named Pierre de Bois had written his own plan for the recovery of the Holy Land called *De Recuperatione Terrae Sanctae,* in which he had recommended and cited the efficiencies that would result from a merger of the Templars and Hospitallers. More recently, a Dominican named Ramon Lull had written a much more detailed plan for the organization of the crusading effort. He proposed that the Knights of the Hospital of St. John of Jerusalem and the Knights of the Temple of Solomon in Jerusalem should be combined into one military order to be called the Knights of Jerusalem. Similarly, he suggested that all of the secular Crusaders be brought together under one commander to be called the *Rex Bellator,* the "War King."

The pope's reaction to the merger concept was favorable. Perhaps because the Hospitallers were gaining new respect from their attack on Rhodes, or perhaps because the order appeared much less controversial, Clement V favored Foulques de Villaret, grand master of the Hospitallers, to become the grand master of the combined orders. As for Philip of France, such a combination would not solve his money troubles unless he could somehow control the treasury and the debt portfolio of the merged orders. His response was that the kings of France should be named the hereditary grand masters of the proposed combination of orders and that he should personally be appointed the *Rex Bellator,* with full authority over and access to the combined treasuries of the merged orders. No one liked his idea.

This was the situation Jacques de Molay sailed into early in 1307 as his fleet of six Templar galleys put into the harbor at Marseilles. His orders from the pope had been to come directly to the papal court at Poitiers and to travel incognito, but those instructions did not suit his personality, nor his perception of his personal importance. He ignored the pope's directives and marched to his Temple fortress at Paris in a medieval parade of power, with a personal escort of sixty knights in red-crossed snow-white robes with banners flying, accompanied by their black-robed squires and sergeants, a contingent of servants, and a pack train that included twelve horses bearing a treasure of over one hundred and fifty thousand gold florins. Incredibly, the proud, gray-bearded master who led the parade had no idea what he was riding into.

To the contrary, he anticipated a warm welcome by Philip of France, who would surely express his gratitude to the grand master for many past favors. Just the year before, Philip had fled from a bloodthirsty mob, angry at the king for debasing the national currency. He had sought refuge in the Paris Temple, where the Knights Templar had guarded his royal person for three full days until the riot died down. The Templars had loaned the king the money he needed for the dowry of his sister, and more recently the money required for the betrothal of his daughter to the English Prince of Wales. When asked, they had guarded the crown jewels and the treasury of France. Grand Master de Molay had broken the Rule of his order to act as godfather to Philip's infant son Robert. Surely Philip could do no less to express his gratitude than to support the Templars in putting aside the plan to merge their order with the Hospitallers and to help them to gain a prominent role in the planning of the next Crusade. It seemed to de Molay that all was going as he expected when he was invited to the royal court, where the assembled nobility of France heard the warm words of praise and welcome heaped upon this unsuspecting grand master by Philip the Fair.

At the Paris Temple, Jacques de Molay told the local officers of his plans for the next Crusade and the arguments he would present to the pope to thwart the attempt to merge the military orders. In return, they told the grand master about the recent spate of rumors of improprieties and sinful conduct within the Templar order. They agreed that the best way to put the rumors to rest was for the grand master to ask Clement V for a formal papal inquiry.

In the belief that he was now fully prepared, de Molay made the trip to the papal court, where he was received by a group of high Church officials, but not by the pope himself. Concerning the next Crusade he had detailed but incomplete plans, because, as he explained, he felt that the definitive plans for the actual invasion should be established as a carefully guarded secret and not committed to writing. As to his own secret plans that would absolutely assure the success of the Crusade, those he would reveal only in person to the pope alone.

As expected, the subject of the proposed merger of the military orders was brought up, and de Molay was ready. He presented a formal document entitled *De Unione Templi et Hospitalis Ordinum ad Clementus Papam Jacobi de Molayo relatio,* a treatise that he had to trust contained his own arguments, since de Molay could not read or write his own native French, much less the Latin of the Church. As to the ridiculous rumors about his holy fraternity, the grand master expressed his supreme confidence that even the most cursory papal inquiry would find those allegations to be totally unfounded, the products of ignorance and envy. He left the meeting pleased that he had met and successfully handled every issue put to him.

As the grand master was presenting his plans, de Nogaret was proceeding with his own plan to bring him down, and his entire order with him. Reportedly a dozen men had been recruited to seek membership in the Templar order and to report back on their initiation rites, but if true, that effort produced nothing usable. The confession of Esquiu de Florian was beginning to prove its value.

The weeks went by with the aging grand master very happy with himself, his order, and the world as he found it. As summer came on, events started to heat up, but they didn't stir de Molay to any action. The anti-Templar rumors were growing stronger, and there had to be some knowledge that trouble was brewing. When a Templar told Hugh de Peraud that he was planning to leave the order, de Peraud encouraged his resignation and told him to act with dispatch because a catastrophe for the order was imminent. De Peraud was a good friend of Philip and a bitter rival to Jacques de Molay, who had defeated him in the grand master election, and he may well have been privy to Philip's thoughts, if not his plans. With no recorded explanation, the Paris master sent an order to every Templar preceptory in France to tighten security and to reveal nothing to anyone regarding the secret rituals or meetings of the order. Several former Templars were taken into the protective custody of the crown, apparently in the fear that they would be murdered if it was suspected that they might discuss what went on in the secret meetings of the order.

Perhaps all these items and more were brought to the attention of the grand master. He would be justified in hearing them without fear, since the Templar order was subject only to the pope and not to any secular monarch, nor to the laws of any land. As members of a holy order, the Templars were exempt from torture, and to top it all they had a strong and experienced fighting force backed by chests of gold. What could there possibly be to fear?

Then, in July, de Nogaret was able to bring wonderful news to his sovereign lord: Edward I of England was dead! The man who could have done the most to thwart Philip's plans, a good friend to the Knights Templar, a cool fox at the bargaining table and a raging tiger on the battlefield, the best king England ever had, was dead. And better still, he was now replaced by a weak-willed young man who was totally enthralled by his handsome homosexual lover. There was nothing to fear from Edward II, whose father had been such a constant source of concern. The continental wars against England must be revitalized, and seizing the treasure of the Templars was now more important than ever.

Philip went to the pope in a great show of reluctance and emotional stress, regretting his duty to present to the Holy Father the shameful evidence of Templar corruption and heresy that had fallen into his hands. A former Templar officer had confessed it all, he moaned, as he produced the confessions of Esquiu de Florian:

The Templars put their order and its selfish interests before the interests of Holy Mother Church and before moral principle. They took a secret oath to defend and enrich their order by any means, without regard for right or wrong. They maintained secret correspondence with the Muslims. In their initiation rites, new members were required to spit or trample on the cross and to deny Jesus Christ. A Templar who attempted to reveal the secrets of the order was murdered. The Templars desecrated the holy sacraments and omitted the words of consecration in the service of the mass. They practiced the absolution of sins by laymen without a priest. The Templars were given permission to engage in sodomy and other homosexual acts. It was through the treachery of the Templars that the Holy Land had been lost. They worshiped satanic idols in the forms of a bearded head and a cat.

That was a great deal for the pope to digest at one time. He apparently had strong doubts as to the truth of the accusations, but he did promise the king that he would mount a formal papal inquiry into the charges. It was not all that Philip had hoped for, but it did provide him a point on which to act. By arresting the Templars he would merely be instigating the inquiry that the pope had called for, as might be expected of a true servant of the Church.

Early in September orders went out to every seneschal of France to organize a military force on the evening of October 12 but, on pain of severe punishment, not to open and read until that time the sealed secret orders enclosed. On September 22, perhaps with some knowledge of what was about to transpire, the archbishop of Narbonne, the king's chancellor, resigned his post and returned the Great Seal. In his place Philip named his faithful servant William de Nogaret. The excommunicated lawyer, orphaned by the Church and dedicated only to the interests of his secular sovereign, took the highest office in the land as the king's chancellor.

His new dignity did not prevent de Nogaret from personally addressing the logistical problems of the pending mass arrest of the Knights Templar, arrests that would include sergeants, men-at-arms, stewards, craftsmen, and servants of the order. Armed with his new authority, he completed his plans to provide prisons and chains for thousands of men in all parts of the one hundred and fifty thousand square miles of the kingdom of France. A small army of scribes was put to work making copies of the allegations against the Templars that would be circulated throughout France on the day of the arrests to calm the fears of the people and to gain their sympathy for the project.

With so many people involved in the preparations, it seems impossible that no news of the impending disaster reached the grand master, but he appears to have been totally relaxed. He was even honored the day before his downfall when he was asked to join the highest nobility of France in acting as a pallbearer at the funeral of Princess Catherine, the deceased wife of Philip's brother Charles of Valois. As de Molay returned to his palace after that day of somber service in the company of kings, dukes, and counts, the seneschals throughout France were opening their sealed orders, as the knights and soldiers they had assembled waited to learn what duties they were about to carry out for their king.

It was not the way of medieval kings to explain or justify their orders to minor officials, but there may well have been some fear that some local seneschal, and even local knights summoned by him, would have formed friendships with Templars in their local preceptories and so be inclined to modify their orders or to postpone action until the startling commands could be confirmed. Just to make certain that every seneschal would understand the orders, the reasons for those orders, and especially the need to carry them out, de Nogaret had composed a letter of explanation. Such a communication to a seneschal from his king was such an extraordinary event that the mere fact of the explanation was a point of drama and proof of the seriousness of the matter at hand:

"A bitter thing, a lamentable thing, a thing horrible to think of, too terrible to hear, a detestable crime, an execrable evil deed, an abominable work, a detestable disgrace, a thing wholly inhuman, foreign to all humanity has, thanks to the reports of several persons worthy of faith, reached our ears, not without striking us with great astonishment and causing us to tremble with violent horror..." and on and on in the same vein. The letter does finally get to the point with the order that "...all the members of the said [Templar] order will be arrested, without exception, imprisoned and reserved for the judgment of the Church..." To get right to the reason for this incredible exercise, it continued "...all their movable and unmovable property will be seized, placed in our hands and faithfully preserved." The phrase "for the judgment of the Church" was defined with orders to immediately call in the good friars of the Inquisition, who were to question the captive Templars as to their alleged crimes "using torture if necessary."

And so it was at dawn of the following day, Friday the Thirteenth in October of 1307, that almost every Templar knight, priest, sergeant, and servant in France was arrested and put in chains. The arresting party at the Paris Temple was led by the king's chancellor in person, probably to assure admittance. The date was ever after regarded as an ominous time, but although for the rest of the world it might become an amusing supersitition, for the Knights Templar that Friday the Thirteenth was the unluckiest day of that or any other year. Their torture began on that same day.

30

A Faith to Die For
1307 to 1311

THERE WERE NOT ENOUGH prisons available for the sudden influx of thousands of men in chains, so makeshift facilities were called into play. Many of the Templars, such as those seized at the Paris Temple, were confined in their own buildings. Every one of those buildings was searched and relieved of any portable items of value. Most welcome to Philip were the chests of gold and silver coins, and the gold and silver religious objects on the altars, of which the most famous was the gold jewel-covered reliquary holding the Templars' own splinter of the True Cross. Other items, such as furniture, ornaments, hangings, weapons, and horses, could be stored where they were. Since the buildings were now held by the forces of Philip the Fair, those items could be removed at leisure.

The only disappointment resulting from the careful searches was the failure to turn up the idols and satanic symbols that would have provided concrete evidence of heretical guilt. A silver head was found with small bones inside, which appeared to have been made to house holy relics. (A legend says that a few days before the arrests a wagonload of hay had been driven out of the Temple carrying precious possessions to safety, but no testimony or documentation exists to take the story out of the world of Templar myth.)

Chancellor de Nogaret had ordered that the torture of the Templars proceed immediately, to get the fast confessions needed to confront the pope. That activity was turned over to Grand Inquisitor Imbert, assisted by Philip's own jailers and executioners. Now that the deed was done, de Nogaret had a complete propaganda program to put into effect. Letters went from Philip to all of the Christian monarchs explaining the French king's actions and urging all rulers faithful to the Church to follow his example. An especially strong letter and a personal envoy went to young Edward II of England, who was scheduled to become Philip's son-in-law just three months later.

Announcements went to every diocese in France, to be read from the pulpits on Sunday, October 15. On that same day de Nogaret met with the clergy of Notre Dame cathedral to encourage their support. He also met with the "masters," the clerical faculty of the University of Paris, to explain the king's actions. Other bulletins cataloging the sins of the Templars were distributed to king's officers in all parts of France, to be read in councils and in the public squares and markets.

When the news of the Templar arrests arrived at the papal court, Clement V was furious. The entire proceedings had been the most flagrant flouting of papal authority. The Church had established the Order of the Temple, which reported only to the Holy Father himself. No one, regardless of rank, title, or motivation, had any right whatsoever to lay hands on the persons or the property of the Knights Templar without the specific permission of the supreme pontiff. He turned loose the full fury of the papal wrath on the guilty king.

Philip responded by launching a propaganda assault against Clement V. Announcements were published all over France condemning the pope for his lenience in the treatment of heretics, for his intention to take all of the Templar wealth for himself and his family, and for his protection of the enemies of God and his Holy Church. As king and pope thundered against each other, Philip went to the papal court backed by a small army.

The pope reminded the king that a papal letter had gone to him two months before in which the pope had clearly stated that he did not believe the charges against the Templars. In rejoinder, Philip claimed a clear remembrance of the pope's reaction when the king had presented those charges. He claimed that Clement had said, "*Fils, tu enquerras diligement de leurs fais, et ce que to feras, to me rescripas*" ("My son, you must look into their deeds with diligent care, and report to me what you make of them"). The king was simply conducting the inquiry the pope had called for. Clement replied that he had meant a quiet inquiry by a papal commission, not arrest and torture. Philip's answer was that prior papal decrees absolutely required secular princes to extend every assistance to the Holy Roman Inquisition, which was exactly what he was doing. Clement's answer was to remove Guillaume Imbert from his post as grand inquisitor of France.

The argument raged for several weeks, with Philip's knights and soldiers strolling about menacingly in their role of overt saber-rattling. A deal was obviously made, with terms we shall probably never know, but the secret sessions of pope and king resulted in a singleness of purpose, with Philip achieving full papal approval and cooperation.

On November 22, Clement V promulgated the bull *Pastoralis preeminentae,* in which he lavished praises on Philip of France as a true son of the Church and loyal defender of the faith. The bull formally recognized the truth of the charges against the Templars and charged all Christian sovereigns to arrest the Templars in their territories and to cause them to be tortured for confessions of heresy. A secular king as well as the supreme priest, Clement V followed his own orders by calling for the immediate arrest of all the Knights Templar in the Papal lands, who were to be turned over to the Inquisition officers there. As part of the agreement, Philip's friend the Dominican brother Imbert was returned to his lofty post as grand inquisitor of France, although there is no indication that the torture of the Templars had been stopped for even a single day during his brief removal from office.

There were basically two types of medieval torture. First was the use of torture as punishment. The man sentenced to be chastised with pain had no way to stop the executioner as that official burned him with a red-hot iron, cut off his nose, ears, or lips, or scourged him with a whip that was frequently tipped with metal. Not until centuries later would merciful authorities limit a flogging to the bare back between neck and waist. In the fourteenth century, the lash could be applied freely to any part of a man's body, including his face and genitals. The other type of torture was that applied to extract information or a confession. The governing factor was the constant reminder that with the right answers the torture would stop. The victim had total control over how long the pain would last. If a man held out because he insisted on staying with the truth, or to prevent his being used as an instrument of betrayal, the pain could go on and on. Unfortunately for the Templars, they were questioned on so many different charges that if they admitted to one charge to stop the pain they would soon find themselves screaming in agony as their jailers proceeded with the next question. Legally, torture by the Inquisition was to be limited to a single session, but the zealous friars developed the concept of a "recess" or "adjournment" that would permit them to torture a man for weeks under the claim that the whole time frame was just "one session."

The object of the Templar torture was clearly to extract confessions, but since a dead man can't confess to anything, it was very important that whatever the degree of agony inflicted it should not bring death. There is no better indication of the enthusiastic brutality of the inquisitors than the fact that thirty-six Templars died under torture during the very first week.

The medieval prison must itself be included as part of the torture process. There were no individual cells except in the case of a secret or very special prisoner. Normally, twenty or thirty men would be confined in a single room, each man chained to a ring in the floor or in a wall. The rooms were frequently underground chambers, with little or no light or ventilation. The prisoners, usually deprived of their clothing, slept on the stone floor. They froze in winter and roasted in the summer. With no sanitary provisions, the stench would itself become a form of punishment. The occasional sloshing of the floor with buckets of water led to the ultimate revulsion in confinement, a French innovation called the *oubliette*. This was a small chamber just under the iron drain cover in the floor. Into this pit went any prisoner slated for special degradation. He was forced to sit in a pit of the blood, excrement, urine, and vomit of his fellow prisoners, which constantly rained on him through the iron grill. He dare not lie down and could not stand up.

The food and water were deliberately revolting. If they were crawling with vermin, so much the better. As a result, the prisoner often became ill, racked with vomiting and diarrhea, with no way to clean himself or the floor under him. As further preparation for the torture, or sometimes as punishment for outbursts of temper or insults to his jailer, he could be deprived of food and water or treated to more painful confinement. He might be forced to stand, with a neck ring located well up the wall, or hung upside down, or hung by his wrists with his hands tied behind him, with weights attached to his ankles, so that he would hang hour after hour with his upper arm bones straining to break free from their confining shoulder sockets.

The inquisitors knew from experience that witnessing the hideous punishment of their fellows had a demoralizing effect on all the other men in the room, which is the reason that they preferred to bring the torture tools into the dungeon rather than take their victims to the torture chambers. It meant that they had to deprive themselves of heavy immovable torture instruments, like the wheel that rotated a man's naked body above a charcoal fire, but they had full knowledge of the use of portable equipment.

The inquisitors had orders to "spare no known means of torture," so they could let their wild imaginations run free. Some Templars had their teeth pulled out one at a time, with a question between each extraction, then had the empty sockets probed to provide an additional level of pain. Some had wooden wedges driven under their nails, while others had their nails pulled out. A common device was an iron frame like a bed, on which the Templar was strapped with his bare feet hanging over the end. A charcoal brazier was slid under his oiled feet as the questioning began. Several knights were reported to have gone mad from the pain. A number had their feet totally burned off, and at a later inquiry a footless Templar was carried to the council clutching a bag containing the blackened bones that had dropped out of his feet when they were burned off. His inquisitors had allowed him to keep the bones as a souvenir of his memorable experience. The hot iron was a favorite tool because it could be easily applied again and again to any part of the body. It could be held a couple of inches away, cooking the flesh while the question was asked, then firmly pressed against the body when the answer came out incorrectly or too slowly.

It is not surprising that this treatment resulted in a number of Templar suicides, or that it produced a profusion of confessions. As the Templar treasurer said, "Under such torture I would willingly confess to having killed God!" Three days after the confessed heretic had made his admissions to stop the torture, he was brought before an officer of the Inquisition and his confession was read back to him, well edited of course, for his confirmation. The grand inquisitor himself conducted such confirmations in Paris, in a room decorated with torture instruments to keep the condemned man's mind on track. If he declined to answer or objected, he could go right back to the hot irons for reinforcement. If he renounced his confession, saying that it had been extracted solely because of the torture, he could be deemed a "relapsed heretic" and be sent off to be burned at the stake, which is exactly what happened to dozens of French Templars who apparently didn't understand how the game was played. But all in all, Philip and de Nogaret were pleased at the way the confessions were piling up. Quite a number of them had come from Templars who had not been tortured. Just listening to the open-throated screams of their brothers with the background of the stink of their burning flesh had been quite enough motivation for some of them to remember all manner of acts of blasphemy and witchcraft.

The confessions stated that in their initiations they had been required to bestow the *Osculum infame,* or "Kiss of shame," on the prior, on his mouth...or on his navel...or below his spine. They had been required to spit on the cross...or to trample on the cross...or to urinate on the cross. Denying Christ, the Templars had worshiped a head, or a head with three faces, or a head with four feet, or a head with just two feet. It was a metal head, or a wooden head, or a human skull set in a reliquary. (A couple of Templars confessed that the head was named Baphomet.) Some confessed that they had also worshiped an idol in the form of a cat, which was red, or gray, or black, or mottled. Sometimes the idol worship required kissing the cat below the tail. Sometimes the cat was greased with the fat from roasted babies. The Templars were forced to eat food that contained the ashes of dead Templars, a form of witchcraft that passed on the courage of the fallen knights. Some said they had to wear a cord next to their skin after the cord had touched the idol.

As they had been ordered to do, Inquisitors got confessions that mass was served without the consecration of the Host, that Templars were allowed to confess to no priests other than their own, that the Templar officers absolved the brothers from sin without recourse to a priest, that no sin, no matter how heinous, was counted as a sin if it benefited the Templar order.

The one infraction of the Rule of the Temple and the canons of the Church that was probably valid in a number of cases—indulgence in homosexual activity—was played down, with only three confessions of all the Templars tortured to admit it. Many did confess that the order encouraged homosexual activities, but on the whole specific confessions of sodomy were not sought, probably because Philip had no desire at this time to offend his royal son-in-law King Edward II of England, who had married Philip's daughter in January 1308. Edward was an active homosexual, and Philip didn't want any wedges driven between himself and the English king, whom Philip was anxious to convert to a more aggressive stance against the Knights Templar.

Edward had received the letter from the pope ordering the arrest and torture of the Templars but had not acted on it. Instead, he had informed the pope that he believed the Templars were innocent and had written letters to share that point of view with other Christian kings. Philip had sent his personal envoy, Bernard Pelletin, to encourage Edward to act, but with no success. Edward had been surrounded by Knights Templar all his life. They had willingly loaned their London facilities to accommodate dozens of young men who had come to London to be knighted along with Edward, then the Prince of Wales, before marching with the prince and his father against the Scots. The English Templars had fought on the English side against the Scottish rebel William Wallace, a war in which the Templar master Brian de Jay had given his life for the English cause. Edward could not accept the accusations against his friends of the Temple.

The papal bull *Pastoralis preeminentae* arrived at the English court on December 15, 1307. Now Edward had to act, but he put off the actual arrests until January 7, a three-week delay that enabled many English Templars to disappear underground. It was not just the English Templars who disappeared, but their treasure as well. Edward's soldiers, expecting to seize a great store of treasure at the London Temple, discovered that the items they could find had a total value of less than two hundred pounds. A half-hearted royal manhunt, aided by the other religious orders, found only two of the fugitive Templars in all of England. Edward did not permit the torture of the Templars who were arrested, which incensed Clement V. The pope demanded that the English Templars be "put to the question," but Edward replied that torture was not part of English jurisprudence, so he didn't even have anyone who knew how to do such things. He was right. For years the English crown had frustrated the papacy and the Dominicans by standing resolutely behind the decision to prohibit the Inquisition from setting up shop in England.

The argument raged between king and pope for three years, until the end of 1310, when Clement V wrote to Edward telling him that he had best look to the fate of his own soul in his refusal to obey the orders of the supreme pontiff. In fairness, the pope was giving the young king one more chance to save himself. The pope accepted the king's excuse that there were no experienced torturers in England, but he was sending ten highly skilled tormentors to Edward, at papal expense, to solve the king's problem. Now there would be no further reason for postponing the tortures for confessions of heresy that the Holy Father had ordered for the Knights Templar. The pope made it clear that as soon as the Dominican torture experts arrived, they were to be put to work, with no hindrance or barrier to the execution of their holy mission. Edward now had no choice, but to his credit he ordered the torture team to effect no mutilations, no permanent bodily injuries, and "no violent effusions of blood."

One can hardly believe the date on the pope's letter. He had taken time from what must have been pressing religious duties during the sacred season to write his demand for the physical torture of the captive knights on Christmas Eve, December 24, 1310. The Christmas gift forced upon the people of England was the introduction of confessions by torture into their legal system. To top it off, the pope further ordered that any person who gave aid or shelter to a fugitive Templar, or who even gave advice and counsel to a fugitive Templar, was to be arrested, excommunicated, and suitably punished. As to those fugitives ,whose number was added to by escapes from the English prisons, they were already condemned. Three years had passed since the original call for their arrests, and the rule for those suspected of heresy was that they had one year to turn themselves in, at which point they were to be excommunicated. If after a year of excommunication they had still not surrendered voluntarily, they were damned as proven heretics. That meant that if a fugitive Templar should be found now, he would not have the mercies of torture and trial, but would be marched directly to death at the stake. All those thundering threats, however, did not result in the unearthing of one more fugitive Templar in Britain.

England was not Pope Clement's only problem. His orders for the maximum possible torture to be applied to the Templars were carried out in the kingdoms of Sicily and Naples and in his own Papal domains, but they were resisted everywhere else. The kingdom of Cyprus informed the pope that their Templars had been arrested and tried but found innocent. Torture had not been used. Clement V angrily ordered that the trials be held again, but only after the Templars had been tortured according to his instructions. To see to that end of the business, he sent a Dominican inquisitor and a Franciscan friar to Cyprus with authority to call on all the Dominicans and Franciscans on Cyprus to help with the questioning. Strangely, no record has survived as to the results of the second trial, nor even that it ever took place.

Scotland was now ruled by Robert Bruce, who had been excommunicated by the Church. When the papal order to arrest the Templars in Scotland arrived at his court, Bruce apparently tossed it in a bottom drawer. It wasn't even published. Legend has it that a few Templar knights who revealed themselves to him were welcomed into Bruce's army.

The German Templars, though few in number, did very well by themselves. As the archbishop of Metz was conducting a judicial inquiry into the matter of the Templars, the door to the council chamber was flung open. In the doorway stood the fierce local preceptor Hugo von Gumbach, in full battle armor surmounted by his flowing white Templar robe. As he stomped into the chamber twenty of his Templar knights followed, fanning out behind him, all armed and ready. Standing in front of the archbishop, von Gumbach loudly proclaimed that Grand Master de Molay was a man of deep faith and personal honor and that he and the Templar order were innocent of all charges. In contrast, Pope Clement V was a completely evil man, who was hereby declared to be deposed because he had been illegally elected. Turning his head to look each member of the council in the eye, von Gumbach declared that all of the Templar knights present were prepared to risk their bodies and their lives in personal trial by combat with their accusers, to let God decide the issue. As the council looked at the challengers, it was obvious that they weren't just willing to fight, they were *eager* to fight. No accuser chose to speak up, and the council quickly adjourned. As it reconvened over the months ahead, the Templars in Germany were found innocent of the charges.

The Christian monarchs of the Iberian Peninsula voiced their objections to the pope for the whole ill-advised affair. They reminded the pontiff that they were actively engaged in incessant warfare against the Muslim armies in Spain and Portugal. They alone were holding the Muslims in check, protecting all of Europe from an Islamic invasion, and the Templars provided strong support in that struggle. The archbishop of Aragon announced that his investigation had proved the Templars were innocent of all charges. Another verdict of innocence came from the kingdom of Castile, where the charges had been investigated by the archbishop of Compostela, and another from the archbishops in Portugal.

In spite of the verdicts of innocence in some lands and the lukewarm pursuit of the Templars in Britain, the torture for confessions of heresy went forward with vigor in Sicily, Naples, and the Papal States, but nowhere with more dedication than in France. A low point for the Templars was the confession of Jacques de Molay. He was an old man now, and the threat of torture was too much to bear. He confessed to denying Christ three times at his initiation. He admitted having been ordered to spit on a crucifix, but he had spit on the floor next to it. He is said to have reacted emotionally to the suggestion of homosexual behavior, whereupon he had been told that there would be no such charges if he would admit to denying Christ.

Hugh de Peraud was a strange figure in the whole affair. He had wanted desperately to be elected the grand master but had been beaten out by de Molay. He was a good friend to King Philip, whom he had accommodated in every way with the Templar funds in his control. Some chroniclers have indicated that he had a private side arrangement with the king. He was apparently well treated and was not tortured, but he confessed to everything. At his own initiation he had denied Christ and kissed his receiver on the mouth. As an officer in charge of initiations he had told candidates to deny Christ, to spit on the cross, and to kiss him on his mouth, his navel, and at the base of his spine. He had informed the initiates that homosexual acts with other Templars were permitted. He had joined other Templars in worshiping an idol made up of a great head with two feet in front and two behind. Most damning of all, he stated that all these things were called for in the secret statutes of the order. He was totally cooperative with the agents of the king.

The confirmed confessions were called in from all of the offices of the Inquisition in the French provinces and in other countries. Templars who tried to recant on the grounds that they had only confessed to stop the torture, and who insisted on maintaining that position, were pronounced relapsed heretics and burned at the stake. An audience of other Templars was always present to witness the writhing, burning, and screaming of their errant brothers, making certain that all learned the lesson and were kept in a state of shattering fear.

Pope Clement V called a great council of the Church to convene in 1310 at the French city of Vienne. The final disposition of the Templar order would be addressed at that time. To prepare for it a papal commission of inquiry convened in Paris on August 7, 1309, under the archbishop of Narbonne, and expressed its willingness to listen to any Templar who cared to defend the order. It was emphasized that the commission would hear charges and defenses only of the Templar order as a whole, not of individual members. Hugh de Peraud appeared, but only to state that since he had already confessed to the guilt of the order, he could not possibly defend it. A Templar knight named Ponsard de Gisi appeared to state that all of the charges against the order were false. He said that his own confessions were extracted by the most cruel tortures and were all false. To prove his point, he showed the commissioners his fingers. His hands had been tied behind his back so tightly that the circulation had been completely cut off. Blood flowed into his hands, but could not get out. As they turned blue and swollen, the built-up blood had burst open the tips of his fingers. He had spent hours in that condition in his dungeon before his torture was even begun.

On November 26 Jacques de Molay appeared, anxious to talk to representatives of the pope, who alone could get him and his order out of the clutches of the king of France. As had all of the Templars who had appeared ahead of him, with the single exception of Hugh de Peraud, de Molay denied the truth of his former confession and denied as well the accusations against the order. He also stated his principal reason for appearing before this council, which was to formally assert that "I challenge your jurisdiction over the Order of the Temple, since it is under the sole authority of the pope himself, so only he can be its judge." Taken aback by this unexpected objection, the archbishop asked if the grand master was going to be the defender of the order. As an illiterate man with no training in ecclesiastic law or proceedings, de Molay felt inadequate as defense counsel for the order. He wanted professional help and funds to pay for that help, as well as travel expenses to get supporting depositions from Christian leaders outside France, all of which could be paid from the Templar treasure seized by Philip.

The archbishop pointed out that the grand master should expect no funds to be provided to him, nor should he expect to be aided by outside counsel. He reminded de Molay that the crime being investigated was heresy, which meant that the usual legal forms of a trial did not have to be followed, and that a suspected heretic had no legal right to representation by lawyers. He then read aloud the formal charges against the Templar order, including specific charges of the denial of Christ and the worship of idols.

De Molay listened in rising anger and repeatedly crossed himself. As the archbishop finished, he cried out that the prelates of the Church might feel safe from the wrath of men, but they were not protected from the wrath of God. The archbishop, who owed his appointment to the diocese of Narbonne to King Philip, was concerned about what might be reported to the king by the royal officers who were watching the proceedings. Prudence demanded that he be observed putting the grand master in his place. He sternly warned de Molay that heretics who retracted their confessions could be handed over to the secular authorities for burning, from which there was no recourse or appeal. De Molay was silenced by the threat of his own death. The archbishop suggested that he take time to consider if he indeed wished to act as the defender of the order. The council adjourned, and Philip's officers hurried off to inform the king of the proceedings.

The grand master appeared again on November 28 and was asked if he had decided to personally conduct the defense of his order. Apparently the time he had spent thinking about it only reinforced de Molay's convictions that the pope alone could judge the Templars, over whom this commission had no legal authority. "I refuse to enter any defense before this commission. I demand to be led before His Holiness. I shall defend the Order from the wicked and false accusations made by its enemies and render to Christ the honor that is due Him.... Let the pope call me before him and I shall defend the Order to the glory of God and His Church."

De Molay was reminded that the pope himself had appointed this commission and had delegated to it the responsibility to investigate the charges, not against individuals, but against the Templar organization. De Molay responded with a recitation of the history of the faith and loyalty of the Templars throughout the Crusades. The king's chancellor, William de Nogaret, who had decided to observe this session in person, had no problem interjecting himself into the proceedings, nor did anyone try to stop him. "The corruption of your Order is notorious. It is stated in the chronicles of St. Denis that your Grand Master de Beaujeu and other Templars did homage to the Sultan, and when the Templars were defeated, the Sultan had attributed that defeat to their vices and sodomy, and to the betrayal of their Christian faith." The grand master answered that the chronicler had lied and defended his predecessor's treaties with the Muslims as necessary to survival: "...nothing else could be done if the land was to be saved..."

Since de Molay held firm his refusal to act as defender of the Templar order except to the person of the pope, the council took a long recess while the captive Templars were contacted to see if any of them would act as the defender. Of about six hundred and fifty Templar knights in Paris, five hundred and forty-six volunteered to defend the order, and reports of more voluntary defenders poured in from other French cities. It was also reported that the Templars were in a high state of excitement over the news that the pope had taken over from the French king. Somehow they believed that, after two and a half years in their filthy dungeons, their lord the pope would not take long now to acknowledge their innocence.

Weeks were spent screening the men who had asked to defend the order. They told the commissioners of the tortures they had endured. One reported that twenty-five of the Templars in his prison had died under torture. Another said that he had been given nothing but bread and water for three solid months. Now the footless Templar was carried before the commissioners so he could show them the fire-blackened bones that had fallen from his feet as they had been burned off by his inquisitors. He wanted to retract the confessions he had made only to stop the unbearable agony of his treatment. One Templar produced a letter from Philip de Vohet, a priest who had been appointed by the commission to take charge of the imprisoned Templars. The letter set forth an order of the pope that any Templar who reversed his confession of guilt should be burned to death, a letter used to intimidate any Templar who had volunteered to defend his order. Called before the commission, de Vohet denied that he had ever seen the letter. When it was pointed out that the letter bore his seal, he said that someone else must have applied it.

The archbishop of Narbonne and two of the other commissioners were essentially creatures of Philip the Fair, but four of them were not, and they were beginning to grow suspicious at the tales of torture, bribery, and trickery. They were reserving judgment.

On March 28 all of the five hundred and forty-six volunteer Templar defenders were assembled in the garden of the palace of the bishop of Paris. The formal charges against the order were read to them, arousing shouts of anger in response. With order restored, the investigative procedure was explained to them, and they were told to choose those who would present their defense.

The Templars had noticed the absence of their grand master, whose orders they would still follow, and asked that he be brought to the gathering. They were told that Jacques de Molay had made it very clear that he would talk to no one but the pope, so he would not be a part of this hearing. With no other choice open to them, their defenders were agreed upon.

They were four in number. Templar knights William de Chambonnet and Bertrand de Sartiges were not learned men, but the other two, who were Templar priests, were men of both learning and experience. Reynaud de Pruino had served as the preceptor of the Temple at Orleans. Peter de Boulogne had very specific experience in Church matters, gained when he had acted as the Templar preceptor in Rome. He quickly became the acknowledged leader of the defense, as he demonstrated that he needed no help from outside lawyers.

At the pretrial hearing on April 7 de Boulogne delivered his opening statement. The willingness to appear before this court was not to be taken as acknowledgment of the authority or jurisdiction of this commission. The Order of the Temple by this appearance did not waive its rights to appeal the judgment of this court to the pope and a formal council of the Church. The Templars would prove that the charges were false and would give that proof in oral testimony, in depositions, and in documentation. Justice required that the defenders be allowed the freedom to travel and access to their own Templar funds to adequately prepare their defense. ''Each and every one of us declare the accusations to be utterly unfounded. It is true that some Templars have admitted them, but only because of torture and suffering.'' He had the names of men who had died under torture. He charged that some men had been bribed to confess and charged that some confessions had been forged and falsified. The Rule that governed the order was not a secret. Not only was it available in writing, but it had been approved in every particular by a succession of popes.

He pointed out that there was no shortage of accusations, but no accusers. Let the accusers come forward to be examined, if any could be found. As to the abominable charge of Templars denying Christ, who could believe such a thing? There was no proof that any Templar had ever denied Christ, but there was a well-documented history of thousands of Templars who died rather than deny Him. Could anyone believe that men would deny the Savior in the security of their meetings, then refuse to deny him in Muslim prisons even to save their own lives? How could anyone stoop to heap scandal on these martyrs of the Church?

He made a point of asking that all laymen be prohibited from attending the hearing, especially the officers of the king of France, whose presence was clearly for the purpose of intimidating witnesses. (Those officers would report to King Philip that this Templar priest Peter de Boulogne was a man who must be stopped. It was obvious to any observer that some of the commissioners were being swayed by his arguments.)

The formal trial began on Saturday, April 11, 1310. The first witnesses were outsiders, whose testimony under examination was shown to be basically hearsay. One man stated that he had heard rumors of "evil practices" in the Templar chapter meetings. Another testified that he had heard a former Templar refer to iniquities in the order, but could not be specific. A former Templar servant said that the knights worshiped an idol, but under questioning could provide no details. One witness had the damning evidence that he had applied for membership in the Knights Templar but had been turned down. Peter de Boulogne could report to his imprisoned brothers that the trial was going well.

When it came time for the prosecutors to present Templar confessions in evidence, de Boulogne objected. True, there were written confessions here from Sicily, Naples, Lombardy, the Papal States, and especially France, but all of those confessions were the products of unbearable torture. He asked that all such confessions be judged inadmissible. He was overruled. He also called attention to the king's officers present at the trial and asked that they be kept away unless testifying as witnesses. The court took the request under advisement. He asked that all men who had testified be put into separate confinement so that they could not communicate with and influence those who had not yet appeared. Request denied.

In spite of the procedural setbacks, de Boulogne was pleased. Most of the outside witnesses had been discredited. Every confession under torture was being identified as such. It was clear that some of the papal commissioners had become suspicious of the whole business. It was clear as well to King Philip and his counsellors, and they were growing concerned. Some drastic action was called for, and someone came up with an answer that was perhaps more drastic than any of them had anticipated.

The archbishop of Sens had died, leaving a vacancy that Clement V had in mind for one of his own friends, but Philip now demanded the right to name the new archbishop. It was a powerful position that exercised clerical authority over the cities of Orleans, Chartres, Meaux, and, by far most important to Philip, the capital city of Paris. The candidate he proposed was Philip de Marigny, bishop of Cambrai, the younger brother of one of Philip's most loyal ministers. Clement V objected on the basis that the bishop of Cambrai was inexperienced and at the age of twenty-two did not even meet the Church's rule of a minimum age of twenty-five for a bishop. Philip countered with the reminder that the minimum-age rule had not kept Clement from naming his own twenty-three-year-old nephew as archbishop of Rouen, and he continued to press the point. The pope finally gave in, and in April 1310 the Templars approached their blackest hour as Philip de Marigny was consecrated as archbishop of Sens. What was expected of him had been clearly spelled out and agreed to in advance. The youthful archbishop was eager to demonstrate his gratitude to the king who had made him the beneficiary of instant power and wealth.

The plan was based on points of Church law. The papal commission had repeatedly made it clear that its mission was to investigate only the Templar order as a corporate entity, and it had no interest or authority in matters involving individual Templars. On the other hand, the popes had long ago assigned to the archbishops full authority to deal with individual heretics in their territories. That meant that Philip, through the archbishop, now had complete and final authority over every individual Templar in the prisons of Paris. It meant that he had the means to completely shatter the proceedings of the papal commission, including the ability to seize the four Templars acting as the defenders of the order.

The new archbishop moved swiftly. He called a council of his bishops for Monday, May 22, for the purpose of declaring the guilt of Templars in his territory and imposing their sentences. The announcement was not public, but the Templars learned about the archbishop's council the day before it was to convene. Although the papal commission had never met on a Sunday, the four Templar defenders sent their urgent pleas to the commissioners for an immediate emergency meeting. When they were assembled, Peter de Boulogne was called upon to explain this extraordinary request. The Templar priest replied: "The pope has set up this commission to investigate the Order of the Temple, and all Templars who wish to defend the order have been invited to appear before you. Most of the brethren have offered themselves as defenders. We are now advised, however, that the Archbishop of Sens has summoned his council for tomorrow to take action against those Templars who have offered to appear for the defense. This can only be for the purpose of preventing them from being heard in defense of the Order."

The archbishop of Narbonne, the president of the council, immediately realized why Philip had engineered the appointment of the youthful archbishop and had no intention of acting at cross purposes to his king. He suddenly remembered that he had promised to celebrate mass on this Sabbath day and hurried out of the room.

The bishop of Trent followed his example, remembering some pressing business of his own, and walked out of the meeting. Those commissioners who stayed behind invited Peter de Boulogne to make his statement.

"We are told," said the Templar defender, "that the Archbishop of Sens and his suffragans [subsidiary bishops] have decided to reopen proceedings against the Templars. As, however, we have been accepted as defenders of the Order before this commission, we claim that, until the commission has completed its inquiry, the Archbishop of Sens is not entitled to proceed against individual Templars. We claim that we are under the protection of this commission, and we ask that the Archbishop should be restrained. His action is irregular and unfair, and will make it impossible for the commission to fulfill its labors."

The commissioners discussed the problem among themselves and finally informed de Boulogne that after the most serious consideration, they could only express their regrets about the Templars' dilemma. It was clear that every archbishop had direct authority over individual heretics, including individual Templars, which had been assigned to him by the Holy Father himself. This commission had no authority to interfere with the archbishop of Sens operating under specific papal authority.

The next morning the papal commission reconvened and proceeded with business as usual, as though nothing had happened. Then in late morning, in the middle of their examination of a Templar servant, a messenger arrived with news that brought the hearing to a halt. The archbishop of Sens had acted, swiftly and viciously. He had summarily announced that all of the Templar prisoners had been consigned to four different categories:

First were those who had confessed to minor transgressions, mostly servants and craftsmen. After suitable penances, which would be assigned to them, they would be set free. Second, those who had confessed to more serious sins would be sentenced to prison terms according to the seriousness of their crimes. The third group was to be made up of those Templars who had stood up under their tortures and had made no confessions at all. They were all sentenced to life in prison.

The fourth group contained the fifty-four Knights Templar who had confessed under torture and had then retracted their confessions, many of whom had testified or would testify before the papal commission. They were ordered to be turned over immediately to the secular authorities to suffer the punishment designated for relapsed heretics: They would all be burned to death at the stake.

The papal commissioners were appalled by the actions of the

archbishop and dispatched emissaries to him to plead the point that his actions were destroying the efforts of the papal commission. Important witnesses had been sentenced to death, and those Templars who would be available to testify would do so in a state of abject terror. They asked the archbishop to postpone his activities until the papal commission had completed its mission. The archbishop responded that he had no desire to interfere with the important work of the papal commission and did not question its authority. In exchange, the commission should not question the archbishop's authority, nor try to interfere with his performance of his duties. In essence, the papal commissioners had been told to go away and to confine themselves to their own responsibilities.

As to the responsibilities of the secular arm, Philip was ready and eager to carry out the orders of the archbishop of Sens. The very next day, in the early morning, the fifty-four condemned Templars were taken from their dungeons. A number of other Templars from each prison were taken with them to witness the majesty of justice. In a field by the Paris gate of Porte Antoine, fifty-four stakes had been set in the ground during the night. The bundles of faggots were piled up nearby.

Most of the knights who were about to die were from noble families, and Philip had invited those families to come and watch their sons, brothers, or cousins being burned to death. After the Templars were chained to their stakes, and as the executioner's assistants were piling the faggots around them, priests went to each man, holding a crucifix in his face, pleading with him to take this last chance to save his soul and his life by confirming his original confessions against his order. Remarkably, not a single Templar would save his life by an act of treachery against the Templar order and his sacred vows. As the executioners lit their torches, the Templars' families were turned loose to add their own pleas to those of the priests. Not a single man would back off his martyrdom, and the soldiers had to tear tearful relatives away from the condemned men as the executioners thrust their flaming torches into the wood piled up to their waists.

Then came a horrible spectacle as flesh began to blister and roast away. Some of the Templars screamed in pain as others called out to them to be resolute, to trust in God. Others fought off the agony long enough to shout out the innocence of their holy order, all to a background of the yells and wails of their friends and relatives. One by one their screams and shouts died out, and the flames consumed what was left of fifty-four dead Knights of the Temple. The king's officers were delighted to report back to King Philip that the Templar witnesses, moving back to their prisons, had to be prodded to move along, so paralyzed were they by revulsion at what they had seen. They moved in raw fear that this same fate was waiting for them if they attempted to retract the confessions that had been tortured out of them.

The other provincial archbishops now saw clearly what their king expected of them, especially in the praise and favor showered by Philip on the bloodthirsty young archbishop of Sens. Not to be left out, the archbishop of Rheims and the archbishop of Rouen, the pope's nephew, called their own councils, sending Templars to prison or to the stake. In all, the archbishops ordered the burning of 120 Templars, and it says something for the strength of their faith that only two of the condemned Templars chose to lie to save their lives.

When the papal commissioners reconvened on November 3, 1310, many witnesses scheduled to be heard were dead, while those Templars who were brought before them stumbled in their speech, trembling in fear. Nor were the four Templar defenders present. In frustration, the commission adjourned until December 27, ordering that the Templar defenders be in attendance. Only two showed up, the secular Templars de Chambonnet and de Sartiges. They protested that they were not learned men and had no knowledge of the law. They asked that the commission not proceed until the two Templar priests, de Pruino and de Boulogne, could be present to actually conduct the defense, which they had done very well to this point. The court informed the two defenders that they would not be seeing de Pruino and de Boulogne again. They had been seized by the council of the archbishop of Sens and sentenced to imprisonment.

Terror gripped the two knights, who pleaded with the court to allow them to resign as Templar defenders, a position that obviously would inevitably lead to punishment and perhaps their deaths. The court accepted their resignations and let them be taken back to their prisons. Later, they learned that somehow the redoubtable Peter de Boulogne, chained in his dungeon, had managed to escape. He was never heard from again, but one must hope that this stalwart man found a life of peace, if not the revenge for which his very soul must have cried out.

The papal commission went ahead, hearing the confessions of men who had watched their brothers burn and now retracted their retractions. All was written out and collected for use by the highest prelates of the Church, who would decide the fate of the Templar order at the Council of Vienne, which the pope had postponed to October 1, 1311. Philip of France would be there, too, with an army.

31

The Destruction of the Temple
1311 to 1314

THE COUNCIL OF VIENNE had been called to plan a new Crusade, to settle the matter of the Knights Templar, to address complaints about the conduct of the clergy, and to discuss any other item the bishops cared to address. The bishops didn't really believe that the Christian world would respond to a call to Crusade, and the subject of stamping out corruption in the Church was uncomfortable because it frequently addressed the behavior and lifestyles of the bishops themselves. The issue that had aroused the major interest of the delegates was everything they had been hearing about the trials of the Templars.

It was not that the bishops and abbots were dedicated to the continued existence of the Order of the Temple. To the contrary, many of them had resented the Templars' privileges, especially those that exempted them from tithes and denied any authority over them to the bishops in whose dioceses they operated. Another sore point was gifts to the Temple. Any market, mill, town, or manor given to the Templars might otherwise have been given directly to the Church, which would put the property and its profits into the care of the local bishops. What aroused their principal concern, however, was the possibility that what had happened to the Templars could happen to them.

Whatever they had witnessed or heard about torture they had dealt with objectively, because the laws of the Church specifically protected the clergy from the ministrations of the Inquisition, but now those laws had been set aside or ignored to work every conceivable agony on the Templars, who were a religious order chartered by the Holy Father himself. Ordained Templar priests had been whipped, burned, and mutilated without regard to their sacred vocations. The grand master ranked as a mitred abbot, the equivalent of a bishop, but that status had not sheltered him. The Templar money and property had been seized as well, so that the wealthiest religious order in the Christian world had been reduced to abject poverty. If this council approved all of those actions, it would establish a dangerous precedent that could threaten the life and the possessions of every prelate in the Church. They surely could not vote in favor of that, and the issue became the primary topic of their private conversations.

The council had brought together twenty cardinals, four patriarchs, about a hundred archbishops and bishops, and an unrecorded number of abbots and priors from all parts of Europe. Every one of them was influenced by the politics of his own country, and some owed their appointments to their own kings. Many were from families with extensive landholdings and had to be careful not to offend their own secular rulers. The prelates of Naples had been told by their king to favor the interests of the king of France. The prelates of the Papal States, especially those from Rome, were largely dedicated to the concept that the pope, the bishop of Rome, should be an Italian, preferably a Roman. They were upset that the papal court was staying away from Rome, but they were well aware of the danger to a French pope who would dare to try to impose his will in the diocese of St. Peter. The Iberian clergy were from a war-torn land of unceasing conflict with resident Muslims, where the monarchs had clearly stated the importance of the Templars to the protection of their kingdoms. The English representatives were acutely aware that their countrymen were not happy with a pope under the domination of their traditional enemy, Philip of France. The assembled high prelates of the Church were anything but a cohesive group.

One matter they could all listen to with interest was the handling of the Templar issue in their respective countries, which only added to their concern and confusion. In all of the Iberian Peninsula the Templars had been found to be innocent of the charges, as they had been in Germany and Cyprus, in spite of the papal bulls asserting that those charges appeared to be true.

The situation in England was not at all clear. Even after the inquisitors sent by Clement V had finally been allowed to torture the Templar prisoners in England, no clear-cut confessions of heresy had been produced. The outside witnesses, mostly members of the monastic orders, had no direct evidence but simply parroted rumors or comments they had heard from others. The most damning confession produced was in the words frequently said by the Templar masters at the end of chapter meetings: "Of those transgressions not brought to light in this meeting, I now absolve you, to the extent that I am able."

As the councils in London and York examined the evidence, they could not find that the Templars were clearly guilty. On the other hand, the pope had said they were guilty, and the archbishops felt bound by the papal decree. The archbishop of Canterbury decided to try a little ecclesiastic plea bargaining, so he went to the English master William de la More at his cell in the Tower of London. The archbishop asked that de la More confess his heresy and express his repentance for his sin. The penance assigned would be very light, the imprisoned Templars would be the beneficiaries of great leniency, and the whole matter could be put to rest. Master de la More was affronted. He took it as a personal insult that anyone could believe that he would deliberately lie about the Templar order just to gain his personal freedom. He flatly rejected the archbishop's proposal.

With the preceptor unmovable in his conviction, the English Church decided to bargain directly with the captive Templars. They were asked about the sin they had witnessed in the granting of absolution at the ends of their meetings by officers who were not ordained priests, who alone could designate God's forgiveness of sin. The Templars objected on the grounds that the transgressions being absolved were violations of their Templar Rule, not sins against God. Besides, the absolution always ended with the words "to the extent that I am able." Well, all that aside, if the Templars would confess to the sin of a layman granting absolution and swear their own condemnation of the Templar heresies charged in the papal encyclicals, they could perform a minor penance and be free men, back in the bosom of the Church. That was too good a bargain to pass up, and most of the English Templars agreed.

They made their confessions in public, then were sent into monasteries to perform their penances. With that done, a few went into the Hospitallers, but most returned to secular lives, with meager pensions based on what the Church felt was the minimum amount required by a monk for food and clothing. They were cautioned that they were still bound by their lifetime oaths of poverty and chastity, but it is difficult to believe that they would have felt bound to those vows. As for those Templars who would not join in the plea bargain, firmly refusing to confess to any Templar guilt, they were sentenced to life imprisonment, but there is no record that those sentences were enforced. William de la More, who would have been in that category, escaped any punishment, as he died in his Tower prison a few months later. The council delegates were told that the king had happily seized the Templar property in England and had no intention of giving it up.

There was one more matter to discuss that would have to interest any bishop or cardinal who dreamed of one day being the pope. Philip of France had never relented in his desire for a posthumous condemnation of Pope Boniface VIII. Bringing down a pope, even a dead one, and finding him guilty of heresy, sodomy, and murder could only damage the entire Church, and the papacy in particular. Boniface's successor Benedict XI had refused to cooperate with Philip in such a horrible project, and his murder may have been related to that refusal. Clement V was no more eager to condemn Boniface than anyone else, but earlier that year Philip, once again accompanied by a small army, had gone to Clement to demand a papal tribunal against Boniface VIII. Clement was coerced into taking some action, and on February 11, 1311, he had caved in to Philip's demand by calling a tribunal of himself and a select group of cardinals to hear the charges, all of which they had heard many times before. William de Nogaret was the biggest embarrassment, because he was still under a ban of excommunication for the Crime of Anagni and shouldn't even have been allowed in the presence of the highest officers of the Church. They were not, however, prepared to tell Philip that his royal chancellor would not be allowed to appear, so de Nogaret became the principal prosecutor.

The witnesses produced by the defense were all clerics, who testified that Boniface VIII was a true son of the Church, legally elected, who brought honor to the Crucified One and His Holy Mother. Their testimony was sober but impassioned. The testimony of de Nogaret's witnesses was wild. They swore that Boniface scorned the sacraments of the Church and desecrated them with a life of depravity. The charges of flagrant homosexuality were repeated, as was the old allegation that he had sexual congress with a demon who lived in his ring. To these was added the new charge that he had beheaded a rooster and spread its blood in a magic circle, calling on Satan to cast spells on his many enemies. He had denied Christ and had rejected the scripture that said His mother was a virgin. He had denied any life after death, saying that the concepts of heaven and hell were promulgated only to control the ignorant. Accusations went on and on, far beyond the abominable charges that had been made before, so that Clement and the cardinals became extremely agitated. Where would this all stop?

Clement finally put an end to this anti-papal madness, but no record was made of how it was done. All that was recorded was that Philip suddenly called off the tribunal by withdrawing the charges. A deal had been cut, probably an assurance that the Templar suppression at the forthcoming council was guaranteed. We do know that some bargain was reached because just before the adjournment of the tribunal, de Nogaret was relieved of his excommunication. Boniface VIII was absolved of all charges, his legal election was confirmed and his dedication to the Church was praised, but at the same time all of Boniface's bulls against Philip and the kingdom of France were retracted and ordered to be removed from the papal records. Philip himself was absolved of any responsibility for the recent conflicts between Church and crown and was declared to be a loyal son of Holy Mother Church, whose every act had been out of concern for the purity of the faith. The fact that many of the statements made about Philip and Boniface were ridiculously contradictory didn't appear to bother Clement or Philip, but the watching world could hardly avoid the conclusion that another bargain had been struck between king and pope. The delegates to the council knew very well of Philip's determination to suppress the Templar order and could have little doubt about the major subject of that bargain.

The Council of Vienne opened on October 1, 1311. True to his bargain with Philip, Pope Clement V opened the council with an angry attack on the Knights Templar. With over two thousand confessions, their guilt could not possibly be open to question. Those confessions had been classified into 127 charges, demonstrating that tedious legal filings with endless repetitions in a veritable orgy of synonyms is not just a recent phenomenon. The reading of those charges droned on endlessly, but they can be grouped to reduce the verbiage to an understandable brief. Essentially, they were these:

1. The Templars renounced God, or Jesus Christ, or His Holy Mother, or the saints. They did this at their initiation or after their initiation. Some of them confessed to believing that Christ had died for his own sins, not for those of others, and did not hold the key to salvation.

2. They denied Christianity by worshiping Satan in the form of a cat.

3. They did not believe in the holy sacraments and omitted from the mass the words of consecration *Hoc est corpus meum* ("This is my body"), so that the host was not consecrated.

4. The Templars spit on or alongside the cross. Sometimes they stamped on the cross. This was their custom on Good Friday.

5. The Templars were absolved of their sins, not by priests, but by their own officers. Grand Master de Molay had personally confessed to this crime.

6. At their initiations new Templars were required to kiss the receiving officer *in umbilico*, on his navel, *in ano seu spina dorsi*,

on his lower spine, and (in what sounds like a bit of Victorian por-
nography) *in virga virili*, on his "manly rod."

7. Initiations were totally secret, with no one present except
members.

8. Homosexual practices were permitted, sometimes encouraged.
Whether the individual Templar took the active or passive role, no
sin was involved, so there was no need for confession and penance.

9. Various idols were worshiped, sometimes represented as the
head of Jesus Christ. The idols were said to bring wealth and good
fortune, to make the earth flower and the trees to bear fruit.

10. Girdles that had touched the idols were worn by the
Templars, sometimes simply a cord, and those who refused to wear
them were imprisoned or secretly murdered.

11. Templars swore never to discuss the secrets of the order, not
even with each other, under threat of imprisonment or death.

12. They were allowed to confess their sins to no priests except
those in their order.

13. Even though fully aware of the grievous sins of their order,
the Templars neglected to object to them, to correct them, or to
report them to Church authorities.

14. The highest Templar officers, the grand master, preceptors,
and visitors (inspectors), had confessed to the guilt of the order.

Many delegates to the council were skeptical. Quite apart from
the fact that the confessions were extracted by torture, where
was the physical evidence? If individual Templars had been
murdered because they told secrets or refused to participate in
heretical practices, where were the bodies? Had the inquisitors failed
to ask where they were buried? If idol worship was so common,
where were the idols?

The charge of sodomy was being overworked. St. Dominic had
accused the Cathars of it. Philip had leveled the same charge at
Boniface VIII. Charges against men in high stations seemed always
to be made in bunches rather than in single charges, and sodomy
always seemed to be included. All of the ecclesiastics at the council
knew of actual homosexual practices by kings, barons, and high
clergymen in their own lands, but no none seemed to care about
those. Secret meetings were no sin: the bishops held plenty of secret
meetings themselves, as did every ruler and pope throughout
history. If a sin, it was not a sin a man should die for. Clement V
thundered on in papal rage that the Knights Templar were so guilty
that they merited no defense. He called for the unanimous vote of
the council to summarily effect the total condemnation of the
Templar order.

The delegates didn't buy it. They expressed their doubts and insisted that the Templars had the right to defend themselves before this council. Clement retorted that when his papal commission had called upon the Templars to defend themselves, none had appeared. The delegates responded that they were well aware that the defenders of the Temple had been seized by the archbishop of Sens, who appeared to be acting more for Philip of France than for the Church. Now they wanted Templar defenders to be invited to appear, with full protection accorded to any men who would answer the call. Only the French archbishops of Sens, Rheims, and Rouen, with a small number of Italian bishops and cardinals, mostly from Naples and the Papal States, agreed with the pope. All of the other delegates favored the council inviting a Templar defense.

Since the pope's supporters were outnumbered more than five to one, Clement V reluctantly gave in to the will of the overwhelming majority and invited any Templar to come to the council to speak for his order. The response was a shock to him and everyone else.

A few days after the announcement, seven mounted and fully armed Knights Templar rode proudly through the gate into Vienne, their brilliant white robes bearing their familiar red Templar cross. They almost appeared to be ghosts of past Templar glory. They asked to be directed to the council, where their leader announced that they were here to defend the Templar order as the duly appointed representatives of between fifteen hundred and two thousand Templars hiding in the forests near the city of Lyons. Although surprised by their appearance, most of the delegates welcomed the Templars and their testimony.

They were not welcomed by Clement V, whose first thought was for his own personal safety. Lyons was just up the Rhône River, about twenty miles from Vienne. It was an ideal place for fugitive Templars to gather, because Lyons had been added to the kingdom of France by force less than two years earlier, and the local population was openly hostile to Philip the Fair. Clement had not given any thought to Templar vengeance on his own person, because most of the Templars he knew of in France were dead or in prison. Everyone knew that some Templars had escaped the trap of Friday the Thirteenth, including a party of knights that had been led away by the preceptor for France and those who had taken the ships from the Templar naval base at La Rochelle, but Clement had never thought there were so many. Now he had been told that a small army of the Templars who hated him were an easy ride away from this almost unguarded city.

The pope ordered that his personal bodyguard be doubled, and in his panic saw to his personal protection by ordering the arrest of the seven Templars. The delegates were incensed that their promise of protection to Templar defenders was so quickly violated and demanded that the Templars be released immediately. Clement felt constrained to turn the Templars loose, but in the absence of any other solution to his sudden dilemma, he adjourned the council until April 3 of the following year, 1312. During the six months' delay he could only pray that King Philip could arrest or disperse the Templars gathered at Lyons. As for the seven Templar knights, they had not been heard but were not going to take the risk of waiting for months to offer their defense. One night they saddled up and rode off to rejoin the fugitive Templars in the forest, perhaps to warn them that their hiding place was now known to Philip of France. In any event, when Philip sent troops to round them up, they didn't find a single Templar around Lyons.

Travel was much too tedious for the delegates to go home and come back, so they spent the winter months in Vienne. Their presence put an unexpected burden on the town, so that food grew scarce and prices went up. Their quarters were damp and cold to men who had not brought cold-weather clothing. They were thoroughly miserable all day long, bored with the prolonged inactivity.

For Philip and his staff, there was plenty of activity. His envoys were busy keeping pressure on a consistory of cardinals that pursued the business of the council during the adjournment and on the pope himself. The Jesuit scholar Norman P. Tanner wrote, "Secret bargains had been made between Clement V and envoys of Philip IV from 17 to 29 February, 1312; the council fathers were not consulted. By this bargaining Philip obtained the condemnation of the Templars. It is most likely that he used a threat that he would bring a public action against Boniface VIII."

Philip gave that threat some substance by calling an assembly of the estates general of France in Lyons a few days later. On March 18 he met with Clement personally and in private. Two days later Clement presented to the consistory of cardinals the bull *Vox in excelso*, disbanding the Templar order in the parliamentary sense of revoking its charter, without finding it guilty of any crime. The result would be the same, and the pope could act alone, with no need to debate the matter in the council or to hear additional testimony, especially any direct Templar defense. The delegates by now were physically miserable and half starved, eager to be away from this ecclesiastic exile and back in their comfortable homes. They were in no mood for a prolonged debate.

When *Vox in excelso* was presented to the council on the opening day of its second session on April 3, 1312, it was quickly approved. Clement soon followed with an announcement that he would call a new Crusade (which never happened) to set the stage for the disposal of the Templar property. Over the ensuing weeks there was a battery of bulls and encyclicals published, which are worth quoting, at least in part. To start with, Pope Clement V presents in *Vox in excelso* the background of the Templar suppression:

"...a little while ago, about the time of our election as supreme pontiff...we received secret intimations against the master, preceptors and other brothers of the order of Knights Templar of Jerusalem and against the order itself. These men had been posted in lands overseas for the defense of the patrimony of our lord Jesus Christ, and as special soldiers of the Catholic faith and outstanding defenders of the Holy Land seemed to carry the chief burden of the Holy Land. For this reason the holy Roman Church honored these brothers and their order with her special support, armed them with the sign of the cross against Christ's enemies, paid them the highest tributes of respect, and strengthened them with various exemptions and privileges. They experienced in many and various ways her help and that of all faithful Christians with repeated gifts of property. Therefore it was against the lord Jesus Christ himself that they fell into the sin of impious apostasy, the abominable vice of idolatry, the deadly crime of the men of Sodom, and various heresies."

Having established the extent to which the Church had extended its support and faith to the Templars, the pope had to address the fact that there were many who did not believe the charges against the order. He sympathized by saying that he, too, had a difficult time accepting their guilt:

"Yet it was not to be expected nor seem credible that men so devout, who were outstanding often to the point of shedding their blood for Christ, who were seen to expose themselves frequently to the danger of death, who even more frequently gave signs of their devotion both in divine worship and in fasting and other observances, should be so unmindful of their salvation as to commit such crimes. The order, moreover, had a good and holy beginning and won the approval of the apostolic see. The rule, which is holy, reasonable and just, had the deserved sanction of that see. For these reasons we were unwilling to listen to insinuation and accusations against the Templars: We had been taught by our Lord's example and the words of canonical scripture."

What had changed the pope's mind about the guilt of the Templars had been the revelations of a faithful son of the Church, bearing the banner of Truth with absolutely no thought of personal gain:

"Then came the intervention of our dear son in Christ, Philip, the illustrious King of France. The same crimes had been reported to him. He was not moved by greed. He had no intention of claiming or appropriating for himself anything from the Templars' property ...." So [putting aside the fact that he had already raped every Templar preceptory in France of every movable item of value], why did he do it? "He was on fire with zeal for the orthodox faith, following in the well-marked footsteps of his ancestors [a reference to St. Louis]. Then, in order to give us greater light on the subject, he sent us much valuable information through his envoys and letters."

The conscientious pope had no choice but to consider the possibility that the accusations were true:

"We were duty bound by our office to pay heed to the weight of such grave and repeated accusations. When at last there came a general hue and cry with the clamorous denunciations by the said king, and of dukes, counts, barons and other nobles, clergy and the people of the kingdom of France, reaching us directly and through agents and officials, we heard a woeful tale—that the master, preceptors and other brothers of the order as well as the order itself had been involved in these and other crimes." There was no mention of torture, of course, but there was at least the admission that the grand inquisitor had been there, apparently as a passive observer: "This seemed to be proved by the many confessions, attestations and depositions of the visitor of France [Hugh de Peraud], and of the many preceptors and brothers of the order in the presence of many prelates and the inquisitor of heresy."

Now the pope had a confession of his own to make. Based on the evidence, there simply was not a legal basis on which the order could be found guilty. The suppression or dissolution of the order would be justified on the basis that the reputation of the order had been so blackened that no one would join it, and that being true it could not fulfull its mission; its purpose could no longer be served. Once again, torture was not mentioned, and the confessions that had been produced by months of indescribable agony were described as "spontaneous":

"...although legal process against the order up to now does not permit its condemnation for heresy by definite sentence under canon law, the good repute of the order had been largely taken away by the heresies attributed to it. In addition, a number of individual members...have been convicted of such heresies, crimes and sins through their spontaneous confessions. These confessions render the order very suspect, and the infamy and suspicion render it detestable to the holy Church of God, to her prelates, to kings and other rulers, and to Catholics in general. It is also believed that from now on there will be no good person who wishes to enter the order, and so it will be made useless to the Church of God and for service to the Holy Land, for which service the knights had been dedicated.''

Although the fact that no one would ever join the order again was given as a major reason for its suppression, the final decree nevertheless forbade anyone to join, on threat of excommunication:

"Therefore, with a sad heart, not by definitive sentence, but by apostolic provision or ordinance [the direct orders of the pope], we suppress, with the approval of the sacred council, the order of Templars, and its rule, habit and name, by an inviolable and perpetual decree. We entirely forbid that any from this time forward should enter the order, or receive or wear its habit, or presume to behave as a Templar. If anyone acts otherwise he incurs automatic excommunication. In addition, we reserve the persons and the property of the Templars for our own disposition and the apostolic see.''

No matter how brutal and outrageous the events of the past few years or how farcical the explanation, the Order of the Poor Fellow-Soldiers of Christ and the Temple of Solomon was finished. Now even to act like a Templar was a crime to be punished.

The decision to suppress the Templar order in the parliamentary sense had been a major compromise on the part of Philip IV. A conviction of heresy would have provided the automatic opportunity to confiscate all of the Templar property in France. Its suppression by revocation of its papal charter meant that there would be no confiscation as such, but that their property could be disposed of by the pope personally. Philip had gone so far as to suggest that the answer was in a new military order to which would be contributed all the personnel, property, and wealth of the Templars and Hospitallers. One of his sons would rule the new order, but instead of being known as the grand master he would have the royal title of king of Syria and Egypt, in anticipation of the ultimate conquest of those territories by the force of Christian arms. No one liked the concept except Philip. The solution agreed upon does indicate that Clement V was not totally dominated by Philip of France, but Philip had enough power and influence to negotiate additional cash for himself as the price of his cooperation.

On May 2 came the bull *Ad providam*, which gave to the Knights Hospitaller of St. John all of the properties of the Knights Templar except those located in Aragon, Castile, Portugal, and the Balearics (Majorca). Philip already had all of the Templars' movables in France, all their treasure, and freedom from his Templar debts, but he had more coming. He got Clement V to agree that the secular monarchs, who after all had just been obeying the pope's orders to them, should be allowed to charge against the Templar properties the cost of arresting and feeding the Templars, the cost of maintaining the properties they had been "holding" for the Church, down even to the cost of the stakes, faggots, and torches required to burn the Templars to death. The arrangement was profitable to the Hospitallers but a cash drain for the next few years, because although they received substantial real estate, they had to part with money to get it.

Four days later, on May 6, came the papal bull *Considerantes*, which dealt with the fates of individual Templars. The pope reserved for himself the judgments and sentencing of Grand Master de Molay; Geoffrey de Charnay, the preceptor of Normandy; Geoffrey de Gonneville, preceptor of Poitou and Aquitaine; and Hugh de Peraud, the visitor of France (and former treasurer) who had cooperated with Philip's officers since the first day. A minor mystery of this bull is that Clement V also reserved for himself the fate of a Templar knight identified as "brother Oliver de Penne." There is no indication of the reason for this special treatment. He may have been an informant, a relative of the pope, or simply from a powerful family. We shall probably never know, since he appears and disappears within the pages of this bull with no further citation anywhere.

All of the other Templars were to be judged and sentenced by provincial councils, which effectively approved the actions of the French archbishops who had imprisoned and burned individual Templars, since it was the archbishops of the Church who called and presided over those provincial councils. The councils were advised to show mercy and compassion except in the cases of relapsed heretics who denied their confessions or those who did not properly express their sincere repentance.

Special consideration was given to those fugitive Templars who had not been caught or had not turned themselves in, perhaps prompted by the pope's memory of his fright at the discovery of the hundreds of escaped Templars who had gathered near Lyons. The usual rule for those suspected of heresy was repeated, but to be dated from this sixth day of May in 1312 to give them one last chance to come forward. It was decreed that all Templars in hiding must surrender themselves to their bishops within one year. Those who did not would suffer excommunication. After one year in that condemned state, if they still had not turned themselves in, they would be decreed to be guilty of heresy with no right of appeal. In other words, any fugitive Templar who did not surrender by May 6, 1314, was automatically subject to death at the stake if he should ever be taken. None of them ever was.

In his subsequent calling of a new Crusade, the pope made another cash concession to Philip of France. He was to be permitted to tax the clergy of France to the extent of 10 percent of their total revenues for six years to provide funds for his Crusade to the Holy Land. Since he never went, it seems safe to assume that he pocketed the money.

Although it had not been on the original agenda, the council did take time to address the excesses of inquisitors, dramatized by the recent torments of the Knights Templar. The Christian world had not experienced such an orgy of mistreatment, torture, and burnings since the Albigensian Crusade years earlier, and the Templars were not of a strange religion but, at least formerly, dedicated sons of the Holy Roman Church. The Inquisition, operated principally by the Dominican order, had functioned in complete independence, freely imprisoning and torturing in any bishop's diocese, without his permission and often without his knowledge. Now the bishops took steps to establish some rules for the conduct of inquisitors.

Any room used as a prison for suspected heretics was to have two keys, one held by the inquisitors and one by a delegate of the bishop, so that neither could approach the prisoners without the other on hand to observe his conduct. No torture was to be applied and no sentence passed without the bishop or his representative present. As an indication of past abuses, inquisitors were enjoined from arresting people for the purpose of extorting money from them. They were told to stop helping themselves to funds that had been provided to feed the prisoners and to gifts brought to suspects by their relatives and friends. To prevent youthful enthusiasm from being applied to the torture process, it was further decreed that from this day forward a man could not be appointed to the office of inquisitor until he had reached forty years of age.

While the rulers did tend to limit excesses in treatment and motivation, they did not place curbs on the torture itself. Those limitations would only begin in the reign of Clement's successor, the controversial Pope John XXII. That pope's limitations brought a complaint from the Dominican inquisitor Bernard de Gui, who said that any boundaries placed on the application of torture would make the Inquisition's assigned task that much more difficult.

The provincial councils quickly disposed of the Templars who had spent the past six years in prison. Those who had staunchly maintained the innocence of the order, making no personal confessions, were sentenced to imprisonment for life. Those who had confessed but had retracted those confessions were now not burned at the stake but sentenced to life in prison. Those who stood by their confessions were called upon for acts of contrition. After their penances were performed they were granted absolution for their sins and released to take whatever roles they could find to supplement the meager pensions granted to them from the Templar properties.

In spite of the formal decree that had wiped out his order, Grand Master de Molay continued to insist on his right to put his case directly to the pope. Clement V, however, had no intention of meeting the grand master face to face. The four high officers languished in their dungeon until the pope finally appointed a commission of three cardinals to conduct a final examination and pronounce a final judgment on them. They could not have been comfortable with the news that the pope had asked the Templar-hating archbishop of Sens to assist the commissioners. He was probably a strong influence on their final sentences.

In the plea bargaining before the final judgment, the four officers had agreed to hold fast to their earlier confessions, in exchange for which they would be shown the mercy and leniency the pope had recommended. They stood in front of the red-clad judges and one at a time confirmed their confessions. Waiting for their lenient treatment, they were horrified to hear the sonorous announcements that condemned them all to imprisonment for life. They were hustled out of the chamber and taken back to their cells. As shocked and angry as they were, they could only advise each other that the probable reward for strong objections to their sentences or retraction of their confessions would be death.

During the ensuing months, sitting in his chains, Jacques de Molay could not have been happy with his own behavior throughout the whole grotesque affair. He had clung to the idea that if he could just get to the pope, he could have the charges removed. He had declined to act as a defender of the order, leaving that responsibility to others. In his advanced years, he had been certain that the torture would kill him and had confessed falsely just to avoid the pain. Now past seventy, he could look back on a long life of service, much of it in rewarding positions of leadership, but he had not acted like a leader during the years that the order needed him the most. He had let down the order and the men who looked to him for guidance. He could only wallow in the deep depression of his failure as a man, as a Templar, and as a grand master.

To top it off with one final humiliation, he was approached with the news that he must make a public declaration of his crimes. There had been emerging an undercurrent of feelings that the Templars had been suppressed in a great act of greed, to get hold of their gold and their properties. At the end, the order had not been found guilty of heresy. The Templars may well have been the victims, not the criminals. To put that kind of destructive rumor to rest, the pope and the king had decided to call an assembly of the people of Paris so they could hear for themselves the confessions of crime and sin from the highest officers of the Templar order.

The whole world was invited to attend the dramatic event. A platform was built in front of the cathedral of Notre Dame to put the Templar criminals in full view of the clergy, the nobles, and the commoners who gathered to watch the final degradation of the Knights Templar. On March 18, 1314, the Templar officers, dressed in their Templar robes for unmistakable identification and in chains to clearly mark them as criminals, were brought to the steps of the platform.

The four officers were herded and prodded up the long flight of steps, two of them past seventy years of age, but nevertheless weighted down with chains. They were lined up in full view of the crowd below as the charges against the Templar order were read in a loud voice. This was Jacques de Molay's last chance to vindicate himself and to clear the order he had commanded and had so neglected in the final years of misery. Perhaps his reaction came on the spur of the moment, or it may have been that he had spent the entire night in prayers for strength, for whatever attempt he might make to recant his confession would most certainly result in his own death, and the most painful death known to the medieval mind. Whatever his motivation, the time had come when he could take no more. As he stepped forward in obedience to the command that he publicly confess to the expectant crowd, he seized the moment and asserted his place in history. He stared at the crowd for a moment as all strained to hear his words, and then he spoke:

"I think it only right that at so solemn a moment, when my life has so little time to run, I should reveal the deception which has been practiced and speak up for the truth. Before heaven and earth and all of you here as my witnesses, I admit that I am guilty of the grossest iniquity. But the iniquity is that I have lied in admitting the disgusting charges laid against the Order. I declare, and I must declare, that the Order is innocent. Its purity and saintliness are beyond question. I have indeed confessed that the Order is guilty, but I have done so only to save myself from terrible tortures by saying what my enemies wished me to say. Other knights who have retracted their confessions have been led to the stake, yet the thought of dying is not so awful that I shall confess foul crimes which have never been committed. Life is offered to me, but at the price of infamy. At such a price, life is not worth having.

I do not grieve that I must die if life can be bought only by piling one lie upon another.''

Inspired by the example of his grand master, Geoffrey de Charnay stepped forward to add his own retraction, declaring the innocence of the Knights Templar, although drowned out by the shouts of the angry crowd. They had to believe what they had just heard, because this was the confession of a dying man! The king's officers and the friars of the Inquisition were confused by the sudden turnaround of the carefully planned drama. They hurried the Templars off the platform, telling the people to disperse and go home.

Philip was outraged that his officers could allow this to happen after all the trouble that had been taken to convince the people of the Templar guilt. The death of the grand master would not correct the situation but at least would keep it from getting worse. Not a moment's delay would be tolerated in putting these relapsed Templar heretics to death. The place chosen was the little island of du Palais in the Seine River, far from people milling in the streets, still talking about the retraction of de Molay. The word leaked out, and soon river boats were carrying to the island those who wanted to witness the last moments of the Templar master. They would report back what they had seen to their families and friends.

Two stakes were set for de Molay and de Charnay. They were stripped of their Templar robes and chained to the stakes while the executioners surrounded them with carefully selected cured wood and charcoal to produce a slow-burning fire of intense heat that would roast the condemned men from the ground up, to prolong their lives and their agony for as long as possible.

As the fire took hold, de Molay and de Charnay shouted out the innocence of the Templar order, calling on God for justice. A legend grew that as Jacques de Molay's body blistered and burned he called down a curse on the king and his family for thirteen generations and on the pope who had condemned the holy order in a betrayal of God's trust. He called upon Philip and Clement V to meet him within the year before the throne of God to answer for their crime. The pope died during the following month, to be followed seven months later by Philip IV.

The next day, when the ashes had grown cold, the charred remains of de Molay and de Charnay were taken down to be disposed of as so much trash, because as excommunicants and heretics they were not entitled to have their remains buried in consecrated ground. Those ashes, however, had taken on a mysterious, even sacred aura. During the night people of Paris swam out to the island to put bits of cinders in their mouths, then swam back with the conviction that they were taking home holy relics. From those cold ashes grew legends, symbols, and even organizations over the centuries ahead that, whether based on fact or fantasy, evidenced a mystic memory of those warrior monks that would not let the Templars die.

Legacy

$\mathcal{T}$HE RULERS OF the kingdoms on the Iberian Peninsula had been angered by the attempts of Philip of France to wipe out the Templar order. Their primary concern was their land wars against the Muslims, who had lived there for five hundred years. They were not about to let Philip IV or anyone else deprive them of the military support of the fighting Knights Templar, who had been helping them to drive the Muslim enemy off the continent of Europe.

In Portugal, King Denis I took both men and properties of the Templars into a new secular order called the Militia of Jesus Christ (or, more popularly, the Knights of Christ) responsible directly to the king. In 1319 the order received the papal blessing of John XXII, who recognized it as a revival of the Knights Templar. Its most famous members were Prince Henry the Navigator and Vasco da Gama. The Knights of Christ used the distinctive red cross patée worn by the Templars, the same cross that artists used to decorate the sails of Columbus's ships, the *Niña*, the *Pinta* and the *Santa Maria*.

The king of Aragon converted his local Templars into a new military order called the Order of Montesa, in honor of Our Lady of Montesa. Before the century was over, it was combined with an older group called the Order of St. George of Alfama. Elsewhere within the Spanish kingdoms the dispossessed Templars, all of whom had been found innocent by the local archbishops, could join the Order of Calatrava in Castile or the Military Order of Alcantara in Leon and Galicia, where membership in the Military Order of Santiago (St. James) could also be sought. This last order had certainly been inspired by the original Templar purpose when it was formed in 1175 to protect the pilgrim roads to the most popular shrine in Europe, that of Santiago de Compostella. Tradition said that this shrine held the body of the Apostle James, which had been brought here after his head was cut off by King Herod Agrippa.

The Templars in Germany could join the Teutonic Knights, and ex-Templars everywhere could seek membership in the Knights Hospitaller of St. John. That order still exists today, although under a different name.

The present ponderous designation of the Hospitallers reflects their long history of survival: The Sovereign Military Hospitaller Order of St. John of Jerusalem, of Rhodes, and of Malta. The Hospitallers completed their conquest of the island of Rhodes in 1310, while the Knights Templar still languished in prison. They continued to provide help in holding the Muslims in check, but more and more as a naval force, rather than as a land army of mounted knights. In 1522 the Hospitallers were driven off Rhodes by the Turks, prompting them to seek another sea base in order to maintain their position as a naval power. In 1530 their search was rewarded when the emperor Charles V granted them the island of Malta. From their new base the Hospitallers acted as a buffer between Christian Europe and Muslim North Africa, earning the popular new name of the Knights of Malta. In 1798 the order lost Malta to Napoleon Bonaparte, who in turn lost it to the British. In 1834 the Knights of Malta established their present headquarters in Rome, where they are regarded by the Vatican as a sovereign power. Since the Hospitallers managed to operate for over five hundred years from their island bases of Rhodes and Malta, it is difficult to avoid speculating on the possible fate of the Templars, had they established a sovereign state by holding on to the island of Cyprus. That property comprised a larger area, and yielded greater revenues, than the two Hospitaller islands combined.

All of the honorable alternatives available to the Knights Templar were, of course, limited to those members who had been found innocent, or who had confessed and then served their prison terms, if any, and had performed the penances prescribed for them by their ecclesiastic judges. The fates of those Templars who had escaped from their prisons, or those who had eluded arrest, were shrouded in mystery. What happened to the Templars who had gathered in the forest near Lyons during the Council of Vienne? Where were the Templar ships that had not been taken, and the Templar knights who commanded them? Where were the English Templars who had used their three-month warning period to go underground? All of those men who escaped arrest were excommunicated and, once the time for turning themselves in expired, were also judged guilty of heresy and doomed to die at the stake if discovered. But they weren't found. Were they just hiding, far from home and under assumed names? Did each fugitive Templar exist isolated from his brothers, or were secret bands formed, who kept in touch with each other for the purpose of mutual protection? Is there any truth behind the legend that in 1314 fugitive Knights Templar fought alongside Scotland's Robert Bruce at the Battle of Bannock Burn? The mystery provided ideal fodder for fantasy and legend, as did the drama surrounding the most memorable event of the Templar suppression, the murder of the last grand master.

A deathbed confession held the highest level of credibility, so the final suicidal words wrung from Jacques de Molay stood not just as a last-minute protestation, but to many were clear proof of the innocence of the whole order. That conclusion was supported by the news that the Knights Templar had been found innocent in Germany, Cyprus, Spain, and Portugal, and in England had been given what, for the time, was a mere slap on the wrist. The grotesque brutality of the Inquisition had been concentrated in France and in the French and papal lands in Italy. To those who believed in the Templars' innocence, Philip IV and Clement V were guilty villains. That great surge of popular speculation caused Church historians of the day to adopt a position that they have never abandoned. King Philip alone, they recorded, was the guilty party, and such cooperation as he received from Pope Clement was exacted through his unceasing pressure upon the pontiff, combined with constant threats. French chroniclers, in response, defended their king by emphasizing that the Templars were unquestionably guilty, arguing that the devout sovereign of France had performed an outstanding service to Christendom in general and to the papacy in particular.

Persistent tales of missing Templar treasure, the disappearance of the ships from the Templar naval base at La Rochelle, the speculations about the activities of Templar fugitives, the whispered revelations of hideous tortures in dank dungeons all worked together to excite men's myth-making propensities. There are many who believe, with no concrete evidence, that one item of Templar treasure that avoided confiscation was the Shroud of Turin. There was magic to be considered, too, in the accusations of the idolatrous worship of heads and cats. The alleged desecrations of the cross may well have led to later stories of trampling, spitting, and urinating on the cross as part of a satanic ritual called the Black Mass.

Then there was the exhilarating prospect of revenge, the first love of storytellers throughout history. Kings, popes, and even gods were known to seek the revenge that to them was the only acceptable form of justice. In the case of the Templars, the first recorded mention of vengeance may have come from the contemporary Italian poet, Dante Alighieri. In his *Purgatorio*, the poet pointed to the sins of Philip IV. Calling the French king "the new Pilate," Dante sought divine retribution for Philip's crimes against Pope Boniface VIII and the Knights of the Temple:

"...I see the fleur-de-lis [of France] enter Anagni and Christ's Vicar made captive...I see the new Pilate so ruthless that this does not sate him, but without law he bears into the Temple with his greedy sails. O my lord, when shall I rejoice to see the vengeance which, hid in thy secret council, makes sweet thy wrath?"

The first act of Templar vengeance, in the minds of many, came with the death of King Philip IV, less than a year after the burning of Jacques de Molay and well within the time frame of the grand master's legendary curse. Philip was out with a hunting party on November 29, 1314, when he was gripped by a sudden seizure. He was carried back to his palace to die, after which his heart was cut out of his body and sent with a holy relic to a monastery near Paris. The relic was a splinter of the True Cross, encased in gold and jewels, which Philip had stolen from the Knights Templar. Common gossip had no problem deciding that the undiagnosed seizure was in fact the result of poison administered to the king in an act of Templar vengeance. Another legend claims that centuries later, during the French Revolution, when the guillotine cut the head off King Louis XVI, a man leapt onto the platform. Plunging his hands into the dead king's blood, the man then flicked the blood out over the crowd, shouting, "Jacques de Molay, thou art avenged!"

Generations of writers have enriched the body of Templar legend, beginning with the crusading minnesinger Wolfram von Eschenbach. In his epic *Parsifal*, Eschenbach portrayed the Templars as part of the Grail family and guardians of the Grail Castle. Sir Walter Scott made Knights Templar the villains of his novels *Ivanhoe* and *The Talisman*. In our own time, *Holy Blood, Holy Grail*, a book published in London in 1982, speculated on a secret role for the original Templars as guardians of a holy royal bloodline emanating from the alleged marriage of Jesus Christ to Mary Magdalene. In 1988 Umberto Eco published his novel, *Foucault's Pendulum*, which had as its central theme the progress of a plot to rule the world, formed six hundred years earlier by a secret society of fugitive Knights Templar.

It is not just in words and whispers that the Templars have lived on, but in formal organizations as well. One historian claims to have identified eighteen different groups that call themselves Templars, although none of them has gained recognition by the Church. Several claim a legitimate descendancy, and at least one modern

Templar order claims to have been founded when Jacques de Molay, from his dungeon, dictated a letter naming a secret successor as grand master, establishing a line that remains unbroken to this day. In World War II, the young men appointed by General "Wild Bill" Donovan's to his staff in the new Office of Strategic Services, feeling like Crusaders, were pleased to refer to their group as the Knights Templar.

It is safe to state that nowhere is the memory of the Knights Templar kept alive with more zeal than in the worldwide order of Free and Accepted Masons, the oldest and largest fraternal society in the world. Freemasonry is the only organization, other than the Templars themselves, to find its principal identity in the Temple of Solomon in Jerusalem. As revealed in London in 1717 and revised during its early years, Freemasonry had just three basic degrees, the highest of which makes a member a Master Mason.

Today, having achieved that status, he can follow a number of paths, of which the most popular in the United States are the two "appendant" systems commonly referred to as York Rite and Scottish Rite.

The York Rite Mason progresses through a series of degrees that culminate in his being made a Masonic Knight Templar. The York Rite Templar commanderies in the United States alone claim over a quarter of a million members. They maintain a national foundation for research into eye diseases of children; and fund cataract surgery for the financially disabled. Scottish Rite Masonry has almost a million members in America, in a system that awards degrees numbered from four through thirty-two. (Explaining why one occasionally hears a man being identified as a "thirty-second degree Mason".) A thirty-third degree does exist; it is not earned automatically but is awarded solely in recognition of meritorious service. In one jurisdiction, the Scottish Rite Mason is made a "Knight Kadosh." *Kadosh* is direct from the Hebrew, and means "holy." The "Holy Knight" of this degree is the Knight Templar. The story of the final days of Grand Master Jacques de Molay, along with a brief history of the Templar order, is recounted to the candidate for the degree. The spirit of the degree is to call upon the initiate to be aware of, and to resolutely oppose, all forms of personal and religious injustice.

An interesting aftermath to the attainment of the level of the Knight Templar in York Rite or the thirty-second degree in Scottish Rite is that the Mason is then eligible to seek membership in the Ancient Arabic Order of the Nobles of the Mystic Shrine, to become a Shriner. The Shriners divide their time between fun and charity (such as their twenty-two free hospitals for burned and crippled children), but they do so in an Arab-Egyptian atmosphere that makes frequent allusions to the Crusades.

The Freemasons also sponsor an organization for tens of thousands of young men between thirteen and twenty-one years old, which memorializes the fallen grand master in its name, the Order of de Molay. Stories recalling the condemnation of the Templar officers and the burning of the last grand master are part of the de Molay ceremonies.

No Masonic body claims direct descent from the original Knights Templar; they usually claim instead to have originated in medieval guilds of cathedral and castle builders. The persistence of legend, however, and the frequent references to the crusading order in Masonic ritual, sent me off into several years of separate research. Although not a Freemason, I became fascinated by the unfolding revelations of Templar roots for Masonic ritual, particularly in regard to Masonic symbols and terminology so ancient that their origins and meanings had been lost to the Freemasons themselves. (The results of that research were published in 1990 in a book titled *Born in Blood: The Lost Secrets of Freemasonry*.)

No book about the Knights Templar should close without citing what is probably the most thoughtful gesture ever made to honor their memory. It was staged by the barristers of the Temple in London, whose connections with the Templars are an interesting bit of history in themselves.

The most valuable property in England awarded to the Hospitallers by Clement V after the suppression of the Knights Templar was the Templar headquarters in London, between Fleet Street and the Thames River, an area still known simply as the Temple. The only surviving Templar structure on the property is the Temple Church. Built of beautiful stone brought from Normandy as ship's ballast, the church was consecrated by Heraclius, the patriarch of Jerusalem, in 1185. The original church is circular, with a larger retangular choir added in 1240.

The Hospitallers already had a London headquarters at Clerkenwell, so they had no real need for the Templar base. They leased it for inns that provided rooms and offices for the trial lawyers who practiced law at the King's Court, just a few yards away through the gate between London and the royal city of Westminster. Its location gave the gate the name of the *Barrière du Temple*, later anglicized to the Temple Bar. Those trial lawyers passing back and forth through the "Bar" became known as "barristers."

In 1534 the Hospitallers lost the property to the crown in the dissolution of the monasteries by Henry VIII, who honored the tenancy of the barristers. In 1608, the "Benchers," the senior barristers of the Temple, purchased the property from King James I, in an agreement under which they promised to assume responsibility for the maintenance of the Temple Church. Seldom has a trust been so conscientiously honored. Not only is the church meticulously maintained, but it was carefully rebuilt after the severe damage inflicted by the Luftwaffe during the London blitz in May 1941.

Holding a unique status, the Temple Church is not a part of any diocese. Its Anglican canon, who bears the title of Master of the Temple, reports directly to the crown. The church is frequently open to visitors, including the penitential cell built into the walls, where the Templar marshal for Ireland was confined in punishment until he starved to death. There is a tomb thought to be that of the patriarch Heraclius, and effigies from the tombs of medieval knights that serve to demonstrate that the barristers of the Inner and Middle Temple are acutely aware of the history of their church.

When General Edmund Allenby led a column of British troops through the gates of Jerusalem in 1917, where no Christian army had set foot since 1244, the barristers of the Temple held a special service. Its highlight was a chivalrous gesture that took place as the barristers processed into the round church of the Templars and placed laurel wreaths of victory on the effigies of the knights, to convey the silent message, "You are not forgotten." And they are not.

Nor will they be.

Grand Masters of Knights Templar

Hugh de Payens	1118 - 1136	Philip de Plessiez	1201 - 1208
Robert de Craon	1136 - 1146	William de Chartres	1209 - 1219
Everard des Barres	1146 - 1149	Pedro de Montaigu	1219 - 1230
Bernard de Trémélai	1149 - 1153	Armand de Perigord	(?) - 1244
André de Montbard	1153 - 1156	Richard de Bures	1245 - 1247
Bertrand de Blanquefort	1156 - 1169	William de Sonnac	1247 - 1250
Philip de Milly	1169 - 1171	Reynald de Vichiers	1250 - 1256
Odo de St. Amand	1171 - 1179	Thomas Berard	1256 - 1273
Arnold de Toroga	1179 - 1184	William de Beaujeu	1273 - 1291
Gerard de Ridfort	1185 - 1189	Tibald de Gaudin	1291 - 1293
Robert de Sablé	1191 - 1193	Jacques de Molay	1293 - 1314
Gilbert Erail	1193 - 1200		

Popes

Urban II	1088 - 1099	Gregory IX	1227 - 1241
Paschal II	1099 - 1118	Celestine IV	1241
Gelasius II	1118 - 1119	Innocent IV	1243 - 1254
Calixtus II	1119 - 1124	Alexander IV	1254 - 1261
Honorius II	1124 - 1130	Urban IV	1261 - 1264
Innocent II	1130 - 1143	Clement IV	1265 - 1268
Celestine II	1143 - 1144	Gregory X	1271 - 1276
Lucius II	1144 - 1145	Innocent V	1276
Eugenius III	1145 - 1153	Adrian V	1276
Anastasius IV	1153	John XXI	1276 - 1277
Adrian IV	1154 - 1159	Nicholas III	1277 - 1280
Alexander III	1159 - 1181	Martin IV	1281 - 1285
Lucius III	1181 - 1185	Honorius IV	1285 - 1287
Urban III	1185 - 1187	Nicholas IV	1288 - 1292
Gregory VIII	1187	Celestine V	1294
Clement III	1187 - 1191	Boniface VIII	1294 - 1303
Celestine III	1191 - 1198	Benedict XI	1303 - 1304
Innocent III	1198 - 1216	Clement V	1305 - 1314
Honorius III	1216 - 1227		

Kings of Jerusalem

Baldwin I	1100 - 1118	Amalric II	1198 - 1205
Baldwin II	1118 - 1131	John of Brienne	1210 - 1125
Fulk	1131 - 1143	Frederick II	1125 - 1228
Baldwin III	1143 - 1162	Conrad	1228 - 1254
Amalric I	1162 - 1174	Conradin	1254 - 1268
Baldwin IV	1174 - 1185	Hugh III	1268 - 1284
Baldwin V	1185 - 1186	John I	1284 - 1285
Guy	1186 - 1190	Henry II	1285 - 1291
Henry	1192 - 1197		

Kings of France

Philip I	1060 - 1108	Louis XIII	1223 - 1226
Louis VI	1108 - 1137	Louis IX	1226 - 1270
Louis VII	1137 - 1180	Philip III	1270 - 1285
Philip II	1180 - 1223	Philip IV	1285 - 1314

Kings of England

William II (Rufus)	1087 - 1100	John	1199 - 1216
Henry I	1100 - 1135	Henry III	1216 - 1272
Stephen	1135 - 1154	Edward I	1272 - 1307
Henry II	1154 - 1189	Edward II	1307 - 1327
Richard I	1189 - 1199		

Kings of Germany and Holy Roman Emperors

Henry IV	1056 - 1106	Conrad IV	1250 - 1254
Henry V	1106 - 1125	Alfonso X	1257 - 1273
Lothar III	1125 - 1137	Rudolf I	1273 - 1292
Conrad III	1138 - 1152	Adolf	1292 - 1298
Frederick I	1152 - 1190	Albert I	1298 - 1308
Henry VI	1190 - 1197	Henry VII	1308 - 1314
Frederick II	1212 - 1250		

Bibliography

ABULAFIA, DAVID. *Frederick II, A Medieval Emperor.* London; 1988.

ADDISON, C.G. *The Knights Templars' History.* New York; 1875.

ARMSTRONG, KAREN. *Holy War.* London; 1988.

ATTWATER, DONALD, ED. *A Catholic Dictionary (The Catholic Encyclopaedic Dictionary).* New York; 1953.

BAINVILLE, JACQUES. *History of France.* New York; 1926.

BALDWIN, JOHN W. *The Scholastic Culture of the Middle Ages 1000-1300.* Lexington, Mass.; 1971.

BARBER, RICHARD. *The Knight and Chivalry.* New York; 1982.

BARRACLOUGH, GEOFFREY. *The Medieval Papacy.* New York; 1968.

BEHA ED-DIN. *The Life of Saladin (1137-1193 A.D.).* Delhi, India; 1988.

BELENITSKY, ALEKSANDR. *Central Asia.* Trans. James Hogarth. Geneva; 1968.

BÉMONT, C. AND MONOD, G. *Medieval Europe from 395 to 1270.* Trans. Mary Sloan. New York; 1902.

BISHOP, MORRIS. *The Middle Ages.* Boston; 1987.

BURMAN, EDWARD. *The Templars, Knights of God.* London; 1986.

CAMPBELL, G.A. *The Knights Templars: Their Rise and Fall.* London; 1937.

CARDINALE, HYGINUS E. *Orders of Knighthood, Awards and the Holy See.* Gerards Cross, Bucks.; 1983.

CAVE, ROY C. AND COULSON, HERBERT H. *A Source Book for Medieval Economic History.* New York; 1965.

CHURCHILL, WINSTON S. *The Birth of Britain.* New York; 1956.

CHAMBERLIN, E.R. *The Bad Popes.* New York; 1986.

COLE, PENNY J. *The Preaching of the Crusades to the Holy Land, 1095 1270.* Cambridge; 1991.

CONTAMINE, PHILIPPE. *War in the Middle Ages.* Oxford; 1990.

COOK, EZRA A. *Revised Knight Templarism Illustrated.* Chicago; 1986.

CROSS, JEREMY L. REV. by Will M. Cunningham. *Templar's Chart.* Philadelphia; 1863.

DAWLEY, POWELL MILLS. *Chapters in Church History.* New York, 1950.

DAWSON, CHRISTOPHER. *Religion and the Rise of Western Culture.* Garden City, N.Y.; 1958.

———, ed. *The Mongol Mission.* Trans. by "a nun of Stanbrook Abbey." New York; 1955.

DE ROSA, PETER. *Vicars of Christ.* New York; 1988.

DUGGAN, ALFRED. *The Story of the Crusades 1097-1291.* New York; 1964.

DUPUY, R. AND TREVOR, N. *The Encyclopedia of Military History.* London; 1970.

DYER, CHRISTOPHER. *Standards of Living in the Late Middle Ages.* Cambridge; 1989.

480

EDBURY, PETER W. AND ROWE, JOHN GORDON. *William of Tyre*. Cambridge; 1988.

EDGE, DAVID AND PADDOCK, JOHN MILES. *Arms & Armor of the Medieval Knight*. New York; 1988.

ERBSTÖSSER, MARTIN. *Heretics in the Middle Ages*. Trans. Janet Fraser. Leipzig; 1984.

EVANS, JOAN, ed. *The Flowering of the Middle Ages*. London; 1966.

FARAH, CAESAR E. *Islam*. Woodbury, N.Y.; 1970.

FERM, VERGILIUS, ed. *An Encyclopedia of Religion*. Patterson, NJ; 1959.

FINK, HAROLD S. *Fulcher of Chartres: A History of the Expedition to Jerusalem 1095-1297*. Trans. Frances Rita Ryan. Knoxville; (n.d.)

FULLER, J.F.C. *The Decisive Battles of the Western World: 480 B.C.-1757*. 2 vols. London; 1970.

FUNK, F.X. *History*. 2 vols. Trans. Luigi Cappadelta. London; 1913.

GABRIELI, ed. and trans. *Arab Historians of the Crusades*. Trans. from the Italian E.J. Costello. Berkeley,; 1969.

GEER, THOMAS H. *A Brief History of Western Man*. New York; 1968.

GHAREEB, EDMUND. *The Kurdish Question in Iraq*. Syracuse, NY; 1982.

GIBBON, EDWARD. *The Decline and Fall of the Roman Empire*. London; 1960.

GIES, FRANCES. *The Knight in History*. New York; 1984.

GIES, JOSEPH AND FRANCES. *Life in a Medieval Castle*. New York; 1979.

GLUBB, SIR JOHN. *Soldiers of Fortune: The Story of the Mamelukes*. New York; 1988.

GROUSSET, RENÉ. *The Empire of the Steppes: A History of Central Asia*. Trans. Naomi Walford. New Brunswick, NJ; (n.d.)

———. *The Epic of the Crusades*. Trans. Noël Lindsay. New York; 1970.

HALLAM, ELIZABETH, ed. *Chronicles of the Crusades: Eye-Witness Accounts of the Wars Between Christianity and Islam*. London; 1989.

HEER, FRIEDRICH. *The Medieval World: Europe 1100-1350*. Trans. J. Sondheimer. London; 1963.

HINNELLS, JOHN R., Ed. *The Penguin Dictionary of Religions*. Middlesex; 1984.

HOLMES, GEORGE, ed. *The Oxford Illustrated History of Medieval Europe*. Oxford; 1990.

HOUSLEY, NORMAN. *The Avignon Papacy and the Crusades 1305-1378*. Oxford; 1986.

HOWARTH, STEPHEN. *The Knights Templar*. New York; 1982.

JOINVILLE AND VILLEHARDOUIN. *Chronicles of the Crusades*. Trans. M.R.B. Shaw. London; 1963.

KEEN, MAURICE. *Chivalry*. New Haven; 1984.

KELEN, BETTY. *Muhammad: The Messenger of God*. New York; 1975.

KINDER, HERMANN AND WERNER, HILGEMANN. *The Anchor Atlas of World History*. Vol. 1. Trans. Ernest A. Menze. Munich; 1964.

LADURIE, EMMANUEL LEROY. *Montaillou: The Promised Land of Error*. Trans. Barbara Bray. New York; 1979.

LAMB, HAROLD. *The Crusades*. Garden City, NY; 1930.

LA MONTE, JOHN I. *Feudal Monarchy in the Latin Kingdom of Jerusalem 1100 to 1291*. New York; 1970.

LANE-POOLE, STANLEY. *A History of Egypt in the Middle Ages*. New York; 1969.

LAPIDUS, IRA M. *A History of Islamic Societies*. New York; 1988.

LIPPMAN, THOMAS W. *Understanding Islam*. New York; 1982.

LOPEZ, ROBERT S. *The Birth of Europe*. New York; 1967.

MAALOUF, AMIN. *The Crusades Through Arab Eyes*. Trans. Jon Rothschild. New York; 1985.

MANSFIELD. *The Arabs*. New York; 1980.

MARSDEN, WILLIAM, Trans. and ed. (Re-ed. Thomas Wright.) *The Travels of Marco Polo the Venetian*. Garden City, NY; 1948.

MARTIN, EDWARD J. *The Trial of the Templars*. New York; 1978.

MARTIN, MALACHI. *The Decline and Fall of the Roman Church*. New York; 1981.

MAYER, HANS EBERHARD. *The Crusades*. Trans. John Gillingham. Oxford; 1988.

McEVEDY, COLIN. *The Penguin Atlas of Medieval History*. London; 1961.

MELTZER, MILTON. *Slavery: From the Rise of Western Civilization to Today*. New York; 1977. (Orig. publ. in 2 vols.; 1971.)

MILLER, D.A. *The Byzantine Tradition*. New York; 1966.

MORIARTY, CATHERINE, ed. *The Voice of the Middle Ages: Personal Letters 1100-1500*. Oxford; 1989.

NEWHALL, RICHARD A. *The Crusades*. New York; 1963.

NICHOLAS, DAVID. *The Medieval West*. Homewood,; 1983.

OLDENBOURG, ZOÉ. *Massacre at Montségur: A History of the Albigensian Crusade*. Trans. Peter Green. New York; 1990.

PARKER, THOMAS W. *The Knights Templars in England*. Tucson; 1963.

PARTNER, PETER. *The Murdered Magicians*. Rochester, VT.; 1987.

PAYNE, ROBERT. *The Dream and the Tomb: A History of the Crusades*. London; 1986.

PETER, EDWARD. *Christian Society and the Crusades 1198-1229*. Philadelphia; 1971.

PICKTHALL, MOHAMMED MARMADUKE. *The Meaning of the Glorious Koran*. (Incl. trans.) New York; (n.d.)

POWELL, JAMES M. *Anatomy of a Crusade 1213-1221*. Philadelphia; 1986.

POWER, EILEEN. *Medieval People*. New York; 1965.

RICE, EUGENE, ed. *The Western Experience: Antiquity to the Middle Ages*. New York; 1974.

RILEY-SMITH, JONATHAN, ed. *The Atlas of the Crusades*. New York; 1991.

ROBINSON, IAN STUART. *The Papacy 1073-1198*. Cambridge; 1990.

ROBINSON, JAMES HARVEY. *Medieval and Modern Times*. New York; 1926.

ROBINSON, JOHN J. *Born in Blood: The Lost Secrets of Freemasonry*. New York; 1990.

RODWELL, J.M., trans. *The Koran*. London; 1957.

ROSS, FRANK, JR. *Arabs and the Islamic World*. New York; 1979.

RUNCIMAN, SIR STEVEN. *A History of the Crusades*. 3 vols. Cambridge; 1951.

SABINI, JOHN. *Islam: A Primer*. Washington, D.C.; 1988.

SCHERMERHORN, ELIZABETH W. *On the Trail of the Eight-Pointed Cross*. New York; 1940.

SEWARD, DESMOND. *The Monks of War*. Frogmore, St. Albans; 1974.

SIMON, EDITH. *The Piebald Standard: A Biography of the Knights Templars*. Boston; (n.d.)

SMAIL, R.C. *Crusading Warfare (1097-1193)*. London; 1956.

STONE, GEORGE CAMERON. *A Glossary of the Consruction, Decoration and Use of Arms and Armor*. New York; 1961.

TANNER, NORMAN P., ed. *Decrees of the Ecumenical Councils*. 2 vols. Washington, D.C.; 1990.

THEIS, DAN. *The Crescent and the Cross*. New York; 1978.

TUCHMAN, BARBARA. *A Distant Mirror: The Calamitous 14th Century*. New York; 1978.

————. *Bible and Sword*. New York; 1984.

TURNBALL, STEPHEN. *The Book of the Medieval Knight*. London; 1985.

VAUGHN, RICHARD, ed. and trans. *Chronicles of Matthew Paris: Monastic Life in the Thirteenth Century*. Gloucester; 1986.

VERNADSKY, GEORGE. *A History of Russia*. New York; 1944.

WALSH, JAMES J. *The Thirteenth, Greatest of Centuries*. New York; 1913.

WATT, W. MONTGOMERY. *The Influence of Islam on Medieval Europe*. Edinburgh; 1972.

WELLS, H.G. *The Outline of History*. 2 vols. New York; 1930.

WILKINSON, FREDERICK. *Arms and Armour*. London; 1978.

WILLIAMS, ANN. *The Crusades*. Harlow, Essex; 1975.

WITTFOGEL, KARL A. *Oriental Despotism*. New York; 1981.

WOLF, JOHN B. *The Emergence of European Civilization*. New York; 1962.

WOOD, CHARLES T. *The Quest for Eternity: Manners and Morals in the Age of Chivalry*. Hanover; 1983.

Index